Studies in Classification, Data Analysis, and Knowledge Organization

Managing Editors
H. H. Bock, Aachen
O. Opitz, Augsburg
M. Schader, Mannheim

Editorial Board
W. H. E. Day, St. John's
E. Diday, Paris
A. Ferligoj, Ljubljana
W. Gaul, Karlsruhe
J. C. Gower, Harpenden
D. J. Hand, Milton Keynes
P. Ihm, Marburg
J. Meulmann, Leiden
S. Nishisato, Toronto
F. J. Radermacher, Ulm
R. Wille, Darmstadt

Springer
*Berlin
Heidelberg
New York
Barcelona
Budapest
Hong Kong
London
Milan
Paris
Santa Clara
Singapore
Tokyo*

Titles in the Series

H.-H. Bock and P. Ihm (Eds.)
Classification, Data Analysis, and Knowledge Organization
(out of print)

M. Schader (Ed.)
Analyzing and Modeling Data and Knowledge

O. Opitz, B. Lausen, and R. Klar (Eds.)
Information and Classification
(out of print)

H.-H. Bock, W. Lenski, and M. M. Richter (Eds.)
Information Systems and Data Analysis
(out of print)

E. Diday, Y. Lechevallier, M. Schader, P. Bertrand,
and B. Burtschy (Eds.)
New Approaches in Classification and Data Analysis
(out of print)

W. Gaul and D. Pfeifer (Eds.)
From Data to Knowledge

H.-H. Bock and W. Polasek (Eds.)
Data Analysis and Information Systems

E. Diday, Y. Lechevallier and O. Opitz (Eds.)
Ordinal and Symbolic Data Analysis

R. Klar and O. Opitz (Eds.)
Classification and Knowledge Organization

Ch. Hayashi, K. Yajima, and H.-H. Bock
Data Science, Classification, and Related Methods

Ingo Balderjahn · Rudolf Mathar
Martin Schader (Eds.)

Classification, Data Analysis, and Data Highways

Proceedings of the 21st Annual Conference
of the Gesellschaft für Klassifikation e. V.,
University of Potsdam, March 12–14, 1997

With 91 Figures
and 41 Tables

 Springer

Professor Dr. Ingo Balderjahn
University of Potsdam
August-Bebel-Str. 89
D-14482 Potsdam, Germany

Professor Dr. Rudolf Mathar
RWTH Aachen
Templergraben 55
D-52062 Aachen, Germany

Professor Dr. Martin Schader
University of Mannheim
Schloß
D-68131 Mannheim, Germany

ISBN 3-540-63909-8 Springer-Verlag Berlin Heidelberg New York

Cataloging-in-Publication Data applied for
Die Deutsche Bibliothek - CIP-Einheitsaufnahme
Classification, data analysis, and data highways: with 41 tables / Ingo Balderjahn; Rudolf Mathar; Martin Schader (eds.). - Berlin; Heidelberg; New York; Barcelona; Budapest; Hong Kong; London; Milan; Paris; Santa Clara; Singapore; Tokyo: Springer, 1998
 (Studies in classification, data analysis, and knowledge organization)
 ISBN 3-540-63909-8

This work is subject to copyright. All rights are reserved, whether the whole or part of the material is concerned, specifically the rights of translation, reprinting, reuse of illustrations, recitation, broadcasting, reproduction on microfilm or in any other way, and storage in data banks. Duplication of this publication or parts thereof is permitted only under the provisions of the German Copyright Law of September 9, 1965, in its current version, and permission for use must always be obtained from Springer-Verlag. Violations are liable for prosecution under the German Copyright Law.

© Springer-Verlag Berlin · Heidelberg 1998
Printed in Germany

The use of general descriptive names, registered names, trademarks, etc. in this publication does not imply, even in the absence of a specific statement, that such names are exempt from the relevant protective laws and regulations and therefore free for general use.

Product liability: The publishers cannot guarantee the accuracy of any information about the application of operative techniques and medications contained in this book. In every individual case the user must check such information by consulting the relevant literature.

Coverdesign: Erich Kirchner, Heidelberg
SPIN 10548628   43/2202-5 4 3 2 1 0 - Printed on acid-free paper

Preface

This volume contains revised versions of 43 papers presented during the 21st Annual Conference of the *Gesellschaft für Klassifikation (GfKl)*, the German Classification Society. The conference took place at the University of Potsdam (Germany) in March 1997; the local organizer was Prof. I. Balderjahn, Chair of Business Administration and Marketing at Potsdam.

The scientific program of the conference included 103 plenary and contributed papers, software and book presentations as well as special (tutorial) courses. Researchers and practitioners interested in data analysis and clustering methods, information sciences and database techniques, and in the main topic of the conference: *data highways and their importance for classification and data analysis,* had the opportunity to discuss recent developments and to establish cross-disciplinary cooperation in these fields.

The conference owed much to its sponsors

- Berliner Volksbank
- Daimler Benz AG
- Deutsche Telekom AG Direktion Potsdam
- Dresdner Bank AG Filiale Potsdam
- Henkel KGaA
- Landeszentralbank in Berlin und Brandenburg
- Ministerium für Wissenschaft, Forschung und Kultur des Landes Brandenburg
- Scicon GmbH
- Siemens AG
- Universität Potsdam
- Unternehmensgruppe Roland Ernst

who helped in many ways. Their generous support is gratefully acknowledged.

In the present proceedings volume, selected and peer-reviewed papers are presented in six chapters as follows.

- Classification and Data Analysis
- Mathematical and Statistical Methods
- World Wide Web and the Internet
- Speech and Pattern Recognition
- Knowledge and Databases
- Marketing

In the first place, we would like to thank the authors for their contributions which made the conference and this volume an interdisciplinary forum for exchanging ideas. Also, we are very grateful to all colleagues who selected and reviewed papers, or chaired sessions during the conference. Furthermore, we are obliged to Marianne Reblin, Michael Feix, Gerrit-John Los (University of Mannheim), and Ingrid Ostlender (Aachen University of Technology) for their diligent efforts in typesetting and reproduction of figures. Finally, thanks are extended to Springer-Verlag, Heidelberg, for the familiar excellent cooperation in publishing this volume.

Potsdam, Aachen, and Mannheim, November 1997   Ingo Balderjahn
                                                            Rudolf Mathar
                                                            Martin Schader

Contents

Part 1: Classification and Data Analysis

Entropy Optimizing Methods for the Estimation of Tables
  U. Blien, F. Graef 3

Automatic Spectral Classification
  N. Christlieb, G. Graßhoff, A. Nelke, A. Schlemminger,
  L. Wisotzki 16

An Approach to Modelling Directional and Betweenness Data
  H. Feger 24

The Application of Random Coincidence Graphs
for Testing the Homogeneity of Data
  E. Godehardt, J. Jaworski, D. Godehardt 35

City-Block Scaling: Smoothing Strategies for Avoiding Local Minima
  P.J.F. Groenen, W.J. Heiser, J.J. Meulman 46

Probability Models and Limit Theorems for Random Interval Graphs
with Applications to Cluster Analysis
  B. Harris, E. Godehardt 54

Labor Supply Decisions in Germany
A Semiparametric Regression Analysis
  W. Kempe 62

A Multiplicative Approach to Partitioning the Risk of Disease
  M. Land, O. Gefeller 73

Multiple Media Stream Data Analysis: Theory and Applications
  F. Makedon, C. Owen 81

Multimedia Data Analysis using ImageTcl
  F. Makedon, C. Owen 87

Robust Bivariate Boxplots and Visualization of Multivariate Data
  M. Riani, S. Zani, A. Corbellini 93

Unsupervised Fuzzy Classification of Multispectral Imagery
Using Spatial-Spectral Features
  R. Wiemker 101

Part 2: Mathematical and Statistical Methods

Some News about C.A.MAN Computer Assisted Analysis of Mixtures
  D. Böhning, E. Dietz 113

Mathematical Aspects of the Feature Pattern Analysis
  M. Brehm 123

A Note on the Off-Block-Diagonal Approximation of the Burt Matrix
as Applied in Joint Correspondence Analysis
  J. Faßbinder 132
A New Look at the Visual Performance
of Nonparametric Hazard Rate Estimators
  O. Gefeller, N.L. Hjort 139
Multilevel Modeling: When and Why
  J. Hox 147
Upper Bounds for the P–Values of a Scan Statistic
with a Variable Window
  J. Krauth 155
A Branch-and-bound Algorithm for Boolean Regression
  I. Leenen, I.V. Mechelen 164
Mathematical Classification and Clustering: From How to What and
Why
  B. Mirkin 172
Heteroskedastic Linear Regression Models – A Bayesian Analysis
  W. Polasek, S. Liu, S. Jin 182
A Heuristic Partial-Least-Squares Approach to Estimating
Dynamic Path Models
  H.G. Strohe 192

Part 3: World Wide Web and the Internet

Using Logic for the Specification of Hypermedia Documents
  E.-E. Doberkat 205
Project TeleTeaching Mannheim – Heidelberg
  W. Effelsberg, W. Geyer, A. Eckert 213
WWW-Access to Relational Databases
  W. Esswein, A. Selz 223
Technology, Data, Relevancy: A Culture-Theoretical Look at the
Internet
  P.M. Hejl 234
Self-Organizing Maps of Very Large Document Collections:
Justification for the WEBSOM Method
  T. Honkela, S. Kaski, T. Kohonen, K. Lagus 245
Segment–Specific Aspects of Designing Online Services in the Internet
  T. Klein, W. Gaul, F. Wartenberg 253
Design of World Wide Web Information Systems
  K. Lenz, A. Oberweis 262
Large WWW Systems: New Phenomena, Problems and Solutions
  H. Maurer 270

Structured Visualization of Search Result List
U. Preiser 277

Part 4: Speech and Pattern Recognition

Application of Discriminative Methods for Isolated Word Recognition
J.G. Bauer 287

Statistical Classifiers in Computer Vision
J. Hornegger, D. Paulus, H. Niemann 295

Speech Signal Classification with Hybrid Systems
Ch. Neukirchen, G. Rigoll 304

Stochastic Modelling of Knowledge Sources
in Automatic Speech Recognition
H. Ney 313

Classification of Speech Pattern Using Locally Recurrent Neural
Networks
H. Reininger, K. Kasper, H. Wüst 335

Part 5: Knowledge and Databases

Information Gathering for Vague Queries Using Case Retrieval Nets
H.-D. Burkhard 345

Characterizing Bibliographic Databases by Content
an Experimental Approach
M. Dreger, S. Göbel, S. Lohrum 355

Medoc Searching Heterogeneous Bibliographic and Text Databases
K. Großjohann, C. Haber, R. Weber 365

Supervised Learning with Qualitative and Mixed Attributes
H. Kauderer, H.-J. Mucha 374

Part 6: Marketing

A Comparison of Traditional Segmentation Methods
with Segmentation Based upon Artificial Neural Networks
by Means of Conjoint Data from a Monte-Carlo-Simulation
H. Gierl, S. Schwanenberg 385

Classification of Pricing Strategies in a Competitive Environment
M. Löffler, W. Gaul 393

Predicting the Amount of Purchase by a Procedure Using
Multidimensional Scaling: An Application to Scanner Data on Beer
A. Okada, A. Miyauchi 401

Author and Subject Index 409

Part 1

Classification and Data Analysis

Entropy Optimizing Methods for the Estimation of Tables

Uwe Blien[1], Friedrich Graef[2]

[1] Institute for Employment Research,
Regensburger Str. 104, D-90327 Nürnberg, Germany

[2] Institute of Applied Mathematics, University of Erlangen-Nuremberg,
Martensstr. 3, D-91058 Erlangen, Germany

Abstract: A new procedure for the problem of recovering tabular data in case of incomplete or inconsistent information is presented. It generalizes the well kown RAS (or IPF) algorithm by allowing a wider class of constraints concerning the table entries such as equalities and inequalities over arbitrary cross sections. The theoretical background of the procedure is outlined and some examples of applications are reported.

1 Introduction

A frequently encountered problem in econometrics, empirical economics, and statistics is that of recovering matrices or multidimensional tables from incomplete information.

To problems of this type usually the RAS procedure (known from input-output analysis) is applied, which is identical to the Iterative Proportional Fitting Algorithm (IPF) used with log-linear models in statistics. With the RAS method a matrix is computed which is structurally similar to a given prior matrix and whose column and row sums attain prescribed values.

The newly developed ENTROP procedure is a generalization of the RAS method. With ENTROP not only values for column and row sums can be prescribed. It may be applied whenever the information about the structure of the matrix (in the following also called *table*) to be estimated is given by a set of linear equations and/or inequalities with respect to the table entries. In addition, an a priori known reference table can be specified. The structure of the table resulting from this computational procedure will be as close as possible to that of the reference table.

ENTROP is a procedure minimizing the relative entropy. The result can be interpreted according to criteria from statistics and formal information theory (Shannon, Weaver (1949), Kullback (1968)). Under certain conditions the table estimated by this method may be interpreted as the most likely one.

ENTROP is an advancement of the entropy maximization procedure of BREGMAN and CENSOR. It is an iterative algorithm of the row action type, i.e. only one out of the total set of constraints is used at each iteration step, and especially well suited for sparse constraints. Thus, problems with large high dimensional tables and with many constraints can be handled even by PCs. Originally the ENTROP procedure had been developed as a tool for the Educational Accounting System of the Institute for Employment Research in Germany. Its purpose is the estimation of large matrices (with approximately 30000 elements) of transition rates between the labour market and the educational system.

Beyond this specific application it may serve many purposes. Typical tasks within the range of applicability of ENTROP are the *disaggregation of data* available only in a summarized form, *the weighting of random samples*, i.e. their adjustment to distributions known from official statistics, the *estimation of tables* from heterogeneous, incompatible and incomplete data, the *computation of transition matrices* of Markov processes, and the *construction of forecasts* (e.g. of the joint distribution of some variables from estimates of their univariate distributions)

2 Computing Tables

The computation of two-dimensional input-output tables may be considered as a representative example for the application of the method. Table 1 illustrates a matrix X^t to be estimated.

Table 1: Input-output matrix X^t

		inputs to industries $1 - J$			Σ
outputs of ind. $1 - I$	x_{11}	x_{12}	$\cdots$	x_{1J}	b_1^r
	x_{21}	x_{22}	$\cdots$	x_{2J}	b_2^r
	x_{31}	x_{32}	$\cdots$	x_{3J}	b_3^r
	$\vdots$	$\vdots$	$\ddots$	$\vdots$	$\vdots$
	x_{I1}	x_{I2}	$\cdots$	x_{IJ}	b_I^r
Σ	b_1^c	b_2^c	$\cdots$	b_J^c	b^{rc}

In input-output analysis the rows of the table are the outputs of industries. The columns are the inputs. The entry at row i and column j is that part of the total output of industry i which is used as input to industry j during a given time period t. In most cases the number of rows I equals the number of columns J. Here, for generality it is assumed that I is not necessarily equal to J.

The unknown values of the elements x_{ij} of X^t have to be estimated from heterogeneous information. If, e.g., the concrete numbers of the row and column totals are given, then the following equations have to be observed:

$$\sum_{j=1}^{J} x_{ij} = b_i^r \text{ for all } i, \text{ and } \sum_{i=1}^{I} x_{ij} = b_j^c \text{ for all } j \qquad (1)$$

Frequently there is some information about the internal structure of X^t which might be drawn from different surveys and other sources. It can be included into the estimation process if is possible to define appropriate linear equations and inequalities. If—as a simple example—an estimate of a single entry x_{ij} stemming from a representative survey is given and it has to be expected that the value is affected by certain random sample and survey errors an inequality of the form

$$b^l \leq x_{ij} \leq b^u \qquad (2)$$

may be adequate where b^l and b^u are the assumed lower and upper limits of the real value corresponding to an error estimate.

By an appropriate choice of these limits information with various degrees of reliability can be handled. The fact that a single x_{ij} is known only from relatively vague judgements of experts can be treated by entering a relatively large difference between b^l and b^u in (2) or by introducing a lower or upper bound only. By contrast, if the given data can be regarded as "hard", for example because they are taken from an overall survey of the population, then by setting $b^l = b^u$ the inequality becomes an equation.

Specifying inequalities to include information affected by sample errors is important, because contradictions between different data sources may lead to intolerable consequences for the whole system which requires the consistency of all accounts.

If only aggregated information on X^t is available, then sums have to be taken into account. The method developed for the estimation of tables works if the information on the table can be given the form of K linear inequalities:

$$\sum_{i=1}^{I} \sum_{j=1}^{J} a_{kij} x_{ij} \leq b_k \qquad (3)$$

for $k = 1 \ldots K$. A system (3) includes inequalities like (2) and—with the a_{kij} being either equal to 0 or to 1—equations like (1). Thus, the row and colummn sums of the tables can also be specified as conditions which must be fulfilled by the estimates.

Under special conditions the system (3) could be solved exactly. In many cases there are not enough inequalities to obtain an exact solution. Thus an estimation procedure has to be applied.

In some cases an estimation can be based on additional information on the structure of the matrix. This is possible if a matrix U^{t-1} for one year is already available, whereas only incomplete and heterogeneous information is given for the adjacent years. If it can be assumed that transition behaviour varies only relatively slightly from year to year, the unknown matrix should be estimated in accordance with the structure of the known matrix.

With a given reference matrix U^{t-1} the estimation problem can be solved if it is possible to redefine it as an optimization problem, e.g. to minimize a distance measure $D(X^t, U^{t-1})$ with the inequalities (3) representing the constraints of the optimization process. Proceeding this way will also be appropriate if the reference matrix U^{t-1} itself is the result of an estimation (then $U^{t-1} = X^{t-1}$), but is based on far more information than is available for the matrix X^t.

3 Minimizing the Relative Entropy

The above description of the estimation problem requires the definition of a distance measure $D(X,U)$ between tables X and U (cf. Blien, Graef (1991, 1992)). After considering the properties of some distance functions, the relative entropy

$$E_u(X) = \sum_{m=1}^{M} x_m \ln\left(\frac{x_m}{u_m}\right) \qquad (4)$$

was chosen. Since the estimation procedure does not rely on a specific ordering of the table entries it is assumed for the following that they are linearly numbered by $m = 1, \ldots, M$ (with $M = I \cdot J$ in case of a two-dimensional table).

Measuring the degree of similarity between two tables by (4) has a long tradition in natural sciences and engineering[1]. Minimizing the relative entropy can also be justified from a statistical viewpoint. If the reference matrix has been normalized such that $\sum_m u_m = 1$, then u_m can be interpreted as the probability of a certain object to be in state m. If a total number $N = \sum_m x_m$ of objects is distributed independendly over the possible states according to this probability law and x_m is the number of objects occupying state m then the probability of the table $X = (x_m)$ follows a multinomial distribution:

$$P(X) = \frac{N!}{x_1! x_2! \ldots x_M!} u_1^{x_1} u_2^{x_2} \ldots u_M^{x_M}$$

The logarithm of $P(X)$ is closely related to the relative entropy $E_u(X)$. Using the Stirling-formula $\ln(s!) \approx s\ln(s) - s$ it can be shown by some algebra that

$$\ln(P(X)) \approx N \ln(N) - E_u(X)$$

---

[1] A particular impressive example is computer tomography in medicine, as the relationship to the problem under discussion is especially clear. In computer tomography x-ray pictures of an organ are taken from various angles. From these photographs a sectional picture of the corresponding organ is made. The resulting picture can be imagined as an extremely finely gridded table which contains the grey values for the individual dots. The x-ray photographs correspond to the row and column sums of the table. The picture is generated with an entropy optimizing algorithm. It shows the organ in question with all details, including any possible pathological changes. Other cases of application for entropy optimizing are pattern recognition in research on artificial intelligence. In particular new approaches usually summarized under the title *neuronal networks* make use of these methods (cf. eg. Hinton, Sejnovski (1987), Kosko (1992)).

The natural logarithm being an increasing function the table X maximizing $\ln(P(X))$ also maximizes $P(X)$. Thus, assuming a stochastically independent placement of the N objects under the specified constraints (5) the table minimizing the relative entropy is asymptotically equal to the table representing the distribution of objects with the highest probability[2].

For arbitrary $u_m \geq 0$ the optimization problem for table estimation may now be stated as follows:

Minimize the function $E_u(X)$ subject to the constraints

$$\sum_{m=1}^{M} a_{km} x_m \leq b_k \quad \text{for } k = 1, \ldots, K \tag{5}$$

and the nonnegativity constraints

$$x_m \geq 0 \quad \text{for } m = 1, \ldots, M \tag{6}$$

The nonnegativity constraints are stated because all elements of X should be equal to or greater than 0 (note that all $u_m \geq 0$ by definition). The general structure of the resulting table can be obtained via the Kuhn-Tucker-Karoush theorem (cf. for example Chiang (1974)). The conditions for the minimum are:

$$\ln\left(\frac{x_m}{u_m}\right) + 1 + \sum_{k=1}^{K} \mu_k a_{km} = 0 \tag{7}$$

$$\mu_k \geq 0 \tag{8}$$

$$\mu_k \left(\sum_m a_{km} x_m - b_k\right) = 0 \tag{9}$$

The μ_k are the dual variables. If we solve (7) for the x_m then

$$x_m = u_m e^{-1} e^{-\sum_k \mu_k a_{km}} \tag{10}$$

From (10) some properties[3] of the estimated table can be seen:

- nonnegativity: all $x_m \geq 0$

- conservation of zeroes: for each $u_m = 0$ the corresponding x_m is also equal to zero.

---

[2] By some algebra it can be shown (cf. Blien, Graef (1991)) that the relative entropy is proportional to another distance measure, to Kullback's *information gain* (cf. Kullback (1968), see also Ireland, Kullback (1968)), which is identical to (4), but defined for probability distributions, i.e. matrices with component sum equal to 1. The information gain is common in applications of the formal information theory (originally founded by Shannon, cf. Shannon, Weaver (1949)). Another term for information gain is *minimum discriminant information*. Haberman (1984) discusses the case of continuous data. Golan, Judge et al. (1996) use information gain minimization for parameter estimation in underdetermined linear models.

[3] There is a growing literature about the properties of estimates obtained by this minimum information principle (see Wauschkuhn (1982), Kullback (1968), Snickars, Weibull (1977), Batten (1983), Batten, Boyce (1986)). One property should be noted: an estimation via this principle is approximately equivalent to an optimization of a weighted sum

4 The ENTROP Algorithm

To estimate a table our task is to minimize the relative entropy (4) under the constraints (5) and (6). There exists a variety of methods known from the theory of nonlinear optimization (cf. Gill, Murray, Wright (1981)) to achieve this, as the relativ entropy has the property of global convexity. To solve the problem some authors have already proposed special applications of the Newton-Raphson algorithm (Wauschkuhn (1982)), geometric programming (Kadas, Klafsky (1976)), stochastic optimization (Ablay (1987)) and simulated annealing (Paass (1988)).

The algorithm finally chosen was designed for the application in the Educational Accounting System (BGR) of the Institute for Employment Research. Since the algorithm exploits the special form of the entropy functional and the constraints, it is very efficient and saves computing time. This special advantage over other methods (e.g. stochastic optimization) is important, because the matrices originated by the BGR are large.

The principle of the ENTROP method is the computation of so called entropy projections. These projections are nonlinear equations originally introduced by Censor (1982)[4] to maximize absolute entropy[5] It can be shown that they may also be applied to minimize the relative entropy with respect to arbitrary reference tables.

The algorithm is an iterative procedure. Its starting values are:

$$\begin{aligned} x_m &= u_m \quad \text{for all } m, \text{ and} \\ \mu_k &= 0 \quad \text{for all } k. \end{aligned} \qquad (11)$$

Every step in the iteration process includes the following operations:

1. Computation of the entropy projection on restriction k: compute a δ so that

$$\sum_m a_{km} x_m e^{\delta a_{km}} = b_k \qquad (12)$$

2. Correction of the sign: If $\delta > \mu_k$, set $\delta = \mu_k$.

3. Updating the values for x_m and μ_k:

$$\begin{aligned} x_m &= x_m e^{\delta a_{km}} \quad \text{for all } m \\ \mu_k &= \mu_k - \delta \quad \text{for all } k \end{aligned} \qquad (13)$$

---

of squares, a modified Chi-square statistic:

$$\chi_Q^2 = \sum_m \frac{(p_m - q_m)^2}{q_m}$$

where the p_m are the normalized x_m's and the q_m the normalized u_m's. This relationship was proved by Kadas and Klafszky (1976, p. 442).

[4]See also Censor and Lent (1981) and Censor (1981). Censor's method is based on a general principle found by Bregman (1967).

[5]The (absolute) entropy of a table is $-\sum_m x_m \ln(x_m)$. It coincides with the negative relative entropy in the case of $u_m = 1$ for all m.

By means of the criteria given by Censor and Lent (1981) it can be shown that the iteration process converges against the solution of (10), (8), and (9), if a solution exists. The procedure is rather simple.

If no reference matrix is present the ENTROP method can also be used. In this case calculations are made with all u_m in the reference table set equal to 1. The method then attempts to occupy the resulting matrix as evenly as possible. Whether this is a reasonable proceeding depends on the specific problem. In this case the optimization of the relative and the absolute entropy are identical (see footnote 4).

5 Generalization of the RAS Method

The ENTROP method contains as a special case the iterative proportional fitting algorithm (IPF) already familiar from loglinear models of statistics (Bishop, Fienberg et al. (1975)). The RAS method (cf. Stone (1962), Bacharach (1970)) used in input-output analysis (also known as the Deming-Stephan algorithm after Deming, Stephan (1940), cf. Bachem, Korte (1979)), is also included, as it is identical with the IPF. Gorman (1963) proved that the RAS method is also a procedure for entropy optimizing.

For the special case that the constraints consist of column and row sum prescriptions only, it can be seen easily that the steps carried out in the RAS method are identical with the computation of entropy projections in ENTROP.

If the constraints are sums

$$\sum_{m \in \mathcal{M}_k} x_m = b_k$$

over cross sections $\mathcal{M}_k$ of table entries the equations (12) can be solved explicitly for δ. Substitution of δ in (13) then results in the recursion

$$x_m^{t+1} = \frac{x_m^t b_k}{\sum_{r \in \mathcal{M}_k} x_r^t} \qquad (14)$$

where t is the respective iteration step. Returning to double-index notation ij for the row and column constraints (1) of input-output analysis the iteration formula (14) reads as

$$x_{ij}^{t+1} = \frac{x_{ij}^t b_j^c}{\sum_r x_{rj}^t} \qquad (15)$$

for column constraints and

$$x_{ij}^{t+1} = \frac{x_{ij}^t b_i^r}{\sum_s x_{is}^t} \qquad (16)$$

for row constraints which is precisely one of the iteration steps of the RAS or the IPF method.

6 Examples of Applications of the ENTROP Procedure

The ENTROP procedure was developed for a task very similar to our example from input-output analysis. It was designed for the *Educational Accounting System* (*Bildungsgesamtrechnung*: BGR) of the Institute for Employment Research (in Germany). To fix ideas a simple application with artificial data will be presented first before giving an overview of the type and size of estimation problems within the framework of the BGR.

6.1 A Simple Example

Assume table 2 to be the input-output matrix of a fictitious economy at time period $t-1$. For the next period t as a first approach assume only the sums of the column entries (the total input to the respective industries) and the row sums (the total output) to be known.

Table 2: Input-output table for time period $t-1$ and totals for period t

		Inputs to industries 1–5					totals	totals at period t
		1	2	3	4	5		
	1	9	71	54	66	11	211	226
outputs	2	20	189	60	53	17	339	372
of	3	31	159	21	25	9	245	333
indu-	4	15	56	0	11	3	85	142
stries	5	1	3	5	5	1	15	50
	6	2	10	51	0	5	68	153
totals		78	488	191	160	46	963	
totals at t		119	638	252	225	42		1276

In estimating the entries of the table for time period t it often is plausible to assume that the basic structure of the relationships between the different industries is nearly constant over time. Thus, the structure of the estimated table should be as similar as possible to that of the a priori matrix of table 2 while at the same time the row entries and column entries should sum up to the quantities known for period t.

It is well known that this can be done with the RAS algorithm. An application of the ENTROP method yields the same result, shown in table 3.

However, the RAS method only permits an estimation using prescribed row and column sums and an a priori matrix. The ENTROP algorithm allows the specification of general linear equations and inequalities serving as restrictions to the estimation. As an example let it be assumed that there exists additional information about the input-output relations for time t. It might

Table 3: Input-output table for time period t, estimated with the ENTROP method on the basis of table 2 and of the column and row totals for period t (the result equals a RAS estimation)

		Inputs to industries 1–5					totals
		1	2	3	4	5	
outputs of industries	1	10.9	78.2	48.2	80.9	7.8	226
	2	24.8	213.4	54.9	66.6	12.3	372
	3	46.5	217.3	23.3	38.0	7.9	333
	4	27.0	91.8	0.0	20.1	3.2	142
	5	3.8	10.4	14.1	19.4	2.2	50
	6	5.9	27.0	111.5	0.0	8.6	153
totals		119	638	252	225	42	1276

be known from a survey that the output of industries 2 and 3 to industries 3 and 4 is at least 250. The output of industry 3 to industry 2 might be less than two times the output of industry 4 to industry 2. This can be stated by two additional inequalities:

$$x_{23} + x_{24} + x_{33} + x_{34} \leq 250 \tag{17}$$
$$x_{32} - 2x_{42} \leq 0 \tag{18}$$

Table 4: Input-output table for time period t, estimated with the ENTROP method on the basis of table 2, the column and row totals of period t and additional information concerning the structure of the table

		Inputs to industries 1–5					totals
		1	2	3	4	5	
outputs of industries	1	14.5	106.4	37.1	58.7	9.3	226
	2	20.5	180.1	**75.7**	**86.6**	9.2	372
	3	41.4	**197.5**	**34.5**	**53.2**	6.3	333
	4	28.5	**98.9**	0.0	11.5	3.0	142
	5	5.4	15.2	11.6	15.0	2.9	50
	6	8.6	39.9	93.2	0.0	11.3	153
totals		119	638	252	225	42	1276

Table 4 shows the result of an application of the ENTROP procedure, which includes table 2 as a reference matrix, the column and the row sums for time period t and the two additional inequalities (17) and (18). The entries affected by (17) and (18) have been emphasized for easy comparison with table 3. Both inequalities are met. The sums of the row entries and column entries are the same as in tables 3 and the structure of table 4 is as similar as possible to that of table 2.

6.2 Application to the Educational Accounting System (BGR)

Demographic accounting approaches provide a means of relating the population in different states at the beginning and the end of a period. Such approaches differ from cross-sectional analyses in that the gross flows of individuals into, within, and out of the states during that period are examined (cf. Stone (1981), Stone, Weale (1986), see also Land, Juster (1981b) and Land, McMillen (1981)).

A system of that kind, the *Educational Accounting System (Bildungsgesamtrechnung - BGR)* was developed by the Institute for Employment Research (IAB) (cf. Blien, Tessaring (1988) and (1992), Tessaring (1986) and (1987), Tessaring et al. (1991) and (1992)). In the BGR the German population is classified according to defined categories: pupils attending different kinds of general and vocational schools, apprentices, students, gainfully employed, unemployed and economically non-active individuals.

Thus, the BGR forms the basis for improved analyses as well as for forecasts on the relationship between education and the labour market. The long-term development of the labour supply in various segments of the labour market can be examined.

The relation between the stocks of adjacent years is given by the inflow-outflow matrix X^t. In X^t the individuals are classified by their opening states in the rows and by their closing states in the columns. An element x_{ij} of this matrix shows the number of people, who change from state i to state j. The so called *stayers*, i.e. x_{ij} with $i = j$ are included as well. The system is consistent, i.e.:

$$\sum_{j=1}^n x_{ij} = b_i^t \text{ for all } i, \text{ and } \sum_{i=1}^n x_{ij} = b_j^{t+1} \text{ for all } j \qquad (19)$$

The b_i^t are the row totals (i.e. the states at t), the b_j^{t+1} the column totals (i.e. the states at $t+1$), n is the number of states.

Most of the BGR stock data were taken from German official statistics. Available transition data, however, stem from surveys and are often incompatible or affected by sample errors. In order to use such heterogeneous and incompatible information to estimate the matrix of the flows of individuals in the BGR the ENTROP procedure was developed.

The matrices estimated by the ENTROP method are very large. Since they contain about 30 000 elements in four dimensions (year t, year $t+1$, sex, age) it is shown that the ENTROP procedure is not restricted to two dimensional tables. The calculations are based on a-priori matrices. Additionally, they use about 2000 inequality and equality restrictions.

The procedure originally was programmed in FORTRAN on a BS2000 mainframe. A program written in C is available as well for Personal Computers running DOS, Windows, or OS/2 and UNIX workstations under the Sun Solaris operating system. The memory management of ENTROP algorithm is so efficient, that PCs can be used for most problems.

Other applications of the ENTROP procedure are in preparation, e.g. an analysis of regional differences of unemployment in Eastern Germany and an analysis of voting mobility.

References

BACHARACH, M. (1970): Biproportional Matrices and Input-Output-Change, Cambridge

BACHEM, A. and KORTE, B. (1979): On the RAS-Algorithm. In: *Computing Vol. 23, 189 ff*

BATEY, P.W.J. and MADDEN, M. (1986) (eds): Integrated analysis of regional systems. London: Pion

BATTEN, D.F. (1983): Spatial Analysis of Interacting Economics. Boston etc.: Kluwer-Nijhoff

BATTEN, D. and BOYCE, D. (1986): Spatial interaction, transportation, and interregional commodity flow models. In: Nijkamp (1986)

BISHOP, Y., FIENBERG, S. and HOLLAND, P. (1975): Discrete Multivariate Analysis: Theory and practice. Cambridge, London

BLIEN, U. and GRAEF, F. (1991): Entropieoptimierungsverfahren in der empirischen Wirtschaftsforschung. In: *Jahrbücher für Nationalökonomie und Statistik 208/4, 399–413*

BLIEN, U. and GRAEF, F. (1992): ENTROP: A General Purpose Entropy Optimizing Method for the Estimation of Tables, the Weighting of Samples, the Disaggregation of Data, and the Development of Forecasts. In: Faulbaum, F. (1992) (ed): *Softstat '91. Advances in Statistical Software 3*. Stuttgart: Gustav Fischer

BLIEN, U. and TESSARING, M. (1988): Die Bildungsgesamtrechnung des IAB. In: Mertens, D. (ed): *Konzepte der Arbeitsmarkt- und Berufsforschung , 3rd ed.*. BeitrAB 70, Nürnberg

BLIEN, U. and TESSARING, M. (1992): Transitions between education and the labour market in Germany. The application of the ENTROP procedure in the Educational Accounting System. *Unpublished paper prepared for presentation at the EALE Conference at the University of Warwick.*

BREGMAN, L. (1967): The relaxation method of finding the common point of convex sets and its application to the solution of problems in convex programming. *USSR Comp. Math. and Math. Phys. Vol. 7/3, 200 ff*

CENSOR, Y. (1981): Row-actions methods for huge and sparse systems and their applications. In: *SIAM Review, Vol. 23*

CENSOR, Y. and Lent, A. (1981): An iterative row-action method for interval convex programming. *Journal of Optimization Theory and Applications, Vol. 34, 321 ff*

CHIANG, A. (1974): Fundamental methods of mathematical economics. (2nd ed.), Tokyo etc.: Mcgraw-Hill Kogakusha

DEMING, W.E. and STEPHAN, F.F. (1940): On a least squares adjustment of a sampled frequency table when the expected marginal totals are known. *The Annals of Mathematical Statistics 11/1, March, 427 ff*

DRENICK, R. and KOZIN, F. (1982) (eds): System Modeling and Optimization. *Lecture Notes in Control and Information Science 38*, Heidelberg etc.: Springer

GOLAN, A., JUDGE, G., and MILLER, D. (1996): Maximum Entropy Econometrics: Robust Estimation With Limited Data. Chichester etc.: Wiley

GORMAN, W. (1963): Estimating Trends in Leontief Matrices. A Note on Mr. Bacharach's Paper. *Discussion paper, Nuffield College*, Oxford

HABERMAN, S.J. (1984): Adjustment by minimum discriminant information. *The Annals of Statistics, 12/3, 971 ff*

HARRIGAN, F. and MCGREGOR, P.G. (1988) (eds): Recent advances in regional economic modelling. London: Pion

HINTON, G.E. and SEJNOWSKI, T.J. (1986): Learning and Relearning in Boltzmann Machines. In: Rumelhart, D.E., McClelland, J.L. et al. (1986) (eds): *Parallel distributed processing.* Vol. 1: Foundations, Cambridge (Mass.), London: MIT Press

IRELAND, C. and KULLBACK, S. (1968): Contingency tables with given marginals. *Biometrika 55, 179 ff*

JUSTER, F.T. and LAND, K.C. (1981) (eds): Social Accounting Systems. Essays on the State of the Art. New York etc.: Academic Press

KADAS, S.A. and KLAFSKY, E. (1976): Estimation of the Parameters in the Gravity Model for Trip Distribution: a New Model and Solution Algorithm, *Regional Science and Urban Economics Vol. 6, 439 ff*

KOSKO, B. (1992): Neural networks and fuzzy systems. Englewood Cliffs: Prentice Hall

KULLBACK, S. (1968): Information Theory and Statistics, 2nd ed., New York: Dover

LAND, K.C. and MCMILLEN, M.M. (1981): Demographic Accounts and the Study of Social Change, In: Juster, Land (1981)

LAND, K.J. and JUSTER, F.T. (1981): Social Accounting Systems: An Overview. In: Juster, Land (1981)

LEVINE, R.D. and TRIBUS, M. (1979) (eds): The maximum entropy formalism. Cambridge (Mass.), London: MIT-Press

NIJKAMP, P. (1986) (ed): Handbook of regional and urban economics, Vol. I: Regional economics. Amsterdam etc.: North-Holland

PAASS, G. (1988): Stochastic Generation of a Synthetic Sample from Marginal Information. *Gesellschaft für Mathematik und Datenverarbeitung, Arbeitspapiere der GMD Nr. 308*. St. Augustin

SHANNON, C.E. and WEAVER, W. (1949): The Mathematical Theory of Communication. Urbana: University of Illinois Press

SLATER, P.B. (1992): Equilibrium and nonequilibrium statistical thermodynamical approaches to modeling spatial interaction dynamics. *Environment and Planning A, vol. 24: 441–446*

SNICKARS, F. and WEIBULL, J. (1976): A minimum information principle. *Regional Science and Urban Economics Vol. 7, 137ff*

STONE, R.N. (1962): Multiple classifications in social accounting. *Bulletin de l'Institut International de Statistique, Vol. 39, No. 3, 215ff*

STONE, R.N. (1981): The Relationship of Demographic Accounts to National Income and Product Accounts. In: Juster, Land (1981)

STONE, R.N. and WEALE, M. (1986): Two populations and their economies. In: Batey, Madden (1986)

TESSARING, M. (1986): Educational accounting in the Federal Republic of Germany. In: Parkes, D.L., Sellin, B. and Tessaring, M.: *Education/ training and labour market policy*. Gravenhage: SVO

TESSARING, M. (1987): Demographic aspects of educational expansion and labour-force development in the Federal Republic of Germany. *European Journal of Population Vol 3: 327–358*

TESSARING, M., BLIEN, U., FISCHER, G., HOFMANN, I. and REINBERG, A. (1990): Bildung und Beschäftigung im Wandel. Die Bildungsgesamtrechnung des IAB. *BeitrAB 126*. Nürnberg

TESSARING, M., REINBERG, A., FISCHER, G. and SCHWEITZER, C. (1992): Übergänge zwischen Bildung, Ausbildung und Beschäftigung und die Entwicklung der Qualifikationsstruktur. *Forthcoming paper*. Nürnberg

THEIL, H. (1967): Economics and Information Theory. Amsterdam

WAUSCHKUHN, U. (1982): Anpassung von Stichproben und n-dimensionalen Tabellen an Randbedingungen. München, Wien: R. Oldenbourg

WILSON, A. (1970): Entropy in urban and regional modelling. London: Pion Ltd.

Automatic Spectral Classification

N. Christlieb[1], G. Graßhoff[2,3], A. Nelke[3], A. Schlemminger[3], L. Wisotzki[1]

[1] Hamburger Sternwarte,
Gojenbergsweg 112, D-21029 Hamburg, Germany

[2] Max-Planck-Institut für
Wissenschaftsgeschichte, Berlin, Germany

[3] Philosophisches Seminar,
Universität Hamburg, Germany

Abstract: In this paper we report on a joint research project between astronomers and philosophers of science. The philosophical and the astronomical goal are described and the astronomical background is shortly reviewed. We present the current status of our development of methods for tackling the relevant classification problems, i.e.: (1) application of Bayes' decision rule for "simple" classification of all spectra in the data base; (2) minimum cost rule classification for compilation of complete samples of rare stellar objects and (3) Bayes classification with application of an *atypicality index* reject criterion for the detection of non-stellar spectra. We report on the discovery of an extremely metal poor halo star by application of method (2) to a small fraction of our data. A method for adequate handling of low signal-to-noise ratio spectra is presented. The classification methods presented are currently applied to a large data base of digital spectra.

1 Introduction

In this paper we report on a joint research project between astronomers and philosophers of science. The former want to develop an instrument which allows a comprehensive classification of astronomical objects on the basis of digital spectra—the astronomical goal, whereas the latter are interested in analysing methods of how such instruments are designed, diagnosed for faults and functionality, and modified for improvement. The philosophical goal is the analysis and modelling of problem solving strategies in scientific research.

The first section of the article will focus on the philosophical goal, whereas in the remaining article we will deal with the details of the methods of automatic classification which have been selected and refined for the application to an astronomical survey.

2 Methodological aspects

The goal of the project *methodology of scientific research strategies* in philosophy of science is the analysis and modelling of problem solving strategies in scientific research. Such analysis requires the study of either historical cases of scientific discovery or of current research. Either have specific difficulties to solve: in historical case studies it is difficult to avoid using retrospective knowledge, and the analysis of current research is difficult to perform, since monitoring problem solving activities requires a drastic selection of such information that is relevant for an understanding of research strategies.

Our philosophical research project aims to develop theories about methods of scientific discovery while participating in research activities of the astronomical project. While the astronomical research is conducted, the methodologists contribute one component for the research instrument, and test predictions about the next strategic steps the astronomers are taking to modify, improve, or apply the research instrument. One member of the astronomical research group (N.C.) documents the various stages of development of the classification techniques in form of written reports. The documentation includes current research goals, decisions between alternative research options and current scientific convictions. On this documentation the methodological analysis will be based.

Current scientific data evaluation techniques are a highly complex blend of theoretical application of classification algorithms, astronomical knowledge and instrumental experience. All such components form a large and complex system of scientific instrumentation that must be controlled and maintained. It has been found that research techniques of such control apply rules of causal reasoning, where the intended functionality, i.e. the classification result of the instrumental system, can be understood as the causal effect and the input data and instrumental components of data analysis as causes for that effect.

The methodological analysis is supported by a computer workbench LINNÉ, which allows a systematic analysis of different classification schemes. It was contributed by the methodologists. In particular the current version of LINNÉ allows to search for the best feature combination, error rate estimation, and visualisation of classification results in a confusion matrix window. It is used for these purposes by the astronomers and will be further extended to support the diagnostic of the classification system.

3 The Hamburg/ESO-Survey

The Hamburg/ESO-Survey (HES) is a quasar survey in the southern hemisphere (Wisotzki et al. (1996)). It is based on objective prism plates taken with a wide-angle telescope at the *European Southern Observatory* (ESO), La Silla, Chile. Each plate corresponds to $5° \times 5° = 25$ square degrees at the sky, i.e. 10×10 full moons fit into one plate. The HES, when completed, will consist of 400 plates, i.e. the total southern hemisphere, excluding the Milky Way.

For the entire survey several million digitised objective prism spectra will have to be processed. Only a small number of them belong e.g. to quasars or other interesting objects. Typical for quasars is a relation of 1 in 5000. The large amount of data obviously can only be treated by automated techniques.

3.1 What are quasars?

Quasars are active galactic nuclei at cosmological distances. They are the intrinsically brightest objects in the universe.

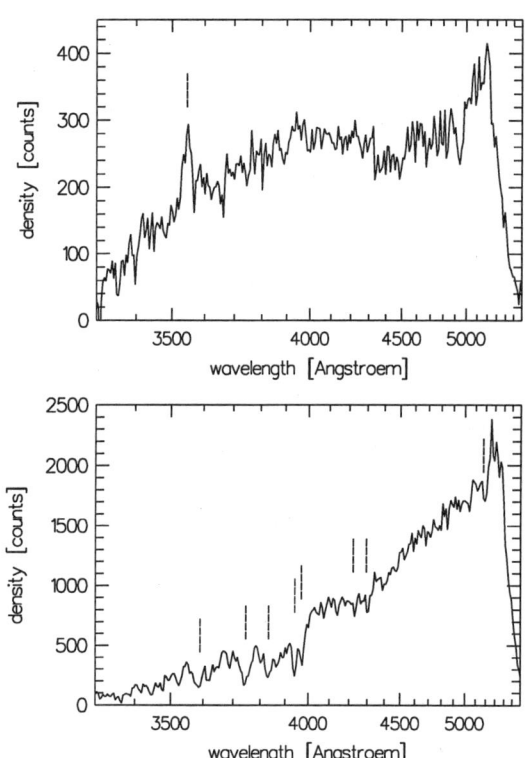

Quasars typically expose the features (cf. spectrum on the right):

Q1 *emission* lines (marked with '|')

Q2 a "blue" continuum

Q3 absorption lines at "random" positions in their spectra.

In contrast to quasars, stars typically have (cf. spectrum on the right):

S1 absorption lines ('|') at *fixed* wavelengths

S2 in most cases a less "blue" continuum then quasars.

4 Scientific interests

In all quasar surveys carried out so far, features Q1 and Q2 have been the main selection criteria for quasar candidates. We call this a *positive selection*, because the objects are searched for by attributes *they have*. Although this selection method has been demonstrated to be very efficient, and in the course of the HES about 1,000 new quasars thus have been found so far, it has been suspected that quasar samples compiled with this method may be *incomplete*. This is mainly because quasars having certain redshifts do not show strong emission lines in the wavelength range covered by the spectra on which the selection is based.

The high resolution of our spectra allows an alternative selection technique.

The basic idea is to identify the "normal" stars, and inspect the remaining set of objects. This set should contain all quasar candidates. With this method, the candidates are selected indirectly, by not having stellar absorption line patterns *(negative selection)*.

Moreover, not only quasars can be found in our data base. There is a variety of rare stellar objects of high scientific interest. We can find, e.g., extremely metal poor halo stars, which belong to the oldest stars in our galaxy and can be used for studies of nucleosynthesis in the early universe.

Last but not least, a large data base of classified "normal" stars can be used for optical identification of objects which have been discovered in other wavelength ranges (radio, infrared, X-ray, etc.).

5 Relevant classification problems

In the table below, the classification problems relevant in the HES are summarised and appropriate decision rules for tackling the problems are given.

problem	decision rule
"simple" classification	Bayes rule
construction of complete samples of rare stellar classes	minimum cost rule
search for objects that do not have stellar absorption line patterns	Bayes rule & reject option

5.1 Estimation of posterior probabilities

For the estimation of posterior probabilities a training set of 671 stellar spectra with high signal-to-noise ratio (S/N) containing 8 classes has been compiled. This was done by comparing the absorption line strengths of the spectra to be classified with the absorption line strengths of standard star spectra. The comparison was done at the computer screen by plotting standard star spectra over each spectrum which had to be classified.

Using Bayes' theorem,

$$p(\omega_i|\vec{x}) = \frac{p(\omega_i)p(\vec{x}|\omega_i)}{\sum\limits_{\forall i} p(\omega_i)p(\vec{x}|\omega_i)},$$

the posterior probabilities $p(\omega_i|\vec{x})$ can be calculated when the class-conditional probabilities $p(\vec{x}|\omega_i)$ have been estimated by means of a learning sample and prior probabilities are determined. The latter has not been done yet so that we assume equal prior probabilities for all stellar classes.

Currently the complete parameter space consists of line strengths of 11 stellar absorption lines which are measured by *template matching*. We assume

	A5–8	A9–F2	F3–6	F7–G0	G1–K0	K1–3	K4–9	SdF
A5–8	27	14	0	0	0	0	0	0
A9–F2	12	48	19	0	0	0	0	0
F3–6	0	7	78	20	2	0	0	10
F7–G0	0	0	22	96	11	0	0	1
G1–K0	0	0	1	2	112	7	0	0
K1–3	0	0	0	0	12	48	15	0
K4–9	0	0	0	0	2	14	54	0
SdF	0	0	12	2	0	0	0	23

Table 1: Confusion matrix of Bayes classification of the learning sample, estimated with the *leaving-one-out* method. In the header row the real classes are given, in the left column the assigned classes. The total rate of misclassification is 185 of 671, or 28 %. Note that nearly all errors are neighbour class errors. The "SdF" is actually a neighbour class of "F3–6".

that the absorption line strengths vectors $\vec{x}$ follow a multivariate normal distribution in all classes i, i.e,

$$p(\vec{x}|\omega_i) = \frac{1}{(2\pi)^{d/2}\sqrt{|\Sigma_i|}} \exp\left\{-\frac{1}{2}(\vec{x} - \vec{\mu}_i)\Sigma_i^{-1}(\vec{x} - \vec{\mu}_i)'\right\}, \quad \forall i. \qquad (1)$$

This assumption has been quantitatively tested by means of univariate Kolmogorov-Smirnov tests and qualitatively by inspection of the feature distributions by eye. It turned out that most features in most classes follow a Gaussian distribution, whereas in some cases the assumption of normality is clearly not valid. It remains to be tested whether the classification results can be improved when non-parametric methods are used for the estimation of the class-conditional probabilities.

5.2 Bayes classification

The confusion matrix of the Bayes classification of the learning sample, using 10 of the 11 features available so far, has been estimated with the leaving-one-out method (cf. Hand (1981)). The total rate of misclassification is 28 %, and the rate of non-neighbour class errors is 1 %. Note that the latter have to be considered for the evaluation of the classifier performance because neighbour class errors only reflect the fact that the classification grid in the learning sample is too dense.

5.3 Minimum cost rule

If one wants to compile a complete sample of a certain class of objects, with moderate contamination of objects of other classes, different types of misclassification have to be weighted differently. Therefore, applying a minimum cost rule in this case is the proper method for classification. The cost or loss L_i for class i is:

$$L_i(\vec{x}) = \sum_{\forall j} c_{ji} p(\omega_j|\vec{x}),$$

where c_{ji} is the *cost factor* for a misclassification of an object of class j to class i, $i \neq j$. Suppose that objects of class A are of interest, and X and Y are any of the other classes. Then three cost factors c_{ij} have to be chosen according to the following pattern:

$$c_{A \to X} \approx 1.0,$$
$$c_{X \to A} \approx 0.2,$$
$$c_{X \to Y} \approx 0.0.$$

Our classification tool LINNÉ allows a convenient iterative, manual adjustment of the loss factors. The error rates are displayed in a confusion matrix window, so that the loss factors can be adjusted according to the classification aim in an iterative trial and error process.

A first test application of the minimum cost rule classification was a search for extremely metal deficient halo stars in a small part of our data base. This already led to the discovery of HE 2319-0852, an extremely metal poor star having [Fe/H] $= -3.5 \pm 0.5$. So far, there are less than 20 objects having [Fe/H] < -3.5 known.

5.4 The problem of noisy spectra

The limiting factor of all astronomical surveys is the stochastic noise N contaminating the signal S received from the survey objects. Fainter sources give lower signals, while on objective prism plates the noise shows only weak dependence of S, so the signal-to-noise ratio (S/N) gets smaller. Theoretically at $S/N = 1$, but in practice much earlier, the signal cannot be analysed anymore.

On the other hand, the number of objects which one can detect in a survey increases rapidly with decreasing signal strength limit $S_{\min}$ to which signals can be analysed. Therefore, we are interested in modelling the low S/N behaviour of spectra on our plates, resulting in a decrease of $S_{\min}$.

We give the following recipe for the treatment of low S/N objects:

1) *Add Gaussian noise stepwise to the learning sample. For a step size of 2, this would give noisy learning samples of e.g. $S/N = 30, 28, \ldots 2$.*

2) *Estimate the parameters of the multivariate normal distribution eqn. (1) independently for all noisy learning samples.*

3) *Classify each object with the appropriate parameter set*, e.g. a spectrum with $S/N = 22$ by using the covariance matrices and mean vectors estimated with the noisy learning sample of $S/N = 22$.

Our tests revealed that the total number of non-neighbour class errors at low S/N is at least by a factor 2 lower when using this technique compared to conventional classification (cf. Fig. 1). For higher S/N, the advantage of the technique is less significant, but the number of misclassification is lower in all cases. The error rates have been estimated in a pseudo *hold out* procedure, i.e. artificial noise has been added independently two times to the original, high S/N learning sample spectra, and after that one noisy sample was taken as training set and the other as test set.

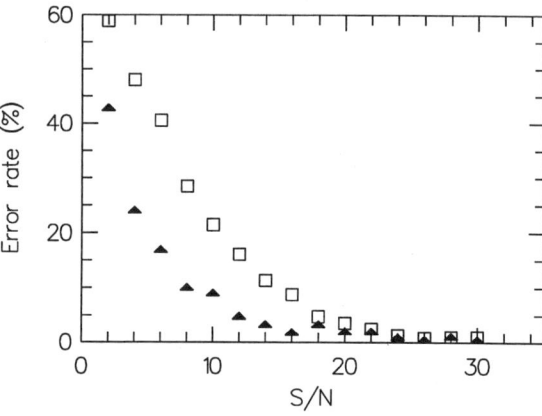

Figure 1: Misclassification rates in percent in dependence of S/N with modelling of the low S/N behaviour of the class-conditional probabilities ('▲') and without modelling of low S/N behaviour ('□').

5.5 Bayes classification with reject option

For the identification of objects not having stellar absorption line patterns, classification with the Bayes rule using a reject criterion is the method of choice. Unfortunately, the "classical" reject criterion, i.e. "Reject an object from classification, if $P(w_i|\vec{x}) < \beta$" does not work in our case. This is so because this criterion is only able to reject objects close to the decision surfaces, whereas we want to reject objects in regions of the parameter space not "covered" by the stellar classes, i.e. objects having negative (= emission lines) or absorption line strengths close to zero.

Therefore we adopted another reject criterion: "Reject an object from classification, if $a.i.(\omega_i; \vec{x}) < \beta$". $a.i.$ is the *atypicality index* suggested by Aitchison et al (1977):

$$a.i.(\omega_i, \vec{x}) = \Gamma\left\{\frac{d}{2}; \frac{1}{2}(\vec{x} - \vec{\mu}_i)\Sigma_i^{-1}(\vec{x} - \vec{\mu}_i)'\right\},$$

where $\Gamma(a;x)$ is the incomplete gamma function and d the number of features used for classification. Using the above reject criterion is of course identical to performing a χ^2 test of the null hypothesis that an object with feature vector $\vec{x}$ belongs to class ω_i at significance level $1 - \beta$.

Bayes classification with the $a.i.$ reject option was applied to a test sample of 203 quasar candidates. The significance level β was adjusted manually by inspecting the distribution of the *a.i.* in the learning sample of stars and in the sample of quasar candidates. β was chosen in a manner were on the one hand only a few quasar candidates were lost and on the other hand the star contamination in the rejected part of the sample was sufficiently low.

The use of the *a.i.* reject option made it possible to compile an almost complete test sample of quasar candidates with only moderate contamination of stars. Only 1 of 203 quasar candidates was not rejected, and the mean star contamination rate is 11 %. Here, again, the results are significantly better when the low S/N behaviour is modelled: The mean star contamination is $\approx 50\,\%$ smaller compared to the conventional method.

6 Conclusions

In the methodological part of this paper, we have presented a concept for the analysis and modelling of problem solving strategies used in an currently running astronomical research project.

In the second part, we have shown that the application of proper methods of automatic classification to a large digital astronomical survey has the potential of producing scientific results of highest interest. This potential has been demonstrated by various tests and some preliminary results:

1) Bayes classification of the learning sample led to a non-neighbour class error rate of 1 % and a total error rate below 30 %.

2) Modelling the low S/N behaviour of the survey spectra led to a highly improved misclassification rate of spectra of faint objects.

3) Bayes classification with application of the *atypicality index* reject option of a test sample of quasar candidates led to the "'rediscovery"' of almost all quasar candidates and moderate star contamination of the sample.

We currently apply the classification methods presented to the large HES data base of digital spectra.

This work was supported by Deutsche Forschungsgemeinschaft under grants DFG-Re 353/40-1 and DFG-Gr 968/3-1.

References

AITCHSION, J., HABBEMA, J. & KAY, J. (1977): A Critical Comparison of Two Methods of Statistical Discrimination, *Applied Statistics, 26(1), 15–25.*

HAND, D. (1981): Discrimination and Classification. Wiley & Sons, New York.

WISOTZKI, L., et al. (1996), The Hamburg/ESO survey for bright QSOs. I. Survey design and candidate selection procedure. *Astronomy & Astrophysics Supplement Series, 115, 227–233.*

An Approach to Modelling Directional and Betweenness Data

Hubert Feger[1]
Department of Psychology
Free University of Berlin

Abstract: A model is introduced to analyze and represent spatially either directly obtained or derived judgments expressing directions in space or betwennness relations among objects. For the two-dimensinal case the construction rules tofind a spatial representation of the object points are given in detail. A small example illustrates the procedure. Consistency tests are reported which allow a differentiated analysis of this kind of cognitive structure. The three-dimensional case is discussed briefly. Finally, it is illustrated how ratings, rankings, and co-occurrence informations are transformed to betweenness data.

1 Purpose and scope of the model

Spatial orientation is based on several information systems. One information base is knowledge of distances between objects. The (ranks of such) distances can be analyzed by MDS and may lead to a "cognitive map" (Tolman 1948, Chase 1986). An other information system is based on directional knowledge which may be retrieved in various ways. We may ask a person to provide judgments from a specified reference point or imagine to be at a reference point and then provide directional judgments. The person may draw a sketch or report verbally the relative direction of several objects as seen from a reference point. The combination of directional and distance information describes the spatial orientation of a person in a more complete and differentiated way. It allows to identify biases, errors, and inconsistencies in detail (Feger 1991, 1996). Therefore, the directional model may be used to study the development of spatial orientation in children,evaluate the effects of training, and detect very early symptoms of mental disturbances.

The purpose of this approach is to identify the location of objects A, B, ..., N using judgments reported from reference points $x_1, x_2, ..., x_m$ if a reference point is located outside of a configuration of object points, or $y_1, y_2, ..., y_m$ for reference points located inside a configuration of object points. The location of a reference point and "inside" and "outside" of a configuration of points will be defined for spaces of a given dimensionality. In the one-dimensional case (cars in a file, products in a queue, life events in careers) we write Ax_1 for the report that A is on one side of x_1, x_1B for B on the other side of x_1, Ax_1B for x_1 between A and B. The location of a reference point is defined as uniquely as possible if one knows which objects are located on both sides (including the empty set for one side of y). The location of an object point A is determined if one knows on which side of any x or y it is located. From observations like Ax one can derive a partial or complete

2 The two-dimensional case

2.1 The fundamental idea

The analytical unit of the two-dimensional case is the triple of points, creating a triangle on the plane. In Fig.1, these points are A, B, C. A line through a pair of these points, A, B, is called the *direction line (AB)*. The direction lines create six open regions and a closed one. The closed region is the area of the triangle ABC. All points in a region are equivalent with respect to the observation of betweenness relations between the three points defining the triangle. In Fig.1, the betweenness judgments originating from the reference points in the open (outer) regions are given as

$x_1 : ACB$,   if form the reference point x_1 the object C is located between A and B with respect to a clockwise ordering

$x_2 : CAB$,   if form the reference point x_2 the object A is located between C and B with respect to the clockwise ordering CAB

...   ...

$x_6 : ABC$,   if form the reference point x_6 the objects are located in the clockwise order ABC .

Note that crossing a direction line interchanges the sequential position of exactly those points which define this direction line. E.g., the regions of $x_1 : ACB$ and $x_6 : ABC$ are adjacent, separated by the direction line (BC).

From a reference point y_1 within the closed region we see the other objects in the clockwise order ACB, or CBA or BAC respectively and note this by $y_1(ACB)$. A difference in *handedness* exists, $(ABC) \neq (ACB)$; thus we derive from (ABC): ABC and BCA and CAB.

2.2 An example

As an example for the two-dimensional case, we test whether the spatial knowledge of a person can be represented as a cognitive map. A student provided from memory his distance and betweenness judgments on the position of 5 German cities: B = Berlin, C = Cologne, H = Hamburg, K = Kassel, and M = Munich. The distance judgments are provided in Tab.1, as km above, and as ranks below the main diagonal (1 = shortest distance).

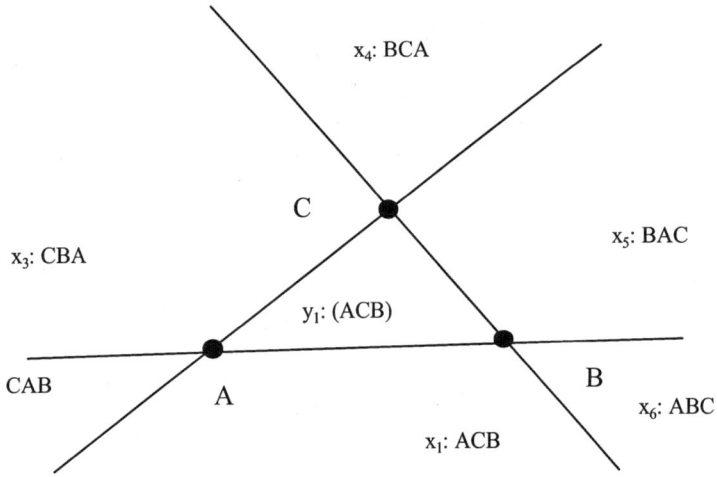

Figure 1: Betweenness judgements with respect to three points

Table 1: Distances and their ranks between German cities

	H	B	K	C	M
H	-	300	400	460	700
B	3	-	250	360	600
K	5	2	-	160	450
C	7	4	1	-	570
M	10	9	6	8	-

Betweenness judgments were collected by asking the student to think that he is located in one of the cities and looks at three other cities. First we ask the student to produce a sketch. Second he is asked to report the order of the other objects (cities) appearing while turning arround clockwise. We obtained the betweenness judgments reported in Tab.2.

Table 2: Betweenness judgments for German cities

from B	KCH	MCH	MKC	MKH
from C	HBK	HBM	BKM	HKM
from H	BKC	BMC	BKM	MKC
from K	CHB	(BMC)	HBM	(MCH)
from M	CHB	CKB	KHB	CKH

2.3 Construction rules in the two-dimensional case

To *derive the position of object points in the plane* we realize (see Feger 1994) that two topologically different configurations of four points in the plane exist. Allowing all possible labellings of the points we find three different quadrilaterals and four different triangles with an inner point (if handedness is taken into account, the number of forms is 14). The notation is A(BCD) for a triangle BCD with A as the inner point, and (ABCD) for a quadrilateral with the diagonals AC and BD. The task is to derive from betweenness judgments which forms are compatible with these judgments. Throughout the paper we assume that all points can be seen and are not obscured or hidden.

We will now provide rules how to test whether a configuration of four points has a specific labelled form. These rules refer either to judgments on three points (if at least one reference point is identical with an object point) or on four points, and they are specified for reference points from the outside of a configuration or from the inside.

Rule 1 (3 points, from outside): *If $x_1 = A$, $x_2 = B$, $x_3 = C$, $x_4 = D$ and if it is reported to see from $x_1 : BCD$, $x_2 : CDA, x_3 : DAB, x_4 : ABC$ then we derive the configuration $(ABCD)$ and note this by "$\to ABCD$".*

In Tab.2 we observe for the quadruple B, C, H, K, $x_1 = B : KCH$, $x_2 = K : CHB$, $x_3 = C : HBK$, and $x_4 = H : BKC$, then we conclude the configuration (BKCH) exists. Correspondingly, for B, C, H, M we derive (BMCH).

Rule 2 (3 points, one point from inside): If $x_1 = B, x_2 = C, x_3 = D, y_1 = A$ and if it is reported to see from $x_1 : CAD$, $x_2 : DAB, x_3 : BAC$, $y_1 : (BCD) \to A(BCD)$.

In Tab.2 for B, C, K, M we observe $x_1 = B : MKC$, $x_2 = M : CKB$, $x_3 = C : BKM$, $y_1 = K : (BMC) \to K(BMC)$. In the same way we derive K(CHM).

For B, H, K, M, neither rule 1 nor rule 2 lead to the identification of a form. If we allow for *error,* we search for a solution with the smallest number of (smallest) changes in the data to obtain a solution. Here, the raw data are the betweenness judgments in Tab.2. One change of a judgment, from M:KHB to M:HKB is sufficient to derive K(BHM). This adjustment was found by visual inspection. A general algorithm to find a solution, representing the data consistently, optimal with respect to the the smallest number of changes in the data, requires a special publication.

Rule 3 (3 points, all from inside): We realize - see Fig.2 - that any y_m, $m = 1...4$, is located in two of the four triangles, each of which is defined by three object points. Therefore, each y must report two judgments on three points with a turn-around (XYZ). Rule 3 is formulated with respect to Fig.2. If it is reported to see from $y_1 : ABC, y_1 : (ABD), y_1 : (ACD), y_1 : BCD \to (ABCD)$.

In Tab.2 we find $y_1 = K$ with CHB, HBM leading here to (BMCH) because we also observe (BMC) and (MCH); a representation is given in Fig 3.

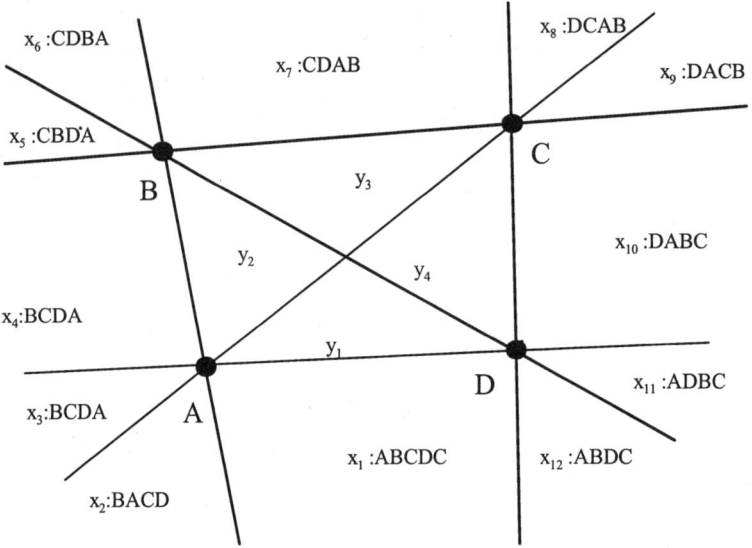

Figure 2: Judgements on four points in the position (ABCD)

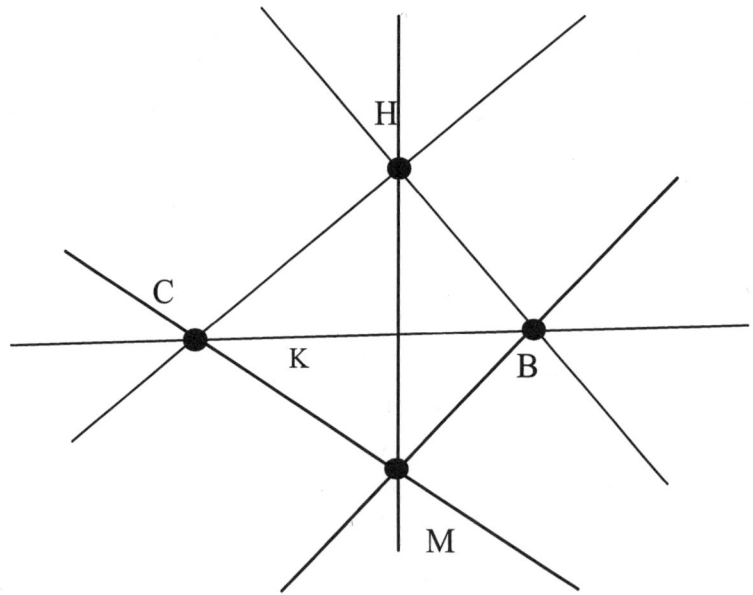

Figure 3: Judgements of y=K

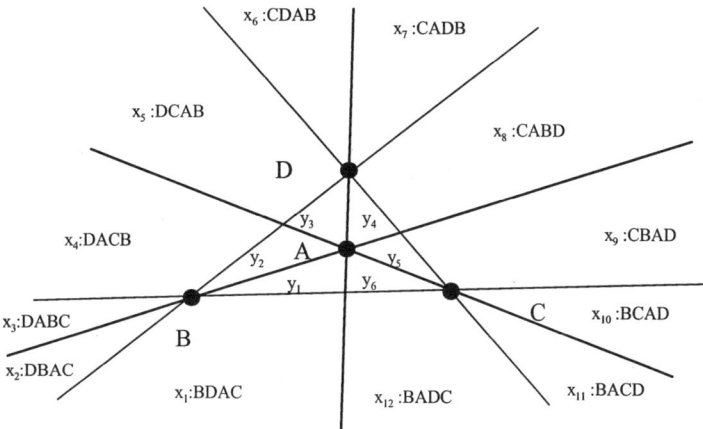

Figure 4: Judgements with respect to four points, triangle with an inner point

Rule 4 (3 points, all from inside): As Fig.4 illustrates, each of the six $y_m, m = 1...6$, is located in two triangles defined by three object points. Always, one triangle is the one with the inner point. With respect to Fig.4 we formulate: If $y_1 : (ACB), y_1 : BDA, y_1 : DAC, y_1 : (BDC) \rightarrow A(BDC)$. In Tab.2, there exists no reference point satisfying the conditions of this rule.

We now turn to judgements on four points. They may be provided directly as a seriation of four object points by a person or an other data source, or the judgment may be derived from four consistent judgments on three points (see below). The usefulness of the four point judgments is apparent in studies with only a limited number of reference points which might even be selectively sampled. Thus, the four point judgments may provide new information, or add redundancy necessary for consistency tests.

Rule 5 (4 points, outside, see Fig.2): If for all x, neither A and C, nor B and D occur together as a pair either at the start or at the end of the reported four point seriation then we conclude the configuration $(ABCD)$ exists.

From the data in Tab.2, we derive four point judgments by testing the consistency (see below) of the three point judgments given from one reference point. E. g., using one of the axiom systems for the betweenness relation, we derive for B the seriation MKCH or B:MKCH. Furthermore, we derive C: HBKM and M: CKHB. K is apparently not a reference point from the outside of B, C, H, M. The judgments of H are inconsistent. Not enough judgments exist to apply rule 5 to the example; to attain the uniqueness one could have used more cities etc. as reference points which are not used as object points.

Rule 6 (4 points, outside, see Fig.4): If for all x, A appears neither as the first nor as the last element $\rightarrow A(BCD)$.

In the example, this is true for K in B: MKCH, C: HBKM, and M: CKHB.

Rule 7 (4 points, inside, see Fig.2). This rule is identical with rule 5 applied to consistent seriations obtained from the inside.

E. g., for y_1 in Fig.2 we derive ABC, (ABD), (ACD), BCD. Realizing that (ABD) is equivalent to ABD or BDA or DAB, and (ACD) to ACD or CDA or DAC, we derive from ABC, ABD, ACD, and BCD the consistent four point seriation ABCD from inside judgments only.

Rule 8 (4 points, inside, see Fig.4): If for all $y_1, ..., y_2$ rule 6 is valid then we conclude the configuration $A(BCD)$ exists.

2.4 Consistency tests in the two-dimensional case

We categorize the consistency tests into three groups, pertaining to (1) the relations between judgments on three points, (2) on four points, and (3) the consistency of the quadruple forms with an overall configuration of all points. In applications, the various consistency tests may be used together to identify errors and biases in the directional orientation system. We first analyze the consistency of the three point judgments with a seriation of four points, using the transitivity of the betweenness relation.

Test 1 (3 points to 4, outside). For any x: If $x_1 : ABC$, $x_1 : ABD$, $x_1 : ACD$, $x_1 : BCD \rightarrow x_1 : ABCD$ (see comments on rule 5).

Test 2 (3 points to 4, inside). For any y: If $y_1 : ABC$, $y_1 : (ABD)$, $y_1 : (ACD)$, $y_1 : BCD \rightarrow y_1 : ABCD$.

For visual, acoustical, and haptical perception these tests warrant a coherent sequence of objects in space if the eye, ear or hand moves around in a turn from one object to the next. The second group of tests insists that four objects form exactly one configuration, no matter from which reference point they are judged.

Test 3 (4 points, outside): For any pair of adjacent reference points x_1, x_2; x_2, x_3; ... ; x_{11}, x_{12}; x_{12}, x_1 and any quadruple A, B, C, D, the for point seriation judgments differ by the interchange of exactly two point adjacent in the seriation. - E. g., in Fig.2, $x_1 : ABCD$ differs from $x_2 : BACD$ by the interchange of A and B, indicating that the direction line (AB) is crossed.

Test 4 (4 points, inside): For any pair of adjacent reference points y_1, y_2, test 3 is valid.

Test 5 (4 points, comparison of forms): For every quadruple A, B, C, D, the form(s) resulting from all x must be the same form(s) as those resulting from all y. (The plural is used because incomplete observations may result in more than one form.)

If the consistency test listed thus far are all passed by a quadruple of object points, and if the observations are redundant enough to apply the construction rules, then one or more forms of a configuration of four object points exist. Then we proceed to the next task:

Test 6 - to analyze whether these forms fit together. We have published a constructive procedure for this test (Feger 1994, chapt. 3.2; Feger, under review). A special case of this procedure is informative for our example. When introducing rule 1, we found for B, C, H, K, the form (BKCH). This part of the analysis did not use any judgments from x = M. However, these judgments can (see Tab.2) consistently be arranged as the seriation M: CKHB. As one aspect of the configuration, this seriation must be consistent with (BKCH) which indeed is the case.

As an additional test, one may compare the subjective representational structure with an objective standard, if it is available, like a geographic map. One may then search for *mistakes* which might indicate that a learning process did not (sufficiently) take place.

2.5 The representation of the data of the example

When illustrating the rules and tests, we collected the following information on the configuration of the cities: 1. (BKCH), 2. = 3. (BMCH), 4. K(BMC), 5. K(CHM), 6. some inconsistent judgments on B, H, K, M, 7. B: MKCH, 8. C: HBKM, 9. M: CKHB. Using those procedures mentioned as test 6, all information - except one three point judgment H: BKM - can be combined to yield the representation of all object points which is identical with Fig.3. Looking at a geographical map, K should be above the direction line (BC). To compare the solution in Fig.3 with the distance data in Tab.1, we first determine the set of admissible forms for every quadruple from distance ranks (see Feger 1994). These forms are reported in Tab.3.

Tab.3: Admissible quadruple forms derived from distance ranks

	.1	.2	.3	.4
1	(BCKH)	B(CHK)	(BHCK)	
2	(BHCM)	(BCMH)	B(CHM)	
3	(BCKM)	(BKCM)	(BCMK)	K(BCM)
4	(BHKM)	(BHMK)	B(HKM)	K(BHM)
5	(CHKM)	(CKHM)	(CHMK)	K(CHM)

From these admissible forms several solutions can be derived. The solution in Fig.3 can be derived from the forms 1.3, 2.1, 3.4, 4.1 and 5.4. The agreement between the distance and direction information may support the interpretation of Fig.3 as a "cognitive map" and allow *to predict* judgments if more cities are added as object points serving as a cross-validation.

3 Notes on the three-dimensional case

Let the points defining the tetrahedron be A, B, C, D. A plane is defined by three points, e. g., A, B, C. Then *a reference point is located* either at the same side as D which is the inner side, or this reference point is located in the half space without D, which is the outer side. The position of a reference point is determined as uniquely as possible relative to a tetrahedron, if it is known with respect to each of the four planes whether this reference point is located on the same side as the point not defining this plane, or on the other side.

In contrast to the analysis of distance data, *chirality* can be identified. One plane of a tetrahedron, say the one defined by A, B, C, can show the orientation (ABC) as seen from the inside of the tetrahedron. Then the orientation (ACB) is seen from the outside. The orientation of all other planes is fixed if the orientation of *one* plane is fixed.

Given a tetrahedron with the points A, B, C, D, and orientation (ABC) from the outside, there exist 15 different regions for reference points. One of them is the inner space (volume) of the tetrahedron, all others are on the outside. Four regions exist on the outer sides of the four planes, four on the tops, and six on the edges. The judgments to be reported by a person located at a reference point in this specific tetrahedron are

from the inside: (ACB), (ABD), (ADC), (BCD);
from the tops: A(BCD), B(ADC), C(ABD), D(ACB);
from the outer sides: A(BDC), B(ACD), C(ADB), D(ABC);
from the edges with the line AB: (ADBC), line AC: (ABCD), line AD: (ACDB), line BC: (ABDC), BD: (ADCB), and line CD:(ACBD).

Moving in a three-dimensional space means crossing planes. Every time a plane is intersected, the perceived topological configuration of the points is changed, including a change in the handedness of at least one triangle.

For five points A, ..., E in a three-dimensional space, two different configurations exist (disregarding handedness for the moment). The configuration either is a tetrahedron (e. g., with B, C, D, E, as defining points) with an inner point (A), written A(BCDE), or it is a double tetrahedron with one common plane (say, defined by B, C, D) and two poles or tops A and E, written AE(BCD). To identify the configuration, one analyzes judgments from all or some reference points with respect to the perceived (or inferred) configuration.

To confirm the assumption that the configuration is E(ABCD) one has to observe from reference points on the outer sides only such betweenness relations which lead to E(ABC), E(ABD), E(ACD), and E(BCD). To confirm the assumption that the configuration is AE(BCD) one must observe that no triangle of points A, E, X, exists (with X either B or C or D) with the two remaining points as inner points. The consistency test for $N > 5$ points now uses all quintuples of object points on every sextuple. The position of three points relative to a plane is tested, e. g., with respect to the plane defined by A, B, C. Then the statements (1) D is on one side, E on the other side of this plane, (2) D is on one side and F on the other side, require that E and F are on the same side of the plane. This testing procedure is - as in the two-dimensional case - constructive.

4 Transformation of ratings, rankings, and co-occurrence data to betweenness information

We assume that rating, ranking, or co-occurrence information is available on N objects. The purpose of the transformation then is to determine for every triple of points A, B, C, which object is between the other two. The assumption on which the transformation will be based is: A seriation of A, B, C, (i. e., A BC or ACB or BAC or their mirror images) reveals a betweenness relation if the data of every data source show a *single peaked distribution* with monotonic descent in both directions (or in only one direction if the peak is located either most to the left or most to the right) over this seriation. E. g., for ratings or polytomous items with categories 1, ..., 4 in their natural order, the following distributions are consistent to the order ABC, given that "1" is the "highest" (e. g., most favorable, best performance etc.) category: 1-2-3, 2-1-4, 3-3-1, 1-1-3, etc., but not 2-3-1, 1-4-1, etc. because they show a dip rather than a peak. For rankings, the same considerations apply.

If the data are dichotomous of the kind "exists = 1" and "does not exist = 0", the same patterns as in one-dimensional parallelogram analysis are acceptable. For the seriation ABC the (partial) patterns 110 and 011 are acceptable while 101 is not, and all other patterns carry no information for the order of this triple of objects. For polytomous items with unordered categories the same principle is used: A seriation of 3 (or more) objects is acceptable if one observes for every data source either xxy or zvv but not uwu. This idea can also be used for co-occurrence data with unordered qualitative attributes. After such a transformation the model of this paper may be applied.

References

CHASE, W. G. (1986): Visual information processing. In: K. R. Boff, L. Kaufman, and J. P. Thomas (eds.): *Handbook of Perception and Human Performance.* Vol.. II. Wiley, New York 28—1-28—71.

FEGER, H. (1991): Depth perception in pictures. *Medienpsychologie, 3,* 124–145.

FEGER, H. (1994): Structure Analysis of Co-occurrence Data. Shaker, Aachen.

FEGER, H. (1996): Positions of objects in space. Their definition and their effects on experience and behavior. In: W. Battmann and S. Dutke (eds.): *Processes of the Molar Regulation of Behavior.* Pabst Science Publishers, Lengerich 55–72.

FEGER, H. (under review). Some applications of FPA in the social and behavioral sciences. In: H. Feger and M. Brehm (eds.): *New Developments in Feature Pattern Analysis* (manuscript available from the author).

FISHBURN, P.C. (1985): Interval Orders and Interval Graphs. Wiley, New York.

TOLMAN, E. C. (1948): Cognitive maps in rats and men. *Psychological Review, 55*, 189–208.

The Application of Random Coincidence Graphs for Testing the Homogeneity of Data

E. Godehardt[1], J. Jaworski[2], D. Godehardt[1]

[1] Klinik für Thorax- und Kardiovaskular-Chirurgie, Heinrich Heine-Universität, Postfach 10 10 07, D-40001 Düsseldorf, Germany

[2] Wydział Matematyki i Informatyki, Uniwersytet im. Adama Mickiewicza, ul. Matejki 48/49, PL-60-769 Poznań, Poland

Abstract: Graph-theoretic classification models provide us with probability models which can be used to study the structure of a data set. In models of random interval graphs or, generally, random coincidence graphs, points are drawn "at random" and joined by lines if their mutual distances are smaller than a threshold d. This is exactly the procedure of finding linkage clusters. We present exact and asymptotic results for properties of those random graphs, especially for the properties that the expected numbers of isolated edges and of isolated vertices remain positive finite as the total number of vertices grows. These properties can serve as test statistics for testing the homogeneity in a data set; they can be used to derive tests for goodness of fit as well.

1 Introduction

Graph-theoretical models are useful when the structure of a data set has to be explored. The similarity matrix induces a labeled graph with the n objects to be clustered as vertices $1, \ldots, n$; two vertices are connected by an edge if and only if the corresponding objects are similar enough. Using the concept of random graphs, we can derive test statistics to test the randomness of the clusters found. This means that we look whether properties found in the graph obtained from the data are likely under the assumption of randomness in the process of drawing vertices and edges.

In medical or biological research, we often deal with quantitative data from the q-dimensional space $\mathcal{R}^q$ with some metric which implies the similarity structure in the data set. Two vertices i and j of the graph generated from the data then are connected by an edge if and only if the mutual distance $d_{i,j}$ between the corresponding data points $\vec{x}_i$ and $\vec{x}_j$ is not greater than a user-defined level d. Every such graph for a distance level d is called a *coincidence graph* (Hafner (1972)). Clusters, which are defined as special subgraphs of such a coincidence graph constructed from the data at a level d are called *clusters at level d* (Bock (1996), Godehardt (1995)).

Bock (1996) describes probability models which can be used for testing the homogeneity within a data set against the alternative of a possible cluster structure. One of them is based on the classical concepts of random graphs, the uniform $\mathcal{G}_{n,N}$-model (Erdős (1961)), and the binomial $\mathcal{G}_{n,p}$-model

(Gilbert (1959)). In both models, the edges are drawn independently and at random, therefore, the triangle inequality for metric data is violated. Moreover, usually the data points are drawn at random and not the distances, or edges as in these models. Therefore, probability models for *random coincidence graphs* are more appropriate for testing the hypothesis of homogeneity in a metric data set than the other two.

Results for the general model of random coincidence graphs are rather cumbersome to derive. Moreover, many of them are of theoretical interest only, since the formulas given, rarely can be used for numerical computations. This holds even for the simplest case, that is if we assume that the data set $\{\vec{x}_1, \ldots, \vec{x}_n\}$ is a realisation of n independent random variables $\vec{X}_1, \ldots, \vec{X}_n$, uniformly distributed in the unit cube (Hafner (1972)). Fortunately, in this case the l-th coordinates of these n vectors generate an interval graph ($1 \leq l \leq q$), and these q interval graphs are independent. This leads to the model of random multigraphs, consisting of several independent graphs as layers.

2 Random Interval Graphs

Throughout this chapter, we restrict ourselves to the study of unit or proper interval graphs, where the vertices are points from the unit interval $[0; 1]$. The following definition as well as the results for random unit interval graphs can be easily generalized to interval graphs on $[a; b]$.

Uniform model $\mathcal{IG}_{n,d}$. *Let $X_1, \ldots, X_n$ be n independent random variables uniformly distributed on the unit interval. A random graph $\mathcal{IG}_{n,d}$ is defined by the vertex set $\mathcal{V} = \{1, \ldots, n\}$, corresponding to the set of these n random variables, and by the edge set $\mathcal{E} = \{(i,j) : |X_i - X_j| \leq d\}$ where $0 < d < 1$. For the n realisations $x_1, \ldots, x_n$ of the random variables, we get a proper or unit interval graph as realisation of $\mathcal{IG}_{n,d}$.*

This definition implies that besides the graph-theoretical properties and characteristics, we can study properties related to the "geometry" of the vertices, that is their realisations $x_1, x_2, \ldots, x_n$, for example the "length" of a connected subgraph.

Let $I_{i,j}$ be the indicator for the presence of an edge between two vertices i and j, and let $I_{i,i} = 0$ for $1 \leq i \leq n$. One can check that for $i \neq j$,

$$\Pr(I_{i,j} = 1) = \Pr((i,j) \in \mathcal{E}) = \Pr(|X_i - X_j| \leq d) = 2d - d^2.$$

Let $U_i = \sum_{j=1}^{n} I_{i,j}$ be the number of vertices connected to a vertex i, that is the degree of this vertex, and let $E = \frac{1}{2} \sum_{i=1}^{n} U_i$ be the number of edges in $\mathcal{IG}_{n,d}$. While n is called the *order* of a graph, E is its *size*. As in the $\mathcal{G}_{n,p}$-model, in the $\mathcal{IG}_{n,d}$-model the size is a random variable. Obviously, the edges of random interval graphs are not independent. For small d, this dependence is not strong. Thus, one can expect some similarities with $\mathcal{G}_{n,p}$ when the edge probabilities $p \sim 2d - d^2$ are small enough. Generally, however, both models differ in many aspects, even for small d.

Other models of random interval graphs are very similar to the model above. In Scheinerman (1988), for example, the distance levels are random variables themselves; n vertices are uniformly distributed on the unit interval, together with n intervals with the chosen vertices as their centers and with their lengths identically and independently uniformly distributed on $[0; r]$. We can define our model in a similar manner with fixed, identical lengths of the intervals. The problems considered here are also related to the theory of random clumps (Kennedy (1976)), coverage problems (Solomon (1976)), and k-spacings (Barbour (1992)).

2.1 Exact Results for Random Interval Graphs

In this part, we state exact results concerning the distributions of some random variables which describe the structure of random interval graphs: the number C_n^k of components of order k, the number C_n^1 of isolated vertices, and the degree U_i of a given vertex. Furtheron, the distribution of the total number C_n of components is given. Conditioning on the events that the point x_i lies either in the inner $[d; 1-d]$ or at the border $[0; d] \cup [1-d; 1]$ of the unit interval, one can derive the following fact about the degree distribution of a given vertex.

Theorem 1. *For a random interval graph $\mathcal{IG}_{n,d}$ with distance level d, the distribution of the degree of any vertex i is given by*

$$\Pr(U_i = l) = \binom{n-1}{l} \left\{ (2d)^l (1-2d)^{n-l} + 2 \int_d^{2d} y^l (1-y)^{n-1-l} dy \right\}$$

for $l = 0, 1, \ldots, n-1$. •

The following three theorems have been proved in Godehardt (1996). First, the factorial moments of the number C_n^k of components of order k are given.

Theorem 2. *The t-th factorial moment for the number of connected components of order k in a random interval graph $\mathcal{IG}_{n,d}$ is given by*

$$\mathrm{E}_t\left(C_n^k\right) = t! \sum_{j=j_0}^{t} \binom{n-kt-1}{t-j}\binom{t+1}{j}$$
$$\times \sum_{i=0}^{(k-1)t} \binom{(k-1)t}{i} (-1)^i (1 - (2t-j+i)d)_+^n$$

with $j_0 = \max\{0, t(k+1) - n + 1\}$, $a_+ = a$ for positive a and $a_+ = 0$ otherwise. •

For $k = 1$, this leads to the distribution of the number of isolated vertices.

Theorem 3. The distribution of the number C_n^1 of isolated vertices in a random interval graph $\mathcal{IG}_{n,d}$ is given by

$$\Pr\left(C_n^1 = r\right) = \sum_{k=r}^{\min\{n-1,\lfloor 1/d \rfloor\}} \binom{k}{r} (-1)^{k-r}$$

$$\times \sum_{j=j_0}^{k} \binom{n-k-1}{k-j} \binom{k+1}{j} (1-(2k-j)d)^n$$

$$+ \binom{n}{r} (-1)^{n-r} (1-(n-1)d)_+^n$$

with $j_0 = \max\{0, 2k - \lfloor 1/d \rfloor, 2k - n + 1\}$, where $a_+ = a$ for positive a and $a_+ = 0$ otherwise. For $1 - td > 0$, the t-th factorial moment is given by

$$\mathrm{E}_t\left(C_n^1\right) = t! \sum_{j=j_0}^{t} \binom{n-t-1}{t-j} \binom{t+1}{j} (1-(2t-j)d)^n$$

with $j_0 = \max\{0, 2t - \lfloor 1/d \rfloor, 2t - n + 1\}$, otherwise it vanishes. ●

The distribution of the number C_n of components is given in the next theorem. From this, the case $C_n = 1$ gives the probability that a random interval graph $\mathcal{IG}_{n,d}$ is completely connected (Godehardt (1996)).

Theorem 4. Let C_n be the number of components in a random interval graph $\mathcal{IG}_{n,d}$. The distribution of this random variable is given by

$$\Pr(C_n = r) = \sum_{j=r-1}^{\min\{n-1,\lfloor 1/d \rfloor\}} \binom{n-1}{j} \binom{j}{r-1} (-1)^{j+r-1} (1-jd)^n$$

for $r = 1, 2, \ldots, \min\{n-1, \lfloor 1/d \rfloor\} + 1$. The t-th factorial moment for the number of components diminished by 1 is $\mathrm{E}_t(C_n - 1) = (n-1)_t (1-td)^n$ whenever $1 - td > 0$, and vanishes otherwise. ●

2.2 Asymptotic Properties

We want to uncover the "typical structures" of random interval graphs at different stages of d. These structures can be described by limit theorems for $n \to \infty$ and $d = d(n)$. Thus, a typical structure of an interval graph at the distance level given by the function $d(n)$ is a property which holds almost surely, that is with probability tending to 1 as $n \to \infty$. We are interested in "threshold functions" for certain properties of $\mathcal{IG}_{n,d}$. Here, by a threshold function for a given property $\mathcal{A}$ we mean a function $d^*(n, c)$ such that, for $n \to \infty$, $\Pr(\mathcal{A}) \to 0$ as $c \to -\infty$ or $c \to 0$, $\Pr(\mathcal{A}) \to 1$ as $c \to \infty$, and $\Pr(\mathcal{A})$ is bounded away from 0 and 1 as c is a constant or c is a positive constant, respectively (Erdős (1961)).

In this paper, we restrict ourselves to direct consequences of the theorems on the exact results of the previous part. More complete studies of asymptotic characteristics of $\mathcal{IG}_{n,d}$ has been given in Godehardt (1996). First, we look at the distribution of the number of components of given order.

Theorem 5. *For sequences $(\mathcal{IG}_{n,d})_{n\to\infty}$ of random interval graphs with $d(n) = \left\{ (c + o(1))/n^k \right\}^{1/(k-1)}$, the distribution of the number C_n^k of components of order k tends to a Poisson distribution with parameter c. For such functions of distance levels and n big enough, interval graphs $\mathcal{IG}_{n,d}$ almost surely do not contain components of any order bigger than k ($k \geq 2$).* •

As a direct consequence of this theorem, for $k = 2$, that means for distance levels $d(n) = (c + o(1))/n^2$, random interval graphs consist almost surely of isolated vertices and a small number of components of order 2 (isolated edges) with no bigger components if n is large enough. Thus, we get for sequences $(\mathcal{IG}_{n,d})_{n\to\infty}$ of random intersection graphs with distance levels as above that the distribution of the number E of edges tends to a Poisson distribution with parameter c, a result which, like the following two theorems, already has been proved in Godehardt (1995).

Theorem 6. *For sequences $(\mathcal{IG}_{n,d})_{n\to\infty}$ of random interval graphs with $d(n) = (c + o(1))/(2n)$, the distribution of the degree U_i of a vertex i tends to a Poisson distribution with parameter c.* •

Theorem 7. *For sequences $(\mathcal{IG}_{n,d})_{n\to\infty}$ of random interval graphs with $d(n) = (\log(n) + c + o(1))/(2n)$, the distribution of the number C_n^1 of isolated vertices tends to a Poisson distribution with parameter e^{-c}. For $d(n) = (\log(n) + c + o(1))/n$, the distribution of the number $C_n - 1$ of components diminished by one, tends to a Poisson distribution with parameter e^{-c}.* •

Note that we do not expect any isolated vertex when the number of components remains finite if n is big enough.

3 Random Coincidence Graphs

In Godehardt (1993, 1994), a multigraph model has been described which is useful to outline clusters in q-dimensional data. We give the definition for metric data only, that means for the case that the similarity matrix is based on distance functions.

Definition. *Let $\{\vec{x}_1, \ldots, \vec{x}_n\}$ be n vectors from the R^q. For each $l = 1, \ldots, q$, define an interval graph $\mathcal{IG}_l$ by the vertex set $\{1, \ldots, n\}$, representing the values $\{x_{1,l}, \ldots, x_{n,l}\}$ of the l-th coordinates of the vectors, and by the edge set $\mathcal{E}_l = \{(i,j)_l : |x_{i,l} - x_{j,l}| \leq d_l\}$. Let these q interval graphs be superposed in q layers. This gives an undirected, completely labelled multigraph $\mathcal{MG}_{q,n,(d_1,\ldots,d_q)} = (\mathcal{V}, \mathcal{E})$, where each vertex $i \in \mathcal{V}$ represents the* point $\vec{x}_i = (x_{i,1}, \ldots, x_{i,q})^T$, and with edge set $\mathcal{E} = \mathcal{E}_1 \cup \ldots \cup \mathcal{E}_q$. Every subset $\mathcal{E}_{i,j} = \{(i,j)_1, \ldots, (i,j)_q\} \cap \mathcal{E} \neq \emptyset$ of edges joining the vertices i and j, is called a connection between i and j. Let s and u be two natural numbers with $1 \leq s \leq u \leq q$. If $s \leq |\mathcal{E}_{i,j}| \leq u$ holds (that means if at least s and at most u edges link the vertices i and j together) then $\mathcal{E}_{i,j}$ is called an (s,u)-connection; for $u = q$, we speak of an s-connection. •

With this definition, we define for natural numbers $1 \leq s \leq q$, the following mapping from multigraphs to graphs: The s-projection $\tilde{\mathcal{G}}$ of a multigraph $\mathcal{MG}_q$ is the graph with the same vertex set $\mathcal{V}$ and exactly those edges (i,j) which are s-connections in the multigraph. Using this mapping $\mathcal{MG}_q \to \tilde{\mathcal{G}}$, we can generalize the definitions commonly used in graph theory to the multigraphs as defined above. For example an s-component of $\mathcal{MG}_q$ is defined by the corresponding component in its s-projection, an isolated vertex in the s-projection is called s-isolated in the original multigraph and so on. Since these generalizations are intuitively clear, we refer to Godehardt (1993, 1994) for more details.

Note that we have a vector $\vec{d}^T = (d_1, \ldots, d_q)$ of possibly different levels. For some applications, the case $s < q$ is useful, since then two points can be considered as similar if their differences are smaller than the levels d_l in at least s of the q coordinates. In this case, the similarity of the points, and thus the cluster structure is not based on a metric as it is discussed for example in Godehardt (1993). Thus, the components or the cliques of the s-projection of level $\vec{d}^T$ of the multigraph $\mathcal{MG}_q$ as the single-linkage, and the complete-linkage clusters, respectively, are of interest in numerical classification.

There is a simple geometrical interpretation of the q-projection of a multigraph $\mathcal{MG}_{q,n,(d,\ldots,d)}$ of distance level $\vec{d}^T = (d, \ldots, d)$, that means with the same d for each dimension: Two vertices i and j are connected by an edge if the maximum or Chebyshev distance between the respective points $\vec{x}_i$ and $\vec{x}_j$ of the R^q is smaller than d. The q-projection of such a multigraph of level $(d, \ldots, d)$ is the coincidence graph (see Hafner (1972)).

Assuming that n vectors are chosen randomly, we arrive at probability models for the multigraphs considered above (see Godehardt (1995)). In this paper, we restrict to the special case of random coincidence graphs on the unit cube.

Uniform model $\mathcal{CG}_{q,n,d}$. Let $\vec{X}_1, \ldots, \vec{X}_n$ be n independent random variables uniformly distributed on the unit cube. A random graph $\mathcal{CG}_{q,n,d}$ is defined by the vertex set $\mathcal{V} = \{1, \ldots, n\}$, corresponding to the set of these n random variables, and by the edge set $\mathcal{E} = \{(i,j) : \|X_i - X_j\| \leq d\}$ where $0 < d < 1$, and $\|\cdot\|$ is the Chebyshev norm. For the n realisations $\vec{x}_1, \ldots, \vec{x}_n$ of the random variables, we get a coincidence graph as realisation of $\mathcal{CG}_{q,n,d}$.

Obviously, a random coincidence graph $\mathcal{CG}_{q,n,d}$ is the q-projection of the superposition of q independent random interval graphs $\mathcal{IG}_{n,d}$; that is, for the same data set as a realisation of the q-dimensional random variables, both construction methods give the same coincidence graph.

As before, let $I_{i,j}$ be the indicator for the presence of an edge (i,j), $U_i = \sum_{j=1}^{n} I_{i,j}$ be the degree of vertex i, and let $E = \frac{1}{2}\sum_{i=1}^{n} U_i$ be the number of edges, now in $\mathcal{CG}_{q,n,d}$. The definition of the q-projection and the independence of the layers imply directly that two vertices i and j in a random coincidence graph $\mathcal{CG}_{q,n,d}$ are connected by an edge with probability

$$\Pr(I_{i,j} = 1) = \prod_{l=1}^{q} \Pr(|X_{i,l} - X_{j,l}| \leq d) = \left(2d - d^2\right)^q.$$

3.1 Exact Results for Random Coincidence Graphs

Using the direct, geometric approach, we can get the probability that a given vertex has the degree l. First, we will restrict ourselves to one of $q+1$ types of regions $Q_0, \ldots, Q_q$ from the unit cube $[0;1]^q$, where Q_k means all points of the cube for which exactly k coordinates are within the distance d from one of the borders of $[0;1]$. Each Q_k is composed of $\binom{q}{k} 2^k$ symmetrical disjoint regions, and Q_0 is the inner region, that is $(d; 1-d)^q$. Therefore, we obtain

$$P_{[k]}(U_i = l) = \Pr\left(\{U_i = l\} \cap \{\vec{X}_i \in Q_k\}\right)$$

$$= \binom{q}{k} 2^k (1-2d)^{q-k} \int_0^d \cdots \int_0^d \left\{(2d)^{q-k}(x_1+d)\cdots(x_k+d)\right\}^l$$

$$\times \left\{1 - (2d)^{q-k}(x_1+d)\cdots(x_k+d)\right\}^{n-1-l} \binom{n-1}{l} dx_1 \cdots dx_k$$

$$= \frac{1}{n}\binom{n}{l}\binom{q}{k}\left(\frac{1}{2d} - 1\right)^{q-k} 2^k$$

$$\times \sum_{i=1}^{n-l} \binom{n-l}{i}(-1)^{i-1} \frac{i}{(i+l)^k}(2d)^{q(i+l)}\left(1 - \frac{1}{2^{i+l}}\right)^k,$$

which, after multiplication by n, gives the expected number of vertices of a given degree l in Q_k. For the special case $l = 0$, we obtain the expected number of isolated vertices in the region Q_k

$$E_{[k]}\left(C_n^1\right) = \binom{q}{k}\left(\frac{1}{2d} - 1\right)^{q-k} 2^k \sum_{i=1}^{n} \binom{n}{i}(-1)^{i-1}\frac{(2d)^{qi}}{i^{k-1}}\left(1 - \frac{1}{2^i}\right)^k.$$

Summing up the probabilities $P_{[k]}(U_i = l)$ over $k = 0, \ldots, q$, we get the generalization of Theorem 1.

Theorem 8. *For a random coincidence graph $\mathcal{CG}_{q,n,d}$, the distribution of the degree of any vertex i is given by*

$$\Pr(U_i = l) = \binom{n-1}{l}\sum_{j=0}^{n-1-l}\binom{n-1-l}{j}(-1)^j (2d)^{q(l+j)}$$

$$\times \left\{ 1 - 2d + \frac{4d}{l+j+1}\left(1 - \frac{1}{2^{l+j+1}}\right) \right\}^q$$

for $l = 0, 1, \ldots, n - 1$. •

The formulas for the expected numbers of vertices of given degree l in a random coincidence graph follow immediately from this theorem. We state the result only for the special case $l = 0$, that is for isolated vertices.

Theorem 9. *For a random coincidence graph* $CG_{q,n,d}$, *the expected number* C_n^1 *of isolated vertices is given by*

$$\mathrm{E}\left(C_n^1\right) = n \sum_{j=0}^{n-1} \binom{n-1}{j} (-1)^j (2d)^{qj} \left\{ 1 - 2d + \frac{4d}{j+1}\left(1 - \frac{1}{2^{j+1}}\right) \right\}^q$$

for given distance level d. •

Unfortunately, the exact distribution of the number of isolated vertices is still not known except for the special case of interval graphs (see Theorem 3).

3.2 Asymptotic Properties

The following theorem on the asymptotic behaviour of random coincidence graphs is a special case of a result from Godehardt (1995). For the proof, we did not use geometrical arguments like those of the proofs of the preceeding two theorems, but the model of the q-projection. Recall that by the definition, we need an edge between vertices i and j in every coordinate to get an edge (i, j) in the q-projection,

Theorem 10. *For sequences* $(CG_{q,n,d})_{n \to \infty}$ *of random coincidence graphs with n vertices and* $d(n) = \{(c + o(1))/n^2\}^{1/q}$ *as the distance level, the distribution of the number E of edges tends to a Poisson distribution with parameter c.* •

The exact results for the expected numbers of isolated vertices in Q_k imply directly that for $d(n) = \frac{1}{2}\{(\log(n) + c + o(1))/n\}^{1/q}$ in the inner region $(d; 1-d)^q$, we have $\mathrm{E}_{[0]}(C_n^1) = n(1-2d)^q(1-(2d)^q)^{n-1} \sim e^{-c}$. For $q = 1$, the ratio $P_{[0]}(U_i = 0)/P_{[1]}(U_i = 0)$ and for $q = 2$, this ratio and $P_{[0]}(U_i = 0)/P_{[2]}(U_i = 0)$ both tend to infinity, which gives $\mathrm{E}(C_n^1) \sim n P_{[0]}(U_i = 0)$. Thus, we can state the following result.

Theorem 11. *For sequences* $(CG_{q,n,d})_{n \to \infty}$ *of random coincidence graphs with* $d(n) = \frac{1}{2}\{(\log(n) + c + o(1))/n\}^{1/q}$ *the expected number of isolated vertices in the region* $Q_0 = (d; 1-d)^q$ *tends to* e^{-c}. *For $q = 1$ or $q = 2$, this is also the limit for the expected numbers of isolated vertices in the unit cube.* •

From the results concerning the largest nearest-neighbor link in the unit q-cube (see Appel (1996) and Dette (1989)), it follows that

$$d(n) = \left(\frac{1}{2q}\frac{\log(n)}{n}\right)^{1/q}$$

is the threshold function for the existence of isolated vertices in random coincidence graphs $\mathcal{CG}_{q,n,d}$. Let us point out that for such threshold distance and $q \geq 3$, there are almost surely no isolated vertices in the inner region Q_0 as $n \to \infty$.

4 Discussion of the Results

The way how to use graph-theoretical based probability models to test the hypothesis of homogeneity against the alternative that we have a cluster structure has been described in Bock (1996) and Godehardt (1993). The disadvantages of the probability models of random graphs $\mathcal{G}_{n,p}$ or $\mathcal{G}_{n,N}$ or multigraphs $\mathcal{MG}_{q,n,p}$ or $\mathcal{MG}_{q,n,p}$, which have been used to derive test statistics are known and have been discussed in those papers. If we can accept a uniform distribution of the random vectors as the hypothesis of homogeneity, then a probability model for random coincidence graphs seems to be the most appropriate one to test the possible cluster structure in a data set.

The results given here, can be used to test whether there is a possible cluster structure hidden in an n-element data set or not. The method is as follows. We can use asymptotic results like those for the distribution of the numbers of isolated edges from Theorems 5 (the one-dimensional case) or 10 (the general q-dimensional case) to find a good distance level $d(n)$. We can use the distance levels from those theorems, since they are threshold functions (which means that for larger d than given by Theorem 10, for example, we expect a rather big number of edges, and for smaller values of d, the edge set will remain empty with probability close to 1 if n is large enough). We generate the coincidence graph of the data for that level d and get the value of the respective random variable (the number of isolated points or isolated edges or other variables in the data). For the one-dimensional case, we may choose the random variable C_n^2, the number of isolated edges (which follows from Theorem 2, see Godehardt (1996)) or the number of isolated vertices from Theorem 3, as test statistic and can determine the region for rejecting the hypothesis of homogeneity for given α. We then will accept a true cluster structure in our data set if the number of isolated edges or of isolated vertices found for this d is too big or too small than that number expected under random conditions of these Theorems. For large sample sizes n, we can use asymptotic results as approximations of the distributions of the respective random variables. For this purpose, it is worth to do some investigations on the functions $o(1)$ to get a good approximation so that the differences between the exact and the asymptotic results are small for sample sizes n, commonly used in applied research.

As in Zhou (1989), the number of edges in a random interval graph together with the procedure outlined here, can be used to derive a goodness-of-fit test to test the hypothesis of a uniform distribution in the one-dimensional case. The same ideas can be applied to q-dimensional data.

In the definition of the coincidence graph, one can use any other distance instead of the Chebyshev one. However, in the life sciences, the Chebyshev distance seems to be the natural one, since usually we look at differences in each coordinate of the data vectors directly (in medicine for example we look at differences in blood pressure, in heart rate and in cholesterol level), and no-one would compare the data of two patients by calculating, for example, their Euclidean distances.

In the life sciences, especially in medical research, it is often tolerated that objects can differ in some variables and still remain "similar" so that one would like to join them by an edge. This leads to the s-projection ($1 \leq s < q$) as defined in the previous chapter. Until now, we could prove only few results for the general q-dimensional case of $\mathcal{CG}_{q,n,d}$, and obviously the research in s-projections is more complicated. Fortunately, in both cases, using the independence between the layers, we can apply the results for the one-dimensional case.

Acknowledgements: This work has been supported by grant no. Go 490/4-3 from the German Research Foundation (DFG).

References

APPEL, M.J.B., RUSSO, R.P. (1996, submitted): The minimum vertex degree of a graph on uniform points in $[0, 1]$. *Journal of Applied Probability.*

BARBOUR, A.D., HOLST, L., JANSON, S. (1992): *Poisson approximations.* Clarendon Press, Oxford.

BOCK, H.H. (1996): Probabilistic models in cluster analysis. *Computational Statistics and Data Analysis, 23, 5–28.*

DETTE, H., HENZE, N. (1989): The limit distribution of the largest nearest-neighbor link in the unit d-cube. *Journal of Applied Probability, 26, 67–80.*

ERDŐS, P., RÉNYI, A. (1960): On the evolution of random graphs. *Publications of the Mathematical Institute of the Hungarian Academy of Sciences, 5, 17–61.*

GILBERT, E.N. (1959): Random graphs. *Annals of Mathematical Statistics, 30, 1141–1144.*

GODEHARDT, E. (1993): Probability models for random multigraphs with applications in cluster analysis. *Annals of Discrete Mathematics, 55, 93–108.*

GODEHARDT, E., HORSCH, A. (1994): Testing of data structures with graph-theoretical models. in: H.H. Bock, W. Lenski, M.M. Richter, (eds.): *Information systems and data analysis (Proceedings 17th Annual Conference of the Gesellschaft für Klassifikation e.V., Kaiserslautern, March 3–5, 1993).* Springer, Berlin – Heidelberg – New York, 226–241.

GODEHARDT, E., HORSCH, A. (1995): Graph-theoretic models for testing the homogeneity of data. in: W. Gaul, D. Pfeifer (eds.), *From Data to Knowledge: Theoretical and Practical Aspects of Classification, Data Analysis and Knowledge Organization (Proceedings 18th Annual Conference of the Gesellschaft für Klassifikation e.V., Oldenburg, March 9-11, 1994)*. Springer, Berlin – Heidelberg – New York, 167–176.

GODEHARDT, E., JAWORSKI, J. (1996): On the connectivity of a random graph. *Random Structures and Algorithms, 9, 137–161*.

HAFNER, R. (1972): The asymptotic distribution of random clumps. *Computing, 10, 335–351*.

KENNEDY, J.W. (1976): Random clumps, graphs, and polymer solutions. In: Y. Alavi, D.R. Lick (eds.): *Theory and Applications of Graphs*. Springer, Berlin – Heidelberg – New York, 314–329.

SCHEINERMAN, E.R. (1990): An evolution of interval graphs. *Discrete Mathematics, 82, 287–302*.

SOLOMON, H. (1976): *Geometric probability*. Society for Industrial and Applied Mathematics, Philadelphia.

ZHOU, X., JAMMALAMADAKA, S.R. (1989): Bahadur Efficiencies of Spacings Tests for Goodness of Fit. *Annals of the Institute of Statistics and Mathematics 41, 541–553*.

City-Block Scaling:
Smoothing Strategies
for Avoiding Local Minima

P.J.F. Groenen[1] , W.J. Heiser, J.J. Meulman

Department of Data Theory, Leiden University,
P.O. Box 9555, 2300 RB Leiden, The Netherlands
(e-mail: groenen@rulfsw.fsw.leidenuniv.nl)

Abstract: Multidimensional scaling (MDS) with city-block distances suffers from many local minima if the Stress function is minimized. In fact, the problem can be viewed as a combinatorial problem, where finding the correct order of the co-ordinates on a dimension is crucial for attaining the minimum. Several strategies have been proposed for arriving at a global minimum of the Stress function. We pay particular attention to Pliner's (1996) smoothing strategy for unidimensional scaling, which smoothes the concave part of the Stress function. We discuss three extensions of this strategy to the multidimensional case with city-block distances. The first extension is shown to lead to problems because it yields a unidimensional solution. A second extension, proposed by Pliner (1986), and a third extension, distance smoothing introduced here, do not have this problem. Numerical experiments with the smoothing strategy have been limited to the unidimensional case. Therefore, we present a comparison study using real data, which shows that the smoothing strategy performs better than three other strategies considered.

1 Introduction

In multidimensional scaling (MDS) the objective is to represent dissimilarities between objects as distances between points in a low dimensional space. Apart from the Euclidean distance, the *city-block* (or L_1) distance is a popular choice. One of the properties of the city-block distance (not shared by the Euclidean distance) is dimensional additivity, that is, the total distance is a sum of the distances per dimension. For an overview of developments in the area of city-block distances, see Arabie (1991). The purpose of least squares MDS can be formalized mathematically as the minimization of the raw Stress function (Kruskal, 1964),

$$\sigma(\mathbf{X}) = \sum_{i<j} w_{ij} \left(\delta_{ij} - d_{ij}(\mathbf{X}) \right)^2, \qquad (1)$$

over the $n \times p$ matrix of coordinates $\mathbf{X}$ of n objects in p dimensions, where w_{ij} are nonnegative weights, δ_{ij} are nonnegative dissimilarities, and $d_{ij}(\mathbf{X})$

---

[1]Supported by The Netherlands Organization for Scientific Research (NWO) by grant nr. 030-56-403 for the 'PIONEER' project 'Subject Oriented Multivariate Analysis'.

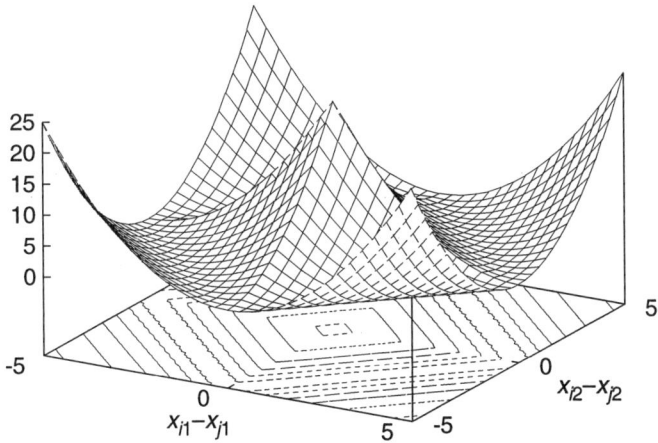

Figure 1: The contribution to $\sigma(\mathbf{X})$ of the term $(\delta_{ij} - d_{ij}(\mathbf{X}))^2$.

is the city-block distance between points i and j defined by

$$d_{ij}(\mathbf{X}) = \sum_{k=1}^{p} |x_{ik} - x_{jk}|. \tag{2}$$

For city-block MDS the Stress function can be written as

$$\begin{aligned}
\sigma(\mathbf{X}) &= \sum_{i<j} w_{ij}\delta_{ij}^2 + \sum_{i<j} w_{ij}d_{ij}^2(\mathbf{X}) - 2\sum_{i<j} w_{ij}\delta_{ij}d_{ij}(\mathbf{X}) \\
&= \sum_{i<j} w_{ij}\delta_{ij}^2 + \sum_{i<j} w_{ij} \sum_{k=1}^{p}(x_{ik} - x_{jk})^2 \\
&\quad + 2\sum_{i<j} w_{ij} \sum_{k<l} |x_{ik} - x_{jk}||x_{il} - x_{jl}| - 2\sum_{i<j} w_{ij}\delta_{ij} \sum_{k=1}^{p} |x_{ik} - x_{jk}| \\
&= \eta_\delta^2 + \eta_k^2(\mathbf{X}) + \eta_{k\neq l}^2(\mathbf{X}) - 2\rho(\mathbf{X}). \tag{3}
\end{aligned}$$

It has been noted by several authors (Heiser (1989), Arabie (1991), Hubert et al. (1992), Groenen and Heiser (1996)) that city-block MDS by minimization of (3) suffers from many local minima. The main concern of this paper is to develop and evaluate strategies that try to avoid local minima. To see why Stress has many local minima, consider the contribution of a single error term for objects i, j to $\sigma(\mathbf{X})$ in two dimensions with $w_{ij} = 1$, i.e., the residual $(\delta_{ij}^2 - [|x_{i1} - x_{j1}| + |x_{i2} - x_{j2}|])^2$, see Figure 1. The sharp ridges give rise to the large number of local minima since they act as a barrier between four potential regions of attraction, due to discontinuities in the direction of change. Some of the best strategies proposed so far use combinatorial approaches (Heiser (1989), Hubert et al. (1992)), where finding the correct order of the coordinates on any dimension is crucial for attaining the overall

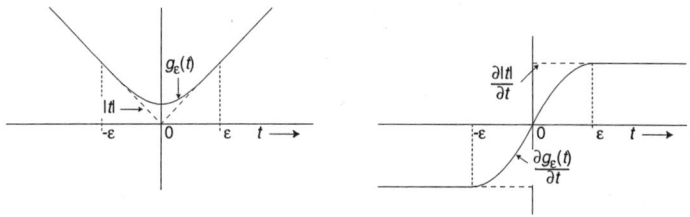

Figure 2: The left panel shows function $|t|$ (dashed line) and its smoothed version $g_\epsilon(t)$ (solid line) and the right panel shows the first derivative of these functions.

minimum. In this paper, we elaborate on a smoothing strategy proposed by Pliner (1986, 1996). The advantage of this approach is that continuous minimization methods can be used instead of combinatorial strategies, which become unpractical for large n. We propose a new smooth loss function that converges to Stress. So far, the smoothing strategy has not been compared to other strategies except for unidimensional scaling. We fill this gap by presenting a small comparison study that investigates the performance of the smoothing strategy relative to competing strategies.

2 The smoothing strategy

The smoothing strategy of Pliner (1986, 1996) smoothes the sharp ridges in the Stress function. It tries to avoid local minima by letting the smooth function gradually approach the original function, while removing the discontinuities in the gradient near the ridges. In unidimensional scaling, Pliner (1996) replaces $-|x_i - x_j|$ in $\rho(\mathbf{X})$ by $-g_\epsilon(x_i - x_j)$, see Figure 2. Here, $g_\epsilon(t)$ is defined by

$$g_\epsilon(t) = \begin{cases} t^2(3\epsilon - |t|)/3\epsilon^2 + \epsilon/3, & \text{if } |t| < \epsilon, \\ |t|, & \text{if } |t| \geq \epsilon. \end{cases} \quad (4)$$

Thus, distances smaller than ϵ are replaced by a smooth function, but large distances remain as they are. For unidimensional scaling, this smoothing strategy turns out to be very successful in reaching global minima (Pliner (1996)).

Instead of $g_\epsilon(t)$, one might as well use other functions that have the property of being smooth if $|t| < \epsilon$, and approach $|t|$ for large $|t| \geq \epsilon$. One such function — well known from robust statistics — is the Huber function (Huber, 1981), which is similar to (4) except that it is quadratic in t for $|t| < \epsilon$. Use of the Huber function in the present context is currently being studied.

The unidimensional smoothing strategy can be generalized to city-block MDS in several ways. Pliner (1996) seems to suggest that smoothing should only be applied to the terms of $\sigma(\mathbf{X})$ containing $-|x_{ik} - x_{jk}|$, i.e.,

$$\sigma_1(\mathbf{X}|\epsilon) = \eta_\delta^2 + \eta_k^2(\mathbf{X}) + \eta_{k \neq l}^2(\mathbf{X}) - 2\rho(\mathbf{X}|\epsilon), \quad (5)$$

where $\rho(\mathbf{X}|\epsilon) = \sum_{i<j} w_{ij}\delta_{ij} \sum_{k=1}^{p} g_\epsilon(x_{ik} - x_{jk})$. Thus, $-\sum_{k=1}^{p} g_\epsilon(x_{ik} - x_{jk})$ smoothes $-d_{ij}(\mathbf{X})$. An important property of (5) is that as ϵ approaches zero, $\sigma_1(\mathbf{X}|\epsilon)$ approaches the original Stress function $\sigma(\mathbf{X})$. However, numerical experimentation with $\sigma_1(\mathbf{X}|\epsilon)$ yielded systematically unidimensional solutions whatever the chosen dimensionality. This property is undesirable because additional dimensions in all practical cases would decrease Stress. Therefore, $\sigma_1(\mathbf{X}|\epsilon)$ cannot be used as a smooth version of Stress for city-block MDS when the rank of $\mathbf{X}$ should be larger than 1.

A second smoothing loss function was proposed by Pliner (1986), i.e., he smoothes every factor $|x_{ik} - x_{jk}|$ by $g_\epsilon(x_{ik} - x_{jk})$ and leaves the quadratic terms $(x_{ik} - x_{jk})^2$ in $\eta_k^2(\mathbf{X})$ of $\sigma(\mathbf{X})$ as they are. This yields the smooth loss function

$$\sigma_2(\mathbf{X}|\epsilon) = \eta_\delta^2 + \eta_k^2(\mathbf{X}) + \eta_{k\neq l}^2(\mathbf{X}|\epsilon) - 2\rho(\mathbf{X}|\epsilon), \qquad (6)$$

where $\eta_{k\neq l}^2(\mathbf{X}|\epsilon) = \sum_{k\neq l} \sum_{i<j} w_{ij} g_\epsilon(x_{ik} - x_{jk}) g_\epsilon(x_{il} - x_{jl})$. This loss function also approaches $\sigma(\mathbf{X})$ as $\epsilon \to 0$ and, in general, retains the rank of the initial configuration.

The smoothing loss function that we propose here is called *distance smoothing*. We replace all factors $|x_{ik} - x_{jk}|$ by $g_\epsilon(x_{ik} - x_{jk})$. Thus, we minimize

$$\begin{aligned}\sigma_3(\mathbf{X}|\epsilon) &= \sum_{i<j} w_{ij} \left(\delta_{ij} - \sum_k g_\epsilon(x_{ik} - x_{jk})\right)^2 \\ &= \eta_\delta^2 + \eta_k^2(\mathbf{X}|\epsilon) + \eta_{k\neq l}^2(\mathbf{X}|\epsilon) - 2\rho(\mathbf{X}|\epsilon), \qquad (7)\end{aligned}$$

thereby smoothing $\eta_k^2(\mathbf{X})$ as well by $\eta_k^2(\mathbf{X}|\epsilon) = \sum_k \sum_{i<j} w_{ij} g_\epsilon^2(x_{ik} - x_{jk})$. The advantage of this adaptation is that the loss function remains least squares, because it is the sum of squared differences of the dissimilarities and the smoothed distances. The minimum of $\sigma_3(\mathbf{X}|\epsilon)$ is not biased to a zero difference of the coordinates (in contrast to $\sigma_1(\mathbf{X}|\epsilon)$), and it has the property that it converges to $\sigma(\mathbf{X})$ as ϵ approaches zero. An even stronger property holds if we assume that all $|x_{ik} - x_{jk}|$ are strictly positive: then there exists an ϵ for which $\sigma_3(\mathbf{X}|\epsilon)$ reduces to $\sigma(\mathbf{X})$.

The smoothing strategy for city-block MDS proposed in this paper is: (a) set ϵ_0, start configuration $\mathbf{X}_0$, and fix the number of smoothing steps $r_{\max}$, (b) for $r = 1$ to $r_{\max}$ do: find minimum $\mathbf{X}_r$ by minimizing $\sigma_3(\mathbf{X}|\epsilon)$ using $\mathbf{X}_{r-1}$ as start configuration; reduce ϵ, i.e., $\epsilon \leftarrow \epsilon_0(r_{\max} - r + 1)/r_{\max}$, (c) minimize $\sigma(\mathbf{X})$ using $\mathbf{X}_{r_{\max}}$ as start configuration. We choose ϵ_0 equal to $2 \max_{1\leq i\leq n}(\sum_{j=1}^n w_{ij})^{-1} \sum_{j=1}^n w_{ij}\delta_{ij}$, thereby adapting Pliner's (1996) recommendation of ϵ_0 for nonidentical weights.

So far, we discussed smoothing for metric city-block MDS. Without much difficulty, smoothing can be extended to *nonmetric* city-block MDS as well. We can proceed as in ordinary nonmetric MDS (see Kruskal (1964), or, e.g., Borg and Groenen (1997)). In smoothing for ordinal city-block MDS one substitutes δ_{ij} by $\hat{d}_{ij}$ in (7), where the $\hat{d}_{ij}$'s are least squares approximates to the distances, constrained to retain the order of the data and have a fixed sum of squares.

3 Performance of the smoothing strategy

To test the performance of our distance smoothing algorithm, we compare it to three other methods: (a) the combinatorial strategy of Hubert et al. (1992), (b) the majorization approach of Groenen et al. (1995), here called "plain majorization", and (c) the MDS program in SYSTAT (Wilkinson (1988)). We used two data sets of Borg and Leutner (1983) on the perception of rectangles which were also analyzed by Hubert et al. (1992). Subjects rated the similarity of pairs of rectangles on a rating scale ranging from 0='equal, identical' to 9='extremely different'. The 16 rectangles varied in width and height (both in four levels). The data set (to which we refer as WH) contains the averaged similarity ratings of 21 subjects. A second set of rectangles was created by varying 'width + height' and 'width − height', thereby emphasizing the area and shape of the rectangles. The average over the similarity ratings of 21 other subjects make up the second data set (the AS data). The data are treated ordinally by the primary approach to ties, which implies that in each step of our smoothing algorithm the proximities are optimally transformed in a least squares way by monotone regression. The figures for SYSTAT and the combinatorial strategy are copied from Hubert et al. (1992). Note that the combinatorial strategy optimized Stress-2, although Stress-1 values are reported. The value of Stress reported is Kruskal's Stress-1 which can be shown to be equal to $(\sigma(\mathbf{X})/\eta_\delta^2)^{1/2}$ if we allow $\mathbf{X}$ to be optimally dilated (see, Borg and Groenen (1997)). To minimize $\sigma_3(\mathbf{X}|\epsilon)$ we have used majorization. Details of this algorithm will be presented in a forthcoming paper (Groenen, Heiser, and Meulman, in preparation).

For each of the two data sets, 100 random starts were fed into our smoothing algorithm, both with 5 and 20 smoothing steps. The minimization of the smoothing function $\sigma_3(\mathbf{X}|\epsilon)$ was stopped whenever the decrease in loss was smaller than 10^{-5}. The stopping criterion in the final minimization of $\sigma(\mathbf{X})$ was set to 10^{-8}.

The results are summarized in Table 1. These results show that the double smoothing strategy with 20 smoothing steps is overall the best strategy. Second best are the 5 step smoothing strategy and the combinatorial method. The worst two methods are plain majorization and SYSTAT. The maximum values of Stress of the smoothing strategies (and from the first quartile upwards for the plain majorization approach) are very high because the transformation obtained by ordinal MDS is degenerated towards equal values for almost all proximities. Therefore, a Shepard diagram (that plots the original proximity values against the transformed values along with the residuals) displays an almost horizontal line. In comparison to 20-step smoothing, the 5-step strategy gives slightly higher Stress values in the summary statistics. For the WH data, 47% had Stress-1 of .0534, and 42% of .0541 using the 20-step smoothing approach, whereas the 5-step version had 33% of .0534, and 84% was smaller than .0565. For the AS data, the 20-step approach had 8% Stress-1 of .0619, and 72% smaller than .0700, whereas the 5-step

Table 1: Summary statistics of Stress-1 values for ordinal city-block MDS on the rectangle data sets WH and AS for 100 multiple random starts. The figures for SYSTAT and the combinatorial strategy (indicated by an '*') are copied from Hubert et al. (1992).

Strategy	Minimum	1st Quartile	Median	3rd Quartile	Maximum
WH data					
plain majorization	.0903	.3594	.3671	.3750	.4001
SYSTAT*	.0665	.1545	.1748	.2992	.3758
combinatorial*	.0537	.0666	.0701	.1368	.1803
smoothing 5 steps	.0534	.0534	.0565	.0565	.3302
smoothing 20 steps	.0534	.0534	.0541	.0541	.3235
AS data					
plain majorization	.1069	.3568	.3660	.3757	.4001
SYSTAT*	.0702	.0783	.1252	.3617	.3804
combinatorial*	.0625	.0699	.0754	.0860	.1078
smoothing 5 steps	.0626	.0668	.0693	.0844	.3294
smoothing 20 steps	.0619	.0644	.0666	.0741	.3294

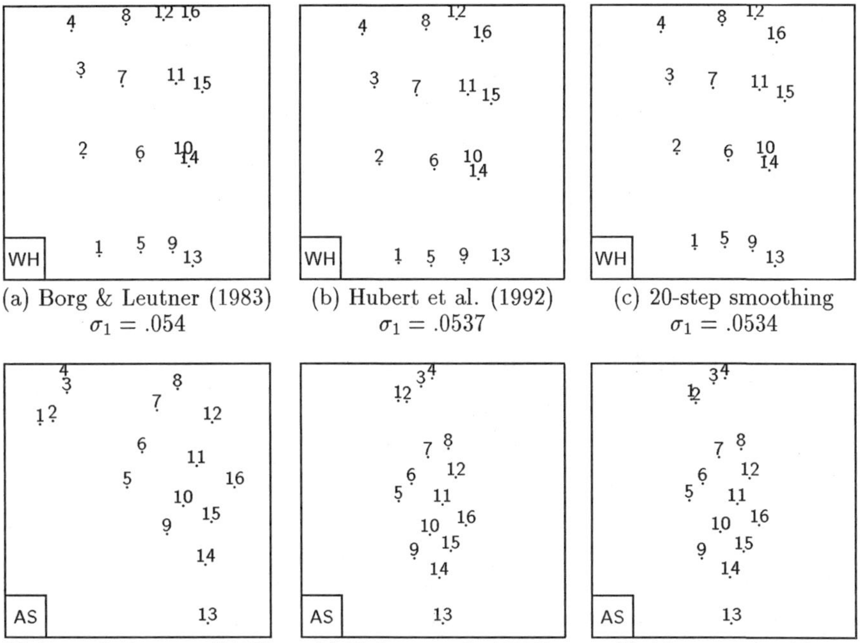

(a) Borg & Leutner (1983)
$\sigma_1 = .054$

(b) Hubert et al. (1992)
$\sigma_1 = .0537$

(c) 20-step smoothing
$\sigma_1 = .0534$

(d) Borg & Leutner (1983)
$\sigma_1 = .064$

(e) Hubert et al. (1992)
$\sigma_1 = .0625$

(f) 20-step smoothing
$\sigma_1 = .0619$

Figure 3: Solutions obtained for WH data (upper panels) and AS data (lower panels) by (a) Borg and Leutner (1983) (left panels), (b) Hubert et al. (1992) (middle panels), and (c) the 20-step smoothing strategy (right panels).

approach found in 3% of the cases Stress-1 of .0626, and 57% smaller than .0700. These results indicate that the smoothing strategies give good local minima in more than half of the searches. Moreover, as the number of steps is increased, the frequency of finding the global minimum also increases.

The (best) configurations found by Borg and Leutner (1983), Hubert et al. (1992), and the 20-step smoothing strategy for the WH data are shown in Figure 3 (upper panels). All three solutions for the WH data reconstruct the grid like structure used for generating the rectangles. The difference between the solutions is either in the positioning of points 12 and 16, or in that of points 1, 5, 9, and 13. For the AS data in Figure 3 (lower panels), the solution found by Borg and Leutner (1983) is considerably different from the solutions found by the combinatorial and the smoothing strategies. Hubert et al. (1992) state that height seems to be much more important than width. Note that the combinatorial solution in panel (e) of Figure 3 only differs from the smoothing solution in panel (f) in the location of point 1.

4 Discussion and conclusions

This paper shows that the combinatorial problem of least-squares city-block MDS can be solved by a smoothing strategy, which is a continuous minimization problem by nature. We have considered three extensions of the basic smoothing strategy suggested by Pliner (1996) for unidimensional scaling. One extension that only smoothes the concave part of the Stress function systematically yields rank-one solutions. However, the distance smoothing strategy proposed in this paper, which smoothes all the absolute value terms in the Stress function, and the strategy of Pliner (1986) give technically correct results.

A comparison study of two real data sets suggests that the distance smoothing strategy gives somewhat better results than the combinatorial strategy of Hubert et al. (1992), and much better results than gradient based methods such as the plain majorization approach of Groenen et al. (1995) and city-block MDS in SYSTAT. Moreover, as the number of smoothing steps is increased, the probability of finding a global minimum also increases.

The distance smoothing strategy can be extended to MDS with Euclidean distances as well. In this way, one would get a method that, hopefully, finds global minima with a much larger probability. Constraints on the configuration in confirmatory MDS as proposed by De Leeuw and Heiser (1980) can be implemented in the majorizing algorithm of smoothed city-block MDS without much difficulty.

In this paper we have regarded the distance smoothing strategy as an approach to find the global minimum in city-block MDS. However, the smoothing function of the absolute value, $g_\epsilon(x_{is} - x_{js})$, can also be viewed as being part of a model. In such a model, differences larger than ϵ are treated as they are, but smaller differences are made somewhat larger. The extreme of a zero difference is transformed by the smoother into a value of $\epsilon/3$. This model approach could be applied if all dissimilarities are by their nature larger than this value.

References

ARABIE, P. (1991): Was Euclid an unnecessarily sophisticated psychologist? *Psychometrika, 56*, 567–587.

BORG, I. and GROENEN, P.J.F. (1997): Modern multidimensional scaling: Theory and applications. New York: Springer.

BORG, I. and LEUTNER, D. (1983): Dimensional models for the perception of rectangles. *Perception and Psychophysics, 34*, 257–269.

DE LEEUW, J. and HEISER, W.J. (1980): Multidimensional scaling with restrictions on the configuration. In P.R. Krishnaiah (eds.): *Multivariate analysis, V.* North Holland Publishing Company, Amsterdam, 501–522.

GROENEN, P.J.F. and HEISER, W.J. (1996): The tunneling method for global optimization in multidimensional scaling. *Psychometrika, 61*, 529–550.

GROENEN, P.J.F., HEISER, W.J., and MEULMAN, J.J. (in preparation): Global optimization in least squares multidimensional scaling: A smoothing approach. Working paper, Department of Data Theory, Leiden, The Netherlands.

GROENEN, P.J.F., MATHAR, R., and HEISER, W.J. (1995): The majorization approach to multidimensional scaling for Minkowski distances. *Journal of Classification, 12*, 3–19.

HEISER, W.J. (1989): The city-block model for three-way multidimensional scaling. In: R. Coppi and S. Bolasco (eds.): *Multiway data analysis.* Elsevier Science, Amsterdam, 395–404.

HUBER, P.J. (1981): Robust statistics. Wiley, New York.

HUBERT, L., ARABIE, P., and HESSON-MCINNIS, M. (1992): Multidimensional scaling in the city-block metric: A combinatorial approach. *Journal of Classification, 9*, 211–236.

KRUSKAL, J.B. (1964): Nonmetric multidimensional scaling: A numerical method. *Psychometrika, 29*, 115–129.

PLINER, V. (1986): The problem of multidimensional metric scaling. *Automation and Remote Control, 47*, 560–567.

PLINER, V. (1996): Metric, unidimensional scaling and global optimization. *Journal of Classification, 13*, 3–18.

WILKINSON, L. (1988): SYSTAT: The system for statistics. SYSTAT Inc., Evanston, IL.

Probability Models and Limit Theorems for Random Interval Graphs with Applications to Cluster Analysis

B. Harris[1], E. Godehardt[2]

[1] Department of Statistics, University of Wisconsin,
1210 W. Dayton St., Madison, Wisconsin 53706-1693, USA
[2] Klinik für Thorax- und Kardiovaskular-Chirurgie, Heinrich Heine-Universität,
Postfach 10 10 07, D-40001 Düsseldorf, Germany

Abstract: Assume that n k-dimensional data points have been obtained and subjected to a cluster analysis algorithm. A potential concern is whether the resulting clusters have a "causal" interpretation or whether they are merely consequences of a "random" fluctuation. In this report, the asymptotic properties of a number of potentially useful combinatorial tests based on the theory of random interval graphs are described. Some preliminary numerical results illustrating their possible application as a method of resolving the above question are provided.

1 Introduction and Summary

Let $F_X(x)$ be a cumulative distribution function on E_k, k-dimensional Euclidean space. We assume that $F_X(x)$ is absolutely continuous with respect to k-dimensional Lebesgue measure and denote the corresponding probability density function by $f_X(x)$. Assume that a random sample of size n has been obtained from $F_X(x)$ and denote the realizations by $x_1, x_2, \ldots, x_n$. In cluster analysis, similar objects are to be placed in the same cluster. We will interpret similarity as being close with respect to some distance on E_k. The relationship between graph theory and cluster analysis has been described in the books by Bock (1974) and Godehardt (1990). Mathematical results related to those used here are given in Eberl and Hafner (1971), Hafner (1972), Godehardt and Harris (1995), Jammalamadaka and Janson (1986), Jammalamadaka and Zhou (1990) and Maehara (1990).

In order to proceed, we need to introduce some notions from graph theory.

2 Graph Theoretic Concepts

A graph $G_n = (V, E)$ is defined as follows. V is a set with $|V| = n$ and E is a set of (unordered) pairs of elements of V. The elements of V are called the vertices of the graph G_n and the pairs in E are referred to as the edges of G_n. With no loss of generality, we can assume $V = \{1, 2, \ldots, n\}$. For the purposes at hand, we choose a distance ρ on E_k and a threshold $d > 0$. Then for $i \neq j$, place (i, j) in E if and only if $\rho(x_i, x_j) \leq d$. Since

$x_1, x_2, \ldots, x_n$ are realizations of random variables, the set E is a random set and the graph G_n is a random graph. In particular, these graphs are generalizations of interval graphs. Specifically, if $I_1, I_2, \ldots, I_n$ are intervals on the real line, then the interval graph $G(I_n)$ is defined by $V = \{1, 2, \ldots, n\}$ and $(i, j) \in E$ if $I_i \cap I_j \neq \emptyset$, $1 \leq i < j \leq n$. Thus, for the model under consideration, if $k = 1$, the intervals I_i are the intervals $[x_i - d/2, x_i + d/2]$, $i = 1, 2, \ldots, n$.

Let $V_m \subset V$ with $|V_m| = m < n$. $K_{m,d}$ is a complete subgraph of order m, if all $\binom{m}{2}$ pairs of elements of V_m are in E. If $m = 1$, then $K_{1,d}$ is a vertex, if $m = 2$, then $K_{2,d}$ is an edge and if $m = 3$, then $K_{3,d}$ is called a triangle. A complete subgraph of order m is said to be a maximal complete subgraph, denoted by $K_{m,d}^*$, if there is no vertex in $V \setminus V_m$ such that adjoining that vertex to V_m results in a complete subgraph of order $m + 1$. A vertex has degree ν, $\nu = 0, 1, 2, \ldots, n - 1$, if there are exactly ν edges incident with that vertex. If $\nu = 0$, then that vertex is said to be an isolated vertex.

3 Probability Distributions for Characteristics of Real Interval Graphs

We now describe the probability that a specified set of m vertices form a $K_{m,d}$ or a $K_{m,d}^*$. With no loss of generality, we can assume that these vertices are labeled $1, 2, \ldots, m$. Then,

$$P\{\max_{1 \leq i \leq n} X_i - \min_{1 \leq i \leq n} X_i \leq d\} = m \int_{-\infty}^{\infty} \{F(x + d) - F(x)\}^{m-1} f(x) \, dx. \quad (1)$$

Similarly,

$$\begin{aligned} P\{\{1, 2, \ldots m\} \text{ is a } K_{m,d}^*\} &= m(m-1) \int_{-\infty}^{\infty} \int_{x_1}^{x_1+d} \{F(x_2) - F(x_1)\}^{m-2} \\ &\quad \times \{1 - F(x_1 + d) + F(x_2 - d)\}^{n-m} \\ &\quad \times f(x_1) f(x_2) \, dx_1 \, dx_2. \end{aligned} \quad (2)$$

The probability that a specified vertex forms a $K_{1,d}^*$ (i.e. is isolated) is

$$P\{1 \text{ is isolated}\} = \int_{-\infty}^{\infty} \{1 - F(x + d) + F(x - d)\}^{n-1} f(x) \, dx. \quad (3)$$

The probability that a specified vertex has degree ν, $\nu = 0, 1, \ldots, n - 1$, is

$$\begin{aligned} P\{1 \text{ has degree } \nu\} &= \binom{n-1}{\nu} \int_{-\infty}^{\infty} \{F(x + d) - F(x - d)\}^{\nu} \\ &\quad \times \{1 - F(x + d) + F(x - d)\}^{n-\nu-1} f(x) \, dx. \end{aligned} \quad (4)$$

4 Asymptotic Properties of Random Interval Graphs

To obtain asymptotic approximations to the above distributions, some assumptions concerning the behavior of the probability density function $f_X(x)$ are needed. Hence we will assume that the probability density function is uniformly continuous on every compact subset of the carrier set for X and let $f'_X(x)$ exist and be uniformly bounded on the carrier set of X. We now examine the asymptotic behavior of the probability distributions introduced in the preceding section, under the conditions $n \to \infty$ and $d \to 0$ (usually, d is a given function of n, $d = d(n)$) and also assuming the regularity conditions for $f_X(x)$ given above.

Let $(A_t)_{t \in T}$ be a family of events depending on the parameter t. We will say that the asymptotic probability of A_t, for $t \to t'$, is p whenever we have $\lim_{t \to t'} P\{A_t\}/p = 1$. Then the asymptotic probability ($d \to 0$ as $n \to \infty$) that the vertices $1, 2, \ldots, m$ form a $K_{m,d}$ is

$$m\, d^{m-1} \int_{-\infty}^{\infty} f^m(x)\, dx. \tag{5}$$

Note that as $d \to 0$, the probability that the specified vertices form a $K_{m,d}$ tends to zero. Formula (5) also tends to zero, but the ratio approaches unity. The asymptotic probability ($d \to 0$ as $n \to \infty$, so that $nd \to 0$) that the vertices $1, 2, \ldots, m$ form a $K^*_{m,d}$ is

$$d^{m-1} \int_{-\infty}^{\infty} f^m(x)\, \{m + (n-m)f(x)[(m-1)d - 2m]\}\, dx. \tag{6}$$

The asymptotic probability ($d \to 0$ as $n \to \infty$, so that $nd \to 0$) that vertex 1 is isolated is

$$1 - 2nd \int_{-\infty}^{\infty} f^2(x)\, dx. \tag{7}$$

The asymptotic probability ($d \to 0$ as $n \to \infty$, so that $nd \to 0$) that vertex 1 has degree ν is

$$\binom{n-1}{\nu}(2d)^\nu \int_{-\infty}^{\infty} f^{\nu+1}(x)\, \{1 - 2nd\, f(x)\}\, dx. \tag{8}$$

5 Asymptotic Poisson and Normal Distributions

In this section, we give specific limiting distributions for the graph theoretic characteristics previously described.

If $n^m d^{m-1} \to \tau > 0$ as $n \to \infty$ and $d \to 0$, then both the number of complete subgraphs of order m and the number of maximal complete subgraphs of order m are asymptotically Poisson distributed with the same mean $\binom{n}{m}md^{m-1}\int_{-\infty}^{\infty}f^m(x)\,dx$ $(m=2,3,\ldots)$. If $n\to\infty$ and $d\to 0$ so that $dn/\ln(n)\to\tau_1>0$, then the number of isolated vertices has an asymptotic Poisson distribution with expected value $n\int_{-\infty}^{\infty}e^{-2ndf(x)}f(x)\,dx$. If $n\to\infty$ and $d\to 0$ so that $n^{\nu+1}d^{\nu}\to\tau_2>0$, then the number of vertices of degree ν $(\nu=2,3,\ldots)$ is asymptotically Poisson distributed with mean $n^{\nu+1}(2d)^{\nu}\int_{-\infty}^{\infty}f^{\nu+1}(x)\,dx$.

For each of these characteristics, limiting normal distributions have also been obtained. Clearly, if the asymptotic Poisson means tend to infinity, then the random variables described above, when suitably normalized, will be asymptotically normally distributed with mean zero and variance unity. Alternatively, the theory of U-statistics can also be successfully exploited to establish normal limits. Due to space limitations, the specific details will be provided in a more extensive manuscript.

6 Multidimensional Extensions

In this section, we assume that $X_1, X_2, \ldots, X_n$ are independent, identically distributed random variables, taking values in E_k, the Euclidean k-space, $k>1$. We assume that these random variables are distributed by the cumulative distribution function $F_X(x)$, where $F_X(x)$ is absolutely continuous with respect to k-dimensional Lebesgue measure and has probability density function $f_X(x)$. We will also assume that an L_p norm is specified on E_k, $1\leq p\leq\infty$. For the mathematical development, the primary difficulty in making the transition to more than one dimension, is that the realizations of the random variables can no longer be ordered.

As before, the vertices $1, 2, \ldots, m$ form a complete subgraph of order m, denoted by $K_{m,d}$, whenever $\rho(x_i, x_j)<d$, $1\leq i,j\leq m$. Let $A(K_{m,d})$ be the event that the vertices $1, 2, \ldots, m$ form a $K_{m,d}$. Let $S(x,r)$ be the ball of radius r with center at x. Let $B(m,d)=\{x_1,x_2,\ldots,x_m:\bigcap\rho(x_j,x_1)<d, j=2,\ldots,m\}$. Let $C(m,d)$ be the event that $x_j\in S(x_1,d/2)$, $j=2,\ldots,m$. It is easy to see that $C(m,d)\subset A(K_{m,d})\subset B(m,d)$. Therefore, we can write

$$P\{C(m,d)\}\leq P\{A(K_{m,d})\}\leq P\{B(m,d)\},$$

and hence

$$\int_{E_k}\left\{\int_{S(x_1,d/2)}\prod_{i=2}^{m}f_X(x_i)\,dx_i\right\}f_X(x_1)\,dx_1\leq P\{A(K_{m,d})\} \qquad (9)$$

$$\leq\int_{E_k}\left\{\int_{B(m,d)}\prod_{i=2}^{m}f_X(x_i)\,dx_i\right\}f_X(x_1)\,dx_1.$$

In a similar manner, we can obtain upper and lower bounds on the probability that a given set of m vertices form a maximal complete subgraph of order m.

It can be shown that these inequalities are adequate for establishing the limiting behavior of the number of complete subgraphs of order m or the number of maximal complete subgraphs of order m. This is accomplished by using indicator functions and the method of moments for establishing Poisson limits and the theory of U-statistics for establishing normal limits. Further, the probability that vertex 1 is of degree $\nu > 0$ is given by

$$P\{1 \text{ has degree } \nu\} = \binom{n-1}{\nu} \int_{E_k} \left\{ \int_{S(x,d)} f_X(y)\, dy \right\}^{\nu} \qquad (10)$$
$$\times \left\{ 1 - \int_{S(x,d)} f_X(w)\, dw \right\}^{n-\nu-1} f_X(x)\, dx.$$

Similarly, the probability that vertex 1 is isolated is given by

$$P\{1 \text{ is isolated}\} = \int_{E_k} \left\{ 1 - \int_{S(x,d)} f_X(y)\, dy \right\}^{n-1} f_X(x)\, dx. \qquad (11)$$

As in the one-dimensional case, in order to obtain uniform approximations to the above integrals, various smoothness conditions on $f_X(x)$ are needed; these include the requirement that $f_X(x)$ is uniformly continuous on every compact set and that the partial derivatives are uniformly bounded. Then, for example, it is possible to establish that the number of complete subgraphs of order m ($m > 1$) will have an asymptotic Poisson distribution whenever $d^{k(m-1)} n^m \to \tau > 0$, as $n \to \infty$ and $d \to 0$.

Remark. Formula (1) is related to a standard formula in the theory of order statistics (see David (1981)). There is, however, one fundamental difference. Let R_n be the range of a random sample $X_1, X_2, \ldots, X_n$ distributed by $F_X(x)$, a cumulative distribution function absolutely continuous with respect to Lebegue measure. Then

$$P\{R_n \leq r\} = n \int_{-\infty}^{\infty} \{F(x+r) - F(x)\}^{n-1} f(x)\, dx.$$

Here the realization is r, whereas d in (1) is a parameter. Our interest is not in the distribution of R_n but rather in the distribution of the number of m-tuples that meet the condition in the left hand side of (1). The limit condition used here, namely, $d \to 0$, is not natural in the theory of order statistics, since that would be equivalent to the range R_n tending to zero. There, the limiting distributions are studied under the assumption $n \to \infty$. •

7 Identification of Mixtures of Distributions

A widely used application of cluster analysis is the detection of mixtures of distributions. Specifically, assume $f_X(x) = \alpha f_1(x) + (1-\alpha) f_2(x)$, with $0 \leq \alpha \leq 1$, where $f_1(x)$ and $f_2(x)$ are distinct probability density functions.

Then, under various conditions on α, $f_1(x)$ and $f_2(x)$, a cluster analysis would be expected to detect two clusters; one cluster consisting largely of data from $f_1(x)$ and the other consisting primarily of data from $f_2(x)$. This leads in a natural way to the following question in statistical inference: Is the data that has been obtained from a homogeneous population (i.e. $\alpha = 0$ or $\alpha = 1$, or equivalently, $f_1(x) = f_2(x)$), or from a non-trivial mixture of two populations?

To illustrate some of the techniques proposed in this report as potential test criteria, the following simple case is treated. Let $f_1(x)$ and $f_2(x)$ be univariate normal distributions. The mean of $f_1(x)$ will be zero and the variance unity, and we will vary the mean μ and variance σ^2 of $f_2(x)$.

For this case, we will calculate the distribution of the number of complete subgraphs of order m and provide specific numerical values for $m = 2$. These values will be "normalized", so that they can be interpreted for all "large" values of n.

Then, the probability that m specified vertices form a $K_{m,d}$ is

$$P\{K_{m,d}\} = m \int_{-\infty}^{\infty} \{F(x+d) - F(x)\}^{m-1} f(x)\, dx,$$

where $f(x) = \alpha f_1(x) + (1-\alpha) f_1(x)$ and $F(x)$ is the corresponding cumulative distribution function. Using the approximation given above, we have

$$P\{K_{m,d}\} \sim 2md^{m-1} \int_{-\infty}^{\infty} f^m(x)\, dx,$$

For the specific case at hand, the mixture of two univariate normal distributions in the above specified form, this gives

$$P\{K_{m,d}\} \sim 2md^{m-1} \sum_{k=0}^{m} \binom{m}{k} \frac{\alpha^k (1-\alpha)^{m-k}}{(2\pi)^{m/2} \sigma^{m-k}} \int_{-\infty}^{\infty} e^{-\frac{kx^2}{2} - \frac{(m-k)(x-\mu)^2}{2\sigma^2}}\, dx. \quad (12)$$

Evaluating the integral, we obtain

$$P\{K_{m,d}\} \sim 2md^{m-1} \sum_{k=0}^{m} \binom{m}{k} \frac{\alpha^k (1-\alpha)^{m-k} e^{-\frac{(m-k)\mu^2}{2} + \frac{(m-k)^2 \mu^2}{2\sigma^2 (k\sigma^2 + m - k)}}}{(2\pi)^{(m-1)/2} \sigma^{m-k-1} (k\sigma^2 + m - k)^{1/2}}. \quad (13)$$

Hence, the expected number of complete subgraphs of order m is approximately given by

$$S_{m,d} \sim 2md^{m-1} \binom{n}{m} \sum_{k=0}^{m} \binom{m}{k} \frac{\alpha^k (1-\alpha)^{m-k} e^{-\frac{(m-k)\mu^2}{2} + \frac{(m-k)^2 \mu^2}{2\sigma^2 (k\sigma^2 + m - k)}}}{(2\pi)^{(m-1)/2} \sigma^{m-k-1} (k\sigma^2 + m - k)^{1/2}}. \quad (14)$$

In a similar manner, we can approximate the variance of $K_{m,d}$, and specifically for $K_{2,d}$, we get

$$\frac{4n^3 d^2}{2\pi \sigma^{m-k-1} (k\sigma^2 + m - k)^{1/2}} \sum_{k=0}^{3} \binom{3}{k} \alpha^k (1-\alpha)^{m-k} e^{-\frac{(m-k)\mu^2}{2} + \frac{(m-k)^2 \mu^2}{2(k\sigma^2 + m - k)}}.$$

Table 1: Table of asymptotic means and variances of the number of edges (both normalized as described in the text).

μ	Means	Variances
0	0.282	0.092
1	0.251	0.072
2	0.193	0.041
3	0.156	0.026
∞	0.141	0.023

Included is a brief table of values for the asymptotic means and variances of the number of edges, when $n^2 d \to \infty$, and hence the asymptotic normal approximations are valid. To provide specific values, we have set $\alpha = 1/2$ and $\sigma^2 = 1$. So that the results can be interpreted for "large n" in general, the means have been normalized by the factor $n^2 d$ and the variance by the factor $4n^3 d^2$. In particular note that when $n^2 d \to \infty$, rescaling the number of edges by this factor, forces the asymptotic variances to zero. Thus, asymptotic consistency of tests for mixtures has been established under the given conditions.

Acknowledgements: This research work has been partly supported by grant no. Go 490/4-3 from the German Research Foundation (DFG).

References

BOCK, H.H. (1974): *Automatische Klassifikation.* Vandenhoeck & Ruprecht, Göttingen.

DAVID, H.A. (1981): *Order statistics.* John Wiley & Sons, New York.

EBERL, W., HAFNER, R. (1971): Die asymptotische Verteilung von Koinzidenzen. *Zeitschrift für Wahrscheinlichkeitstheorie und verwandte Gebiete, 18, 322–332.*

GODEHARDT, E. (1990): *Graphs as structural models.* Vieweg, Braunschweig.

GODEHARDT, E., HARRIS, B. (1995): Asymptotic properties of random interval graphs and their use in cluster analysis. *University of Wisconsin Statistics Department Technical Report (submitted for publication).*

HAFNER, R. (1972): Die asymptotische Verteilung von mehrfachen Koinzidenzen. *Zeitschrift für Wahrscheinlichkeitstheorie und verwandte Gebiete, 21, 96–108.*

JAMMALAMADAKA, S.R., JANSON, S. (1986): Limit theorems for a triangular scheme of U-statistics with applications to interpoint distances. *Annals of Probability 14, 1347–1358.*

JAMMALAMADAKA, S.R., ZHOU, X. (1990): Some goodness of fit tests in higher dimensions based on interpoint distances. In: *Proceedings of the R.C. Bose Symposium on Probability, Statistics and Design of Experiments, Delhi 1988.* Wiley Eastern, New Delhi, 391–404.

MAEHARA, H. (1990): On the intersection graph of random arcs on the cycle. In: M. Karoński, J. Jaworski, A. Ruciński (eds.): *Random Graphs '87.* John Wiley & Sons, New York – Chichester – Brisbane, 159–173.

Labor Supply Decisions in Germany –
A Semiparametric Regression Analysis

Wolfram Kempe[1]

Institut für Wirtschaftsforschung Halle, Abteilung Arbeitsmarkt
D-06038 Halle, Germany

Abstract: This paper analyzes labor supply decisions of married women in order to identify differences between East and West Germany. The semiparametric General Additive Model (GAM) was chosen to avoid assumptions about the functional type of correlation and to discover characteristics in behavior. The estimator is based on a partial integration following Linton and Nielsen (1995). The analytical features of the new estimator are easier to determine than in the traditional backfitting algorithm. This analysis unveiled significant differences of labor supply behavior among East and West Germany.

1 Introduction

The estimation of labour supply is a main field of research for quantitative labour economists. A number of studies for former West Germany exists from the beginning of the 1990s (see Merz (1990), Strøm and Wagenhals (1991), Stobernack (1991)). They used data from the Socio-Economic Panel (SOEP) of the German Institute for Economic Research (DIW) in Berlin. The results indicate a distinctive variability in decision patterns for married women. This paper attempts to identify differences in labour market participation of women in East and West Germany. Historically labour market participation of women in the GDR was significantly higher than in the FRG. One might suppose that this pattern has not completely disappeared after unification. Yet it is empirically not clear to what extent functional relationships of labour supply determination are similar in East and West.

This study uses nonparametric regression to avoid assumptions about the functional relationship between determinants of labour supply and response variable. The method rests on the principle of local averaging and suffers from the curse of dimensionality. One way to deal with it is to apply Additive Models (AM). The assumption of separability reduces the regression dimension to one.

Since the response variable (participation) is binary a parametric link-function is required. This combination of nonparametric and parametric methods belongs to the (semiparametric) class of Generalized Additive Models (GAM, see Hastie and Tibshirani (1991)). This paper uses the recently de-

---

[1] I gratefully acknowledge the support from Stefan Sperlich (Special Research Unit SFB 373 'Quantification and Simulation of Economic Processes' at Humboldt-University Berlin) for the computational implementation of the integration estimator.

veloped integration estimator of Linton and Nielsen (1995) to implement the nonparametric AM[2].

The paper has the following structure: Section 2 and 3 present the model and the estimation procedure. Section 4 introduces the data used and the variables. Section 5 discusses the estimation results.

2 The Model

The generalization of the multivariate linear regression $Y = X^T\beta + \varepsilon$ leads to

$$Y = c + \sum_{j=1}^{p} g_j(X_j) + \varepsilon, \qquad (1)$$

$E(\varepsilon_i) = 0$. The linear parameters β_j are replaced by functions g_j which are not necessarily linear. The regression function is

$$m(x) = E(Y|X = x) = c + g_1(x_1) + \ldots + g_p(x_p) \qquad (2)$$

where $X = (x_1, \ldots, x_p)$ is a vector of explanatory variables observed in the data, c is a constant. The unknown functions $\{g_j(\bullet)\}_{j=1}^{p}$ fulfill the condition $E_{X_j} g(X_j) = 0$. They are univariate and describe the relative explanatory power of each variable x_j. These functions are estimated separately using nonparametric kernel density estimators (see Härdle (1990)). Asymptotically, the single p-dimensional estimation is thereby reduced to p one-dimensional estimations.

The graphical presentation of the p dimensions of the analysis is straightforward: The p plots - one for each function - show the marginal effects of the variables x_j on the response variable Y.

In theory all variables sum to a value of the response variable for each individual in the sample. In practice, this realization of the response variable is not observed and therefore called latent variable Y^*:

$$Y^* = c + \sum_{j=1}^{p} g_j(X_j) + \varepsilon. \qquad (3)$$

ϵ is the stochastic error component with distribution: $\epsilon \sim N(0, \sigma_\varepsilon^2)$. It is assumed to be independent of X.

The *observed* response variable Y is dichotomous: Participation or non-participation in the labour market. Latent and observed variable are related: If the latent variable Y^* is above a threshold value α the observed variable Y indicates participation ($Y = 1$), and non-participation ($Y = 0$) otherwise. Equation (2) fails to hold in the case of a binary choice dependent variable. $E(Y|X = x)$ is the probability of participation in the labour market for

---

[2]Using the well-known backfitting algorithm has the severe drawback that its asymptotic properties can not be computed in practice.

women. But it does normally not fall in the range $[0,1]$ if model (1) is used. Introducing a link function G which has support over $[0,1]$ gives the Generalized Additive Model[3] of the form

$$m(x) = E(Y|X = x) = G(c + \sum_{j=1}^{p} g_j(X_j)). \quad (4)$$

The assumption ($\varepsilon \sim N(0, \sigma_\varepsilon^2)$) implies that the link function is normally distributed[4]. Denoting the Normal $\Phi(\bullet)$ the model (using eight explanatory variables) can be written

$$m(x) = E(Y|X = x) = \Phi(c + \sum_{j=1}^{8} g_j(x_j)).$$

3 Estimation Procedure

The standard procedure for Generalized Additive Models[5] is backfitting, an iterative optimization with initialization values, an algorithm and a terminal condition. For a model of the form $E(Y|X) = c + \sum g_j(X_j)$ the initialization values are determined in a first step: $\hat{g}_1^{(0)}, \hat{g}_2^{(0)}, \ldots, \hat{g}_p^{(0)}$. The second step estimates the functions g_j. Note that $E(g_j(X_j)) = 0 \; \forall j$ implies $\hat{c} = E(Y|X)$. It uses the principle of partial residuals (Gauss-Seidel-algorithm):

$$\begin{aligned}
\hat{g}_1^{(1)} &= Y - \hat{c} - \hat{g}_2^{(0)} - \ldots - \hat{g}_p^{(0)}, \\
\hat{g}_2^{(1)} &= Y - \hat{c} - \hat{g}_1^{(1)} - \hat{g}_3^{(0)} - \ldots - \hat{g}_p^{(0)}, \quad (5)\\
&\vdots \\
\hat{g}_p^{(1)} &= Y - \hat{c} - \hat{g}_1^{(1)} - \ldots - \hat{g}_{p-1}^{(1)}.
\end{aligned}$$

The iteration ends when the terminal condition is fulfilled[6]: $|\hat{g}_j^{(l)} - \hat{g}_j^{(l-1)}| < \alpha$. The procedure has some undesirable properties: The results are influenced by the order of estimation and the choice of initial values. It is not known if convergence has actually been achieved when the iteration is stopped. The terminal condition is intuitively chosen. The estimator is analytically not tractable in practice [7].

Recently, an analytical approach for the class of additive models[8] has been

---

[3] see Hastie und Tibshirani (1991).
[4] see Ronning (1991), S. 8ff.
[5] Introducing a link function in the GAM is irrelevant for the nonparametric estimation of the functions g_j. Hence analyzing the Additive Model is sufficient.
[6] For a detailed discussion see Hastie and Tibshirani (1991).
[7] A complete presentation and discussion is given in Härdle and Hall (1993).
[8] The results hold regardless of the inclusion of a link function for the Generalized Additive Models.

developed by Linton and Nielsen (1995): Their estimator is based on integration to reduce the dimension of the regression[9].

The expectation of the function $g_j(\bullet)$ can be written as $\int g_j(\omega) f_j(\omega) d\omega = 0$. The function f_j is the marginal distribution of x_j. The regression function is

$$m(x_1, \ldots, x_p) = c + \sum_{j=1}^{p} g_j(x_j).$$

One can integrate out $(p-1)$ dimensions using the joint distribution f_{-j} because the following holds

$$g_j(x) + c = \int m(x_1, \ldots, x, \ldots, x_p) f_{-j}(x_1, \ldots, x_p) \prod_{s \neq j} dx_s, \quad (6)$$

where f_{-j} is the joint distribution of $X_{i1}, \ldots, X_{i(j-1)}, X_{i(j+1)}, \ldots, X_{ip}$. Equation (6) is an expectation and can be estimated by $\hat{g}_j(x) = \frac{1}{n} \sum_{i=1}^{n} m(\bullet)$. A multivariate Nadaraya-Watson estimator is used to determine the function $m(\bullet)$. This leads to

$$\begin{aligned}\hat{g}_j(x) &= \frac{1}{n} \sum_{i=1}^{n} \widehat{m}(X_{i1}, \ldots, X_{i(j-1)}, x, X_{i(j+1)}, \ldots, X_{ip}) \\ &= \frac{1}{n} \sum_{i=1}^{n} \left[\frac{\sum_{l=1}^{n} [\prod_{s \neq j} L_{h'_n}(X_{ls} - X_{is})] K_{h_n}(X_{lj} - x) Y_l}{\sum_{t=1}^{n} [\prod_{s \neq j} L_{h'_n}(X_{ts} - X_{is})] K_{h_n}(X_{tj} - x)} \right] \end{aligned} \quad (7)$$

h_n is the binwidth of the kernel K that belongs to the jth dimension we want to analyze. The binwidths h'_n belong to the kernels L of all other dimensions $s \neq j$.

The integration estimator has the disadvantage that it requires the (at least two) parameters h_n and h'_n to be chosen. But this is outweighed by the advantages: The asymptotic distribution of the bias, the variance and the convergence rate can be determined. Since the derivatives of the additive functions become estimable elasticities and rates of substitution can be derived[10]. Furthermore, the results in Section 5 include confidence intervals.

Chen, Härdle, Linton and Severance-Lossin (1995) have shown that the integration estimator is consistent and asymptotically normal. Variance and bias of backfitting and integration estimator have been examined through simulations. They show that the former procedure performs better with respect to the overall regression function $\widehat{m}$[11] while the latter is superior in the individual additive functions $\hat{g}_j$. This is a distinctive practical advantage because one is interested in the separate interpretation of each explanatory variable. Two practical problems remain to be resolved: the choice of the binwidth can lead to over- or undersmoothing. And the estimation is not

---

[9] see also Chen, Härdle, Linton and Severance-Lossin (1995).
[10] see Severance-Lossin and Sperlich (1995).
[11] The reason is that backfitting includes an estimate of the residuals; see (5).

robust at the margins due to sparse data which results in wide confidence intervals. Therefore outliers must be excluded from the analysis.

Another problem has to be taken into account: sample selection bias. The variable wage is a main determinant of labour supply. However its influence on individual decisions can not be measured for individuals out of work. But estimation with the subsample of employed individuals is not consistent because the subsample is not randomly chosen.

Heckman (1979) has suggested the following remedy for the selection bias: Using the whole sample of employed and unemployed a correction variable λ[12] is estimated. It represents the probability of belonging to the group of employed[13].

In a second step $\hat{\lambda}$ and other variables are used to estimate the wage level which could theoretically be earned by the unemployed. This completes the vector of wages for all individuals in the sample. The last step is to estimate the Generalized Additive Model.

Hence the estimation process has three stages:

1. The reduced GAM estimation for the variable $\hat{\lambda}$.

$$\hat{\lambda} = f(\text{CHILD, EDUC, UNEMPL, JOBEXP, RENT, INCHUSB, FHHINC})$$

2. OLS for the variable wage to correct for sample selection.

$$\hat{w} = f(\hat{\lambda}, \text{EDUC, UNEMPL, JOBEXP})$$

3. The complete GAM.

$$Y = f(\hat{w}, \text{AGE, EDUC, RENT, UNEMPL, CHILD, INCHUSB, FHHINC})$$

4 Variables and Data

The dependent variable Y is the employment status:

$$Y = \begin{cases} 0 & \text{individual is not working} \\ 1 & \text{individual is employed (including part-time employment)} \end{cases}$$

The explanatory exogenous variables X are

- WAGE: wage per hour was calculated from net income and specified working hours

- AGE: Age of the individual.

---

[12] This variable is often denoted as the inverse of Mills' ratio.
[13] see Franz (1996) p.69ff for a discussion.

- EDUC: Qualification is the sum of years in formal education (e.g. a university degree counting for five years). This gives a quasi-continous quantitative measure.

- RENT: This variable is included because the cost of accommodation is the single biggest expenditure of a household. Mortgage payments are used for home owners.

- UNEMPL: the unemployment rate of the Bundesland is included as a regional indicator for the state of the economy.

- CHILD: Number of children according to the definition of the SOEP (under age of 16).

- INCHUSB: The net income of the husband.

- FHHINC: This variable includes all other sources of income to the household like pensions, benefits, allowances, capital gains and rent from properties. It can be negative due to payments to divorcees, and dependent relatives outside the home.

The data comes from the survey No.10 of the SOEP in 1993. It covered 13200 individual of age 16 and over. The focus of this paper is on married women between 25 and 60[14]. Students, apprentices and pensioners were excluded. Individuals with missing values for one or more variables were also excluded (around 13%). Missing values occured to the same extent for all variables which makes a systematic bias from the exclusion highly unlikely. The analysis looks at labour supply decisions in East and West Germany separately: The two datasets contain data of 1283 West German women and data of 958 East German women respectively.

5 Results

The two samples reveal significant differences in labour supply of West and East German women. The results for the West German sample confirm conventional considerations about labour supply decisions and their explanation. But the East German sample deviates in various variables. The biggest differences were found for the variables wage, children and income of husband. Variations were also found with respect to education.

Figures (1) to (4) display the corresponding nonparametric functions g_j for East and West[15]. The presentation includes connected confidence intervals

---

[14]The standard definition of the work force is 15 to 65 years. The narrower definition excluded mostly individuals in education and early retirement.

[15]The variables age, rent, unemployment and other sources of income do seem to have rather similar influence on labour supply in East and West. Space limitations preclude their presentation. See Kempe (1996) provides an extensive treatment.

at the 10% level[16] (dashed line). 1 to 2% of the data have been truncated at the margins because data sparsity would lead to disproportionately wide confidence intervals.

Each figure contains four pictures: Two additive functions can be found in the top row. The results for the West German women are on the left and for the East German Women on the right respectively. Below, corresponding density functions for the explanatory variable are displayed.

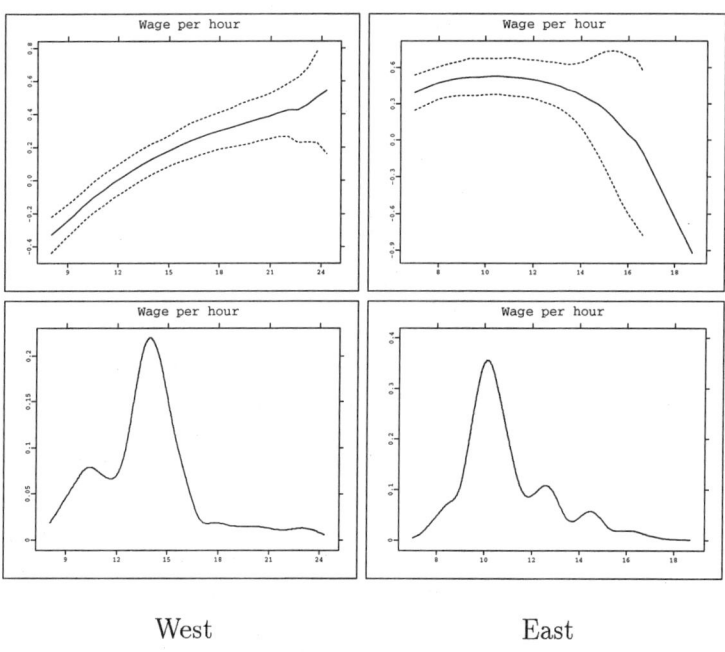

West   East

Figure 1: Variable *WAGE*

Participation in the labour market was positively related with wage in the West German sample. Higher remuneration prospects make it more attractive to take up employment. The relationship is almost linear. The narrow confidence intervals indicate robustness of the result. In contrast, the function for the East shows a negative quadrative form. The tendency to work is relatively high at the bottom end of the income scale and rises further in the middle range. For higher wage however the labour market participation of East German women sharply declines. Note that the SOEP counts individuals receiving unemployment benefits as non-participants of the labour market. It seems that the higher the prospective wage due to educational background and experience the more difficult it was to find an employer.

---

[16]The estimated regressor wage (Heckman procedure) can be expected to increase the uncertainty. However, lack of measurement does not allow to quantify it adequately in the graphs.

It is important to remember that unemployment in East German regions reached (first time) its highest levels in 1992/1993. The standard positive relationship between participation and wage must have been overlaid by an irregular effect. This irregularity could be the devaluation of human capital acquired in another political system. Note that the relatively wide confidence intervals also allow for a straight line with zero slope. This means that a change in prospective wage would not be associated with a change in labour supply !

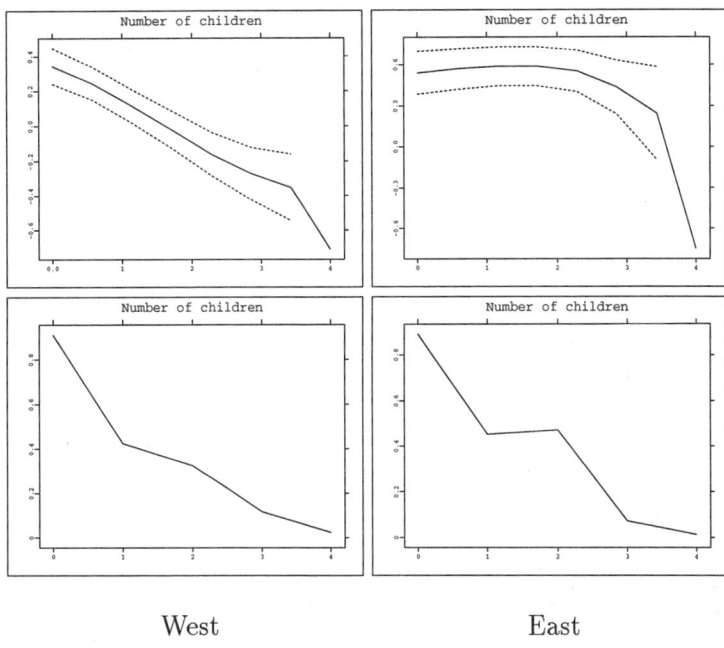

West   East

Figure 2: Variable *CHILD*

A second main factor affecting the decision of women to seek employment are children in the household (Figure 2). The estimated function for West German women shows a clear linear negative relationship. This is consistent with standard findings. The Eastern sample again gives a quite different picture. Up to two children do not seem to impair the labour supply of their mothers. It is worth remembering that working mothers were a normal phenomenon in the GDR - a pattern that seems to prevail. This matches with the fact that nursery-schools are still more wide-spread and cheaper in the East than in the West of Germany - a legacy of the GDR that has at least partly survived unification. Furthermore, lower East German wages might 'force' both parents to seek employment to match the financial needs of having children. But the sharp kink downward in the graph illustrates that the compatibility of having children (three and more) and having a job is clearly limited - even for East German women.

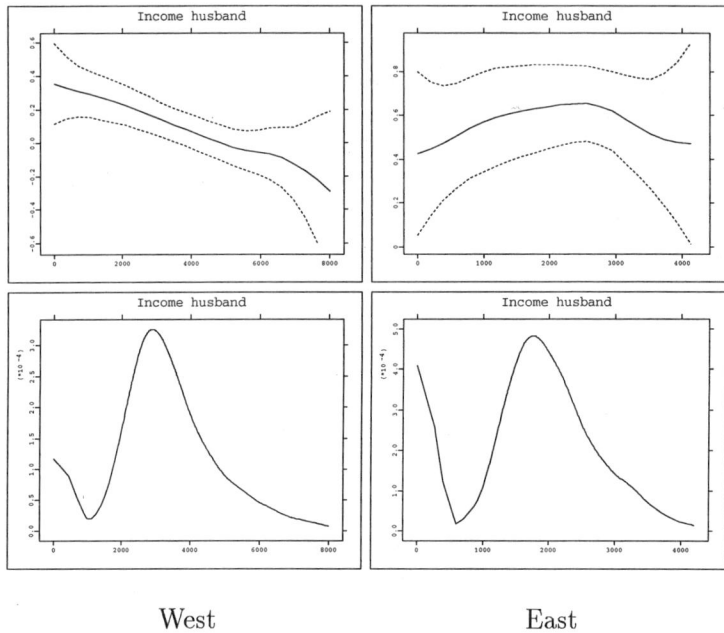

West   East

Figure 3: Variable *INCHUSB*

Figure 3 shows the connection between the income of the husband and labour supply of the wife. For West Germany the curve is strictly downward sloping: The more he earns the less attractive the labour market is to her. East German results tell a different story. The function is slightly positively sloped in the range from low to middle income of the husband. This range represents the biggest proportion of the sample. Note however the width of the confidence bands which makes the result not very reliable. Income differences were levelled in the GDR and are still relatively small which make women seek employment independently of the income of their partner. Since couples often belong to the same age cohort and social strata their earnings develop parallely.

The influence of the variable qualification (see figure (4)) on labour supply bears no surprise. The Western sample states a positive relationship between education and employment: Investment in human capital seeks to obtain pay-offs. Deviating from this is the negative slope of the function for highly qualified East German women. The explanation is again the irregular devaluation of human capital which made it difficult for individuals with high qualification of GDR vintage to find appropriate employment under Western conditions.

The results for the remaining variables are reported without graphical presentation: Positive other sources of income tend to reduce employment of women. Negative source of incomes (payments of the household to persons

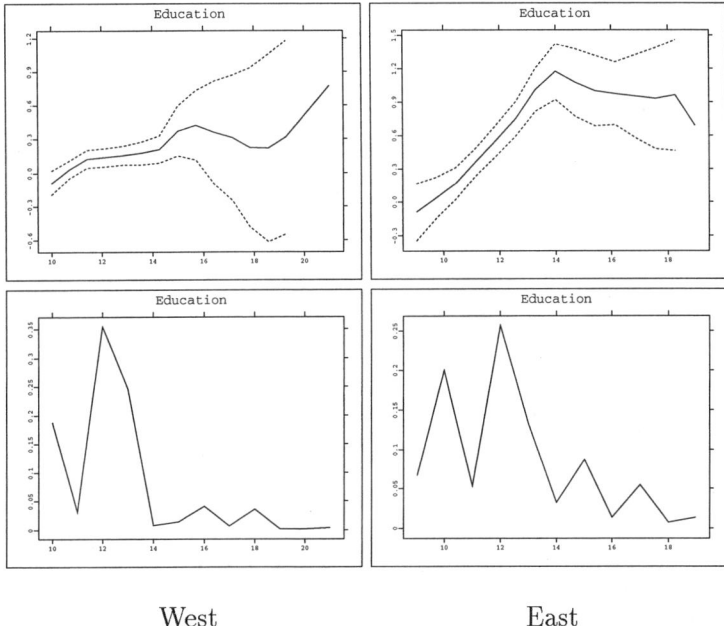

Figure 4: Variable *EDUC*

outside it) raise occupational activities. The results are roughly the same for both samples which is surprising if one considers the absolute difference of accumulated wealth per household between East and West.

Expenditure for accomodation has a strong positive influence on the economic activity of women in the West. This tendency is weaker in the East German sample. In 1992/93 Eastern rents had only begun to rise and were still well below Western levels.

The well-known results of labour supply with respect to age cohorts are confirmed with one exception: The decline of employment among women beyond their middle age is stronger in the East German sample. This finding is supported by relatively narrow confidence bands.

Regional unemployment does not play a significant role in the determination of labour supply - neither in the Western nor in Eastern sample. But the high aggregation level of the Länder might obscure relationships that would be visible in a more detailed disaggregation. However the survey of 1993 was the last to include informations about the regional origin of individuals.

Summary: The application of a nonparametric model has produced a detailed picture of the differences in labour supply determination for East and West German women. The nonparametric approach has revealed that East German labour supply deviates in various aspects from conventional findings.

References

CHEN, R.; HÄRDLE, W.; LINTON, O.B.; SEVERANCE-LOSSIN, E. (1995): Nonparametric Estimation of Additive Separable Regression Models. *SFB 373 Discussion Paper Nr. 50/95, Berlin.*

DEUTSCHES IINSTITUT FÜR WIRTSCHAFTSFORSCHUNG (1993): Das Sozio-ökonomische Panel, Benutzerhandbuch Bd. I und II, Version November 1993, DIW, Berlin.

FRANZ, W. (1996): Arbeitsmarktökonomik, Springer-Verlag, Heidelberg.

HÄRDLE, W. (1990): Applied Nonparametric Regression, Econometric Monograph Series 19, Cambridge University Press.

HÄRDLE, W.; HALL, P. (1993): On the Backfitting Algorithm for Additive Regression Models, *Statistica Neerlandica, 47, 43-57.*

HÄRDLE, W.; KLINKE, S.; TURLACH, B.A. (1995): XploRe – an interactive statistical computing environment, Springer-Verlag, New York.

HASTIE, T.J.; TIBSHIRANI, R.J. (1991): Generalized Additive Models, Monographs on Statistics and Applied Probability 43, Chapman and Hall, London.

HECKMAN, J.J. (1979): Sample Selection Bias as a Specification Error, *Econometrica, 47, 153-161.*

KEMPE, W. (1996): Das Arbeitsangebot verheirateter Frauen in den neuen und alten Bundesländern - Eine semiparametrische Regressionsanalyse, *Universität Potsdam, Wirtschafts- und Sozialwissenschaftliche Fakultät, Statistische Diskussionsbeiträge Nr. 2/96, Potsdam.*

LINTON, O.B.; NIELSEN, J.P. (1995): A kernel method of estimating structured nonparametric regression based on marginal integration, *Biometrika, 82, 93-100.*

MERZ, J. (1990): Femal Labor Supply: Labor Force Participation, Market Wage Rate and Working Hours of Married and Unmarried Women in the Federal Republic of Germany, *Jahrbücher für Nationalökonomie und Statistik, 207, 240-270.*

RONNING, G. (1991): Mikroökonometrie, Springer-Verlag, Berlin.

SEVERANCE-LOSSIN, E.; SPERLICH, S. (1995): Estimation of Derivative for Additive Seperable Models, *SFB 373 Discussion Paper Nr.60/95, Berlin.*

STOBERNACK, M. (1991): Das Arbeitsangebot in der Bundesrepublik Deutschland – Eine Schätzung auf der Basis des Sozio-ökonomischen Panels, *Jahrbücher für Nationalökonomie und Statistik, 208, 625-641.*

STRØM, S.; WAGENHALS, G. (1991): Female Labour Supply in the Federal Republic of Germany, *Jahrbücher für Nationalökonomie und Statistik, 208, 575-595.*

A Multiplicative Approach to Partitioning the Risk of Disease

M. Land, O. Gefeller

Department of Medical Statistics,
University of Göttingen, D-37073 Göttingen, Germany

Abstract: Analysing the interrelations between several exposure factors that affect the risk of developing a disease is an important aim in epidemiological studies. The relative risk is the perhaps most popular parameter for quantifying the strength of such interrelations. The paper introduces the concept of factorial relative risks as one possibility of generalizing the relative risk parameter to the context of several interrelated exposures. An axiomatic justification of the new parameter is given and it is outlined that the factorial relative risk of a single exposure factor in a multifactorial setting is a measure of its individual contribution to the joint effect of all considered exposures.

1 Introduction

The epidemiological parameter preferred for assessing the strength of the association of an exposure with a given disease is the *relative risk*. It is defined as the ratio of the risk of disease among the exposed to the risk of disease among the unexposed. However, in order to understand and describe the complex interrelations between disease and possible risk factors realistically, several exposure factors of prime interest as well as further covariables should be incorporated into the analysis simultaneously. This paper introduces the *factorial relative risk* parameter as an appropriate generalization of the concept of relative risk from the context of one exposure factor of prime interest to those situations where several exposures of prime interest have to be considered and the etiologic importance of all single exposures has to be quantified simultaneously. Such questions play an important role when deciding on compensation claims where the plaintiff (e.g. a worker) developed a disease that is suspected to be closely related to some risk factors (e.g. occupational agents) he was exposed to by the responsibility of the defendant (e.g. the employer). In such disputes, usually the fact has to be taken into consideration that in addition to the factors which the defendant is responsible for, the plaintiff's behaviour might have contributed to the damaging of health. In that case epidemiological methods should provide aids for quantifying the contributions of all considered exposures to the risk of disease in order to find justifiable tools for evaluating that share of the amount in dispute that the plaintiff has to bear himself (Christoffel and Teret (1991)). Methodological solutions to this legal problem have already been proposed. They are predominantly based on the *probability of causation* (Lagakos and Mosteller (1986)), the *expected years of life lost* (Robins and

Greenland (1991)) or the *partial attributable risk* (Eide and Gefeller (1995), Land and Gefeller (1997)), respectively. In contrast to these approaches the concept of factorial relative risk focuses on the multifactorial analysis of the individual risk of developing a given disease. In order to be more precise on this issue, let the term *joint relative risk of all exposures* denote the ratio of the risk of disease among those people that are exposed to all factors at the same time to the risk of disease among the unexposed. The factorial relative risk of a single exposure now quantifies its individual multiplicative contribution to the joint relative risk of all considered exposures.

The paper provides an axiomatic derivation of the factorial relative risk parameter. Desirable properties of the parameter are axiomatically established before an exact definition is given in paragraph 3. The process of defining this new risk parameter is concluded at the end of the same paragraph by proving that a parameter satisfying all conditions exists and is even uniquely determined.

2 Definitions and Notation

The basic parameters for defining measures to quantify the interrelations between n dichotomous exposure factors $E_1, \ldots, E_n$ and a disease of interest are the following elementary probabilities:

1) the probability of developing the disease and being simultaneously exposed to several factors at the same time is denoted by $P(D \cap E)$ or simply by p_E, where E is a suitably chosen subset of $\{E_1, \ldots, E_n\}$ which specifies the set of factors that the person is simultaneously exposed to;

2) the probability of not developing the disease while being exposed to a subtotal $E \subset \{E_1, \ldots, E_n\}$ of exposures is analogously denoted by $P(\overline{D} \cap E)$ or simply by q_E.

Each vector $\mathbf{p} = (p_E, q_E)_{E \subset \{E_1, \ldots, E_n\}}$ of elementary probabilities satisfies $0 \leq p_E, q_E \leq 1$, $E \subset \{E_1, \ldots, E_n\}$, and $\sum_{E \subset \{E_1, \ldots, E_n\}} p_E + q_E = 1$. For technical reasons, however, the extreme cases of any component of such a vector being 0 or 1 will be excluded from the derivation of the concept. Hence, the following considerations focus on the system Θ_n of all vectors of elementary probabilities whose components are elements of the interval $]0; 1[$.

The relative risk of being simultaneously exposed to several factors is called their *joint relative risk* and is defined as

$$RR_E = \frac{P(D|E)}{P(D|B)} = \frac{p_E \cdot (p_B + q_B)}{p_B \cdot (p_E + q_E)}, \qquad (1)$$

where E has the same interpretation as in 1), $P(D|E)$ denotes the risk of disease conditional on being exposed to exactly all those factors that are included in E and $P(D|B)$ denotes the risk of disease conditional on being exposed to none of the factors $E_1, \ldots, E_n$ (the *background risk*). The terms $ER_E = RR_E - 1$, $E \subset \{E_1, \ldots, E_n\}$, are called *joint excess risks*.

Example: Suppose the association of the risk of developing lung cancer with the dichotomized exposure factors S (ever having smoked daily), Q (ever having been occupationally exposed to quartz dust) and R (ever having been occupationally exposed to radon) is to be assessed. In that situation $RR_{\{A,R\}}$, for example, quantifies the proportional change in disease risk associated with being exposed to quartz dust and radon while never having smoked daily. The effect of smoking, for instance, can be assessed by estimating $RR_{\{S\}}$. However, the effect of smoking might be influenced by occupational exposures. Therefore, it is interesting to assess the additional effect of smoking with respect to four different combinations of occupational exposure: being exposed to *(i)* Q and R, *(ii)* R alone, *(iii)* Q alone, *(iv)* neither Q nor R. This leads to four stratum–specific relative risks of smoking, denoted by $RR_S^{Q,R}$, RR_S^R, RR_S^Q and $RR_S^\emptyset$, respectively. This consideration can be generalized as follows.

Suppose that E_i is one of the considered exposure factors and let all combinations of the remaining exposure factors form 2^{n-1} strata of the population, each one identified with an appropriate subset $E \subset \{E_1,\ldots,E_n\} \setminus \{E_i\}$ which includes all factors different from E_i that the people in the corresponding stratum are exposed to. The *stratum–specific relative risk* for an exposure E_i and a stratum-specifying set $E \subset \{E_1,\ldots,E_n\} \setminus \{E_i\}$ is defined as

$$RR^E_{E_i} = \frac{P(D|E \cup \{E_i\})}{P(D|E)} = \frac{p_{E \cup \{E_i\}} \cdot (p_E + q_E)}{p_E \cdot (p_{E \cup \{E_i\}} + q_{E \cup \{E_i\}})}. \tag{2}$$

In order to emphasize the fact that the terms RR_E and $RR^E_{E_i}$ depend on the underlying vector $\mathbf{p} = (p_E, q_E)_{E \subset \{E_1,\ldots,E_n\}}$ of elementary probabilities they are sometimes denoted by $RR_E(\mathbf{p})$ or $RR^E_{E_i}(\mathbf{p})$, respectively. Furthermore, the brackets "{" and "}" are sometimes dropped when specifying a selection of factors or a subset $E \subset \{E_1,\ldots,E_n\}$, respectively.

On the basis of these notations the next paragraph provides an axiomatic definition of the factorial relative risk parameter.

3 The Factorial Relative Risk

Like the joint and stratum–specific relative risk parameters, the factorial relative risks of single exposures should be functions of the underlying vectors of elementary probabilities and thus are formally defined in Definition 3 as components FRR_{E_i}, $i=1,\ldots,n$, of an n–dimensional parameter function $FRR : \Theta_n \to \mathbb{R}^n$, as detailed below. Each factorial relative risk FRR_{E_i} is supposed to reduce the complex information that is contained in a parameter vector $\mathbf{p} \in \Theta_n$ in order to quantify the "exposure–specific" contribution of factor E_i to the joint relative risk of all exposures. The meaning of the term "exposure–specific" in the context of factorial relative risks, however, needs to be clarified. This is done in the following by reducing the consideration to the special case of two factors E_1 and E_2.

The assumption that the association between factor E_1 and the disease is indepedent from being exposed to factor E_2 (and vice versa) is often referred to as the "absence of interaction" and can be formalized in at least two different ways (Rothman (1986)) by demanding E_1 and E_2 to satisfy either

1. $RR_{E_1}^{E_2} = RR_{E_1}^{B}$ (which is equivalent to $RR_{E_1,E_2} = RR_{E_1} \cdot RR_{E_2}$) or

2. $RR_{E_1,E_2} - RR_{E_2} = RR_{E_1} - RR_B$
   (which is equivalent to $ER_{E_1,E_2} = ER_{E_1} + ER_{E_2}$).

The first case reflects a multiplicative understanding of the term "absence of interaction", whereas the second case arises from an additive conception of the same term. The following derivation of the concept of factorial relative risks, however, is based upon the multiplicative interpretation of the state of absence of interaction. Whenever E_1 and E_2 interact, their exposure–specific effects are not completely determined by the terms RR_{E_1} or RR_{E_2} but are partly included in the joint relative risk RR_{E_1,E_2}. In that sense, the effect of interaction aggravates a clear division of the joint risk of both factors into exposure–specific components. Since the parameter FRR is supposed to quantify the *exposure-specific* contributions to the joint risk it is a natural idea to demand this parameter to remove the disguising effects of interaction. Therefore, the factorial relative risks ought to satisfy $RR_{E_1,E_2} = FRR_{E_1} \cdot FRR_{E_2}$ in all situations. The following definition transfers this idea to the case of n exposures being incorporated into the analysis.

Definition 1: A parameter function $\psi : \Theta_n \longrightarrow \mathbb{R}^n$ is a *factorization of the relative risk* whenever the parameters $\psi_1, \ldots, \psi_n$ multiply up to the joint relative risk $RR_{E_1,\ldots,E_n}$, i.e.:

$$\psi_1(\mathbf{p}) \cdot \ldots \cdot \psi_n(\mathbf{p}) = RR_{E_1,\ldots,E_n}(\mathbf{p}) \qquad \forall \mathbf{p} \in \Theta_n. \qquad (3)$$

A simple example of a parameter function that satisfies equation (3) can be obtained from a successive incorporation of factors into the analysis of their joint relative risks. At first the relative risk of a single exposure factor (the first one according to a specific order) is calculated. After that, the relative risk of the second factor according to the same order is calculated and it is based on that subpopulation that is already exposed to the first factor. Carrying out this algorithm up to the point where the relative risk of the last factor is calculated for that subpopulation that is already exposed to all preceding factors leads to a vector of n stratum–specific relative risks, called *sequential relative risks*. They can formally be defined for each factor E_i by

$$SRR_{E_i}^{\pi} = \begin{cases} RR_{E_i}^{E_{\pi(1)},E_{\pi(2)},\ldots,E_{\pi(j-1)}} & \text{if } i \neq \pi(1) \\ RR_{E_i} & \text{if } i = \pi(1) \end{cases}, \qquad (4)$$

where π is that permutation of the integers $1,\ldots,n$ that characterizes the order of incorporating the exposures into the analysis. Furthermore, j is chosen to indicate the position of E_i according to that order of factors, i.e.: $\pi(j) = i$. For a given exposure E_i and a fixed permutation π the sequential relative risk of that factor thus quantifies the proportional change in risk associated with being exposed to E_i conditional on already being exposed to all preceding factors. The following example illustrates the calculation of sequential relative risks and emphasizes the fact that using this risk parameter for comparing the importance of different exposure factors for the risk of developing a disease is a particular problematic matter.

Example: Suppose E_1, E_2 and E_3 are dichotomous exposure factors affecting a given disease. Table 1 shows the components of a hypothetical vector $(p_E, q_E)_{E \subset \{E_1, E_2, E_3\}} \in \Theta_3$ of elementary probabilities. The same table includes the resulting joint relative risks as well as the stratum–specific relative risks.

Table 1: Hypothetical vector $(p_E, q_E)_{E \subset \{E_1, E_2, E_3\}}$ of elementary probabilities and the resulting joint and stratum–specific relative risks

E	B	$\{E_1\}$	$\{E_2\}$	$\{E_3\}$	$\{E_1,E_2\}$	$\{E_1,E_3\}$	$\{E_2,E_3\}$	$\{E_1,E_2,E_3\}$
p_E	0.025	0.020	0.023	0.017	0.018	0.015	0.005	0.014
q_E	0.275	0.130	0.177	0.133	0.082	0.025	0.035	0.006
RR_E	1.000	1.600	1.380	1.360	2.160	4.500	1.500	8.400
$RR^E_{E_1}$	1.600*		1.565†	3.309◊			5.600‡	
$RR^E_{E_2}$	1.380*	1.350†		1.103◊		1.867‡		
$RR^E_{E_3}$	1.360	2.813	1.087		3.889			

The analysis of the values displayed by Table 1 shows that being exclusively exposed to the first factor, for instance, is associated with a higher increase in risk than being exclusively exposed to the second factor (compare the values which are indexed by ⋆). Furthermore, the additional exposure to the first factor (conditional on already being exposed to the second factor) is associated with a higher increase in risk than vice versa. This can be seen by comparing the values indexed by †. Finally, comparing the stratum–specific relative risks of factor E_1 to the corresponding stratum–specific relative risks of E_2 (corresponding values are indexed by ◊ or ‡, respectively), leads to the same result: the increase in risk associated with being exposed to E_1 is higher than the increase in risk associated with E_2, no matter which stratum is considered. However, the method of calculating sequential relative risks (according to $\pi = (1\ 3\ 2)$) assigns a higher risk value to factor E_2 than to E_1: $SRR^\pi_{E_1} = 1.600$, $SRR^\pi_{E_2} = 1.867$ and $SRR^\pi_{E_3} = 2.813$. From an epidemiological point of view this seems to be absurd. In a more formal way, however, it can be stated that the parameter function given by equation (4) is not monotone in stratum–specific relative risks in the sense of the following definition.

Definition 2: A parameter function $\psi : \Theta_n \longrightarrow \mathbb{R}^n$ is *monotone in stratum–specific relative risks* if it satisfies the conditions *(i)* and *(ii)* as detailed below.

(i) Let $\mathbf{p} \in \Theta_n$ and let $E_i, E_j \in \{E_1, \ldots, E_n\}$. If $RR^E_{E_i}(\mathbf{p}) \geq RR^E_{E_j}(\mathbf{p})$ holds for all $E \subset \{E_1, \ldots, E_n\} \setminus \{E_i, E_j\}$ then $\psi_i(\mathbf{p}) \geq \psi_j(\mathbf{p})$.

(ii) Let $E_i \in \{E_1, \ldots, E_n\}$ and let $\mathbf{p}_a, \mathbf{p}_b \in \Theta_n$. If $RR^E_{E_i}(\mathbf{p}_a) \geq RR^E_{E_i}(\mathbf{p}_b)$ holds for all $E \subset \{E_1, \ldots, E_n\}$ then $\psi_i(\mathbf{p}_a) \geq \psi_i(\mathbf{p}_b)$.

The consequences of demanding an n–dimensional risk parameter to satisfy the conditions (i) and (ii) given in Definition 2 are discussed in the following. Suppose that the strength of association (in terms of relative risk) between disease and exposure E_i is stronger in each stratum of the population than the strength of association between disease and E_j. Whenever (i) holds for a parameter function a risk value is assigned to E_i that is at least as high as that value that is assigned to E_j. Note that the sequential relative risks do not satisfy this condition, as can be seen from the example above.

Now suppose that the parameter vectors $\mathbf{p}_a$ and $\mathbf{p}_b$ represent different groups A and B of a population (e.g. the groups of men and women), and suppose further that E_i is an exposure factor whose stratum–specific relative risks are higher in group A than in group B, no matter which stratum is considered. Whenever (ii) holds for a parameter function, the risk value that is assigned to E_i with respect to group A is at least as high as the risk value for the same exposure in group B.

Monotonicity in stratum–specific relative risks is a particular important feature of those risk parameters that are devoted to the task of assessing the importance of single exposures in a multifactorial framework. Therefore, the factorial relative risk parameter ought to satisfy this condition and is thus defined as follows.

Definition 3: The *factorial relative risk* is a parameter function which is monotone in stratum–specific relative risks and factorizes the relative risk.

Note, however, that Definition 3 gives no evidence for the existence of a factorial relative risk parameter. Moreover, Definition 3 does not answer the question whether the factorial relative risk is uniquely defined. The following theorem provides an answer to both questions. It states that the factorial relative risk of an exposure E_i is uniquely defined by Definition 3 as a weighted geometric mean of its stratum–specific relative risks.

Theorem: There exists exactly one factorial relative risk parameter. The n–dimensional parameter is denoted by $FRR = (FRR_{E_1}, \ldots, FRR_{E_n})$ or by $FRR(\mathbf{p}) = (FRR_{E_1}(\mathbf{p}), \ldots, FRR_{E_n}(\mathbf{p}))$, $\mathbf{p} \in \Theta_n$, respectively. The factorial relative risk of an exposure E_i is given by

$$FRR_{E_i} = \sqrt[n!]{\prod_{E_i \notin E} \left(RR^E_{E_i}\right)^{|E|! \cdot (n-|E|-1)!}}, \qquad (5)$$

where $|E|$ denotes the number of factors contained in $E \subset \{E_1, \ldots, E_n\}$.

Proof: The fact that the parameter FRR satisfies Definition 3 is easily proved. However, the purely technical proof of that statement is not given here. In order to prove the statement of uniqueness it is shown that

$$\psi_i(\mathbf{p}) = FRR_{E_i}(\mathbf{p}), \quad \forall \mathbf{p} \in \Theta_n, \tag{6}$$

holds for all $E_i \in \{E_1, \ldots, E_n\}$ whenever $\psi : \Theta_n \to \mathbb{R}^n$ is any parameter function that satisfies the definitions 1 and 2. For all $\mathbf{p} \in \Theta_n$ the mapping $E \mapsto \ln(RR_E(\mathbf{p}))$, $E \subset \{E_1, \ldots, E_n\}$, can be viewed as a pseudo-Boolean function (Hammer and Holzmann (1992)). Therefore, there exist unique coefficients $\alpha_H(\mathbf{p}) \in \mathbb{R}$, $B \neq H \subset \{E_1, \ldots, E_n\}$, satisfying

$$\ln(RR_E(\mathbf{p})) = \sum_{B \neq H \subset E} \alpha_H(\mathbf{p}), \quad \forall E \subset \{E_1, \ldots, E_n\}. \tag{7}$$

The integer $\deg(\mathbf{p})$ is defined for all $\mathbf{p} \in \Theta_n$ as the number of subsets $H \subset \{E_1, \ldots, E_n\}$ with $\alpha_H(\mathbf{p}) \neq 0$. Equation (6) is now proved by induction with respect to $\deg(\mathbf{p})$. If $\deg(\mathbf{p}) = 0$, equation (7) implies that $RR_E(\mathbf{p}) = 1 \ \forall E \subset \{E_1, \ldots, E_n\}$. Hence, $RR_{E_i}^E(\mathbf{p}) = 1$ holds for all $E_i \in \{E_1, \ldots, E_n\}$ and $E \subset \{E_1, \ldots, E_n\}$. Since ψ satisfies condition (i) of Definition 2, we have $\psi_1(\mathbf{p}) = \ldots = \psi_n(\mathbf{p})$. Moreover, ψ factorizes the joint relative risk. Thus, $\psi_i(\mathbf{p}) = 1 = FRR_{E_i}(\mathbf{p})$ holds for all $i = 1, \ldots, n$. Now suppose, equation (6) is proved for all $\hat{\mathbf{p}} \in \Theta_n$ with $\deg(\hat{\mathbf{p}}) \leq k$ for some integer $k < 2^n - 1$ and let $\mathbf{p} \in \Theta_n$ with $\deg(\mathbf{p}) = k+1$. The set $\{E_1, \ldots, E_n\}$ can be divided into two subsets $\mathcal{E} = \bigcap_{\alpha_H(\mathbf{p}) \neq 0} H$ and $\mathcal{F} = \{E_1, \ldots, E_n\} \setminus \mathcal{E}$. Suppose $\mathcal{F}$ includes an exposure factor E_i. Then choose any $\tilde{p}_B$ from the interval $]0; \delta \cdot 2^{-n}[$, where $\delta = \min\{\exp(-\sum_{E_i \in H \subset E} \alpha_H(\mathbf{p})) | E \subset \{E_1, \ldots, E_n\}\}$. Furthermore, define $\tilde{p}_E := \tilde{p}_B \cdot \exp(\sum_{E_i \in H \subset E} \alpha_H(\mathbf{p}))$ and $\tilde{q}_E = (1/2^n) - \tilde{p}_E$, $E \subset \{E_1, \ldots, E_n\}$. It can easily be proved that $\tilde{\mathbf{p}} = (\tilde{p}_E, \tilde{q}_E)_{E \subset \{E_1, \ldots, E_n\}}$ is an element of Θ_n and that

$$\ln(RR_E(\tilde{\mathbf{p}})) = \ln\left(\frac{\tilde{p}_E(\tilde{p}_B + \tilde{q}_B)}{\tilde{p}_B(\tilde{p}_E + \tilde{q}_E)}\right) = \ln\left(\frac{\tilde{p}_E}{\tilde{p}_B}\right) = \sum_{E_i \in H \subset E} \alpha_H(\mathbf{p}) \tag{8}$$

holds for all $E \subset \{E_1, \ldots, E_n\}$. Since $E_i \in \mathcal{F}$, there exists a subset $H \subset \{E_1, \ldots, E_n\}$ with $\alpha_H \neq 0$ and $E_i \notin H$. Therefore, $\deg(\tilde{\mathbf{p}}) < \deg(\mathbf{p})$ follows from (7), (8) and from the definition of $\deg(\cdot)$. Now the identity $\ln(RR_{E_i}^E(\mathbf{p})) = \ln(RR_{E_i}^E(\tilde{\mathbf{p}}))$ can be shown for all $E \subset \{E_1, \ldots, E_n\} \setminus \{E_i\}$ by using (7), (8) and the identity $RR_{E_i}^E = RR_{E \cup \{E_i\}}/RR_E$. Since ψ as well as FRR are monotone in stratum-specific relative risks, we have $\psi_i(\mathbf{p}) = \psi_i(\tilde{\mathbf{p}})$ and $FRR_{E_i}(\mathbf{p}) = FRR_{E_i}(\tilde{\mathbf{p}})$. Moreover, $\psi_i(\tilde{\mathbf{p}}) = FRR_{E_i}(\tilde{\mathbf{p}})$ holds by induction. Hence, (6) is proved for all $E_i \in \mathcal{F}$. Since ψ and FRR both satisfy Definition 1, the proof can be completed by showing that

$$\psi_j(\mathbf{p}) = \psi_k(\mathbf{p}) \text{ and } FRR_{E_j}(\mathbf{p}) = FRR_{E_k}(\mathbf{p}) \ \forall E_j, E_k \in \mathcal{E}. \tag{9}$$

Equation (7) and the definition of $\mathcal{E}$ imply that $RR_E(\mathbf{p}) = 1$ whenever $E_j \notin E$ or $E_k \notin E$. Hence, $RR_{E_j}^E(\mathbf{p}) = 1 = RR_{E_k}^E(\mathbf{p})$ holds for all $E \subset \{E_1, \ldots, E_n\}$, $E_j, E_k \notin E$. Finally, (9) follows from the fact that ψ and FRR both are monotone in stratum-specific relative risks. □

4 Conclusion

The factorial relative risk has been introduced as a new risk parameter that quantifies the individual contributions of single exposure factors to the joint relative risk of several exposures that are considered simultaneously in a multifactorial setting. It has been shown that the factorial relative risk of an exposure E_i is a weighted geometric mean of its stratum–specific relative risks. Furthermore, it has been proved that apart from the factorial relative risk there is no other parameter that factorizes the joint relative risk in the sense of Definition 1 and is monotone in stratum–specific relative risks. The first condition can be interpreted as a model–based axiom which is closely related to a multiplicative conception of the principle of interaction. An analogon to the factorial relative risk parameter which is supposed to satisfy an additive conception of interaction can easily be derived by applying a general method of risk partitioning (Land and Gefeller (1997)) to the task of additively dividing up the joint excess risk of all considered exposures into exposure–specific components. The factorial relative risk is not meant to elucidate the "true" type of interaction, but it serves as a measure of disease/exposure association that facilitates the comparison of different exposure factors with respect to the strength of their individual association with disease while simultaneously taking account of all combined effects of exposures in the actual multifactorial context.

Acknowledgements: This work is supported by a grant of the Deutsche Forschungsgemeinschaft (grant no. Ge 637/3-1).

References

CHRISTOFFEL, T., TERET, S.P. (1991): Epidemiology and the Law: Courts and Confidence Intervals. *American Journal of Public Health, 81, 1661–1666.*

EIDE, G.E., GEFELLER, O. (1995): Sequential and Average Attributable Fractions as Aids in the Selection of Preventive Strategies. *Journal of Clinical Epidemiology, 48, 645–655.*

HAMMER, P.L., HOLZMANN, R. (1992): Approximations of Pseudo-Boolean Functions; Applications to Game Theory. *Zeitschrift für Operations Research, 36, 3–21.*

LAGAKOS, S.W., MOSTELLER, F. (1986): Assigned Shares in Compensation for Radiation-Related Cancers. *Risk Analysis, 6, 345–357.*

LAND, M., GEFELLER, O. (1997): Variations on the Shapley Solution for Partitioning Risks in Epidemiology. In: O. Opitz and R. Klar (eds.): *Classification, Data Analysis and Knowledge Organization.* Proc. 20th Conf. GfKl, Freiburg, Springer, Heidelberg (in press).

ROBINS, J., GREENLAND, S. (1991): Estimability and Estimation of Expected Years of Life Lost due to a Hazardous Exposure. *Statistics in Medicine, 10, 79–94.*

ROTHMAN, K.J. (1986): Modern Epidemiology. Little, Brown, Boston.

Multiple Media Stream Data Analysis: Theory and Applications

F. Makedon, C. Owen

Dartmouth Experimental Visualization Laboratory
6211 Sudikoff Labs
Dartmouth College, Hanover, NH, 03755, USA
devlab@cs.dartmouth.edu

Abstract: This paper presents a new model for multiple media stream data analysis as well as descriptions of some applications of this model. This model formalizes the exploitation of correlations between multiple, potentially heterogeneous, media streams in support of numerous application areas. The goal of the technique is to determine temporal and spatial alignments which optimize a correlation function and indicate commonality and synchronization between media streams. It also provides a framework for comparison of media in unrelated domains.

1 Introduction

This paper presents a new model for multiple media stream data analysis. Many common approaches to media data analysis can be described as "monomedia" approaches in that they focus on a single media stream. Examples include content based browsing of video by Arman et. al. (1994) and speech retrieval by Brown et. al. (1996). This work is important and complicated. However, many applications can benefit from analysis of multiple media streams. In such applications it is the relationship between streams which is important as opposed to the relationship between a query and a single stream.

For the purpose of this research, multiple media stream data analysis is considered to be the derivation of temporal and spatial relationships between two or more media streams. One example is the correlation of lip motion to speech audio — the audio provides clues as to the motion of the lips. If the two streams can be spatially synchronized (moving lips located), several applications become possible. The audio can be used to predict the lip motion, allowing joint audio-video data compression, and the speaker can be physically located in the image sequence, providing locality cues for speaker recognition and robotic navigation.

An important application for multiple media stream data analysis is cross-modal information retrieval. Some media are far more difficult to query than others. The technology for very complicated information retrieval in text has been in place for many years. Speech, on the other hand, is very difficult to query. Locating words in audio streams is prone to all of the problems of open vocabulary word spotting and, therefore, requires relatively new technologies which are often proud to quote accuracy numbers in the 60% range (Brown, et. al. (1996)). If a textual transcription for recorded speech and its temporal alignment to the speech audio is available, a query into that text can be used to locate a desired speech segment. Computing the alignment between these two streams is an application of multiple media stream data analysis. The transcription provides a useful query mechanism for the audio: each query in the text is then used to locate the appropriate speech segments. The fundamental basis of cross-modal information retrieval is that one media is queried to produce a result in another. The underlying requirement is automatic synchronization.

Multiple media stream analysis is a relatively new area. Some early projects included alignment of newly recorded voice audio to degraded voice audio, a technique used for motion picture dubbing. This work is described along with many other unsolved application areas by Chen, et. al. (1995a). The ViewStation project included cross-modal retrieval of close-captioned video, which falls into the script-tight category described in this paper (Lindblad (1994)). Chen, et. al. (1995) illustrate joint audio-video coding based on audio prediction of lip motion in order to achieve higher compression levels.

2   Multiple media stream data analysis

This paper presents a general model for multiple media stream data analysis. This model provides a basis on which to build more practical models including a discrete formulation and a ranked results formulation. There are two primary goals of this analysis: spatial and temporal synchronization. Temporal synchronization derives the modification of the timing of one or more of the media streams in order to maximize the correlation. An example is the alignment of two similar audio streams using speed variation techniques so as to align the voices. In many applications one media will be considered to be on a reference time frame and others temporally adjusted to achieve synchronization to that media. This is particularly the case when one media is in real time (measured in seconds) and the others are only causal in nature. Some applications get temporal synchronization for free and are only concerned with spatial synchronization.

Spatial synchronization is the second goal. This is a spatial translation of contents at a point in time in order to maximize correlation. This may consist of spatial warping or selection. Warping is the adjusting of parameters in order to rearrange a media element temporally or spatially. As an example, some motion analysis techniques attempt to compute the optimal spatial warping of images so as to cancel the motion from frame to frame. Selection can be considered to be warping wherein all of the unselected components of the media are omitted. Lip motion location by correlation with speech audio selects the particular moving components of the image sequence that represent the lips.

2.1 Continuous formulation

Equation 1 is the continuous formulation for multiple media stream data analysis.

$$\eta = \arg \max_{\tau_i \in T_i, \psi_i \in \Psi_i, i=1...N} \int_{-\infty}^{\infty} \rho(\psi_1(\mu_1 \circ \tau_1, t), ..., \psi_N(\mu_N \circ \tau_N, t)) dt \quad (1)$$

There are a large number of variables in this model. The model assumes N media streams are to be correlated, with functions $\mu_1, ..., \mu_N$ representing the media streams. The model assumes a media stream is a function of time. This is not a major restriction in practical discrete applications, as discussed in the next subsection. Each function τ_i is a temporal synchronization function and T_i is the set of possible temporal translation functions for stream i. These functions represent the possible time warpings of the media stream in order to achieve temporal synchronization. A selected temporal warping function τ_i must be a member of T_i.

ψ_i is a domain translation function and Ψ_i the set of all domain translation functions for stream i. A domain translation function translates complicated and highly redundant media data to a common and optimized comparison domain, where ρ, referred to as the correlation function, is used to produce the computed result η.

Domain translation is an important element of the model. It is difficult to construct appropriate correlation functions with disparate media parameters; as an example, what does it mean to compare audio, a one-dimensional function, to video, a two-dimensional function? However, comparison of estimated lip movement in audio to motion vectors in video is much more easily realized. Even when the media are the same, they may be too complicated to correlate directly. For this reason, it is specified in this model that all media be translated to a common domain for comparison by the correlation function ρ.

In many cases ρ is some derivative of simple statistical correlation. Applications of multiple media stream correlation undertaken at the DEVLAB have favored complicated domain translation and simple correlation.

It is important to note that the result of this computation is not the maximization of the integral, but, rather, the functions which achieve this maximization. This model specifies a structure for defining and selecting functions which maximize the correlation. The resulting functions indicate necessary temporal and spatial correlations. The set of temporal translation function results $\tau_{i,i=1,...,N}$ indicate the appropriate temporal synchronization for maximum correlation. The set of domain translation function results indicate the appropriate spatial synchronization for maximum correlation.

There are several unique characteristics of this model which should be noted. The parameters of the spatial synchronization function are time and the composition of the media function and the temporal synchronization function. This allows flexibility in the construction of the spatial synchronization function because it can compute synchronization based on a neighborhood of the time point. Many technologies, including simple filtering, require access to a neighborhood like this.

2.2 Additional formulation

Equation 2 is the discrete formulation for multiple media stream data analysis. This is derived from the continuous formulation with the constraint that the media functions $\mu_{i,i=1,...,N}$ are discrete functions.

$$\eta = \arg \max_{\tau_i \in T_i, \psi_i \in \Psi_i, i=1...N} \sum_{-\infty}^{\infty} \rho(\psi_1(\mu_1 \circ \tau_1, t), ..., \psi_N(\mu_N \circ \tau_N, t)) \quad (2)$$

This model is compatible with non-temporal media provided the media is causal. As an example, text is not temporal, but does have a definite ordering. This ordering can be considered to be equivalent to a temporal ordering in the model. The temporal synchronization functions are not restricted to those requiring inverses, and can be used to reorder content if necessary (as in media presentations where content is repeated).

The most extreme case of non-temporal media is hypertext, wherein content can be represented as a graph with media nodes and navigation edges. This case is not supported by this model and would require modifications to account for the navigation edges.

2.3 Computational approaches

These models provide a basic modularization and theoretical description of the multiple media stream data analysis and correlation problem. They do not specify the functions to use for any particular application. This paper describes how appropriate functions have been selected for several applications.

3 Text-to-speech synchronization

A major project at the DEVLAB is Speak Alexandria. The goal of Speak Alexandria is information retrieval in speech-based media, any media which is predominately human speech. Such media is very common and can be queried using simple text queries. Speech-based media can be divided into three types: script-less, script-light, and script-tight. Script-less media is media for which no transcription exists (live recordings, etc.). Script-tight media is media for which a tightly synchronized transcription exists (such as close-captioned video). Script-less media requires voice recognition technologies for query processing and is not the subject of this paper. Script-tight content is a simple application of cross-modal information retrieval.

Script-light media is speech-based audio content for which an unaligned transcription exists. This is a surprisingly large category of content including broadcasting, dramatic performances, and court proceedings. This content can be queried efficiently provided the synchronization between the text and the speech can be computed. There are significant advantages in treating script-light material as cross-modal information retrieval rather than applying the same techniques used for script-less content. The script can drive voice recognition tools with the words that exist in the content rather than attempting to automatically recognize the text and produce a new transcription. Much higher accuracy is possible using this approach.

This application has two media streams. μ_1 represents the text and μ_2 represents the audio. In this application the temporal synchronization function τ_2 is the identity function, i.e. the text will be aligned to the speech. The alignment is easily invertible to provide speech to transcription retrieval if necessary (given a location in the audio, provide the written transcription at that point).

Ψ_1 is implemented by converting the text to a biphone graph. Phonemes are units of pronunciation in language. Biphones represent the transition between phonemes (as well as a context independent "middle" of the phoneme). This is a common technology used in voice recognition (See Rabiner (1993)). A directed graph is constructed of biphone translations of the words in the text wherein edges represent the possible biphone transitions. In the current implementation an optional .pau (pause) biphone is placed between words. Since many words have multiple pronunciations ("the" for example), the graph has multiple paths. In addition, bypass edges are included to model errors in the transcription (skipped or substituted content). This constructed graph is called a *transcription graph* and is represented in the multiple media stream correlation model as Ψ_1. It is a goal of the computation to select the correct path ψ_1 through this graph for the speech audio. The duration of individual biphones is not known, so explicit edges are added to each node which loop back to the node itself.

Ψ_2 is implemented using speech recognition tools which convert audio into a sequence of biphone probabilities. This process is beyond the scope of this paper, but is described in detail in Rabiner (1993). In summary, audio is blocked into finite frames and the probability of any given biphone at that point is time is computed. In the current implementation 536 biphone probabilities are computed for each audio frame. These vectors are treated as a lattice where each $\psi_2 \in \Psi_2$ is a left-to-right path through the lattice. The optimal ψ_2 is a path which is valid in the transcription graph and maximizes the total path probability. Clearly, ψ_1 and ψ_2 must correspond.

The temporal synchronization function τ_1 is computed from the path ψ_1 through the transcription graph. In effect, these parameters are computed simultaneously. Computation of this path can be performed using the Viterbi algorithm, which is described in Rabiner (1993). In order to prevent numeric underflow, all probabilities are computed as logarithms. In this implementation, $\rho(\alpha, \beta) = \alpha + \beta$. Several enhancements of the Viterbi algorithm have been included in this application including modification of probabilities in the transcription graph over time to force interpolation and path pruning (beam searching) to decrease computational complexity.

4 Summary

This paper describes multiple media stream correlation, a general model for the spatial and temporal alignment of multiple media streams. This model provides a framework for research on retrieval and analysis algorithms which work on more than one media stream, gaining useful and important information from the relationships between these streams. It is a technique with an open future, and the basis for much DEVLAB research at this time.

References

ARMAN, F., DEPOMMIER, A. and HSU, A., and CHIU, M.Y. (1994): Content-based browsing of video sequences. Proc. of ACM Multimedia'94, 97-103, San Francisco, CA.

BROWN, M. G., FOOTE, J. T., JONES, G. J. F., SPARCK JONES, K. and YOUNG, S. J. (1996): Open-vocabulary speech indexing for voice and video mail retrieval. *Proc. of Multimedia'96*, 307-316, Boston, MA.

BLOOM, P. J. and MARSHALL, G. D. (1984): A Digital Signal Processing System for Automatic Dialogue Post-Synchronization. *SMPTE Journal, Volume 93, Number 6, June, 1984, 566-569.*

CHEN, T. and RAO, R. (1995): Audio-Visual Interaction in Multimedia: From Lip-Syncronization to Joint Audio-Video Coding. *IEEE Circuits and Devices*, 11(6), November, 1995, 21–26.

CHEN, T. and RAO, R. (1995a): Cross-Modal Prediction in Audio-Visual Communication. *Proc. ICASSP'96*, Atlanta, GA, May, 1996.

LINDBLAD, C. J. (1994): A programming system for the dynamic manipulation of temporally sensitive data. MIT/LCS/TR-637, Massachusetts Institute of Technology.

RABINER, L. and JUANG, B.-H. (1993): *Fundamentals of Speech Recognition*, Signal Processing Series, PTR Prentice Hall, Englewood Cliffs, NJ.

Multimedia Data Analysis using ImageTcl

F. Makedon, C. Owen

Dartmouth Experimental Visualization Laboratory
6211 Sudikoff Labs
Dartmouth College, Hanover, NH, 03755, USA
devlab@cs.dartmouth.edu

Abstract: IMAGETCL is an new system which provides powerful Tcl/Tk based media scripting capabilities similar to those of the ViewSystem and Rivl in a unique environment that allows rapid prototyping and development of new components in the C++ language. Powerful user tools automate the creation of new components as well as the addition of new data types and file formats. Applications using IMAGETCL at the Dartmouth Experimental Visualization Laboratory (DEVLAB) include multiple stream media data analysis, automatic image annotation, and image sequence motion analysis. IMAGETCL combines the high speed of compiled languages with the testing and parameterization advantages of scripting languages.

1 Introduction

Multimedia applications require the efficient manipulation of media data (video, images, audio, etc.). The IMAGETCL multimedia development environment has been created to facilitate multimedia data analysis research (Owen (1996)). Typically, development of new technologies for multimedia data analysis has been complicated by many factors. Algorithms are usually concerned with processing sequences of image frame data or audio samples. However, prototypes of new algorithms must deal with complicated media file formats, mixed compression techniques, temporal sequencing of data, and pipelining issues required to deal with the large volumes of data. All of these issues ride like baggage on the back of the multimedia algorithm developer. IMAGETCL provides layers of abstraction which mask these issues from the developer while still providing a fast and efficient environment for algorithm testing. It manages implementation layers automatically and provides algorithms under design with data in simple forms (vectors of audio data, matrices of image data). A small, yet flexible, set of standard media data types simplifies this process.

While IMAGETCL does not theorize new algorithms, it is a great aid to the other stages of development. Algorithm implementation is in C++, which provides a clean, easy to use, object oriented environment. The most unique feature of IMAGETCL is its support for simplified implementation of algorithms in a modern **compiled** language. Test procedures can be rapidly prototyped and easily altered in the Tcl scripting language. This is a fairly common approach in research software systems due to its inherent flexibility. Test

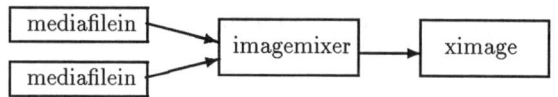

Figure 1: Example of an IMAGETCL application as a graph.

procedures are often highly instrumented and parameterized. Instrumentation provides monitoring of the algorithm operation both for analysis and debugging. Parameter adjustments are performed to tune the algorithm implementation and to test effectiveness and robustness.

Multimedia data is highly stochastic in nature and it is difficult to theorize away the problems of noise and media sampling. Hence, experimental development and demonstration of results is very important. Experimental media can be collected easily in an IMAGETCL site and provided using the IMAGETCL Media Database (ItMD). The popular Tcl/Tk development environment is available for user interface design. Since Tcl/Tk is an interpreted language, user interface design and experiment procedure development can occur rapidly. New compilations of the test program are not required when user interface changes are made.

Several systems have been developed for multimedia software design and prototyping. VideoScheme, also developed at the Dartmouth Experimental Visualization Laboratory (DEVLAB), utilized the Scheme programming environment as a rapid prototyping system for digital video editing and analysis (Matthews (1993)). VideoScheme heavily influenced the genesis of IMAGETCL. MIT's ViewStation is another powerful multimedia environment which is also Tcl/Tk based (Lindblad (1994)). IMAGETCL uses a data-flow structure very similar to that of the ViewStation. Cornell's Rivl system abstracts away most of the media parameters, including resolution and timing and provides very powerful media manipulation tools (Swartz (1995)).

2 ImageTcl Components

The most basic element in IMAGETCL is the media manipulation object. Objects are created by IMAGETCL commands and are connected into a directed graph, (which may be cyclical) where the nodes are objects and the edges are connections. Objects are the data processing elements. Figure 1 illustrates an image combination application, where two video files are combined (possibly with a cross fade) and displayed. In this figure the `mediafilein` objects are sources of data from files and `ximage` is a data sink which is a display window on the screen. The `imagemixer` object is both a sink and a source, accepting two channels of media data as input and producing a mixed media stream as output.

This structure is similar to the ViewStation design (Lindblad (1994)). Objects are typically general-purpose elements in the graph which perform a generic function. A module is associated with an object to provide detailed algorithmic functionality. In addition to objects and modules, IMAGETCL has data types which are described below, and system commands, commands which provide control functionality in the system, but do not create new graph objects.

The flow of data packets within the graph is managed entirely by IMAGETCL. Data pipe-lining and packet queuing is transparent to the algorithm designer. A source object program simply transmits packets to a source channel. Sink object programs provide a virtual function which is called when a new packet becomes available. A process scheduler balances execution among the graph nodes.

2.1 Media File and Live Media Support

Most application development involves processing media from files since such tests are easily repeatable. For this reason IMAGETCL supports a wide variety of multimedia file formats, including WAVE, audio/video interleaved (AVI), Sun rasterimage, PPM, PGM, AIFF, and even some specialty medical image formats such as IMGF. IMAGETCL uses a plug-in module system for media file support, making it easy to extend the system with new media file formats. Real-time video and audio I/O is also supported. Video and audio provided in real time by computer interfaces is often useful for demonstrations of multimedia applications. Live media also provides a limitless data source; it is not uncommon for workstations to have a permanent connection to cable television for raw test data.

2.2 ImageTcl Data Types and Processing

IMAGETCL supports a set of data types for media data. The media data format is the form in which the actual media data is stored. A set of basic media types are explicitly selected by the algorithm developer. This approach promotes efficiency and accuracy, avoiding computationally intensive and potentially error contributory implicit data conversion. Data type conversion components are standard in IMAGETCL and can easily be applied to data not in a desired format. Some example IMAGETCL data types include fixed and floating point color and monochrome images, digital audio, generic matrices and vectors, and special data types such as the YV data type which supports an image sequence as a three dimensional matrix. A powerful vector and matrix class library provides superclasses and manipulation tools for many of these data types. Matrix and vector manipulation can be directly applied to media data. There is no need to copy data out of data objects into intermediate storage.

There are many standard image and audio processing operations that algorithm developers call upon in development and don't wish to write anew for each project. IMAGETCL has a wide variety of such operations as built-in components. These can be used at both the script level and in C++ code. A small sampling of these components includes image cropping, warping, edge enhancement, and edge detection. Several optical flow algorithms are provided as well as FFT and arbitrary flow field generation.

2.3 Automatic Prototyping Tools

A powerful feature of IMAGETCL is automatic component creation. Supplying a C++ class library and an integrated environment does not necessarily lead to rapid algorithm development. A developer must create new classes for the components derived from any of several base classes, the ancestors in an object-oriented environment with inheritance. Selecting the correct base class and knowing which functions to supply would be a burden on the prototyping process and result in a lot of useless code copying and deleting. The IMAGETCL Interactive Component Creation utility allows for the simple creation of a new component by simply filling out a form. All files necessary to build and include this component are then generated automatically. Simple information about the new command, module, or data type is provided by the user before the component files are generated. The new component provides shells for all necessary procedures.

IMAGETCL is a highly modular system, a fundamental feature of any large software system, particularly rapid prototyping environments. Automatic System Build Tools allow an application to be built using any desired combination of components. Inclusion of components naturally creates larger systems, requiring larger compile and link times. Because IMAGETCL applications can be built using a subset of available components, the development process can be accelerated. A smaller system can be developed which will compile and link much quicker. In addition, it is very easy to add new components to the system one at a time when there is no interrelationship between them.

3 Applications

IMAGETCL is a standard development environment in the DEVLAB and has been used in many multimedia projects including video and audio analysis, speech recognition and synchronization, and medical imagery. This section describes a few applications in these diverse areas in which IMAGETCL has been a major component.

A major research concern at the DEVLAB has been the study of human communication. Of particular interest is the visual language: American Sign Language (ASL) (Sternberg (1996)). There are three major categories of automation that have been addressed: cut detection, pause detection, and non-manual (facial) component motion analysis. The first two of these categories are concerned with video segmentation for efficient manipulation and categorization.

3.1 Video Cut Detection

ASL research video has several unique characteristics. Each utterance sequence is produced as a unit with recording starting at the beginning of the first utterance. This results in cuts between utterances. If cuts can be detected automatically, the video segmentation required for easy access to individual utterances can be derived in advance, saving manual work.

In IMAGETCL a new command called cutdetect was created using the Interactive Component Creation utility. This command creates "generic" video cut detection objects. Modules for the command can be created in a similar fashion so that several cut detection algorithms can be implemented and compared. Experiments performed on digital video in the DEVLAB media database occur in three basic steps: (1) an algorithm is written in C++, (2) test scripts are written in Tcl, and (3) Tk and Tix are used to write a simple user interface.

This application demonstrates the importance of the IMAGETCL approach. The algorithms must manipulate pixels, performing frame comparisons and creating color histograms to detect the changes indicating a cut. Since each algorithm uses a differing approach, no standard command for image histogram or comparison could have performed these operations, and processing all of this data (230,400 bytes of data per frame, 30 frames per second, for nearly 7 megabytes per sequence second of processing) in interpreted code would have been too slow.

A major problem in all of these algorithms is parameterization. Numerous parameters must be "tweaked" during performance comparisons, including histogram bucket counts, detection thresholds, and frame support counts. Had these parameters been compiled in the algorithm source, each change would have entailed a time-consuming re-compilation. Certainly there are alternatives to this approach; for example, the parameters could be supplied by user input for each run. This approach, while useful, will be prone to error and limit reproducibility of experiments. It would have been possible to place these parameters in files and read them, but that would have added additional programming complexity. In IMAGETCL , these parameters are supplied by the interpreted script. They can be easily changed and the program immediately restarted.

3.2 Video Pause Detection in American Sign Language

An alternative approach to segmentation of video sequences is video pause detection. Each sign language utterance can be further segmented by detecting the times when the signer paused between elements of the utterance. Indeed, this is an important issue in the study of ASL. Pauses are not a simple segmentation means for terms, just as they are not a segmentation means for spoken sentences. The characterization of pauses is an important linguistic research goal.

Pause detection can be likened to inverted cut detection. Cut detection searches for changes between frames which cannot be accounted for by normal motion or variance in image content. Such changes are, by definition, gross changes. Pause detection, on the other hand, searches for sections of minimal change. A major distinction between the two techniques is that pauses have duration, but cuts do not.

3.3 Motion Analysis in American Sign Language

A significant component of the linguistic study of sign language is the study of non-manual components as shown in Bahan (1996). Non-manual components are elements of the language not involving the hands. It is usually assumed that sign language is entirely based on hand movement. However, this is not the case — movement of the eyes and head and facial expressions are also critical components.

DEVLAB researchers are currently exploring motion analysis techniques for tracking the head and facial components in SignStream video. Though this work is too preliminary to be reported in detail here, it is based on a hierarchical derivation of the video motion and construction of affine motion tracks.

References

BAHAN, B. J. (1996): *Non-manual realization of agreement in American sign language*, Ph.D. Thesis, Boston University.

LINDBLAD, C. J. (1994): A programming system for the dynamic manipulation of temporally sensitive data. MIT/LCS/TR-637, Massachusetts Institute of Technology.

LIU, X. and OWEN, C. B. and MAKEDON, F. S., Automatic video pause detection filter, Technical Report PCS-TR97-307, Dartmouth College, 1997.

MATTHEWS, J., GLOOR, P. and MAKEDON, F. (1993): VideoScheme: A programmable video editing system for automation and media recognition. *Proc. of ACM Multimedia'93*, Anaheim, CA.

OWEN, C. B. (1996): IMAGETCL multimedia development environment, http://devlab.dartmouth.edu/imagetcl/.

STERNBERG, M. L. A. (1996): *Essential ASL*, HarperPerennial Press, New York.

SWARTZ, J. and SMITH, B. C. (1995): A Resolution Independent Video Language. Proc. ACM Multimedia'95, San Francisco, CA.

TENNENHOUSE, D. et. al. (1993): The ViewStation Collected Papers. Massachusetts Institute of Technology Technical Report MIT/LCS/TR-590.

Robust Bivariate Boxplots and Visualization of Multivariate Data

M. Riani, S. Zani, A. Corbellini

Istituto di Statistica, Facoltà di Economia, Univ. of Parma, Italy

Abstract: Zani *et al.* (1997) suggested a simple way of constructing a bivariate boxplot based on convex hull peeling and B-spline smoothing. This approach leads to define a natural, smooth and completely non parametric region in $I\!R^2$ which retains the correlation in the data and adapts to differing spread in the various directions. In this paper we initially consider some variations of this method. The proposed approach shows some advantages with respect to that suggested by Goldberg and Iglewicz (1992), because we do not need to estimate either the standard deviations of the two variables or a correlation measure. Furthermore we also show how, in presence of p-dimensional data, the data visualization method based on the construction of the scatterplot matrix with superimposed bivariate boxplots in each diagram can become a very useful tool for the detection of multivariate outliers, the analysis of multivariate transformations and more generally for the ordering of multidimensional data.

1 Introduction

Recently Goldberg and Iglewicz (1992) proposed a method of constructing a bivariate boxplot based on ellipses. This approach needs to estimate two location parameters, the ratio of the standard deviations of the two variables and a measure of correlation. Two additional parameters are required if one wants to keep into account the differing spread in the various directions. In addition one unit is always forced to lie on the boundary which defines the outer contour. The approach of Zani *et al.* (1997), which is based on convex peeling and B-splines, seems to overcome these problems because in this last case the construction of the outer region which allows for differing spread simply needs an estimate of the bivariate centroid. Furthermore, in this method no unit is forced to lie on the outer contour.

The structure of the paper is as follows: in section 2 we resume shortly our proposal for a bivariate boxplot considering some modifications. In section 3 we claim that for p-dimensional data the construction of a bivariate boxplot for each pair of variables can help to find an initial clean data set free from outliers and influential observations, which can act as a starting point in the forward search techniques for the detection of multivariate outliers or the analysis of multivariate transformations. Section 4 concludes.

2 Construction of a bivariate boxplot

In this section we recall shortly the main steps of the suggested approach, introduce some modifications and present a new application. The suggested method is based on the following 3 steps:

Step 1: *definition of the inner region*

The inner region (hinge) is the two dimensional extension of the interquartile range of the univariate boxplot. In one dimension we take the length of the box which contains 50% of the values. In two dimensions we look for a similar region centred on a robust estimator of location, containing a fixed percentage of the data. A natural and completely non parametric way of finding a central region in $I\!R^2$ is through the use of the so called convex hull peeling (Bebbington, 1978). Barnett (1976) suggested that "the most extreme group of observations in a multivariate sample are those lying on the convex hull (with those on the convex hull of the remaining sample, the second most extreme group, etc.)". The output of the peeling is a series of nested convex polygons (hulls). We call the $(1 - \alpha)\%$-hull the biggest hull containing not more than $(1 - \alpha)\%$ of the data. Usually, even if the outermost hull assumes very different shapes and is influenced by outliers, the 50%-hull seems to capture the correlation of the two variables.

In order to obtain a smooth inner region we suggest to draw a B-spline curve inside the 50%-hull previously formed. A B-spline is an interpolation curve which is constructed from polynomial pieces joined at certain values of x, the knots (see Eilers and Marx (1996) for the properties and the computational details about the construction of the B-spline curves). In our application we consider a cubic curve. Let $x_1, \cdots, x_k, x_{k+1} = x_1$ denote the x coordinates of the vertices of the 50%-hull and $x'_1, \cdots, x'_k, x'_{k+1} = x'_1$ the position of the knots. We construct every polinomial piece between two adjacent knots x'_j and x'_{j+1} ($j = 1, 2, \ldots, k$) using a four points control system based on $x_{j-1}, x_j, x_{j+1}, x_{j+2}$.

This leads us to define the inner region as follows:

Definition - *We call "inner region" the portion of the space which lies inside or at the boundary of the B-spline curve (hinge) superimposed on the 50%-hull.*

As an illustration of our method we use the data plotted in Figure 1. On the x axis we have the average per capita taxable income of the 341 municipalities of Emilia-Romagna (a region in the north of Italy). On the y axis we have the unemployment rate. The bulk of the data, as expected, shows a negative correlation. However, there are many points which seem to depart from the robust regression line drawn through the distribution of the data. Figure 1 also gives the most extreme hull, the 75%-hull and the 50%-hull. This figure shows that while the shape of the outermost hull is influenced by some extreme observations, the 75% hull already seems to capture the correlation in the data and the 50% is centred on the bulk of the data. On the 50%-hull we have superimposed a B-spline curve. This inner region is surely free from outliers and robust, but at the same time it keeps the correlation

Figure 1: Plot of the unemployment rate versus the average per capita taxable income in the 341 municipalities of Emilia-Romagna (Italy) with outermost, 75% and 50%-hulls. A B-spline curve has been superimposed on the 50%-hull and two 50% trimmed LS lines have been drawn.

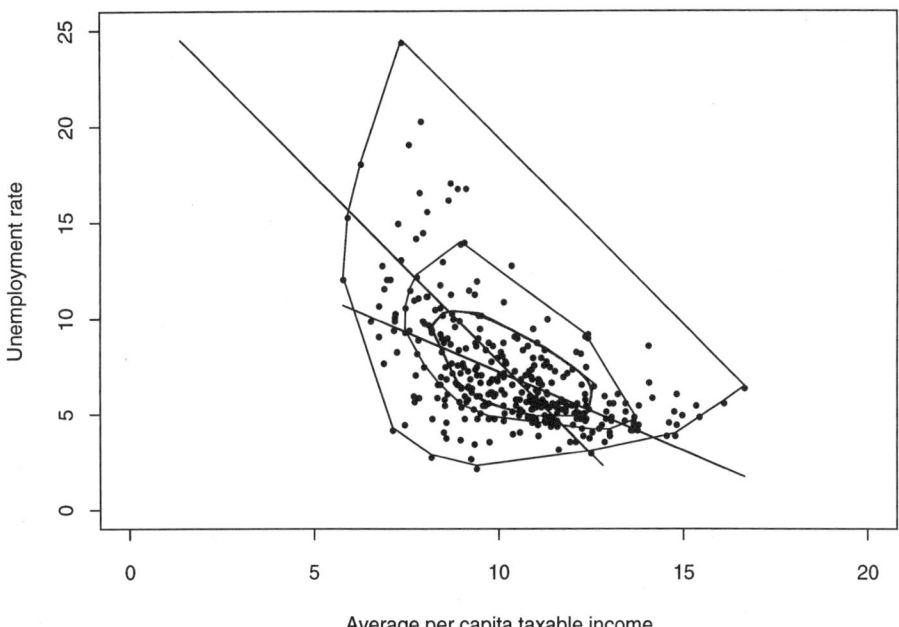

in the data and it allows for different spreads in the various directions.

Step 2: *definition of the robust centroid*

In order to find a robust centroid we have several viable alternatives: centre of the innermost hull, minimization of the L_1 norm in $I\!R^2$ (Small, 1990), intersection of two least median of squares lines (Rousseeuw and Leroy, 1987), point with maximal depth (Ruts and Rousseeuw, 1996).

Zani et al. (1997) used the arithmetic means of the observations inside the inner region. In this work we use the intersection of the two least squares (LS) lines built with the observations forming the inner region (50% trimmed LS lines). This latter approach, which exploits the efficiency properties of the least squares estimators and the natural trimming offered by the hulls, has the additional advantage of taking into account the relation between the two variables. In Figure 1 we have also drawn the two 50% trimmed LS lines.

Step 3: *definition of the outer region*

Once we have found a robust bivariate centre and a curve containing half of the data (hinge) we must devise a criterion in order to build an outer contour which discriminates between "good" and "bad" observations.

In the traditional univariate boxplot we define as outliers those observations which lie outside the following interval: $[x_{0.25} - 1.5 \times IR, x_{0.75} + 1.5 \times IR]$ where IR is the interquartile range ($IR = x_{0.75} - x_{0.25}$). As is well known, if the data come from the normal distribution, the former interval contains 99.3% of the values.

In two dimensions, in order to allow a degree of asymmetry, we suggest to build a bivariate outer contour using a multiple of the distance of the hinge from the robust centre. The purpose is to find a contour which leaves outside the (small) proportion of the data which can be considered as atypical. Furthermore, under the hypothesis of bivariate normality, this contour can be interpreted as a probability contour at $(1-\alpha)$ level with very small α (say close to 0.01). Lastly this contour is robust to departures from normality. Zani et al. (1997) show that in a bivariate normal distribution, in order to find an outer contour which leaves outside a percentage of observations close to 1%, we must multiply the distance of the hinge to the robust centre by 1.58. This coefficient (which we call l) is independent of the correlation parameter ρ of the bivariate normal distribution.

Our inner region is defined through a spline which always lies inside the 50%-hull and therefore it contains a little bit less than 50% of the values. Zani et al. (1997) give a table with the theoretical and empirical coefficients (using Monte-Carlo method) which enable us to pass from an inner region to an outer contour containing respectively 75%, 90%, 95% and 99% of the observations in a bivariate standard normal distribution. The coefficient (l) which asymptotically leaves outside the outer contour a percentage of observations equal to 1% is 1.68. Using this value we obtained the outer region plotted in Figure 2.

The graph shows that the shape of the outer region (which is completely non parametric and smooth) retains the correlation in the data and at the same time it adapts to the differing spread of the data in the differing directions[1].

Note that the spread of the data from the robust centroid is not symmetric, therefore a robust confidence ellipse does not seem appropriate to summarize the data.

Remark: In order to construct the outer region we do not need to estimate either the standard deviations of the two variables or a correlation measure. In addition, no unit is forced to lie on the line which defines the outer contour. These are clearly advantages with respect to the proposal of Goldberg and Iglewicz (1992).

3 Visualization of multivariate data

In presence of p-dimensional data, we suggest to construct the scatterplot matrix with superimposed bivariate boxplots in each diagram. In ex-

---

[1] The program to build our bivariate boxplot was developed under S-Plus version 3.2 except for the routine of computation of the B-spline coefficients which was written under pure C. Upon request the authors will provide the C and S-Plus source code. We can be contacted at Zani@ipruniv.cce.unipr.it and statdue@ipruniv.cce.unipr.it.

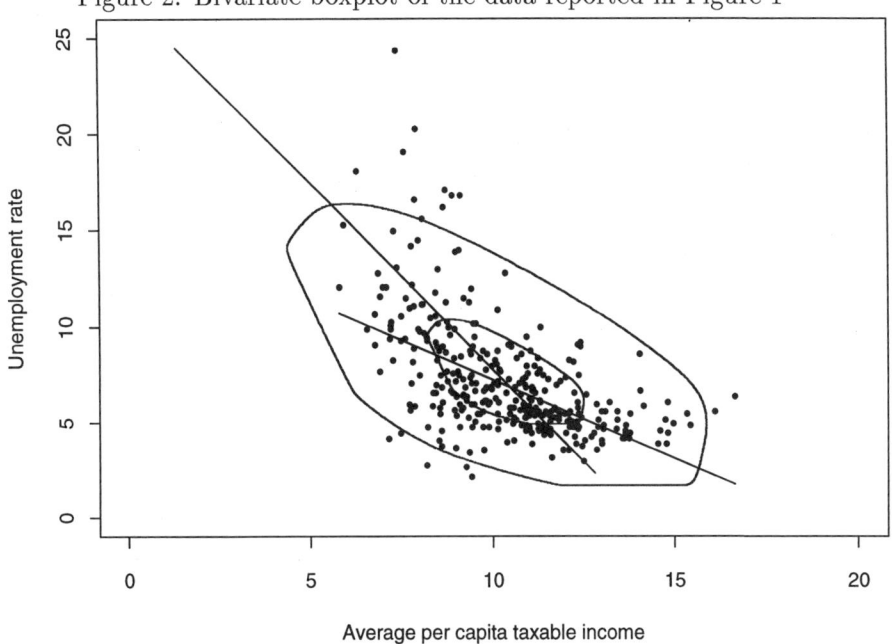

Figure 2: Bivariate boxplot of the data reported in Figure 1

ploratory analysis of the data, where cogent graphical summaries are at a premium, highlighting the position of the units (Venables and Ripley, 1994) which lie at least once outside the bivariate boxplots can give us interesting informations. This method of data visualization can also become a very useful tool for the detection of multivariate outliers, the analysis of multivariate transformations and the ordering of multidimensional data.

Usually in the modern procedures for the detection of multivariate outliers we define a clean data set (basic subset) free from outliers of dimension $p+1$ and iteratively include the units in the clean data set until a stopping rule is satisfied (e.g. Hadi, 1992). One problem is the choice of the clean data set with which to start the forward iterative insertion. For example Atkinson (1994), in order to avoid this choice, suggested to extract a subset of observations at random and to repeat the forward search several times. With p dimensional data the construction of bivariate boxplots for each pair of variables enables us to define as "bivariate clean data sets" the subsets containing the units inside the $1 - \alpha$ outer contours.

A natural definition of the multivariate initial basic subset is the following (Riani and Zani, 1996):

Definition - *We call the initial basic subset of multivariate clean observations the one formed by the intersection of the subsets of bivariate clean data in each of the $p(p-1)/2$ pairs of variables.*

The threshold of 1% which has been used in Figure 2 can conveniently be decreased in order to increase the probability that the initial clean data set is free from outliers. The observations which lie at least once outside the outer contour can be considered as potential outliers and can be removed from the basic subset.

Usually outliers form a small part of the overall sample. Therefore it is not sensible to start the forward search with a clean data set of dimension $p+1$ especially when the sample size is large. The former criterion, which enables us to start with a basic subset of a certain dimension, provides computational savings and simplifications in the analysis of potential outliers.

Figure 3: Scatter plot matrix of four economic indicators (Average per capita taxable income, Unemployment rate, Labour force index, Industrialization index) in 341 municipalities and bivariate boxplots with 90% outer contours. (Intersection of straight lines corresponds to robust centroid).

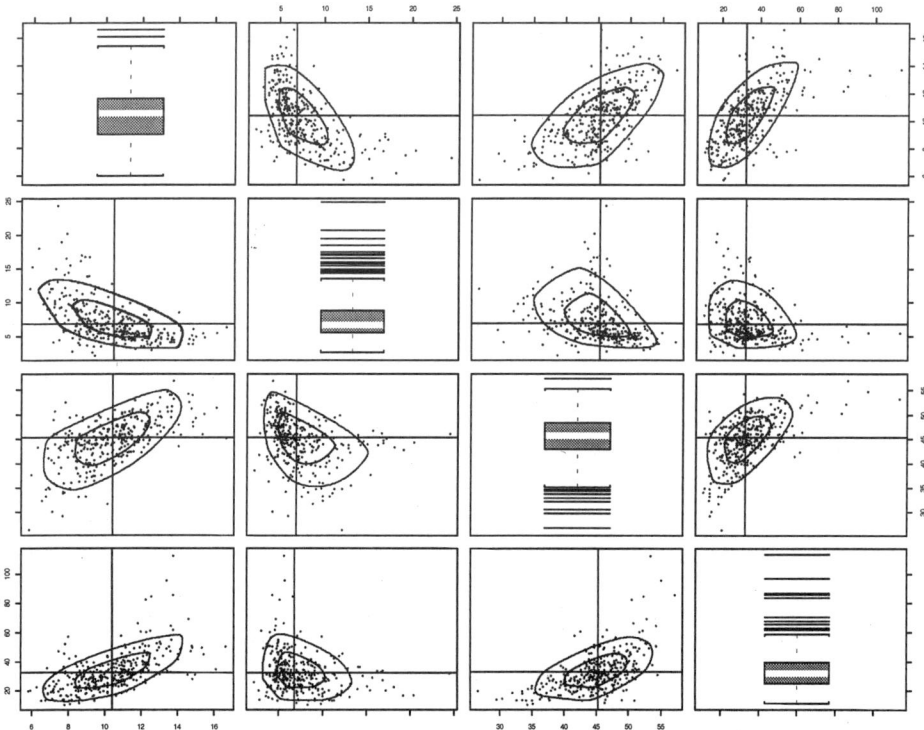

As an illustration of the suggested method for the detection of multivariate outliers and the analysis of multivariate transformations, let us consider this example: the data reported in Figure 1 belong to a four dimensional data set in which the third variable is a labour force index and the fourth is an industrialization index (data published in Zani (1996) and available on request). Figure 3 reports the bivariate boxplots for each pair of variables using 90% outer regions and the univariate boxplots on the main diagonal. As Figure 3 shows, the distribution of some of these variables is highly asymmetric. As the hypothesis of bivariate normality is not satisfied, the effective number of observations which lie outside the outer regions is slightly greater than 10%.

Once we have found an initial basic subset (from now on BSB) we can calculate Mahalanobis distances (MD) using a centroid based on the statistical units forming this subset. In this case the number of units belonging to BSB is equal to 228. This number however can conveniently be decreased or increased simply modifying the coefficient used to build the outer region. The number of times in which every unit not belonging to BSB lies outside the outer contours provides preliminary informations about its degree of outlyingness and gives a criterion for the multivariate ordering of extreme observations.

The units belonging to the group of potential outliers (from now on NBSB) are iteratively included in the initial basic subset. At each step of the forward search we can monitor particular Mahalanobis distances. For example Riani and Zani (1996) found that the monitoring of the minimum of MD among the units belonging to NBSB and the gap between the minimum of the distances of NBSB and the maximum of the units in BSB are very useful tools for detecting masking and swamping effects (Barnett and Lewis, 1994) and gain further insight into the structure of the data.

The construction of a bivariate boxplot for each pair of variables can be very helpful also for the analysis of multivariate transformations. Since it is the extreme observations which provide the evidence for transformation, the initial clean data set defined as above will provide a good start to the search for many values of the transformation parameter. This approach has been suggested by Riani and Atkinson (1997) for the analysis of multivariate transformations. These authors found that the monitoring at each step of the forward search of the maximum likelihood estimates of the transformation parameters coupled with the analysis of the likelihood ratio are very powerful tools for the choice of multivariate transformations.

4 Conclusions

In this paper we have initially explored some modifications of the method of constructing a bivariate boxplot suggested by Zani et al. (1997). The output of the analysis is an inner region (hinge) containing about 50% of the data and an outer region (fence) which (a) is completely non parametric, (b) whose shape doesn't need parameters to estimate, (c) is smooth, (d) is robust to the presence of clusters of outliers and (e) under the hypothesis of bivariate normality can be interpreted as a 99% contour.

In section 3 we have shown how the construction of the scatterplot matrix with superimposed bivariate boxplots in each diagram can be a very useful tool in multivariate data visualization. Furthermore this method can be used for defining an initial clean data set, which can then act as a starting point in the usual forward search techniques for the detection of multivariate outliers or the analysis of multiple transformations.

References

ATKINSON, A.C. (1994): Fast very robust methods for the detection of multiple outliers, *JASA, 89*, 1329-1339.

BARNETT, V. (1976): The ordering of multivariate data, (with discussion), *JRSS, Series A, 139*, 318-339.

BARNETT, V. and LEWIS, T. (1994): *Outliers in Statistical Data*, 3rd edn., Wiley, New York.

BEBBINGTON, A.C. (1978): A method of bivariate trimming for robust estimation of the correlation coefficient. *Appl. Statist., 27*, 221-226.

EILERS, P.H.C. and MARX, B.D. (1996): Flexible Smoothing with B-splines and Penalties, *Statistical Science, 11*, 89-121.

GOLDBERG, K.M. and IGLEWICZ, B. (1992): Bivariate extensions of the boxplot, *Technometrics, 34*, 307-320.

HADI, A.S. (1992): Identifying multiple outliers in multivariate data, *JRSS, B, 54*, 761-771.

RIANI, M. and ZANI, S. (1996): An iterative method for the detection of multiple outliers. Proceedings of the Conference: *Analysis of Multidimensional Data*, Napoli, (in press).

RIANI, M. and ATKINSON, A.C., (1997): *A Unified Approach to Multivariate Transformations and Multiple Outlier Detection*, mimeo, London School of Economics and Political Science.

RUTS, I. and ROUSSEEUW (1996): Computing Depth Contours of Bivariate Point Clouds, *Computational Statistics and Data Analysis, 23*, p. 153-168.

ROUSSEEUW, P.J. and LEROY, A. (1987): *Robust Regression and Outlier Detection*, Wiley, New York.

SMALL, C.G. (1990): A survey of multidimensional medians, *Intern. Stat. Rev., 58*, 263-277.

VENABLES, W.N. and RIPLEY, B.D. (1994): *Modern Applied Statistics with S-PLUS*, Springer Verlag, Berlin.

ZANI, S. (1996): *Measures of Quality of Life*, (in italian), Franco Angeli, Milano.

ZANI S., RIANI, M. and CORBELLINI, A. (1997): Robust Bivariate Boxplots and Multiple Outlier Detection, submitted for publication to *Computational Statistics and Data Analysis*.

Unsupervised Fuzzy Classification of Multispectral Imagery Using Spatial-Spectral Features

Rafael Wiemker

II. Institut für Experimentalphysik, Universität Hamburg,
KOGS / Informatik, Vogt-Kölln-Str. 30, D-22527 Hamburg, Germany,
http://kogs-www.informatik.uni-hamburg.de/~wiemker

Abstract: Pixel-wise spectral classification is a widely used technique to produce thematic maps from remotely sensed multispectral imagery. It is commonly based on purely spectral features. In our approach we additionally consider additional spatial features in the form of local context information. After all, spatial context is the defining property of an image. Markov random field modeling provides the assumption that the probability of a certain pixel to belong to a certain class depends on the pixel's local neighborhood. We enhance the ICM algorithm of Besag (1986) to account for the fuzzy class membership in the fuzzy clustering algorithm of Bezdek (1973). The algorithm presented here was tested on simulated and real remotely sensed multispectral imagery. We demonstrate the improvement of the clustering as achieved by the additional spatial fuzzy neighborhood features.

1 Introduction

Spectral classification is a widely used technique to produce *thematic maps* from remotely sensed multispectral imagery. The *classification* or *labeling* of each pixel relies on its spectrum or *spectral signature*, which consists of n spectral values of the spectral bands $i = [1 \ldots n]$ of wavelength λ_i. The similarity between an observed spectral vector $\mathbf{x} = [\ldots, x(\lambda_i), \ldots]^t \in \mathbb{R}^n$ and a given reference spectrum $\mathbf{m}$ is commonly evaluated by the *spectral distance* $d = \|\mathbf{x} - \mathbf{m}\|$ in the feature space. The n-dimensional spectral feature space is spanned by the radiance or reflectance signals $x(\lambda_i)$ as received in the n spectral bands of the sensor or camera.

Given the set of all observed spectral vectors $\mathbf{x}$ corresponding to the pixels of a particular multispectral image, unsupervised clustering algorithms are employed to find k cluster centers in the spectral feature space $\mathbb{R}^n$ around which the observed spectra are scattered. Each pixel of the image can then be classified (labeled) to the class to which its spectral distance is minimal.

Most classification techniques applied in multispectral remote sensing (Richards 1993) rely on purely *spectral* features and consider only one pixel at a time. More recently, a method for utilizing additional contextual information from neighboring pixels has been derived from Markov random field modeling (Besag 1986). This 'ICM-algorithm' has been shown to improve classification results on multispectral imagery (Solberg et al. 1996). So far, this spectral-spatial labeling approach has been used in conjunction with supervised classification only, *i.e.*, the reference classes were established from training data by the analyst. In this paper we describe the effects of incorporating spatial context information into *unsupervised* clustering techniques such as the hard and fuzzy k-means algorithms.

2 Hard and Fuzzy Clustering with Spectral and Spatial Features

All k-means algorithms or 'migrating means'-algorithms work iteratively. Also, all k-means algorithms, as used in multispectral image classification, determine for each pixel the Euclidean distance $d(\mathbf{x}|\mathbf{m}_c) = \sqrt{\sum_i (x_i - m_{c,i})^2}$ between the spectral vector $\mathbf{x}$ and the respective mean spectrum $\mathbf{m}_c$ of each class ω_c ($c = 1, ..., k$) in the spectral feature space which is spanned by the n spectral bands i of the imaging sensor ($i = 1, ..., n$), where $x_i = x(\lambda_i)$.

The hard k-means algorithm (Ball and Hall 1967) assigns each pixel to the class ω_c to which the spectral distance $d(\mathbf{x}|\mathbf{m}_c)$ is minimal. Then the k cluster centers $\mathbf{m}_c$ are recomputed as the means of all pixels which currently belong to the respective class. The process is repeated until convergence.

The fuzzy k-means algorithm (originally 'c-means', Bezdek 1973) relies on a fuzzy membership $p_{\text{spec}}(\mathbf{x}|\omega_c)$ which is inversely proportional to the spectral distance $d(\mathbf{x}|\mathbf{m}_c)$:

$$p_{\text{spec}}(\mathbf{x}|\omega_c) = \frac{d^{-1}(\mathbf{x}|\mathbf{m}_c)}{\sum_{c'} [d^{-1}(\mathbf{x}|\mathbf{m}_{c'})]} \quad , \quad \sum_{c=1}^{k} p_{\text{spec}}(\mathbf{x}|\omega_c) = 1 \quad . \tag{1}$$

The algorithm iterates two alternating steps: (a) updating the membership weights $p_{\text{spec}}(\mathbf{x}|\omega_c)$, and (b) re-estimating the cluster centers $\mathbf{m}_c = \sum_{\mathbf{x}} p_{\text{spec}}(\mathbf{x}|\omega_c) \mathbf{x} / \sum_{\mathbf{x}} p_{\text{spec}}(\mathbf{x}|\omega_c)$. In contrast to the hard k-means, *all* pixels are used for the computation of each cluster center, weighted with their respective fuzzy membership $p_{\text{spec}}(\mathbf{x}|\omega_c)$. Convergence to a local minimum of a global objective function has been shown (Bezdek 1981).

Considering contextual image information, we use Markov random field modelling, and assume that the conditional spatial probability $p_{\text{spat}}(\mathbf{x}|\omega_c)$ of pixel $\mathbf{x}$ depends only on the pixels $\mathbf{x}'$ in its spatial neighborhood $\mathcal{N}(\mathbf{x})$ (Li 1995). As the neighborhood $\mathcal{N}(\mathbf{x})$ we here use a $l \times l$ window around pixel $\mathbf{x}$ except the pixel itself.

For the interaction between neighboring pixels, Besag (1986) has suggested a neighborhood potential $U(\mathbf{x}) = \sum_{\mathbf{x}' \in \mathcal{N}(\mathbf{x})} [1 - \delta(\mathbf{x}, \mathbf{x}')]$, with $\delta(\mathbf{x}, \mathbf{x}') = 1$ for equal classes $\omega(\mathbf{x}) = \omega(\mathbf{x}')$, and 0 otherwise.

In this paper we use a refined 'fuzzy' neighborhood potential $U(\mathbf{x}|\omega_c)$, based on the current memberships $P(\omega_c|\mathbf{x}')$ (defined in Eq. 4) of the neighboring pixels $\mathbf{x}'$. The potential $U(\mathbf{x}|\omega_c)$ and then the spatial membership $p_{\text{spat}}(\mathbf{x}|\omega_c)$ are defined as

$$U(\mathbf{x}|\omega_c) = \sum_{\mathbf{x}'\in \mathcal{N}(\mathbf{x})} [1 - P(\omega_c|\mathbf{x}')] \qquad (2)$$

$$p_{\text{spat}}(\mathbf{x}|\omega_c) = \frac{1}{Z} e^{-\beta U(\mathbf{x}|\omega_c)} \quad , \quad \sum_{c=1}^{k} p_{\text{spat}}(\mathbf{x}|\omega_c) = 1 \qquad (3)$$

where $\beta > 0$ is a factor to weight the influence of the spatial context. The spatial membership $p_{\text{spat}}(\mathbf{x}|\omega_c)$ for class ω_c is large if the neighboring pixels $\mathbf{x}'$ have large memberships $P(\omega_c|\mathbf{x}')$ for the same class ω_c, and small if they tend to belong to other classes $\omega_{c'}$. Computation of the normalization constant Z is unnecessary here, as it cancels out in Eq. (4). The joint spectral-spatial membership $P(\omega_c|\mathbf{x})$ of pixel $\mathbf{x}$ to belong to class ω_c then is defined to be :

$$P(\omega_c|\mathbf{x}) = \frac{p_{\text{spec}}(\mathbf{x}|\omega_c) \cdot p_{\text{spat}}(\mathbf{x}|\omega_c)}{\sum_{c'} [p_{\text{spec}}(\mathbf{x}|\omega_{c'}) \cdot p_{\text{spat}}(\mathbf{x}|\omega_{c'})]} \quad , \quad \sum_{c=1}^{k} P(\omega_c|\mathbf{x}) = 1 \quad . \quad (4)$$

Using the additional spatial features, we again can perform hard and fuzzy k-means clustering, depending on whether the cluster centers are re-estimated from only those pixels currently assigned to each cluster, or from all pixels using their current memberships as weights.

3 Results on Simulated and Remotely Sensed Multispectral Imagery

In order to evaluate the effect of the additional contextual memberships (Eq. 3), we have simulated a test image with $n = 2$ spectral bands and $k = 2$ spectral classes ω_1 and ω_2 (Fig. 1). The spectral vectors $\mathbf{x} = [x_1, x_2]^t$ of each class are scattered randomly around the two cluster centers $\mathbf{m}_{\omega_1}$ and $\mathbf{m}_{\omega_2}$, forming uncorrelated Gaussian distributions. In the original spectral feature space the two clusters (Fig. 1, right, true cluster centers marked by crosses) are almost indistinguishable by eye appraisal due to the extreme scatter. The root mean square scatter of both clusters is equal to the Euclidean distance between the cluster centers.

A number of runs was performed with four different algorithms. The number of clusters $k = 2$ and random initial centers (seed coordinates) for the cluster centers were supplied. The resulting classification accuracies (i.e., the relative number of correctly labeled pixels) and the cluster center estimation accuracy (mean relative deviation of coordinates between true and estimated class centers) are given in Table 1. Typical classification results of each method are shown in Fig. 2. We observe that the fuzzy k-means performs slightly better in the estimation of the class center coordinates, but not in the classification. Also, the hard k-means is improved by the additional spatial features in classification, but not in cluster center accuracy. For fuzzy k-means with additional contextual memberships, however, the results indicate clearly that not only the classification results are improved, but that also the coordinates of the cluster centers are estimated with significantly improved accuracy.

Good convergence of the iterative algorithm can be achieved by starting the iteration with $\beta = 0$, *i.e.*, without spatial influence, and then increasing β gradually towards $\beta = 1$. For each intermediate β-value, convergence is waited for before the spatial influence is increased (Fig. 4).

Another interesting observation is that the classification and cluster center accuracy does not deteriorate when the number of classes k is over-estimated. We performed another series of runs with $k = 3$ and $k = 4$ and random cluster seeds provided. With a fuzzy k-means on purely spectral features this decreases the classification accuracy as well as the cluster center estimation (Fig. 3). In contrast, with contextual fuzzy k-means the superfluous classes are basically not populated at all, and the centers of the actually existing Gaussian distributions are found correctly. Classification and cluster center accuracy with over-estimated $k = 4$ clusters is indeed the same as for the correct $k = 2$ case (Table 1, bottom line).

The fuzzy clustering with purely spectral features on the one hand, and with spectral-spatial features on the other hand, was applied to remotely sensed multispectral scanner imagery (flight altitude 300 m) with $n = 10$ spectral bands. The airborne line scanner of DAEDALUS, Inc., is operated on board of a Do 228 aircraft by the German Aerospace Research Establishment (DLR).

Some examplary classification results can be inspected in Fig. 5. The classification results which utilize both spectral and spatial features appear smoother and without grainy, pixel-size noise. Note that not only the pixel-wise classification but also the cluster centers differ when utilizing additional spatial features. The such established clusters are clearly better suitable for thematic image segmentation (see e.g. the forest areas in Fig. 5, top).

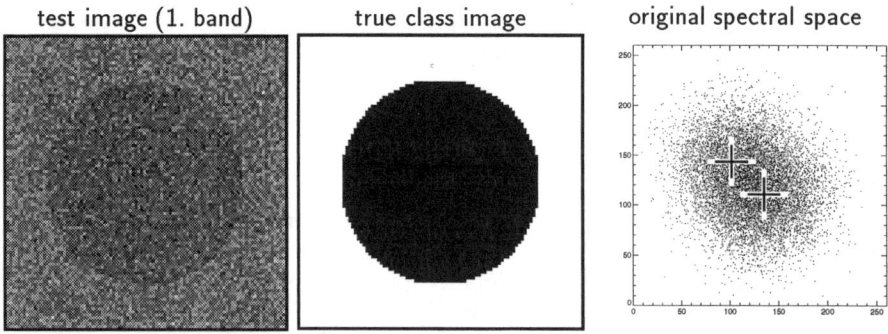

Figure 1: Simulated test image (left) with $n = 2$ spectral bands and $k = 2$ spectral classes (center) with rms scatter equal to the distance between the cluster centers in the spectral feature space (right).

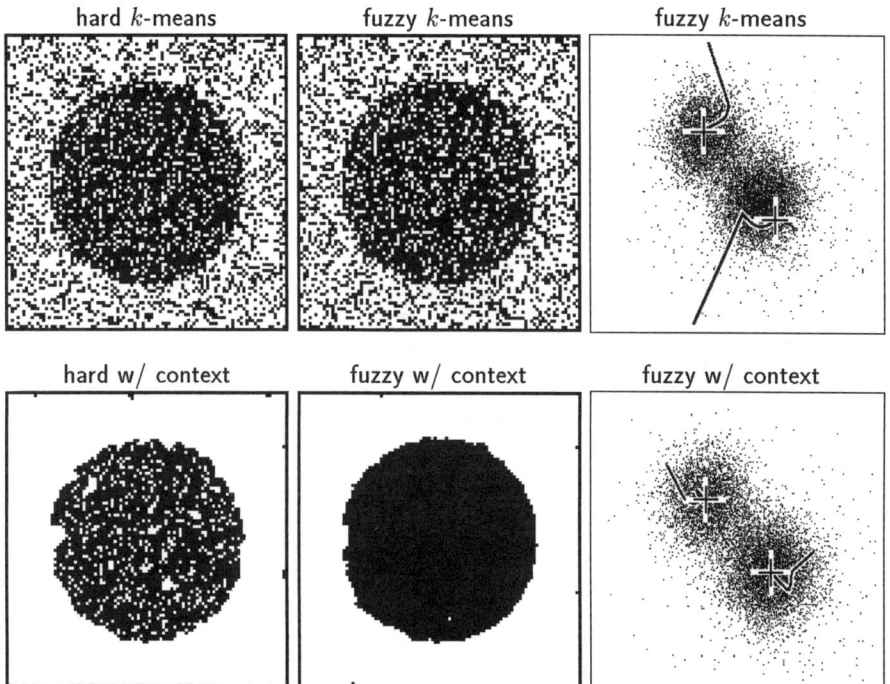

Figure 2: Typical classification results of the various algorithms (left and center). On the right-hand side, estimated cluster centers are depicted in the spectral feature space. The path of the migrating means from random seeds is indicated by solid lines. (For improved visualization, the original feature space was magnified and the scatter reduced.)

algorithm	classification accuracy (correctly classified pixels)	cluster center accuracy (deviation from true centers)
hard k-means	75% (± 1%)	5% (± 1.5%)
with context	91% (± 1%)	5% (± 1.5%)
fuzzy k-means	75% (± 1%)	3.5% (± 1%)
with context	**99%** (± 1%)	**0.3%** (± 0.1%)

Table 1: Results on simulated data. Accuracy of cluster center estimation and classification for various algorithms. Error margins are estimated from several runs with random cluster seeds.

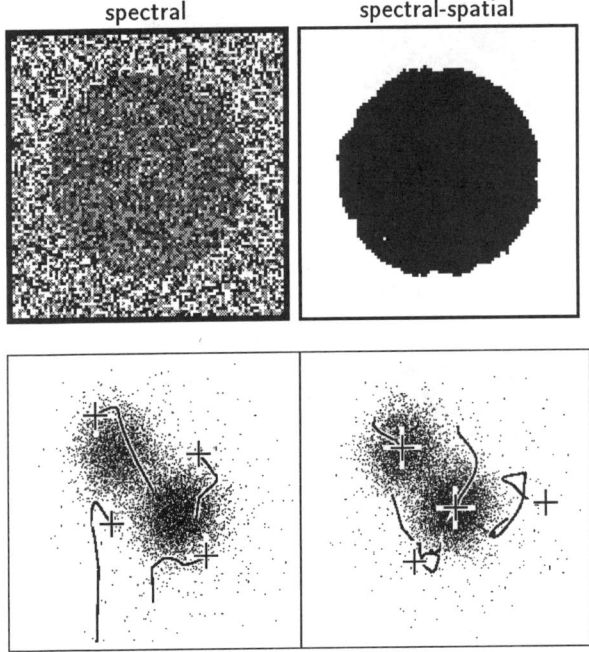

Figure 3: Typical classification results (top), and cluster centers found (bottom), with over-estimated $k = 4$ (instead of the correct $k = 2$) for fuzzy k-means clustering, on purely spectral (left) and spatial-spectral features (right). On the right-hand side, estimated cluster centers are depicted in the spectral feature space. The path of the migrating means from random seeds is indicated by solid lines. (For improved visualization, the original feature space was magnified and the scatter reduced.)

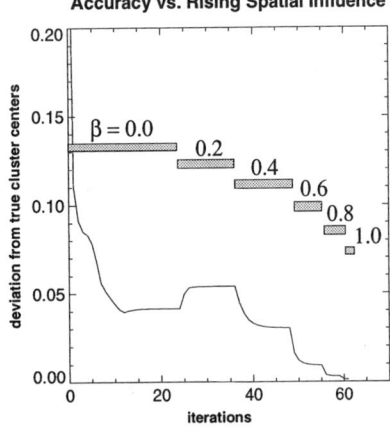

Figure 4: Typical iteration process. Convergence is achieved for each level of spatial influence β. The spatial influence is raised gradually and yields increasing accuracy of the cluster center estimation.

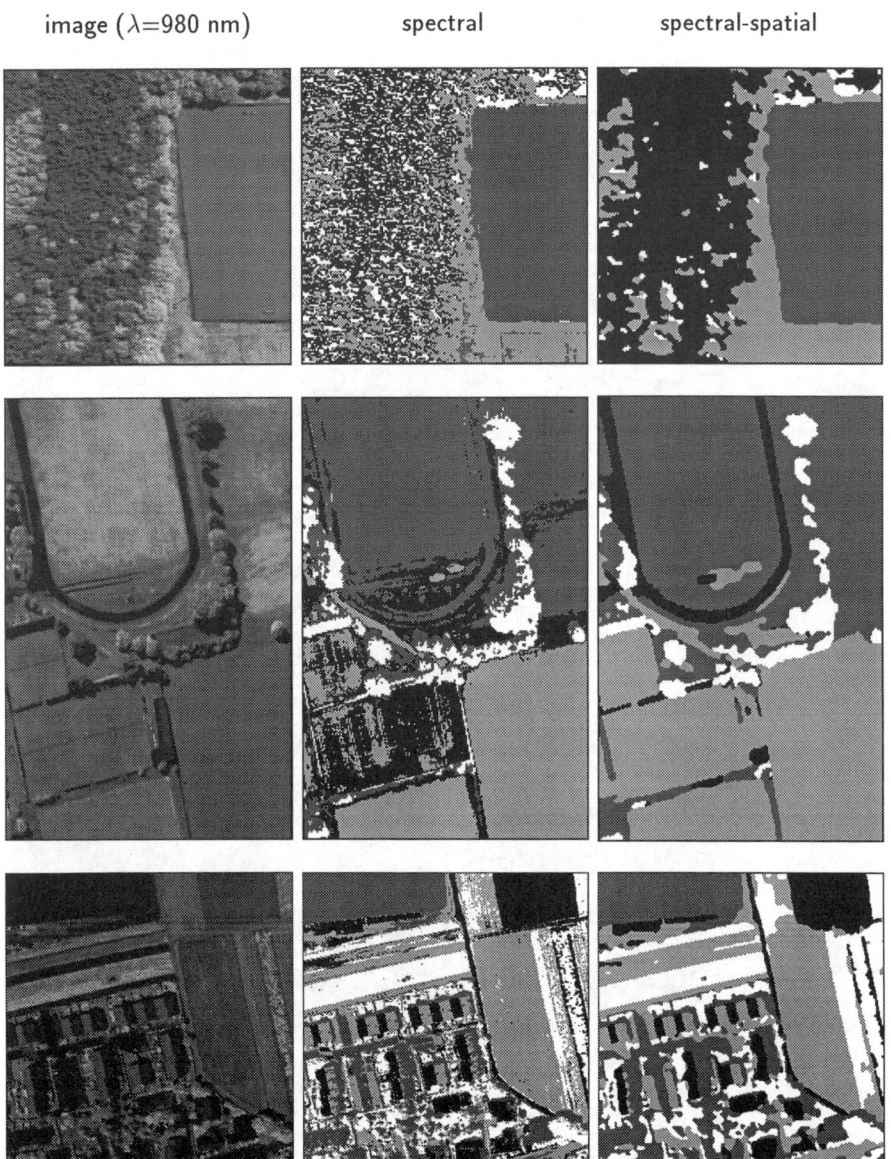

Figure 5: Multispectral aerial imagery of Nürnberg with $n = 10$ spectral bands ($\lambda_1 = 435$ nm, $\lambda_{10} = 2215$ nm), unsupervisedly classified by fuzzy k-means clustering into $k = 4$ classes (recorded in 1995, 300 m altitude, atmospherically corrected, various scales).

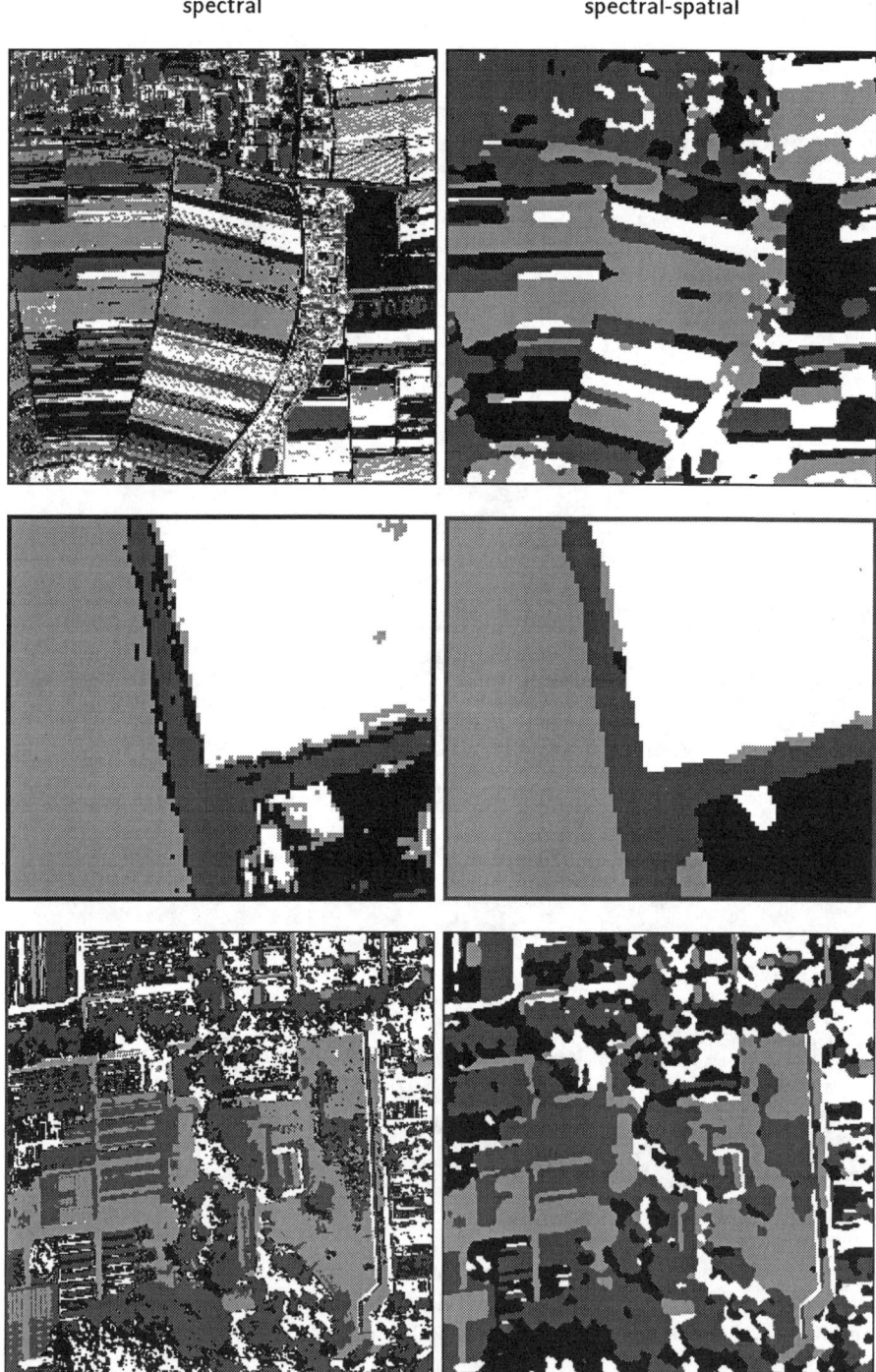

Figure 5b: Multispectral aerial imagery of Nürnberg with $n = 10$ spectral bands ($\lambda_1 = 435$ nm, $\lambda_{10} = 2215$ nm), classified by fuzzy means clustering into $k = 4$ classes (recorded in 1995, 300 m altitude, atmospherically corrected).

4 Conclusions

We have tested the effects of using spatial context features in addition to spectral features for unsupervised clustering and classification of multispectral imagery. Our observations with simulated and remotely sensed multispectral imagery can be summarized as follows:

▷ The additional use of spatial features can significantly improve the classification (labeling) results of unsupervised clustering. The full benefits of additional spatial features are experienced when used in conjunction with fuzzy clustering (in contrast to hard clustering).

▷ Moreover, also the accuracy of the cluster center coordinates as estimated by unsupervised clustering is significantly improved when using additional spatial features in conjunction with *fuzzy k*-means.

▷ The additional spatial features avoid effectively the deteriorating effect of over-estimating the number of clusters k. The cluster centers are found accurately by fuzzy k-means clustering even if the spectral feature space in fact contains fewer than k clusters of Gaussian distribution.

References

BALL, G. and HALL, D. (1967): A Clustering Technique for Summarizing Multivariate Data. *Behavioral Sciences, 12, 153–155.*

BESAG, J. (1986): On the statistical analysis of dirty pictures. *Journal of the Royal Statistical Society B, 48, 3, 259–302.*

BEZDEK, J.C. (1973): Fuzzy Mathematics in Pattern Classification. PhD-thesis, Applied Math Center, Cornell University, Ithaca.

BEZDEK, J.C. (1981): Pattern Recognition with Fuzzy Objective Function Algorithms, Plenum Press, New York.

LI, S.Z. (1995): Markov Random Field Modeling in Computer Vision, Springer, Tokyo.

RICHARDS, J.A. (1993): Remote Sensing Digital Image Analysis. Springer, Heidelberg, New York.

SOLBERG, A.H.S., TAXT, T., and JAIN, A.K. (1996): A Markov Random Field Model for Classification of Multisource Satellite Imagery. *IEEE Transactions on Geoscience and Remote Sensing, 34, 1, 100–134.*

Part 2

Mathematical and Statistical Methods

Some News about C.A.MAN
Computer Assisted Analysis of Mixtures

D. Böhning, E. Dietz

Department of Epidemiology, Free University Berlin
Fabeckstr. 60-62, Haus 562, 14195 Berlin, Germany

Abstract: The paper reviews recent developments in the area of computer assisted analysis of mixture distributions (C.A.MAN). Nonparametric mixture distribution modelling heterogeneity in populations can become the standard model in many biometric applications since it also incorporates the homogeneous situations as a special case. The approach is nonparametric for the mixing distribution including leaving the number of components (subpopulations) of the mixing distribution unknown. Besides developments in theory and algorithms the work focuses in various biometric applications.

1 Introduction

The importance of *mixture distributions*, their enormous developments and their frequent applications over the recent years is due to the fact that mixture models offer natural models for unobserved population heterogeneity. What does this mean? Suppose we are dealing with the case that a one-parametric density $f(x, \lambda)$ can be assumed for the phenomenon of interest. Here λ denotes the parameter of the population, whereas x is in the sample space X, a subset of the real line. We call this the *homogeneous case*. However, often this model is too strict to capture the variation of the parameter over a diversity of subpopulations. Let the parameters of the various subpopulations be denoted by $\lambda_1, \lambda_2, ..., \lambda_k$ where k denotes the number (possibly unknown) of subpopulations. We call this situation the *heterogeneous case*. In contrast to the homogenous case, we have the same type of density in each subpopulation j, but a potentially different parameter: $f(x, \lambda_j)$ is the density in subpopulation j. In the sample $x_1, x_2, ..., x_n$ it is not observed, however, from which subpopulation the observations are coming from. Therefore, we speak of *unobserved heterogeneity*. Let a latent variable Z describe the population membership. Then the joint density $f(x, z)$ can be written as $f(x, z) = f(x \mid z)f(z) = f(x, \lambda_z)p_z$, where $f(x \mid z) = f(x, \lambda_z)$ is the density conditionally on membership in subpopulation z. Therefore, the unconditional density $f(x)$ is the *marginal density*

$$f(x, P) = \sum_{z=1}^{k} f(x, z)f(z) = \sum_{j=1}^{k} f(x, \lambda_j)p_j \qquad (1)$$

where the margin is taken over the latent variable Z. Note that p_j is the probability of belonging to the j-th subpopulation having parameter λ_j. Therefore, the p_j are subject to the constraints $p_j \geq 0$, $p_1 + ... + p_k = 1$. Note that

(1) is a mixture distribution with *kernel* $f(x, \lambda)$ and *mixing distribution*

$$P = \begin{pmatrix} \lambda_1 & \cdots & \lambda_k \\ p_1 & \cdots & p_k \end{pmatrix}$$

in which weights $p_1, \cdots, p_k$ are given to parameters $\lambda_1, \cdots \lambda_k$. Estimation is done conventionally by maximum likelihood, that is we have to find $\hat{P}$ which maximizes the log-likelihood $l(P) = \sum_{i=1}^{n} log f(x_i, P)$. $\hat{P}$ is called the *nonparametric maximum likelihood estimator* (Laird (1978)). The software package C.A.MAN (Böhning et al.(1992)) provides the NPMLE for P:

$$\hat{P} = \begin{pmatrix} \hat{\lambda}_1 & \cdots & \hat{\lambda}_{\hat{k}} \\ \hat{p}_1 & \cdots & \hat{p}_{\hat{k}} \end{pmatrix}$$

Note that also the number of subpopulations k is estimated.

Many applications are of the following type: Under standard assumptions the population is homogeneous, leading to a simple, one-parametric and natural density. If these standard assumptions are violated because of population heterogeneity, mixture models can capture these additional complexities easily. Therefore, C.A.MAN offers most of the conventional densities such as normal (common unknown or known different variances), Poisson, Binomial, Geometric, Exponential among others. To demonstrate these ideas we start with a simple example which has recently found its entry into the textbook "Advanced Methods of Marketing Research" (Bagozzi (1995)). After that we give a short overview in which directions the recent developments of C.A.MAN have taken place.

1.1 An Introductory Example

Data are from a new product and concept test, leading to a variable of interest $X = \#$ *individual packs of hard candy purchased within the past seven days*. Figure 1 shows its distribution.

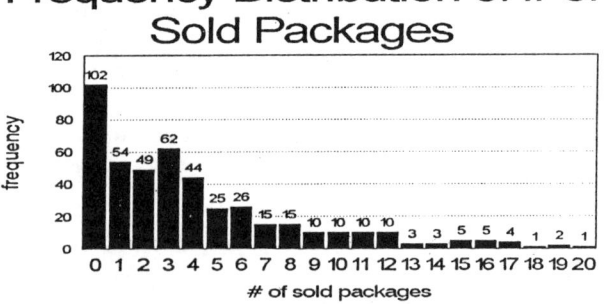

Figure 1: Distribution of Sold Packages

Typically, the assumption of a Poisson distribution is done for count data. The heterogeneity analysis provided by C.A.MAN delivers a five component mixture distribution as shown in Figure 2.

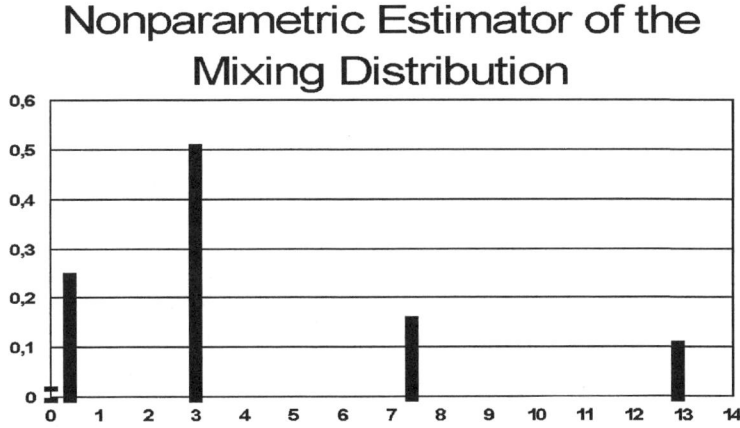

Figure 2: NPMLE of Mixing Distribution for Candy Data

These components can easily be interpreted. The two low components correspond to stores with no or almost no sale of the new product, together about 30% of all stores. There are about 50% with a mean sale of 3 packages, 15% with about 7.5 packages, and 10% with the large number of 13 packages.

2 Developments in C.A.MAN

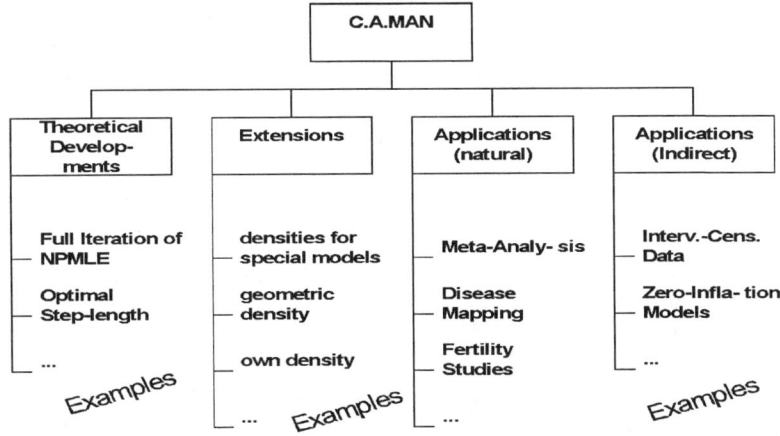

Figure 3: Some Developments in C.A.MAN

Developments in the area of Computer Assisted Analysis of Mixtures have been taking place in various areas as indicated un Figure 3. There have been theoretical developments, algorithmic developments, and developments in direct and indirect applications, the latter meaning developments deviating from the natural genesis of the mixing distribution as capturing population heterogeneity. In the sequel we will give a short overview on these developments.

2.1 Some Elements of Theory

Historically, the strong results of nonparametric mixture distributions are based on the fact that the log-likelihood l is a concave functional on the set of all discrete probability distributions Ω. It is very important to distinguish between the set of all discrete distributions and the set Ω_k of all distributions with a fixed number of k support points (subpopulations). The latter set is not convex. For details see Böhning, Schlattmann and Lindsay (1992). The major tool for achieving characterizations and algorithms is the directional derivative at P in the direction Q, for both P and Q in Ω:

$$\Phi(P,Q) = \lim_{\alpha \to 0} \frac{l((1-\alpha)P + \alpha Q) - l(P)}{\alpha} = \sum_{i=1}^{n} \frac{f(x_i, Q) - f(x_i, P)}{f(x_i, P)}$$

In particular, for one-point mass Q_λ at λ (the vertex of the simplex), the directional derivative is:

$$D_P(\lambda) = \Phi(P, Q_\lambda) = \sum_{i=1}^{n} \frac{f(x_i, \lambda) - f(x_i, P)}{f(x_i, P)} = \sum_{i=1}^{n} \frac{f(x_i, \lambda)}{f(x_i, P)} - n.$$

The determining part in this directional derivative, namely $\frac{1}{n}\sum_{i=1}^{n} \frac{f(x_i,\lambda)}{f(x_i,P)}$ is called the *gradient function* and denoted by $d(\lambda, P)$. We have the general mixture maximum likelihood theorem (Lindsay (1983a,b), Böhning (1982)):

1. $\hat{P}$ is NPMLE if and only if $D_{\hat{P}}(\lambda) \leq 0$ for all λ or, if and only if $\frac{1}{n}\sum_{i=1}^{n} \frac{f(x_i,\lambda)}{f(x_i,P)} \leq 1$ for all λ

2. $D_{\hat{P}}(\lambda) = 0$ for all support points λ of $\hat{P} = \begin{pmatrix} \hat{\lambda}_1 & \cdots & \hat{\lambda}_k \\ \hat{p}_1 & \cdots & \hat{p}_k \end{pmatrix}$

Secondly, the concept of the directional derivative is important in developing reliable converging algorithms (for a review see Böhning 1995). Historically, the vertex direction method (VDM) is of interest. In this method convex combinations $(1-\alpha)P + \alpha Q_\lambda$ are considered, for which the log-likelihood increase (as a function of the step-length α and the vertex direction Q_λ) $l((1-\alpha)P + \alpha Q_\lambda) - l(P)$ is desired to be made as large as possible. A first-order approximation $\alpha D_P(\lambda)$ of this difference leads to the maximization of $D_P(\lambda)$ in λ. Having found a vertex direction with maximum increase one can choose a monotone or optimal step-length α to achieve an update $(1-\alpha)P + \alpha Q_\lambda$.

The VDM is usually slow in its convergence behavior. A faster method (also now used as the standard method in C.A.MAN) is the vertex exchange method (VEM). The basic idea here is to exchange good vertex directions against bad ones already in support of the current mixing distribution. The VEM is defined by $P + \alpha P(\lambda^*)\{Q_\lambda - Q_{\lambda^*}\}$, where $P(\lambda^*)$ is the weight of the bad support point λ^* and α in [0,1] is a step-length. Good and bad support points are identified again by means of the directional derivative. Again, one tries to optimize the gain in the log-likelihood $l(P+\alpha P(\lambda^*)\{Q_\lambda - Q_{\lambda^*}\}) - l(P)$. Now, consider a first order approximation of this difference: $\alpha P(\lambda^*)\{D_P(\lambda) - D_P(\lambda^*)\}$. Clearly, this is maximized if $D_P(\lambda)$ is maximized in λ and $D_P(\lambda^*)$ is minimized in the support of P. Choosing an optimal or monotonic step-length completes the VEM. For details or different methods see Böhning (1989, 1995) or Lesperance and Kalbfleisch (1994).

For the practical realization in C.A.MAN we recall that the goal is to maximize $l(P)$ in the simplex Ω of all probability distributions P on parameter space λ. We call the solution of this problem the fully iterated nonparametric maximum likelihood estimator and this solution is achieved in C.A.MAN into two phases (in which phase II is new). In phase I an approximating grid $\lambda_1, ..., \lambda_L$ ($L \leq 50$) is chosen and $l(P)$ is maximized in the simplex Ω_{GRID} of all probability distributions P on grid $\lambda_1, ..., \lambda_L$ with one of the algorithms described above. For example, we can choose the observed data values as approximating grid, in the introductory example L=21 different values of sold number of packages were observed: $\lambda_1, ..., \lambda_L = 0, 1, 2, ..., 20$. As potential choice of initial weights the observed relative frequencies or unifrom weights: $p_i = 1/21$ could be used.

In phase II, all grid points which are left with positive weights as a result of the optimization process in phase I are used as initial values for the EM algorithm (Dempster et al. (1977)) to produce the fully iterated NPMLE.

2.2 Meta-Analysis and Heterogeneity

Meta-analysis can be defined as the quantitative analysis of a variety of single study results with the intention of an integrative presentation. Often in epidemiology or clinical trials we have as a measure of interest the Odds-Ratio Ψ, or equivalently the log (Odds-Ratio) $\lambda = log(\Psi)$. Then the following situation forms the basis for any meta-analysis. We have n independent studies with estimates: $\hat{\lambda}_1, ..., \hat{\lambda}_n$, from which a pooled estimate $\hat{\lambda}_{pool} = w_1 \hat{\lambda}_1 + ... + w_n \hat{\lambda}^n$ is computed. The weights w_j are frequently chosen proportional to $1/var(\hat{\lambda}_j)$. There exists an extensive debate on the pros and cons of meta-analysis (see the review article of Dickersin and Berlin 1992). Besides many arguments in favour of meta-analysis most importantly it seems that it is becoming more and more part of the scientific method of providing evidence in favour or against a certain hypothesis or argument.

One question of debate in meta-analyis is whether individual study estimates of effect can validly be pooled into a common estimate of effect. This is conveniently put as the question of homogeneity or heterogeneity of study results. Homogeneity is conventionally investigated by diagnostic tests such as the χ^2-test of homogeneity. If there is evidence for heterogeneity, then the problem remains how to proceed. The mixture approach provides an elegant solution for this problem in that it models the heterogeneity distribution in a nonparametric way. The underlying assumption in most forms of meta-analysis is that of a normal distribution for the effect estimate $\hat{\lambda}_i \sim N(\lambda_i, \sigma_i^2)$, with $\sigma_i^2 = var(\hat{\lambda}_i)$. Note that it is important to allow for different variances since the sample sizes will differ from study to study. In the simplest case of homogeneity ($\lambda_1 = \lambda_2 = \cdots = \lambda_n = \lambda$) the MLE of λ corresponds to the pooled estimator. If the population is heterogeneous we must assume the existence of subpopulations with parameter λ_j receiving weight p_j for the j-th subpopulation. Consequently, the density of $\hat{\lambda}_i$ corresponding to (1) is

$$\sum_{j=1}^{k} f(x, \lambda_j) p_j = \frac{1}{\sigma_i} \sum_{j=1}^{k} \phi((x - \lambda_j)/\sigma_i) p_j$$

Here, ϕ is the standard normal density $\phi(x) = \exp(-x^2/2)/\sqrt{2\pi}$. Note also that k is not assumed to be known. If the NPMLE provides k=1, one can conclude, that there is no evidence for unobserved heterogeneity.

If a χ^2-test for heterogeneity is used, it remains frequently unclear how to proceed if this test is significant. The C.A.MAN approach offers a constructive solution in that an estimation of heterogeneity is provided. It is also possible to classify studies into the various subpopulations using the maximum posterior distribution as a classification rule.

2.3 Disease Mapping

Disease mapping can be defined as a method for displaying the spatial distribution of disease occurrence, the most prominent forms being the variety of existing cancer atlases. A conventional biometric method used frequently to construct disease atlases is based on the SMR (standardized mortality ratio) = O/E, where O is the observed number of deaths and E is the expected number for a given region. E is computed on the basis of an external standard population. Then it is conventionally assumed that in area i the observed number of deaths O_i follows a Poisson distribution Po with parameter λE_i:

$$f(x_i, \lambda) = Po(o_i, \lambda E_i) = \exp(-\lambda E_i)(\lambda E_i)^{o_i}/o_i! \qquad (2)$$

Here, $x_i = o_i/E_i$ is the observed SMR, whereas λ is the theoretical SMR. In recent years, we have developed out of C.A.MAN a WINDOWS-program by the name DISMAP (Schlattmann and Böhning (1992, 1996)), solely for the purpose of disease mapping. This program attempts to improve the goodness of fit for the data at hand by replacing (2) by a mixture model

$$O_i \sim \sum_{j=1}^{k} f(x_i, \lambda_j) p_j = \sum_{j=1}^{k} Po(o_i, \lambda_j E_i) p_j$$

Here, the number of subpopulations k (which is equal to the number of colors in the map) is estimated by the program. This is a great advantage. Conventional methods such as the percentile method choose a fix number of colors without considering the data at hand. The method used in DISMAP is also superior to P-value based methods, which sometimes lead to maps not showing the differences in the disease risk in the different areas but the differences in their population sizes.

Crude rate estimators have been also criticized for some time in the connection with disease mapping (see Clayton and Kaldor (1987)) and stabilized estimators, usually in the context of empirical Bayes estimation, have been proposed and used. However, the usage of the nonparametric estimator of the underlying heterogeneity as basis for the construction of the map appears to be of recent novelty.

2.4 Likelihood Ratio Test and Number of Components

Although the nonparametric estimation of the heterogeneity distribution provides an estimate of the number of components itself, it is sometimes requested to use the likelihood ratio test for testing whether a reduced number of components is likewise sufficient. It is well known (Titterington, Smith, and Makov (1985), McLachlan and Basford (1988)) that conventional asymptotic results for the null distribution of the likelihood ratio statistic do not hold, since the null hypothesis is situated on the boundary of the alternative hypothesis. In some cases theoretical results are available (Böhning et al. (1994)), but in other cases simulation results must be used. In general, a parametric Bootstrap procedure can be used (McLachlan (1992)), and it was pointed out recently that this approach is leading to valid statistical inference (Feng and McCulloch (1996)).

2.5 Interval-Censoring and C.A.MAN

In this contribution emphasis has been put on direct applications of mixture modeling, in which the mixture distribution arises as the natural model for (latent) population heterogeneity. The problem of finding the nonparametric maximum likelihood estimate for the distribution function of a survival time under interval-censoring is an example of an indirect application of mixture modeling, where mixing is on indicator variables instead of densities. To demonstrate the details let T be the time until a certain event occurs and $Pr(T \leq t) = F(t)$ its distribution function. T is allowed to be *interval censored*, e.g. T ∈ (L, R] that is, it is only known that the event has occurred between time point L and time point R. This situation occurs for example in repeated testing for occult events (as in tumorgenesis). The contribution of the i-th interval $(L_i, R_i]$ to the likelihood is $Pr\{T_i \in (L_i, R_i]\} = Pr\{L_i < T_i \leq R_i\} = F(R_i) - F(L_i)$. Let $s_0, \cdots, s_m$ the uniquely ordered different values of $\{L_1, \cdots, L_n, R_1, \cdots, R_n\}$. The contribution to the likelihood of any interval can be written uniquely as the sum of all contributions to the likelihood of neigbouring intervals. This leads to the following full likelihood:

$$\prod_{i=1}^{n}(F(R_i) - F(L_i)) = \prod_{i=1}^{n}\sum_{j=1}^{m}\alpha_{ij}[F(s_j) - F(s_{j-1})] = \prod_{i=1}^{n}\sum_{j=1}^{m}\alpha_{ij}p_j,$$

where $F(s_0) = 0$, $\alpha_{ij} = 1$, if $(s_{j-1}, s_j] \subseteq (L_i, R_i]$ and 0 otherwise and $p_j = F(s_j) - F(s_{j-1})$. Note that $p_j \geq 0$ for all j=1,...,m, and $p_1 + .. + p_m = 1$. Thus, the NPMLE $\hat{p}$ is maximizing $l(p) = \sum_{i=1}^{n} log(\sum_{j=1}^{m} \alpha_{ij}p_j)$ subject to the restrictions given above. This likelihood is easily identified as a mixture likelihood though here mixing is not on densities, but on indicator functions. For details see Böhning, Schlattmann, and Dietz (1996) and Gentleman and Geyer (1994).

2.6 C.A.MAN and Covariates

Currently, there is no option for handling covariates in C.A.MAN. Although some of the variables considered here are inherently adjusted for covariates (such as the SMR), analysis of additional covariates is often desirable. Mixture modeling with covariates leads to the area of mixed generalized linear models. One of the authors has developed a variety of macros in GLIM, which allow the fitting of mixed generalized linear models, when the number of components is fixed in advance (see Dietz (1992), Dietz and Böhning (1996)). If the number of components is estimated itself, we are in the class of nonparametric mixed generalized linear models, which we are considering in forthcoming work.

2.7 Other Applications

There is not enough space in this paper to present all kinds of novel C.A.MAN applications of the last years. Two of them should be mentioned at least.
The first one is the analysis of fecundability studies. Using a mixture of geometric distributions for the cycle numbers in which pregnancy is reached, unobserved heterogeneity of fertility can be taken into account. The respective C.A.MAN routine incorporates the problem of censoring, that is the problem that no pregnancy occurs in the study period.
The second application is the estimation of a (prevalence) rate in a population if it is clustered (e.g., an animal population is occuring in herds). If there is a heterogeneity of clusters, the variance of the usual rate estimator is underestimated. Using the results of a mixture analysis by C.A.MAN on

the cluster level leads to an adjusted variance estimate of the pooled rate of interest.

3 Availability

The package C.A.MAN is available from the authors free of cost by sending an E-mail to the following address: boehning@zedat.fu-berlin.de.

Acknowledgments

This research is supported by Deutsche Forschungsgemeinschaft. The work of Dankmar Böhning is under additional support of BIOMED2 grant on Disease Mapping and Risk Assessment.

References

BAGOZZI, R. P. (1995): Advanced Methods of Marketing Research. Cambridge (Mass.), Blackwell.

BÖHNING, D. (1982): Convergence of Simars algorithm for finding the maximum likelihood estimate of a compound Poisson process. *Annals of Statistics 10, 1006 – 1008.*

BÖHNING, D. (1989): Likelihood inference for mixtures: geometrical and other constructions of monotone step-length algorithms. *Biometrika 76, 375–383.*

BÖHNING, D. (1994): A note on test for Poisson overdispersion. *Biometrika, 81, 418–419.*

BÖHNING, D. (1995): A review of reliable maximum likelihood algorithms for the semi-parametric mixture maximum likelihood estimator. *Journal of Statistical Planning and Inference, 47, 5–28.*

BÖHNING, D., SCHLATTMANN, P., and LINDSAY, B.G. (1992): Computer Assisted Analysis of Mixtures (C.A.MAN): Statistical Algorithms. *Biometrics 48, 283–303.*

BÖHNING, D., DIETZ, E., SCHAUB, R., SCHLATTMANN, P. and LINDSAY, B.G. (1994): The distribution of the likelihood ratio for mixtures of densities from the one-parametric exponential family. *Annals of the Institute of Statistical Mathematics 46, 373–388.*

BÖHNING, D., SCHLATTMANN, P. and DIETZ, E. (1996): Interval Censored Data : A note on the nonparametric maximum likelihood estimator of the distribution function. *Biometrika 83, 462–466.*

CLAYTON, D. and KALDOR, J. (1987): Empirical Bayes estimates for age-standardized relative risks. *Biometrics 43, 671–681.*

DEMPSTER, A.P., LAIRD, N.M., and RUBIN, D.B.(1977): Maximum likelihood estimation from incomplete data via the EM algorithm (with discussion). *Journal of the Royal Statistical Society B 39, 1–38.*

DICKERSIN, K. and BERLIN, J.A. (1992): Meta-analysis: state-of-the-science. *Epidemiologic Reviews 14, 154-176*.

DIETZ, E. (1992): Estimation of Heterogeneity - A GLM-Approach. In: Fahrmeir, L. ,Francis, F.,Gilchrist, R., Tutz, G. (Eds.), Advances in GLIM and Statistical Modeling. Lecture Notes in Statistics, Springer Verlag Berlin, 66-72.

DIETZ, E. and BÖHNING, D. (1996): Statistical Inference Based on a General Model of Unobserved Heterogeneity. In: Fahrmeir, L., Francis, F., Gilchrist, R., Tutz, G. (Eds.), Advances in GLIM and Statistical Modeling. Lecture Notes in Statistics, Springer Verlag Berlin, 75-82.

FENG, Z.D. and McCULLOCH, C.E. Using Bootstrap likelihood ratios in finite mixture models. *Journal of the Royal Statistical Society B 58, 609-617*.

GENTLEMAN, R. and GEYER, C.J. (1994): Maximum likelihood for interval censored data: Consistency and computation. *Biometrika 81, 618-623*.

LAIRD, N.M. (1978): Nonparametric maximum likelihood estimation of a mixing distribution. *Journal of the American Statistical Association 73, 805-811*.

LESPERANCE, M. and KALBFLEISCH, J.D. (1992): An algorithm for computing the nonparametric MLE of a mixing distribution. *Journal of the American Statistical Association 87, 120-126*.

LINDSAY, B.G. (1983a): The geometry of mixture likelihoods, part I: a general theory. *Annals of Statistics 11, 86-94*.

LINDSAY, B.G. (1983b): The geometry of mixture likelihoods, part II: the exponential family. *Annals of Statistics 11, 783-792*.

McLACHLAN, G.F. and BASFORD, K.E. (1988): Mixture Models. Inference and Applications to Clustering. New York, Marcel Dekker.

McLACHLAN, G. J. (1992): Cluster Analysis and related techniques in medical research. *Statistical Methods in Medical Research 1, 27-49*.

SCHLATTMANN, P. and BÖHNING, D. (1993): Mixture Models and Disease Mapping. *Statistics in Medicine 12, 943-50*.

SCHLATTMANN, P., DIETZ, E., and BÖHNING, D. (1996): Covariate adjusted mixture models with the program DismapWin. *Statistics in Medicine 15, 919-929*.

Mathematical Aspects of the Feature Pattern Analysis

Michelle Brehm

Department of Psychology
Free University of Berlin

Abstract: The Feature Pattern Analysis (FPA), as introduced by Feger (1988), is a method which analyzes a set of observed patterns with respect to co-occurrence. The mathematical formalism of the FPA and the several logically equivalent alternative forms of its representation as geometrical configurations, sets of contingencies and sets of prediction rules are described. Mathematical conditions for the uniqueness and existence of Type I and Type II FPA-solutions are discussed. A fast algorithm is developed to construct a two dimensional FPA-solution using Hasse-diagrams.

1 Introduction

The FPA, as a model, is based on the analysis of contingencies using the lowest contingencies fitting the data. The present paper describes the mathematical formalism of the FPA. Simple signed pseudohyperplane-arrangements turn out to be an appropriate object to represent FPA-solutions geometrically. As mathematical objects FPA-solutions can be regarded as oriented matroids with additional properties. The usefulness of introducing pseudohyperplane-arrangements for modelling FPA-solutions instead of Feger's first attempt to consider ordinary hyperplane-arrangements (i.e. straight lines arrangements for K = 2), is discussed.

In the two-dimensional case it is essential to regard different types of FPA-solutions. For Type I FPA-solutions it is required that each region corresponds to exactly one observed pattern, i.e. a vector of attributes. For a Type II FPA-solution also "empty" regions are allowed, where the corresponding pattern has not been observed. The description of FPA-solutions by a Hasse-diagram as a dual representation of a pseudoline-arrangement viewed as a planar graph is used to develop an algorithm to construct a two dimensional FPA-solution. The algorithm has polynomial running time. The correctness of the algorithm and the necessity and sufficiency of the conditions proposed by Feger (1994) are briefly discussed. Formal proofs can be found in Brehm (1995) and Brehm (1996 b).

2 Description of the data and notations

The starting point is a set $I\!P$ of observed patterns (data) described by n-tuples $(x_1, ..., x_n)$, or words $x_1...x_n$, being realisations of a vector $(A_1, ..., A_n)$

of n dichotomous items (attributes) A_i which may occur in the two categories $a_i, \bar{a}_i$, i.e. $x_i \in \{a_i, \bar{a}_i\}$. Lower case letters such as $x_i, y_i, \ldots$ will always be used as variable symbols for the realisations of the i-th item A_i and $\bar{x}_i, \bar{y}_i, \ldots$ then denote the opposite category of $x_i, y_i, \ldots$. Lower case letters such as u, v will be also used as variable symbols for patterns $(u_1, \ldots, u_n), (v_1, \ldots, v_n)$, i.e. for realisations of $(A_1, \ldots, A_n)$.

The third order contingencies will appear throughout the paper as a major tool characterising the data. A *third order contingency* is defined as every triple (x_i, x_j, x_k) of one and the same pattern $x = (x_1, \ldots, x_n)$. The set of those third order contingencies which have been observed together in at least one pattern will be called the *set of third order contingencies* of the data set $\mathbb{P}$ and will be denoted by $M(\mathbb{P})$.

3 The general FPA-model

An *FPA-solution* is a **geometric representation** of the set of observed patterns $\mathbb{P}$ (vectors of attributes) in terms of regions, called *cells*, in a space of minimal dimension k. These regions are separated by pseudohyperplanes, each dividing the space in two half spaces corresponding to the opposite categories of a single item of the pattern.

A formal definition of oriented pseudohyperplane-arrangements in general can be found in the mathematical literature on oriented matroids (see Björner et. al, 1993). Oriented pseudohyperplane-arrangements are generalisations of arrangements of affine hyperplanes in the k-dimensional space.

In the one- dimensional case ($k = 1$) the cells are intervals and the pseudohyperplanes are points separating the intervals. In the two-dimensional case ($k = 2$) the cells are polygons (with possibly curved edges). Each pseudoline separates the space into two regions which correspond to the two categories of the item. Each cell is the intersection of n pseudohalfplanes each of which corresponds to the categories of the items. Thus from an oriented pseudoline-arrangement one obtains immediately a set of patterns. For additional illustration and motivation see Feger (1994).

4 The mathematical FPA-model

We represent a mathematically supported approach to solve the problem of analysing co-occurrence data by introducing the notion of oriented pseudohyperplanes.

The formal definition of a simple oriented (signed) pseudoline-arrangement is given as follows:

Definition 4.1 A *simple oriented* (signed) *pseudoline-arrangement* $\mathcal{A}$ in the Euclidean plane E^2 is a family of simple unbounded oriented curves in E^2, such that any two curves intersect in exactly one point, and no three curves meet in one point.

For convenience, we drop the words "simple" and "oriented (signed)" and refer briefly to pseudoline-arrangements. Considering the data set $I\!P$ of observed patterns, we identify the pseudolines with the items and the two pseudohalfplanes, separated by such a pseudoline, with the corresponding pair of categories of that item. Consequently, the cells are identified with patterns, bounded by the corresponding pseudolines. The notion of a third order contingency can be introduced also in the context of a pseudoline-arrangement $\mathcal{A}$. We call a triple of categories an *associated third order contingency* of a pseudoline-arrangement $\mathcal{A}$ if there exists a cell u in the pseudoline-arrangement $\mathcal{A}$ such that this triple of categories is part of u. The set of all third order contingencies associated to $\mathcal{A}$ will be denoted by $M(\mathcal{A})$.

In the construction of the precise mathematical model of a geometric representation of the data by a pseudoline-arrangement one has to distinguish three types of FPA-solutions:

Definition 4.2 Given a set of observed data (patterns) $I\!P$

a) a **two dimensional Type I FPA-solution** (Complete data structure) is defined as a (simple signed) pseudoline-arrangement $\mathcal{A}$ in the (affine) plane such that each observed pattern corresponds to exactly one cell and, conversely, each cell corresponds to an observation.

b) a **two dimensional Type II FPA-solution** (Incomplete data structure) is defined as a pseudoline-arrangement $\mathcal{A}$ in the (affine) plane, such that the set $M(I\!P)$ of third order contingencies derived from the observed data and the set $M(\mathcal{A})$ of third order contingencies associated with the arrangement $\mathcal{A}$ coincide, i.e. $M(I\!P) = M(\mathcal{A})$.

c) a **two dimensional Type III FPA-solution** (Sparse data structure) is defined as a pseudoline-arrangement $\mathcal{A}$ in the (affine) plane such that the set $M(I\!P)$ of third order contingencies being derived from the observed data is a subset of the third order contingencies $M(\mathcal{A})$ associated with $\mathcal{A}$, i.e. $M(I\!P) \subseteq M(\mathcal{A})$.

The mathematical theory of pseudoline-arrangements has been intensively studied since 1950, see Ringel (1956, 1957), Grünbaum (1972) and others. The axiomatisation of the geometrical and combinatorial properties of the pseudoline-arrangements and their generalisations to pseudohyperplane-arrangements initiated the theory of oriented matroids (see Björner et al (1993)).

We note that the relation between the oriented matroid and a simple arrangement of pseudo-lines, i.e. a two dimensional Type II FPA-solution $\mathcal{A}$ can be derived from the topological representation theorem of Lawrence and Folkman (1978). The following theorem yields the connection of FPA-solutions to the established theory of oriented matroids.

Theorem 4.4 A two dimensional Type II FPA-solution $\mathcal{A}$ can be represented uniquely as a rank 3 oriented matroid.

Pseudoline-arrangements have been also considered by Bokowski (1994) and Bokowski and Kollewe (1992) to represent concept lattices (Formal Concept Analysis). Bokowski defines a context which allows a geometric representation as an arrangement of pseudolines to be a pictorial context.

4.5 Pseudolines instead of straight lines

A definition of the regions (cells) by oriented hyperplanes and in the special case of dimension two, by oriented straight lines instead of pseudolines, is not appropriate, because there are simple pseudoline-arrangements which are not stretchable, i.e. which can not be realised by arrangements of straight lines (see Bokowski et al. (1989) for a proof). In general it is theoretically and algorithmically a very difficult problem to decide whether a pseudoline-arrangement is stretchable.

It is known that there cannot exist a local characterisation for pseudoline-arrangements to be stretchable, i.e. realisable by straight lines. This implies in particular that there cannot exist a recursive algorithm for constructing FPA-solutions by straight lines, and more generally, by oriented hyperplanes. However, there are such algorithms for constructing FPA-solutions based on the set of third order contingencies from a given data set (see Brehm (1995) and (1996 a)), and thus, the difficult realization problem for oriented matroids can be avoided in the mathematical model.

Most important, however, is the fact that applications and interpretations in psychology, including the visualisation of the data in terms of cells, are not affected if curved lines (pseudolines) are used as boundaries of the cells instead of straight lines.

5 Uniqueness of Type II FPA solutions for incomplete data structures

To answer the question how many solutions exist if the set of order contingencies is given, we need the zero-cell-criterion first proposed by Feger (1994).

Definition 5.1: The data set satisfies the *zero cell condition* if for each triple A_i, A_j, A_k of the items $A_1, ... A_k$ precisely seven of the eight combinatorially possible third order contingencies are contained in the data set and precisely one is not contained, which is then called the *zero-cell* $N(A_i, A_j, A_k)$ of A_i, A_j, A_k.

The *zero cell condition* of the third order contingencies assures the uniqueness of the two-dimensional Type II FPA-solution. Thus the unique model provided by a FPA-solution permits an unequivocal interpretation of the data in these terms. In general, the order of the contingencies used in the analysis determines the minimal dimension of the representation space and may be interpreted accordingly. In order to get a simpler formulation of the uniqueness theorem and its proof we define an admissible pattern (n-tuple).

Definition 5.2 A pattern $u = (u_1, ... u_n)$ will be called *admissible* with respect to the data set $I\!P$ if no third order contingency of u is a zero cell of the data set, i.e. if

$$u_i u_j u_k \neq N(A_i, A_j, A_k) \text{ for all } A_i, A_j, A_k, \quad i, j, k = 1, ..., n.$$

It turns out that a set of third order contingencies of a data set satisfying the zero cell condition admits at most one pseudo-line-arrangement (see Brehm (1996a), for a proof). Here, two pseudoline-arrangements are considered as equal if they have the same set of cells.

Uniqueness Theorem 5.3 A pseudoline-arrangement $\mathcal{A}$ is uniquely determined by the set $M(\mathcal{A})$ of its associated third order contingencies. The set of admissible n-tuples coincides with the set of cells of the pseudo line-arrangement.

From the Uniqueness Theorem it follows immediately that a two dimensional Type II FPA-solution is uniquely determined by the observed data set $I\!P$.

Definition 5.4 If a given set M of third order contingencies coincides with the set of third order contingencies $M(\mathcal{A})$, i.e. $M = M(\mathcal{A})$, $\mathcal{A}$ will be called a *realization* of M, or $\mathcal{A}$ is an *admissible* Type II FPA-solution for M, or $\mathcal{A}$ is *compatible* with M.

In the higher dimensional case ($k > 1$) this uniqueness theorem is essentially a mathematical consequence of the theorem of Helly. In particular, the elementary proof of the uniqueness theorem shows that the uniqueness theorem is a direct consequence of the zero cell condition, if the observed data set is representable by a pseudoline-arrangement.

Furthermore, the proof of the uniqueness theorem shows that the construction of the pseudoline-arrangement and hence also the problem whether a realization compatible with the observed data exists, can be done recursively. If the items are represented by straight lines instead of pseudo lines, the above statement is no longer valid.

6 Existence and construction of FPA-solutions

We developed a fast algorithm for the construction of a two dimensional Type II FPA-solution. The technical details and the correctness of the algorithm will be presented in Brehm (1996 b).

Starting with a set of observed data the algorithm constructs a uniquely determined Type II FPA-solution recursively one item after the other.

For the construction we use the geometric representation of a pseudoline-arrangement as a planar graph described by the associated Hasse-diagram. The cells of the pseudoline-arrangement $\mathcal{A}$ coincide with the vertices of the corresponding Hasse-diagram. Two vertices are joined in the Hasse-diagram, if and only if they are separated by a pseudoline. We describe the Hasse-diagram by the sequence of its level sets.

These level sets appear extremely useful for the construction of a correct and fast algorithm for FPA-solutions:

- First, one has to choose a pair of complementary cells. Then, in every step of the recursion, the associated Hasse-diagram is constructed, starting with 3 arbitrary items.

- In the step from i to $i+1$, one has to determine those cells, which are separated by the new pseudoline A_{i+1} in the Hasse-diagram H_i.

  The new pseudoline A_{i+1} is represented by a path in the Hasse-diagram H_i. This path will be constructed by deriving an order relation "<" from the one dimensional zero-cells $N_{A_{i+1}}$. This relation describes the order of the intersections of the other pseudolines with the new pseudoline A_{i+1}.

- The new Hasse-diagram of the pseudoline-arrangement of the items $A_1, ..., A_{i+1}$ is constructed by doubling the cells along the path. Thereby some patterns above the path representing A_{i+1} are shifted to the next higher level. A test condition warrants that the new patterns can be inserted compatibly with the data set and that the vertices and edges fit together, yielding a plane Hasse-diagram H_{i+1} and hence a two-dimensional pseudoline-arrangement.

6.1 Algorithm.

Input: The data set $I\!P$ of observed patterns
Output: A planar Hasse-diagram and the associated Type II FPA-solution .

The algorithm introduced in 6.1 is correct, i.e. the algorithm constructs a pseudoline-arrangement uniquely from the data if a pseudoline-arrangement exists at all, otherwise it stops indicating for the given data set a pseudoline-arrangement does not exist.

The algorithm is fast because the input is of magnitude n^3 after deducing the third order contingencies from the observed data and it takes about n^4 operations to find a solution (see Brehm (1996 b)).

7 Necessary and sufficient conditions for the existence of a Type II FPA-solution

As we showed in Brehm (1996 b) Feger's zero cell condition and a more precise version of the consistency condition for zero cells turned out to be as necessary and sufficient for the existence of an FPA-solution.

Definition 7.1 The data set satisfies the *consistency condition* if and only if for all quadruples A_i, A_j, A_k, A_l of four dichotomous items, satisfying the zero cell conditions, the categories of the items in the four zero cells appear in the following combination (up to permutation and reorientation) where $x_i \in A_i = \{a_i, \bar{a}_i\}$:

	Items	A_i	A_j	A_k	A_l
	$N(A_i, A_j, A_k)$	$\bar{x}_i$	x_j	$\bar{x}_k$	–
Zero-cell	$N(A_i, A_j, A_l)$	$\bar{x}_i$	x_j	–	$\bar{x}_l$
	$N(A_j, A_k, A_l)$	–	x_j	$\bar{x}_k$	x_l
	$N(A_i, A_k, A_l)$	$\bar{x}_i$	-	x_k	$\bar{x}_l$

Table 7.1

This can also be formulated as follows:

In the four zero cells exactly two of the four items appear in just one category ($\bar{x}_i$ and x_j in Table 7.1). The two categories which appar in exactly one zero cell (x_k and x_l) appear in two different zero cells ($x_j \bar{x}_k x_l$ and $\bar{x}_i x_k \bar{x}_l$).

Theorem 7.2. For a given data set $\mathbb{P}$ of observed patterns $x = (x_1, ..., x_n)$ a two dimensional Type II FPA-solution exists, if and only if all third order contingencies, i.e. all triples (x_i, x_j, x_k) from the observed patterns $x \in \mathbb{P}$, satisfy the zero cell condition and all quadruples (x_i, x_j, x_k, x_l) from the observed patterns $x \in \mathbb{P}$ satisfy the consistency condition.

8 How to interpret an FPA-solution

We have found a geometric representation of the data which can be exploited in different ways. Through coincidence, condensation and visualisation one wants to develop new hypotheses about the understanding of the subject under consideration. Moreover the FPA-solution is a model. The most essential condition for this model is the zero-cell condition. This condition is a part of the model specification and can be verified empirically. The variation of the observed complex patterns are reduced to contingencies of a minimal order. The dimension of a solution is uniquely determined by the structure within the data. It is the result of the data analysis and can be interpreted accordingly.

A one-dimensional FPA-solution is a generalisation of a Guttman scaling. Scaling is here the specification of the sequence of the observed patterns (attribute vector of the objects). In this sense the one-dimensional FPA solution can be viewed as a pair of linear orders on the set of observed patterns. A two dimensional FPA-solution as a generalisation of a multidimensional Guttman scaling, can be regarded as a two dimensional scaling in the following sense. After choosing a pair of complementary patterns, which should correspond to extreme situations from a psychological point of view, the FPA-solution determines a unique planar Hasse-diagram. Its underlying graph is the dual graph of the pseudoline-arrangement, regarded as a graph. The lowest and largest elements of the Hasse-diagram correspond to the initial pair of patterns. One quantitative (psychological) dimension is given by the vertical direction in the Hasse-diagram, representing the partial order on the set of patterns. The second (psychological) dimension can be constructed by the fact that on every level of the Hasse-diagram the patterns are (linearly) ordered from left to right. This means that the objects on every level of the Hasse-diagram may be quantified if the subject under consideration supports such an interpretation.

The FPA is also a model for the prediction of observations on two levels. On one level the zero cells can be interpreted through several equivalent logical reformulations see Feger (1994). The set of zero-cells in an FPA-solution then corresponds to a consistent set of prediction rules. On the second level the empty cells within a Type II or Type III FPA-solution may be used to predict further observations.

References

BJÖRNER, A., LAS VERGNAS, M., STURMFELS, B., WHITE, N., ZIEGLER, G.M. (1993): *Oriented Matroids*, Cambridge University Press, Cambridge.

BOKOWSKI, J. (1994): *On Recent Progress in Computational Synthetic Geometry*. Preprint TH Darmstadt.

BOKOWSI, J., KOLLEWE, W. (1992): On Representing Contexts in Line Arrangements, *Order, 8, 393-403*.

BOKOWSKI, J., STURMFELS, B. (1989): *Computational Synthetic Geometry*, Springer Verlag, Berlin - Heidelberg - New York

BREHM, M., (1995): *Grundlagen der Feature Pattern Analysis*, Master Thesis.

BREHM, M., (1996 a): The Representation of Feature Pattern Analysis-solutions as Pseudoline-arrangements. In H. Feger and M Brehm, (eds.), (Under Review) *New developments in Feature Pattern Analysis* .

BREHM, M., (1996 b): Existence and Construction of FPA-solutions. In H. Feger and M Brehm, (eds.), (Under Review) *New developments in Feature Pattern Analysis* .

FEGER, H. (1988): Spatial Representations of Feature Patterns. In H. H. Bock (eds.), *Classification and Related Methods of Data Analysis (pp. 431-437)*. Amsterdam: North Holland.

FEGER, H. (1994): *Structure Analysis of Co-occurrence Data*. Aachen: Shaker Verlag.

GRÜNBAUM, B. (1972): Arrangements and spreads, *CBMS Regional Conference Series in Math., 10, Amer. Math. Soc, Providence, R.I.*

FOLKMAN; J.and LAWRENCE J., (1978): Oriented Matroids, *J. Combinatorial Theory, Ser. B, 25, 199-236.*

RINGEL, G. (1956): Teilungen der Ebene durch Geraden oder topologische Geraden, *Math. Zeitschrift, 64,* 79–102.

RINGEL, G. (1957): Über Geraden in allgemeiner Lage, *Elemente der Mathematik, 12,* 75–82.

A Note on the Off-Block-Diagonal Approximation of the Burt Matrix as Applied in Joint Correspondence Analysis

Johannes Faßbinder

Institut für Medizinische Informatik, Biometrie und Epidemiologie
ME der Universität GHS Essen

Abstract: Joint correspondence analysis (JCA) is a commonly applied variation of multiple correspondence analysis (MCA) where the block-diagonal part of the Burt matrix is not considered in the fit. Examples shown here underline that this approach may in some cases lead to ambiguous results which may violate desirable properties of the representation.

1 Introduction

Correspondence analysis was designed as a tool to evaluate two-way contingency tables by methods resembling principle component and factor analysis, with the main difference that the cell entries are used both as data to be approximated by lower-dimensional matrices and weights used for fitting. The desire to extend the method to multi-way contingency tables was obvious, and several approaches to generalize the method were designed. The most obvious one was performing a correspondence analysis on the original incidence matrix. De Leeuw (1984) remarked that this way only one-way interactions are modelled, and that the same space is spanned when analyzing the Burt matrix instead.

The Burt matrix contains the two-way marginal tables between each pair of variables. Additionally, in cells of combinations between categories of the same variable it contains entries corresponding to the marginal frequencies (for identical categories) or zeroes (for different categories of the same variable). The lower-dimensional approximation to the Burt matrix by help of singular value decomposition was named multiple correspondence analysis (MCA). While Benzécri (1990, §IV 0.5.5) argued that the total variation of the Burt matrix cannot be fully explained by a lower-dimensional approximation and suggested an alternative measure to describe the percentage explained by the approximation, Greenacre (1988) suggested that the entries not belonging to two-way contingency tables should be not fitted at all and instead be assigned zero weight. This method of off-block-diagonal fitting has in later publications been given the name joint correspondence analysis (JCA).

1.1 Nomenclature

The incidence matrix N is defined as a matrix whose elements are either 1 or 0. The column vectors $c_1, \ldots c_J$, called "categories" are arranged in sub-matrices $v_1, \ldots v_q$ with $\sum_{v_i} c_j = \underline{1}\, \forall i \in \{1, \ldots, q\}$ ($\underline{1}$ denoting a vector of ones) where $\#v_i \geq 2$. The incidence matrix is arranged such that categories of the same variable appear in subsequent columns.

Let the incidence matrix N be collapsed into a Burt matrix (or Burt's table) $B = N^\mathsf{T} N$. This matrix will have entries $n(j_i)$ on the main diagonal, 0 in cells (j_1, j_2) when j_1 and j_2 belong to the same variable (henceforth called "on the block-diagonal") v_{q_i} and $n(j_1, j_2)$ when the categories belong to different variables. Before approximating a lower-rank matrix, B it is centered and weighted by being transformed into $\tilde{B} = D_r^{-1}(B - nrr^\mathsf{T})D_r^{-1}$, where $r = B\underline{1}$ and $n = \underline{1}^\mathsf{T} B\underline{1}$. The approximation is obtained through a generalized singular value decomposition (for the exact procedure, see for example Greenacre (1984) or Greenacre (1988)). The categories (or columns) will then be represented by points in a space with dimension of at most $J - q$.

Let Q be a symmetric block-diagonal matrix with zeroes in all cells off the block-diagonal, and arbitrary values in cells on the block-diagonal restricted by $Q^\mathsf{T}\underline{1} = 0$. In joint correspondence analysis, let L be the solution of a lower-dimensional approach to $\tilde{B}^* := \tilde{B} + Q$, where both the elements of Q and L are obtained through a least squares problem minimizing $\sum_{(i,j)\in\{1\ldots J\}^2}(l_{ij} - \tilde{b}^*_{ij})^2$, whereas in multiple correspondence analysis only the elements of L are obtained such as to minimize $\sum_{(i,j)\in\{1\ldots J\}^2}(l_{ij} - \tilde{b}_{ij})^2$.

2 Motivation of off-block-diagonal approximation

When suggesting the alternative approach of off-block-diagonal fitting of Burt's table, Greenacre (1988) gave some arguments supporting the approach and later backed up these arguments by applying MCA to a hypothetical data set (Greenacre (1991)).

The main argument is that the classical approach lacked the desirable feature of fitting only the two-dimensional marginal tables by minimizing the χ^2-statistic. The block-diagonal matrices contribute to the statistic with a term that has no statistical interpretation, inflates the variation and introduces additional dimensions which are not of direct interest. This holds especially when the number of categories is large compared to the number of variables. By trying to fit the block-diagonal matrices, especially different categories of the same variables are fitted with an artificial distance between each other.

A feature of classical correspondence analysis is that the distributional equivalence of two categories of the same variable, i.e. the identity of profiles with respect to the categories of the other, results in both columns being fitted to the same point in the graphical representation. It is even possible to merge the two columns to one without changing the coordinate system (Benzécri (1990)). This principle clearly does not transfer to multiple correspondence analysis when the main diagonal is considered to be of interest.

The off-block-diagonal fitting approach solves this problem and indeed includes simple correspondence analysis as a special case.

3 Problems with off-block-diagonal fitting

Whereas off-block-diagonal fitting has some desirable properties for the comparison between categories of the same variable, the argument changes when comparing categories of different variables. As an example, we consider two categories of different variables highly correlated to each other, so that most observations carrying feature c_{j_1} belonging to variable v_{q_1} will have feature c_{j_2} belonging to variable v_{q_2}. Table 1 shows an excerpt of Burt's table where $n(j_1) \approx n(j_1, j_2)$, and $n(j_2) \approx n(j_1, j_2)$. Obviously, as column c_{j_1} and c_{j_2} represent mostly the same observations, their profile with respect to the other variables will also be similar. Hence, a dissimilarity measure between the two columns will be small even if the main diagonal entries are considered in the fit, so one would not expect an unnecessarily enlarged dissimilarity that can be mitigated by putting no weight on the block-diagonal elements.

Table 1: Excerpt of Burt's table: Two categories of different variables

	...	c_{j_1}	c_{j_1+1}	...	...	c_{j_2}	c_{j_2+1}	...	...
...	⋱	⋮	⋮	⋱	⋱	⋮	⋮	⋱	⋱
c_{j_1}	...	$n(j_1)$	0	...	...	$n(j_1, j_2)$	$n(j_1, j_2+1)$	...	...
c_{j_1+1}	...	0	$n(j_1+1)$	...	...	$n(j_1+1, j_2)$	$n(j_1+1, j_2+1)$	...	...
...	⋱	⋮	⋮	⋱	⋱	⋮	⋮	⋱	⋱
...	⋱	⋮	⋮	⋱	⋱	⋮	⋮	⋱	⋱
c_{j_2}	...	$n(j_1, j_2)$	$n(j_1+1, j_2)$	...	...	$n(j_2)$	0	...	...
c_{j_2+1}	...	$n(j_1, j_2+1)$	$n(j_1+1, j_2+1)$	...	...	0	$n(j_2+1)$	...	...
...	⋱	⋮	⋮	⋱	⋱	⋮	⋮	⋱	⋱
...	⋱	⋮	⋮	⋱	⋱	⋮	⋮	⋱	⋱

It is clear that agreement of observations between two categories of different variables is a sufficient but not necessary condition for a similar profile with respect to the other categories. We consider now a situation as in table 1 where there is distributional equivalence between categories with respect to the other variables, but the observations in the two categories do not agree. Furthermore, the number of categories of the variables of interest be 2, so the entries $n(j_1, j_2)$, $n(j_1+1, j_2)$, $n(j_1, j_2+1)$, $n(j_1+1, j_2+1)$ comprise a 2×2 marginal table of any form that allows distributional equivalence with respect to the other variables. Finally we require this table to be symmetric. As the two categories do not agree in observations, we would expect them to yield two different points in the representation space. A lower-dimensional approximation $B + Q$ where the block-diagonal elements can be chosen freely allows the choice of $n(j_1) + q(j_1) = n(j_2) + q(j_2) := n(j_1, j_2)$, $n(j_1, j_1+1) + q(j_1, j_1+1) = n(j_2, j_2+1) + q(j_2, j_2+1) := n(j_1+1, j_2)$. Now the two columns c_{j_1} and c_{j_2} are equal and will be fitted to the same point in the representation space, regardless of how their relation to each other is given by their marginal table, as long as this marginal table is symmetric. In this respect categories of different variables are treated the same way as categories of the same variable. Before an off-block-diagonal fit is attempted, it seems advisable to check if this treatment is desired.

4 Example

It has been demonstrated that two categories of different variables can be fitted to one point by an off-block-diagonal approximation if their profile over the other variables is identical. It can be argued that Greenacre's approach of joint correspondence analysis suggests a predefined numerical iteration rule that finds a local minimum, whereas there might well be other methods that find different local minima, which are not under consideration of joint correspondence analysis.

A numerical example will demonstrate that, with use of the predefined algorithm, Burt's table can be changed to a matrix of lower rank by changing the block-diagonal elements, thus allowing a lower-rank "approximation" with a loss of 0, producing a result, however, which does not preserve the symmetry which is originally, by construction, there. This example uses approximation as suggested in Greenacre (1988), page 462, bottom, which is basically an iterative fit of L and Q by singular value decomposition.

Let a $2 \times 2 \times 2$ contingency table be given as in table 2. Read "catq_1:k" as "category k of variable q_1". The respective profile vector is named $c_{q_1:k}$. Its Burt's table is given as in table 3. The profiles of the first and second variable with respect to the third are identical. The representation in a MCA plot is thus that the distance between $c_{1:1}$ and $c_{3:1}$ is identical to the distance between $c_{2:1}$ and $c_{3:1}$. A desirable feature of another graphic representation would be that this symmetry between $c_{1:1}$ and $c_{2:1}$ with respect to $c_{3:1}$ is preserved. This feature is automatically fulfilled if a lower-dimensional matrix is constructed as described in the previous section.

If, however, one chooses to obtain L through the iterative approach as given in Greenacre (1988), one obtains a 2-dimensional matrix $L = B + Q$ as in table 4. This matrix fulfils the criterion of being a lower-dimensional positive semidefinite approach, with a global minimum as the sum of squared difference is equal to 0. Leaving aside that the block-diagonal elements are rounded to one decimal, it can be verified that the centered matrix $\tilde{B}*$ has rank two. Here, obviously $c_{1:1}$ and $c_{2:1}$ are not fitted to the same point.

Table 2: Hypothetical example of a 2 × 2 × 2-table

Subtable: cat3:1

1st var.	2nd variable		
	cat2:1	cat2:2	Σ
cat1:1	35	5	40
cat1:2	10	10	20
Σ	45	15	60

Subtable: cat3:2

1st var.	2nd variable		
	cat2:1	cat2:2	Σ
cat1:1	10	10	20
cat1:2	5	35	40
Σ	15	45	60

Table 3: Burt's table of example data

	cat1:1	cat1:2	cat2:1	cat2:2	cat3:1	cat3:2
cat1:1	60	0	40	20	45	15
cat1:2	0	60	20	40	15	45
cat2:1	40	20	60	0	45	15
cat2:2	20	40	0	60	15	45
cat3:1	45	15	45	15	60	0
cat3:2	15	45	15	45	0	60

Instead, the resulting plot has been "flattened" so $c_{3:1}$ had to "choose" which of $c_{1:1}$ and $c_{2:1}$ to approach, thus violating the symmetry between $c_{1:1}$ and $c_{2:1}$. Clearly, the matrix given by $(c_{2:1}, c_{2:2}, c_{1:1}, c_{1:2}, c_{3:1}, c_{3:2})$ is also a solution of the problem that violates the symmetry condition. Its plot would look the same, only with the points belonging to the first and the second category exchanged, which would naturally lead to a different interpretation. The two diagrams in figure 1 indicate that the plot of Burt's table as in table 4 gives a distorted picture of the original symmetry.

Table 4: Possible fit of Burt's table

	cat1:1	cat1:2	cat2:1	cat2:2	cat3:1	cat3:2
cat1:1	49.1	10.9	40	20	45	15
cat1:2	10.9	49.1	20	40	15	45
cat2:1	40	20	74.6	−14.6	45	15
cat2:2	20	40	−14.6	74.6	15	45
cat3:1	45	15	45	15	16.9	43.1
cat3:2	15	45	15	45	43.1	16.9

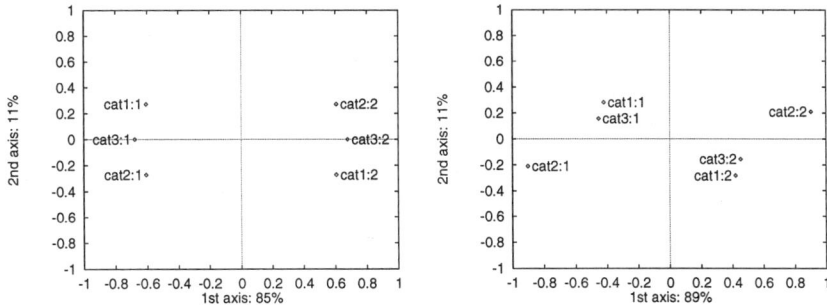

Figure 1: Plot of normal MCA fit and off-block-diagonal fit

5 Discussion

It has been shown that there are examples where a lower-dimensional off-block-diagonal approximation of Burt's table gives ambiguous results and the resulting plots can become highly volatile. While it can be argued that these examples will not exactly occur in practice, one can imagine situations close to table 2, i.e. two variables behaving roughly symmetrical with respect to the rest. This symmetry might be highly disturbed when fitting an off-block-diagonal approximation.

It is interesting to note that in the hypothetical examples given in Greenacre (1991) the distribution of every variable except the last one was chosen to be wholly balanced with respect to one another (i.e. each marginal table had the same entries, stemming from a "balanced 2^4 factorial design") so the difference between the categories could only be explained by their distribution over the last variable. Without the last variable all categories were indistinguishable from one another, so we should expect that all categories be plotted on the same point without being artificially "driven away" from one another by the main block-diagonal. In the examples chosen here, however, there is a difference between categories of different variable, conveyed by their marginal table showing clear dependency. This difference should correspond to a distance in the plot which might be levelled down by the freely chosen entries in the block-diagonal.

A solution to this problem might lie in trying out approximations where the block-diagonal elements have a lower weight which is still greater than 0. Bailey and Gower (1990) proved that in this case a positive semidefinite approximation to a symmetric matrix has rank at least as high as the number of positive eigenvalues of the original matrix, so unwanted collapsing of dimensions could not happen here. However, this was shown for attaining different weights to the main diagonal only, not for a block-diagonal.

The off-block-diagonal fit or joint correspondence analysis approach should not be applied generally. If one is interested in finding similarities between categories of *the same* variable, it is definitely a viable approach to use an approximation which does not take the block-diagonal elements into account. When interested in similarities between categories of *different* variables, the block-diagonal even has an interpretation and one might want to not at all exclude it from the analysis.

Acknowledgement

I would like to express my gratitude to an anonymous referee whose advice helped me a lot clarifying my thoughts.

References

BAILEY, R.A. and GOWER, J.C. (1990): Approximating a Symmetric Matrix. *Psychometrika, 55.4, 665-675.*

BENZÉCRI, J.-P. (1990): Correspondence Analysis Handbook. Marcel Dekker, New York.

DE LEEUW, J. (1984): Canonical Analysis of Categorical Data. DSWO Press, Leiden.

GREENACRE, M.J. (1984): Theory and Applications of Correspondence Analysis. Academic Press, New York.

GREENACRE, M.J. (1988): Correspondence Analysis of Multivariate Categorical Data by Weighted Least Squares. *Biometrika, 75, 457-467.*

GREENACRE, M.J. (1991): Interpreting Multiple Correspondence Analysis. *Applied Stochastic Models and Data Analysis, 7, 195-210.*

A New Look at the Visual Performance of Nonparametric Hazard Rate Estimators

O. Gefeller[1], N.L. Hjort[2]

[1] Department of Medical Statistics, University of Göttingen,
Humboldtallee 32, D–37073 Göttingen, Germany

[2] Department of Mathematics and Statistics, University of Oslo,
P.B. 1053 Blindern, N–0316 Oslo, Norway

Abstract: Nonparametric curve estimation by kernel methods has attracted widespread interest in theoretical and applied statistics. One area of conflict between theory and application relates to the evaluation of the performance of the estimators. Recently, Marron and Tsybakov (1995) proposed *visual error criteria* for addressing this issue of controversy in density estimation. Their core idea consists in using integrated alternatives to the Hausdorff distance for measuring the closeness of two sets based on the Euclidean distance. In this paper, we transfer these ideas to hazard rate estimation from censored data. We are able to derive similar results that help to understand when the application of the new criteria will lead to answers that differ from those given by the conventional approach.

1 Introduction

In various areas of applied and theoretical statistics nonparametric curve estimation by kernel methods has attracted widespread interest during the last two decades. Without imposing any distributional assumptions on the observed data, structural information, for example, on the underlying density functions, some interesting functionals of the density (like the hazard rate) or regression curves, can be obtained by "smoothing" the empirical mass of the observations to some neighbouring environment around the observed data points. Starting with the pioneering work by Rosenblatt (1956) and Parzen (1962), nowadays a vast literature on the properties of kernel methods can be found (for recent textbooks see Wand and Jones (1995), Härdle (1991)). Important progress has been made recently in a variety of issues (for example, bandwidth selection, boundary behaviour, software implementation), mostly originating from research in density estimation, the simplest situation. However, it has been criticised repeatedly that there is an obvious gap between theory and application with respect to the evaluation of the performance of the nonparametric estimators. The estimated curves that are judged to be "good" from theoretical reasoning (based on their distance to the true curve in terms of the classical norms on function spaces, mostly L_2) do not satisfy applied statisticians as their "graphical fit" can be substantially poorer than that of other estimators which are more appealing from a graphical notion but exhibit larger deviations from the true curve in L_2-norm. To address this issue of conflict, Marron and Tsybakov

(1995) proposed new *visual error criteria* for assessing the performance of nonparametric density estimators. The core idea of this concept consists of using integrated alternatives to the Hausdorff distance for measuring the closeness of two sets of points based on the usual Euclidean distance.

The aim of this paper is twofold: first, we review this interesting approach and describe the basic properties of the visual error criteria in section 2 and 3. Second, in the following sections 4 and 5 of this paper, we apply the criteria to nonparametric hazard rate estimation from censored data via kernel estimators. The evolving area of hazard rate estimation is a promising field for these new ideas, because, due to the application-orientated interpretation of hazard rates in practical survival analysis, qualitative aspects of smoothing performance should be preferred to the exclusive consideration of L_2-fit. As a first step into this direction, we derive similar results as in the density context showing that a suitable asymptotic bridge can be built between expected visual error criteria and conventional integrated mean squared errors ($MISE$), incorporating some weight function depending on the derivative of the hazard rate In the final section we discuss advantages and disadvantages of this approach and point to future work needed to broaden the understanding of the concept.

2 Conventional L_p-norm Criteria

The conventional approach for measuring the distance between some "true" curve h and its estimate $\widehat{h}$ relies on the application of classical mathematical norms on function spaces. The most popular representative of this approach is the L_2-norm. The distance between two functions in terms of the L_2-norm is then defined as

$$L_2(\widehat{h}, h) := \int \left[\widehat{h}(x) - h(x)\right]^2 dx\,.$$

Alternatively, other variants of the broad class of L_p-norms such as, for example, $L_1(\widehat{h}, h) := \int |\widehat{h}(x) - h(x)| dx$ and $L_\infty(\widehat{h}, h) := \sup_x |\widehat{h}(x) - h(x)|$ have also been proposed, but are less often used. All measurements of distance based on the various L_p-norms have one fundamental property in common: they focus completely on the *vertical* discrepancy between the curves at all points x belonging to the support of the functions (typically in cases of lifetime data, the support is some subset of $\mathcal{R}_+$).

A striking graphical example that the concentration on vertical discrepancy can contradict the visual notion of distance between curves has been provided by Kooperberg and Stone (1991). Their example shows a "true" bimodal curve that is approximated by two very different estimates. The key element of this example is that the visually more appealing estimate that recovers the bimodal structure but with some imprecision in the location of the second peak is clearly inferior in terms of all L_p-norms to the other estimate that only recovers the first peak and "smoothes away" the lower second peak. The reason for this contradiction between graphical impression and mathematical L_p-norm analysis is obvious: as the distances between the curves are only assessed vertically, no L_p-norm criterion realises that the first estimate is "structurally correct", although quite incorrect with respect to localising the second peak, and thus penalises the estimate in both regions of vertical discrepancy, the region of the true second peak and that of the estimated second peak, whereas the "oversmoothed" estimate is penalised only once, in the region of the true peak. Any remedy to this problem has to drop the strict reliance on vertical distances and has to offer another way of conceptualising discrepancies between curves.

3 Visual Error Criteria

One such alternative approach of measuring the discrepancy between curves has been developed by Marron and Tsybakov (1995) who termed their measures *visual error criteria*. The starting point for the derivation of these criteria consists in treating curves not as pointwise collections of the values of functions $\widehat{h}$ and h of a single variable at fixed $x \in \mathcal{R}_+$ but instead as sets in $\mathcal{R}^2$ that are defined by their corresponding "graphs". The graph of some function h is defined as the set $G_h := \{(x,y), x \in \mathcal{R}_+, y = h(x)\} \subset \mathcal{R}^2$. Some planar distance between the sets G_h and $G_{\widehat{h}}$ can now replace the conventional vertical distance between h and $\widehat{h}$ for fixed $x \in \mathcal{R}_+$. The basis of the definition of a planar distance is the notion of distance from a point to a set, defined as

$$d((x,y), G_h) := \inf_{(x^*,y^*) \in G_h} \|(x,y) - (x^*, y^*)\|_2$$

and giving the shortest distance from some fixed point (x,y) to any element in the set G_h, where $\|\cdot\|_2$ denotes the usual Euclidean distance. By allowing (x,y) to vary and take on all elements in the set $G_{\widehat{h}}$, a set of distances between between G_h and $G_{\widehat{h}}$ is defined, formally introduced as $\mathcal{M}(G_h, G_{\widehat{h}}) := \{d((x,y), G_{\widehat{h}}) : (x,y) \in G_h\}$. A variety of different ways to summarise the complete information in $\mathcal{M}(G_h, G_{\widehat{h}})$ when defining a real-valued one-dimensional distance are now conceivable. In analogy to the L_2-norm criterion based on quadratic vertical distances we first consider the two versions of the quadratic visual error criteria:

$$VE_2(h \longrightarrow \widehat{h}) := \left[\int d((x, h(x)), G_{\widehat{h}})^2 dx\right]^{1/2}$$

$$VE_2(\widehat{h} \longrightarrow h) := \left[\int d((x, \widehat{h}(x)), G_h)^2 dx\right]^{1/2}$$

As the planar distances are asymmetrical in nature, both versions have to be distinguished since they are not identical in general. However, a symmetrised version of VE_2 can also be defined by simply averaging the two versions, in a Pythagorean way, as follows

$$SE_2(\widehat{h}, h) := \left[VE_2(h \longrightarrow \widehat{h})^2 + VE_2(\widehat{h} \longrightarrow h)^2\right]^{1/2}$$

As for the L_p-norm criteria, similar asymmetrical and symmetrical visual error criteria can also be defined for the non-quadratic distances (by simply integrating over $d((x, h(x)), G_{\widehat{h}})$ and $d((x, \widehat{h}(x)), G_h)$, respectively, yielding $VE_1(h \longrightarrow \widehat{h})$ and $VE_1(\widehat{h} \longrightarrow h)$, respectively) and maximal distance (by considering $\sup(\mathcal{M}(G_h, G_{\widehat{h}}))$ and $\sup(\mathcal{M}(G_{\widehat{h}}, G_h))$, respectively, yielding $VE_\infty(h \longrightarrow \widehat{h})$ and $VE_\infty(\widehat{h} \longrightarrow h)$, respectively). The symmetrical version of the two variants of VE_∞ given by $SE_\infty(\widehat{h}, h) := \max\{VE_\infty(h \longrightarrow \widehat{h}), VE_\infty(\widehat{h} \longrightarrow h)\}$ is also known for a long time as the Hausdorff distance. Thus, all other visual error criteria described in this section can be viewed as integrated alternatives to the Hausdorff distance.

It has to be kept in mind that the other symmetrised versions (SE_2 and SE_1) are — in a mathematical sense — not "distances" on the corresponding function space as they do not satisfy the triangle inequality (see Marron and Tsybakov (1995) for an illustrative counterexample). For the practical application of these criteria, lacking this mathematical property does not seem to be a serious drawback.

4 Kernel Estimation of the Hazard Rate

The evolving area of hazard rate estimation from censored data comprises a promising field for the application of the visual error criteria as qualitative aspects of smoothing performance are of primary interest here. In this section the necessary background about the statistical setting and some known asymptotic results concerning kernel estimators of the hazard rate are briefly summarised. More detailed reviews on this subject can be found in Gefeller and Michels (1992), Andersen et al. (1993) and Hjort (1996).

Suppose $T_1, \ldots, T_n$ refer to i.i.d. nonnegative failure times with distribution function F and density function f, and $C_1, \ldots, C_n$ denote i.i.d. nonnegative censoring times with distribution function G and density function g. Assume further that failure times T_i and censoring times C_i are independent for all $i = 1, \ldots, n$. Under this setting of the so-called *random censorship model*, which is the simplest and most important special case of models for censored failure time data in the framework of counting process models, the observed data consist of the bivariate sample $(X_1, \delta_1), \ldots, (X_n, \delta_n)$, where $X_i := \min(T_i, C_i)$ and $\delta_i := I\{T_i \leq C_i\}, i = 1, \ldots, n$. The censoring indicator δ_i provides the information whether the observed X_i refers to a true failure time ($\delta_i = 1$) or to a censoring time ($\delta_i = 0$).

The hazard rate $h(x) := \lim_{\Delta x \to o}(1/\Delta x) \cdot P(x \leq T_i < x + \Delta x | T_i \geq x)$, $x \geq 0$, has the application-orientated flavour that it can be nicely interpreted as the instantaneous risk of observing the failure event of interest at time x. In a variety of applications ranging from survival analysis in a medical context to reliability testing in industrial settings the hazard rate is thus used extensively as a methodological tool to describe variations in risk over time. In these applications qualitative aspects of the structure of the hazard rate are more interesting than the precise location and height of peaks of the function.

The most prominent nonparametric approach to estimate the hazard rate is given by the kernel estimator with a fixed bandwidth which is defined as

$$\widehat{h}(x) := \sum_{i=1}^{n} \frac{\delta_{(i)}}{n-i+1} \cdot \frac{1}{b} \cdot K\left(\frac{x - X_{(i)}}{b}\right)$$

where $\delta_{(i)}$ refers to the censoring indicator corresponding to the i-th element of the order statistic of the observed failure times, $K(\cdot)$ denotes the kernel function (satisfying standard conditions, see below), and the bandwidth parameter b has to be positive. Several variations of this kernel estimator have been suggested allowing the bandwidth to vary with x, for example, the nearest neighbour kernel estimator (Gefeller and Dette (1992)), the local-bandwidth kernel estimator (Müller and Wang (1994)) or the variable kernel estimator (Schäfer (1985)). For the rest of this paper attention is focussed on the simplest case of the fixed-bandwidth kernel estimator. Modifications for the local-bandwidth and the nearest neighbour kernel estimator are straightforward; however, the variable kernel estimator poses the additional complexity that expressions for the $MISE$ have not been derived yet and thus conditions under which the results of following section might be transferred to the variable kernel estimator are not yet explicitly available.

A variety of results on the asymptotic behaviour of $\widehat{h}$ ranging from different proofs of consistency to sophisticated elaborations on the optimal order of convergence can be found in the literature. For the purpose of this paper it is sufficient to restrict the attention to a result on the asymptotic $MISE$ which can be easily decomposed into integrals over a squared bias ($\mu^2(\cdot)$) and a variance part ($\sigma^2(\cdot)$). The necessary technical assumptions for the asymptotics to work can be stated as follows:

(K) The kernel function $K(\cdot)$ has to defined on a compact support $[a,b] \subset \mathcal{R}$ as a bounded symmetrical probability density function having a second derivative that is Lipschitz continuous on $[a,b]$.

(H) The hazard rate h has to be twice continuously differentiable and square integrable on $\mathcal{R}_+$.

(B) The sequence of bandwidths b_n has to approach zero at a rate slower than n^{-1}. The convergence rate in this situation is optimised for the bandwidth sequence $b_n = C_0 \cdot n^{-1/5}$, with $C_0 > 0$ denoting a special constant.

Given that (K), (H) and (B) hold it has been shown that for $n \to \infty$ the

MISE can be written as follows (omitting asymptotically vanishing terms):

$$\begin{aligned}
MISE(\widehat{h}, h) &= \int E\left[\widehat{h}(x) - h(x)\right]^2 dx \\
&= \int \left(\left[\frac{b_n^2}{2} h''(x)\beta(K)\right]^2 + \frac{h(x)\alpha(K)}{nb_n(1 - F(x))(1 - G(x))}\right) dx \\
&=: \int \left(\mu^2(x) + \sigma^2(x)\right) dx
\end{aligned}$$

where $\alpha(K)$ and $\beta(K)$ denote constants depending on the kernel function ($\alpha(K) := \int K^2(u) du$, $\beta(K) := \int u^2 K(u) du$). This result demonstrates the well-known problem in selecting an appropriate bandwidth, often termed the "variance-bias trade-off". For the bias to decrease one needs to select a small bandwidth, however, taking this parameter small means automatically an increase in the variance. The variance-bias trade-off is in accordance with the intuitive understanding of smoothing as a technique to reveal the underlying structure of the data by reducing the "noise" (variance) at the expense of some "oversimplification" (bias). More details on these general aspects of smoothing and on the technical details of the derivation of asymptotic results in a general counting process framework can be found in the monograph by Andersen et al. (1993).

5 Asymptotic Properties of Visual Error Criteria Applied to Hazard Rate Estimation

The standard asymptotic results on the properties of the kernel estimator $\widehat{h}$ consider only distances between $\widehat{h}(x)$ and $h(x)$ at fixed $x \in \mathcal{R}_+$ and thus exhibit the drawback of measuring error only vertically as discussed previously. In this section we analyse the asymptotic behaviour of the quadratic versions of the visual error criteria that is essentially determined by the asymptotics of the distances $d((x, \widehat{h}(x)), G_h)$ and $d((x, h(x)), G_{\widehat{h}})$, respectively. To this end, consider for fixed $x_0 \in \mathcal{R}_+$ the distances as sequences of nonnegative random variables $D_n^1(x_0)$ and $D_n^2(x_0)$, respectively. In the context of density estimation Marron and Tsybakov (1995) derived a result on the convergence in probability of $D_n^1(x_0)$ and $D_n^2(x_0)$, respectively, for $n \to \infty$. In the proof they used a combination of primarily geometric arguments that can be directly transferred to the hazard rate context. The only density-specific step concerned the convergence in probability of the kernel estimator for the derivative of the density to the true derivative of the density. The same property, i.e. $\widehat{h}'(x_0) \xrightarrow{P} h'(x_0)$ for fixed x_0 as $n \to \infty$, holds for the kernel estimator of the hazard rate as can be checked easily. Thus, analogous to the density context analysed in Marron and Tsybakov (1995),

$$n^{2/5} \cdot \left(D_n^i(x_0) - \frac{|\widehat{h}(x_0) - h(x_0)|}{\sqrt{1 + [h'(x_0)]^2}}\right) \xrightarrow{P} 0$$

holds in the hazard rate context for $i = 1, 2$ as $n \to \infty$. This result allows to build an asymptotic bridge between the expected squared visual error criteria and the conventional approach as follows:

$$\begin{aligned} E\left[VE_2(\widehat{h} \to h)^2\right] &= \int d((x, \widehat{h}(x)), G_h)^2 dx \\ &= \int E\left(D_n^1(x)^2\right) dx \\ &\approx \int \frac{E\left([\widehat{h}(x) - h(x)]^2\right)}{1 + [h'(x)]^2} dx \\ &\approx \int \frac{\mu^2(x) + \sigma^2(x)}{1 + [h'(x)]^2} dx \quad . \end{aligned}$$

Here the first two equalities are given by the definition of the quantities, the first approximation utilises the asymptotic result on D_n^1 and the last approximation results from plugging in the asymptotic MSE expression given in the previous section (a similar line of reasoning leads to the same asymptotic result for $E[VE_2(\widehat{h} \to h)^2]$). When defining $w(x) := (1 + [h'(x)]^2)^{-1}$, the final expression above can also be viewed as the standard asymptotic representation of a weighted $MISE$ employing the special weight function $w(\cdot)$. This shows that expected squared visual error corresponds asymptotically to a weighted $MISE$, and inspection of the weight function allows to infer in which situations the two concepts of measuring discrepancy between curves will contradict each other. For example, for hazard rates of exponentially distributed failure times both error concepts give identical answers, but for hazard rates with regions where $|h'(x)|$ is large $E[VE_2(\cdot)^2]$ and $MISE$ can disagree remarkably. This finding corresponds with the motivating example given in section 2 and the intuitive understanding of the deficiencies of the L_2-approach in situations where functions reveal several peaks.

Although the asymptotic expressions derived above for $E[VE_2(\widehat{h} \to h)^2]$ and $E[VE_2(h \to \widehat{h})^2]$ are the same, details of the proof in Marron and Tsybakov (1995) suggest that the asymptotics might come into action later for $VE_2(h \to \widehat{h})$ than for $VE_2(\widehat{h} \to h)$. This should also be reflected in a different finite sample behaviour of the two criteria which needs further investigation. From the findings on the two asymmetrical versions of squared visual error it follows immediately that for the symmetrised criterion $SE_2(\widehat{h}, h)$ it can be shown that, for $n \to \infty$, $E[SE_2(\widehat{h}, h)^2]$ tends to twice the same weighted $MISE$ as above.

6 Discussion

The standard approach when evaluating the performance of a functional estimate uses some L_p-norm to quantify its distance to the true function. As demonstrated in this paper, there are several situations in which this approach contradicts the graphical notion of discrepancy between curves since all L_p-norms consider only vertical distances and neglect aspects of qualitative similarities. Thus, the new concept of visual error criteria has been discussed as an alternative method to evaluate the visual appropriateness of functional estimates. In the context of hazard rate estimation from censored data it has been shown that application of these criteria corresponds asymptotically to a weighted version of the conventional $MISE$. A more detailed analysis of the finite properties of visual error criteria is, however, needed to expand the knowledge about advantages and disadvantages of this new concept. Visual error criteria represent an attractive first step into the direction of rethinking the mathematical evaluation of the performance of functional estimates, but they require further elaboration — and perhaps some modification — prior to their routine application.

References

ANDERSEN, P.K., BORGAN, Ø., GILL, R.D., KEIDING, N. (1993): *Statistical Models Based on Counting Processes.* Springer-Verlag, New York.

GEFELLER, O., DETTE, H. (1992): Nearest neighbour kernel estimation of the hazard function from censored data. *Journal of Statistical Computation and Simulation, 43, 93-101.*

GEFELLER, O., MICHELS, P. (1992): Nichtparametrische Analyse von Verweildauern. *Österreichische Zeitschrift für Statistik und Informatik, 22, 37-59.*

HÄRDLE, W. (1991): *Applied Nonparametric Regression.* Cambridge University Press, Boston.

HJORT, N.L. (1996): New methods for hazard rate estimation. In: *Proceedings of the 17th Rencontre Franco-Belge de Staticiens, Université de Marne-la-Vallée,* p. 20-24.

KOOPERBERG, C., STONE, C.J. (1991): A study of logspline density estimation. *Computational Statistics & Data Analysis, 12, 327-347.*

MARRON, J.S., TSYBAKOV, A.B. (1995): Visual error criteria for qualitative smoothing. *Journal of the American Statistical Association, 90, 499-507.*

MÜLLER, H.G., WANG, J.L. (1994): Hazard rate estimation under random censoring with varying kernels and bandwidths. *Biometrics, 50, 61-76.*

PARZEN, E. (1962): On the estimation of a probability density and mode. *Annals of Mathematical Statistics, 33, 1065-1076.*

ROSENBLATT, M. (1956): Remarks on some nonparametric estimates of a density function. *Annals of Mathematical Statistics, 27, 832-837.*

SCHÄFER, H. (1985): A note on data-adaptive kernel estimation of the hazard function in the random censorship situation. *Annals of Statistics, 13, 818-820.*

WAND, M., JONES, M. (1995): *Kernel Smoothing.* Chapman & Hall, London.

Multilevel Modeling: When and Why

J. Hox

University of Amsterdam/Utrecht University,
Amsterdam/Utrecht, the Netherlands

Abstract: Multilevel models have become popular for the analysis of a variety of problems. This chapter gives a summary of the reasons for using multilevel models, and provides examples why these reasons are indeed valid. Next, recent (simulation) research is reviewed on the robustness and power of the usual estimation procedures with varying sample sizes.

1 Why we need multilevel models

Multilevel models are specifically geared toward the analysis of data that have a hierarchical or cluster structure. Such data arise routinely in various fields, for instance in educational research with pupils nested within schools, family studies with children nested within families, medical research with patients nested within physicians or hospitals, and biological research, for instance the analysis of dental problems with teeth nested within different mouths. Clustered data may also result from a specific research design. For instance, in large scale survey research the data collection is usually, for economic reasons, organized in some sort of multistage sampling design that results in clustered or stratified design. Another example are longitudinal designs; one way of viewing longitudinal data is as a series of repeated measurements nested within individual subjects.

Older approaches to the analysis of multilevel data, such as reviewed in Huetnner and Van den Eeden (1982) generally ignore the question, aggregate or disaggregate all data to a common level, and subsequently apply standard analysis methods. The problems created by this approach were recognized, but were considered statistically intractable.

The magnitude of the statistical problem can be illustrated by a simple example from sample surveys. Survey statisticians have long known that the extend to which the samples are clustered affects the sampling variance. In his classic work, Kish (1965) analyzes this problem in detail. He defines the design effect (*deff*) as the ratio of the operating sampling variance to the sampling variance that applies to simple random sampling. Thus, *deff* is the factor with which the simple random sampling variance must be multiplied to provide the actual operating sampling variance. Kish (1965) describes how *deff* can be estimated for various sampling designs. In simple cluster sampling with equal cluster sizes *deff* equals $(1+\text{rho}(n_{\text{clus}}-1))$ where rho is the intraclass correlation and n_{clus} is the common cluster size. It is clear that *deff* equals one only when either the intraclass correlation is zero, or the cluster size is one. In all other situations *deff* is larger than one, which implies that standard statistical formulas will underestimate the sampling variance, and therefore lead to significance tests with an inflated alpha level. Using *deff*, the standard statistical formulas can be adjusted to reflect the true sampling variance. If such adjustments are made, the impact of cluster sampling on the operating alpha level proves itself often rather large. For example, Barcikowski (1981) examines the effect of cluster sampling on the actual alpha level of a *t*-test performed at a nominal alpha level of 0.05. With a small intraclass correlation of rho=0.05 and a cluster size of 10, the operating alpha level is 0.11. With larger intraclass correlations and larger cluster sizes, the operating alpha level increases rapidly. For another example, we look at the effect of cluster sampling in educational research. In educational research, data is often collected from classes. Assuming a common class size of 25 pupils, and a intraclass correlation for school effects of rho=0.10, the operating alpha level is 0.29 for tests performed at a nominal alpha level of 0.05! Clearly, **not** adjusting for clustered data produces totally misleading significance tests.

The examples given above are confirmed by simulation research by Tate and Wongbundhit (1983). They generate data for a multilevel regression model, and conclude that the estimates of the regression coefficients are unbiased, but have a much larger sampling variance than ordinary least squares (OLS) methods would produce. Again, significance tests ignoring the multilevel structure of the data would produce spuriously significant effects.

2 The multilevel regression model

The multilevel regression model is known in the research literature under a variety of names, such as 'random coefficient model,' 'variance component model,' and 'hierarchical linear model.' It assumes hierarchical data, with one response variable measured at the lowest level and explanatory variables at all existing levels. Conceptually the model is often viewed as a hierarchical system of regression equations. For example, assume we have data in J groups or contexts, and a different number of individuals N_j in each group. On the individual (lowest) level we have the dependent variable Y_{ij} and the predictor X_{ij}, and on the group level we have the predictor Z_j. Thus, we have a separate regression equation in each group:

$$Y_{ij} = \beta_{0j} + \beta_{1j} X_{ij} + e_{ij}. \tag{1}$$

The β_j are modeled by predictors at the group level:

$$\beta_{0j} = \gamma_{00} + \gamma_{01} Z_j + u_{0j}, \tag{2}$$
$$\beta_{1j} = \gamma_{10} + \gamma_{11} Z_j + u_{1j}. \tag{3}$$

Substitution of (2) and (3) in (1) gives:

$$Y_{ij} = \gamma_{00} + \gamma_{10} X_{ij} + \gamma_{01} Z_j + \gamma_{11} Z_j X_{ij} + u_{1j} X_{ij} + u_{0j} + e_{ij} \tag{4}$$

In general there will be more than one predictor at the available levels. Assume that we have P predictors X at the lowest level, indicated by the subscript p (p=1..P), and Q predictors Z at the highest level, indicated by the subscript q (q=1..Q). Then, equation (4) generalizes to:

$$Y_{ij} = \gamma_{00} + \gamma_{p0}X_{pij} + \gamma_{0q}Z_{qj} + \gamma_{pq}Z_{qj}X_{pij} + u_{pj}X_{pij} + u_{0j} + e_{ij} \quad (5)$$

The estimators generally used in multilevel analysis are Maximum Likelihood (ML) estimators, with standard errors estimated from the inverse of the information matrix. These standard errors are used in the Wald test; the test statistic $Z=parameter/(st.error)$ is referred to the standard normal distribution to establish a p-value for the null-hypothesis that in the population that specific parameter is zero.

Computing the Maximum Likelihood estimates requires an iterative procedure. The procedure starts with reasonable starting values for the various parameters, often single level OLS estimates. After one iteration, we have Generalized Least Squares (GLS) estimates. When the iterative process has converged, we have ML estimates. GLS estimates require much less computing time, which makes them attractive for computer-intensive procedures like simulation and bootstrapping. Also, it may be possible to obtain GLS estimates in situations where the iterative procedure does not converge (cf. Goldstein, 1995, p23).

Two different varieties of Maximum Likelihood estimation are commonly used in multilevel regression analysis. The one is Full Maximum Likelihood (FML); in this method both the regression coefficients and the variance components are included in the likelihood function. The other is Restricted Maximum Likelihood (RML); here only the variance components are included in the likelihood function. The difference is that FML treats the estimates for the regression coefficients as known quantities when the variance components are estimated, while RML treats them as estimates that carry some amount of uncertainty (Goldstein, 1995). Since RML is more realistic, it should, in theory, lead to better estimates, especially when the number of groups is small (Bryk & Raudenbush, 1992). FML has two advantages over RML: the computations are simpler, and a likelihood ratio test can be used to test for differences between two nested models that differ with respect to the regression coefficients. With RML only differences in the random part (the variance components) can be tested this way.

The usual assumptions are that the residual errors at the lowest level e_{ij} have a normal distribution with a mean of zero and a common variance σ^2 in all groups. The second level residual errors u_{0j} and u_{pj} are assumed to be independent from the lowest level errors e_{ij}, and to have a multivariate normal distribution with means of zero. Other assumptions, identical to the usual assumptions of multiple regression analysis, are fixed predictors and linear relationships. The standard errors generated by the ML procedure are asymptotic, meaning that we need fairly large samples at all levels.

3 The accuracy of parameter estimates

The assumptions stated above generate questions about the accuracy of the various estimation methods when these assumptions are false. Most research in this direction uses simulation methods, and investigates the accuracy of the fixed and random parameters with small sample sizes and nonnormal data. Comparatively less research investigates the accuracy of the standard errors used to test specific model parameters.

3.1 Accuracy of fixed parameters and their standard errors

The regression coefficients appear generally unbiased, for OLS, GLS, as well as ML estimation. OLS estimates have a larger sampling error; Kreft (1996), reanalyzing results from Kim (1990) estimates that they are about 90% efficient. The OLS based standard errors are known to be severely biased downward, which was illustrated in the introduction section. The asymptotic Wald tests used in most multilevel software assume either large samples (of groups) or equal group sizes.

The power of the Wald test for the significance of the individual level regression coefficients depends mostly on the total sample size. The power of tests of higher level effects and cross-level interactions depends more strongly on the number of groups than on the total sample size. Both simulations (van der Leeden & Busing, 1994; Mok, 1995) and analytic work (Snijders & Bosker, 1993) suggest a trade-off between sample sizes at different levels. For accuracy and high power a large number of groups appears more important than a large number of individuals per group. Bryk and Raudenbush (1992) argue that the test statistic should rather be referred to a Student distribution with J-p-1 degrees of freedom (number of groups - number of parameters estimated - 1), citing simulations by Fotiu (1989). Simulations by Van der Leeden & Busing (1994) and Van der Leeden et al. (1997) suggest that when assumptions of normality and large samples are not met, the ML estimates are still unbiased, but the standard errors are somewhat biased downward. GLS estimates of fixed parameters and their standard errors are somewhat less accurate, but workable.

3.2 Accuracy of random parameters and their standard errors

Estimates of the error variance at the lowest level are generally accurate. The group level variances are generally underestimated, with FML somewhat more that with RML. GLS variance estimates are less accurate than ML estimates, and for accurate estimates many groups (>100) are needed (Busing, 1993; Van der Leeden & Busing, 1994; Afshartous, 1995).

The asymptotic Wald test for the variance components implies the unrealistic assumption that they are normally distributed. For this reason, other approaches have been advocated, among which estimating the standard error for sigma (the square root of the variance, and using the likelihood ratio test. Bryk & Raudenbush (1992) advocate a chi-square test based on the OLS residuals. The literature contains no comparisons between these methods. Simulations by Van der Leeden et al. (1997) show that the standard errors used for the Wald test are generally estimated too small, with RML more accurate than FML. Symmetric confidence intervals around the estimated value also do not perform well. Van der Leeden et al. show that the bootstrap is a promising alternative to obtaining more accurate variance estimates, standard errors, and confidence intervals, provided the bootstrapping method samples cases and not residuals.

3.3 Accuracy and sample size

With increasing sample sizes at all levels, estimates and their standard errors become more accurate. Kreft (1996) suggests a rule of thumb which she calls the '30/30 rule.' To be on the safe side, researchers should strive for at least 30 groups with at least 30 individuals per group. From the various simulations reviewed above, this seems sound advice if the interest is mostly in the fixed parameters. For certain applications it may be wise to modify this rule of thumb. Specifically, if there is strong interest in cross-level interactions, the number of groups should be larger, which leads to a 50/20 rule: about fifty groups with about 20 individuals per group. If there is strong interest in the random part, the variance and covariance components, the number of groups should be considerably larger, which leads to a 100/10 rule: about 100 groups with about 10 individuals per group.

These rules of thumb take into account that there are costs attached to data collection, so if the number of groups is increased, the number of individuals per group decreases. In some cases this may not be a realistic reflection of costs. For instance, in school research the extra cost will be incurred when an extra class is included. Testing only part of a class instead of all pupils will usually not make much difference. Given a limited budget, an optimal design should reflect the various costs of data collection. Snijders and Bosker (1994) discuss the problem of choosing sample sizes at two levels while taking costs into account.

4 Analysis of proportions and binary data

Multilevel analysis of proportions is uses a generalized linear model with a logit link, which gives us the model:

$$\text{logit}(\pi_{ij}) = \gamma_{00} + \gamma_{10} X_{ij} + U_{0j} \tag{6}$$

The observed proportions P_{ij} are assumed to have a binomial distribution with known variance:

$$\text{var}(P_{ij}) = (\pi_{ij}(1-\pi_{ij}))/n_{ij} \qquad (7)$$

This variance may be modeled by including the predictor $s_{ij} = \sqrt{var(P_{ij})}$ in the random part, with associated variance constrained to one. The π_{ij} are estimated by prediction from the current model. If the variance term is not constrained to one, but estimated, we can model over- and underdispersion. If the extrabinomial variation is significantly different from one, this is usually interpreted as an indication that the model is misspecified, for instance by leaving out relevant levels, interactions among predictors, or in time series data by not allowing autocorrelation in the error structure.

Most programs rely on a Taylor expansion to linearize the model. The programs VARCL and MLn use a first-order Taylor expansion and marginal (quasi) likelihood (MQL1: P_{ij} predicted by fixed part only). MLn also offers the options of a second-order expansion and predictive or penalized (quasi) likelihood (PQL2: P_{ij} predicted by both fixed and random part).

Simulations by Rodriguez & Goldman (1995) show that marginal quasi likelihood with first-order Taylor expansion underestimates both the regression coefficients and the variance components, in some cases quite severely. Goldstein and Rasbash (1996) compare MQL1 and PQL2 by simulating data according to the worst performing dataset of Rodriguez and Goldman. In their simulation, the means of the MQL1 estimates for the fixed effects, from 200 simulation runs, were underestimated by about 25%. The means of the MQL1 estimates for the random effects were underestimated by as much as 88%. Moreover, 54% of the level 2 variances were estimated as zero, while the population value is one. For the same 200 simulated datasets, the means of the PQL2 estimates for the fixed effects underestimated the population value by at most 3%, and for the random effects by at most 20%. None of the PQL2 variance estimates was estimated as zero. It appears that predictive quasi likelihood with second order Taylor expansion is sufficiently accurate for the regression coefficients, and in many cases good enough for the random parameters. However, with some data sets the PQL2 algorithm breaks down, and it is recommended to start with the simpler MQL1 approach to obtain good starting values for the more complicated PQL2 approach.

If anything, the analysis of proportions and binomial data requires larger samples that needed for normally distributed data. For proportions very close to 0 or 1 and small numbers of groups, estimation using Gibbs sampling is coming into use (cf. Goldstein, 1995, p45).

5 Conclusion

As multilevel modeling becomes more widely used, it is important to gain an understanding of its limitations when the model assumptions are not fully met. This chapter, after establishing the need for multilevel modeling when data have a complex (hierarchical) error structure, focusses mostly on the effects of the sample sizes at different levels on accuracy and power of the statistical tests. A review of the available literature shows that estimates and tests for the regression coefficients are accurate with samples of modest sizes, but estimates and tests of the variances are not.

References

AFSHARTOUS, D. (1995): Determination of Sample Size for Multilevel Model Design. Paper, AERA Conference, San Francisco, 18-22 april 1995.

BARCIKOWSKI, R.S. (1981): Statistical Power with Group Mean as the Unit of Analysis. *Journal of Educational Statistics, 6, 267-285.*

BRYK, A.S. and RAUDENBUSH, S.W. (1992): Hierarchical Linear Models. Sage, Newbury Park, CA.

BUSING, F. (1993): Distribution Characteristics of Variance Estimates in Two-level Models. Department of Psychometrica and research Methodology, Leiden University, Leiden.

FOTIU, R.P. (1989): A Comparison of the EM and Data Augmentation Algorithms on Simulated Small Sample Hierarchical Data from Research on Education. Unpublished doctoral dissertation, Michigan State University, East Lansing.

GOLDSTEIN, H. (1995): Multilevel Statistical Models. Arnold, London.

GOLDSTEIN, H. and RASBASH, J. (1996): Improved Approximations for Multilevel Models with Binary Responses. Multilevel Models Project, University of London, London.

KIM, K.-S. (1990): Multilevel Data Analysis: a Comparison of Analytical Alternatives. Ph.D. Thesis, University of California, Los Angeles.

KISH, L. (1965): *Survey Sampling. Wiley, New York.*

KREFT, ITA G.G. (1996): Are Multilevel Techniques Necessary? An Overview, Including Simulation Studies. California State University, Los Angeles.

MOK, M. (1995): Sample Size requirements for 2-level Designs in Educational Research. Multilevel Models Project, University of London, London.

RODRIGUEZ, G. and GOLDMAN, N. (1995): An Assessment of Estimation Procedures for Multilevel Models with Binary Responses. *Journal of the Royal Statistical Society, A-158, 73-90.*

SNIJDERS, T.A.B. and BOSKER, R. (1993): Modeled Variance in Two-level Models. *Journal of Educational Statistics, 18, 273-259.*

TATE, R. and WONGBUNDHIT, Y. (1983): Random versus Nonrandom Coefficient Models for Multilevel Analysis. *Journal of Educational Statistics, 8, 103-120.*

VAN DEN EEDEN, P. and HUETTNER, H.J.M. (1982): Multi-level Research. *Current Sociology, 30, 3, 1-117.*

VAN DER LEEDEN, R. and BUSING, F. (1994): First Iteration versus IGLS/RIGLS Estimates in Two-level Models: a Monte Carlo Study with ML3. Department of Psychometrica and research Methodology, Leiden University, Leiden.

VAN DER LEEDEN, R., BUSING, F., and MEIJER, E. (1997): Applications of Bootstrap Methods for Two-level Models. Paper, Multilevel Conference, Amsterdam, April 1-2, 1997.

Upper Bounds for the P–Values of a Scan Statistic with a Variable Window

J. Krauth

Department of Psychology,
University of Düsseldorf, D–40225 Düsseldorf, Germany

Abstract: It is asked if n independent events occurring in a given time interval are clustered or if, alternatively, the null hypothesis of a uniform distribution can be adopted. A simple scan statistic defined to be the maximum number of events within any sub–interval (or window) of given length has been used as test statistic in this context. Nagarwalla (1996) described a modification of this scan statistic, based on a generalized likelihood ratio statistic, which no longer assumes that the window width is fixed a priori. Unfortunately, the distribution of this statistic is not known and a simulation procedure had to be applied. In this paper a quite simpler statistic is proposed which can be considered as an approximation of Nagarwalla's statistic. For this new statistic, upper bounds for the upper tail probabilities are given. Thus, the new test can be performed without recourse to a simulation. Furthermore, no restrictions on the cluster size are imposed. The procedure is illustrated by examples from epidemiology.

1 The simple scan statistic and its modification by Nagarwalla (1996)

We consider n independent identically distributed random variables $Y_1, \ldots, Y_n$ which correspond to times of occurrence of n events in an interval $[t_L, t_U]$ with $t_L < t_U$, and would like to test the null hypothesis H_0 of a uniform distribution on the interval $[t_L, t_U]$ against an alternative hypothesis H_1 of clustering in this interval. Considering the linear transformation

$$X_i = \frac{Y_i - t_L}{t_U - t_L} \text{ for } i = 1, \ldots, n, \tag{1}$$

we can restrict our considerations to the unit interval $[0, 1]$, without loss of generality.

A well-known statistic for the test problem above is the simple *scan statistic*

$$N(d) = \sup_{x \in [0, 1-d]} N(x, d), \tag{2}$$

where $N(x, d)$ is the number of those random variables from $\{X_1, \ldots, X_n\}$ which lie within the window $[x, x + d]$ with a given width $d\, (0 < d < 1)$. In other words, the interval $[0,1]$ is *scanned* by a moving window of width d to find the maximum number of events within such a window. A realization of $N(x,d)$ is denoted by $n(x,d)$.

According to Neff and Naus (1980), the use of the scan statistic can be traced back at least to Silberstein in the year 1939. A justification of the scan statistic was given by Naus (1966) who considered densities of the form

$$\begin{aligned} f(y) &= a & \text{for} \quad b \leq y \leq b+d \\ &= \frac{1-ad}{1-d} & \text{for} \quad 0 \leq y < b \text{ or } b+d < y \leq 1, \end{aligned} \qquad (3)$$

where b $(0 \leq b \leq 1-d)$ is an unknown constant. It can be shown (Naus (1966)) that the test based on $N(d)$ is a generalized likelihood ratio test for testing the null hypothesis $H_0 : a = 1$, corresponding to the uniform distribution, against the clustering alternative $H_1 : 1 < a \leq 1/d$. Thus, the scan statistic can be considered optimum for situations of clustering with a density which is constant except for a rectangular peak.

An obvious drawback of the scan statistic is the necessity to fix the window width d before knowing the data. Otherwise, the level of the scan test would not be controlled. By choosing a value of d which is too large or too small the power of the test may be impaired and existing clusters may remain unrecognized. For these reasons, Nagarwalla (1996) reconsidered the derivation by Naus (1966) of the generalized likelihood ratio test for the test problem H_0 versus H_1. For a known constant value of d the m. l. estimate for a is obtained by maximizing the function

$$a^{n(b,d)} \left(\frac{1-ad}{1-d} \right)^{n-n(b,d)} \qquad (4)$$

with respect to a. The maximum is achieved at $\hat{a} = n(b,d)/(nd)$, if $n(b,d) \geq nd$ and at $\hat{a} = 1$ otherwise. With respect to the test problem above, we only need to consider the case $\hat{a} > 1$, i. e. only the case $n(b,d) > nd$ is of interest. Thus, H_0 is rejected for large values of

$$G(d, n(b,d)) = \left(\frac{n(b,d)/n}{d} \right)^{n(b,d)} \left(\frac{1 - (n(b,d)/n)}{1-d} \right)^{n-n(b,d)}. \qquad (5)$$

For a fixed value of d the function $G(d, n(b,d))$ is increasing in $n(b,d)$. Thus, the test based on the classical scan statistic $N(d)$ is equivalent to the generalized likelihood ratio test.

Nagarwalla (1996) observed that for fixed values of $n(b,d) = 1, \ldots, n-1$, $G(d, n(b,d))$ is a convex function of d, for $0 < d < 1$. The minimum value of $G(d, n(b,d))$ is obtained at $d = n(b,d)/n$ and for $d \to 0$ we find $G(d, n(b,d)) \to \infty$. Thus, by choosing d small enough, we can always reject the null hypothesis. This is not astonishing, because with d close to zero each of the n events can be considered as a cluster of its own. As one way to encounter this difficulty, Nagarwalla (1996) proposed to reject the null hypothesis for large values of the test statistic

$$\Lambda = \sup_{n(b,d) \geq n_0,\, 0 < d < n(b,d)/n,\, 0 \leq b \leq 1-d} G(d, n(b,d)), \tag{6}$$

and called Λ a *scan statistic with a variable window*.

In contrast to Nagarwalla (1996), we would not call the test based on (6) a generalized likelihood ratio test, because such a test obviously does not exist for the original situation where no additional restrictions were imposed on d or $n(b,d)$, respectively. Instead of fixing in an arbitrary way a window width (d), Nagarwalla (1996) fixes arbitrarily a minimum cluster size (n_0). Depending on the choice of n_0, just as for the choice of d, different results may arise for the same set of data.

Because Nagarwalla (1996) could not derive the null distribution of Λ or find a function g which is strictly monotonic on the set of possible values of Λ such that $g(\Lambda)$ has a known distribution, he proposed a simulation test. In contrast, we derive upper bounds for the P–values of a test based on a statistic which approximates the statistic in (5).

2 An alternative test statistic

Obviously, the basic idea of the test statistic of Nagarwalla (1996) is to compare for each sub–interval $[b, b+d]$ and each possible choice of interval length d the estimate $n(b,d)/n$ of the probability of occurrence of an event within this interval with the probability d of such an occurrence under the null hypothesis H_0. Thus, a candidate for a simpler test statistic could be

$$\Lambda^\star = \sup_{0 < d \leq n(b,d)/n,\, 0 \leq b \leq 1-d} \left\{ \frac{n(b,d)}{n} - d \right\}. \tag{7}$$

In contrast to Nagarwalla's statistic, $\Lambda^\star$ takes only values in the interval $(0,1)$. In particular, for $d \to 0$ we get $\Lambda^\star \to 1/n$.

The computation of the statistic $\Lambda^\star$ can be facilitated considerably because not all possible values of $d \in (0,1)$ must be considered. For that purpose we write $\Lambda^\star$ as

$$\Lambda^\star = \max_{\substack{1 \leq i \leq n \\ i \leq j \leq n}} \left\{ \frac{i}{n} - \left(x_{(j)} - x_{(j-i+1)} \right) \right\}, \tag{8}$$

where $x_{(1)}, \ldots, x_{(n)}$ are realizations of the order statistics $X_{(1)}, \ldots, X_{(n)}$ defined by $X_{(1)} < X_{(2)} < \ldots < X_{(n)}$.

Though, obviously Λ^* is not identical to Λ, it can be considered as a reasonable approximation to Λ. To see this, we consider the function $G(d, n(b,d))$ defined in (5). By setting $f = n(b,d)/n$ G takes the form

$$G(d, f) = \left(\frac{f}{d}\right)^{nf} \left(\frac{1-f}{1-d}\right)^{n(1-f)} = \left[\left(\frac{f}{d}\right)^{f} \left(\frac{1-f}{1-d}\right)^{1-f}\right]^n. \tag{9}$$

Because we assumed $f > d$, we can consider instead of $G(d, f)$ the function

$$H(d, f) = \left(\frac{f}{d}\right)^{f} \left(\frac{1-f}{1-d}\right)^{1-f} = G(d,f)^{1/n} \tag{10}$$

which is a strictly monotonic function of $G(d, f)$. This holds also for

$$h(d, f) = \ln H(d, f) = f \ln \frac{f}{d} + (1-f) \ln \frac{1-f}{1-d}. \tag{11}$$

Next, we consider the reparametrization $u = 1 - 2f$, $v = 1 - 2d$ with $-1 \leq u < 1$, $-1 < v < 1$ with inverse $f = 0.5(1-u)$, $d = 0.5(1-v)$. This results in

$$h(v, u) = 0.5(1-u) \ln \frac{1-u}{1-v} + 0.5(1+u) \ln \frac{1+u}{1+v}. \tag{12}$$

If we exclude for a moment the case $u = -1$ which is equivalent to $n(b,d) = n$ we can expand the logarithms and derive

$$\begin{aligned}
h(v, u) &= 0.5 \left\{ (1-u) \left[-\left(u + \frac{u^2}{2} + \frac{u^3}{3} + \ldots \right) + \left(v + \frac{v^2}{2} + \frac{v^3}{3} + \ldots \right) \right] \right.\\
&\quad \left. + (1+u) \left[\left(u - \frac{u^2}{2} + \frac{u^3}{3} - \ldots \right) - \left(v - \frac{v^2}{2} + \frac{v^3}{3} - \ldots \right) \right] \right\}\\
&= 0.5 \left\{ u^2 + v^2 - 2uv + \frac{1}{6}u^4 - \frac{2}{3}uv^3 + \ldots \right\}\\
&= 0.5(u-v)^2 + o(\max\{|u|, |v|\}^4)
\end{aligned} \tag{13}$$

where

$$0.5(u-v)^2 = 2(f-d)^2 = 2\left(\frac{n(b,d)}{n} - d\right)^2. \tag{14}$$

Because we assumed $(n(b,d)/n) > d$, $h(v, u)$ is approximately a monotonic function of $(n(b,d)/n) - d$. Thus, $(n(b,d)/n) - d$ can be used approximately instead of $G(d, n(b,d))$ and therefore the test statistic Λ can be approximated by the simpler test statistic $\Lambda^\star$. If all events cluster in a small sub–interval it may happen that the supremum is achieved at $n(b,d) = n$. However, this case was also excluded in Nagarwalla's argumentation.

Considering (13), we find that the approximation of Λ by $\Lambda^\star$ will be good only for u and v near 0, i. e. for $f = n(b,d)/n$ and d near to 0.5. In other cases the two statistics may differ considerably.

3 Upper bounds for the P–values of the new statistic

Obviously, it holds

$$\Lambda^\star \geq \max_{1 \leq j \leq n} \left\{ \frac{1}{n} - \left(x_{(j)} - x_{(j-1+1)}\right) \right\} = \frac{1}{n}, \tag{15}$$

i. e., the minimum value of $\Lambda^\star$ is given by $1/n$ and is achieved for $i = 1$, i. e., for the case of single–event clusters. If we set, e. g., $x_{(j)} = (j - 0.5)/n$ for $j = 1, \ldots, n$, the value $\Lambda^\star = 1/n$ is actually attained. Thus, we can conclude (if $x_{(j)}$ is replaced by $X_{(j)}$ for $j = 1, \ldots, n$) that

$$P\left(\Lambda^\star \geq \frac{1}{n}\right) = 1 \tag{16}$$

holds. For $n \geq 2$, we consider now the test statistic

$$T = \max_{\substack{2 \leq i \leq n \\ i \leq j \leq n}} \left\{ \frac{i}{n} - \left(x_{(j)} - x_{(j-i+1)}\right) \right\}, \tag{17}$$

and we have for $t > 1/n$ (if $x_{(j)}$ is replaced by $X_{(j)}$ for $j = 1, \ldots, n$)

$$P(\Lambda^\star \geq t) = P(T \geq t), \tag{18}$$

i. e., we can replace $\Lambda^\star$ by T if $t > 1/n$. In contrast to Nagarwalla's test statistic no minimum cluster size is fixed.

It holds

$$
\begin{aligned}
P(T \geq t) &= P\left(\max_{\substack{2 \leq i \leq n \\ i \leq j \leq n}} \left\{\frac{i}{n} - \left(X_{(j)} - X_{(j-i+1)}\right)\right\} \geq t\right) \\
&= P\left(\bigcup_{i=2}^{n} \bigcup_{j=i}^{n} \left\{\frac{i}{n} - \left(X_{(j)} - X_{(j-i+1)}\right) \geq t\right\}\right) \\
&= P\left(\bigcup_{i=2}^{n} \bigcup_{j=i}^{n} \left\{X_{(j)} - X_{(j-i+1)} \leq \frac{i}{n} - t\right\}\right) \\
&\leq \sum_{i=2}^{n} P\left(\bigcup_{j=i}^{n} \left\{X_{(j)} - X_{(j-i+1)} \leq \frac{i}{n} - t\right\}\right).
\end{aligned}
\qquad (19)
$$

With

$$
c_i = \frac{i}{n} - t, \; A_i = \bigcup_{j=i}^{n} \left\{X_{(j)} - X_{(j-i+1)} \leq c_i\right\} \text{ for } i = 2, \ldots, n \qquad (20)
$$

we thus have

$$
P(T \geq t) \leq \sum_{i=2}^{n} P(A_i). \qquad (21)
$$

Obviously, we get $P(A_i) = 0$ for $c_i \leq 0$.

Upper bounds for $P_{H_0}(A_i)$ were derived by Berman and Eagleson (1985) and Krauth (1988).

With the notation

$$
B(n, i, p, q) = \sum_{j=i}^{n} \binom{n}{j} p^j q^{n-j} \text{ for } p, q \in \mathbb{R} \qquad (22)
$$

the two Berman–Eagleson bounds are given by

$$
P_{H_0}(A_i) \leq (n - i + 1) B(n, i - 1, c_i, 1 - c_i) =: b_{1i}, \qquad (23)
$$

$$
\begin{aligned}
P_{H_0}(A_i) &\leq B(n, i-1, c_i, 1 - c_i) \\
&\quad - (n-i)(-1)^i B(n, i-1, -c_i, 1 - c_i) =: b_{2i},
\end{aligned}
\qquad (24)
$$

and the Krauth bound by

$$\begin{aligned}
P_{H_0}(A_i) \leq\ & B(n, i-1, c_i, 1-c_i) - (-1)^i B(n, i-1, -c_i, 1-c_i) \\
& +(-1)^i(n-i-1)[nc_i\, B(n-1, i-2, -c_i, 1-c_i) \\
& +(i-2)B(n, i-1, -c_i, 1-c_i) \\
& +0.5n(n-1)c_i^2\, B(n-2, i-2, -c_i, 1-c_i) \\
& +n(i-2)c_i\, B(n-1, i-1, -c_i, 1-c_i) \\
& +0.5(i-1)(i-2)B(n, i, -c_i, 1-c_i)] =: b_{3i}.
\end{aligned} \qquad (25)$$

The inequality $b_{1i} \geq b_{2i} \geq b_{3i}$ holds. The bound b_{1i} is valid for $0 < c_i < 1$, the bound b_{2i} for $0 < c_i \leq 0.5$ and the bound b_{3i} for $0 < c_i \leq 0.5$ and $i \geq 2$. Improvements of these bounds are given in Glaz (1989, 1992, 1993), but they are more complicated.

If for an observed value $t > 1/n$ of the test statistic T we have

$$P_{H_0}(T \geq t) \leq \alpha \qquad (26)$$

with a given significance level α, the null hypothesis H_0 can be rejected and a clustering seems to exist. This is also the case if an upper bound of $P_{H_0}(T \geq t)$ does not exceed α. A crude upper bound for $P_{H_0}(T \geq t)$ is given by

$$P_{H_0}(T \geq t) \leq \sum_{i=2}^{n} b_{1i}. \qquad (27)$$

This bound can be improved by replacing b_{1i} in all those cases by b_{3i} where $0 < c_i \leq 0.5$ holds. For $t \geq 0.5$ or $i \leq (n+2)/2$ we have always $c_i \leq 0.5$ and may replace each bound b_{1i} by the better bound b_{3i}. However, for $(1/n) < t < 0.5$ and $i > (n+2)/2$ values of c_i with $c_i > 0.5$ may occur for which the better bounds b_{2i} and b_{3i} may not be applicable.

4 Examples from epidemiology

The data of our first example (cf. Table 1) consists of the days of certain birth defects for $n = 35$ cases observed in a hospital in Birmingham, U.K., between 1 January 1950 and 31 December 1955 ($t_L = 0$, $t_U = 2191$). It was first published by Knox (1959) and reanalyzed by Weinstock (1981). Nagarwalla (1996) set $n_0 = 5$ and got with 9999 replications a simulated P-value of $P = 0.0058$. The author identified as the most likely cluster the set of 15 cases starting with the case on day 1233.

Table 1: Days of birth for $n = 35$ cases of oesophageal atresia or tracheo-oesophageal fistula as given in Table 1 of Nagarwalla (1996)

170	316	445	468	938	1034	1128	1233	1248	1249	1252
1259	1267	1305	1385	1388	1390	1446	1454	1458	1461	1491
1583	1699	1702	1787	1924	1974	2049	2051	2067	2075	2108
2151	2174									

Here, a cluster is defined by the set of cases within a window which results if the width and the position of the window is fixed. The most likely cluster corresponds to that choice of a window for which the largest value of the test statistic is found. Likewise, the second most likely cluster etc. is defined by that choice of the window for which the second largest value etc. of the test statistic results.

Our test yielded $T = 0.370516$ which corresponds to the 28 cases beginning with the case on day 1233. The crude bound based on the b_{1i} yielded 0.003697 corresponding to a significant result. Values of c_i with $c_i > 0.5$ resulted for $i = 31, \ldots, 35$. If we replace in all other cases b_{1i} by b_{3i}, we find the better bound 0.002585.

It is interesting to note that the second most likely cluster corresponds for our test to the 26 cases starting at day 1233, the third most likely cluster to the 25 cases starting at day 1233, and only the fourth most likely cluster to the 15 cases starting at day 1233 as in Nagarwalla (1996) . If we restrict the maximum cluster size to 24 we find Nagarwalla's cluster with $T = 0.310817$, the crude bound 0.047021 and the better bound 0.026803, i. e., with this restriction our procedure seems to be inferior with respect to power in comparison with Nagarwalla's test.

The data of our second example (cf. Table 2) is taken from several Newcastle hospitals from 1 January 1950 through 31 December 1958 ($t_L = 0$, $t_U = 3287$). It was first published by Knox (1959) and reanalyzed by Weinstock (1981). Our test yielded $T = 0.303485$ which corresponds to the 49 cases starting with the case on day 1718. The crude bound based on the b_{1i} yielded 0.001089 indicating a significant result. Values of c_i with $c_i > 0.5$ resulted for $i = 51, \ldots, 63$. If we replace in all other cases b_{1i} by b_{3i} we get the better bound 0.000648.

Table 2: Days of birth for $n = 63$ cases of oesophageal atresia or tracheo-oesophageal fistula in the Newcastle region as given in Table 2 of Weinstock (1981)

46	372	377	422	504	528	597	675	698	1056	1143
1292	1301	1317	1718	1724	1794	1834	1843	1856	1862	1865
1878	1909	1910	1912	1940	1962	2026	2029	2080	2128	2144
2197	2219	2260	2325	2329	2332	2336	2384	2461	2518	2528
2603	2626	2691	2692	2789	2819	2832	2923	3070	3071	3084
3096	3101	3148	3177	3182	3211	3254	3277			

References

BERMAN, M. and EAGLESON, G.K. (1985): A Useful Upper Bound for the Tail Probabilities of the Scan Statistic when the Sample Size is Large. *Journal of the American Statistical Association, 80, 886–889.*

GLAZ, J. (1989): Approximations and Bounds for the Distribution of the Scan Statistic. *Journal of the American Statistical Association, 84, 560–566.*

GLAZ, J. (1992): Approximations for Tail Probabilities and Moments of the Scan Statistic. *Computational Statistics & Data Analysis, 14, 213–227.*

GLAZ, J. (1993): Approximations for the Tail Probabilities and Moments of the Scan Statistic. *Statistics in Medicine, 12, 1845–1852.*

KNOX, G. (1959): Secular Pattern of Congenital Oesophageal Atresia. *British Journal of Preventive Social Medicine, 13, 222–226.*

KRAUTH, J. (1988): An Improved Upper Bound for the Tail Probabilities of the Scan Statistic for Testing Non–random Clustering: In: H.H. Bock (ed.): *Classification and Related Methods of Data Analysis.* Elsevier Science Publishers, Amsterdam, 237–244.

NAGARWALLA, N. (1996): A Scan Statistic with Variable Window. *Statistics in Medicine, 15, 799–810.*

NAUS, J.I. (1966): A Power Comparison of Two Tests of Non–Random Clustering. *Technometrics, 8, 493–517.*

NEFF, N.D. and NAUS, J.I. (1980): The Distribution of the Size of the Maximum Cluster of Points on a Line. Selected Tables in Mathematical Statistics. Volume VI. American Mathematical Society, Providence.

WEINSTOCK, M.A. (1981): A Generalised Scan Statistic Test for the Detection of Clusters. *International Journal of Epidemiology, 10, 289–293.*

A Branch-and-bound Algorithm for Boolean Regression

Iwin Leenen, Iven Van Mechelen

University of Leuven

Abstract: This paper proposes a branch-and-bound algorithm to trace disjunctive (conjunctive) combinations of binary predictor variables to predict a binary criterion variable. The algorithm allows for finding logical classification rules that can be used to derive whether or not a given object belongs to a given category based on the attribute pattern of the object. An objective function is minimized which takes into account both accuracy in prediction and cost of the predictors. A simulation study is presented in which the performance of the algorithm is evaluated.

1 Introduction

In various research contexts one faces the problem to look for the connection between a criterion variable and a set of predictor variables. If both the criterion and the predictors are binary (0/1), one can look for connections based on a logical combination of the predictors (such as a disjunction or a conjunction, with or without negations). Within a classification context, in which the binary criterion may be thought as category membership and the binary predictor variables as binary features, this problem comes down to finding appropriate classification rules. Depending on the application, two cases can be distinguished:

In a first case there is a perfect connection between predictors and criterion. This implies that for one and the same combination of values on the predictor variables only a single value on the criterion has been observed. Such a perfect connection can be described by means of a family of logical expressions (including an expression in disjunctive normal form). Within this family one may be interested in finding the least complex expressions, complexity being measured in terms of, for example, the total number of predictors included in the expression and their total occurrence frequency. This is the classical minimization problem of Boolean functions (see Korfhage (1966)), which, amongst others, is relevant for the context of the design of electronic switching circuits. Several algorithms have been proposed to solve this problem (e.g., Biswas (1975), Halder (1978), McCluskey (1965), Sen (1983)).

In a second case there is not a perfect connection between predictors and criterion. This case typically occurs within the context of empirical prediction problems (see, Lbov (1982), McKenzie et al. (1992), Ragin et al. (1984), Van Mechelen (1988)). In this case again an optimal logical predictive combination can be looked for, optimality now including two aspects:

(a) the complexity of the logical expression (see above), and (b) the number of prediction errors (i.e., the sum of the numbers of false positives and false negatives, which optionally can be differentially weighted). The objective function that is optimized typically consists of a combination of those two aspects.

This paper addresses an instance of the second type of logical prediction problems, namely *Boolean regression*. Within the class of simple disjunctive (or, alternatively, conjunctive) expressions, Boolean regression looks for the predictive combination that optimizes an objective function as described above. Boolean regression is both used as a stand-alone technique and as part of more complex algorithms, in particular Boolean factor analysis (Mickey et al. (1983)) and hierarchical classes analysis (De Boeck and Rosenberg (1988), Van Mechelen et al. (1995)). Existing algorithms for Boolean regression are based on a greedy heuristic (e.g., Van Mechelen (1988), Van Mechelen and De Boeck (1990)). The solutions yielded by these greedy algorithms, although being satisfactory in many applications, are not necessarily optimal in terms of the objective function. A new, branch-and-bound, algorithm was therefore developed, which is described in the present paper.

The remainder of this paper is organized as follows: In the next section (Section 2), the branch and bound algorithm for Boolean regression is described; Section 3 reports the results of a simulation study set up to explore the performance of the algorithm and the factors that determine the computing time.

2 A Branch-and-bound algorithm for Boolean regression

Given the values of N observations on a binary criterion C and a set P of n binary predictors $p_1, p_2, \ldots, p_n$, the aim of Boolean regression is to find a simple disjunctive or conjunctive combination of predictors that has minimal value on some objective function.

The objective function penalizes for both prediction errors and the complexity of the logical expression. The parameters involved in it, all being nonnegative numbers, are the following:

1. $c_1, \ldots, c_n$: a cost parameter for each of the n predictors.

2. D^-: the cost parameter for one false negative prediction error (an observation for which the logical expression yields 0, whereas its criterion value equals 1).

3. D^+: the cost parameter for one false positive prediction error (an observation for which the logical expression yields 1, whereas its criterion value equals 0).

We further denote the number of false negatives by N_{D-} and the number of false positives by N_{D+}. For a disjunctive (conjunctive) expression, defined by a subset W of the predictors, the value on the objective function is defined as:

$$f(W) := D^- N_{D-} + D^+ N_{D+} + \sum_{\substack{i \\ p_i \in W}} c_i \tag{1}$$

Note that from the definition 1 of the objective function and from the equivalence of, on the one hand,

$$(p_{i_1} \wedge p_{i_2} \wedge \cdots \wedge p_{i_k}) \iff C$$

and, on the other hand,

$$(\neg p_{i_1} \vee \neg p_{i_2} \vee \cdots \vee \neg p_{i_k}) \iff \neg C$$

(with $\wedge, \vee, \neg, \iff$ denoting logical and, or, not, and equivalence, respectively), it follows that an algorithm yielding optimal disjunctive combinations can also be used to yield optimal conjunctive combinations (and vice versa); for this it suffices to apply the disjunctive algorithm with $\neg C$ as the criterion, $\neg P_1, \ldots, \neg P_n$ as predictors, D^+ as cost per false negative error and D^- as cost per false positive error. Therefore, in the remainder of this paper we will limit ourselves to the disjunctive case.

In order to find an optimal disjunctive combination, a tree with 2^n nodes corresponding to the subsets of P is constructed. The tree has $n+1$ levels, labeled 0 through n, with at level k all subsets of P with k elements. For each node in the tree, some order $\succ$ is defined on the set of its child nodes (see below). The parent-child relations of the tree may be recursively defined as follows. The children of the single node at level 0, representing the empty set, are all singletons. In order to define the children of a node W at level k, $k > 0$, we denote the parent of W by V; the children of W then are the sets $W \cup C^{(i)}, \forall C^{(i)} \succ W$, with $C^{(i)}$ being a child of V.

The algorithm passes through this tree by means of a recursive procedure. This procedure starts from the empty set at the root of the tree. When applied on a node S of the tree, the procedure further performs essentially two tasks. First, $f(S)$ is compared to the minimum value for f found so far; the set for which this minimum value was reached will further be denoted by M. If $f(S) < f(M)$ then M is replaced by S. Second, the children W of S are evaluated, in ascending order, with respect to the following bounding function:

$$f^+(W) := D^+ N_{D+} + \sum_{\substack{i \\ p_i \in W}} c_i$$

This function f^+ returns a lower bound on f for all possible extensions of W; for, false positives cannot be corrected by extending a disjunctive expression. Hence, the subtree descending from W has not to be examined if $f^+(W) \geq f(M)$. If $f^+(W) < f(M)$ the recursive procedure is applied to W.

From the preceding it should be clear that the algorithm necessarily yields an optimal solution. For, it checks all predictive combinations, except for a number of combinations that are known to be less than optimal.

It should also be clear that the performance of the algorithm would benefit from finding in an early stage a set M with a low value on the objective function. In this respect it was found out that an ordering of the children of each node based on their values on f^+ is very efficient. In a simulation study such an ordering resulted in significantly lower execution times compared with a fixed ordering and with an ordering based on the values on f or a weighted sum of the values on f^+ and f.

Algorithm

PROCEDURE FindOptimalExtension (S, T);

Step 1 *Improve lower bound*

If $f(S) < f(M)$ then $M \leftarrow S$

Step 2 *Construct new sets by adding, in turn, all predictors not in T to S*

If $P \setminus (T \cup S) = \emptyset$ then goto step 4

For all $p_i \in P \setminus (T \cup S)$ do $S^{(i)} \leftarrow S \cup \{p_i\}$

Step 3 *Branch*

Reorder the sets $S^{(i)}$ such that $f^+(S^{(i)}) \leq f^+(S^{(i+1)})$ for all i

$i \leftarrow 1$

While $(f^+(S^{(i)}) < f(M))$ do

    a FindOptimalExtension $(S^{(i)}, T)$

    b $T \leftarrow T \cup \{p_i\}$

    c $i \leftarrow i + 1$

Step 4 *End*

PROGRAM

Step 1 *Initialize*

$M \leftarrow \emptyset$

Step 2 *Search tree*

FindOptimalExtension $(\emptyset, \emptyset)$

In the description of the algorithm above, it should be noticed that S and T are local variables, getting a new memory address at each call of the procedure FindOptimalExtension. On the contrary, the variable M is global and has the same memory address throughout the complete execution of the algorithm.

3 Simulation results

The proposed algorithm has been implemented in Turbo Pascal and tested in an extensive simulation study. More in particular, the effect of four input characteristics was examined, which were systematically varied in a completely crossed design:

1. the *number of predictors* with 6 levels (viz., 1, 2, 4, 8, 12 and 15)

2. the *number of observations* with 5 levels (v.i.z., 20, 50, 100, 500, 1000)

3. the *proportion of ones in the predictors* with 4 levels (v.i.z., 0.20, 0.40, 0.60, 0.80)

4. the *proportion of observations to which error was added* with 6 levels (v.i.z., 0.00, 0.01, 0.02, 0.05, 0.10, 0.20)

For each of the $6 \times 5 \times 4 \times 6 = 720$ combinations in the design, 50 random samples were analyzed, which resulted in 36 000 runs.

Each simulation run implied the execution of the following steps:

1. all predictors were assigned random 0/1-values on each of the observations

2. a random subset of the predictors was selected

3. the selected predictors were used to assign to each observation a criterion value of 1 if at least one of the predictors equaled 1, and a value of 0 otherwise

4. error was added by complementing the criterion value of some observations (0 turned into 1, and vice versa)

These data were submitted to the algorithm described above, the execution time being the output variable. Simulations were done on an IBM-compatible PC with Cx486DX processor (40 Mhz CPU clock) and numeric co-processor.

The main conclusions that can be drawn from this simulation study are the following:

1. Increasing the number of predictors has an exponential effect on execution time. This is to be expected from an analysis of the algorithm as adding a predictor generally implies evaluating an extra node on all levels of the search tree. The upper left graph in Figure 1 illustrates this finding for the analyses with 500 observations, a proportion of ones in the predictors of .60 and a 5% error rate. (In this and all following cases, the graphs for the other conditions are similar.)

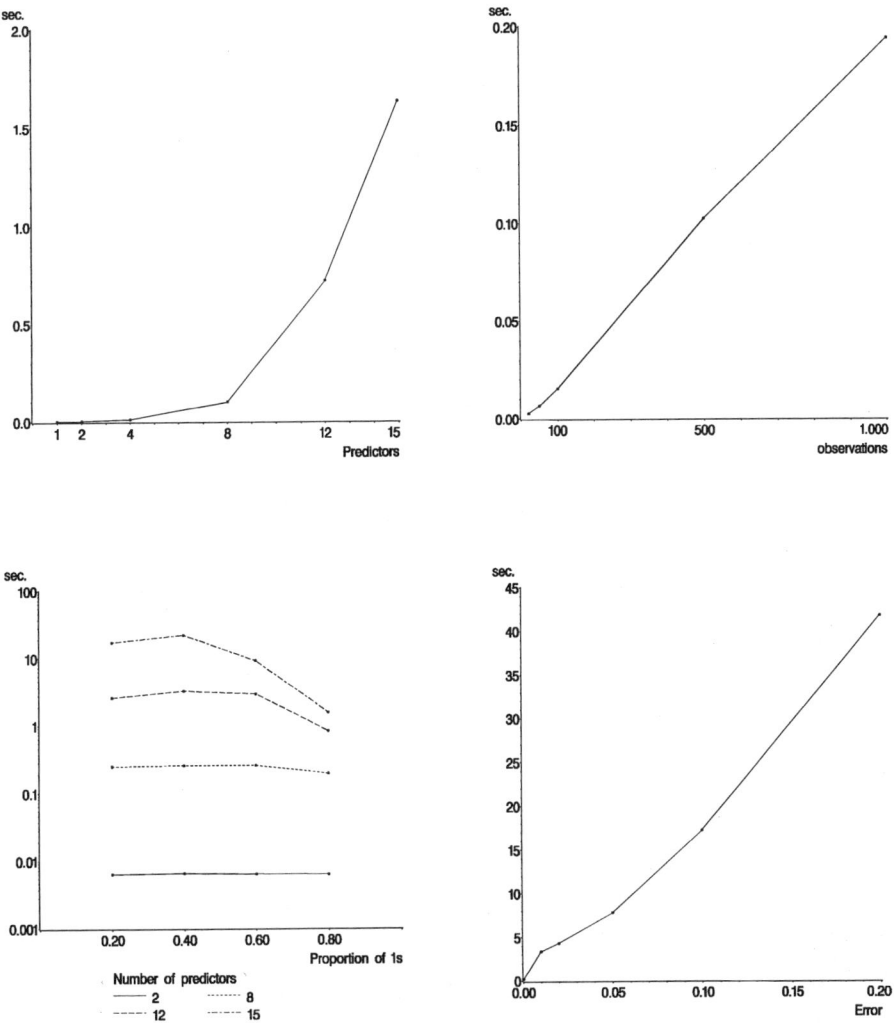

Figure 1: Upper left: Mean execution time as a function of the number of predictors. Upper right: Mean execution time as a function of the number of observations. Bottom left: Mean execution time as a function of the proportion of ones in the predictors and the number of predictors. Bottom right: Mean execution time as a function of the amount of error in the criterion.

2. The number of observations has a linear effect on execution time. This finding follows from the fact that evaluating a set of predictors on either f or f^+ requires comparing the predicted value with the criterion value on each observation. The upper right graph in Figure 1 illustrates this for the analyses with 8 predictors, a proportion of ones in the predictors of .80 and a 10% error rate.

3. For small numbers of predictors execution time does almost not vary as a function of the proportions of ones in the predictors. For larger numbers of predictors, however, execution time decreases significantly with an increasing proportion of ones. The bottom left graph in Figure 1 shows this interaction between number of predictors and proportion of ones for the analyses with 1000 observations and a 10% error rate. The time axis is logarithmically scaled to allow of a simultaneous representation of the four predictor conditions.

4. Very fast execution times were observed with errorfree data. For the other error levels the amount of error has an almost linear effect on execution time. Indeed, the less error in the data, the more probable it is that a global minimum can be obtained in an early stage. This enhances the possibilities for bounding and, thus, results in lower execution times. The bottom right graph in Figure 1 illustrates this finding for the analyses with 1000 observations, 15 predictors and a proportion of ones in the predictors of .20.

References

BISWAS, N.N. (1975): Introduction to logic and switching theory. Gordon and Breach, New York.

DE BOECK, P. and ROSENBERG, S. (1988): Hierarchical classes: Model and data analysis. *Psychometrika, 53, 361–381.*

HALDER, A.K. (1978): Grouping table for the minimisation of n-variable Boolean functions. *Proceedings of the Institution of Electric Engineers London, 125, 474–482.*

KORFHAGE, R.R. (1966): Logic and algorithms. Wiley, New York.

LBOV, G.S. (1982): Logical functions in the problems of empirical prediction. In P.R. Krishnaiah and L.N. Kanal (eds.): *Handbook of statistics (Volume 2)*. North Holland, Amsterdam, 479-491.

MCCLUSKEY, E.J. (1965): Introduction to the theory of switching circuits. McGraw-Hill, New York.

MCKENZIE, D.P., CLARKE, D.M., and LOW, L.H. (1992): A method of constructing parsimonious diagnostic and screening tests. *International Journal of Methods in Psychiatric Research, 2, 71-79.*

MICKEY, M.R., MUNDLE, P., and ENGELMAN, L. (1983): Boolean factor analysis. In W.J. Dixon (ed.): *BMDP statistical software.* University of California Press, Berkeley, 538-546.

RAGIN, C.C., MAYER, S.E., and DRASS, K.A. (1984): Assessing discrimination: A Boolean approach. *American Sociological Review, 49, 221-234.*

SEN, M. (1983): Minimization of Boolean functions of any number of variables using decimal labels. *Information Sciences, 30, 37-45.*

VAN MECHELEN, I. (1988): Prediction of a dichotomous criterion variable by means of a logical combination of dichotomous predictors. *Mathématiques, Informatique et Sciences Humaines, 102, 47-54.*

VAN MECHELEN, I., and DE BOECK, P. (1990): Projection of a binary criterion into a model of hierarchical classes. *Psychometrika, 55, 677-694.*

VAN MECHELEN, I., DE BOECK, P., and ROSENBERG, S. (1995): The conjunctive model of hierarchical classes. *Psychometrika, 60, 505-521.*

Mathematical Classification and Clustering: From How to What and Why

B. Mirkin[1]

DIMACS, Rutgers University,
P.O.Box 1179, Piscataway, NJ 08855-1179 USA
and CEMI, Moscow, Russia

Abstract: Although some clustering techniques are well known and widely used, their theoretical foundations are still unclear. We consider an approach, approximation clustering, as a unifying framework for making theoretical foundations to some popular techniques. The questions of interrelation of the models with each other and with some other methods (especially in contingency and spatial data analyses) are also discussed.

1 Introduction

Clustering has emerged as a set of ad hoc techniques and still suffers of insufficient theoretical support. A clustering theory must suggest a unifying framework for different methods, which should include:

1. Foundations and limits of applicability to clustering techniques;

2. Interrelations between different concepts and techniques in and out of clustering;

3. A basis for suggesting solutions to newly emerging problems and applications in data processing.

To the moment, we can distinguish three areas of growth in theoretical clustering: (a) probabilistic modeling, especially concerning the mixture-of-distributions considerations; (b) abstract algebraic modeling studying particular types of cluster and data structures; and (c) approximation clustering which will be considered in this paper.

In Section 2, some most popular heuristical clustering techniques ("how"s) are considered. In Section 3, three cluster structures (single cluster, partition, and cluster hierarchy) are employed for approximation of the data by either of the structures, so that local search optimization algorithms give a substantiation and, also, restrictions to the heuristical techniques ("why"s and "what"s). In Section 4, a data scatter decomposition is exploited to relate the approximation model to co-occurence data analysis and conceptual clustering. Section 5 is devoted to applying the approximation approach to some more recent problems in massive data processing.

---

[1] The research was supported by the Office of Naval Research under grants number N00014-93-1-0222 and N00014-96-1-0208 to Rutgers University.

2 Some Most Used Clustering Techniques

2.1 Entity Based Clustering

Though several different data formats can be distinguished quite clearly, only the column-conditional data format will be considered in this paper. Such a data table is presented as a matrix $X = (x_{ik})$, $i \in I, k \in K$, where I is the set of entities, K is the set of variables, and x_{ik} is the value of variable $k \in K$ at entity $i \in I$. The number of entities will be denoted by N and number of the variables by n.

Let us remind three most popular geometric clustering techniques.

K-Means

The algorithm, in its "parallel" version, starts with choosing a set of m tentative centroids $c_1, ..., c_m$. Then two updating steps are reiterated until the output is not varied anymore. The steps are: (1) updating of the clusters with the so-called *minimal distance rule*, i (2) updating of the centers (centroids) of the clusters found.

Hierarchic Clustering

Hierarchic entity-based clustering methods are considered within two major families: of sequential fission (agglomeration) or fusion (division) methods that construct the hierarchy level-by-level, from bottom to top (agglomerative clustering) or from top to bottom (divisive clustering). Divisive clustering, so far, has not received much attention.

Seriation

This group of methods is based on a preliminary ordering (seriation) of the entities by adding them one-by-one, each time minimizing the dissimilarity between an entity and the initial fragment of the ordering, with subsequent cutting of the ordering to produce clusters.

The methods show How to do computation; the major drawbacks are related to that there is not much to say about What and Why (goals, choice of parameters, and interpretation issues).

2.2 Conceptual Clustering

This approach is supposed to overcome some of the drawbacks of the geometric clustering. The data matrix is considered as a set of its columns (the variables), and a decision tree is produced with sequential splitting its nodes (corresponding to subsets of entities) by the variables.

To decide which class S and by which variable is to be split, the following two goodness-of-split criteria are widely used:

1. *Twoing Rule* (Breiman et al. (1984)) applied when split of S is made

into two subclasses, S_1 and S_2, only:

$$tw(y, S_1, S_2) = \frac{p_1 p_2}{4}[\sum_u |p(u/S_1) - p(u/S_2)|]^2 \quad (1)$$

where u are the categories of a target variable y.

2. *Category Utility Function* (Fisher (1987)) applied when there is a set of categorical variables Y and the split is made into any number T of subclasses $S_t, t = 1, ..., T$:

$$CU(Y, \{S_t\}) = \sum_{y \in Y}[\sum_{u_y}\sum_t \frac{p_{u_y t}^2}{p_t} - \sum_{u_y} p_{u_y}^2]/T \quad (2)$$

where p_{u_y} and $p_{u_y t}$ are the frequencies of observing a category u_y of $y \in Y$ or a pair (y_u, S_t).

3 Approximation Clustering

3.1 Cluster Structures and Their Linear Representation

In the approximation approach, the $N \times n$ data matrix $X = (x_{ik})$ itself is considered as a vector in an $(N \times n)$-dimensional space to be approximated by a cluster structure of which the following three types will be considered below.

(A) Single Cluster. Every subset $S \subseteq I$ can be one-to-one assigned with its binary indicator $s(i)$ which is equal to 1 if $i \in S$ and 0 if $i \in I - S$. Supplied with an n-dimensional "center" vector, c, the single cluster matrix can be defined as $sc^T = (s(i)c_k)$.

(B) Partition. Any partition $S = \{S_1, ...S_m\}$ of I can be one-to-one assigned with a binary $N \times m$ matrix $s = (s_{it})$ where $s_{it} = 1$ if $i \in S_t$ and $= 0$ if $i \notin S_t$. The columns of s are obviously mutually orthogonal. Supplied with a set of m n-dimensional center vectors, $c_1, ..., c_m$, being rows of $m \times n$ matrix, c, the partition cluster matrix is sc.

(C) Binary Hierarchy. This is a nested set, S_W, of clusters $S_w \subseteq I$ such that: (a) $I \in S_W$, (b) $\{i\} \in S_W$ for all $i \in I$, and (c) each nonsingleton cluster is union of exactly two other clusters called children. Every nonsingleton cluster $S_w \in S_W$ is assigned with its nest indicator, $\phi_w(i)$, which is equal to a_w for i in one and to b_w for i in the other of children of S_w. The values of a_w and b_w are chosen so that ϕ_w is centered and normed:

$$a_w = \sqrt{\frac{n_{w2}}{n_{w1}n_w}}, \text{ and } b_w = -\sqrt{\frac{n_{w1}}{n_{w2}n_w}} \quad (3)$$

where n_w, n_{w1}, and n_{w2} are cardinalities of S_w and its two children, S_{w1} and S_{w2}, respectively.

It turns out, vectors ϕ_w are mutually orthogonal, which makes the set $\Phi = \{\phi_w\}$ an orthonormal basis of all N-dimensional centered vectors. Any data matrix, Y (preliminarily column-centered), can thus be decomposed by the basis:

$$Y = \Phi C \qquad (4)$$

so that

$$C = \Phi^T Y \qquad (5)$$

that is,

$$c_{wk} = \sum_{i \in I} \phi_{iw} y_{ik} = \sqrt{\frac{n_{w1} n_{w2}}{n_w}} (y_{w1k} - y_{w2k}), \qquad (6)$$

where y_{w1k} and y_{w2k} are the averages of k-th variable in S_{w1} and S_{w2}, respectively.

3.2 Bilinear Clustering Model

Let us fix a cluster structure (single cluster, partition, or cluster hierarchy) and present it by a matrix $Z = (z_{it})$ where columns z_t correspond to clusters. Let us consider the following bilinear model expressing observed values y_{ik} via (partly) unknown elements of the cluster structure (z_t or/and c_t) plus residuals, e_{ik}:

$$y_{ik} = \sum_t c_{tk} z_{it} + e_{ik} \qquad (7)$$

The model, in matrix terms, is $Y = ZC + E$. The least-squares fitting criterion leads to the optimal estimate of the load matrix equal to $C = (Z^T Z)^{-1} ZY$.

As it is described in Mirkin (1996), the three geometric clustering algorithms above appear to be local search techniques for approximation of the data with single clusters (seriation), partitions (K-Means) and hierarchies (both agglomerative and divisive clustering). The local search techniques (that are one-by-one adding/removing in single cluster clustering, alternating minimization in partitioning, and sequential fitting in hierarchical clustering) provide also for restricting the principal parameters of the methods (the similarities/distances used, stopping criteria, etc.). Let us discuss, in brief, a model-based divisive clustering strategy.

3.3 Hierarchic Clustering

Let us denote by y_w vector of the averages of the variables in S_w, $w \in W$. Equation (6) implies that the Euclidean norm squared, (c_w, c_w), is

$$\mu_w^2 = \frac{n_{w1} n_{w2}}{n_w} d^2(y_{w1}, y_{w2}) \qquad (8)$$

where $d(x, y)$ is the Euclidean distance between vectors x, y.

When the hierarchy is partly unknown, equation (7) implies

$$(Y,Y) = \sum_{t=1}^{m} \mu_t^2 + (E, E) \tag{9}$$

so that finding an optimal Φ requires maximizing $\sum_{t=1}^{m} \mu_t^2$. The problem is hard, which leads us to do optimizing sequentially, each time maximizing only one μ_t^2 which is exactly the Ward's criterion (Ward (1963)). Splitting can be done by a version of K-Means algorithm.

4 Some Interrelations

4.1 A Decomposition

Some interconnections between approximation clustering criteria and parameters of the algorithms are discribed in Mirkin (1996), Chapters 4, 5 and 6. Here we consider a few corollaries to the least-squares decomposition of the data scatter due to the bilinear partitioning model. When c_t are optimal for given z_t ($t = 1, ..., m$):

$$\sum_{i,k} y_{ik}^2 = \sum_t \sum_k c_{tk}^2 \sum_i z_{it}^2 + \sum_{i,k} e_{ik}^2 \tag{10}$$

Term

$$v(k,t) = c_{tk}^2 \sum_i z_{it}^2 = c_{tk}^2 |S_t| \tag{11}$$

shows contribution of a variable-cluster pair to the data scatter and can be considered as a cluster-specific evaluation of the salience of a variable, k (Mirkin (1997)).

4.2 Category-to-Cluster Measures

In the case when k is a category presented originally by a zero-one column subsequently standardized with subtracting its average, p_k, and dividing by $\sqrt{p_k}$ (Poisson normalization) or by 1 (no normalization) category-to-cluster contribution becomes equal to $(p_{kt} - p_t p_k)^2 / (p_t p_k)$ or $(p_{kt} - p_t p_k)^2 / p_t$, respectively. These measures can be used for data mining as those depending on normalization of the categories.

4.3 Contingency Coefficients as Contributions

Summing up the category-to-cluster contributions with regard to both clusters and categories we can see that the contribution of a pair (nominal variable, cluster partition) is expressed with well-known indices of contingency between the nominal variables, one of which is the Pearson chi-squared coefficient, the other, the reduction of proportional prediction error. Amazingly, it is the method of data standardization which determines which of them is produced as the contribution-to-scatter.

4.4 Criteria for Conceptual Clustering

The category utility function $CU(Y, \{S_t\})$ (2) is proved to be proportional to the sum of contributions of nonnormalized categories. This means that CU is just a specific case of the least-squares partitioning criterion.
Criterion μ_w^2 for splitting in bilinear hierarchical clustering, applied to nominal variables, is equal to

$$\mu_w^2 = n_w p_1 p_2 \sum_u |p(u/S_1) - p(u/S_2)|^2 \tag{12}$$

which much resembles the twoing rule criterion but has a geometrical meaning as well.

5 Approximation Clustering Based Solutions to Some Problems in Massive Data Processing

5.1 Non-Standard Clustering

5.1.1 Robot-Planning Clustering

A robotic device, put into a real-world environment, must learn and classify the nearest part of the world in more detail than more distant objects. That means that clustering should related to a reference point so that the nearer to that point, the less the cluster diameters. Such an algorithm can be produced with sequential fitting the bilinear partitioning model (Mirkin (1996), section 4.3)

5.1.2 Extending Conceptual Clustering to Mixed Data

When both quantitative and nominal variables are present, the cluster-to-variable contribution to the square data scatter is equal to the so-called correlation ratio (squared) of a quantitative variable with regard to the cluster partition. This allows extend the conceptual clustering splitting/pruning rules to the mixed data case.

5.1.3 Box Clustering

When the data entries are comparable or even summable (aggregable) across the data table, analysis of interconnections between row items and column items can be made based on the concept of box-cluster. Box cluster is a pair of subsets, V of rows and W of columns, whose elements are all pair-wise interconnected. The approximation clustering approach can be extended to this case as was done in Mirkin, Arabie and Hubert (1995).

5.1.4 Aggregating Contingency and Mobility Tables

Contingency (co-occurrence) data usually have been considered in the socio-economics studies; currently, they emerge as a tool in analyzing large data sets in informatics. The problem of aggregating of this kind of data can be naturally put in the approximation framework correspondence-wisely (see Mirkin (1996), sections 5.6 and 6.4, and references therein).

5.2 Machine Learning: Concepts, Feature Extraction and Constructive Induction

Due to its simplicity, the cluster-specific contribution weight (11) can be employed for machine learning of predefined or constructed classifications in very large data sets. A typical problem of finding a good description to predefined classes involves finding the most salient variables for each of the classes with creating approximate conjunctive conceptual descriptions to each class. In the case when the pregiven variables allow only a poor conceptual description, new, compound, variables should be generated with arithmetic operations (as a constructive induction step, see Wnek and Michalski (1994)) to find a better description of the classes.

Applied to the well known Iris data set (150 specimens belonging to 3 Iris genera classes and described by 4 nondiscriminating variables, $w1$ to $w4$), this strategy leads to the following results. The approximate conjunctive concepts (restricted to have no more than 2 conjunctive terms involving only variables $w2$ to $w4$) are: $w2/w3 \geq 1.77$ (class 1, PE=0), $0.33 \leq w2/(w3*w4) \leq 0.76$ & $9.9 \leq w3*w3*w4 \leq 42.5$ (class 2, PE=0.02), and $7.5 \leq w3*w4 \leq 15.87$ & $0.38 \leq w2/w3 \leq 0.63$ (class 3, PE=0.02). The PE, precision error, here is just the proportion of false positives (entities satisfying a description but not belonging to the corresponding class). Taking the space of four variables from these concepts, $w2/w3, w2/(w3*w4), w3*w3*w4, w3*w4$, we can see how "cohesive" the classes have become by applying a clustering method to the specimens in this space. Bilinear clustering produces 3 clusters which differ from the predefined ones by only 8 instances of class 3 joined to class 2 (Mirkin (1997)).

5.3 Hierarchies as Multiresolution Analysis Devices

The concept of binary hierarchy suits into the so-called spatial data structures: digitalized intervals, rectangles or hyper-rectangles consisting of one-, two- or three- dimensional pixels ordered according to the coordinate axes

(Samet, 1990). Let us consider I a unidimensional pixel set, for the sake of simplicity.

5.3.1 Compression/Decompression of Spatial Data

In the problems of data compression, the hierarchy layers (which are obtained by cutting the tree at any level) can be exploited for approximate compression of the data. More specifically, with a layer $L_m = \{L_{mt}\}$ taken, a data vector $f = (f_i)$, $i \in I$, can be substituted by the vector of within class averages, $f_{mt} = \sum_{i \in L_{mt}} f_i/|L_{mt}|$, which is considered as the data at m-th level of resolution. The smaller m, the coarser the resolution; the larger m, the finer the resolution.

The layers can be trivially used for recalculating the averages while running along the hierarchy bottom-up. It is not difficult also to exploit the hierarchy for recalculating the averages running up-down along the hierarchy. Let us save, for every cluster S_w, in addition to f_w, the between-split difference $d_w = f_{w1} - f_{w2}$. The formulas

$$f_{w1} = f_w + \frac{n_{w2}}{n_w}d_w, \quad f_{w2} = f_w - \frac{n_{w1}}{n_w}d_w \qquad (13)$$

provide for calculating the average values in L_{m+1} by the averages of L_m. This allows to make decompression of the data in a fast way.

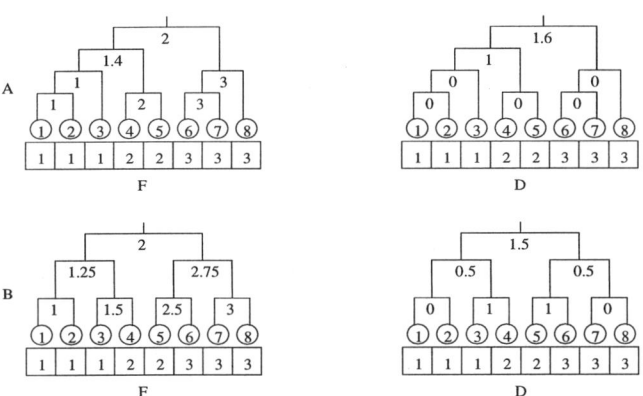

Figure 1: Compression and decompression of the boxed data with two hierarchies, A and B.

In Figure 1, two hierarchies, A and B, are exploited for compressing a vector f whose values are the boxed digits: F version keeps all the averages, D all the differences. It can be seen that hierarchy A provides for a safer data compression: only one average, f_0 in F, and two differences, 1.6 and 1, are needed to decompress the data entirely. Thus, adjusting the hierarchy to the data may lead to better processing them.

5.3.2 Multiresolution Approximation and Wavelets

This methodology can be put in the linear space framework as follows.

Let us define, for the partition at any layer L_m, corresponding binary matrix whose columns give a basis of the corresponding subspace, V_m. Let us denote by D_m the subspace generated by the nest indicator vectors, $\phi_{mt}(i)$, of non-singleton classes in L_m. It appears, for any m ($m = 1, ..., q$), subspace D_{m-1} is the orthogonal complement of V_{m-1} in V_m so that $V_{m-1} \oplus D_{m-1} = V_m$.

This can be "decoded" into interconnection between coefficients of decompositions of the vector f through subspaces of different levels. It appears (Mirkin (1998)) that the equations above - in the case of a complete binary hierarchy (as B in Figure 1) - are exact parallel to those emerging in the so-called theory for multiresolution approximation involving the box scale and Haar wavelet functions (see, for example, reviews by Mallat (1989) and Kay (1994)). The (discrete) wavelet theory involves two basic constructions: a multiresolution approximation of the space of all square-integrable real-valued functions L^2 and a dilation/translation family of functions $\chi_{mt} = 2^{m/2}\chi(2^m x - t)$ obtained from a so-called *scale* function $\chi(x)$ (which integrates to unity) with m "doubling" dilations of the space and translation of the origin by t. Graphs of the box and Haar functions are shown in Figure 2.

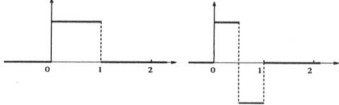

Figure 2: Graphs of the box and Haar functions.

5.3.3 Quadtrees and Bihierarchies

A striking parallel also emerges between a natural extension of the binary hierarchy concept onto the planary digitallized rectangles and that of quadtree (Burt and Adelson (1983)), a device exploited for safe encoding the images (Mirkin (1998)).

6 Conclusion

Our claim is that the least-squares approximation clustering covers a substantial part of clustering to meet issues raised in the Introduction. Especially important seems that this model can be employed in newly emerged challenging areas of processing and learning massive data sets because of simple and fast computations involved. The formulas for down-up and top-down calculations along binary hierarchies hold for any hierarchies, which allows to drop off the standard requirements of the multiresolution wavelet-based analysis: the classes can be of different cardinalities and be spatially discontinuous. This may give some computational advantages when processing data of a predefined format (as documents or images of a body organ).

References

BREIMAN, L., FRIEDMAN, J.H., OLSHEN, R.A., and STONE, C.J. (1984): Classification and Regression Trees. Wadswarth International Group, Belmont, Ca.

BURT, P.J., and ADELSON, E.H. (1983): The Laplacian pyramid as a compact image code. *IEEE Transactions on Communications V COM-31, 532-540.*

FISHER, D.H. (1987): Knowledge acquisition via incremental conceptual clustering. *Machine Learning, 2, 139-172.*

JAIN, A.K. and DUBES, R.C. (1988): Algorithms for Clustering Data. Prentice Hall, Englewood Cliffs, NJ.

KAY, J. (1994): Wavelets. *Advances in Applied Statistics, 2, 209-224.*

MALLAT, S.G. (1989): Multiresolution approximations and wavelet orthonormal bases on $L^2(R)$. *Transactions of the American Mathematical Society, 315, 69-87.*

MIRKIN, B. (1996): Mathematical Classification and Clustering. Kluwer Academic Press, Dorderecht.

MIRKIN, B. (1997): Concept learning and feature selecting based on square-error clustering. *Machine Learning* (to appear).

MIRKIN, B. (1998): Linear embedding of binary hierarchies and its applications. In: B. Mirkin, F. McMorris, F. Roberts and A. Rzhetsky (eds.): *Mathematical Hierarchies and Biology. DIMACS AMS Series.* American Mathematical Society, Providence (to appear).

MIRKIN, B., ARABIE, P., and HUBERT, L. (1995): Additive two-mode clustering: the error-variance approach revisited. *Journal of Classification, 12, 243-263.*

SAMET, H. (1990): The Design and Analysis of Spatial Data Structures. Addison-Wesley Series on Computer Science and Information Processing. Addison-Wesley Publishing Company, Amsterdam.

WARD, J.H., Jr (1963): Hierarchical grouping to optimize an objective function, *Journal of American Statist. Assoc., 58, 236-244.*

WNEK, J. and MICHALSKI, R.S. (1994): Hypothesis-driven constructive induction in AQ17-HCI: A method and experiments, *Machine Learning, 14, 139-168.*

Heteroskedastic Linear Regression Models
A Bayesian Analysis

W. Polasek, S. Liu, S. Jin

Institute of Statistics and Econometrics
University of Basel
Holbeinstrasse 12, 4051 Basel
Switzerland
e-mail: wolfgang@iso.iso.unibas.ch

Abstract: Heteroskedastic linear regression models with linear and non-linear multiplicative and additive specifications are analysed. A Bayesian estimation approach based on natural conjugate priors and a Markov Chain Monte Carlo (MCMC) method is proposed. The numerical computation is done using the Gibbs and Metropolis sampling algorithm. Simulated data sets are examined. The marginal likelihood analysis is proposed to compare among specifications for modelling the heteroskedasticity.

1 Introduction

Heteroskedastic models have been first comprehensively analysed by Goldfeld and Quandt (1972), and many proposals for estimating the effects of independent variables on the residual variances of the regression model have been published. Little work was done on the small sample properties of the estimators in a heteroskedastic model (for a survey on heteroskedastic regressions see Neudecker, Polasek and Liu, 1995). For a Bayesian analysis see e.g. Surekha and Griffiths (1989) and for recent work on ARCH, GARCH, and VAR-VARCH models, see e.g. Polasek and Kozumi [1996]. The recently developed Markov Chain Monte Carlo methods (see Gelfand and Smith [1990]) make a complete Bayesian analysis now possible. Also, with the tools of Bayes tests and the marginal likelihood (see e.g. Chib [1995]) we can use new ways of model selection within the Bayesian framework.

In this paper we propose the Gibbs and Metropolis sampling algorithm (see e.g. Tierney [1994], or Chib and Greenberg [1995]) to simulate the posterior distribution for $\theta' = (\beta', \alpha')$ in the linear heteroskedastic model given as $y_i \sim N(\mathbf{x}_i'\beta, \mathbf{z}_i'\alpha)$, $i = 1, \ldots, n$. Also, we extend the model for several non-linear cases of the form $y_i \sim N[\mathbf{x}_i'\beta, g(\mathbf{z}_i'\alpha)]$, where $g(\cdot)$ can be an exponential function or a Box-Cox transformation for positive z-variables like $g(z, \lambda) = \frac{z^\lambda - 1}{\lambda}$ for $z > 0$.

The plan of the paper is the following:

In section 2, first we develop the basic settings for the Bayesian heteroskedastic regression model. We derive the so-called full conditional distributions. In the linear specification we take the Goldfeld-Quandt estimator with its asymptotic covariance matrix in the Metropolis step. For the power function parameter in the Box-Cox model we suggest a grid search. In the multiplicative specification we choose Harvey's (1976) estimator as a proposal distribution in the Metropolis step. In the additive (or quadratic) specification we adopt the one discussed in

Fomby et al. (1984). Furthermore, we derive a general formula of the marginal likelihood for heteroskedastic linear regression models.

In section 3, we illustrate the techniques by examples of simulated data sets. We use the Gibbs and Metropolis sampling algorithm to produce sequences of drawings for θ, and describe the marginal posterior distributions by histograms. Also, we analyse different parameterisations of the heteroskedastic model and compare then by the marginal likelihood criterion.

In the last section we conclude with final remarks.

2 Inference and analysis

2.1 The heteroskedastic linear regression model

We consider the following heteroskedastic regression model with linear and non-linear multiplicative or additive specifications (see e.g. Fomby et al. [1984]):

$$y_i = \mathbf{x}_i'\beta + u_i, \tag{1}$$

where y_i is the dependent variable, $\mathbf{x}_i$ is a $k \times 1$ vector of independent variables, β is a $k \times 1$ parameter vector, u_i is an error term, and the expected value of u_i is $E(u_i) = 0$, $i = 1, ..., n$. The error variances

$$D(u_i) = \sigma_i^2 = g(\mathbf{z}_i'\alpha), \qquad i = 1, \ldots, n \tag{2}$$

depend on further covariates and a known function $g(.)$ specifying the heteroskedastic variance structure. An example for $g(\mathbf{z}_i'\alpha)$ is $exp(\mathbf{z}_i'\alpha)$. In the next section we show how to estimate the Bayesian heteroskedastic model by a MCMC approach.

2.2 The MCMC algorithm

A good survey on different MCMC techniques can be found in e.g. Tierney (1994). We establish the Bayesian formulation of the heteroskedastic model (1) - (2) with informative prior distributions for α and β as follows:

$$y_i \sim N(\mathbf{x}_i'\beta, \sigma_i^2), \quad i = 1, \ldots, n \tag{3}$$
$$\mathbf{y} = (y_1, \ldots, y_n)', \quad n \times 1, \tag{4}$$
$$\sigma_i^2 = g(\mathbf{z}_i'\alpha), \tag{5}$$
$$\mathbf{X} = (\mathbf{x}_1, \ldots, \mathbf{x}_n)', \quad n \times k, \tag{6}$$
$$\mathbf{Z} = (\mathbf{z}_1, \ldots, \mathbf{z}_n)', \quad n \times q, \tag{7}$$
$$\Sigma = diag(\sigma_1^2, \ldots, \sigma_n^2), \quad n \times n, \tag{8}$$
$$\beta \sim N[\mathbf{b}_*, \mathbf{H}_*], \quad k \times 1, \tag{9}$$
$$\alpha \sim N[\mathbf{a}_*, \mathbf{G}_*], \quad q \times 1. \tag{10}$$

Here $g(.)$ is known, (9) - (10) are the (independent) prior distributions for $\theta = (\beta', \alpha')'$, and the star-index refers to known hyperparameters.

Then the joint distribution of $\mathbf{y} = (y_1, \ldots, y_n)'$ and $\theta' = (\beta', \alpha')$ is

$$p(\mathbf{y}, \theta) = \prod_{i=1}^{n} N[y_i \mid \mathbf{x}_i'\beta, \sigma_i^2] \cdot N[\beta \mid \mathbf{b}_*, \mathbf{H}_*] \cdot N[\alpha \mid \mathbf{a}_*, \mathbf{G}_*]. \tag{11}$$

We have the full conditional distribution for β
$$p(\beta \mid \mathbf{y}, \alpha) = N[\mathbf{b}_{**}, \mathbf{H}_{**}], \qquad (12)$$
with
$$\mathbf{H}_{**}^{-1} = \mathbf{H}_{*}^{-1} + \mathbf{X}'\Sigma^{-1}\mathbf{X}, \qquad (13)$$
$$\mathbf{b}_{**} = \mathbf{H}_{**}[\mathbf{H}_{*}^{-1}\mathbf{b}_{*} + \mathbf{X}'\Sigma^{-1}\mathbf{y}]. \qquad (14)$$

The proposal distribution for α in the Metropolis step is
$$\alpha \sim N[\hat{\alpha}, \hat{\mathbf{V}}], \qquad (15)$$
where the parameters $\hat{\alpha}$ and $\hat{\mathbf{V}}$ of this normal distribution are chosen in the following way

(i) in the linear case $\sigma_i^2 = \mathbf{z}_i'\alpha$: For (15) we use the Goldfeld-Quandt estimator $\hat{\alpha}$ and its asymptotic covariance $\hat{V}$
$$\hat{\alpha} = (\mathbf{Z}'\mathbf{Z})^{-1}\mathbf{Z}'(\hat{\mathbf{u}} \otimes \hat{\mathbf{u}}), \qquad (16)$$
$$\hat{\mathbf{u}} = \mathbf{y} - \mathbf{X}\hat{\beta}, \qquad (17)$$
$$\hat{\mathbf{V}} = 2(\mathbf{Z}'\mathbf{Z})^{-1}\mathbf{Z}'\hat{\Sigma}^2\mathbf{Z}(\mathbf{Z}'\mathbf{Z})^{-1}, \qquad (18)$$
$$\hat{\Sigma} = diag\,(\mathbf{z}_1'\hat{\alpha}, \ldots, \mathbf{z}_n'\hat{\alpha}) > 0, \qquad (19)$$

where $\otimes$ indicates the Hadamard product (see e.g. Polasek, Liu and Neudecker [1996]).

Note: It is known that $\hat{\alpha}$ in (16) is asymptotically normally distributed with mean α and covariance matrix $\mathbf{V} = 2(\mathbf{Z}'\mathbf{Z})^{-1}\mathbf{Z}'\Sigma^2\mathbf{Z}(\mathbf{Z}'\mathbf{Z})^{-1}$. Amemiya's (1977) feasible GLS estimator of α is asymptotically normally distributed with mean α and covariance matrix $\mathbf{A} = 2\,(\mathbf{Z}'\Sigma^{-2}\mathbf{Z})^{-1}$. Because $\mathbf{V} \geq \mathbf{A}$ (see e.g. Polasek, Liu and Neudecker [1996]) we choose $\hat{\mathbf{V}}$.

(ii) in the power function case $\sigma_i^2 = \mathbf{z}_i'\alpha$ with $\mathbf{z}_i$ to be introduced in (24) below: For (15) we use
$$\hat{\alpha} = (\mathbf{Z}'\mathbf{Z})^{-1}\mathbf{Z}'(\hat{\mathbf{u}} \otimes \hat{\mathbf{u}}), \qquad (20)$$
$$\hat{\mathbf{u}} = \mathbf{y} - \mathbf{X}\hat{\beta}, \qquad (21)$$
$$\hat{\mathbf{V}} = c\,(\mathbf{Z}'\mathbf{Z})^{-1}\mathbf{Z}'\hat{\Sigma}^2\mathbf{Z}(\mathbf{Z}'\mathbf{Z})^{-1}, \qquad (22)$$
$$\hat{\Sigma} = diag\,(\mathbf{z}_1'\hat{\alpha}, \ldots, \mathbf{z}_n'\hat{\alpha}), \qquad (23)$$
$$\mathbf{z}_i = (\mathbf{x}_{i1}^{p_1}, \ldots, \mathbf{x}_{iq}^{p_q})', \qquad (24)$$

where c in (22) can be any positive constant and the prior distribution for the exponents p_j is an uniform distribution $p_j \sim Unif\,(p_{j,1*}, p_{j,2*})$ with two known constants $p_{j,1*}$ and $p_{j,2*}$, $j = 1, \ldots, q$. Here the parameter vector is $\theta' = (\beta', \alpha', p')$.

(iii) in the exponential case $\sigma_i^2 = \exp(\mathbf{z}_i'\alpha)$: For (15) we use
$$\hat{\alpha} = (\mathbf{Z}'\mathbf{Z})^{-1}\mathbf{Z}'(\log\,\hat{\mathbf{u}} \otimes \hat{\mathbf{u}}), \qquad (25)$$
$$\log(\hat{\mathbf{u}} \otimes \hat{\mathbf{u}}) = (\log \hat{u}_1^2, \ldots, \log \hat{u}_n^2)', \qquad (26)$$
$$\hat{\mathbf{u}} = \mathbf{y} - \mathbf{X}\hat{\beta}, \qquad (27)$$
$$\hat{\mathbf{V}} = 4.9348\,(\mathbf{Z}'\mathbf{Z})^{-1}, \qquad (28)$$
$$\hat{\Sigma} = diag\,[exp\,(\mathbf{z}_1'\hat{\alpha}), \ldots, exp\,(\mathbf{z}_n'\hat{\alpha})]. \qquad (29)$$

Note:
Harvey (1976) shows that the asymptotic covariance matrix for $\hat{\alpha}$ in (26) is $\mathbf{V} = 4.9348 \cdot (\mathbf{Z}'\mathbf{Z})^{-1}$. The maximum likelihood estimator $\hat{\alpha}_{ML}$ would obtain the asymptotic Cramer-Rao lower bound $\mathbf{C} = 2\,(\mathbf{Z}'\mathbf{Z})^{-1}$. Since $\mathbf{V} \geq \mathbf{C}$, we choose $\hat{\mathbf{V}}$ as in (28) for the Metropolis step.

(iv) in the additive case $\sigma_i^2 = (\mathbf{z}_i'\alpha)^2$: For (15) we use the Glejser-type estimator (see Fomby et al. (1984) for details) with the parameters

$$\hat{\alpha} = (\mathbf{Z}'\mathbf{Z})^{-1}\mathbf{Z}'|\hat{\mathbf{u}}|, \tag{30}$$

$$\hat{\mathbf{u}} = \mathbf{y} - \mathbf{X}\hat{\beta}, \tag{31}$$

$$\hat{\mathbf{V}} = \frac{1-c^2}{c^2}(\mathbf{Z}'\mathbf{Z})^{-1}\mathbf{Z}'\hat{\Sigma}\mathbf{Z}(\mathbf{Z}'\mathbf{Z})^{-1}, \tag{32}$$

$$\hat{\Sigma} = diag\,[(\mathbf{z}_1'\hat{\alpha})^2,\ldots,(\mathbf{z}_n'\hat{\alpha})^2], \tag{33}$$

where $|\hat{\mathbf{u}}|$ is the absolute value of $\hat{\mathbf{u}}$ and $c = (2/\pi)^{1/2}$.
Again, the idea is to use the classical approximate distributional results as a proposal distribution in the Metropolis step.

A proposal in the Metropolis step means that we switch to α_{new}, the new sample of the proposal distribution with probability

$$prob = min\,[1, \frac{p(\alpha_{new})}{p(\alpha_{old})}]$$

or else we keep α_{old}, the old value (and $p(.)$ is the probability density function given in (11) and β is the current sample).

2.3 Marginal likelihood

Now we derive the marginal likelihood for all cases of the heteroskedastic model. In a Bayesian analysis the marginal likelihood is obtained from the joint distribution of the data $\mathbf{y}$ and the parameter θ by integrating out θ: $f(\mathbf{Y}) = \int f(\mathbf{Y}, \vartheta)d\theta$. If this is not possible in closed form, one needs numerical methods.

Consider the following heteroskedastic linear model

$$y_i \sim N[\mathbf{x}_i\beta, \sigma_i^2], \quad i = 1,\ldots,n, \tag{34}$$

$$\sigma_i^2 = g(\mathbf{z}_i'\alpha). \tag{35}$$

The likelihood function is given by

$$f(\mathbf{y}\mid\alpha,\beta) = (2\pi)^{-\frac{n}{2}}|\Sigma|^{-\frac{1}{2}}exp\{-\frac{1}{2}(\mathbf{y}-\mathbf{X}\beta)'\Sigma^{-1}(\mathbf{y}-\mathbf{X}\beta)\} \tag{36}$$

$$\text{with } \Sigma = diag\,(g\,(\mathbf{z}_1'\alpha),\ldots,g\,(\mathbf{z}_n'\alpha)) > 0. \tag{37}$$

Based on the prior distribution

$$\beta \sim N[\mathbf{b}_*, \mathbf{H}_*], \quad \alpha \sim N[\mathbf{a}_*, \mathbf{G}_*] \tag{38}$$

the joint distribution is

$$f(\mathbf{y},\alpha,\beta) = (2\pi)^{-\frac{n}{2}}|\Sigma|^{-\frac{1}{2}}N[\mathbf{a}_*,\mathbf{G}_*]\cdot exp\{-\frac{1}{2}(\mathbf{Q}+\mathbf{\Delta})\}$$
$$\cdot exp\{-\frac{1}{2}(\beta-\mathbf{b}_{**})'\mathbf{H}_{**}^{-1}(\beta-\mathbf{b}_{**})\}(2\pi)^{-\frac{k}{2}}|\mathbf{H}_*|^{-\frac{1}{2}} \quad (39)$$

with

$$\mathbf{H}_{**}^{-1} = \mathbf{H}_*^{-1} + \mathbf{X}'\Sigma^{-1}\mathbf{X}, \quad (40)$$
$$\mathbf{b}_{**} = \mathbf{H}_{**}[\mathbf{H}_*^{-1}\mathbf{b}_* + \mathbf{X}'\Sigma^{-1}\mathbf{y}], \quad (41)$$
$$\mathbf{Q} = (\mathbf{y}-\mathbf{X}\mathbf{b}_{GLS})'\Sigma^{-1}(\mathbf{y}-\mathbf{X}\mathbf{b}_{GLS}), \quad (42)$$
$$\mathbf{b}_{GLS} = (\mathbf{X}'\Sigma^{-1}\mathbf{X})^{-1}\mathbf{X}'\Sigma^{-1}\mathbf{y}, \quad (43)$$
$$\mathbf{\Delta} = (\mathbf{b}_*-\mathbf{b}_{GLS})'[(\mathbf{X}'\Sigma^{-1}\mathbf{X})^{-1}+\mathbf{H}_*]^{-1}(\mathbf{b}_*-\mathbf{b}_{GLS}). \quad (44)$$

Integrating out β from the joint distribution $f(\mathbf{y},\beta,\alpha)$ involves the following normal integral

$$\int exp\{-\frac{1}{2}(\beta-\mathbf{b}_{**})'\mathbf{H}_{**}^{-1}(\beta-\mathbf{b}_{**})\}d\beta = |\mathbf{H}_{**}|^{\frac{1}{2}}(2\pi)^{\frac{k}{2}}. \quad (45)$$

Thus, we obtain

$$f(\mathbf{y},\alpha) = \int f(\mathbf{y},\alpha,\beta)d\beta \quad (46)$$
$$= (2\pi)^{-\frac{n}{2}}|\Sigma|^{-\frac{1}{2}}N[\mathbf{a}_*,\mathbf{G}_*]\cdot exp\{-\frac{1}{2}(\mathbf{Q}+\mathbf{\Delta})\}\cdot|\mathbf{H}_*|^{-\frac{1}{2}}|\mathbf{H}_{**}^{-1}|^{-\frac{1}{2}} \quad (47)$$

with $|\Sigma| = \prod_{i=1}^{n} g(\mathbf{z}_i'\alpha)$.
The marginal likelihood $f(\mathbf{y})$ can be determined as an average of the simulation output ($j=1,\ldots,M$ repetitions in the stochastic integration)

$$f(\mathbf{y}) = \int f(\mathbf{y},\alpha)d\alpha \quad (48)$$
$$= (2\pi)^{-\frac{n+q}{2}}|\mathbf{H}_*|^{-\frac{1}{2}}|\mathbf{G}_*|^{-\frac{1}{2}}\cdot\frac{1}{M}\sum_{j=1}^{M}\{|\Sigma_j|^{-\frac{1}{2}}|\mathbf{H}_{**j}^{-1}|^{-\frac{1}{2}}\}$$
$$\cdot exp\{-\frac{1}{2}(\mathbf{Q}_j+\mathbf{\Delta}_j+\mathbf{A}_j)\} \quad (49)$$

with

$$\mathbf{A}_j = (\alpha_j-\mathbf{a}_*)'\mathbf{G}_*^{-1}(\alpha_j-\mathbf{a}_*) \quad (50)$$
$$\mathbf{Q}_j = (\mathbf{y}-\mathbf{X}\mathbf{b}_j)'\Sigma_j^{-1}(\mathbf{y}-\mathbf{X}\mathbf{b}_j) \quad (51)$$
$$\mathbf{\Delta}_j = (\mathbf{b}_*-\mathbf{b}_j)'[(\mathbf{X}'\Sigma_j^{-1}\mathbf{X})^{-1}+\mathbf{H}_*]^{-1}(\mathbf{b}_*-\mathbf{b}_j) \quad (52)$$
$$\mathbf{b}_j = (\mathbf{X}'\Sigma_j^{-1}\mathbf{X})^{-1}\mathbf{X}'\Sigma_j^{-1}\mathbf{y} \quad (53)$$
$$\Sigma_j = diag(g(\mathbf{z}_1'\alpha_j),\ldots,g(\mathbf{z}_n'\alpha_j)) > 0. \quad (54)$$

3 Examples

Now we illustrate the techniques discussed in Section 2. We constructed four data sets according to the following models (with $u_i \sim N(0, \sigma_i^2)$ and $z_i = x_{i2}$ as in Judge et al. [1988]):
(i) The linear model ($\theta' = (\beta_0, \beta_1, \alpha)$):

$$y_i = 10 + x_{i2} + u_i, \quad i = 1, \ldots, 100, \tag{55}$$
$$\sigma_i^2 = 0.004 z_i > 0. \tag{56}$$

(ii) The power function model ($\theta' = (\beta_0, \beta_1, \beta_2, \alpha_1, \alpha_2, p_1, p_2)$):

$$y_i = 10 + x_{i2} + x_{i3} + u_i, \quad i = 1, \ldots, 100, \tag{57}$$
$$\sigma_i^2 = -2 + 0.3 z_i^2 > 0. \tag{58}$$

(iii) The exponential model ($\theta' = (\beta_0, \beta_1, \beta_2, \alpha_1, \alpha_2)$):

$$y_i = 10 + x_{i2} + x_{i3} + u_i, \quad i = 1, \ldots, 100, \tag{59}$$
$$\sigma_i^2 = exp(-2 + 0.3 z_i). \tag{60}$$

(iv) The additive model ($\theta' = (\beta_0, \beta_1, \beta_2, \alpha_1, \alpha_2)$):

$$y_i = 10 + x_{i2} + x_{i3} + u_i, \tag{61}$$
$$\sigma_i^2 = (-4 + 0.3 z_i)^2, \quad i = 1, \ldots, 100. \tag{62}$$

The MCMC sampling results for the four models are shown in Figures 1-4, respectively. The results upon the marginal likelihood criterion for each case and each data set are shown in the Table 1.

The MCMC converges quite fast and we show the marginal distributions for the four models of the simulated data sets in Figures 1-4. Except for the power function example the marginal distributions are rather symmetric. The "flat distribution" of p_1 in Figure 2 is a redundant output of the general computer model, since the constant has exponent 1. All calculations are estimation outputs of the Basel package (see Jin [1996]).

Table 1: Marginal likelihood analysis

	Log of marginal likelihood for		
Simulated data for	linear case	power function case	exponential case
linear case	-119.37	-124.34	-174.89
power function case	-128.35	-126.65	-193.48
exponential case	-185.62	-190.77	-98.24

From Table 1 we see that our analysis upon the marginal likelihood criterion works quite well. The linear model is best for linearly simulated samples, the power function model selects the power function data, and the exponential model the exponential data set. By choosing the model with the maximum marginal likelihood, we select the correct model form for the simulated data set correspondingly.

4 Conclusion

In this paper we have developed a straightforward approach to Bayesian modelling of heteroskedasticity. This involves a Metropolis step in the MCMC estimation algorithm. The heteroskedastic model with known function $g(.)$ covers a variety of specifications, like the exponential, the additive or the power function cases, in addition to the linear case. To discriminate different models we have used the so-called marginal likehood criteria of Chib (1995) which can be used for Bayes test as well. In the simulated data examples we have demonstrated the flexibility of this new Bayesian approach. We can recommend MCMC approaches as an alternative to the classical way of modelling heteroskedasticity which is rather ad hoc and diverse with respect to estimation methods (for a recent survey on some of them, see also Polasek, Liu and Neudecker [1996]). For an unknown function $g(.)$ a so-called semi-parametric Bayesian modelling strategy has to be used.

5 References

AMEMIYA, T. (1977): A note on a heteroscedastic model. *Journal of Econometrics* 6, 365-370.

CHIB, S. (1995): Marginal likelihood from the Gibbs output. *Journal of the American Statistical Association* 90, 1313-1321.

CHIB, S. and GREENBERG, E. (1995): Understanding the Metropolis-Hastings Algorithm. *American Statistician* 49, 327-335.

FOMBY, T.B., HILL, R.C. and JOHNSON, S.R. (1984): *Advanced Econometric Methods.* Springer-Verlag, New York.

GELFAND, A.E. and SMITH, A.F.M. (1990): Sampling based approaches to calculating marginal densities. *Journal of the American Statistical Association* 85, 398-409.

GOLDFELD, S.M. and QUANDT, R.E. (1972): *Nonlinear Methods in Econometrics.* North-Holland Publishing Company, Amsterdam.

HARVEY, A.C. (1976): Estimating regression models with multiplicative heteroscedasticity. *Econometrica* 44, 460-465.

JIN, S. (1996): The BASEL package, ISO-WWZ, University of Basel, Switzerland. *ftp://iso.iso.unibas.ch/pub/basel.*

JUDGE, G.G., HILL, R.C., GRIFFITHS, W.E., LÜTKEPOHL, H. and LEE, T.C. (1988): *Introduction to the Theory and Practice of Econometrics.* 2nd. edn., Wiley, New York.

NEUDECKER, H., POLASEK, W. and LIU, S. (1995): The Heteroskedastic Linear Regression Model and the Hadamard Product-A Note, *Journal of Econometrics* 68, 361-366.

POLASEK, W. and KOZUMI, H. (1996): The VAR-VARCH model: A Bayesian approach. *Modelling and Prediction,* Honoring Seymour Geisser, ed. by Lee, J.C., Johnson, W.O. and Zellner, A., Springer, New York, 402-422.

POLASEK, W., LIU, S. and NEUDECKER, H. (1996): Heteroskedastic Linear Regression Models. *WWZ-Discussion Paper. Nr. 9608*, University of Basel, Switzerland.

SUREKHA, K. and GRIFFITHS, W.E. (1989): Additive and multiplicative heteroskedasticity : A Bayesian analysis with an application to an expenditure model, *Journal of Quantitative Economics* 5, 43-58.

TIERNEY, L. (1994): Markov Chains for Exploring Posterior Distributions. *Annals of Statistics* 22, 1701-1762.

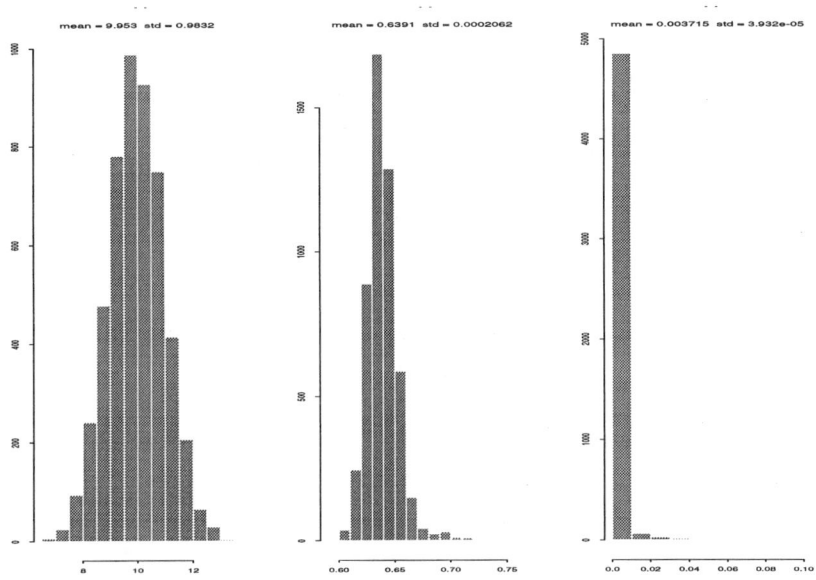

Figure 1: Marginal distributions for β_0, β_1, and α in the linear case

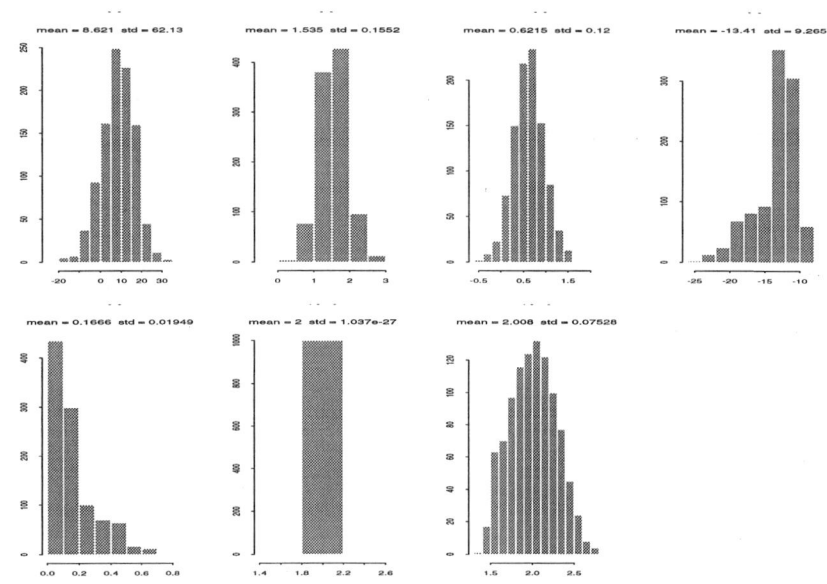

Figure 2: Marginal distributions for $\beta_0, \beta_1, \beta_2, \alpha_1, \alpha_2, p_1$, and p_2 in the power function case

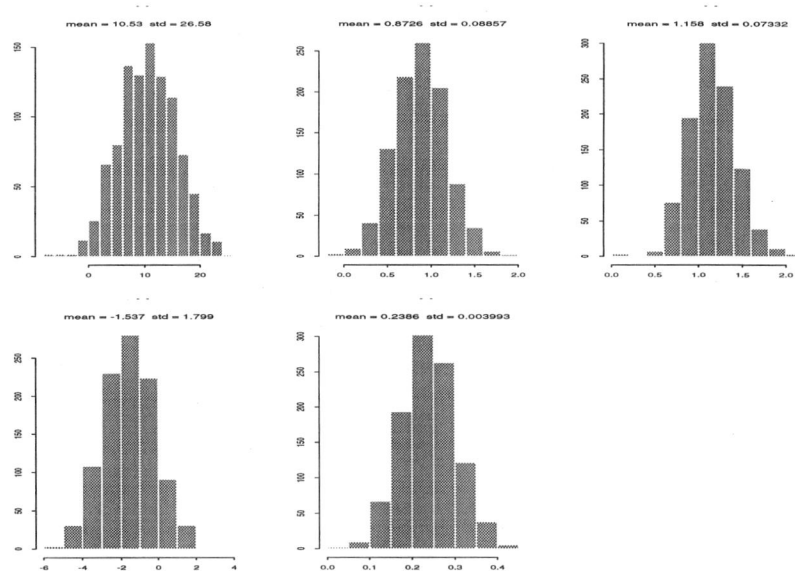

Figure 3: Marginal distributions for $\beta_0, \beta_1, \beta_2, \alpha_1$, and α_2 in the exponential case

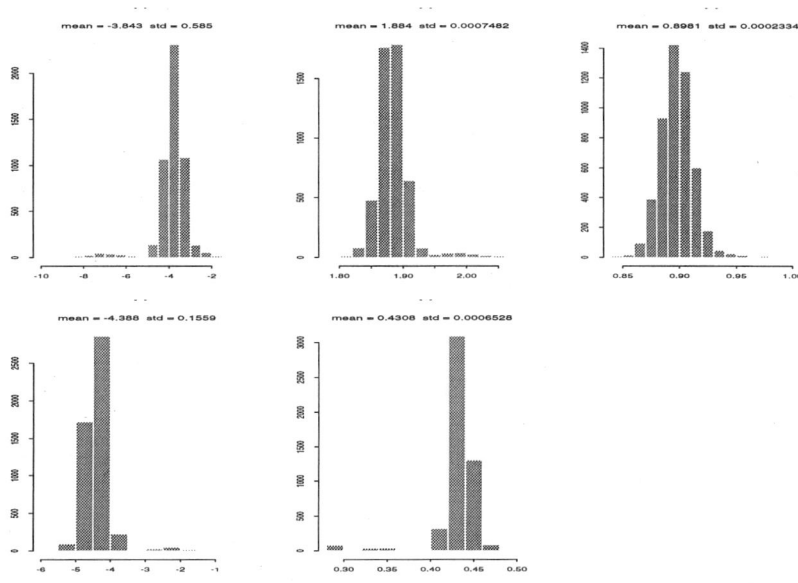

Figure 4: Marginal distributions for $\beta_0, \beta_1, \beta_2, \alpha_1,$ and α_2 in the additive case

A Heuristic Partial-Least-Squares Approach to Estimating Dynamic Path Models

Hans Gerhard Strohe

Lehrstuhl für Statistik, Universität Potsdam, Germany

Abstract: An approach to dynamic modelling with latent variables is proposed. It has been developed on the base of H. Wold's Partial Least Squares (PLS). An operator matrix containing the lag operator L is substituted for the path coefficient matrix of Wold's static PLS model. On what is called the dynamic PLS model (DPLS) the original PLS estimation algorithm is virtually applicable. Lagged and leaded latent variables are used in the iterative process of estimating the weights of the manifest variables. The path coefficients are estimated by OLS or an appropriate dynamic modelling method The redundancy coefficient allows to measure the forecasting validity. DPLS has been programmed in PC-ISP/DGS© . Some properties of DPLS will be shown by simulation.

1 Introduction

In addition to the well known estimation and confirmation approach for path models, LISREL by Jöreskog and Sörbom (e.g. 1987), the partial least squares (PLS) algorithm by H. Wold (1973) has gained popularity as an instrument of analysis and forecasting in sociometrics and econometrics during recent years. The PLS approach to path models is data oriented and mostly descriptive or explorative, the model being defined purely by an algorithm.
A PLS model involves M observable, "manifest" variables (MV) y^m (m=1, ..., M) and K<M latent, i.e.not directly observable variables (LV) η^k (k=1, ..., K). The latter are assumed to be certain constructs composed from those MVs. Furthermore, the LVs are assumed to be connected with each other by the linear inner or structural model:

$$\eta_t = \mathbf{b}_0 + \mathbf{B}\eta_t + \nu_t \tag{1}$$

where $\eta_t = \left(\eta_t^1, \eta_t^2 ... \eta_t^K\right)'$ is the column vector of the scores of all latent variables $\eta^1,...,\eta^k$ for one case t (t = 1, ..., T). **B** is a triangular K×K matrix of path coefficients with zero diagonal and $\mathbf{b}_0$ is a location parameter vector usually set equal zero. The error term ν_t has zero expectation.

What is called the outer or measurement model describes the assumed linear relations between the MVs and the LVs:

$$y_t = p_0 + P\eta_t + \varepsilon_t \quad (loadings\ relation) \qquad (2)$$

with a block diagonal M×K matrix P of path coefficients and a zero expectation disturbance term ε_t. Again the location parameters p_0 are usually transformed to zero. The latent variables are taken to be weighted sums of manifest variables with a block diagonal weight matrix W:

$$\eta_t = W'y_t \quad (weight\ relations) \qquad (3)$$

The iterative estimation of the weights W is the main aim of Wold's PLS algorithm. The procedure is to start with more or less arbitrarily chosen weights W. The next stage involves the calculation of proxies η^{k*} for the latent variables η^k. η^{k*} is a weighted sum of all LVs directly connected with η^k.

Finally new weights $W = (\omega_{mk})$ are estimated by OLS regression between the MVs and the approxies. The scores of the LVs being approximately known after stopping the iteration process, we can easily estimate the parameter matrices B and P by OLS, using model equations 1 and 2 respectively.

More details about PLS are given by Lohmöller (1989) who is the author of the PLS computer programme LVPLS (Lohmöller 1984).

In section 2 a PLS-like approach to a class of dynamic models with latent variables will be suggested. The way to use these models for prediction will be shown, and a measure for goodness of fit will be deduced. Then, a computer programme for dynamic partial least squares modelling will be presented. The final section will show a small three-block model with an autoregressive distributed lag relation between the LVs and offer the results of a Monte Carlo simulation study in order to demonstrate some properties of the estimator.

2 The Dynamic Partial Least Squares Model

2.1 The Dynamic Path Model

The dynamic form of the structural model can be transformed into the exterior shape of the "normal" PLS model:

$$\eta_t = F\eta_t + \nu_t \qquad (4)$$

where

$$F = B + CL \qquad (5)$$

is a matrix containing the lag operator L with $L\eta_t = \eta_{t-1}$. On what we call now the dynamic PLS model (DPLS)

$$\eta_t = \mathbf{F}\eta_t + \nu_t$$
$$\mathbf{y}_t = \mathbf{P}\eta_t + \varepsilon_t$$
$$\eta_t = \mathbf{W}'\mathbf{y}_t \tag{6}$$

the original PLS alogrithm is applicable. Initially, Boolean design matrices $\mathbf{D}_B$, $\mathbf{D}_C$ and $\mathbf{D}_P$ corresponding to the unlagged and lagged dependencies in the inner model 6 and to the outer model, i.e. to the zero restrictions for the coefficient matrices $\mathbf{B}$, $\mathbf{C}$ and $\mathbf{P}$, must be fixed. The inner model can be illustrated by a path diagram, including additional arrows for the lagged relationships (dotted arrows in fig.1). The inner design matrix $\mathbf{D}_B$ contains the digit one where there is a connection between two LVs in the path model and consists of zeros elsewhere. Similarly, the lag design matrix $\mathbf{D}_C$ consists of ones and zeros corresponding to whether or not there is assumed to be first order lagged (auto-)regression between latent variables. $\mathbf{D}_P = [d_{mk}]$ is the outer design matrix corresponding to whether or not a variable y^m of $\mathbf{Y}$ belongs to the block of a certain latent variable i.e. a row η^k of $\mathbf{H}$.

2.2 PLS Estimation with Dynamic Inner Approximation

For simplicity the symbols for the empirically estimated LVs and coefficients will not be distinguished from those for the corresponding theoretical quantities in this section. In order to estimate the weight matrix $\mathbf{W}$, the following steps will be repeatedly executed:

1. Initial representation of the latent variables as components of the manifest variables with chosen starting values for the matrix $\mathbf{W}$

$$\eta_t = \mathbf{W}'\mathbf{y}_t \tag{7}$$

2. Standardization of the LVs to unit variance

$$\eta_t := \sqrt{T}\,(\mathbf{I} \ast \mathbf{HH}')^{-\frac{1}{2}}\,\eta_t \tag{8}$$

where
$$\mathbf{H} = (\eta_1, \eta_2, ..., \eta_T), \tag{9}$$

is the K×T matrix of all time scores of η_t for t = 1, ..., T. Element-wise multiplication of matrices is denoted by $\ast$.

3. Calculation of "neighbourhood" variables corresponding to the inner path model:
$$\eta_t^* = \mathbf{F}^*\eta_t \tag{10}$$
$$\mathbf{F}^* = \mathbf{B}^* + \mathbf{C}^*L + \mathbf{C}^{*\prime}L^{-1} \tag{11}$$

that means
$$\eta_t^* = \mathbf{B}^*\eta_t + \mathbf{C}^*\eta_{t-1} + \mathbf{C}^{*\prime}\eta_{t+1} \qquad (12)$$

where $\mathbf{B}^*$ and $\mathbf{C}^*$ are suitable inner weighting matrices, e.g.:

$$\mathbf{B}^* = (\mathbf{D}_B + \mathbf{D}_B') * \mathbf{R} \qquad (13)$$

$$\mathbf{C}^* = \mathbf{D}_C * \mathbf{A} \qquad (14)$$

with $\mathbf{D}_B$ and $\mathbf{D}_C$ being the design matrices for the inner model.

$$\mathbf{R} = \mathbf{H}\mathbf{H}'/T \qquad (15)$$

$$\mathbf{A} = \mathbf{H}\left(L\mathbf{H}\right)'/T \qquad (16)$$

are the correlation matrix and the first order autocorrelation matrix of LVs, respectively, with

$$\mathbf{H} = (\eta_1, \eta_2, ..., \eta_T), \qquad (17)$$

$$L\mathbf{H} = (\eta_0, \eta_1, ..., \eta_{T-1}) \qquad (18)$$

4. New values of the weight matrix $\mathbf{W}$ are gained by OLS estimation:

$$y_t^m = \omega_{mk}\eta_t^{k*} + v_t^{mk} \quad \text{if } d_{mk}=1 \quad \text{(Wold's Mode A)} \quad (19)$$

where $\mathbf{D}_P = [d_{mk}]$ is the outer design matrix.

5. The estimated coefficients ω_{mk} are substituted for the previous elements of the weight matrix $\mathbf{W}$

$$\mathbf{W} := [\omega_{mk}].$$

Using this new weight matrix we continue the procedure by repeating step 1. The iteration process is stopped when subsequent estimations of the LVs η_t in step 2 do not relevantly differ from the previous ones.
Then the coefficient matrices $\mathbf{B}$ and $\mathbf{C}$ of the inner model 4

$$\eta_t = (\mathbf{B} + \mathbf{C}L)\eta_t + \mathbf{v}_t \qquad (20)$$

can be estimated by a suitable method for dynamic models, such as OLS, GLS, Cochrane-Orcutt, ECM etc. The loadings $\mathbf{P}$ of the outer model 2 are estimated by simple OLS.

2.3 Prediction and Goodness of Fit

By substituting 4 for y_t in 2 we obtain

$$\begin{aligned} y &= \mathbf{P}\boldsymbol{\eta}_t + \boldsymbol{\varepsilon}_t \\ &= \mathbf{PF}\boldsymbol{\eta}_t + \mathbf{P}\boldsymbol{\nu}_t + \boldsymbol{\varepsilon}_t \end{aligned} \qquad (21)$$

Then substituting 6 for $\boldsymbol{\eta}_t$, we have

$$\mathbf{y}_t = \mathbf{PFW}'\mathbf{y}_t + \mathbf{P}\boldsymbol{\nu}_t + \boldsymbol{\varepsilon}_t \qquad (22)$$

or

$$\mathbf{y}_t = [\mathbf{PBW}'\mathbf{y}_t + \mathbf{PCW}'\mathbf{y}_{t-1}] + [\mathbf{P}\boldsymbol{\nu}_t + \boldsymbol{\varepsilon}_t] \qquad (23)$$

Using this prediction formula, we can construct a goodness-of-fit criterion. From 21 it follows that the predictable part of $\mathbf{y}_t$ is $\mathbf{y}_t^* = \mathbf{PF}\boldsymbol{\eta}_t$. Let $\mathbf{Y}^* = (\mathbf{y}_1^*, ..., \mathbf{y}_T^*)$ denote the whole predicted data matrix, $\mathbf{H} = (\boldsymbol{\eta}_1, ..., \boldsymbol{\eta}_T)$ the matrix of the LVs, and $\mathbf{R}$ the empirical correlation or covariance matrix of $\mathbf{H}$. Then the empirical covariance of these predictions is

$$\begin{aligned} cov(\mathbf{Y}^*) &= \mathbf{P}\,\mathbf{F}\,cov(\mathbf{H})\,\mathbf{F}'\,\mathbf{P}' \\ &= \mathbf{P}\,\mathbf{F}\,\mathbf{R}\,\mathbf{F}'\,\mathbf{P}' \end{aligned} \qquad (24)$$

$$\begin{aligned} cov(\mathbf{Y}^*) &= \mathbf{P}(\mathbf{B}+\mathbf{C}L)\mathbf{H}\,\mathbf{H}'\,(\mathbf{B}+\mathbf{C}L)'\mathbf{P}'/T \\ &= (\mathbf{PBHH}'\mathbf{B}'\mathbf{P}' + \mathbf{PC}(L\mathbf{H})\mathbf{H}'\mathbf{B}'\mathbf{P}' + \mathbf{PBH}(L\mathbf{H})'\mathbf{C}'\mathbf{P}' \\ &\quad + \mathbf{PC}(L\mathbf{H})(L\mathbf{H})'\mathbf{C}'\mathbf{P}')/T \\ &\approx \mathbf{PBRB}'\mathbf{P}' + \mathbf{PBAC}'\mathbf{P}' + \mathbf{PCRC}'\mathbf{P}' + (\mathbf{PBAC}'\mathbf{P}')' = \mathbf{G}^* \end{aligned} \qquad (25)$$

with $\mathbf{A}$ being the first order autocorrelation matrix. The inconsiderable inaccurracy of the last relationship arises from tiny differences that might occur between the covariances of the latent variables $\mathbf{HH}'/\mathbf{T}$ and those of the lagged LVs $(L\mathbf{H})(L\mathbf{H})'/T$.

It is easy to see that $\mathbf{G}^*$ contains in its diagonal the variances of the predictable part, or what Lohmöller (1989) calls the "redundant" part, of the MVs.

Following Lohmöller again we calculate the ratio of two diagonal matrices

$$\mathbf{G} = (\mathbf{I} * \mathbf{G}^*)(\mathbf{I} * \boldsymbol{\Sigma}_y)^{-1} \qquad (26)$$

where $\boldsymbol{\Sigma}_y$ denotes the empirical covariance matrix of the manifest variables. The entries in the diagonal of G are ratios expressing to what extent the variance of each manifest variable is reproduced by the variance of the predictable part, i.e. by the model.

The average of these measures

$$G^2 = trace\ \mathbf{G}/M \qquad (27)$$

is the redundancy coefficient or average redundancy and is used for the evaluation of the goodness of fit of the model.

2.4 The Computer Programme DPLS

A computer programme for DPLS has been written by F. Geppert (1995) using the command language of the PC-ISP/DGS statistics system. This programme is controlled by a dialogue asking for the number of MVs, the number of LVs, the outer design matrix $\mathbf{D}_W$, and the dependencies among the LVs, i.e. the inner design matrix $\mathbf{D}_B$. Furthermore, for each variable one must name the lagged variables (inclusing of itself) on which it depends, corresponding to the inner design matrix $\mathbf{D}_C$. The MVs data matrix to be analysed can be keyed in by any text procesor, data bank programme or statistics programme creating an ASCII file or by the "input" command of the programme ISP/DGS which is used when one runs DPLS.

DPLS produces the weight matrix $\mathbf{W}$ for the MVs to be combined into a LV, the corresponding matrix $\mathbf{P}$ of the loadings, the unlagged path coefficient matrix $\mathbf{B}$ and the lagged path coefficient matrix $\mathbf{C}$. In addition, DPLS gives the scores of the LVs and the redundancy as a goodness-of-fit measure. More details on DPLS can be found in Strohe/Geppert (1997).

3 A Simulation Study

On the basis of this programme a series of simulations has been done. For simplicity, an example of a dynamic three-latent-variables model will be considered (figure 1, the dotted arrows denote lagged relationships.):

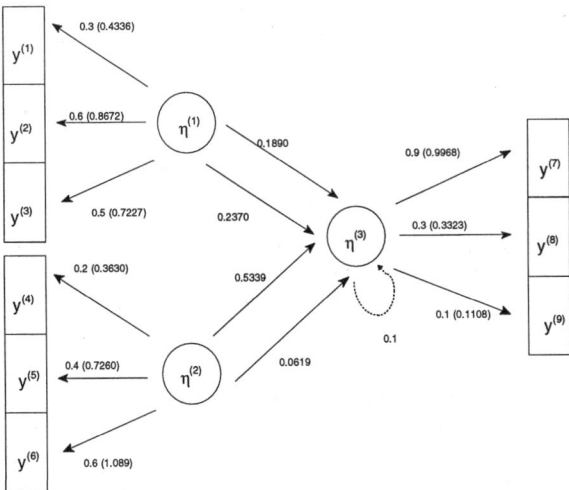

Figure 1: Three-block path model for a three-LV dynamic model

$$\eta_t^3 = b_1\eta_t^1 + b_2\eta_t^2 + c_1\eta_{t-1}^1 + c_2\eta_{t-1}^2 + c_3\eta_{t-1}^3 + \nu_t \qquad (28)$$
$$y_t^m = p_{m1}\eta_t^1 + \varepsilon_t^m \text{ for m=1,...,3}$$
$$y_t^m = p_{m2}\eta_t^2 + \varepsilon_t^m \text{ for m=4,...,6}$$
$$y_t^m = p_{m3}\eta_t^3 + \varepsilon_t^m \text{ for m=7,...,9}$$

In order to examine the assymptotic properties of the DPLS approach, a simulation study on the basis of this three-block dynamic path model with LVs was effected. The loadings, weights, lagged and unlagged path coefficients were fixed according to the following matrices:

$$\mathbf{P} = \begin{bmatrix} 0.3 & 0 & 0 \\ 0.6 & 0 & 0 \\ 0.5 & 0 & 0 \\ 0 & 0.2 & 0 \\ 0 & 0.4 & 0 \\ 0 & 0.6 & 0 \\ 0 & 0 & 0.9 \\ 0 & 0 & 0.3 \\ 0 & 0 & 0.1 \end{bmatrix}, \mathbf{W} = \begin{bmatrix} 0.434 & 0 & 0 \\ 0.867 & 0 & 0 \\ 0.723 & 0 & 0 \\ 0 & 0.363 & 0 \\ 0 & 0.726 & 0 \\ 0 & 1.089 & 0 \\ 0 & 0 & 0.997 \\ 0 & 0 & 0.332 \\ 0 & 0 & 0.111 \end{bmatrix},$$

$$\mathbf{B} = \begin{bmatrix} 0 & 0 & 0 \\ 0 & 0 & 0 \\ 0.189 & 0.534 & 0 \end{bmatrix}, \mathbf{C} = \begin{bmatrix} 0 & 0 & 0 \\ 0 & 0 & 0 \\ 0.237 & 0.062 & 0.1 \end{bmatrix}$$

In the first part of the study, the errors were assumed to be normal distributed. The error variances of the inner or outer model vary within the range from 0.0 to 0.1. In the second part, the errors of the inner and outer model were assumed to have a β-distribution with parameters p varying between 1 and 10 and q equalling 10-p in order to represent assymmetric error distributions with varying skewness.

The aim of both parts of this simulation was to analyse the changes in the parameter estimates caused by the varying shape of the error distribution. For each model, i.e. each parameter combination under consideration, MVs time series with a length of 200 data points each were generated 500 times by the usage of the ISP/DGS random number generator.

Thus 500 replications of the MVs data matrix were available for each model version, the errors being normal or β-distributed and having zero mean.

By means of the programme DPLS and within the framework of ISP/DGS, weights, loadings, lagged and unlagged path coefficients were estimated for each data matrix. For each group of 500 data matrices, average parameter estimations, standard deviations, mean quadratic errors, and the biases of the estimations were calculated.

The latter were plotted as functions of the varying error variances of the model or as functions of the changing parameters of the β-distribution. Figure 2 shows those of changing error variances with normal distribution. Figure 3 shows the biases for the model with β-distribution.

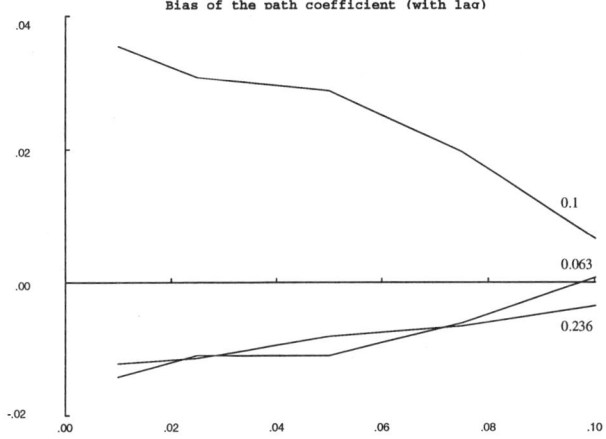

Figure 2: Bias of the lagged coefficients (normal errors)

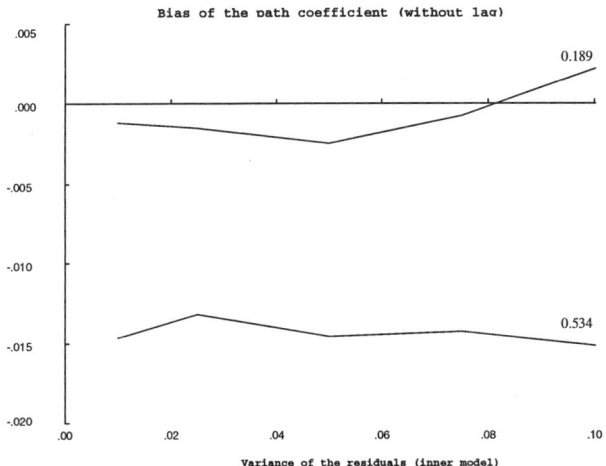

Figure 3: Bias of the unlagged coefficients (normal errors)

The main results are:

- The average of the estimated path coefficients does not change significantly with changing inner model error variances.

- The standard errors and the mean squared errors of the estimates increase almost linearly with increasing inner or outer model errors.

- The absolute biases of the estimated lagged path coefficients decrease if the inner model errors increase, while the bias of the estimates of the unlagged coefficients does not show any definite trend (Fig.2, Fig.3).

- The absolute biases of the estimated lagged and unlagged path coefficients increase with increasing outer model error.
- There is no clear tendency of over- or underestimating the path coefficients (Fig.2 to 5).
- The skewness of an asymmetric error distribution does not significantly influence the bias of the estimates (Fig. 4, Fig 5).

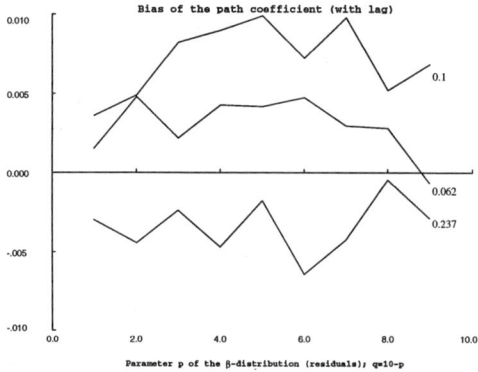

Figure 4: Bias of the lagged coefficients (β-distribution)

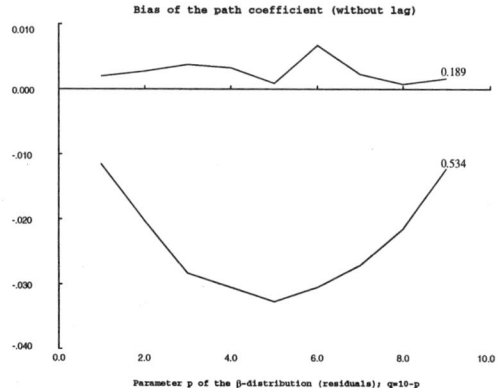

Figure 5: Bias of the unlagged coefficients (β-distribution)

4 Conclusions

Approaches to dynamic latent variables models on the base of ML estimations demand the definite determination of the error distribution. More robust methods such as LVPLS are not well suited to the particular structure of dynamic models.

DPLS (Partial least squares for dynamic path models with LVs) is an promising tool for exploratory analysis of latent variables path models with autoregressive and distributed lag terms. There is no need to assume a certain error distribution of the model.

It will be particularly useful for models with large numbers of MVs and only a few LVs. In these cases it provides models much more parsimonious than vector autoregressive models directly concerning the MVs.

DPLS model redundancy is an effective measure for model evaluation. The aims of modelling with DPLS should be data exploration and forecasting. DPLS is not suitable for confirmative or causal analyses of dependencies. Because of gaps in theoretical knowledge about distributional properties, significance tests are at present not yet appropriate for DPLS models. First simulation studies indicate that the methode is very effective in finding the true parameters given and that the estimates obtained by DPLS are empirically consistent and not relevantly biased.

References

GEPPERT, F. (1996): Bearbeitung, Programmierung, Simulation und Anwendung eines PLS-Algorithmus für einfache dynamische Modelle mit latenten Variablen. Diploma thesis supervised by H. G. Strohe, Universität Potsdam.

JÖRESKOG, K.G. and SÖRBOM, D. (1987): LISREL VII Program Manual. International Educational Services, Chicago.

LOHMÖLLER, J.-B. (1984): LVPLS 1.6 - Program Manual (Latent Variables Path Analysis with Partial Least Squares Estimation). Zentralarchiv für empirische Sozialforschung, Universität Köln.

LOHMÖLLER, J.-B. (1989): Latent Variable Path Modelling with Partial Least Squares. Heidelberg.

MATHES, H. (1993): Der PLS-Ansatz für die Analyse von Pfadmodellen; Mathematical Systems in Economics. Anton Hain, Frankfurt/Main.

PC-ISP (1992): Users Guide and Command Descriptions, Datavision AG, Schweiz.

STROHE, H.G. (1993): Weiche Modellierung umweltökonomischer Zusammenhänge; in: Allgem. Statistisches Archiv 77, p. 281-310.

STROHE, H.G. (1995): Dynamic Latent Variables Path Models - An Alternative PLS Estimation. Statistische Diskussionsbeiträge Nr. 1, Universität Potsdam.

STROHE, H.G. and GEPPERT, F. (1997): DPLS - Algorithmus und Computerprogramm für dynamische Partial-Least-Squares-Modelle. Statistische Diskussionsbeiträge Nr. 7, Universität Potsdam.

WOLD, H. (1973): Nonlinear Iterative Partial Least Squares (NIPALS) Modelling - Some Current Developement; in P.R. Krishnajah (Ed.), Multivariate Analysis (Vol. 3, p. 383-407), New York; Academic Press.

Part 3

World Wide Web and the Internet

Using Logic for the Specification of Hypermedia Documents

Ernst-Erich Doberkat

Chair for Software Technology
University of Dortmund
D-44221 Dortmund

Abstract: We describe an approach to the specification of hypermedia systems using first order logic. The static part concerning the document structure is described using Horn Clauses, the dynamic part uses Smolka's feature logic. The linguistic mechanisms for a hypermedia description language are outlined, it is emphasized that an object oriented approach is helpful.

1 Introduction

Even a casual user of the Internet observes that the way WWW pages are organized cannot possibly represent the *ultima ratio* in this field. This is so since these pages often appear as more than slightly chaotic, not indicating any principle of well structuring the considerable amount of information which is presented. Experience indicates that maintenance may sooner or later become a serious problem, quite similar to software that is not constructed according to the sound principles of software engineering. Experience also indicates that once program systems exceed a certain size, maintenance ought to be done through a specification rather than operating on the program text directly.

We argue that hypermedia systems become unmanageable, whenever their complexity is beyond a certain threshold. Although complexity is not measured in terms of size only, the size of a system is indicative of its complexity. Hence hypermedia systems exceeding a certain size should be specified first, and only then implemented. This paper proposes a certain style of specification for such systems, viz, using first order logic. A hypermedia system is characterized conceptually through the static document structure, indicating the static parts of a document and relating these parts to each other. This is done through a description of the document hierarchy (a section consists of several subsections etc.) and by a specification of what parts should be linked to other parts of a document. Although the linked structure depends on the document's context, the structural properties may be described by abstracting away the content. Again, this is similar to program structure: the program manifests its behavior through certain actions which usually are data dependent; nevertheless a static description of its structure captures its essential properties. It turns out that Horn clauses in an object-oriented framework are useful for specifying the static structure.

Browsing a hypermedia system means that starting from a particular position a particular link is selected and travelled. Thus the browsing behavior is characterized by a selection rule for links. Link selection depends on link properties, hence browsing is described through specifying properties of links, i.e. through link attributes. Feature logic provides a suitable description machinery for doing this.

This suggests three views for a hyperdocument: the structural view emphasizes document hierarchy and adopts a specialization-oriented point of view, the link-oriented view focuses on the description in terms of a directed graph which is built up through Horn Clauses, and finally the browsing view tells the user how to travel the document. These views permit custom tailoring a hyperdocument. E.g., the same graph may be travelled in different ways, customizing the browsing behavior, and the same hierarchic structure may be instantiated with different linked structures.

Several authors deal with architectural aspects of hypermedia systems and address the problem of navigating through such a system. The work on HDM Garzotto et al. (1993) stresses the analogy of hypertext and of software construction. Navigating through a hypermedia system is systematically explored in Furuta and Stotts (1989); that paper describes browsing explicitly by attaching a timed colored Petri net to a hyperdocument. Traversing a link is modeled as firing a transition. The *Content-Based Hypermedia* approach (CBH) by Grosky et al. (1994) permits the user to make use of metadata to browse through a collection of media objects. The metadata derive from media objects which in turn are based on images and videos. Depending on attribute values and interest, the user decides what to see next. In this way paths through the hypermedia systems are generated. Bieber and Kimbrough (1994) argue for a logic description of what they call *second generation* of hypertext systems. Link traversal is not specified by separate rules, the link a user may travel next is infered from the context at run time.

The approach proposed here is intended to be of practical use, thus we present the ideas in terms of a programming language called DoDL (document description language) - in fact, a prototypical implementation exists, which compiles a DoDL specification and a set of documents that fit the typing constraints into a collection of HTML pages. The techniques for this compilation are described in Doberkat (1996a).

The next section describes DoDL in greater detail, focussing on the hierarchical structure together with a specification of links. Then we discuss the specification of the browsing behavior after briefly introducing Smolka's feature logic. The reader interested in further details may wish to consult Doberkat (1996a,b), in particular with respect to evaluating a specification (i.e., generating a hyperdocument) and further aspects of structuring hyperdocuments using a device called **token**.

2 DoDL - The Basic Constructions

Documents are described as instantiations of classes, so that classes carry the structural information. Each document should belong to a class, the only predefined class is dbUnit indicating a persistent document taken from some outside repository. The pattern for a class is given through the following skeleton, each part of which is optional

```
class <name> is
      <other_name> with  -- inheritance is indicated here
      declare ...        -- local classes
      documents ...      -- local objects
      constraints ...    -- class properties
      browsing ...       -- local browsing behavior
end <name>;
```

Hierarchical declarations are formulated through the device of declaring local classes and instantiating them in the declare and documents section, resp. The constraints section formulates properties of the class using Horn clauses. This includes asserting and retracting links and attributes, the browsing section indicates how instances of the class are travelled. Documents are typed, the type indicating the class a document belongs to. Naming observes the visibility rules of black structured languages. Constraints and browsing sections containing logical clauses and thus adhering conventions from logic programming. Inheritance is hinted at in the pattern above through <other_name> with. The effect is that each of the sections in class <other_name> is augmented through the corresponding section in the class declaration under consideration. Note that inheriting means adding, so that properties of an inheriting class are extended (but not overwritten), yielding a powerful but conceptually simple approach to inheritance akin to the one realized e.g. in the BETA programming language. Finally it should be noted that we need to anchor links; the central abstraction is that of a *position* resembling an anchor in the Dexter model but disregarding any physical layer.

The discussion of the browsing behavior is postponed to section 4. Documents are bound to classes and have to be provided with values, which are composed through the composition rules indicated in a class declaration from primitve building blocks like texts, graphics etc. Value transmission is done in a separate binding section yielding a PROLOG program which in turn generates a directed attributed graph.

3 Features

Features are abstractions of properties, each feature term may be interpreted informally as a set of entities which satisfy these properties. This logic has been investigated by Smolka (1992) in the context of knowledge presentation.

A *feature system* $\mathcal{F} = (F, A, X)$ consists of a finite set F of features, a finite set A of atoms and a set X of free variables. Feature terms are constructed recursively from features, variables and atoms. Their syntax is given in the following table:

a	atom
x	variable
$p : S$	selection
$p \uparrow$	divergence
$p \downarrow q$	agreement
$p \uparrow q$	disagreement
$\bot$	bottom
$\top$	top
$S \sqcap T$	intersection
$S \sqcup T$	union
$\sim S$	complement
$\exists x.S$	existential quantification

(here $p, q \in F$, S and T are feature terms). We will use $S \to T$ as shorthand for $\sim S \sqcup T$.

A *feature algebra* (D, φ) is a set D and an interpretation φ such that each feature $f \in F$ is interpreted as a partial map $f^\varphi : D \to D$, different atoms are interpreted differently, and atoms have no features. Assign each variable $x \in X$ a value $\alpha(x) \in D$, then an assignment and an interpretation together yield the set-valued semantics S_α^φ of a feature term, e.g. disagreement has the semantics $(p \uparrow g)_\alpha^\varphi = \{d \in D; \forall e \neq e' \in D : (d, e) \in p^\varphi \land (d, e') \in g^\varphi\}$ and selection is assigned $(p : S)_\alpha^\varphi := \{d \in D; \exists e \in S_\alpha^\varphi : (d, e) \in p^\varphi\}$.

Identifying terms with the same semantics under each interpretation and each variable assignment yields a Boolean algebra of feature terms with subsumption as a partial order.

4 Specifying the Browsing Behavior

The browsing semantics is a description of the traversal of a document. Such a description should be provided on a sufficiently high level, it should integrate well with the specification of the linked structure of a hyperdocument, and it should address links through properties rather than as separate entities.

A formalism which describes the browsing behavior should address properties of nodes and links in a hyperdocument. Intuitively, these properties are closed under the usual Boolean operations, hence so should be their description. Thus the usual Boolean operators (and, or, not, quantification) should be available. In particular, negation is necessary: one certainly wants to specify e.g. that a user should be able to traverse a class of links which do *not* have a particular property.

A selection rule indicates what links may be traversed. Suppose a user visits a node, e. g., the target of a link he has traveled last, and should be shown now how to proceed further. One of the alternatives is selected, the current node is changed accordingly. Traversing a link may change attribute values: the user may be charged or getting credits for traversing it, or a counter associated with the link may change. Consequently, traveling along a link may lead to a reevaluation of attributes, so that the selection of links may change from step to step. Note, however, that the selection rule is defined as a static rule.

A selection rule specifies a set of edges that may be traversed next through feature terms. Since we bind these rules to classes, they constitute local rules (in particular, different instances of the same class then show the same browsing behavior). Features are derived from the attributes of nodes and of links, as will be shown now.

The structure generated from the **constraints** of a DoDL specification is a directed graph the nodes and edges of which carry attributes. More formally

$$\mathcal{G} = (N, E, s, t, A_N, A_E)$$

is an *attributed graph* with N as set of nodes, and E as set of edges; $s, t : E \to N$ are maps yielding the sources and the targets, resp., of edges. Attributes are taken from the sets A_N and A_E. They are partial maps, from nodes and edges, resp., to some range.

We will focus on edges, the attributes on nodes may be shifted to edges: a node attribute $\beta : N \to R_\beta$ defines edge attributes $\beta_s : E \to R_\beta$ and $\beta_t : E \to R_\beta$ upon setting $\beta_s := \beta \circ s$ resp. $\beta_t := \beta \circ t$. Note that these attributes also constitute partial maps.

Because of this construction we may (and do) assume that we have attributes on edges only. Associate with each attribute μ a feature $\tilde{\mu}$, then $\mathcal{F}_1 := (\tilde{A}_E, \emptyset, M)$ is a feature system in the sense of sect. 3, where $\tilde{A}_E := \{\tilde{\mu}; \mu \in A_E\}$ is the set of associated features. We will not use free variables, the set M of atoms is the union of all ranges. The straightforward interpretation (D, φ) of $\mathcal{F}_1$ is furnished by $D := E \cup M$ and by $k^\varphi :=$ if $k = \tilde{\mu} \in \tilde{A}_E$ then μ else if $k = a \in M$ then a fi.

Considering some examples, $(\tilde{\beta}_s : a) \sqcap (\tilde{\mu} : b) \sqcap (\tilde{\delta}_t : \top)$ denotes all edges e the μ-attribute of which has the value b such that $\beta(s(e)) = a$ and $\delta(t(e))$ is defined (where β_s, δ_t are derived from attributes on nodes). The feature term $(\mu_1 \downarrow \mu_2) \to (\tilde{\beta}_s : a_1 \sqcup ... \sqcup a_k) \sqcup (\tilde{\delta}_t \uparrow \tilde{\mu}_s)$ denotes all edges e which have the property that if the μ_1- and the μ_2-attribute agree on e, then the β-attribute on its source has one of the values $a_1, ..., a_k$ or the δ-attribute on its target has a value different from the μ-attribute on its source.

The browsing behavior is specified then through the selection rule discussed above. The selection rule in turn is a feature term constructed from the attributes available on nodes and links.

DoDL's inheritance mechanism applies to the **browsing** section, thus an inheriting class may add in particular browsing specifications through special-

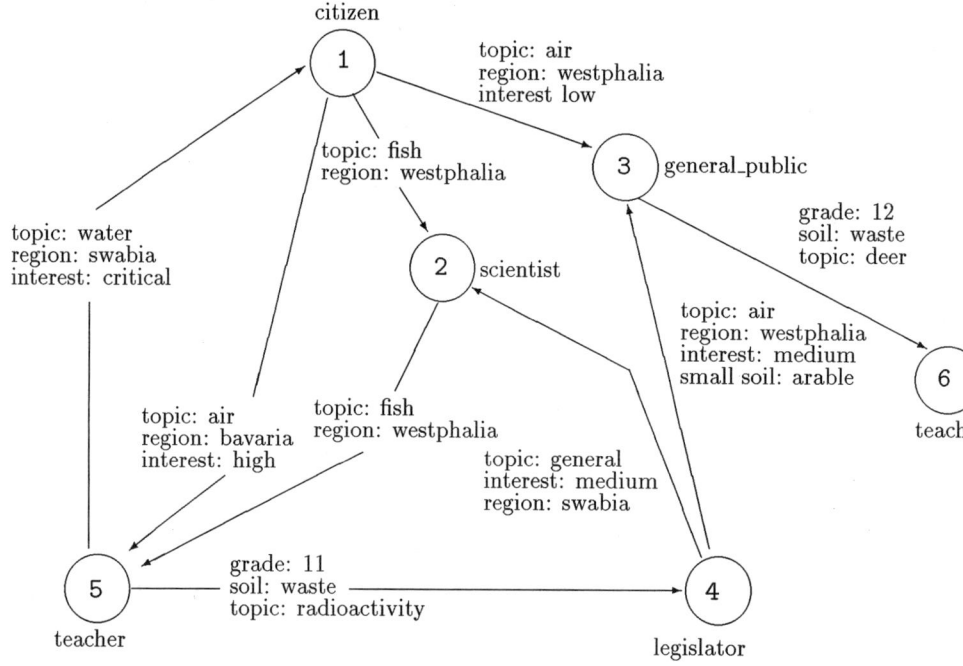

Figure 1: Graph for a Simple Environmental Hypertext

ization. In this way one class may serve as a basis for specifying a multitude of ways for browsing. Inheriting a browsing specification implies specializing it, this complies with the view of inheritance as a mechanism for specialization.

We will demonstrate working with feature terms with some examples now. The feature term $(window_s : \top) \sqcap (window_t : \top) \sqcap (window_s \uparrow window_t)$ selects all links for which both the source and the destination have their **window** attribute defined, albeit with different values.

Consider the class **Env** which results in the graph given in Fig. 1 when suitably elaborated. No browsing behavior has been specified for **Env**. Specialize **Env** to

```
class Env1 is Env with
    browsing ((citizen_s: ⊤ ⊔ teacher_s: ⊤) ⊔ legislator_s: ⊤))
             ⊓ (general_public_t: ⊤)
end Env1;
```

then this would select the links

$$\{\overline{15}, \overline{13}, \overline{43}, \overline{54}, \overline{36}\}$$

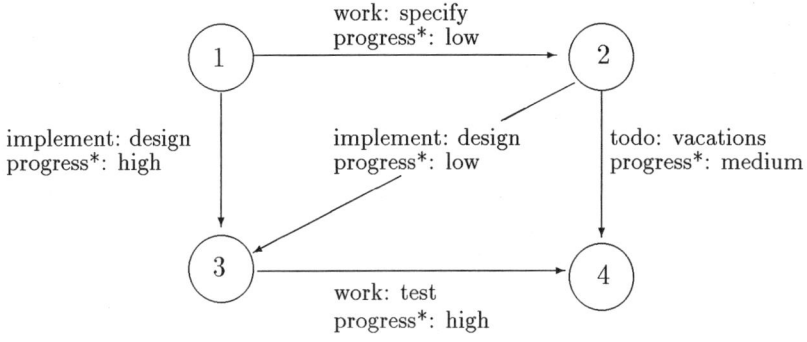

Figure 2: Dynamic Attribute Values

($\overline{ab}$ denoting the edge between positions a and b).
The attributes considered so far are static, so a dynamic evaluation is not necessary. Consider, however, the attributed graph from Fig. 2.
The attribute **progress** may change over time, thus a browsing rule involving it may result in different values. The following rule illustrates this:

$$
\begin{aligned}
S := \quad & (progress : \{low, medium, high\}) & \sqcap \\
& ((progress : low) \to (work : specify)) & \sqcap \\
& ((progress : medium) \to (todo : vacations)) & \sqcap \\
& ((progress : high) \to (work : test))
\end{aligned}
$$

Suppose the **progress** attribute evaluates to **low**, then

$$S \sqcap (progress : low) = (progress : low) \sqcap (work : specify),$$

thus the link $\overline{12}$ is selected (**progress: medium** selects $\overline{24}$, and link $\overline{34}$ is selected by **progress: high**). Consequently, it depends on the value of **progress** which link may be taken.
This example also demonstrates a useful technique for selecting links conditionally, quite apart from dynamic attributes. If an attribute a has the values $x_1, ...x_k$, and the value x_i should have the effect that feature term S_i is selected, then the whole selection may be described with the term

$$R := (a : \{x_1, ..., x_n\}) \sqcap (((a : x_1) \to S_1) \sqcap \cdots \sqcap ((a : x_n) \to S_n)),$$

since from the absorption law $S \sqcup (S \sqcap T) = S$ it is easy to see that $R \sqcap (a : x_j) = (a : x_j) \sqcap S_j$ holds.

5 Conclusion and Further Work

We suggest a method for specifying hyperdocuments using first order logic within the framework of an object oriented approach. We feel that logic for describing the structure of a hyperdocument and for the specification of traversal yields a high-level specification that is concise yet readable. Hence maintaining such a document relieves the author from addressing petty details, directing his attention to the structural aspects of authoring a hyperdocument. The present experience with DoDL indicates that it may serve well as a tool for rapid prototyping of hypertext systems.

Further work will address version and configuration control for hypermedia systems, an investigation of issues pertaining to dynamically changing attributes, and will finally address semantic questions modelling DoDL-documents through a blend of F-logic and transaction logic.

References

M. P. BIEBER and S. O. KIMBROUGH (1994). On the logic of generalized hypertext. *Decision Support Systems, 11:241 – 257.*

E.-E. DOBERKAT (1996a): A language for specifying hyperdocuments. *Software – Concepts and Tools, 17:163 – 172.*

E.-E. DOBERKAT (1996b): Browsing a hyperdocument. Technical report, Chair for Software Technology, University of Dortmund.

R. FURUTA and P.D. STOTTS (1989): Petri-net-based hypertext: Document structure with browsing semantics. *ACM Transactions on Information Systems, 7:3 – 29.*

F. GARZOTTO, P. PAOLINI, and D. SCHWABE (1993): HDM – a model-based approach to hypertext application design. *ACM Transactions on Information Systems, 11:1 – 26.*

W. I. GROSKY, F. FOTOUHI, I. K. SETHI, and B. CAPATINA (1994): Using metadata for the intelligent browsing of structured media objects. *ACM SIGMOD RECORD, 23(4):49 – 57.*

G. SMOLKA (1992): Feature-constrained logics for unification grammars. *Journal of Logic Programming, 12:51 – 87.*

Project TeleTeaching Mannheim - Heidelberg

Wolfgang Effelsberg, Werner Geyer, Andreas Eckert

University of Mannheim Germany

effelsberg@pi4.informatik.uni-mannheim.de

Abstract: The technology needed for teleteaching is widely available today. Interest focuses on the use of multimedia technology and high-speed networks to disseminate course content and work and deepen understanding on the part of the students. The Universities of Mannheim and Heidelberg are engaged in a joint pilot project to develop and test new technologies for teleteaching in a digital network. High-capacity multimedia workstations and PCs are linked via ATM to enable access over the network to lectures, exercises and stored teaching materials. The departments of education and psychology of the two universities are scientifically advising and evaluating the project.

1 Introduction

Inauguration of the new course of study in Computer Engineering ("Technische Informatik") at the University of Mannheim gave the final nudge for instigating the joint teleteaching project with the University of Heidelberg. The required courses in physics are currently not available at the University of Mannheim and the establishment of a faculty of physics solely for this purpose was out of the question. Conversely, while the University of Heidelberg allows students to minor in Computer Science in a variety of fields, the number of courses in computer science available is insufficient. Mutual aid was thus an obvious alternative. Generally it can be said that the University of Heidelberg and the University of Mannheim are predestined for such a cooperative venture due to their geographic proximity and their complementary spectrum of courses.

The main goal of the teleteaching project between the universities of Mannheim and Heidelberg is the improvement in the number and type of courses available at either institution. On the one hand, a broader spectrum of teaching activities at both universities is envisioned, while on the other it is hoped that the use of multimedia teaching aids (animation, visualization of technical calculations, 3-D models, etc.) will enrich and intensify the transfer of knowledge. Teleteaching aims to supplement rather than to replace current methods of teaching and learning.

2 TeleTeaching Scenarios

Several teleteaching scenarios are under investigation within the course of the project. In all cases the latest multimedia technology is in use, with transmission over an ATM high-speed network. The high bandwidth of ATM allows the integrated transmission of video, audio and data streams of high quality and in both directions. Thus the project also fosters development of further innovative applications for high-speed networks.

2.1 Scenario 1, Remote Lecture Room (RLR)

The initial pilot phase began with the installation of multimedia equipment in one auditorium respectively at the University of Mannheim and the University of Heidelberg. In each of the two auditoriums there is one camera focused on the instructor, and a second camera focused on the students. The instructor uses a multimedia workstation rather than an overhead projector. Its screen contents are projected by an RGB projector as a large image in the local auditorium. The transparencies used in the presentation are prepared for the computer. This enables the use of graphics and pixel images in color. Midterm planning includes the use of video clips, particularly animated scenes, the visualization of algorithms and processes, and 3-D models that can be controlled interactively. Later on, a second RGB projector will project the image of the audience in the remote auditorium on to a side or the rear wall of the local auditorium. Figure 1 depicts the Remote Lecture Room scenario.

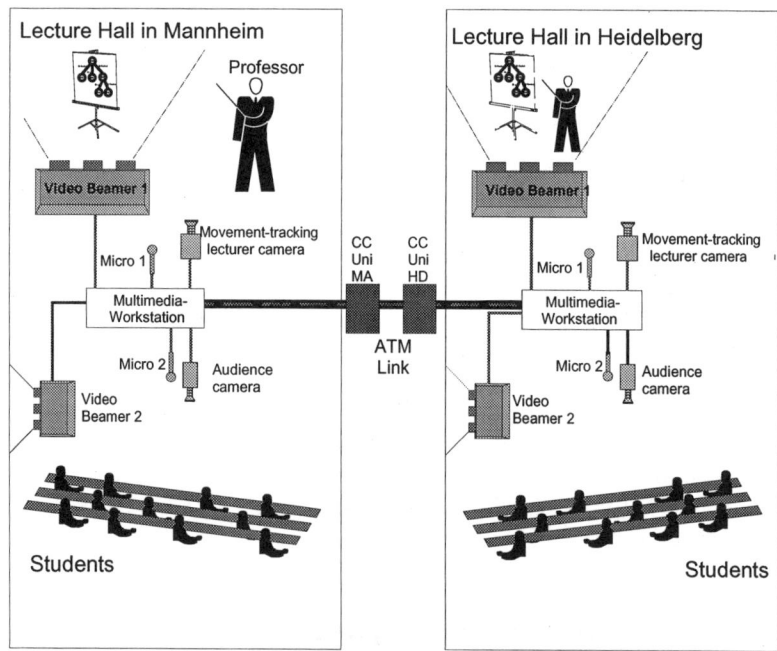

Figure 1: Remote Lecture Room (RLR) scenario

During a lecture, three data streams are activated and transmitted: the video and audio from the instructor's camera, and the "whiteboard image". At the same time, two channels will be activated on the remote end: the video and audio of the audience. While lecturing, the instructor is able to see the students at the remote site on the screen of the local workstation. Any questions they ask there are heard by everyone in the local auditorium. Students in both auditoriums are able to see the "whiteboard image" (better: digital lecturing board) as a large image. The same equipment (hardware and software) is used in the auditoriums in both universities, so that transmissions of courses can take place in either direction.

2.2 Scenario 2, Remote Interactive Seminar (RIS)

A small seminar room is equipped with a multimedia workstation and a high-speed network link. The transmission of the data streams is similar to that in the first scenario (RLR). Equipment costs are much lower, since it is much easier in small rooms to attain high-quality levels of image and sound. Advanced level seminars are offered each semester on an inter-university basis, whereby students will be able to engage in inter-site discussions. This scenario bears a strong resemblance to that of the traditional videoconference.

During the winter semester 1996/97 a teleseminar entitled "Digital Money" was conducted jointly by the universities of Mannheim, Karlsruhe and Freiburg in the RIS scenario. Each university was responsible for four lectures.

2.3 Scenario 3, Interactive Home Learning (IHL)

Currently in the planning stages is the Home Learning scenario, in which students can participate in lectures online from a PC via ISDN. Interactivity is available here as well.

The realization of multicast groups via ISDN poses a technical challenge. In order to efficiently support a greater number of participants, it is important that the network know the multicast group and support it with a protocol. Much work still has to be done to this end. Another challenge is the adjustment of the quality of audio and video to the various bandwidths. Hierarchical coding of video would be desirable, so that each participant can be served with the optimum bandwidth and quality of image. Unfortunately such hierarchical coding does not yet exist. And finally, new graphical user interfaces must be developed for the instructors. It is still unclear how to best present a large number of students at their home workplaces on the instructor's screen and how best to call on them, when they have a question or comment.

Figure 2 illustrates the three online scenarios RLR, RIS and IHL.

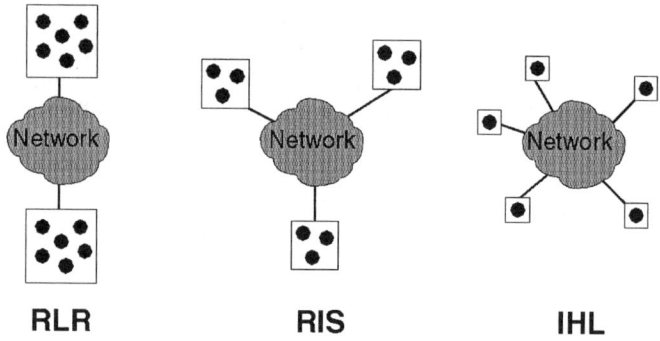

Figure 2: The Three Online Scenarios

2.4 Scenario 4, Offline Distance Learning (ODL)

Making relatively minor extensions to the equipment enables the simple (analog) recording of lectures for later digitalization, compression and storage on a large disk server. A video server will be established that will have an index of video recordings suitable for digital remote retrieval. During preparation for exams, the student can dial up the video-on-demand service and call up the material components to be reviewed. In the ideal setting, almost every lecture will have been "revised" after the fact. Errors made during the lecture or long pauses will have been edited out of the video. Additional interactive learning materials will also be available. A number of tools for the efficient authoring of multimedia materials "on the fly" are currently being developed at the University of Freiburg.

The preparation, storage and network-wide transmission of multimedia learning materials is not very well understood yet; many research issues are still open, for example the automatic indexing of digital videos, the optimal scheduling of videos on distributed servers, or real-time transmission protocols in packet-switched networks. (Bernhardt and Biersack (1994), Rangan and Vin (1993), Effelsberg et al. (1994))

3 Application Software

Application software used in the project is in the form of the MBONE tools, which are very popular in the Internet: sdr (Session Directory, LBL), vat (Visual Audio Tool, LBL), vic (Video Conferencing Tool, LBL and ICSI), and wb (Shared Whiteboard, LBL and ICSI). These are already in widespread use in the U.S.A. and an active user community sees to continual further development. By using Multicast-IP the communication with several end points can be carried out at the same time (Deering and Cheriton (1990)).

We consider multicast support within the network to be an essential prerequisite for the scenarios Remote Interactive Seminar and Interactive Home Learning.

4 Educational Support and Evaluation

Educational support and evaluation is carried out by the Department of Education in Mannheim and the Department of Psychology in Heidelberg. The primary goals are an on-going assessment of the learning success and the media-didactic advice of the educators.

Medial solutions to date, such as the exchange of videocassettes or traditional television transmissions, do not allow the "remote student" any influence on the instruction by means of questions or contributions to the discussion (Niegemann (1995)). The instructors lack feedback on the reception of their lecture and on any remaining questions students might have. Teleteaching can deliver a solution to such basic educational issues: Teaching activities are transmitted with the opportunity for instructors and students to interact. To date there is little first-hand experience in Europe with such a form of university education

An important function of the educational-psychological support and evaluation lies in the extensive formative and summative assessment of tele-activities and multimedia learning aids. Formative denotes the evaluation accompanying such measures for the purpose of optimization. A summative evaluation consists of the final evaluation of a measure with regard to the realization of its formulated goals. Evaluative studies in the course of the TeleTeaching Project are structured according to the evaluation model of Wittmann (Wittmann, 1990). This model permits a careful analysis of the efficacy of variables with a potential influence on the intervention measures. It connects research issues and goals with advance information on the users and frames of reference (predictors), questions as to study design and potential effects of measures.

5 Multimedial Teaching Materials

The accompanying development of multimedial teaching materials (video clips, animated scenes, simulation programs with interactivity, etc.) is essential; it is foreseen for all teleteaching activities between Mannheim and Heidelberg. Only in this manner can the potential for new technology be used optimally. Springer-Verlag Heidelberg brings important experience to bear.

Of particular interest are simulations that students can operate on their own. Volume models of the human cranium, for example, can be prepared for a lecture in anatomy. These can be rotated in three-dimensional space and dissected into their components, giving students a much more precise idea of space than that offered by illustrations in an anatomy textbook. Or, supplementary to a physics lecture on harmony oscillations, for example, there would be a PC simulation model, by means of which students could alter such parameters as the spring constant, and the damping factor and observe the resultant effects. These two multimedia learning aids already exist today and they deliver an excellent idea of the potential borne by new media in the field of education (Springer Verlag URL: http://www.springer.de).

The creation of such teaching materials entails an immense effort; experts estimate that approximately 200 hours of preparation are required for one hour of lecture time, in addition to the fact that most instructors have not learned to deal with the new media. While the writing of a scientific paper or textbook is considered part of the standard repertoire of a scientist and is practiced during university studies and in the preparation of one's doctoral thesis, the planning and production of an instructional video, an interactive hypermedia document or interactive learning software represent new challenges. Teamwork affords a chance to streamline the individual effort involved: Several colleagues, who all hold similar lectures at different universities, can collaborate, each developing multimedia instructional and learning materials to cover a subsection of the entire topic. A second alternative is "authoring on the fly": Video, audio and "whiteboard" annotations are recorded while the lecture is in progress. The raw material gleaned with relatively little effort can be extended by written materials and deposited on a server for call-up.

6 Experience

During the summer semester 1996 a complete course on computer networks was transmitted regularly from Mannheim to Heidelberg in the Remote Lecture Room scenario. Brief descriptions of our initial experiences from both a technological and an educational-psychological stance, as well as from the standpoint of the instructor, follow.

6.1 Technology Experience

Definitely positive was the transmission of an electronic transparency image with the aid of the shared whiteboard wb. This posed no technical problem at all and the quality received by the students was good. Audio quality was also very good, aside from phase-wise disturbance. Audio coupled with whiteboard annotations is of primary importance in transmitting instructional content in the field of computer science, whereby video is more important with regard to raising the social presence. The video image of the instructor was transmitted in H.261 format at a frame rate of approx. 16-17 fps. Higher frame rates were not attainable because the workstation had to do the encoding and decoding of all streams in software. The end systems, rather than the bandwidth of the network, were the bottleneck.

In summary, first transmission of a complete lecture was considered to be quite successful with regard to technology despite the minor problems that occurred. Modifying the routing of the network link between Mannheim and Heidelberg, largely solved the audio dropouts by the end of the semester. The primary factor for the success of future activities of this type, however, lies in the possibility of reserving bandwidth on the network.

6.2 Educational and Psychological Evaluation

Figure 3 illustrates the evaluation program carried out during the semester. Data were gathered throughout one semester by means of a total of four written questionnaires, sample interviews and participatory observation both on-location and at the remote site. In addition, advance information about the participants (for example, courses similar in content that they had already completed, their motivational structure, etc.) and for later reference, information with regard to their reasons for dropping out, was gathered by means of electronic questionnaires installed on the WWW. Data were gathered on motivation, concentration, comprehension difficulties, rating of the lecture, acceptance of the remote situation, evaluation of technical aspects of the transmission, etc. As an additional, semi-experimental variation, the instructor changed location midterm for a period of four lectures (moving from Mannheim to Heidelberg). Thus both groups, who differed with regard to the potential variables of influence such as course of study, advance knowledge, motivation and relevance of the lecture contents for examinations, could be studied under both conditions (remote and on-location). The interview intervals were (1) at the beginning of the semester (predictors), (2) directly prior to instructor's change of location, (3) directly prior to instructor's change back to the original location, and (4) at the end of the semester.

At first sight, both groups already differed strongly at the outset. The students in Mannheim demonstrated more advanced knowledge and a motivational profile more strongly oriented to the examination in that subject. This is not surprising, as computer science, the category of the lecture transmitted, is a full course of study in Mannheim, whereas it is an elective only for students of mathematics or physics in Heidelberg.

Of the 139 students participating in Mannheim at the beginning of the semester, 80 remained at semester's end. The number of students decreased continually over the course of the semester, whereby a sharp drop can be observed at the time of the instructor's change of location to Heidelberg. On the Heidelberg end, 22 students were enrolled at the beginning of the semester, dropping to merely 5 by the end of the semester. Here, a drop of approximately 60% occurred in approximately the fourth week of lectures. Results to date from questionnaires (electronic and paper) and interviews permit the assumption that especially the minimal relevance of the lecture for students in Heidelberg with regard to their examinations is responsible for the drop in attendance. In favor of this interpretation is that fact that

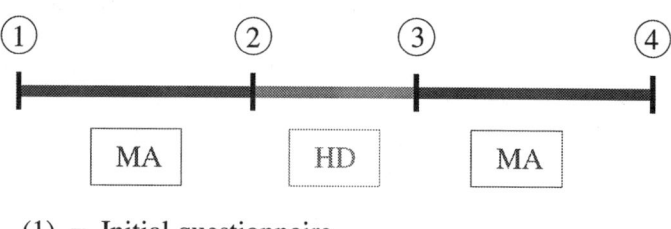

(1) = Initial questionnaire
(2) = Milestone 1 questionnaire
(3) = Milestone 2 questionnaire
(4) = Final questionnaire

MA = Lecture in Mannheim
HD = Lecture in Heidelberg

Figure 3: Educational Evaluation

neither was the teleteaching technology negatively rated, nor did the lecture fail to satisfy. Quite the opposite was true: data indicate that although the technical disturbances occurring at the beginning of the semester, among them particularly the audio transmission, were criticized, teleteaching as such was well appreciated on the remote end. Finally, the lecture was rated all in all by both sides as good to very good.

The interactivity (questions put to the instructor, etc.) was minimal on both ends, which was to be expected in a "traditionally" structured lecture setting with a very large number of students. However, the students did not seem to exhibit much of a need for more interaction with the instructor. In comparing both groups, it is apparent that students at the remote site felt less free to ask questions, which was ascribed on the one hand to the technical barriers (questions via microphone after prior handraising), and on the other to their uncertainty as to "interfering" from Heidelberg in the course of the lecture in Mannheim.

6.3 Instructor's Experience

There is little experience on the part of instructors in Germany with teleteaching; use of the new technology is unfamiliar. Interesting specific experiences can be described for the three media: audio, video and electronic whiteboard respectively.

The *audio transmission* posed the fewest problems. On-location the usual auditorium neck-microphone was used. The quality of the audio was generally good. Unfamiliar was only the use of the student microphones for questions during the lecture: while in the local auditorium, questions during a purely local lecture can be put without the aid of a microphone since the acoustics are good, in the remote auditorium the students had to make their way to the microphone or else had to be given a portable microphone. To have equipped all seats in both auditoriums with individual microphones would have been prohibitively expensive.

Use of the *video equipment* was made significantly easier by having a student aide to operate the camera in the local auditorium. Our experience shows that the instructor cannot carry out this job, since it distracts too much from the main didactic task.

In lectures on computer science, annotations on the whiteboard are an important means of communication (pointing, writing, developing small drawings interactively, etc.). Thus the freedom of movement on the part of the instructor is considerably restricted. In other fields, where the freedom to gesticulate and facial expression of the instructor are important, a camera operator on-location could be very important. We plan trial of *object-tracking* software in connection with a tilt/swivel mount for the camera; by this technique an instructor could automatically always be kept in the scene.

If the instructor has experience with computers, handling the *whiteboard* ought not to be too difficult. The graphical user interface is easy to learn. Particularly annotation (pointing, marking, framing, writing) is easy to learn and was put rapidly into effective use. Construction of small graphics with the mouse was also easy. However, the ability to enter and edit mathematical formulae was sorely missed.

The educational advisors in the auditorium ascertained that the concentration on the part of the students always rose noticeably when something on the whiteboard was developed "live". For this reason we recommend the increased use of *half-ready transparencies*, which can then be completed during the lecture, perhaps even in interaction with the students. A prerequisite is the advance preparation and availability to students of the (ready and half-ready) transparencies, which was the case in our project (via WWW).

In disciplines which use neither transparencies nor a blackboard, but primarily declamation, little difficulty should be encountered in teleteaching. A slight but manageable adjustment must be made by an instructor who is used to working with overhead transparencies (these can be loaded into the whiteboard as PostScript files), but who has little experience with computers. We expect acceptance problems above all in those areas in which the blackboard classically plays a role in the scientific culture, such as in mathematics, or in areas in which the PC or workstation are even today unknown entities.

7 Conclusion

Initial experiences within the project are very encouraging. The number of surprising and interesting results encountered in such a short time is amazing. Once the early problems with the audio and whiteboard had been solved, the technology posed few problems. The quality of video, however, continues to be a problem.

The educational advice and evaluation proved extraordinarily helpful and interesting. These constitute a central component of the project. Within the next few months we will be instituting a third scenario (Home Learning) and gathering new experiences. At the same time the development of active elements (animated scenes, video clips, etc.) continues.

For up-to-date information please refer to URL http://www.informatik.uni-mannheim.de/informatik/pi4/projects/teleTeaching/

References

BERNHARDT, Ch. and BIERSACK, E. (1994): A Scalable Video Server: Architecture, Design and Implementation. *Research Memorandum, Institut Eurecom, Sophia Antipolis.*

DEERING, S.E. and CHERITON, D.R. (1990): Multicast Routing in Datagram Networks and Extended LANs. *ACM Trans. Computer Systems, Vol. 8, No. 2, 85-110.*

EFFELSBERG, W., LAMPARTER, B. and KELLER, R. (1994): Application Layer Issues for Digital Movies in High-Speed Networks. *O. Spaniol, A. Danthine, W. Effelsberg (eds): Architecture and Protocols for High-Speed Networks, Kluwer Academic Publishers, Boston, 273-292.*

HOCHMUTH, M. and WILDENHAIN, F. (1995): ATM-Netze: Architektur und Funktionsweise. *Tomson's Aktuelle Tutorion, Bd. 10, International Tomson Publishing.*

MALY, K, OVERSTREET, C.M., ABDEL-WAHAB, H., GUPTA, A.K., KUMAR, M. and SRIVASTAVA, R. (1995): Performance Trade-offs for a Multimedia Distributed Application. *Proc. High-Performance Networking VI, Ramon Puigjaner (ed.), Chapman & Hall, London, 181-192.*

NIEGEMANN, H. M. (1995): Computergestütze Instruktion in Schule, Aus- und Weiterbildung. *Theoretische Grundlagen, empirische Befunde und Probleme der Entwickung von Lernprogrammen. P. Lang-Verlag, Frankfurt/Main, Bern.*

DE PRYCKER, M. (1993): Asynchronous Transfer Mode: Solution for Broadband ISDN. *Ellis Horwood, 1993.*

RANGAN, P.V. and VIN, H.M. (1993): Efficient Storage Techniques for Digital Continuous Media. *IEEE Trans. on Knowledge and Data Engineering*

SPRINGER VERLAG URL: http://www.springer.de *Available from Springer-Verlag, Abteilung Elektronische Medien, Tiergartenstrae 17, 69121 Heidelberg*

WITTMANN, W. (1990) Brunswick-Symmetrie und die Konzeption der fünf Datenboxen – Ein Rahmenkonzept für umfassende Evaluationsforschung. *Zeitschrift für Pädagogische Psychologie, (4)1990, 241-251*

WWW-Access to Relational Databases

W. Esswein[1], A. Selz[2]

[1,2] Lehrstuhl für WI, insb. Systementwicklung,
Technische Universität Dresden, D-01062 Dresden, Germany
http://www.tu-dresden.de/wwwise/

Abstract: After a general discussion of Web Database Connectivity this paper presents a concept for a transaction-based Web-frontend for relational databases. The prototype was developed in Objective-C using NeXT's WebObjects and allows consistent operations even across different database systems. The future work will focus on views, workflows, and user administration.

1 Introduction

Data management in companies normally was not designed from scratch, but has grown for many years. This is why a lot of different legacy systems with numerous user interfaces can be found. HTML offers a single interface which many employees already know because of the popular web browsers. Especially table-oriented views can be done easily.
The Chair of System Engineering explores in its Intranet-project concepts for a flexible information- and communication-structure in companies, and the possibilities for their realisation with internet-like tools. The present prototype uses NeXT's powerful tool "WebObjects" for the communication between the Web and the relational database management systems. The WWW-server and WebObjects communicate exclusively via the Common Gateway Interface (CGI), which allows the use of any WWW-server. As no browser-specific HTML-extensions have been used, any browser that understands tables can navigate the system.
The meta-information is retrieved from a simple data dictionary which contains essential information about the database: The names of all entity-types, the names and data-types of their attributes, and the relationship-types between the entity-types.
These data are available after having performed the analysis-part of the database engineering process, i. e. as a SERM (Structured Entity-Relationship-Model) (Sinz(1987)). The relationship-types are used for navigating the database. The user can navigate either to a view of the whole entity-set, or only to those entities, that are related to the entity selected in the previous table.
Insert-, update- and delete-operations can be performed by HTML-forms. In the case of a consistency violation, the operation is rejected with a qualified error message.
This prototype is the basis for further research work, esp. an automatic generation of more complex user interfaces from data structures, and the generation of workflow systems.

2 Dynamic Page Generation

HTML-Pages can be designed as forms and allow the user to send data to the server. These data can be used as input for scripts or programs. The WWW-server passes them on via the Common Gateway Interface (CGI) or a server-specific API (Application Programming Interface). "The Common Gateway Interface (CGI) is a standard for interfacing external applications with information servers, such as HTTP or Web servers. A plain HTML document that the Web daemon **retrieves** is **static**, which means it exists in a constant state: a text file that doesn't change. A CGI program, on the other hand, is **executed** in real-time, so that it can output **dynamic** information." (CGI)

Unlike static HTML-pages, which are simply sent to the requesting browser, **CGI Scripts** are executed upon request. The result of the execution must comply with the CGI standard and normally returns plain HTML.

To the Web server, a **CGI Wrapper** looks like a normal CGI Script. But its execution involves one more step: A CGI Wrapper communicates with another program before sending output to the Web server.

Some Web servers offer a **server specific API** (Application Programming interface). Programs can communicate with the server via this API and so improve execution speed by bypassing the CGI.

3 Common WWW-Access To Databases

WWW-access to databases is normally made possible through **CGI Wrappers** (cf. Figure 1). A CGI program gets requests from the Web server and answers them after communicating with a DBMS. The CGI Wrapper transforms the Web server requests into DBMS queries. The query results are transformed into HTML and sent back to the Web server.

These CGI Wrappers are all **DBMS-specific**. This means that for ev-

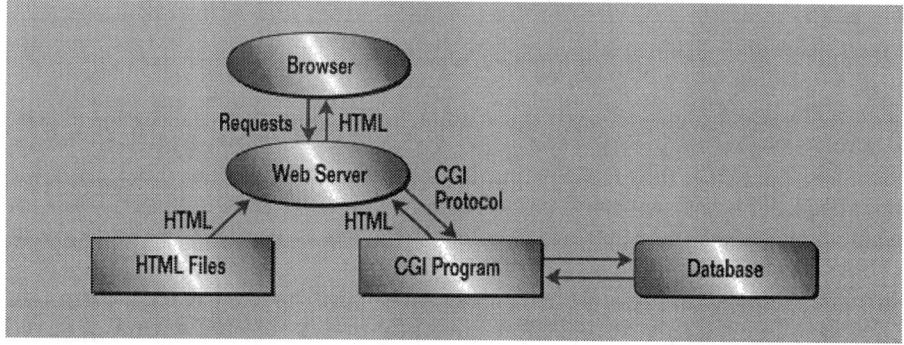

Figure 1: Communication of WWW-Browsers with Database-Applications (Frank (1995))

ery DBMS you need a different CGI program with a different functionality, a different syntax etc. Engineering of DBMS-independent Web-Database-Applications is not possible. So these systems do not offer a suitable platform for open information structures.

Most of the common CGI wrappers for database access **do not support the transactional concept**. This means that there is no way of guaranteeing that the database is in a consistent state after an operation has been performed.

Although some of the CGI wrappers offer support for PERL scripts or other executables, the **integration of programming languages is very poor**: none of them really integrates structured or even object-oriented programming (Pyung-Chul (1996)). So there is a need for alternatives that allow the use of software engineering principles and offer seamless integration of Web user interfaces and structured or object-oriented programming.

4 Transactional Access via Meta Information

Before a database is implemented, a conceptual model should be developed. The prototype assumes the existence of an Entity-Relationship-Model or Structured-Entity-Relationhsip-Model for all databases to be explored. They contain all the necessary information for the generic browser.

4.1 ERM or SERM

The (very simplified) model of a trading company will be used as an example: Customers place orders, and the order items refer to articles. The bills consist of bill items which in turn refer to the order items. Note the SERM cardinality, which is always (1,1) from right to left. From left to right, it is (0,1) for single lines, (1,1) for double lines, (0,*) for single-lined arrows, and (1,*) for double-lined arrows. Key inheritance always goes from left to right. The corresponding ERM would do as well but integrity constraints are less obvious there.

SERM Example

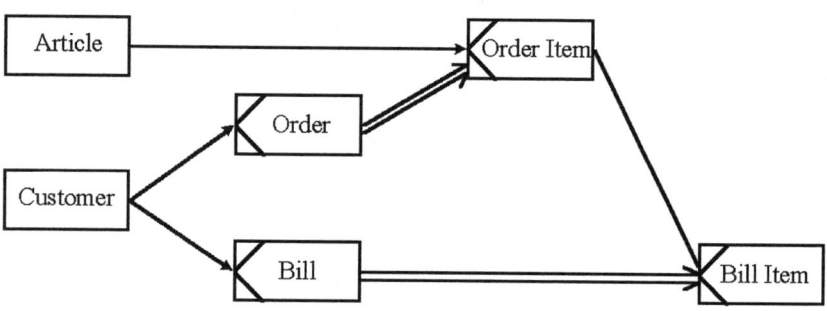

Figure 2: Simplified SERM Example of a trading company

4.2 Fulfilment of Integrity Constraints

The four basic operators Select, Insert, Update, and Delete must comply with the model's integrity constraints. Select is uncritical as it does not modify the data. For semantic reasons a modification of primary keys or of inherited foreign keys is never allowed. So update here is uncritical, too. Insert and Delete, however, may only be performed, if the database is in a consistent state afterwards. Here are some of the example's restrictions:

- An order item may only be inserted if the corresponding order and the corresponding article exist in the database.

- An article may only be deleted if there are no order items referring to it.

- A customer may only be deleted if there are no orders and no bills referring to it.

- An order may only be inserted together with at least one order item belonging to it.

As the browser only processes one entity at a time, the last item means, of course, that no order can be inserted at all. A more complex transaction would be necessary to perform this task. See 4.6 Outlook for more information

4.3 Notation of Meta Information

The meta information (= the conceptual data model) which is necessary for navigating the databases is stored in the form of NeXT's Enterprise Object Model - a textual representation of entity-types, their attributes, and their relationship-types (Next (1995)). The model was extended by some elements to be able to store SERM-specific information and links over DBMS-borders. The use of the Enterprise Object Model has several advantages over other specifications:

- The Enterprise Object Model is part of the software development environments NeXTSTEP and OpenSTEP. This allows applications to be deployed on NeXT's machOS, Sun's Solaris, and Microsoft's WindowsNT.

- Tools for the creation and modification (like the EOModeler) are already available and thus reduce the need for own tool construction.

- The elements of the EOModel are seamlessly integrated into Objective-C.

- The EOModel can be used directly for accessing rDBMSs from Objective-C via adaptors. At present adaptors are available for Sybase, Oracle, Informix, miniSQL, and ODBC.

- NeXT's WebObjects Enterprise allows a Web database connectivity in Objective-C via the EOModel.

4.4 Architecture

The generic database browser "wiseweb" is a WebObjects Enterprise Application and therefore complies with the following architectural model:

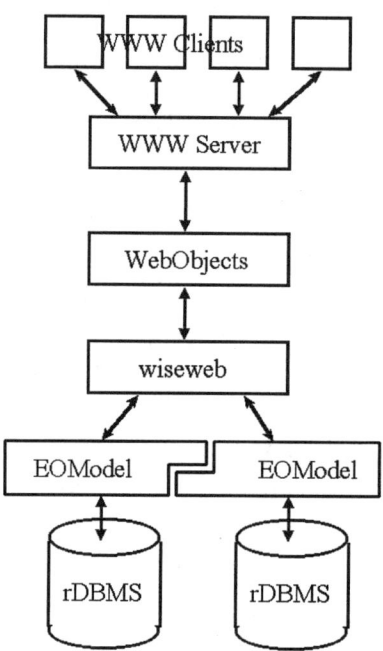

Figure 3: The architecture of wiseweb

The user accesses a Web server with a WWW-Client like Netscape, OmniWeb, etc via HTTP. The request is then passed via CGI or API (cf. 2 Dynamic Page Generation) to the WebObjects system. The WebObjects system handles the communication with wiseweb. Wiseweb performs database operations via the related Enterprise Object Models and passes the results back to the WebObjects system. Here they are transformed into HTML and handed over to the Web server which in the end returns the response to the requesting WWW-client.

4.5 Features

Wiseweb can access any database described by an (extended) EOModel for which an EOAdaptor exists. This means that as soon as conceptual modeling has been done, the databases can be created and populated consistently (with the restriction of the (1,*)-relationships). Or, if the conceptual model is created for legacy databases, these can instantly be navigated. Wiseweb offers a table view of entity-sets, showing the entities' attribute values, and links to their relationships' original and destination entities. It assumes that each entity-type of the conceptual model is mapped to exactly one relation (= one table in the database). Generalization is not supported yet.

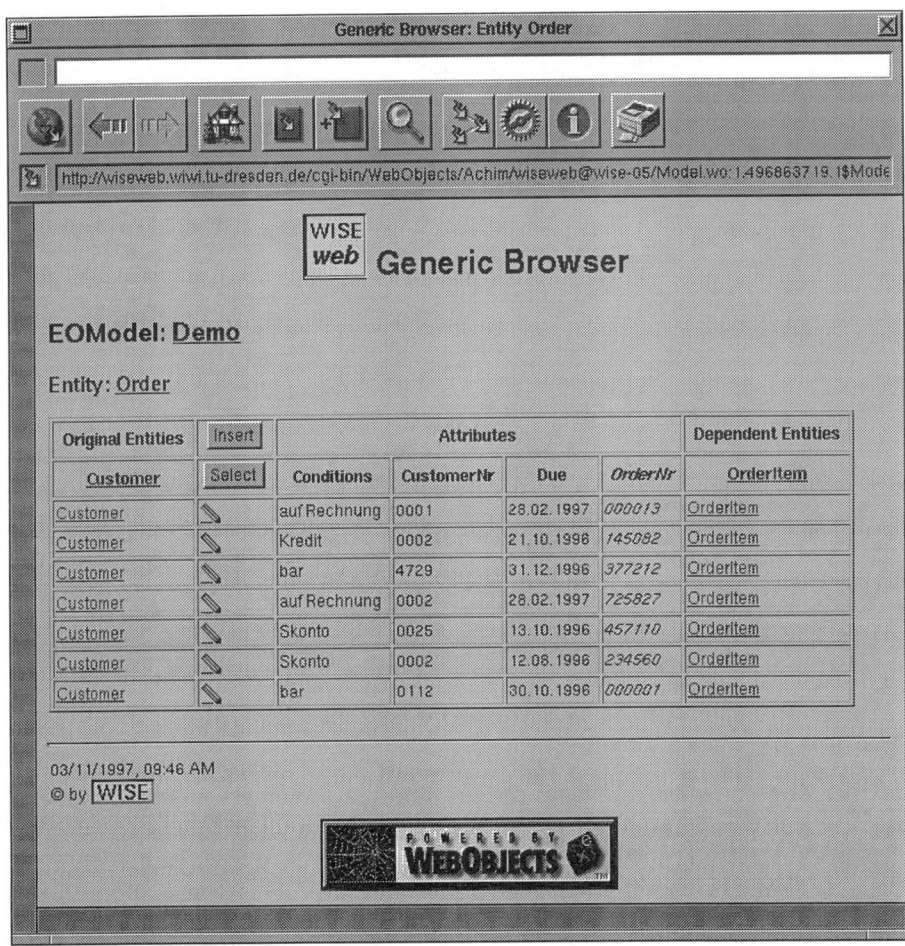

Figure 4: Table view for entity type Order

The user has several options here:
He can navigate through the databases on type level or on instance level. By clicking on an entity-type's name in the table header he can navigate on entity-type level. If he chooses for example **OrderItem**, he gets a new table showing all the entities of the type OrderItem. By clicking on an entity-type's name in the table body, he navigates on instance level. Choosing OrderItem in the second row, for example, raises a new table with the order items having OrderNr = 145082.

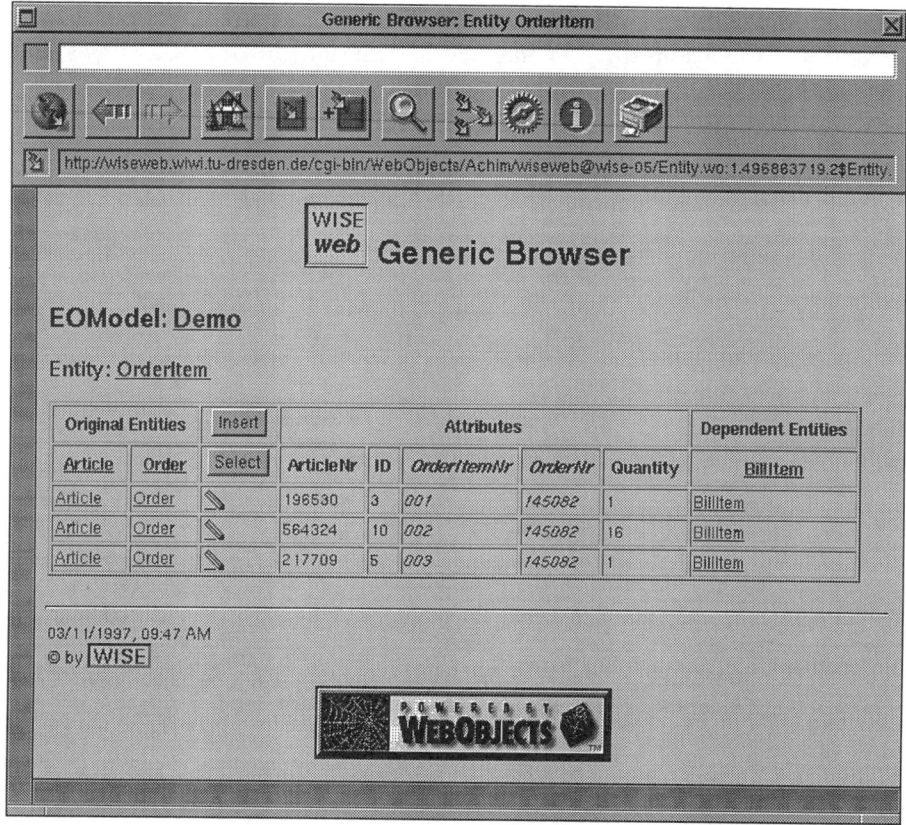

Figure 5: Table view for entity type OrderItem with OrderNr = 145082

In this way the user can view the original entity-types or entities (= the entities that are located left of the actual one in the SERM), as well as the dependent entity-types or entities (= the entities that are located right of the actual one in the SERM). The underlying DBMS is transparent to the user! In the example the user can choose the article of order item 002, being unaware of the fact that he now operates on a miniSQL database on host wise-05 instead of an oracle database on host wise.

With the Select-Button, a query by example can be performed to select certain entities for display (cf. Figure 6). The operators can be selected from Popup-Buttons, the arguments are entered in text fields. The query is stored during one session and automatically applied whenever this entity-type is selected.

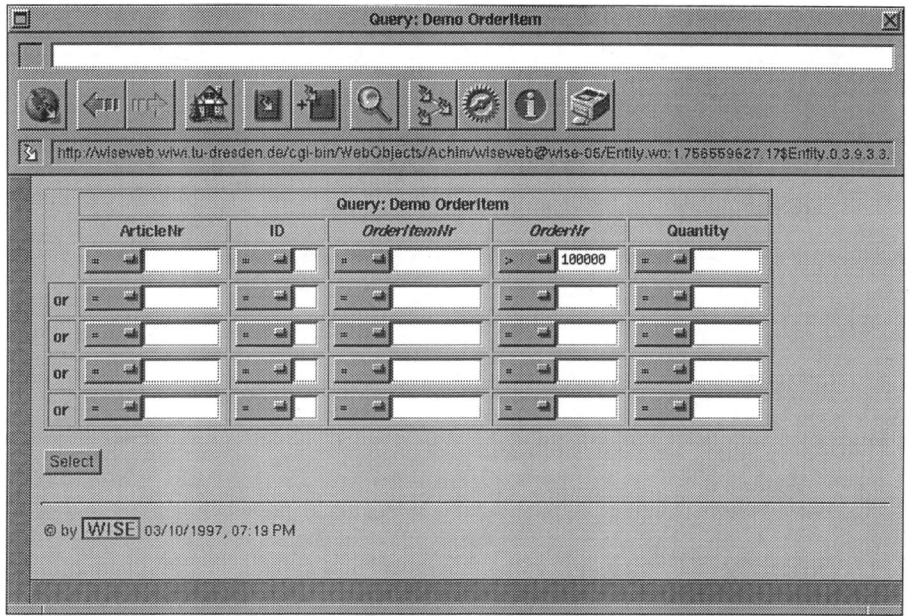

Figure 6: Query for entity type OrderItem

Insert, update, and delete operations are performed from a form-based single-entity window which is reached by clicking on the Insert-Button or any of the Edit-Icons in the table view (cf. Figure 7). For semantic reasons primary keys and inherited foreign keys cannot be modified. For example, a modification of an order item's order nr is not allowed. If the user ever wanted to do this, he would have to delete the order item and create a new one with the new order nr.

The transactional concept prevents integrity violations. If a user wanted to delete an order's only order item, the operation would be rejected because of the (1,*)- relationship-type from order to order item and a warning would be displayed. Or, if he wanted to insert an order item with an article nr that does not exist, the operation would be rejected as well with a suitable warning. Again, this integrity constraint is preserved even across database systems.

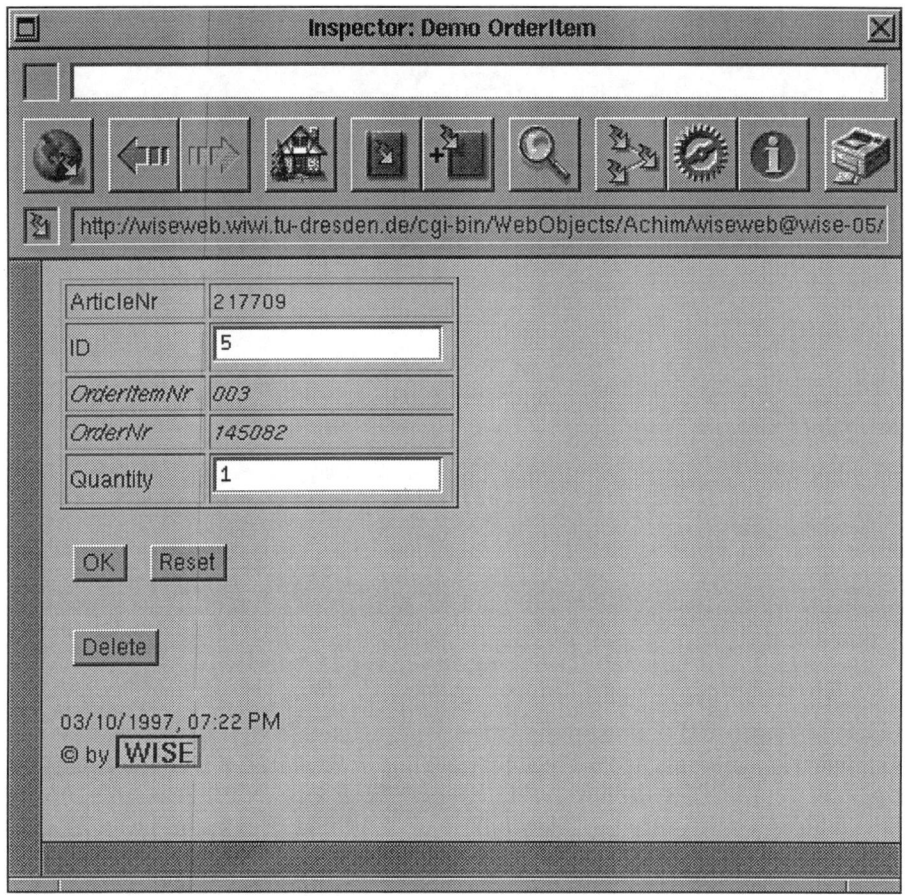

Figure 7: Record view for entity type OrderItem

4.6 Outlook

As we have seen, not all database operations can be performed consistently on single entity-types or entities. As soon as (1,*)-relationship-types are involved, insert and delete can not always be done with elementary transactions. So the next step in the wiseweb project is to allow the definition of views as parts of the conceptual data model. Transactions can then be performed within a view and thus include more than one entity-type, as long as a consistent state is guaranteed at the transaction's end. Such a view must include at least its root entity-type, the other entity-types belonging to it, the attributes to be displayed, the relationship-types included, and the valid operators. Tools for creating and modifying these views will be developed as well.

The views could then be linked together in order to represent simple workflows. The views and the workflows must have interfaces to specific logic and to other applications. Again, tools for creating and maintaining the workflows must be developed, too.

A flexible **user administration** must be implemented on four levels: the database level, the view level, the workflow level, and the user level. The functions available for the user are deducted from the rights on all four levels.

All these activities are performed on the conceptual level, but you can immediately go into the databases and work consistently with them. You will even have working prototypes of workflow systems with no extra programming and no additional software required on your computer.

References

CGI: Common Gateway Interface.
http://hoohoo.ncsa.uiuc.edu/cgi/intro.html, WWW 03/07/97

FRANK, M. (1995): Database and the Internet. *DBMS Vol. 8, No. 13.*
http://www.dbmsmag.com/f19512.html, WWW 03/07/97

NEXT Computer, Inc. (1995): Enterprise Objects Framework Release 1.1. Online Documentation

PYUNG-CHUL, K. (1996): WWW-DBMS-Gateways.
http://grigg.chungnam.ac.kr/~uniweb/documents/www_dbms.html.
WWW 03/10/97

SINZ, E. J. (1987): Datenmodellierung betrieblicher Probleme und ihre Unterstützung durch ein wissensbasiertes Entwicklungssystem.
Habilitationsschrift, presented at Universität Regensburg

Technology, Data, Relevancy: A Culture-Theoretical Look at the Internet

Peter M. Hejl

Institut für empirische Literatur- und Medienforschung (LUMIS)
University of Siegen, D-57068 Siegen, Germany

Abstract: The Internet is a medium that gives access to an unknown amount and quality of knowledge. This knowledge is, moreover, stored in several ways and distributed over several continents. As a potential source for problem-solving, this knowledge cannot be ignored. Clearly enough, the Internet and its users share important characteristics with other socio-cultural systems. Assuming this parallel, three points seem to be particularly interesting: the problem of access, the problem of meaning, and the problem of relevancy. My discussion of these problem areas first with respect to culture in general and then with respect to the Internet seeks both to enlarge the discussion and to substantiate a proposition that opposes the idea of an "information overload" suggested by the title of this conference. The proposition says: "Information overload" is a phenomenon of stress. It results, at least partially, from our insistence to cling to solutions determined by what we take to be the very nature of the object itself. As a result, we tend to ignore behavioral strategies that evolved to cope with relevancy problems.

1 The culture-theoretical perspective

There are numerous definitions of culture.[1] For the present purpose, the most helpful approach seems to be one that draws on discussions from evolutionary anthropology.[2] I therefore speak of "culture" to designate the repertory of generalized knowledge used by a population to inform its communicative and practical behavior.

"Knowledge" includes concepts or constructs of reality as well as norms, evaluations, or concepts related to what is understood as "rational" in (equally) culturally defined contexts. Cultural knowledge is learned and "spreads" via learning. Although cultural knowledge can be conceived as a specific level of analysis characterized by a certain autonomy, it is nevertheless related to problems of physical survival, of selecting mates for reproduction, and of social success.

1.1 Culture as a repertory of knowledge

To conceptualize culture as a repertory implies several decisions.

---

[1] KROEBER/KLUCKHOHN as early as 1952 analyzed some 150 more or less different definitions of culture. Their number has probably grown since.

[2] Cf. e.g. DURHAM/BOYD/RICHERSON, 1997 and HEJL, 1993b for a more detailed discussion of the author's position.

1. If the elements of "culture" are defined as knowledge-units, then the repertory consists of ideational entities that have to be distinguished from their physical substrata (c.f. "media") and from their "applications". As "application" suggests some degree of consciousness, it seems more appropriate to speak either of "instantiation" (e.g. scientific models or approaches to problem solving) or of "objectivization" (technical artifacts, objects of art, etc.). A particular painting, a book, or a scientific solution, is therefore not considered to be "part of" cultural domains like artistic painting, literature, or science. But, obviously enough, the cultural knowledge of these fields is required both to produce and to identify these "objects" as products of the art-system, the literary system or the scientific system.

2. Cultural entities are spread by "horizontal" and "vertical" learning processes. "Horizontal" spreading takes place among members of the same generation (e.g. in fashion), whereas "vertical" communication occurs mainly between parents and children. The agents of cultural knowledge are always individuals forming a society or groups within it.

3. No individual or group knows, or has access to, the total amount of cultural knowledge. Access to culture is always selective and subject to various influences.

4. Finally, conceptualizing culture as a repertory opposes the tradition that sees culture as a kind of system, e.g. as a fixed set of entities with more or less constant relations holding between them. Nevertheless, the repertory concept does not exclude the concept of cultural system altogether. Such systems are, however, seen as embedded in the larger repertory. Scientific paradigms, religions, ideologies, political programs, etc. may in fact be understood as systems within culture. Both their formation and their development might be explained using concepts like self-organization or self-regulation.

1.2 The problem of access

Cultural knowledge is passed on both spontaneously via living in a family system itself a constituent of a greater societal network, or through the action of specialized institutions like schools and universities. Following loosely the differentiation of modern societies, cultural knowledge is itself differentiated. Although there is a kernel of ideational entities everyone has to know and to use in daily life if he is to be accepted as a "normal" member of his particular society, there are other parts of the repertories that vary to a great extent between particular individuals. But, however great these differences might be, to participate in a cultural domain normally requires to meet certain requirements.

These requirements generally include the capacity and the readiness to act in a specific way, as well as the knowledge of a particular language or jargon. Both imply a set of shared reality constructs and concepts. Through reference to these behavior and communication particular to a specific cultural domain "make sense" to the participants. Moreover, joining a cultural domain quite often means investing considerable amounts of money to it and/or to achieve an advanced level of knowledge.

On the whole, participation in specialized cultural domains seems to be controlled by requirements and restrictions that belong to five not always clearly differentiated categories:

1. Technical, procedural, and especially media-related knowledge requirements. (What language is needed? What resources are required and how are they to be handled?)

2. Domain-specific knowledge requirements. (What knowledge is needed to participate in the processes particular to a specific domain and to distinguish between "relevant" and "not relevant" processes?)

3. Social restrictions (What knowledge is deemed important by those already "in" the system that its control is taken to be essential for the particularity of the domain (insider-outsider)?)

4. Judicial restrictions (What are the restrictions enforced by law for reasons e.g. of secrecy or protection of human rights?)

5. Economic restrictions (What are the economic restrictions that limit the access to a cultural domain?)

1.3 The function of culture

Culture can be understood as a second system of inheritance.[3] Through storage, transmission qua learning,[4] and transportation by media, culture allows living conditions to change much faster than biological evolution could do. As culture can change faster, it allows, compared to the biological level, both greater adaptation and innovation.

Despite this flexibility, culture remains related to basic biological and hence social functions. This can be seen if one looks at what attracts our attention or what we find beautiful or interesting.[5] Literature, the media, television production and, of course, publicity, are dominated by a small number of topics: (1) Sexuality, reproduction and love, (2) Competition, (3) Struggle for power, (4) Survival under difficult conditions. If we look into science as a

---

[3] Cf. BOYD/RICHERSON, 1985 as a major contribution on dual inheritance.

[4] Cf. on the ambiguities of "transmission" in the context of genetics, behavioral biology, and sociology HEJL/FALK/HENDRICHS/JABLONKA, 1997.

[5] Cf. the contributions from a variety of fields in BARKOW/COSMIDES/TOOBY, 1992.

cultural domain that seems to be rather far from these occupations, the dominating points of interest do not change very much. There are disciplines involved in questions of physical health, others try to produce knowledge useful to a better understanding of the world we live in and to exploit its resources more effectively. Finally, a whole group of disciplines, and not the youngest ones if we include theology and jurisprudence, is interested in understanding and regulating social relations. Even if a certain - culturally produced - disagreement about all this exists, these are the topics we find interesting and entertaining. Leaving out sexuality because science has so far practically been a mono-sex-domain, we have no difficulties finding the aspects of competition, struggle for power, and survival (at least metaphorically: "publish or perish) in the functioning of science as well, as sociologists of science have amply demonstrated.[6]

2 Culture and media

If culture is conceived of as a repertory of ideational entities, the difference between culture and media becomes obvious. "Knowledge" refers ultimately to the states and dynamics of our brains which, as organs, are involved in the generation and regulation of behavior. Media are means to store, transport and process representations of knowledge and of communicative events (thoughts, requests, indications, promises, evaluations, etc.). A media system is therefore a socio-technical system that (1) produces, transports, and processes medial representations of knowledge and of communicative events and/or that (2) produces part of what it medially represents.

3 Data and meaning

Although knowledge is "stored" in media, the representation of such knowledge does not carry its meaning like a backpack from the human sender to the human receiver. It does not "re-produce" by itself what it is thought to signify. The basis of all meaning in communication lies in a repertory of cultural knowledge sender and receiver of a message share. This repertory also includes partial knowledge about media and their use. This is the precondition for all coding and decoding in communication.

Because of its cultural knowledge the receiver identifies a message written on paper as a text and not as black spots. If he knows the language, he can read the text and eventually understand it. But what does "understand" mean? A reader attributes meaning to a message by establishing a relationship between the message and his own repertory of knowledge. As a result, we may say: As far as sender and receiver possess the same cultural

---

[6]Cf. as one of the classical contributions MERTON/LEWIS, 1971. Many aspects of science and technology as fields that participate in the controversies of our societies are presented in JASANOFF, 1995.

knowledge, the same reality constructs, and the same competence in using media, decoding will be very much like the reverse process of coding. In this case, communication will be successful.

4 Culture and media from a historical perspective

The importance of culture and media becomes obvious if we look both at European history and at the technological perspectives of our time.

The transformation of European feudal societies into democratic and capitalist societies involved profound changes in the production of knowledge, in the kind of knowledge people asked for, and in the access to knowledge. During the Middle Ages the focus was on religious and military knowledge. With the transition to early modern times economic, administrative, and technological/scientific knowledge became more and more important. In the Middle Ages the precursors of this knowledge were concentrated in the church. With the formation of cities a new social basis for this knowledge developed. The formation of modern societies with a more democratic organization of its internal functioning can be described as a parallel process with respect to culture and media. New cultural domains developed, i.e. new domains of general knowledge. At the same time, the criteria of access to culture changed from traditional orientations like descent, tradition, and faith to economic and meritocratic principles. Collective orientations were progressively replaced by individualistic ones. The individual as social actor entered the scene.

The central media in this transformation were paper and writing. More exactly, it was printing that, for the first time in history, allowed a massive storage of language. The printing press allowed storing and transporting encoded language together with scientific and technical notations and signs. Ideas, concepts, arguments, etc. could be brought to many people at a relatively low price.[7] Reading and writing became basic competencies to become a participant - a "user" - of this international network for the exchange and, not to forget, the entertainment by means of written communication.

5 The Internet as a socio-cultural system

Given this outline of culture, its social basis, and its function we can understand the Internet together with its users as a socio-cultural system. Its components are the users as far as they participate in the activities of the net as a result of their cultural knowledge and of the extent to which they

---

[7] The spread of Protestantism is linked to the use of the printing press as a mass medium. E. L. Eisenstein 1979, 1, 303 mentions that the 30 publications Luther produced between 1517 and 1520 probably sold in more than 300000 copies.

master the requirements needed for that participation. The organization of the system is given by the Internet itself that functions as the medium of mostly communicative interactions between the components. With respect to its type of organization, the Internet is a heterarchical or polycentrical system. The border of the system is simply formed by the difference between users and not-users. The problems of access, of the relation between data and information, and the relevancy question can now be discussed in this frame of reference.

5.1 The problem of access

To participate in the Internet, a number of technical and economic preconditions have to be met. They tend to be ignored both in the public discussion about the "information society" around the corner and, not very surprisingly, in the beautiful scenarios potential producers of related goods and services distribute so generously. To use the potential of worldwide communication via computers, the primary condition is, of course, the availability of computers. Moreover, they have to be linked somehow to form a net which can be connected to the Internet. This presupposes an advanced economic and administrative environment only highly industrialized societies can provide (cf. (Dyrkton (1996)). Finally, an advanced level of education is required. It allows developing technical and communicative competencies that are the basis of active communication via media.

These "fundamentals" already exclude the majority of today's world population. Even if we assume a rapid decline of the prices for the technical part of these requirements, it will last a long time until living standards have risen high enough to free resources for such an exotic interest like worldwide communication.

Another barrier are the technical competencies users still need for what is euphemistically called "net surfing." Surely, believing the claims of great software producers, their products are already so much adapted to the needs of lay consumers that "plug and play" is enough. But everybody who has tried to upgrade his favorite text processor knows that he may easily be confronted with a situation where he will experience the limits of his technical competence. Moreover, the "normal user" just cannot afford, and is not interested in wasting, the time required to become such an expert for computers, networks, and telecommunication that he can do without professional help. Today, however, computer experts still seem to ignore that users are normally just users - and experts for some other topic. For them, the computer, be it an isolated one or one that is connected to some network, is just a promise to solve their problems more effectively. The importance technical problems still play is demonstrated by the 29% of Internet users who work in computer related professions.[8] Moreover, in Europe, especially in Germany, a high percentage of users enter the net from their office. This

---

[8]The Internet Agency, WWW Nutzer Umfrage, Oktober 1995-März 1996.

suggests an additional important number of users who get technical support by experts via computer centers, etc.[9] Given these scant figures, it seems nor very risky to assume that using the Internet even in technologically advanced countries depends on the availability of technical support.

To use the Internet finally demands linguistic competencies. Although there is a certain offer of services and activities in greater national languages, English is needed to participate in worldwide communication. Hence all native speakers of English are privileged.[10] This might well be one of the reasons[11] why, at the turn of 1995/96, approximately 85% of the Internet users lived in the USA, Canada, and Mexico. Looking at the distribution of linguistic competencies in Europe reveals that the Dutch and the Scandinavians usually have a high standard in English, whereas South-Europeans tend to be less competent. The combination of linguistic capacities with a strong economy explains the massive use of the Internet in the Netherlands, Scandinavia, and Switzerland, all European front-runners in early 1996.[12]

Relying on my experience, it seems that even the linguistically best qualified section of the population, students, experience English as an obstacle to the use of the Internet - even after eight to nine years of English at school. But even so, the advantage higher education confers is important. A relatively high percentage of German Internet users have higher-level education. Fittkau/Maass report for the end of 1996 78% German users with the Abitur. A third of all Internet users in Germany are students.

Finally, all languages and cultures are disadvantaged that do not use the Latin alphabet.

5.2 Data and meaning

The Internet is more than just a worldwide data bank. But it includes a huge amount of representations of knowledge in the form of texts, web-pages that allow to identify authors, and, of course, data banks. In addition, it allows to contact users who eventually have access to the knowledge one is looking for. Only to access this knowledge requires already a highly specialized amount of knowledge. As a medium, the net provides symbol sequences or graphic

---

[9] According to The Internet Agency, 28% US Americans enter the net via an employer-paid modem. The corresponding figure for Europe is 43%. Fittkau/Maass report for Germany 21% Internet users having neither a private computer nor a modem. According to the same authors, 38% have an employer-paid access and 45% enter the net from universities or schools.

[10] The importance of English has some interesting aspects with respect to the relation between culture and media. If languages are just considered media, then the dominance of a particular language gives an advantage to all those who master the particular media. This advantage results exclusively from their media competence and not from what they have to say. If we assume additionally, that language encodes reality constructs, concepts, etc., then the dominance of a language gives an advantage to the culture that is expressed by this very language.

[11] Other reasons are, of course, the economic and technological importance of the USA and Canada and the sheer number of native English-speakers.

[12] DER SPIEGEL, March, 1996.

or audiovisual data. By relating them to factual or procedural knowledge, these data are transformed into information. Of course, every user controls only his part of the larger repertory of knowledge. As experience from work with data banks shows, we are not only inconsistent with our classifications but the meaning of words and concepts changes with changing contexts. In combination with the language problems already mentioned, considerable difficulties are encountered when using the Internet in a professional context where efficiency is important. These problems are amplified by the fact that most search engines, if not looking only for words, assume a logic of objective classification. Without denying its usefulness, this approach is often not very satisfying because it abstracts from the variety of practical goals served by the search.

Such general abstraction from contexts is apparently experienced by numerous users as problematic who use the Internet mainly as a medium of communication. For net-chatting as well as for tele-conferencing, the obligations due to restrictions imposed by the technical setup of camera and micro or by the medium of written language are felt to be disturbing. The "emoticons" are interesting in this respect. These little pictures formed by signs of the ASCII code symbolize facial expressions that appear in normal communication as nonverbal comments on verbal communication. Representing facial expressions, they specify, underline what is important, mark what is meant ironically, etc. Put shortly, they help to establish a context that makes communication more precise.

6 The problem of relevancy

If producers and users of Internet offers possess the same cultural repertory, coding and decoding of messages is unproblematic. But this does not yet solve the problem of relevancy nor will this situation be achieved in a near future. If we assume that the Internet will continue to grow, then there will be more and more participants with different cultural backgrounds in the net. With the Internet becoming more and more international, the decoding of messages will become more and more difficult unless a parallel process of reducing cultural pluralism takes place.

The angelic conviction that the increase in communication and the sheer "speaking together" will by itself solve problems resulting from cultural differences seems to be a mere expression of naivety. Conflicts are not only solved by talk, they also result from communication and the differences of interests, convictions, norms, etc. that are part of it.

But there seem to be other and perhaps more fundamental aspects to the problem of relevancy.

1. The model of encoding/decoding seems to be not complex enough to explain processes of communication

2. The mere growth of the Internet will aggravate problems of selection in an unprecedented way.

As Sperber and Wilson (1987) argue, in addition to encoding/decoding it has to be assumed that the participants in a communication factually claim the relevancy of their message for the addressee. Communication is seen as a two step process. After decoding there is a second step, in which the receiver of a message determines its relevancy in more or less conscious inferential processes. Based on assumptions about the economy of thought, the authors propose and discuss that relevancy is determined in that incoming messages are selected and evaluated according to the greatest number of ideational entities they will affect and with respect to the effort their processing requires. Relevance is hence not specified as a property of messages as such, but by its relation to cognition.

If one accepts these considerations as a starting point, one has to assume that, "surfing" through the Internet, we use cognitive mechanisms for determining the relevance of what we encounter, that are only learned to a certain extent. The reason is that we have to deal with numerous decisions in a short time and that we continuously encounter new data. To deal with them, we resort to evolved behavioral strategies that were advantageous to cope exactly with this type of situation. They are "switched on" when cues are present that signal the necessity of extremely effective selection procedures.

The selection pressure just mentioned will even increase if we look into the foreseeable future of the Internet. We might assume that only China and India had developed the scientific, technological etc. capacities that correspond with those in countries like Australia, Europe, North America and some other Asian countries. In addition, we speculate that the use of the Internet had started to stagnate at the present level in countries today connected by it. Finally, we add that the actual capacities of the net in its old parts remain more or less the same. Even under these extremely conservative assumptions the data offer would increase by a factor of approximately 2.3. This figure already suggests that, in a not too distant future, queries in the net will yield such high numbers of potentially adequate findings that neither our time nor our cognitive capacities will suffice to deal with them in an "objective" way. A situation might come when we will have, at least for some topics, no rational search strategies based on an "objective" analysis of the field we explore.

The English Biologist R. I. M. Dunbar argued in several papers that the group-size of non-human primates is a function of the relative size of their neo-cortex. He furthermore gathered evidence that the group size for humans to expect from these estimates corresponds to what we know about societies of a stone-age level. Of course, due to social differentiation, the development of corresponding languages, and media allowed humankind to overstep this limitation. But Dunbar presents a whole list of human groups whose size can be related to these measures.

Faced with the necessities to select, we do not "fall back" but quite naturally use strategies that belong to the older parts of our behavioral repertoire. They take into account that the basic problem of humans is not to know how the "objective world" really is but to survive in it. Here are just three of such strategies put into a maxim-like form:

1. Repeat what worked in the past. (We tend to stay with the search engines we know or with data banks where we think we got interesting results.)

2. Imitate the successful. (We ask experts and ignore to what extent they use the same maxims)

3. Keep an eye on important actors. (We take up the work and orientation of authors we think important or who hold powerful positions in the system to which our work is related)

That we encounter old behavior in the Internet is also underlined by the fact that three thirds of its users do not turn to the Internet for work purposes or in order to extract information on some subject. They are interested in the Internet as a medium of entertainment. Hence, we find more and more modes of presentation in the Internet attractive to animals relying as heavily on their eyes as we do: colors and movements. This continuity also holds for the topics that fascinated humans from the very beginnings: sexuality, emotions, fights, etc., and that have already lead to the formulation of various "netethics": Behind new technology is our evolutionary ancestry.

References

BARKOW, J. H., COSMIDES, L. and TOOBY, J. (eds.) (1992): The Adapted Mind. Evolutionary Psychology and the Generation of Culture. Oxford University Press, New York, Oxford.

BOYD, R. and RICHERSON, P. J. (1985): Culture and the Evolutionary Process. University Press of Chicago, Chicago, London.

DUNBAR, R. I. M. (1993): Coevolution of neocortical size, group size, and language in humans. Behavioral and Brain Sciences 16, 681-694.

DURHAM, W. H., BOYD, R. and RICHERSON, P. J. (1997): Models and Forces of Cultural Evolution. In: Maasen, S., Mitchell, S., Richerson, P. J. and Weingart, P. (eds.): Human - By Nature. Between Biology and the Social Sciences. Erlbaum Ass., Hillsdale, 299-326.

DYRKTON, J. (1996) Cool Runnings: The Coming of Cybereality in Jamaica. In: R. Shields (ed.): Cultures of Internet. Virtual Spaces, Real Histories, Living Bodies. Sage, London, 249-57.

HEJL, P. M. (1993): Culture as a Network of Socially Constructed Realities. In: Rigney, A. and Fokkema, D. (eds.): Cultural Participation. Trends since the Middle Ages. J. Benjamins, Amsterdam, Philadelphia, 227-250.

HEJL, P. M., HENDRICHS, H.; FALK, R. und JABLONKA, E. (1997): "Complex Systems: Multilevel and Multiprocess Approaches". In: Weingart, P., Mitchell, S. D.; Richerson, P. J. und Maasen, S. (Hg.): Human - By Nature. Between Biology and the Social Sciences. Erlbaum Ass., Hillsdale, 387-425.

JASANOFF, S. et al. (eds.) (1995): Handbook of Science and Technology Studies. Sage, Thousand Oaks, London, New Delhi.

KROEBER, A. L. and KLUCKHOHN, C. (1952): Culture: A Critical Review of Concepts and Definitions. Vintage Books, New York.

MERTON, R. K. and LEWIS, R. (1971): The Competitive Pressures (I): The Race for Priority. Impact of Science on Society, 21, 2, 151-161.

SPERBER, D. and WILSON, D. (1987): Prcis of Relevance: Communication and Cognition. Behavioral and Brain Sciences, 10, 697-754.

Self-Organizing Maps of Very Large Document Collections: Justification for the WEBSOM Method

T. Honkela, S. Kaski, T. Kohonen, K. Lagus

Neural Networks Research Centre
Helsinki University of Technology
P.O.Box 2200, FIN-02015 HUT, Finland

Abstract: Powerful methods are needed for interactive exploration and search from collections of miscellaneous textual documents that are available in the electronic media. Searching from text documents has traditionally been based on keywords and Boolean expressions. With the WEBSOM method a document collection may be organized into a map display that provides an overview of the collection and facilitates interactive browsing. Interesting documents can be retrieved by a content addressable search. The WEBSOM method is based on using the Self-Organizing Map algorithm for automatically learning relevant structures in the text and for organizing the document collection.

1 Introduction

The WEBSOM is an explorative full-text information retrieval method and a browsing tool developed in our laboratory. In the WEBSOM similar documents become mapped close to each other on the document map, like the books on the shelves of a well-organized library. The self-organized document map offers an overall view of the underlying document space. The user may view any area of the map in detail by simply clicking the map image with the mouse. The WEBSOM browsing interface is implemented as a set of HTML documents that can be viewed using a graphical WWW browser. The potential of the WEBSOM method has been demonstrated in case studies where articles from Usenet newsgroups have been organized. Some demonstrations of the WEBSOM are also available at the WWW address *http://websom.hut.fi/websom/*.

In this article the problems any intelligent information retrieval system must face are first discussed. The WEBSOM method is then described briefly. Finally, the motivations for the WEBSOM method are discussed in detail by relating it to the information retrieval and data mining methodologies.

2 Motivation for intelligent information retrieval

Modern information technology has not changed the basic setting in text document management: natural languages are used for communication between individuals with varying background, knowledge, and ways to express themselves. Different words and phrases are used for expressing similar objects of interest. Information retrieval based on keywords may fail because of many reasons including the differences between the authors of the documents. Some of the specific problematic areas are described below.

2.1 Inflected word forms and compound words

The morphology of analytical languages like English is rather simple and there are only minor difficulties caused by the inflected word forms and compound words. On the contrary, for instance German texts contain a lot of compounds that make a straightforward string-to-string comparison problematic. Finnish, on the other hand, is a good example of a language in which a single word may have thousands of inflections.

Typing errors degenerate the search results as well: the string used in the query does not match the incorrectly typed string of the text.

2.2 Variation in expression and contextuality

Ambiguous words and expressions in the texts lower the precision of information retrieval. The search term "morphology", for instance, may retrieve documents related to linguistics, biology, mathematics, physics, geology, image analysis, etc. Ambiguity might be described as a one-to-many relation between the words and reality. The reference to the world may also be graded, which is taken into account in the theory of fuzzy sets. On the other hand, the relation mentioned above may be many-to-one, i.e., there may be many ways for expressing the same idea. Distinct words, i.e., lexical items, have one or several basic meanings listed in the dictionaries. However, the actual meaning of a word in a text is determined by the context where it appears. Traditional systems that are based on keywords have no means for tackling this phenomenon.

3 WEBSOM method in a nutshell

The WEBSOM method and the browsing system has been described in detail in (Honkela et al. 1996, Kaski et al. 1996, Kohonen et al. 1996, Lagus et al. 1996). Related SOM-based approaches to information retrieval and data mining have been described, e.g., by Lin et al. (1991), Merkl et al. (1994), and Scholtes (1991).

The organization of documents onto a map is performed using the Self-Organizing Map algorithm (Kohonen 1982, 1995), in much the same way as any kind of data is organized using the SOM. The difficulty, however, lies in how to construct such numerical representations for documents (i.e. the document vectors) that they contain the relevant information about the contents of the documents. A rather commonly used method in text retrieval is to encode a document as the histogram of its words. In this representation, the information of relative word order in the document is lost but efficiency of representation is gained. However, in large document collections the vocabularies may become prohibitively large: the number of the "slots" in the histogram equals the size of the vocabulary, thus forcing also the length of each document vector to equal the size of the vocabulary. Furthermore, in the word histogram any two words are treated as "dissimilar" as any other two words. Thus information of, e.g., synonymity or other similarity relationships between words is lost. In WEBSOM, instead of using word histograms to encode documents, *word category histograms* are used. The words are clustered with the so-called "self-organizing semantic maps" (Ritter and Kohonen 1989), utilizing the statistics of the textual contexts of words to provide information on their relatedness. This way the size of the word histograms can be reduced to a fraction. At the same time the semantic similarity of the words becomes expressed in the closeness of the word categories on the "semantic map", and it can therefore be taken into account in encoding the documents. The basic processing architecture of the WEBSOM method is presented in Fig. 1.

Computational speedups have been developed for creating very large maps. In the largest experiments published so far (Kohonen 1997), the word category map contained 315 units with 270 inputs each, and the document map had 104 040 neurons with 315 inputs each. The number of documents used for training the map in the experiment was 1 124 134.

4 Approaches for document search and exploration

When investigating a large document collection it would be beneficial to have a set of different tools available. Any tool has its own area of application for which it is especially well suited. We shall next present an overview of a sample of different methods that may be used in searching and exploring textual document collections.

4.1 Information retrieval

In the purest form of information retrieval (IR) the user gives a set of cues, and the system retrieves a set of documents that best match the given cues. The cues are typically keywords and search expressions. In the extreme case the cue may be formed of the document itself or of parts of it. Then

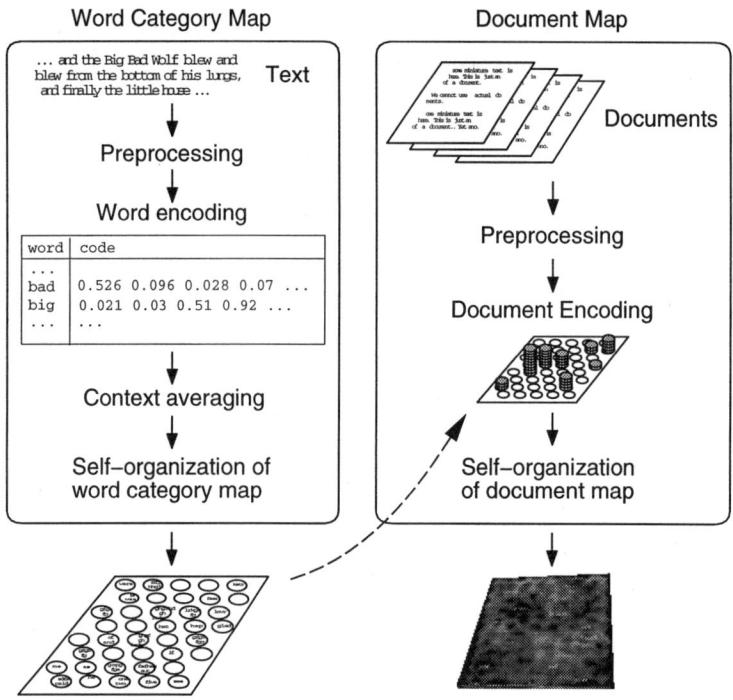

Figure 1: The basic architecture of the WEBSOM method. Words are organized onto the word category map based on the statistics of their contexts in a large and representative text material. The document map is organized based on documents encoded using the word category map. Both maps are produced with the SOM algorithm.

the retrieval system will correspond to a rudimentary form of a *content-addressable memory*. The system tries to *complement* the missing parts of the document.

The simplest keyword-based methods of information retrieval can also be viewed as content-addressable memories. In these methods the cue consists of a selected set of terms which the retrieved documents must contain; the system completes the rest of the document.

More advanced but yet quite standard methods allow one to join the keywords with Boolean logic operators. These methods may be seen to impose an elementary structure on the documents that are searched for, a structure that is expressed in terms of logical expressions. It may also be possible to search for documents based on *markup*, i.e. elements that have been inserted to describe the internal structure of the document (such markup is used, for example, in documents written using HTML language). These possibilities, however, suffer from weaknesses related to their symbolic nature: the problems related to ambiguity, contextuality, and variation in expression that were discussed in Sec. 2.2 are relevant also here.

4.1.1 WEBSOM method in information retrieval

The alternative route towards enhancing the capabilities of IR systems is to match the documents to some graded cues instead of the keywords. The cues may, for instance, refer to sets of synonymous words. The synonyms can be looked up from a thesaurus, or even learned from the text material automatically. In the WEBSOM system the word category map forms a kind of a thesaurus: the different word categories that are formed automatically may contain synonyms, closely related words, and different inflected forms of the words.

The WEBSOM system compares the documents based on their *word category histograms*, whereby the words belonging to the same category will be treated as synonyms. To make the encoding tolerate even more variation in the expressions used by different authors, *similar* words could be treated similarly. In WEBSOM this can be achieved by "smoothing" the word category histogram so that the occurrence of a word in a document will be assumed replaceable not only by the synonymous words occurring in the same category, but by closely related words as well, albeit at different probabilities.

There exist also other document encoding schemes which try to take into account the relations of different words in the encoding. In the latent semantic indexing (LSI) method (Deerwester et al. 1990) each word is encoded with a vector which reflects the co-occurrence of the words in the same documents. The vectors are formed by applying the singular value decomposition (SVD) to a matrix whose each column describes how many times each word has occurred in one document. The documents will thereafter be encoded as the centroids of the vectors corresponding to the words that occur in them.

Another related method has been used in the HNC's MatchPlus system (Gallant et al. 1992). No detailed empirical comparison between the quality of the different methods has been done yet. The WEBSOM has the computational advantage that the word category map can be computed off-line, whereby the encoding of the documents themselves can be done faster than with the alternative methods.

4.1.2 Interactivity

Information retrieval tools differ in how they approach interaction with the user. There are the "question and answer" tools, where the user has to learn a certain search language in which to state queries, and the system simply performs the given search and produces results. The next step is to allow natural language queries, and let the system do a little more work to interpret the questions, but it still just answers given questions. A more discussing and active approach is also possible. The system may ask specific questions about the query in a discussing manner, suggest synonyms etc. For example AltaVista, the Digital's Web search engine, has taken a more active role: based on search words written by the user, the system suggests classes of several related keywords, synonyms etc., by which the user may limit or broaden the search. This is one way to attack the "vocabulary problem", i.e., that the user may not come up with all the relevant, possibly synonymous search terms that are used in the documents of interest. In these examples the interaction is always textual. In approaches concentrating on visualization, also graphical or visual interaction is possible.

4.2 Data exploration

In information retrieval the documents will be ordered in a list according to the goodness of their match with the query. This is probably the best order if the query was well constructed and reflects accurately the material to be searched. If the query is not well-formed, however, the order of the documents, which is determined by the goodness of the match, may not reveal very interesting structures in the data.

When nothing is known of a document collection the only possibility seems to be to provide a view or different views to it. With a view we refer to any kind of a visual representation of the collection; the purpose of a view is to *aid the user in exploring* the collection. There is no reason why the view should be an ordered list like in the keyword searches; two- or even three-dimensional views where each document attains a location in the two- or three-dimensional space, respectively, are much more intuitive. In contrast to most information retrieval methods which treat each document separately, with the aid of such a view the document collection could be utilized in a more flexible manner. Instead of treating the documents one by one, the structures of the whole collection, i.e., clustering structures and other relations could be illustrated. In the WEBSOM system the documents become organized on a usually two-dimensional lattice which provides a groundwork for visualizing both the relative locations of the documents and the clustering structures in the document collection.

When nothing is known of the interests of the explorer, the data exploration methods should form an overview of the document collection using only a bottom-up approach. For instance, in the WEBSOM system the only essential assumption of the structure of the documents seems to be that they consist of words. The system should be able to construct views which aid in the exploration based only on the statistical knowledge the systems learn from the document collection. In the most intuitive types of views similar kinds of documents are presented close to each other. After something interesting is found, other interesting documents will most likely be found nearby.

Dynamic construction of different views, based on the actions of the user, would probably be the most versatile approach for exploring a document collection. One might want to change the viewpoint dynamically based on what has been learned from the collection, and as the goals of browsing become more focused during the browsing. However, there are two possible problems with dynamic changes of the viewpoint. For very small document collections consisting of a maximum of a few thousands of documents, different views can possibly be computed quickly. With most methods, however, the amount of computation quickly increases as the document collection becomes larger. Perhaps an even more severe problem is that for large document collections consisting of, say, one million documents, it will take a long time for the user to get acquainted with even a single view, no matter how well constructed it is. For these reasons, the basic approach in WEBSOM is to construct a single view of the document collection, a view which the user can become accustomed to while exploring the collection. The more familiar the user becomes with the document landscape, the more useful the map becomes as a tool for visualizing new information.

It is of course necessary to update the view of the collection every now and then, but the key idea is to provide the user with an intuitive landscape of the document collection. On the document landscape nearby locations contain documents that have similar contents.

4.3 Different approaches used together

Each of the different approaches used in information retrieval and data mining have their own areas of excellence. Therefore, probably the most useful approach is to use several methods together in a flexible manner. In such a system the WEBSOM is useful not only as a document browsing tool, but also as a platform that provides a familiar landscape of the document collection. The results provided by the other information retrieval and data mining methods can then be more easily understood by referring to the document landscape provided by the WEBSOM. Results of more classical information retrieval methods, for instance keyword searches, can be visualized on the WEBSOM document map: the map nodes can for instance be colored according to how many matching documents the node contains, and the user can then interpret the results easily based on the map display. Furthermore, true content-addressable search can be implemented simply by encoding the document used as the query in the same manner as the documents in the collection have been encoded, and thereafter positioning the query on the map. Similar documents are then found in the nearby map locations.

References

DEERWESTER, S., DUMAIS, S.T., FURNAS, G.W., and LANDAUER, K.T. (1990): Indexing by latent semantic analysis. *Journal of the American Society for Information Science, 41, 391-407.*

GALLANT, S.I., CAID, W.R., CARLETON, J., HECHT-NIELSEN, R., PU QING, K., and SUDBECK, D. (1992): HNC's MatchPlus System. *ACM SIGIR Forum, 26, 2, 34-38.*

HONKELA, T., KASKI, S., LAGUS, K., and KOHONEN, T. (1996): Newsgroup Exploration with WEBSOM Method and Browsing Interface. Technical Report A32, Helsinki University of Technology, Laboratory of Computer and Information Science, Espoo, Finland.

KASKI, S., HONKELA, T., LAGUS, K., and KOHONEN, T. (1996): Creating an Order in Digital Libraries with Self-Organizing Maps. *Proc. of WCNN'96, World Congress on Neural Networks,* Lawrence Erlbaum and INNS Press, Mahwah, NJ, 814-817.

KOHONEN, T. (1982): Self-Organized Formation of Topologically Correct Feature Maps. *Biological Cybernetics, 43, 59-69.*

KOHONEN, T. (1995): *Self-Organizing Maps.* Springer, Heidelberg.

KOHONEN, T. (1997): Exploration of very large databases by self-organizing maps. *Proc. ICNN'97, International Conference on Neural Networks,* IEEE Service Center, Piscataway, NJ, PL1-PL6.

KOHONEN, T., KASKI, S., LAGUS, K., and HONKELA, T. (1996): Very Large Two-Level SOM for the Browsing of Newsgroups *Proc. ICANN'96, International Conference on Artificial Neural Networks,* Springer, Berlin, 269-274.

LAGUS, K., HONKELA, T. KASKI, S., and KOHONEN, T. (1996): Self-Organizing Maps of Document Collections: A New Approach to Interactive Exploration. *Proc. KDD'96, 2nd Int. Conf. on Knowledge Discovery and Data Mining,* AAAI Press, Menlo Park, CA, 238-243.

LIN, X., SOERGEL, D., and MARCHIONINI, G. (1991): A self-organizing semantic map for information retrieval. *Proc. 14th Ann. Int. ACM/SIGIR Conf. on R & D in Information Retrieval, 262-269.*

MERKL, D., TJOA, A. M., and KAPPEL, G. (1994): A self-organizing map that learns the semantic similarity of reusable software components. *Proc. ACNN'94, 5th Australian Conf. on Neural Networks, 13-16.*

RITTER, H. and KOHONEN, T. (1989): Self-organizing semantic maps. *Biological Cybernetics, 61, 241-254.*

SCHOLTES, J. C. (1991): Unsupervised learning and the information retrieval problem. *Proc. IJCNN'91, Int. Joint Conf. on Neural Networks,* IEEE Service Center, Piscataway, NJ, 18-21.

Segment–Specific Aspects of Designing Online Services in the Internet

T. Klein, W. Gaul, F. Wartenberg

Institut für Entscheidungstheorie und Unternehmensforschung,
Universität Karlsruhe (TH), D-76128 Karlsruhe, Germany

Abstract: The success of Internet services depends on, e.g., the identification and description of relevant user segments and efforts to establish segment-specific attraction. In contrast to other Internet surveys the approach discussed here takes into consideration behavioral aspects of potential users related to the design of online services in the World Wide Web (Web for short). Preference data have been collected using a technical realization of online pairwise comparisons of selected homepages together with association data concerning indicators for homepage valuation and data on attitudes towards Web site features. Segment-specific results concerning Web site design aspects will be reported.

1 Introduction

In an empirical study the analysis of association data concerning indicators for homepage valuation, of attitudes and preferences of Internet users, and their active behavior concerning online services is taken into consideration to identify relevant dimensions for designing Web sites within different user segments. Aspects of *advertising effectiveness* which are traditionally founded on a passive one-to-many communication model of mass media are used together with Web site features to explain what could be called *online effectiveness* of Internet services. The research goals can be described as follows: (1) identification of relevant dimensions for the valuation of online services in the Web, (2) identification of user segments with similar attitudes and wishes, and (3) derivation of segment-specific characteristics for the description of segments identified.

2 Aspects of Designing Web Sites

Considering the Internet and especially the Web as an information and communication tool for marketing activities, questions concerning the creation of attractive and effective online services become more and more important. To get some clues for an optimal configuration, it is helpful to compare first–time Web site contacts with "normal" advertising contacts in such a medium. Positive attitudes towards such a service may be caused if users follow available hyperlinks or repeatedly visit the corresponding Web site. Therefore, successful attempts to make first–time visitors to activate further hyperlinks can be interpreted as indicators for a main goal of offering commercial Web sites: Turning first–time visitors to regular users. This kind of success can be used for a definition of *online effectiveness* of a Web site. Of course, it appears difficult to measure such a phenomenon but there are at least two ways to increase online effectiveness: First, by an attractive design of the homepage (which – in most cases – constitutes the initial contact page) "consumers" are motivated to activate hyperlinks on this Web site. Second, by providing appropriate benefits (which can be very different and depend on the special online service) "customers" are attracted to come back. We will concentrate on the first aspect and regard the initiation of point–and–click operations as an important goal of a Web site. In this context the question remains which possibly unknown dimensions underlying the design of a Web site influence online effectiveness.

To get useful indicators for such dimensions a closer look to Web-specific aspects for designing online services is of interest. Tab. 1 gives an overview over important characteristics, their essentials, and possible recommendations that have to be taken into account within the process of designing Web sites (see, e.g., Angell and Heslop (1995), Bornman and v. Solms (1993), Krol (1994)). The multimedia ability of the Web offers a variety of design features. Especially the intensified usage of images and graphical elements may lead to a different valuation of Web sites by users who have, e.g., the restricted bandwidth of customary internet connections in mind.

Characteristics	Essentials	Recommendations
client-server-architecture	active selection of information desired	incorporation of affective and cognitive pull-elements
dynamic distributed network	access to different information resources	incorporation of network navigation support facilities
integration of services	email, news, ftp, telnet, internet relay chat, ...	incorporation of the most important internet services
multimedia ability	text, images, graphic, sound, video	consideration of variable degrees of technical pretension
international scope	different language versions	target group specific adaption of cultural aspects
availability of contents	time- and space-independent call of service functions	guaranty of service quality and information actuality
hypermedia CMEs[1], interactive access and communication	hypertext and hypergraphic, machine and person interactivity	appropriate representation of the non-linear structure of information flow, consideration of the depth of interactions

Tab. 1: Characteristics, essentials, and recommendations concerning Web site design aspects

---

[1]Hoffman and Novak (1996) define a hypermedia *computer-mediated environment* (CME) in a summarizing way as a "dynamic distributed network, potentially global in scope, together with associated hardware and software for accessing the network, which enables consumers and firms to (1) provide and interactively access hypermedia content (i.e. "machine interactivity") and (2) communicate through the medium (i.e. "person interactivity")."

For further classification it is helpful to divide the whole design process into different levels. On a technical level, system-specific features of the hard- and software environment, e.g., performance and compatibility with respect to browsers, are normally perceived by users in an indirect way. On a representation level, the visual and therefore directly perceivable design can be composed of the following main components: optical design (on a perception level), content design (on a context level), and interactive design (on a navigation and communication level) (see, e.g., Resch (1996, p. 151) for a similar classification).

Optical design is closest to the design of classical media such as print ads or television spots. As users navigate through the Web resp. a single Web site using point-and-click motions, which are available via appropriate navigation elements, interactive design builds the new and most exciting component. Therefore, visualization of navigation structures on the representation level is of importance. Furthermore, a valuation of navigation elements together with optical design features delivers precious hints, whether a user would activate further links or not. In Tab. 2 a classification of Web site features which should be taken into consideration (see, e.g., Alpar (1996, p. 142) for a general listing of such features) is given.

Web Site Features	Description	Examples
design features	directly perceivable features rather without content relation	usage of images and graphical elements, text and background colours, ... for optical upgrading
entertaining features	directly perceivable features with content relation	usage of images and graphical elements for advancing the reception of information, animations, multimedia, ...
navigation features	directly perceivable features with navigation functions	usage of symbols resp. navigation bars, imagemaps, internal search functions, ... for navigation support
structural features	indirectly perceivable meta-features with orientation functions	usage of images, lists and tables, headings, ... for structuring pages

Tab. 2: Classification of Web site features on the representation level

A main problem with respect to designing online offers in the Internet arises from the various possibilities of creating just a single page resp. a complete Web site and from the different preferences and attitudes of users towards single Web site features. Thus, the goal to identify relevant dimensions for valuating Web sites has to be combined with an appropriate classification of user segments with similar preferences and attitudes.

Of course, aspects of *advertising effectiveness* have to be incorporated into the analysis in order to achieve reliable results. Based on the construct *attitude towards ads*, which is similar to *acceptance of ads* (see, e.g., Neibecker (1990) for a detailed discussion), stable dimensions for measuring advertising effectiveness and corresponding indicators are known for quite some time, e.g., liking, credibility, information content, attention, and degree of innovation (see Kroeber-Riel et al. (1977)) or entertainment, personal importance, displeasure, and warmth (see Aaker and Bruzzone (1981)). The "hierarchy-of-effects order of the single-item best measures" for predicting ad's sales effectiveness leads to some additional dimensions for online effectiveness, e.g., preference and buying intention (see Rossiter and Eagelson (1994)). Especially the measure buying intention can be transferred to the online situation when the "purchase" of a Web page is interpreted as activating a link on it.

3 Research Design

A detailed description of the study will be given in the following. The research goals – formulated in the introduction – can be motivated further by the questions (1) "Which Web site features contribute to a positive attitude towards online design of Web pages?", (2) "Which Web site features increase the probability of activating further hyperlinks?", and (3) "Is it possible to find segment specific differences concerning questions (1) and (2)?". The objects in our study are so-called homepages (the central starting point into a Web site – only in exceptional cases users enter a Web site via an external link or a bookmark not using the homepage). Obviously, an understanding of "consumer behaviour" is crucial for the success of designing a Web site as a whole. To achieve appropriate judgements the platform of the empirical study was the Web itself. Hyperlinks to our online questionaire have been placed at different locations – especially, on multiplicator services like search engines – to increase the chances for the survey to be based on a representative sample. It was embedded into the so-called *Karlsruher Marktplatz* (see Gaul, Klein, Wartenberg (1997)), an integrative platform with heterogeneous services and predominant regional content. Thus, a larger proportion of respondents from the Karlsruhe area was expected.

In a pretesting step association data were collected for 13 selected homepages of German electronic malls[2]. 17 indicators corresponding to the dimensions for measuring advertising effectiveness as discussed before were used. To keep the final online survey small six representatives of homepages were chosen. In a similar way, the number of indicators of the relevant dimensions was reduced to seven by forming "indicator bundles" for homepage valuation via property fitting (see Gaul and Baier (1994)) and selected classes of indicators for the Web site features of Tab. 2 were used. Tab. 3 gives an overview over items considered for the final online survey in relation to the topics mentioned in the discussion concerning Web site design aspects.

---

[2]In spring 1996, when the study was initiated, in Germany just about 20 homepages of virtual market-places concerning more or less professional collections of services and hyperlinks were present in the Internet. At that time, electronic malls did not have the comprehensive functions of virtual market-places known at present.

Topics	Items Considered for the Online Survey
homepage objects[3]	Sektor (Aachen), Electronic Mall Bodensee, Hansa (Hamburg), Karlsruher Marktplatz, MVV (Mannheim), Marktplatz Deutschland (München)
indicators for homepage valuation[4] (measure dimension in brackets)	well done (liking); new (attention and degree od innovation); clearly arranged (confusion); appealingly designed (design); diverting, enjoyable (entertainment); activating links (interactivity)
Web site features (feature class in brackets)	background colours/images, text colours, livening up images, images as main design features, transparent / animated GIFs[5], new techniques, corporate design (design features); images as entertaining features, animations, sound/video, prizes, chats, email possibility, actual value adding services, hotlists (entertaining features); graphical links, textual links, hierarchical navigation path, content page, 'what's new' page, search index (navigation features); small page extent, much information at first sight, headings, horizontal rules, images for content classification, lists/tables (structural features);

Tab. 3: Topics and items considered for the online survey

The main online survey consisted of four parts. After a short introduction pairwise comparison data[6] concerning the homepage objects were collected by a sequentially and automatically designed presentation procedure. In the second part of the questionaire the participants had to score statements on a seven-stage rating scale with respect to the seven indicators for homepage valuation identified at the pretest. This scoring process was supported by always available thumbnails[7] of the original homepages allowing an "aided recall"–procedure for obtaining the corresponding association data. It goes without saying that the order of presentation of the paired comparisons in the first part as well as the homepages in the second part had been randomized. The third part consisted of judgements concerning attitudes towards the Web site features listed in Tab. 3. Finally, the participants were asked for some personal data (e.g., age, sex, profession and main reasons for Web usage).

---

[3]In the following, homepage objects will be named after the underlined city resp. region for which the corresponding online services are offered.

[4]Indicators for the dimensions credibility, information content, personal importance, displeasure, and warmth mentioned before were not embedded into the research design.

[5]Transparent GIFs are images with transparent background colours. Their usage avoids the disturbing rectangular shape especially of inline hypergraphics. Animated GIFs are sequences of images which are automatically and repeatedly displayed by the browser.

[6]Pairwise comparisons have never been realized before in a online survey. Important technical aspects like same scale of the objects shown, constant time of view, and same left–right–positions have been taken into consideration.

[7]Thumbnails are small scaled – normally as large as a stamp – versions of clickable inline images which can be enlarged for a closer look via activation.

In a period of two months in spring/summer 1996 over sixhundred online users visited the Web pages of our survey, but due to the seemingly pretentious and comprehensive task of 15 paired comparisons, e.g., only 170 preference data sets were completed. The evaluations for this paper are based on 96 overall data sets without any missing values. These overall data sets contain preference data indicating more general impressions mainly based on affective dimensions, association data describing affective and cognitive dimensions for homepage valuation, and attitudes towards more cognitive ratings concerning Web site features.

4 Empirical Results

An evaluation of the sociodemographic data from the last part of the survey revealed that the overall profile of the participants is quite similiar to other recent German Internet surveys. As expected, a regional preponderance was observed which, however, was not significant for segment-specific differences.

Various data analysis techniques were applied to the overall data sets according to the proposals of the knowlegde based system WIMDAS-PS (see Gaul and Schader (Hrsg.) (1994)). A hierarchical cluster analysis based on data concerning attitudes towards the Web site features listed in Tab. 3 yielded a stable two-class solution, which was further improved by an exchange algorithm and resulted in two clusters of 58,3% (segment 1) and 41,7% (segment 2) of the respondents as shown in Fig. 1. A comparison of the segment-specific profiles with the total average profile revealed that segment 1 rates design and entertainment features higher than segment 2. Respondents of segment 2 seem to be more information-oriented ("searchers"), a fact which corresponds to the already observed "experiential and goal-directed behavior in a CME" (see Hoffman and Novak (1996)), while members of segment 1 can be characterized as entertainment-oriented ("surfers"). Younger, male students dominate in the "surfers" segment, whereas the "searchers" have a higher percentage of salaried employees, are older and can be characterized by a higher share of females. A strengthened Web usage for personal and business research and the major readiness for online shopping of the information-oriented users is also remarkable. Moreover, the characterization of this classification confirms hints concerning differences in attitudes towards the usage of the Web as indicated in chapter 2.

An analysis of segment-specific preferences and outcomes with respect to the indicators of homepage valuation – based on paired comparisons and aggregated association data from the second part of the survey – can be used for the visualization of preference structures of these two segments. For this purpose a wandering ideal point model (see Bckenholt and Gaul (1986)) has been applied to a two-dimensional quasi-internal representation of the situation as provided via the $MARK^2MAN$ system (see Gaul and Baier (1994)). Fig. 2 shows that especially in segment 1 a preference for "Karlsruhe" can be stated. With respect to the distance to the ideal point of segment 2, "Aachen", "Bodensee", and "Karlsruhe" appear quite similar. The incorporation of property vectors with respect to the indicators for homepage valuation confirms the entertainment-orientation of segment 1. The property vector for "diverting" is directed to the ideal point of segment 2.

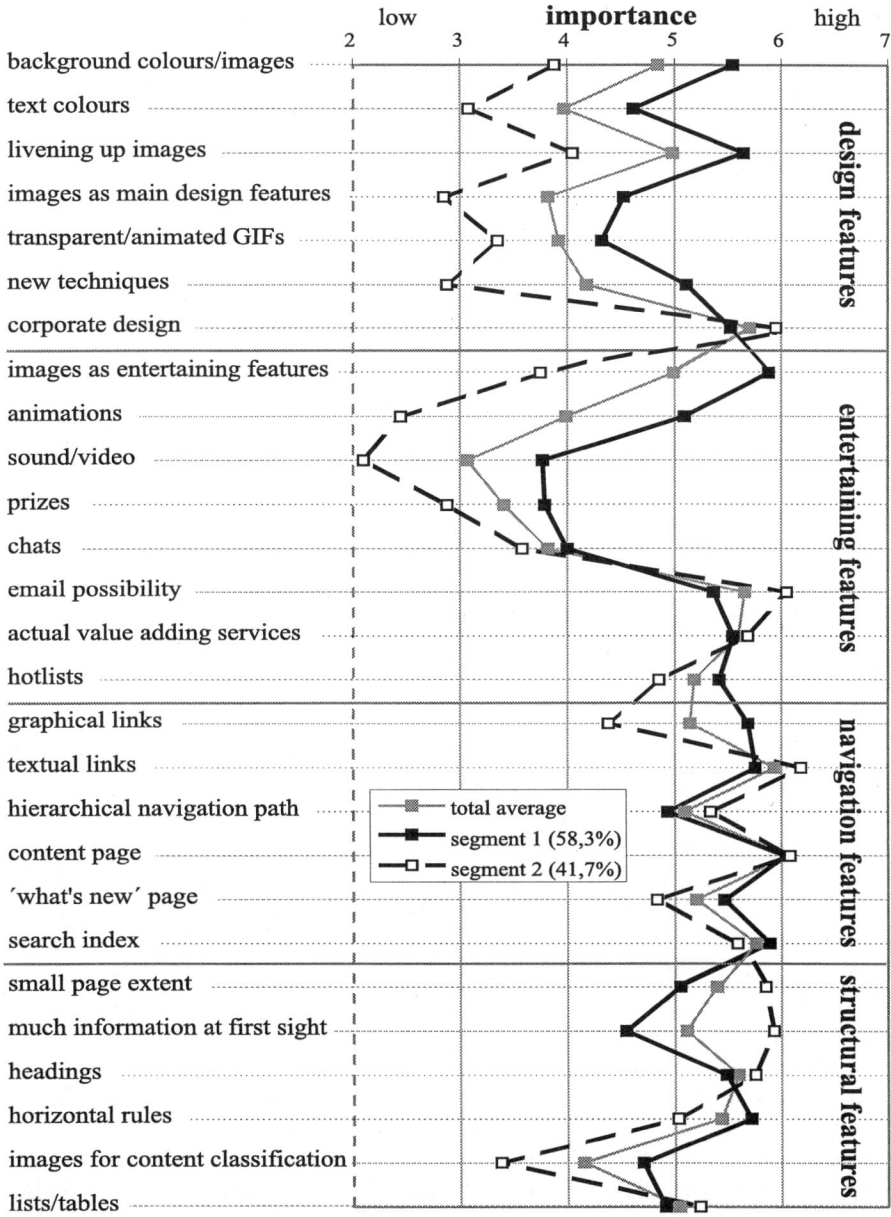

Fig. 1: Segment-specific profiles of Web site features considered

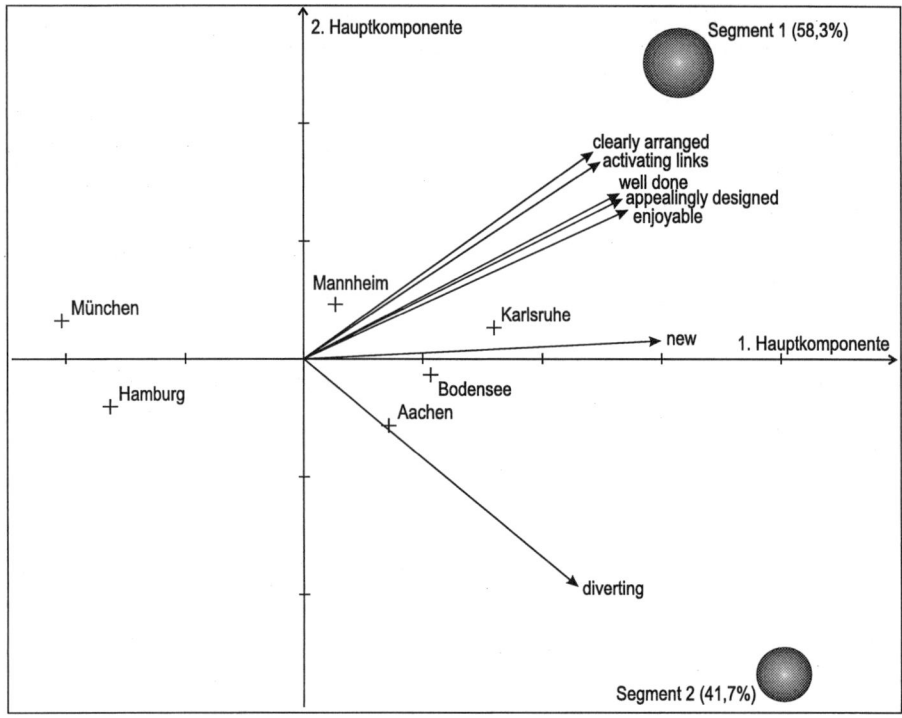

Fig. 2: Two-dimensional quasi-internal solution of the wandering ideal point model

5 Conclusions and Outlook

Because of page restrictions only selected results of an online survey concerning virtual market-places in the Internet have been reported. A segmentation based on attitudes towards Web site features has yielded an interpretable and well-founded solution, that reflects the motivation of two main user groups to "surf" or "search" in the Web. An analysis of the association data has shown that the indicators selected – based on previous research to measure advertising effectiveness and on additional online-specific Web site features – are quite suitable for getting a grip on online effectiveness, whereas the absence of content aspects in our final research design can be a crucial point for an appropriate representation of more information-oriented users. In order to make the design of a Web site successful the target group (with respect to the user segments identified in this study) should be defined at an early stage in the development phase. Either a more entertainment- or a more information-orientated approach should be followed. Research based on available data concerning observed behaviour of Internet users, e.g., via an appropriate evaluation of so-called access log-files will allow a deeper insight into design specific aspects for online services.

Acknowledgement

Thanks are due to A. Roppert for his valuable programming activities during the whole *Karlsruher Marktplatz* project.

References

AAKER, D.A., BRUZZONE, D.E. (1981): Viewer Perceptions of Prime-Time-Television Advertising, *Journal of Advertising Research*, 21 (5), 15–23.

ALPAR, P. (1996): Kommerzielle Nutzung des Internet, Springer, Heidelberg.

ANGELL, D., HESLOP, B. (1995): The Internet Business Companion, Addison-Wesley, New York.

BCKENHOLT, I., GAUL, W. (1986): Analysis of Choice Behavior via Probabilistic Ideal Point and Vector Models, *Applied Stochastic Models and Data Analysis*, 2, 202–226.

BORNMAN, H., VON SOLMS, S.H. (1993): Hypermedia, Multimedia and Hypertext – Definitions and Overview, *Electronic Library*, 11 (4/5), 259–268.

GAUL, W., BAIER, D. (1994): Marktforschung und Marketing Management, 2nd Edition, Oldenbourg, München.

GAUL, W., KLEIN, T., WARTENBERG, F. (1997): Elektronische Marktplätze als Marketing–Plattform im Internet – Integrierte Online–Präsenz steigert die Akzeptanz, *Office Management*, 45 (4), May 1997, 41–45.

GAUL, W., SCHADER, M. (Hrsg.) (1994): Wissensbasierte Marketing–Datenanalyse, Peter Lang, Frankfurt am Main.

HOFFMAN, D.L, NOVAK, T.P. (1996): Marketing in Hypermedia Computer-Mediated Environments: Conceptual Foundations, *Journal of Marketing*, 60 (July), 50–68.

KROEBER-RIEL, W., BARG, C.D., WIMMER, R.M. (1977): Bericht über den psychophysiologischen Test (PPP) der dor-flüssig-Werbung, *Forschungsbericht des Instituts für Konsum- und Verhaltensforschung*, Universität des Saarlandes.

KROL, E. (1994): The Whole Internet User's Guide & Catalog, O'Reilly & Associates, Sebastopol.

NEIBECKER, B. (1990): Werbewirkungsanalyse mit Expertensystemen, Physica, Heidelberg.

RESCH, J. (1996): Marktplatz Internet, Microsoft Press, Unterschleissheim.

ROSSITER, J.R., EAGLESON, G. (1994): Conclusions from the ARF's Copy Research Validity Project, *Journal of Advertising Research*, 34 (3), 19–32.

Design of World Wide Web Information Systems

K. Lenz, A. Oberweis

Lehrstuhl für Wirtschaftsinformatik II,
Universität Frankfurt/Main, D-60054 Frankfurt/Main, Germany

Abstract: Public global networks as for example the internet with the world wide web represent more and more a suitable platform for distributed information systems. Yet, the lack of methods for conceptual modelling (as known for the database design) often leads to quick and dirty implementations with uncontrollable data, data redundancies and data inconsistencies. In this paper, we present a method for the conceptual modelling of information systems within the world wide web. Starting from an extended Entity Relationship model, a page link scheme can be derived according to a classification of web pages and their links.

1 Introduction

With its growing acceptance and use public global networks represent more and more a suitable platform for distributed information systems. An example is the internet and the world wide web (WWW), the globally distributed public hypermedia information system on the internet. Specific problems and methods for the design of distributed information systems on the internet may be easily transferred to other online services such as CompuServe or America Online.

In the WWW multimedia information can be retrieved directly by specifying a unique address, the URL (uniform ressource locator), via search engines, by navigation, that is following certain pointers between chunks of information, or by specification, that is navigation following a given hierarchy. The information consumer therefore can individually determine his method of accessing the information he searches for and of handling the information flooding. The information supplier on the other hand may support quick and easy information retrieval by providing information in a structured way and in the right context to the information consumer. But facing the mass of information, the information supplier may want to present in the web, he has to develop the information system very carefully, paying attention to all phases of the development process. Nowadays, the implementation phase is already supported by various tools as for example HTML-editors, database interfaces or tools for visualizing the structure of the information system. Until now, methods for the design of information systems only exist for specific problems (Isakowitz et al. (1995), Garzotto et al. (1996), Goll (1996)). In practice, the lack of comprehensive methods for conceptual modelling still leads to quick and dirty implementations with difficult information management, inconsistencies and uncontrollable redundancies.

In this paper, we present a method for the conceptual modelling of a web information system using an extended Entity Relationship model. For that purpose we extend existing methods for database design for the design of web information systems.

In the next section we present the page link model which allows the modelling of information and its interrelated pointers. The derivation of a page link scheme for a simple university example will be described in section 3. Finally a brief outlook on future work is given.

2 Page Link Model

For the conceptual modelling of web information systems, we propose a graphical modelling language similar to the Entity Relationship model for the database design. It allows to model aspects of the real world independently from implementation aspects. The language consists of two modelling constructs: chunks of information, the web pages, and their interrelated pointers, the links. Because web information systems are based on hypertext techniques, the page link model has to combine net like structures of the linked multimedia information and the hierarchical structure of supplementary navigational help ('go one page up', 'go to homepage' etc.).

In the following, we describe the components of the page link model in detail.

2.1 Web Pages

In order to reduce the number of real world objects to be modelled and thereby to increase readability of the page link scheme, all web pages of the same type, with identical structure and comparable information content form a class of web pages: the page type. In the scheme, the page type is represented by a rectangle with the page type name in it (see Figure 1 (a)). The specific web pages are instances of the page type.

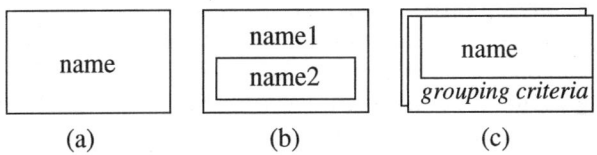

Figure 1: Graphical representation of page types

Ergonomical aspects play an important role for the design of web information systems so that some ergonomical considerations may or even should be anticipated during the phase of conceptual modelling: If, for example, information that is to be presented on one web page is too small (in the sense of disproportionate high retrieval time and costs), it should be integrated into another web page. For example, one would not create an own address web page for staff members whose addresses are not very detailed, but include the address on their home page. The page link model therefore allows aggregation of page types (here 'staff' and 'address'). The graphical representation is shown in Figure 1 (b).

For the same reason, it may be useful to combine all instances of a page type on one single web page and thus create information lists (for example a list of all staff members) which can be grouped by arbitrary criteria. The corresponding graphical representation, two overlapping rectangles, can be seen in Figure 1 (c). The grouping criteria is only indicated when the list has been grouped.

2.2 Links

In analogy to web page classification, links between web pages of the same page type with comparable navigation characteristics are collected to one link type. Links with comparable navigation characteristics, i.e. especially links of the same link type, must belong to the same class of links. Links can be classified with respect to

- whether they are a part of a specific link pattern,
- their semantics,
- their validity for special groups of users,
- whether they can be (locally) administrated,

and other criterias. In this paper, we concentrate on the first two classification criterias. The first classification is the most relevant for the page link model. The classes and their graphical representation in a page link scheme are shown in Figure 2. An index link between two page types means that starting from a web page of the first page type, we can navigate to an index page and there have bidirectional links to several web pages of the second page type. In contrast, the guided tour link allows to visit several web pages of the second page type one after another with an extra web page as starting and ending point. The index guided tour link combines both navigation structures (Isakowitz et al. (1995)).

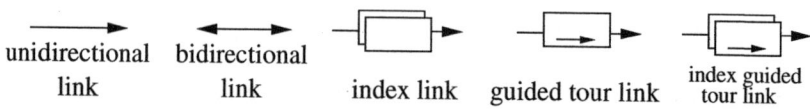

Figure 2: Classification of links

Due to their different semantics, we distinguish content links and structural links. Data, other applications or meta-information can be accessed from the context via content links whereas structural links serve as supplementary navigation possibilities. Structural links are graphically represented by dashed lines.

3 Derivation of a Page Link Scheme

The basis for a page link scheme is an extended Entity Relationship diagram (Schlageter and Stucky (1983)). The Entity Relationship model is widely accepted for the conceptual modelling of database systems. But it is also very suitable for the derivation of the page link scheme, because relationships between objects of the real world indicate a link between the information concerning those objects. However additionally, a hierarchical order has to be found for the page link scheme to support structural navigation and for example the file management. Finally, the information system can be implemented according to the page link scheme.

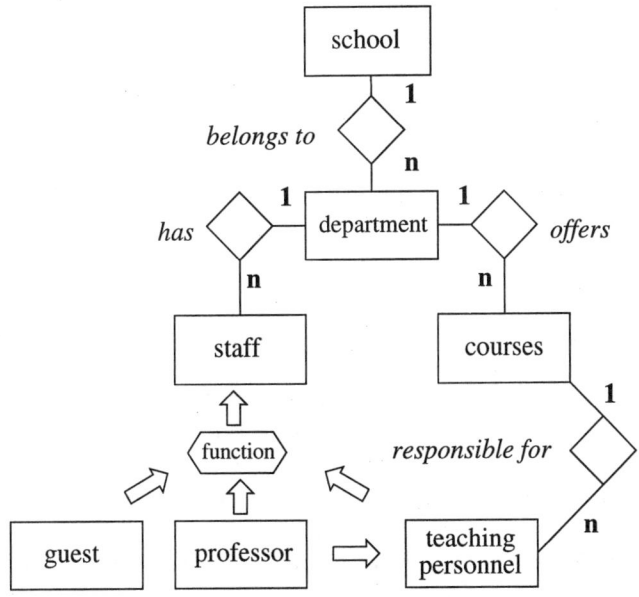

Figure 3: Simple Entity Relationship diagram for a department

The Entity Relationship diagram of Figure 3 shows an extract of the university world: a department (belonging to a school) wants to present its staff and courses in a web information system. The staff of the department consists of the teaching personnel, the professors who belong to the teaching personnel (but have to be modelled explicitely, because they may have additional attributes or relationships compared to the teaching personnel), and finally the guests (specialization in the ER-scheme). The department offers several courses for which the teaching personnel is responsible (one-to-many relationships of the ER-scheme).

The further explanation of the single steps of deriving a page link scheme will be based on this example.

3.1 Step 1: Page Types

First, we create a corresponding page type for each entity type of the ER-scheme. For all page types, we then have to consider if ergonomical aspects imply some modifications. For each entity of the type 'staff', only few information would be presented on a corresponding web page: The more detailed information can be retrieved on the web page which corresponds to the entity of one of the specialized entity types 'guest', 'professor' or 'teaching personnel'. Here, a list page for all staff members is very useful and, in addition, we group all list entries by *function*. Thus, we create a page type 'staff' with the graphical representation of Figure 1 (c) and a single instance, the list page. In contrast, it makes no sense to have such a list page for the courses. Too much information on one page can be confusing for the information consumer. The graphical representation of all other page types therefore corresponds to that in Figure 1 (a).

Now, the page link scheme has to be completed by the links.

3.2 Step 2: Content Links

We derive the content links from the relationships (including the specialization) of the ER-scheme. For one-to-one relationships or specializations, we create a bidirectional link between the corresponding page types, for one-to-many relationships a unidirectional link and an index link. Moreover, the index page of the index link can be an own web page as shown in Figure 4 (a) or an anchor on a web page of the page type from which the link starts (Figure 4 (b)).

For many-to-many relationships, we consequently create two index links in both directions.

In order to complete the page link scheme by structural links, we then have to derive a hierarchical structure from the ER-scheme.

3.3 Step 3: Derivation of a Hierarchy

In the beginning, we mark those entity types which do not directly belong to our application and whose corresponding web pages are not under our control ('school' and 'guest' in our example). They will not be part of the hierarchy. Afterwards, we determine a primary entity type (the 'home page')

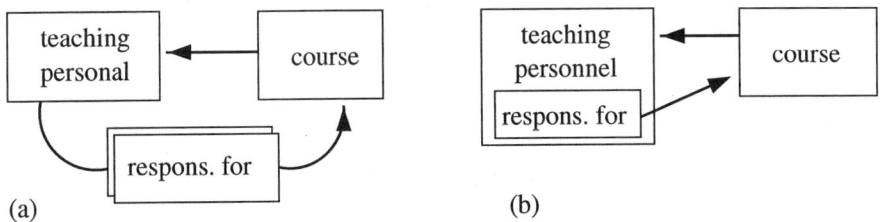

Figure 4: One-to-many relationship 'teaching personnel is responsible for courses'

whose corresponding page type is going to be the root of the hierarchy tree. As long as there are still entity types left whose corresponding page types are not yet nodes of the tree, we continue searching *subordinated* entity types for all leafs. An entity type E' is called subordinated to an entity type E if there exists a one-to-one or a one-to-many relationship from E to E' or if E' is a specialization of E. For example, the entity type 'staff' is subordinated to 'department' and 'professor' is subordinated to 'staff', being a specialization of it. The page type of the subordinated entity type becomes the child of that page type.

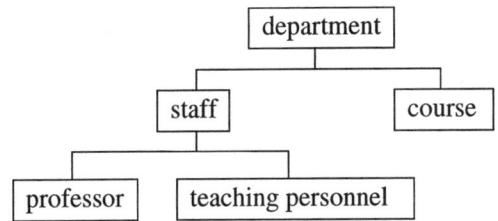

Figure 5: Hierarchy for the university example

This procedure does not lead to a unique hierarchy tree. For example, an entity type can be located in the same depth of the tree, but in different branches. As we have no sort of ordering of the relationship types of the entity relationship model (which could help to resolve the ambiguities), it is left to the developer to decide for one specific hierarchy.

The hierarchy in Figure 5 can now be used to create structural links and as a unique ordering to store the web pages during the implementation phase.

3.4 Step 4: Structural Links

The page link scheme is being completed by structural links if no corresponding content link of the same class already exists. However, with regard to the design of the user interface, the modelling of the link as both content link and structural link can be reasonable. For example, a link can have two anchors on a web page, one within the context (for the content link) and one as a navigation button in the page header (for the structural link).

The structural links are derived from the page type hierarchy as follows: for each page type, unidirectional links to the page types corresponding to the root and the parent node must be created. Optionally, we can create a unidirectional link to all page types which are brother nodes (in our example between 'staff' and 'course'). Further, we can create an index link from a page type to itself (for example if the page for a member of the teaching personnel contains a list of the other teaching personnel).

The complete page link scheme for our university example is shown in Figure 6. The structural links are represented by the arrows with dashed lines. Furthermore a link (between 'school' and 'department') is shown whose anchor is on a page of an external application and therefore can not be (locally) administrated.

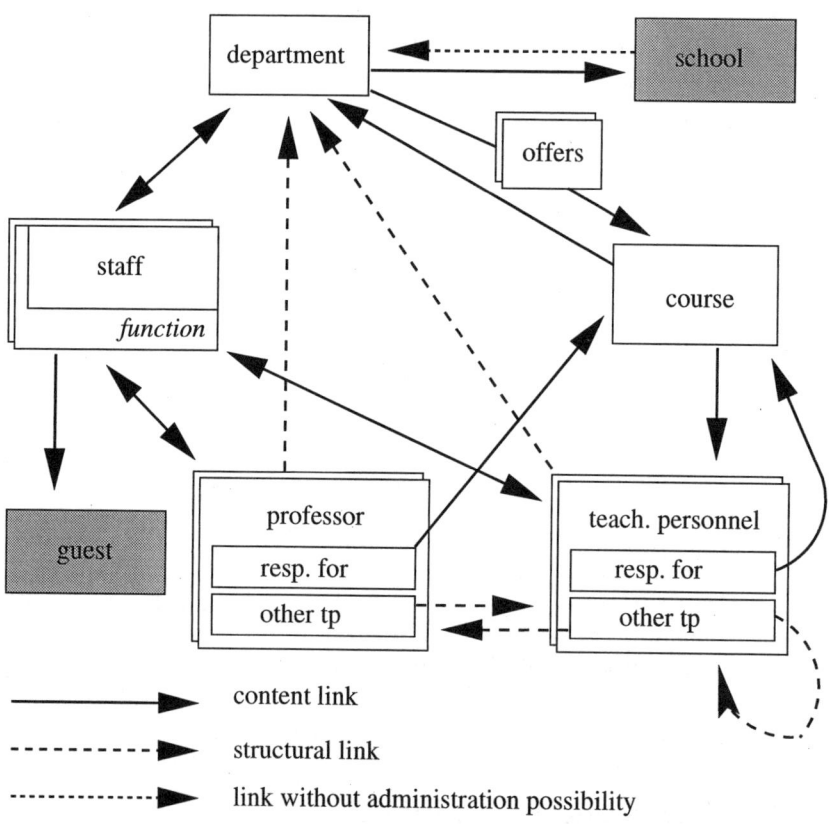

Figure 6: Page link scheme for the diagram of Figure 3

4 Future Work

In this paper we have described some data modelling concepts for the design of world wide web based information systems. The concepts are integrated into INCOME/STAR (Oberweis et al. (1994)) which is a collection of methods and tools for the cooperative development of distributed information systems.

In the future, some aspects of the page link model must be refined. The page link model always must be adapted to new standards or extended standards for the world wide web like for example frames and layers in HTML. Furthermore the modelling of user interfaces has to be discussed in more detail: e.g., the use of templates or the representation of different link classes.

References

GARZOTTO, F., PAOLINI, P., and SCHWABE, D. (1995): HDM - A Model-Based Approach To Hypermedia Application Design. *ACM Transactions on Information Systems, 11, 1-26.*

GOLL, S. (1996): Methode und Werkzeug zur modellbasierten Hypertext-Entwicklung. Verlag Görich & Weiershäuser GmbH, Marburg. (in german)

ISAKOWITZ, T., STOHR, E., and BALASUBRAMANIAN, P. (1995): RMM: A Methodology for Structured Hypermedia Design. *Communications of the ACM, 8, 34-44.*

OBERWEIS, A., SCHERRER, G., and STUCKY, W. (1994): INCOME/STAR: Methodology and tools for the development of distributed information systems. *Information Systems, 19 (8), 641-658.*

SCHLAGETER, G. and STUCKY, W. (1983): Datenbanksysteme: Konzepte und Modelle. B. G. Teubner, Stuttgart.

Large WWW Systems: New Phenomena, Problems and Solutions

H. Maurer

Institute for Information Processing and Computer Supported New Media,
Graz University of Technology, A-8010 Graz, Austria

Abstract:

This paper is a compact written version of an invited paper presented on the occasion of the 21st Annual Meeting of the German Society for Classification. It is structured into three parts. In the first we try to show how WWW is starting to influence all kinds of areas of our lives, and in doing so new and unforeseen phenomena and problems arise. In the second part we explain how modern WWW systems are starting to reduce the problems discussed. And in the last part we analyse a number of statements often made about WWW that - when carefully analysed - turn out to be superficial, if not incorrect. We do not include many references to written papers, but rather pointers to further information on the WWW.

1 WWW is penetrating the world

At the time of writing (May 1997) some 500.000 WWW servers are active (see http://www.altavista.digital.com). (Note that here and in what follows I refer to information on the WWW by using the "Uniform Resource Locator" - the URL - as it is used in all WWW browsers. For brevity's sake I will, however, omit the prefix http:// indicating what kind of protocol is used. Hence, in what follows I would just write www.altavista.digital.com instead of the "full" http://www.altavista.digitial.com used above.) On the 500.000 WWW servers mentioned we find an incredible wealth of information and services, ranging from literature to arts, from music to movies, from "touristic" pictures to virtual museums (www.doc-donna.dlr.de/dcc), from schedules of trains or planes to news of all kinds, from electronic shopping malls to discussion groups, from telebanking to telebooking, form cartographic information to scientific papers, from curricula to lecture material; and the list could be extended arbitrarily. A few concrete examples will help to demonstrate the breadth of information. There is the vectorised map of the world that allows us to zoom into any location on the world down to street level (www.mapquest.com), the train information system of the German railway that goes far beyond Germany (www.hacon.de), the flight information on all scheduled commercial flights world-wide (www.lufthansa.de), the 8 GB large multimedia presentation of Austria (www.aeiou.at), the largest online bookshop of the world with over 2,5 million titles (www.amazon.com), the electronic version of the New Zealand National Library (timeframes.natlib.govt.nz), electronic journals from scientific (www.iicm.edu/jucs) to general ones (www.spiegel.de). What is surprising about above information sites is not that they exist, but how many of them exist and with incredibly huge quantities of information. Of course, the WWW also contains rather unorthodox information like life sports news (www.sportsline.com), very comprehensive information on movies (hollywood.com), interactive stories (www.narrative.com), virtual cemeteries (virtual29.com/garden/cemetery.html), personal columns (www.webpersonals.com), digital multimedia postcards (www.kodak.com), virtual driving schools (www.stimmt.at) or reminder services (www.neverforget.com). Altogether it is fair to say: you can find just about anything on the WWW, if you have the time, and if you are not totally frustrated by the chaos you will encounter.

The time factor, i.e. the slow speed with which information often is loaded is, of course, a question of available bandwidth, and the situation varies from place to place and even from hour to hour. Frustrated users in Europe avoid accessing large information in the US during (European) late afternoon, when Europe is still at work, and US has already started: a Sunday morning (European time) with the US can be up to 100 times faster than the same session on, say, a Wednesday afternoon! Cynics have started to re-interpret WWW as World Wide Waiting, rather than World Wide Web!

It is interesting to note that communication bottle-necks are usually not caused by technology, but by pricing. A typical example is the new transatlantic fibre TAT 12/13: its 5 Gbit capacity allows 300.000 simultaneous ISDN calls, its construction required around US$ 750 million. Looking at current phone tariffs and assuming a usage of TAT 12/13 at close to full capacity the $ 750 million would be recouped within a single week! Thus, if dropping phone charges by a factor of 100 would assure that TAT 12/13 runs fully loaded this fibre would be just as good an investment as it is today, when it runs at a meagre few percent capacity. The lesson that should be learnt from this, but has not been learnt yet, is: to create lots of WWW traffic usage of WWW has to become less expensive and this would be beneficial for all, also from a commercial point of view.

However, as has been hinted at earlier, WWW users do not only suffer from low transmission speeds but also from the fact that it is often hard to find the desired information. To help in this process of locating information often so-called search engines (that index all WWW servers by regularly sending "harvesting robots" through them) are used. Unfortunately in many cases they lead to information overkill. Searching e.g. for "Potsdam" results in some 100.000 entries, too many to really check them systematically. Thus, the question arises how the ranking is performed in such lists. Without going into details, documents that have a frequent occurrence of a word compared to the length of the document are basically ranked higher with respect to this word (although other criteria are also used). This has led to the phenomenon that some information providers repeat a word very often to obtain a high ranking. Indeed the first ones to use this trick were various "erotic" information providers who created pages that would contain the word "sex" hundreds of time, but quite well hidden: like at the end of the HTML page in tiny red letters on a red background. Other providers, notably a number of religious groups, have started to use the same trick.

A different method to locate information is to try to guess URL's: www.toyota.com, www.quelle.com, www.spiegel.de, www.lufthansa.de indeed lead to what one might expect, i.e. to Toyota, Quelle, Spiegel, and Lufthansa, respectively. However, www.spiegel.com leads to a shoe shop, www.sacher.com not to the famous hotel in Vienna, www.aua.com not to Austria Airlines (AUA), and www.louvre.com to an artist selling her paintings for US $ 400,- a piece, not to the Louvre in Paris. When I tried to register www.hyperg.com for the WWW-server system that was developed by my group in Graz the URL was already taken. I could have purchased the URL for a fairly large amount of money, but rather than supporting what I have started to call "URL piracy" we changed the name Hyper-G to Hyperwave. It is worth noting that international efforts to avoid URL piracy in the future are indeed starting to be successful, so URL piracy will soon just be a story to tell associated with the emergence of a new system.

2 How can one administer the chaotic Web?

One of the main problems encountered with large WWW servers is that the administration gets more and more difficult, as the amount of data increases. It is a simple matter to start a small WWW server and input a few cute HTML pages with e.g. some text and pictures; however as the amount of information grows it becomes surprisingly hard to keep information consistent and up-to-date. It is very easy to forget to remove obsolete pages; yet often pages are removed (or often just moved from one directory to another) with other pages pointing to them. This tends to lead to "broken links" that can drive users crazy when, again, the message "Object not found. Error 404" appears as the result of clicking on a link that no longer is valid. As documents are added, changed and deleted the structure of the information on servers tends to get less and less transparent. Users "get lost" in the maze of links, don't find entries they know they exist (since they just located them hours ago), etc. The Austrian proverb: "It is easy to become father. It is not easy to be a father" remains, unfortunately, valid if you replace "father" by "webmaster".

To avoid the problems mentioned WWW server systems are necessary with sophisticated data- and link management support. One such system was developed by a team headed by me with an effort of over 100 person years in the period 1991 - 1996. It is now available as a commercial product Hyperwave (www.hyperwave.de) from a company based in Munich, while R+D work continues in a separate company in Graz, Austria. Here is a very brief summary of the most important aspects of Hyperwave: documents and groups of documents ("collections") can have arbitrary attributes; links are not uni-directional, embedded in HTML documents and without attributes, but are bi-directional, stored in a separate link database and can have at-

tributes like other objects; information can be structured in a variety of ways; it is even possible that different user groups have completely
different views of the same database; access control and billing mechanisms are integrated, as well as search engines, new navigational techniques and automatic support for multilinguality.

The concept of attributes eases the location of documents and allows the system to automatically perform certain actions that would ordinarily require much manual work. Typical instances are the deletion (or reclassification) of documents after their expiration date, the opening of documents at a predefined moment in time, the extraction of documents not modified for a long time, etc. Also, the fact that arbitrary attributes can be defined makes it much easier to map relational databases into Hyperwave, since the relations can be modelled using the attribute structure. This, together with the fact that large amounts of "legacy data" reside (and will continue to reside) in relational databases gives Hyperwave a decisive advantage over other WWW server solutions. The generalised link concept of Hyperwave proves beneficial in more ways than can be described in a few sentences. Some examples must suffice: using the fact that links are bi-directional and are kept in a separate database allows the system to assure automatic link integrity, i.e. the message "Object not found. Error 404" cannot occur in a Hyperwave server, or in a "tribe" of co-operating Hyperwave servers. Structuring information eliminates many unnecessary and undesirable links (much like structure in programming languages reduces the need for goto's, and structure in data management the need for explicit pointers!); it also improves usability and permits different users to see different links, a rather essential point: the assumption that all persons of an organisation want to see the same information with the same priority (from general manager to sales personnel, from researcher to administrator) is plain ludicrous, yet is a currently accepted WWW wisdom since no WWW system before Hyperwave offered any chance for alternatives. Summarising, Hyperwave assists server managers in a democratic way, improving efficiency by up to 80%. It also makes WWW servers more transparent and easier to use.

Hyperwave, by the way, obtained BYTE's "Best of the Show" Award, and the Award "Best Product" (Internet Category) at CeBit'97 against a competition of 6.800 exhibitors and 35.000 products for the very reasons just mentioned: Hyperwave is currently the only technology that massively supports data- and link management of large amounts of information even across physical server boundaries. Concerning the CeBit'97 award and the reasons leading to it, see www.byte.com/special/cebit97.htm or www.iicm.edu/hyperwave.cebit. For more on Hyperwave as such please consult www.hyperwave.de or www.iicm.edu/hyperg. The "classical" book on Hyperwave is [Maurer 1996]. [Maurer 1997] explains in detail, why large WWW servers cannot do without databases and why such databases are particularly easy to integrate into Hyperwave.

3 Some claims concerning WWW - and why they are wrong

In this section we will discuss five statements that are heard over and over, and yet are at least doubtful if not plain wrong.

(1) WWW is becoming the largest information system of the world.

This is not wrong, but it is only half the truth: WWW as mere information system would never become important or be as important as it already is. It is the communicative components (Emails, Chats, Forms, Transactions, Discussion groups, ...) that will prove to be the really driving forces.

(2) WWW will allow us soon, supported by "intelligent agents", to select the best offer for any product we want.

Whoever is stating this is dreaming a beautiful dream, not more. The market has always been very resistant against "comparison shopping" and will continue to do so. In the same way as there are first hard cover and later soft cover versions of most books (to collect higher prices from those who "just can't wait"), or in the same way as the same product is often offered with minimal differences (preventing direct comparisons), in the same way WWW will be full of special offers, "frequent buyer" programs, and many other schemes not even yet invented: to carefully select will remain a complex job, hated by some, loved - like a game - by others. By the way, "differential pricing" is not always directed against consumers, it can also work for them. One of my favourite stories is the one concerning a high quality fast laser printer. It was produced in two versions: one very fast and expensive, the second artificially slowed down by adding an extra chip (!) but much cheaper. If this sounds crazy, it was actually beneficial both for the company and the consumers: the company sold much larger quantities; the customers requiring the fast printer, could buy them - due to the large quantity produced - at a lower price than if the slow version would not have been built; customers requiring a high quality printer of moderate speed were also happy. Even in business not everything has to be a war: there are also win-win situations!

(3) Electronic publishers have to decide whether to publish on CD-ROM or WWW.

This is a fundamental error. Publishers should always pursue both approaches in parallel in a way that creates not (or little) extra effort. And this is possible: if publishers produce a fancy WWW site on a Hyperwave server they can burn it - including all structuring and search mechanisms - on a CD-ROM with little extra effort.

(4) WWW makes everyone a publisher.

Photocopiers have not turned everyone into a publisher. The WWW won't either. To provide homogeneous informations and to carry out administrative functions will remain as important as always was the case. When locating information on the WWW it is often hard to verify its authenticity: if, e.g., there are two WWW servers describing different restaurants as "three star", how can you trust such ratings if there is nobody who has reliably visited all of the restaurants mentioned? It has to be realised that information as such is of no value, unless we know the source and we can judge the authority of the source. Surely, if we read a contribution concerning an arbitrary topic we will take it more serious or less serious depending on whether it has appeared in the Bildzeitung, the Frankfurter Allgemeine or Penthouse!

(5) WWW will lead to selective reading (of e.g. daily newspapers) and selective payment.

All persons with a rudimentary knowledge of basic economics will know that this statement must be wrong: products with small variable costs (i.e. when the costs are fairly independent of the number of customers) always lead to "bundling", not "unbundling". To put it differently, it is indeed likely that we will read more selectively but we won't pay for what we read, but for a bundle of information.

A small and naive example will demonstrate conclusively why this is the case. Let us assume a newspaper is covering three main topics: sports, politics and entertainment. Let us further assume that we have 3 persons A, B and C with different profiles of interest: A is willing to spend daily 50 cents on sports, and B and C daily 50 cents for politics and entertainment, respectively; however, all of the three would only spend 20 cents on each of the other topics. If the newspaper is offered electronically there are three pricing strategies:

(a) For each topic the newspaper charges 50 cents (high price policy). In this case A, B and C will only pay for and read their favourite topic, i.e. the newspaper will make 3 x 50 = 150 cents.

(b) For each topic the newspaper charges 20 cents (low price policy). In this case A, B and C will pay for and read all topics, i.e. the newspaper will make 3 x 20 x 3 = 180 cents.

(c) The newspaper does not offer the topics separately, but as a bundle for 90 cents. Now all of A, B, C have acceptable conditions, but the newspaper makes 3 x 90 = 270 cents.

WWW will bring many new phenomena: a few have been briefly described above. Many more statements will be made concerning WWW that sound superficially convincing, but do not hold up to reality, as was explained in (1) – (5).

References

MAURER, H. (1996): Hyper-G now HyperWave: The Next Generation Web Solution; Addison-Wesley, London

MAURER, H. (1997): Datenbanken, Interaktivität und Benutzerprofile im WWW; Proc. DIK'97, Düsseldorf, dpunkt Verlag Heidelberg.

Structured Visualization of Search Result List

U. Preiser

Siemens AG ZT IK 1
D-81739 München, Germany

Abstract: Information highways are being built around the world. The impact on the business of companies like Siemens is tremendous. New techniques for information processing are required. The integration of features for navigation, in addition to the static presentation, enables the user to find the relevant information by browsing through the information space. By structured visualization, which means to represent the information in form of a 3-D net, the "Kontextgestalt", the user gets an overview of the relevant topics the information set is concerned about.

1 Introduction

During the past years the growing networks (Internet and Intranet) resulted in a large number of potential possibilities to access information sources. This availability produces a vast amount and also a large variety of information. Therefore, it is necessary to provide specified functions for information systems, which will visualize the complex information bases and their structure. Although while today large bases of data and knowledge are being maintained, the man-machine interface is, by its textual command orientation, still not sufficiently adjusted to human perception (visual sense !) and orientation. The approach by "Kontextgestaltgebung" realizes an easy and intuitive way to visualize large data and knowledge bases and therefore results in an easier way to access information by retrieval and processing. *Remark:* The German word "Kontextgestalt" is very hard to translate into English. Its meaning is something like context shape and its plural is "Kontextgestalten". The meaning of the German word "Kontextgestaltgebung" is something like building a "Kontextgestalt".

The techniques of contextual information processing by 3D-visualization are supported by the principle "contextual correlation $\cong$ spatial proximity". Because of their visual sense, human beings are most familiar with the three-dimensional euclidian space (in the following called 3D-space). Therefore spatial proximity as a metaphor for contextual coincidence or similarity is especially memorable. Any electronic source of information can be described in a suitable way by means of an application specific terminology in the form of formal contexts. In this case, a formal context consists of the information units called "objects and attributes" and a binary relation (incidence relation) between objects and attributes. It is possible to deduce specific contextual measures for objects and attributes from such a formal context by using the formal incidences. These measures are either called formal similarity of two objects or formal equivalency of two attributes. In a scaled space, information units (objects respectively attributes) can be represented as points in the sphere by using suitable norms respectively by distance measures. They are arranged in a way that the spatial distances, which are defined by the suitable norm, will equal the contextual distances (spatial proximity). The embedding of a context in such a space, will therefore maintain similarity and equivalency. The arrangement of the context in the 3D-space is made by an approximate transformation which represents contextual proximity by a useful spatial representation (i.e. contextual correlation $\cong$ spatial proximity). Thereby a complex formal context is represented in an easily conceivable way, and its processing by means of search and navigation in space is made possible. This metaphor is used in a demonstrator for obtaining a structured visualization of search results. Thereby the search results can be received either from Internet-based search engines or from local data bases. The information is domain specific, a fact which influences the selection of the attributes used. The goal is to offer the user a structured preparation of the search results in the 3D-sphere instead of a pure listing. Therefore the user will be able to quickly identify relevant information, without having to view all search results.

2 Method and Metaphor

In most situations of data analysis the data records (obtained by measurements, interviews, collections ...) can be described by an application specific conceptual language. In this case, the data records will be represented by objects and their observed attributes in the form of so called "formal contexts", which are known from the formal concept analysis. A (single valued) formal context $K = (G, M, I)$ consists of the following information units (Wille (1984)):

1. a set G of objects

2. a set M of attributes

3. a binary relation (incidence relation) $I \subseteq G \times M$
   between objects and attributes

The relation gIm between an object g and an attribute m is interpreted as "the object g has the attribute m" or "m belongs to g". Such single valued formal contexts exist for example in literature data bases: The attribute set consists of the relevant descriptors and the assigment of the descriptors to supply the incidence relation. The data records which are to be evaluated, often exist in the form of a table whose rows are seen as objects and whose columns are qualified or quantified attributes. This situation is described by an multivalued Kontext $K = (G, M, W, I)$, where W is called the attribute expression. $I \subseteq G \times M \times W$ is a ternary relation, so (g, m, w)

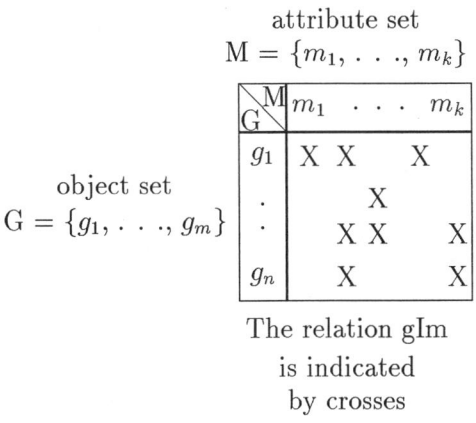

Figure 1: Description of a Formal Context

∈ I is to be read as "the object g has the attribute m with the value w". Such multivalued contexts can be changed into single valued contexts by the method of conceptual scaling, with a loss controlled by the conceptual language of scales. In practice, this means, for example, that the statement of the multivalued context "At the second measurement the pressure was 42 bar" is changed into the "At the second measurement the pressure was very high" in the single valued context. The interpretation "very high" takes the place of the value "42 bar". The attributes and the conceptual scales define a language, which will connect the existing data to an application specific semantic, so that the usability of the relevant situation is being considered. To control the terminology conceptual scales, other (if necessary application specific) methods and techniques like thesauri or semantic networks can be used.

2.1 Kontextgestalten and Information Spaces

This chapter is an overview of the formal and theoretical bases for the Kontextgestaltgebung which is an embedding of formal contexts into so called *information spaces*. The semantic of the information space, in comparison to the vector space model will not be generated by the semantic interpretation of the coordinate axis, but it is based on the distance concept. This semantic will be deduced by the principle "contextual correlation ≅ spatial proximity".

2.2 Formal Aspects of the Embedding of a Context

The information space, in which the contexts will be embedded is an affine metric space S with a set P of picture elements. *Remark:* One can imagine an affine space as a vector space shifted by a selected vector. To obtain a

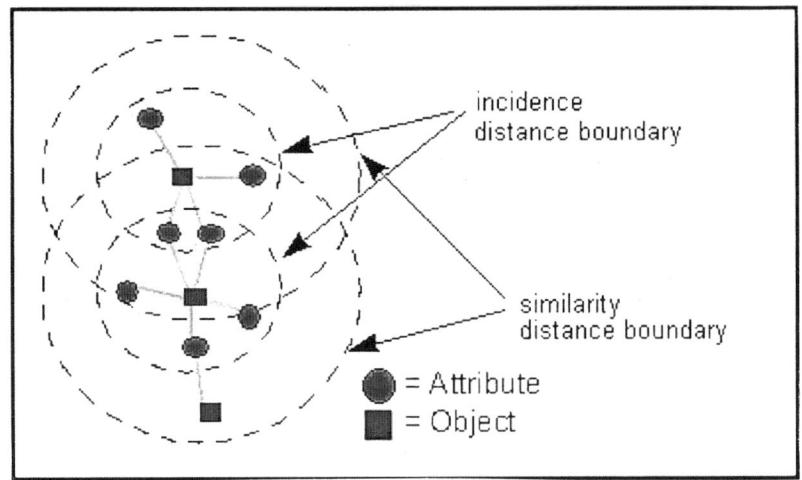

Figure 2: Illustration of a Kontextgestalt

semantic which can be used to embedd a context for this affine space, the picture elements, pairs and sets of picture elements have to be interpreted as elements or properties of context. The Kontextgestalt as an embedding of a context with finite sets of object and attributes in such an affine information space is represented as a triple $F=(P_G, P_M, L)$ with P_G respectively P_M is called the set of object resp. attribute points and L is called the set of incidence lines. For an embedded context K and its corresponding Kontextgestalt F, there are surjective mappings $\pi_G: G \to P_G$, $\pi_M: M \to P_M$, $\pi_I: I \to L$, which assign the elements of the context to the elements of the Kontextgestalt. The set of the incidence lines L is only used for graphical presentation of the Kontextgestalt.

2.3 Interpretation of the Principle "Contextual Correlation ≅ Spatial Proximity"

Figure 2 illustrates a simple Kontextgestalt. Therein the geometrical form cube represents an object and a sphere represents an attribute. The line between a cube and a sphere indicates that the attribute belongs to this object. All attributes of an object have to be within the so called incidence distance boundary. The principle "contextual correlation ≅ spatial proximity" means that objects which are correlated in any way, i.e. they have common attributes, are in a closer environment. This environment is defined by the similarity distance boundary as illustrated in figure 2.

2.4 Approximate Embedding of a Context

Based on the interpretation, the procedure of the Kontextgestaltgebung can be described by words in the following manner: "Distribute both the objects and attributes within the information space in such a way that the interpretated relations (similarity, equivalency, incidence) deduced from the distances of these points correspond with the relations in the formal context". This procedure has to consider three spatial constraints for the object-object-, attribute-attribute-, and object-attribute-pairs.

The similarity and equivalency measure, which was introduced in the description of the constraints is a contextual measure for the similarity of object respectively the equivalency of the attributes in dependency of their attributes respectively objects.

The similarity measure of two objects is calculated by three numbers:

1. the number of attributes belonging to both objects,
2. the number of attributes belonging to none of the objects and
3. the number of attributes belonging to only one of the objects.

It characterizes the formal similarity by real values between 0 and 1. The value 0 means no similarity which is defined by the lack of common attributes. The value 1 describes the formal similarity, which is defined by having only attributes in common.

The equivalency measure of two attributes is also calculated by three numbers:

1. the number of objects both attributes belongs to,
2. the number of objects none of the attributes belongs to and
3. the number of objects only one of the attributes belongs to.

It characterizes the formal equivalency by real values between 0 and 1. The value 0 means no equivalency which is defined by the lack of common objects. The value 1 describes the formal equivalency, which is defined by having only objects in common.

1. the distance of two objects has to correspond to their similarity measure if they are similar. If not, the distance has to exceed the similarity distance boundary
2. the distance of two attributes has to correspond to their equivalency measure if they are equivalent. If not, the distance has to exceed the equivalency distance boundary
3. the distance of an object and an attribute has to be smaller than the incidence distance boundary if the attribute belongs to the object; else the distance has to exceed the non-incidence boundary.

The similarity and equivalency measure is a contextual measure for the similarity of object respectively the equivalency of the attributes in dependency of their attributes respectively objects.

The procedure of the Kontextgestaltgebung has the task to determine the distribution of the object and attribute representation in the 3D space, so that the constraints are fulfilled. In doing so the following two problems occur:

1. Conventional procedures to solve such constraint systems are normally very complex.

2. Typically, at the embedding of contexts in the graphically three dimensional information space, all of the constraints can not be fulfilled. In comparison with the spaces observed by the vector space model in which every attribute builds a (logical) dimension, the 3D-space possesses only three dimensions.

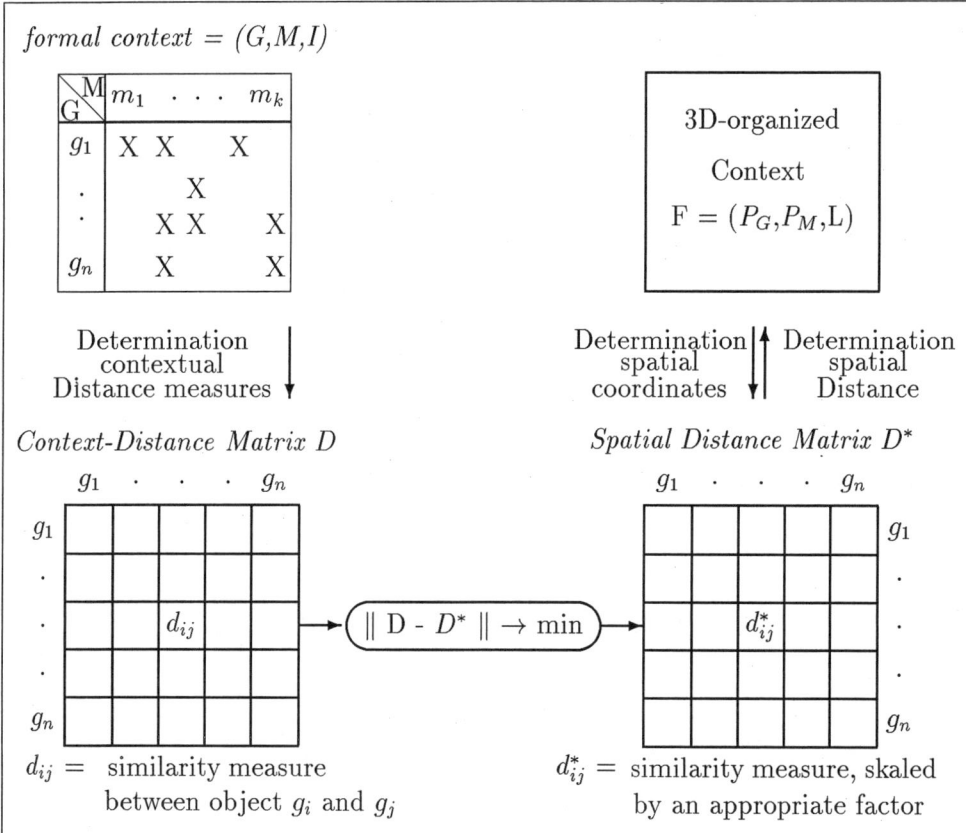

Figure 3: Kontextgestaltgebung

When embedding the context into the 3D-information space the task is to satisfy as many constraints as possible in the best way. This is in short nothing else than to solve an optimization problem.

The procedure of Kontextgestaltgebung is illustrated in figure 3.

3 Application

The method described in the chapters before was implemented in a tool called KOAN. This abbreviation stands for the German word *Kontextanalysator* and means in English the analysis of a context. It is a tool to retrieve and visualize the structure of large information and data bases. It was used in several application areas such as software reengineering, planning and analysis like in the scenario technique and the power plant technology for alarm surge interpretation.

In a new field KOAN is used to retrieve medical information from local sources and from the internet. The problem herein is that the search results provided by standard search engines are less expressive. First, they are oriented according lists without providing a inherent structure, i.e. which documents deal with the same topics. Another disadvantage is the size of the result list. Either there are only a few entries or there is a mass of retrieved results.

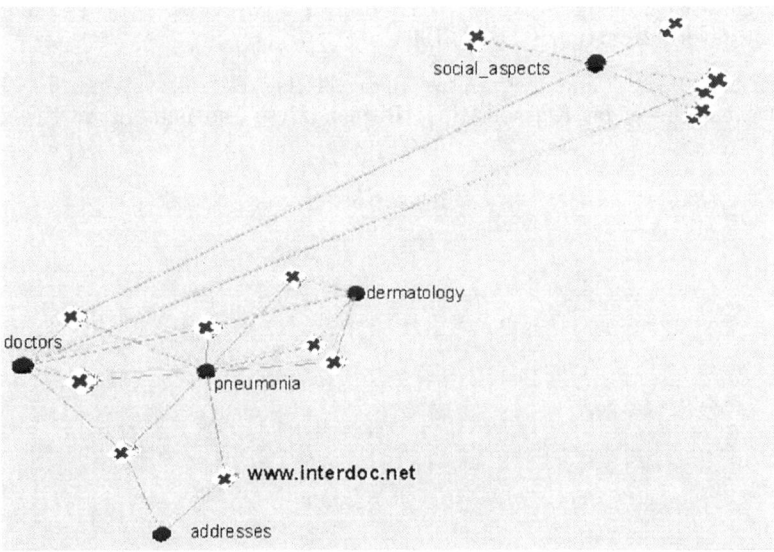

Figure 4: Illustration of a Search Result

The aim of the project is to provide the search and presentation of information in a structured form to get a fast overview of the connections between these documents. Therefore first a search mask is offered to the user by which the search item can be provided to the system. After obtaining the results a background process produces the connections between the results such that the most significant topics that are addressed by the documents build the attribute set. Then this context can be visualized in an OpenGL based implementation of a KOAN viewer which supplies the 3D-functionalities like zooming, shifting or rotating and it provides the user to select interesting

documents which are presented at a standard internet browser.
In figure 4 a search result is illustrated. The cubes are textured with a red cross to indicate the medical content.

Acknowledge

I want to give my best thank to Th. Führing, K. Jacoby, R. Michelis, J. Panyr and L. Pfefferer.

References

FÜHRING, TH., JACOBY K., MICHELIS R., PANYR J. (1994): Kontextgestaltgebung: Eine Metapher zur Visualisierung von und Interaktion mit komplexen Wissensbeständen. Nachtrag Schriften zur Informationswissenschaft Bd. 16; von Rauch (et.al.) Mehrwert von Information: Professionalisierung der Informationsarbeit (Proc. des 4. Internationalen Symposiums für Informationswissenschaften (ISI '94) in Graz, Österreich, 2-4. November 1994) Konstanz: Universitätsverl. Konstanz (UVK), 1994

WILLE, R. (1984): Liniendiagramme hierarchischer Begriffssysteme. In: Bock, H.H: Anwendungen der Klassifikation: Datenanalyse und numerische Klassifikation.

Part 4

Speech and Pattern Recognition

Application of Discriminative Methods for Isolated Word Recognition

Josef G. Bauer

Siemens AG
ZT IK 5
81730 Munich, Germany
Josef.Bauer@mchp.siemens.de

Abstract: This paper describes a Hidden Markov Model based system for automatic recognition of isolated digits over telephone lines. For an LDA based linear feature transformation the classes to discriminate are choosen to be the HMM states. For MCE training this selection of classes is compared to the usage of the lexical words treated as classes. Experiments show that for MCE based reestimation of model parameters the latter choice is more appropriate, although in the case of Maximum Likelihood trainined parameters the correlation between Word Error rate and State Error rate is quite high.

1 Introduction

In spite of their well known limitations **H**idden **M**arkov **M**odel based speech recognition systems are currently one of the best performing means for automatic speech recognition. One aspect that is rarely described by standard HMMs is the correlation in the time sequence of acoustic feature vectors.

Maximum Likelihood based methods are only proven to lead to optimal classification performace if the applied stochastical model describes the underlying stochasitic process correctly. One way to cope with this restriction is the application of discriminative training methods that can compensate for some of the limitation of HMMs (Bahl (1993)).

In section 2 and 3 we describe the baseline HMM-based **M**aximum **A** **P**osteriori (MAP) classifier that makes use of a cepstral speech feature vector and is trained using the **M**aximum **L**ikelihood (ML) criterion. Sections 4 and 5 illustrate how **L**inear **D**iscriminant **A**nalysis (LDA) and **M**inimum **C**lassification **E**rror (MCE) training are applied to the speech recognition system in order to enhance the classification performance. After giving some experimental results in section 6 we draw some conclusions in section 7.

2 System Overview

2.1 Feature Extraction

The speech signal is digitized with a sampling rate of 8000 samples per second which is sufficient for telephone speech that usually has a bandwidth from 300 to 3800 Hz. A 51 dimensional feature vector $\vec{x}_t$ is computed every 10 ms from a 25 ms speech portion. This feature vector contains 24 cepstral coefficients and the logarithmic short time signal energy. The other 26 components consist of first and second order time derivatives of the smoothed cepstral coefficients and energy. Details on feature extraction can be found in Hauenstein (1995).

The result of the feature extraction process is a set of T feature vectors $X = \{\vec{x}_1, \vec{x}_2, \ldots, \vec{x}_{T(X)}\}$ for an utterance that serves as the input for a HMM-based classifier.

2.2 HMM Based MAP Classifier

The classifier has to discriminate between I classes C_i. In our case the $I = 11$ classes correspond to the eleven digit words used in American English (zero, oh, one, ..., nine). Each of the 11 words is modeled by a left to right Hidden Markov Model λ_i. Following a Maximum A Posteriori decision rule the recognizer has to select the class with the highest a posteriori probability $p(C_i|X)$. Of course this probability can only be approximated using the applied speech models. The resulting classification rule can be rewritten as

$$C^{MAP}(X) = \mathrm{argmax}_i \{p(X|\lambda_i)p(C_i)\}. \tag{1}$$

$p(C_i)$ can be ignored in case of isolated digit recognition. The conditional probabilities $p(X|\lambda_i)$ can (approximately) be computed by means of the Viterbi algorithm.

The topology of the models in the described system is motivated by a context dependent phonetic representation of the lexical words (diphones). The mean number of states per model is 18. Transition probabilities between states are not trained but set to empirical values that allow self loops, next state transitions and one state skips for all states.

Two one-state silence models are added to the basic states of the word models in order to model silence before and after uttering a digit word.

The state specific emission probabilities are modeled by mixtures of Gaussian probability density functions. For reduction of the system complexity all variance matrices of the Gaussian densities are set to a constant matrix $\Sigma = diag(\sigma_o^2)$.

3 ML Parameter Estimation

During Maximum Likelihood training one tries to find a parameter set Λ_{ML} so that the probability of producing the feature sequences $\{X^r\}$ from a set of training samples is maximized.

$$\Lambda_{ML} = \mathrm{argmax}_\Lambda \prod_r p(X^r|\lambda_{C(X^r)}) \tag{2}$$

Here, only the models $\lambda_{C(X^r)}$ for the correct class of each training pattern X^r are taken into account.

In the described system only the mean vectors of the Gaussian densities $\vec{\mu}^i_{s,m}$ have to be estimated. The mean vectors are initialized by a clustering algorithm using a given suboptimal alignment between feature vectors and models states. In an iterative procedure new alignments are computed using the Viterbi algorithm and the means are adjusted following the Maximum Likelihood criterion.

4 LDA

Using Linear Discriminant Analysis (Haeb-Umbach (1993)) a single linear transformation matrix A can be computed that is applied to the cepstral feature vectors $\vec{x}$: $\vec{x}_{LDA} = A \cdot \vec{x}$.

For the resulting feature vector $\vec{x}_{LDA}$ the objective function

$$J = \frac{sp(S_B)}{sp(S_W)} \qquad (3)$$

reaches a maximum. S_B and S_W are the scatter between and the scatter within matrices of the resulting feature vector.

To apply LDA classes must be selected for which (at least approximately) Gaussian distributions can be assumed. In the case of Hidden Markov Models for speech recognition the classes must only represent short portions of speech that are approximately stationary. For this reason the selection of words for LDA classes is not appropriate. In the described system we choose the states of the HMM as classes for the LDA.

We apply a two step procedure for the computation of the LDA matrix. First features are decorrelated and whitened. The decorrelation of features is very helpful for the applied type of density modeling because the errors produced by neglecting variance and covariance modeling are reduced. In a second step the between class discrimination measure $sp(S_B)$ is maximized. As the eigenvalue system of S_B is ordered according to eigenvalues the resulting feature vector is ordered in terms of class discrimination. Therefore the resulting feature vector can be reduced in size without major loss of discriminant information.

5 MCE Parameter Estimation

The basic idea of Minimum Classification Error is to minimize a differentiable approximation of the error rate on a set of training samples $\{S^r\}$ (Chou (1992)).

Given the models m_i we define a misclassification measure for a pattern S:

$$d(S, \Lambda) = -g(S, m_c) + g_k(S, m_k) \qquad (4)$$

where $g(S, m_c)$ is the log likelihood score of the correct ($c = C(S)$) model. $\log p(S|m_c)$ and $g(S, m_k)$ is the score of the best competitive model ($k = \text{argmax}_{i \neq c} p(S, m_i)$). A positive value of d indicates that the pattern S was misclassified because the model m_k gave a higher probability than the correct model m_c.

A sigmoid function is used to form a differentiable measure $l(S, \Lambda)$ that is correlated with the classification error for the specific pattern S:

$$l(S, \Lambda) = \frac{1}{1 + e^{-\gamma d(S,\Lambda)}} \quad (5)$$

The objective function of MCE training is formed as the mean value of $l(S, \Lambda)$ for the whole set of training patterns $\{S^r\}$:

$$l(\Lambda) = \frac{1}{R} \sum_{r=1}^{R} l(S^r, \Lambda) \quad (6)$$

As $l(\Lambda)$ approximates the error rate on the training set a parameter set Λ_{MCE} is found to minimize $l(\Lambda)$.

$$\Lambda_{MCE} = \operatorname*{argmin}_{\Lambda} l(\Lambda) \quad (7)$$

For the described system Maximum Likelihood trained system parameters are taken as start values for MCE training. Using the General Probabilistic Descent method the means of the Gaussian densities are reestimated in an iterative procedure:

$$\Lambda_{n+1} = \Lambda_n - \epsilon_n U_n \nabla l(\{S^r\}, \Lambda_n) \quad (8)$$

Taking the identity matrix for U_n and setting $\epsilon_n = \epsilon_0 = const$ we end up with a simple gradient search that showed sufficient convergence in all experiments (n is the iteration index).

One major difference between ML and MCE training is that for a training pattern not only the correct model but all other models are taken into account.

The MCE frame work is not based on any assumptions for the kinds of models that are applied. In the given tasks there seem to be two reasonable choices for the models: one can choose either the HMM states (as for LDA) or the whole HMMs for the words as the classes to discriminate between.

5.1 MStateE

In the following we will call the selection of states for the MCE classes **Minimum State Error** training. In the above notation the training patterns S consists of single feature vectors $\vec{x}$. The state specific Gaussian mixtures are the models m_i.

As for LDA an alignment of the feature vectors $\vec{x}$ to the model's states is necessary. As MCE training is an iterative procedure we do not use one fixed alignment but rather for our experiments we computed a new alignment for each iteration.

For practical reasons we ignore the silence state for the MStateE training as this class has a much higher frequency of occurrence in the set of training patterns and has minor influence on the word recognition performance.

5.2 MWE

In Minimum Word Error Training we select the whole word-specific HMMs as classes for MCE training. Here the HMMs λ_i play the role of the class models m_i and each training patterns S^r consists of a sequence of feature vectors X^r.

For every utterance the probabilities $p(X|\lambda_i)$ as well as the different alignments of the feature vectors to the model states have to be determined. Given this information the model parameters of the correct model and the best competitive model are reestimated.

6 Experiments

In the described experiments we used the so called American English Voice Mail database (Klisch (1996)), specificly a subset of those utterances only containing isolated digits. All utterances were recorded over public telephone lines in the United States of America from approximately 900 different native speakers. The database was divided into a training set with 689 speakers and a disjoint test set with 228 speakers. We have to remark here that the utterances in the test set have been manually reviewed in full detail, while this was not performed for the training set. Although this leads to more realistic recognition rates on the test set, it can result in a higher recognition performance than for the training set.

The applied model topology leads to 77 different Gaussian mixtures for the inner word states and one for the silence state. A total number of 200 Gaussian densities was used for all experiments.

For the baseline system feature vectors with 51 components based on cepstral coefficients were used. The HMM parameters were estimated during 10 iterations of ML based Viterbi training. The system gave an word error rate of 5.4% on the test set.

Using the baseline system an alignment between states and feature vectors was generated and used for computation of the LDA matrix.

Based on the LDA transformed feature vector $\vec{x}_{LDA}$ new model parameters were estimated during 10 ML iterations. Figure 1 shows the the word error and the state error rate on the training set for the LDA transformed feature vector. For the computation of the state error rate only those feature vectors that were not aligned to silence were taken into account.

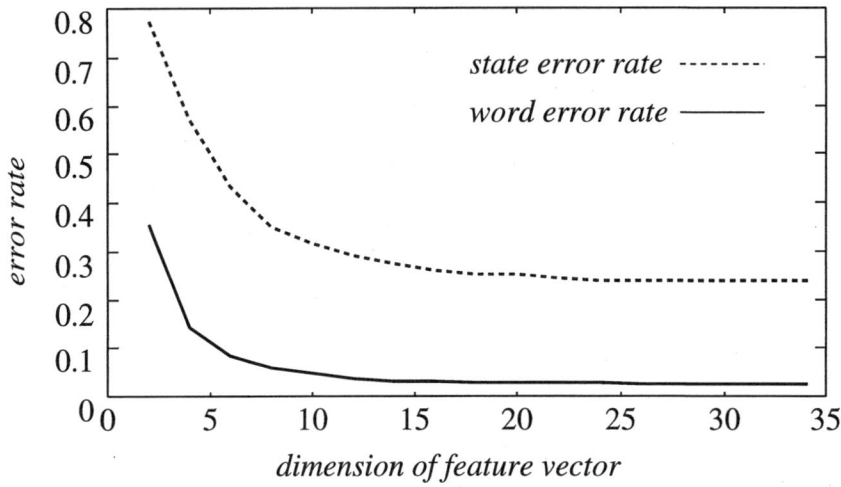

Figure 1: Word and state error rates on the training set for different sizes of the LDA transformed feature vectors

For all following experiments only the first 24 components of $\vec{x}_{LDA}$ were used. The achieved word error rate of the ML trained system on the test set was 2.0%.

With the initial model parameters taken from the ML trained models 20 iterations of MStateE training were performed. As for ML training only the mean vectors of the Gaussian densities were reestimated. The state error rate on the training set reduced from 23.2% to 18.9%. For both the training and the test set the word error rates were not significantly reduced with MStateE training. The exact reduction was from 2.7% to 2.5% word errors on the training set and from 2.0% to 1.9% word errors on the test set.

In the final experiment we applied 20 iterations of MWE training to the ML trained LDA feature based models. The resulting model showed a reduction of the word error rate from 2.7% to 0.7% on the training set and from 2.0% to 1.0% on the test set. We found an increase from 23.2% to 26.1% on the training set in state error rate.

Table 1 summarizes the error rates for the different setups.

	training set word errors	training set state errors	test set word errors
Baseline/ML	6.4%	39.5%	5.4%
LDA/ML	2.7%	23.2%	2.0%
LDA/MStateE	2.5%	18.9%	1.9%
LDA/MWE	0.7%	26.1%	1.0%

Table 1: Comparison of error rates for the training set and the test set. Baseline/ML: Maximum Likelihood training and cepstral features, LDA/ML: ML training using LDA transformed features, LDA/MWE: LDA features and Minimum State Error training, LDA/MWE: LDA features and Minimum Word Error training.

7 Summary and Discussion

Although standard first order HMMs have certain limitations they can provide reasonable classification performance for real world speech recognition tasks. With the use of some simplifications they can also be implemented with little computational costs in such applications. On the other hand the poor ability of such simple speech models to describe the speech production process correctly can lead to non-optimal performance when applying standard methods such as Maximum Likelihood parameter estimation of model parameters.

In a first step we applied a linear feature transformation based on Linear Discriminate Analysis. The classes considered here were the states of the HMMs. The objective function was therefore correlated with the ability to discriminate between the short portions of speech which were described by Gaussian mixtures. One important property of the transformed features (that did actually not result from improved class discriminance) was the decorrelation and variance whitening of the feature vector components. In the described system variances and covariances were assumed to have these properties. This reduced the mismatch between the probability distributions of the speech models and the transformed features. The other property of the LDA transformed features were an improved discrimination when using only a fraction of all feature vector components. In our experiments it was possible to reduce the computational costs of the overall system by almost 50%, while the error rate was also reduced by approximately 50%.

Although the use of LDA transformed features made our speech models more appropriate for describing the underlying stochastic process of speech production, other phenomena like correlation in time are not covered and lead to non optimal recognition performance. Using the framework of Minimum

Classification Error training model parameters could be adjusted to lead to a local minimum of an approximation of the error rate on a set of training patterns. The flexibility of the approach allowed application of this method for different kinds of class definitions. In our experiments we used the states of the HMMs (as for LDA) or alternatively the whole HMMs (respectively the words) as the classes to discriminate between.

In different experiments using the LDA transformed features we applied MCE training either for discrimination of the states (MStateE) or words (MWE). We found that it was possible to reduce the amount of state errors by approximately 20% with MStateE training, though this had no significant influence on the achieved word error rates. This might be surprising as we found that for ML training there exists a strong correlation between state error rate and word error rate. On the other hand one has to remark that with LDA transformed features there is little mismatch between the density modeling of the states and the described features. Other modeling problems might have a greater influence on the word recognition performance.

Applying MWE training, we found a reduction of the word errors of about 70% on the training set and 50% for the test set. It is remarkable that for this training method the achieved state error rate (on the training set) was more than 10% higher in comparison with the ML training and approximately 40% higher than with the MStateE training.

We conclude here that MWE as a more global training criterion is able to outperform MStateE due to its strong correlation to the applications goal: discrimination between lexical words.

References

BAHL, L.R. et al. (1993): Estimating Hidden Markov Models Parameters So As To Maximize Speech Recognition Accuracy. *IEEE Transactions on SAAP, Vol1, NO. 1, January 1993*

CHO, W., JUANG, B.H., LEE, C.H. (1992): Segmental GPD Training of HMM Based Speech Recognizer. *Proceedings ICASSP 92*

HAEB-UMBACH, R., GELLER, D., NEY, H. (1993): Improvements in Connected Digit Recognition Using Linear Discriminant Analysis And Mixture Densities. *Proceedings ICASSP 1993*

HAUENSTEIN, A., MARSCHALL, E. (1995): Methods for Improved Speech Recognition over Telephone Lines. *Proceedings ICASSP 95*

KLISCH, R. (1996): The Voice Mail Digits and Their Performance on ICSI's Hybrid HMM/ANN System. *technical report, International Computer Science Institute*

Statistical Classifiers in Computer Vision

J. Hornegger, D. Paulus, H. Niemann[1]

Lehrstuhl für Mustererkennung (Informatik 5),
Universität Erlangen, Martensstraße 3, D-91058 Erlangen, Germany

Abstract: This paper introduces a unified Bayesian approach to 3–D computer vision using segmented image features. The theoretical part summarizes the basic requirements of statistical object recognition systems. Non–standard types of models are introduced using parametric probability density functions, which allow the implementation of Bayesian classifiers for object recognition purposes. The importance of model densities is demonstrated by concrete examples. Normally distributed features are used for automatic learning, localization, and classification. The contribution concludes with the experimental evaluation of the presented theoretical approach.

1 Introduction

Classification in computer vision is commonly dominated by geometrical, model–based approaches (Faugeras (1993)). Heuristics for many algorithms in image processing restricted to the given problem domain and motivated by associated applications are reported in the literature. Herein, model–based image analysis provides the scientific framework for matching algorithms and for understanding the information process. The comprehensive goal is to describe the intrinsic character of images in a symbolic or parametric manner.
Bayesian methods have provided solutions to various classical problems in pattern recognition. Especially the progress in the field of speech processing is substantially based on the application of statistical methods. The general use of Bayesian classifiers is motivated by several aspects: they show optimality in a decision theoretic sense under a 0–1 cost function (Duda and Hart (1973)). Furthermore, statistical methods can deal with uncertainty in a natural manner, have a well elaborated mathematical theory, and provide a unified framework within which many different tasks can be considered. For that reason, we favor model–based computer vision algorithms which apply statistical discriminants or, at least, close approximations of Bayesian classifiers.
In this paper, we present a probabilistic framework for 3–D vision: statistical methods for object modeling, algorithms for the automatic estimation of model parameters — even in the presence of incomplete and disturbed training data —, classification rules, and localization methods for 3–D objects using 2–D views. The introduced model densities show several degrees

---
[1]The authors wish to thank the German Research Foundation (DFG), who partially funded the work reported here under grant SFB 182.

of freedom, and standard hidden Markov models or mixtures of densities can be derived by specialization. The experiments prove that the classification and pose estimation task for 3–D objects using real image data can be treated statistically.

A general discussion of Bayesian image analysis (section 2) is followed by a statistical description of objects and their appearance in scenes (section 3). The object recognition and localization problem is formalized (section 4), and experimental results for these problems are given (section 5).

2 Bayesian Image Analysis

There exists a wide range of model–based methods for computer vision. Model–based statistical algorithms, in general, require the stages model selection, sampling, parameter estimation, and goodness–of–fit. The main difference between standard geometrical techniques and probabilistic modeling schemes is due to the fact that Bayesian image analysis methods make use of statistical models to incorporate both, general and object specific prior knowledge. The object recognition problem is understood as the assignment of a subset of observed image features to a pattern class Ω_κ ($1 \leq \kappa \leq K$), which characterize one object or a set of objects. Statistical classifiers known from pattern recognition theory require feature vectors c of fixed dimensions and a probabilistic description of pattern classes. For an observed feature vector, the Bayesian decision rule is

$$\lambda = \operatorname*{argmax}_{\kappa} p(\Omega_\kappa|c) = \operatorname*{argmax}_{\kappa} p(\Omega_\kappa)p(c|\Omega_\kappa) \quad , \qquad (1)$$

i.e., we decide for that class with highest a posteriori probability. The basic problem for the implementation of statistical classifiers is the definition of adequate a posteriori probabilities. It is a priori not obvious how this statistical concept can be applied to solve 3–D object recognition and pose estimation problems. The required generalization of (1) is guided by the ground rules of Bayesian image analysis approaches stated by Besag (1993), which are commented in the following:

1. *Underlying images, scenes or features have to be characterized by prior probabilities.*

   These statistical measures define the *prior knowledge*; they describe, for instance, the probabilities for the appearance of objects, for the permitted pose parameters or for specific configurations of objects in the scene. The prior knowledge also allows to incorporate prior geometrical information for object recognition. At this point we do not consider the observable features, yet.

2. *Joint probability density functions for observations have to be defined.*

   The statistical behavior of *observable features* has to be defined by a probability density function. This statistical measure describes the probability that a set of features appears, if a special object is present. If the features vary with the object's pose, this density function depends on the position and orientation of objects, too.

3. *Prior probabilities and the joint density functions are combined to find the probability density function.*

   The *combination* of prior probabilities and the feature specific joint density functions results in a probability measure, which can be applied to recognition and pose estimation. This probability measure is called *model density* and describes a traditional form of regularization. The observable features and prior knowledge equally contribute to these model densities, and form the basic mathematical concept for model generation, pose estimation, and classification.

4. *Definition of an inference strategy which allows the efficient computation of a posteriori probabilities for classification.*

   The *evaluation* of a posteriori probabilities is necessary for applying the Bayesian decision rule. Efficient methods are required for the computation of a posteriori probabilities. If hidden Markov models are used, for example, the inference algorithm utilizes the efficient forward–backward algorithm (Rabiner and Juang (1993)).

These guidelines constitute the recipe for the introduction of statistical models for 3–D object recognition purposes.

3   Statistical Modeling of 3–D Objects

The Bayesian framework for 3–D object recognition based on 2–D images has to incorporate the following elements: prior knowledge, rotation and translation of objects, self–occlusion, projection from the model into the image space, and statistical modeling of errors and inaccuracies caused by varying illumination, sensor noise or segmentation errors.

Here, we will not consider single pixels or grid models, but restrict the statistical modeling on segmented images. We assume that the image $[f_{i,j}]$ is transformed into a set of D_{image}–dimensional feature vectors, i.e., the segmentation operator $\mathcal{S}$ defines the mapping

$$\mathcal{S} : [f_{i,j}] \mapsto \boldsymbol{O} \quad , \tag{2}$$

where $\boldsymbol{O} = \{\boldsymbol{o}_k \in \mathbb{R}^{D_{\text{image}}} | 1 \leq k \leq m\}$. Within the segmentation step points, lines, regions or other features can be computed. The number of observed, which are projected to the 2–D image plane is not constant for different images. The cardinality of $\boldsymbol{O}$ depends on the viewing direction, on the applied segmentation algorithm, and on the lighting conditions. Due to the projection, the range information and the assignment between image and model features is lost. The statistical model generation, classification, and localization are limited to these projected feature vectors $\boldsymbol{O}$. In general, model densities of 3–D objects appearing in images embody three principal components: the uncertainty of observed feature vectors, the dependency of features on the object's pose, and the correspondence between image and model features. The statistical description of an object belonging to class Ω_κ is defined by the density $p(\boldsymbol{O}|\boldsymbol{B}_\kappa, \boldsymbol{R}, \boldsymbol{t})$, and discrete priors $p(\Omega_\kappa)$, $1 \leq \kappa \leq K$, if only single objects appear, or $p(\Omega_{\kappa_1}, \Omega_{\kappa_2}, \ldots, \Omega_{\kappa_q})$ for multiple object scenes. Here, $\boldsymbol{O}$ represents the set of observed feature vectors, and the parameter set $\boldsymbol{B}_\kappa$ contains the model-specific parameters, which model the statistical behavior of features as well as the assignment. The parameters $\boldsymbol{R}$ and $\boldsymbol{t}$, however, symbolize the rotation, translation, and the projection from the model space into the image plane.

The major problem now is the explicit definition of $p(\boldsymbol{O}|\boldsymbol{B}_\kappa, \boldsymbol{R}, \boldsymbol{t})$. Generally, we distinguish between the 3–D model and the 2–D image space. The observable D_{image}-dimensional image features are characterized by $\boldsymbol{O} = \{\boldsymbol{o}_1, \boldsymbol{o}_2, \ldots, \boldsymbol{o}_m\}$. The corresponding D_{model}-dimensional features in the model space are denoted by $\boldsymbol{C}_\kappa = \{\boldsymbol{c}_{\kappa,1}, \boldsymbol{c}_{\kappa,2}, \ldots, \boldsymbol{c}_{\kappa,n_\kappa}\}$, where in general $n_\kappa \neq m$ due to segmentation errors and occlusion.

Example: *If a 3–D cube is characterized by its corners, $\boldsymbol{C}_\kappa$ includes the 3–D corners. The 2–D image features $\boldsymbol{O}$ are the projected 3–D corners of the model.*

Let us assume the parametric density of the model feature $\boldsymbol{c}_{\kappa,l_k}$ corresponding to $\boldsymbol{o}_k$ is given by $p(\boldsymbol{c}_{\kappa,l_k}|\boldsymbol{a}_{\kappa,l_k})$. A standard density transform results in the density $p(\boldsymbol{o}_k|\boldsymbol{a}_{\kappa,l_k}, \boldsymbol{R}, \boldsymbol{t})$, which characterizes the statistical behavior of the feature $\boldsymbol{o}_k$ in the image plane dependent on the object's pose parameters $\boldsymbol{R}$ and $\boldsymbol{t}$.

Example: *If normally distributed 3–D model features are present, then $\boldsymbol{a}_{\kappa,l_k}$ includes the 3–D mean vector $\boldsymbol{\mu}_{\kappa,l_k}$ and the (3×3) covariance matrix $\boldsymbol{\Sigma}_{\kappa,l_k}$. Let the affine transform $\boldsymbol{o}_k = \boldsymbol{R}\boldsymbol{c}_{\kappa,l_k} + \boldsymbol{t}$ define the mapping from the model into the image space. The image feature $\boldsymbol{o}_k$ is again normally distributed with mean vector $\boldsymbol{R}\boldsymbol{\mu}_{\kappa,l_k} + \boldsymbol{t}$ and covariance matrix $\boldsymbol{R}\boldsymbol{\Sigma}_{\kappa,l_k}\boldsymbol{R}^T$.*

An assignment function ζ_κ defines a discrete mapping, which yields for an observed feature $\boldsymbol{o}_k$ the index $l_k \in \{1, 2, \ldots, n_\kappa\}$ of the corresponding model feature $\boldsymbol{c}_{\kappa,l_k}$, i.e., $\zeta_\kappa(\boldsymbol{o}_k) = l_k$. A set of observed features can thus be associated with the assignment vector $\boldsymbol{\zeta}_\kappa = (\zeta_\kappa(\boldsymbol{o}_1), \zeta_\kappa(\boldsymbol{o}_2), \ldots, \zeta_\kappa(\boldsymbol{o}_m))^T$, which is considered to be a random vector, i.e., the classical matching problem is also modelled statistically. The discrete probability of this random vector is denoted by $p(\boldsymbol{\zeta}_\kappa)$. The probability density function for observing the set of features $\boldsymbol{O}$ thus is,

$$p(\boldsymbol{O}|\boldsymbol{B}_\kappa, \boldsymbol{R}, \boldsymbol{t}) = \sum_{\boldsymbol{\zeta}_\kappa} p(\boldsymbol{\zeta}_\kappa) \prod_{k=1}^{m} p(\boldsymbol{o}_k|\boldsymbol{a}_{\zeta_\kappa(\boldsymbol{o}_k)}, \boldsymbol{R}, \boldsymbol{t}) \quad , \qquad (3)$$

wherein the non observable assignment is eliminated by marginalization, i.e., we sum over all assignments $\boldsymbol{\zeta}_\kappa$. The evaluation of (3) is computationally bounded by $\mathcal{O}(n_\kappa^m m)$. If pairwise statistically independent assignments are assumed, this complexity reduces to $\mathcal{O}(n_\kappa m)$, and we get a product of density mixtures. Hidden Markov models are derived from (3), if statistically dependent assignments of first order are assumed and the feature transform is omitted. The inference strategy for this case is bounded by $\mathcal{O}(n_\kappa^2 m)$ (Hornegger (1996)).

This flexible formalism of model densities can easily be applied to use multiple views for pose estimation or classification. Assume there are N different views yielding the feature sets ${}^1\boldsymbol{O}, {}^2\boldsymbol{O}, \ldots, {}^N\boldsymbol{O}$. The correct pose parameters are denoted by $\boldsymbol{R}$ and $\boldsymbol{t}$. The images are grabbed by a camera, which is mounted on a calibrated robot arm. Thus, the approximate extrinsic parameters ${}^\varrho\boldsymbol{R}$ and ${}^\varrho\boldsymbol{t}$ for each view ${}^\varrho\boldsymbol{O}$ are known. These parameters can be expressed in terms of sums using the viewed object's pose $\boldsymbol{R}$ and $\boldsymbol{t}$:

$$ {}^\varrho\boldsymbol{R} \;=\; \boldsymbol{R} + \Delta^\varrho\boldsymbol{R} \quad \text{and} \quad {}^\varrho\boldsymbol{t} \;=\; \boldsymbol{t} + \Delta^\varrho\boldsymbol{t} \;. \qquad (4)$$

The density for multiple observations thus is

$$ p({}^1\boldsymbol{O}, {}^1\boldsymbol{O}, \ldots, {}^N\boldsymbol{O} | \boldsymbol{B}_\kappa, \boldsymbol{R}, \boldsymbol{t}) \;=\; \prod_{\varrho=1}^{N} p({}^\varrho\boldsymbol{O} | \boldsymbol{B}_\kappa, \boldsymbol{R} + \Delta^\varrho\boldsymbol{R}, \boldsymbol{t} + \Delta^\varrho\boldsymbol{t}) \;, (5) $$

if statistically independent views are presupposed. The use of multiple views will improve the discriminating power of the observed features, because the more data are available for pose estimation and classification, the more reliable results can be expected, even if calibration results will not provide the exact parameters.

4 Statistical Object Recognition

The automatic generation of model densities includes different components: the definition of the structure and the computation of free parameters. The number of model features, the distribution of single features, the mapping from the model into the image space and the dependency of assignments characterize the structure. A practical solution of automatic structure generation is an open research problem (Hornegger (1996)). Nevertheless, there exist algorithms for the estimation of the parameter set $\boldsymbol{B}_\kappa$, if the structure of the model density is defined; the computation of $\boldsymbol{B}_\kappa$ for each object class Ω_κ, $\kappa = 1, 2, \ldots, K$ includes the estimation of the discrete probabilities $p(\boldsymbol{\zeta}_\kappa)$, which model the assignment function, and $\{\boldsymbol{a}_{\kappa,l} \,|\, l = 1, \ldots, n_\kappa\}$, which characterizes single model features. The available training data consist of features, which are projected model features. The depth information as well as the assignment function are missing. Therefore, the computation of $\boldsymbol{B}_\kappa$ corresponds to an incomplete data estimation problem. An established method which can deal with this type of parameter estimation problems is provided by the Expectation Maximization algorithm (Dempster et. al. (1977)). For normally distributed point features, for instance, there exist closed form iteration formulas which allow the estimation of mean vectors from projections. The interested reader will find the complete derivation of several training algorithms for normally distributed point and line features in Hornegger (1996). The probabilistic modeling of objects makes the application of the Bayesian decision rule (1) possible, but some extensions are required. Instead of a single vector a set of features $\boldsymbol{O}$ is given. Furthermore, the pose parameters are part of the probability density functions. The modified Bayesian decision rule, which allows the statistical classification of objects thus is

$$\lambda = \underset{\kappa}{\operatorname{argmax}}\ p(\Omega_\kappa|\boldsymbol{O}) = \underset{\kappa}{\operatorname{argmax}}\ p(\Omega_\kappa) p(\boldsymbol{O}|\boldsymbol{B}_\kappa, \boldsymbol{R}, \boldsymbol{t})\ . \qquad (6)$$

Since rotation and translation of objects is a priori unknown, $\boldsymbol{R}$ and $\boldsymbol{t}$ are free parameters. A posteriori probabilities $p(\Omega_\kappa|\boldsymbol{O})$ cannot be evaluated explicitly. The pose estimation stage has to compute the best position and orientation before the class decision is possible; the estimation of $\boldsymbol{R}$ and $\boldsymbol{t}$ corresponds to the maximization problem

$$\{\widehat{\boldsymbol{R}}, \widehat{\boldsymbol{t}}\} = \underset{\boldsymbol{R},\boldsymbol{t}}{\operatorname{argmax}}\ p(\boldsymbol{O}|\boldsymbol{B}_\kappa, \boldsymbol{R}, \boldsymbol{t})\ . \qquad (7)$$

This parameter estimation task is associated with a global optimization problem of a concave multimodal likelihood function. Probabilistic optimization routines are discussed in Hornegger (1996) which allow practically efficient solutions.

5 Experimental Results

The experimental evaluations examine several aspects: we compare standard methods for pose estimation with the introduced statistical approach, show the improvement of pose estimation results using multiple views, and discuss the recognition rates based on a test set including 1600 randomly chosen views of simple polyhedral objects (Figure 1). All experiments run on an HP 9000/735 (99 MHz, 124 MIPS).

Figure 1: Polyhedral 3–D objects

First a comparison of pose estimation techniques based on the geometrical alignment method of Huttenlocher (1993) and the statistical approach was

number of processors	2	3	4	5	6
speed–up	1.7	2.8	3.5	3.9	4.2

Table 1: Parallelization of pose estimation

3–D object	recognition rate [%]		run time per image [sec]	
	points	lines	points	lines
Ω_1	47	44	466	1882
Ω_2	78	82	485	2101
Ω_3	58	36	465	1933
Ω_4	89	76	471	1520
average	68	59	472	1859

Table 2: Run time and recognition rate of 3–D experiments

done using 49 test images. The statistical pose estimation algorithm requires 80s using global optimization, and the alignment method needs 70s in average. The correct pose is computed for 45 images using the statistical approach (see Figure 2). The alignment method failed for 11 images. This experiment shows that the statistical approach can compete with geometrically based methods both with respect to reliability and run time. The computation time for pose estimation is crucially influenced by the global optimization module and its efficiency. The parameter space of continuous model densities is easily partitioned into disjoint subsets which can be considered independent from each other. The use of four processors, for instance, results in a speed–up of 3.5. Table 1 summarizes the speed–up for increasing numbers of processors.

The use of multiple views for pose estimation shows remarkable improvements regarding the correct pose parameters. We run experiments using 400 views and the correct pose parameters increased from 96% to 100%. Existing ambiguities considering a single image are eliminated with a second view, but the average computation time using two views instead of one is three times higher. In average it takes 420s to compute the right position.

The recognition results using 1600 test images of objects shown in Figure 1 are summarized in Table 2. It is distinguished between point and line features.

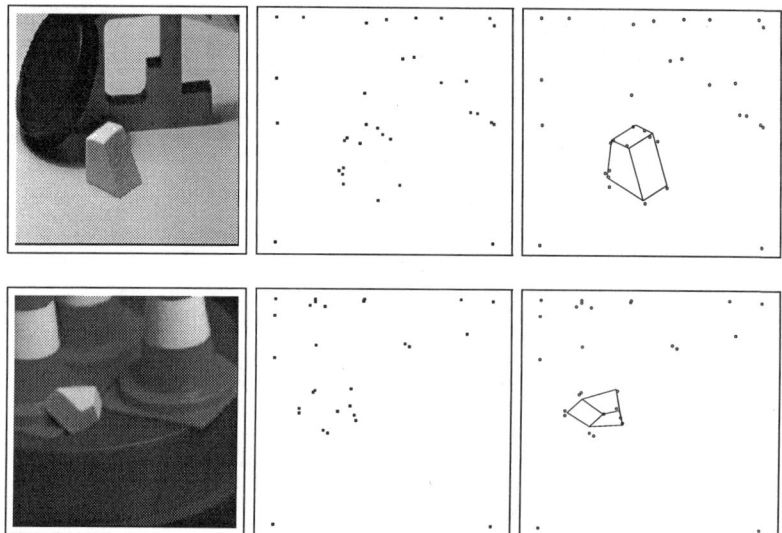

Figure 2: Examples of scenes with heterogeneous background (left: gray-level image, middle: segmentation result, right: estimated pose)

6 Summary and Conclusions

In this paper, we proposed a framework for Bayesian image analysis. We presented a coherent approach to both modeling single features and the probabilistic characterization of the assignment function between image and model features. The introduced concept of model densities combine assignment, rotation, translation, projection of features, and prior knowledge in a unified manner. The model generation process has to deal with incomplete data estimation problems, whereas the pose computation corresponds to a maximum likelihood estimation. Due to the statistical nature of the introduced modeling scheme, the implementation of Bayesian classifiers for object recognition is made possible. Experimental results with real data show the practical use of statistical classifiers in computer vision.

Indeed, with respect to computer vision applications statistical methods are still in its infancy, but the implemented and evaluated applications show that there is a considerable potential for future development and research.

References

BESAG, J. (1993): Towards Bayesian Image Analysis In: K.V. Mardia and G.K. Kanji (eds.): *Statistics and Images*, volume 1. Carfax Publishing Company, Abingdon, 107–119.

DEMPSTER, A., LAIRD, N. and RUBIN, D. (1977): Maximum Likelihood from

Incomplete Data via the EM Algorithm *Journal of the Royal Statistical Society, series B (Methodological), volume 39, number 1, 1–38.*

DUDA, R. and HART, P. (1973): Pattern Classification and Scene Analysis. John Wiley & Sons, New York.

FAUGERAS, O. (1993): Three–Dimensional Computer Vision – A Geometric Viewpoint. MIT Press, Cambridge, Massachusetts.

HORNEGGER, J. (1996): Statistische Modellierung, Klassifikation und Lokalisation von Objekten. Shaker, Aachen.

HUTTENLOCHER, D. (1993): Recognition by Alignment In: A.K. Jain and P.J. Flynn (eds.): *Three-Dimensional Object Recognition Systems*. Elsevier, Amsterdam, 311–324.

RABINER, L. and JUANG, B.-H. (1993): Fundamentals of Speech Recognition. Prentice Hall, Englewood Cliffs, NJ.

Speech Signal Classification with Hybrid Systems

Ch. Neukirchen, G. Rigoll

Faculty of Electrical Engineering, Department of Computer Science,
Gerhard-Mercator-University Duisburg,
D-47057 Duisburg, Germany

Abstract: This paper gives a brief overview on two successful hybrid approaches that combine artificial neural networks and Hidden Markov Models for speech signal classification tasks. At first, a short description of traditional stochastic-based Hidden Markov Model speech recognizers with different kinds of emission probabilities are given. The first proposed hybrid approach uses a neural network that approximates arbitrary emission densities in a model-free way. The second hybrid system uses discrete models and a neural network that is trained to work as optimal vector quantizer. The paper compares both systems and integrates them in the traditional stochastic model framework. Speech recognition results are given for the speaker-independent continuous speech ARPA resource management database.

1 Introduction

Research during recent years has shown that Hidden Markov Models (HMMs) are the most successful approach for the recognition of speaker-independent continuous speech. By using context dependent HMMs, very high recognition accuracies have been achieved also in large vocabulary tasks. The main goal in training such kind of system is to estimate the parameters of a discrete or a continuous density model in order to fit the acoustic feature vectors.

In parallel to the traditional HMM systems, hybrid NN/HMM approaches combining both, HMM technology and artificial neural networks, have been developed to achieve State-of-the-Art performance. These hybrid systems take advantage of the neural network training algorithms that are discriminative by nature. Furthermore the hybrid speech recognizers typically make less strong assumptions about the probability densities of the acoustic features compared to the traditional HMM systems.

In the following a short overview on traditional HMM based speech recognition using (semi-)continuous and discrete models is given. We then give an integration of two popular hybrid speech recognition approaches in the traditional HMM framework. Finally, these approaches are compared and recognition results for the speaker-independent resource management task are given.

2 Traditional HMM systems for speech classification

In current speech classification systems at first the speech signal is typically divided into overlapping frames with a frame rate around 10ms. For signal analysis, suitable features like cepstral coefficients, filter-bank parameters, PLP parameters, signal energy and temporal derivatives etc. are extracted from each frame. The temporal sequence X of the acoustic feature vectors $\mathbf{x}(n) \in X$ (with $1 \leq n \leq N$) is modeled by a Hidden Markov Model (HMM). The HMM is described by the probabilities a_{ij} of transition from state S_i to state S_j and by the emission probability densities $p(\mathbf{x}|S)$ of generating a feature vector $\mathbf{x}$ in state S. Since the true probability densities are unknown several assumptions about the $p(\mathbf{x}|S)$ must be made in the HMM framework. A very general assumption is to use a mixture of J_S different basic densities $p(\mathbf{x}|m_j, S)$ for the HMM emission probabilities. It can be shown that any arbitrary probability density can by modeled by a mixture of Gaussians. In the speech recognition community this approach is referred to as *continuous* HMM system with the HMM emission densities given by:

$$p(\mathbf{x}|S) = \sum_{j=1}^{J_S} p(\mathbf{x}|m_j, S) \cdot P(m_j|S) \qquad (1)$$

Most commonly Gaussians are used as basic densities and the $P(m_j|S)$ are called the mixture weights. The system parameters i.e. the means and the variances of the Gaussians and the mixture weights are determined during maximum likelihood HMM training via the forward-backward algorithm.

The so called *semi-continuous (tied mixture)* system can be derived from the approach given above by using a large pool of J different basic Gaussian densities that are shared among all the states of all HMMs. Thus the emission probabilities are given by:

$$p(\mathbf{x}|S) = \sum_{j=1}^{J} p(\mathbf{x}|m_j) \cdot P(m_j|S) \qquad (2)$$

Typically the semi-continuous systems use less parameters compared to the untied continuous systems and the parameters can be better estimated in a robust way when the amount of training data is limited.

A third classical approach are *discrete* HMM systems. In a discrete system the continuous feature space is subdivided by a vector quantizer (VQ) into J different partitions. Most commonly the VQ is constructed by an unsupervised cluster algorithm like k-means or LBG. In this case the j-th VQ-partition is associated with the label m_j and any feature vector in the j-partition is mapped on m_j. Thus the VQ maps the sequence of continuous acoustic feature vectors $X = \{\mathbf{x}(1), \ldots, \mathbf{x}(N)\}$ on a temporal sequence of discrete VQ-labels $\hat{M} = \{\hat{m}(1), \ldots, \hat{m}(N)\}$ (with $\mathbf{x}(n) \to \hat{m}(n)$). This sequence of labels is modeled by an HMM that uses the (discrete) emission probability $P(m_j|S)$ for generating the discrete label $\hat{m} = m_j$ by state S.

In practice the discrete HMMs work faster than the continuous systems because calculation of $P(m_j|S)$ can be done rapidly by table lookup compared to the slow calculation of the $p(\mathbf{x}|S)$ in the (semi-)continuous case. On the other hand the usage of a VQ in the discrete HMM case causes an information loss due to the quantization error that leads to a degradation of recognition rates that can be avoided by the continuous models.

3 Hybrid speech recognition systems

3.1 Neural network as probability estimator

One possible drawback of traditional continuous HMMs is the assumption that the acoustic feature distributions can be modeled by mixtures of Gaussians; what is not true for a small number of mixture components. The usage of a neural network offers a way to incorporate model-free methods for density approximation that avoids these assumptions. For speech recognition simple layered structures of nodes and connecting weights like multilayer perceptrons (MLP), radial basis functions (RBF) and recurrent networks have been used successfully. Such kind of neural network uses the n-th feature vector $\mathbf{x}(n)$ (along with some acoustic context $\mathbf{x}(n-t)\ldots\mathbf{x}(n+t)$) as network input. The neural network has J different output nodes, the internal activation of the j-th output node is denoted $f_j(\mathbf{x}(n))$ and the output of the network at node j is given by the softmax function, introduced by Bridle (1990):

$$O_j(\mathbf{x}(n)) = \frac{\exp(\frac{f_j(\mathbf{x}(n))}{T})}{\sum_{i=1}^{J}\exp(\frac{f_i(\mathbf{x}(n))}{T})} \qquad (3)$$

Thus the outputs have the property to be positive and to sum up to unity, what allows an interpretation as probabilities. The parameter T in eqn. (3) is usually set to unity.

Typically the neural networks are trained in a supervised fashion using a method like backpropagation that needs a target vector at the network output for each training pattern. In the case of training hybrid speech recognizers these target classes are the HMM states associated with the training vectors; in the following we assume that the n-th training sample $\mathbf{x}(n)$ was generated by (i.e. belongs to the class of) HMM state $S(n)$. Thus the number of NN output nodes J must be equal to the total number of different HMM states and the ideal target of the j-th output node when the n-th training pattern is presented at the NN input would be be $\delta_{j,S(n)}$.

One suitable training criterion of such NN would be the minimization of the error between the NN outputs and targets that is given by:

$$E = \frac{1}{2}\sum_{n=1}^{N}\sum_{j=1}^{J}(O_j(\mathbf{x}(n)) - \delta_{j,S(n)})^2 \qquad (4)$$

The derivative of eqn. (4) with respect to a NN weight denoted by θ that can be obtained by the backpropagation method is given by:

$$\frac{\partial E}{\partial \theta} = \frac{1}{T} \sum_{n=1}^{N} \sum_{l=1}^{J} \frac{\partial f_l(\mathbf{x}(n))}{\partial \theta} \cdot A_l^{(E)}(\mathbf{x}(n)) \quad (5)$$

with

$$A_l^{(E)}(\mathbf{x}(n)) = O_l(\mathbf{x}(n)) \cdot \sum_{j=1}^{J} (O_j(\mathbf{x}(n)) - \delta_{j,S(n)}) \cdot (\delta_{j,l} - O_j(\mathbf{x}(n))) \quad (6)$$

Here the expression $\frac{\partial f_l(\mathbf{x}(n))}{\partial \theta}$ depends on the internal structure of the NN (i.e. number of different layers, recurrent nodes, etc.)

Another well known training criterion that fits very well with the softmax activation function is the minimization of the cross-entropy between the network outputs and the targets for several output nodes:

$$J = -\sum_{n=1}^{N} \sum_{j=1}^{J} \delta_{j,S(n)} \log(O_j(\mathbf{x}(n))) \quad (7)$$

In this case the derivative is given by a very simple expression that is similar to eqn. (5) but eqn. (6) is replaced by:

$$A_l^{(J)}(\mathbf{x}(n)) = O_l(\mathbf{x}(n)) - \delta_{S(n),l} \quad (8)$$

For both cases, error minimization and cross-entropy minimization, it has been shown (see Bishop (1995)), that the NN outputs can be interpreted as an approximation of the posterior class probability, if the objective function is globally minimized. In the case of speech signal classification that means:

$$O_j(\mathbf{x}(n)) = P(S_j|\mathbf{x}(n)) \quad (9)$$

i.e. the j-th network output is the probability that the network input $\mathbf{x}(n)$ was generated by the HMM state S_j. These posterior probabilities can be transformed into scaled likelihood densities by dividing by the a priori state probability $P(S_j)$ that can be obtained by counting in the training samples, yielding:

$$p(\mathbf{x}|S_j) = c \cdot \frac{O_j(\mathbf{x})}{P(S_j)} \quad (10)$$

In a hybrid speech recognition system the scaled likelihood densities can be used as HMM emission densities by incorporating eqn. (10) instead of eqn. (1).

Hence, such hybrid system makes only weak assumptions about the form of parametric density that is used as HMM emission probability. Instead of this the neural network, that makes use of its parameters (i.e. weights) in a very efficient (parallel) way, can model a large variety of different (scaled) emission densities. The main disadvantage of such hybrid speech recognition system is the identity between the number of HMM states and the number of NN output nodes; because with a large number of states (when using triphone HMMs there are several thousand states) the size of the neural network becomes impractical. Therefore, common systems that use neural networks as probability estimators are based on monophone HMMs. For usage with triphone HMMs the NNs must be split up.

3.2 Neural network as vector quantizer

In section 2. the concepts of semi-continuous modeling and discrete modeling are treated independently. By introducing an alternative hybrid approach that uses a neural network as vector quantizer the discrete HMMs can be integrated in the (semi-) continuous density model framework.

As shown above in a discrete model the VQ maps the feature vector $\mathbf{x}(n)$ on the discrete label $\hat{m}(\mathbf{x}(n))$ with $\hat{m}(\mathbf{x}(n)) = m_j$ if $\mathbf{x}(n)$ is in the j-th VQ-partition. Therefore the probability of generating a label m_i for a given $\mathbf{x}$ is $P(m_i|\mathbf{x}) = \delta_{m_i, \hat{m}}$. Application of the Bayes rule leads to the probability density of $\mathbf{x}$ in the j-th partition:

$$p(\mathbf{x}|m_j) = \frac{P(m_j|\mathbf{x}) \cdot p(\mathbf{x})}{P(m_j)} = \begin{cases} \frac{p(\mathbf{x})}{P(m_j)} & \text{if } m_j = \hat{m}(\mathbf{x}) \\ 0 & \text{else} \end{cases} \quad (11)$$

This can be combined with the emission probability density of the semi-continuous HMM (eqn. (2)) yielding a continuous density for a VQ-based HMM:

$$p(\mathbf{x}|S) = \frac{p(\mathbf{x})}{P(\hat{m}(\mathbf{x}))} \cdot P(\hat{m}(\mathbf{x})|S) \quad (12)$$

From eqn. (12) follows that in the VQ case the modeled state dependent continuous density $p(\mathbf{x}|S)$ is piecewise proportional to the state independent density $p(\mathbf{x})$ for all different HMM states S with $\frac{P(\hat{m}(\mathbf{x})|S)}{P(\hat{m}(\mathbf{x}))}$ as weighting factor. This is a constraint that may limit the modeling power of discrete models. On the other hand in eqn. (12) the expression $\frac{p(\mathbf{x})}{P(\hat{m}(\mathbf{x}))}$ is equal for all different HMM states S. Thus during classification (when the $p(\mathbf{x}|S)$ are compared) only $P(\hat{m}(\mathbf{x})|S)$ must be evaluated and compared. Therefore the system can handle any form of the state independent density $p(\mathbf{x})$ since it is actually not needed in the calculations.

For classifier training the speech vector samples may be used to learn the parameters of the HMMs as well as the parameters of the vector quantizer. In the following it is assumed that the n-th training vector $\mathbf{x}(n)$ is mapped by the VQ on the discrete label $\hat{m}(n) = \hat{m}(\mathbf{x}(n))$. There are K different HMM states S_k ($1 \leq k \leq K$); the state that generated the n-th acoustic sample vector is denoted $S(n)$. Again θ describes the set of VQ parameters and the state independent density $p(\mathbf{x}(n))$ is assumed independent from the parameters θ. The widely used training criterion for HMMs is the maximum likelihood (ML) objective function that leads with eqn. (12) to:

$$\theta_{ML} = \underset{\theta}{\operatorname{argmax}} \prod_{n=1}^{N} p_\theta(\mathbf{x}(n)|S(n)) = \underset{\theta}{\operatorname{argmax}} \prod_{n=1}^{N} \frac{P_\theta(\hat{m}_\theta(n)|S(n))}{P_\theta(\hat{m}_\theta(n))} \quad (13)$$

Eqn. (13) defines an objective for designing an optimal vector quantizer in the ML sense. To allow a simple interpretation eqn. (13) can be transformed into: $argmax_\theta(H(\hat{M}) - H(\hat{M}|S)) = argmax_\theta(H(S) - H(S|\hat{M}))$. That is the maximization of the mutual information (MMI) between the stream S of HMM states and the stream of labels $\hat{M}$ generated by the VQ. Because the stream of HMM states S does not depend on the VQ parameters, eqn. (13) can be rewritten as:

$$\underset{\theta}{\operatorname{argmin}}\left(H(S|\hat{M}_\theta)\right) = \underset{\theta}{\operatorname{argmin}}\left(-\sum_{k=1}^{K}\sum_{j=1}^{J} P_\theta(S_k, \hat{m}_j) \cdot \log \frac{P_\theta(S_k, \hat{m}_j)}{\sum_{r=1}^{K} P_\theta(S_r, \hat{m}_j)}\right) \quad (14)$$

In the following for vector quantization a Winner-takes-all (WTA) neural network will be used. As in the previous section any kind of NN topology (i.e. MLP, RBF, recurrent nets, etc.) can be applied. The Winner-takes-all rule selects the output node with the highest internal activation $f_j(\mathbf{x})$ as VQ label $m_j = \hat{m}(\mathbf{x})$. Thus in contrast to section 3.1, here the individual NN output activations are not considered, we are just interested in the decision boundaries formed by the winning nodes of the neural network. The output of the j-th node according to the WTA rule can be interpreted as probability of generating the VQ label m_j given an acoustic vector $\mathbf{x}$ at the NN input, that is (as shown above): $O_j(\mathbf{x}) = P(m_j|\mathbf{x}) = \delta_{m_j, \hat{m}(\mathbf{x})}$ During NN training with gradient information, finite derivatives are needed, thus the crisp WTA output activation must be approximated by the softmax function (eqn. (3)) with a quite small choice for the parameter T. These outputs can be used to calculate the probabilities that are contained in the MMI objective function (eqn. (14)) by averaging over all training samples:

$$P(S_k, \hat{m}_j) = \frac{1}{N}\sum_{n=1}^{N} \delta_{S_k, S(n)} \cdot O_j(\mathbf{x}(n)) \quad (15)$$

Calculating the derivative of eqn. (14) with respect to a neural network weight θ yields an expression similar to eqn. (5) but eqn. (6) is replaced by:

$$A_l^{(H)}(\mathbf{x}(n)) = -\frac{1}{N}O_l(\mathbf{x}(n)) \cdot \sum_{j=1}^{J} \log P(S(n)|m_j) \cdot (\delta_{j,l} - O_j(\mathbf{x}(n))) \quad (16)$$

In spite of the similarities in the topological structure and the expression for calculating the derivatives in training between the MMI-VQ neural network presented here and the traditional NNs of section 3.1 there are some important differences: In the MMI-VQ-NN the number of output nodes J can be chosen arbitrarily and may be larger or even smaller than the number of HMM states K. Thus, in this kind of hybrid system, triphone HMMs with several thousand states can be applied easily. Furthermore, there are no targets presented to the NN output nodes during training. Instead of this, the network finds the optimal outputs in a self-organizing way by considering all training samples simultaneously.

4 Speech recognition experiments and results

To compare the different approaches presented above, word recognition rates of three popular speech recognition systems for a standard speech database are given here.

The first system is the state-of-the-art HTK speech recognizer representing a continuous HMM approach that uses mixtures of Gaussians as emission probability densities (for details see Woodland and Young (1993)). As acoustic features 12 mel-cepstral coefficients plus relative signal power plus their first and second temporal derivatives are used. The stream of feature vectors is modeled by ca. 2300 tied-state context dependent word-internal triphone HMMs. Each HMM consists of three states with strict left-to-right topology. Each state uses five Gaussians per mixture density, comprising ca. 1 million parameters.

The second system is a hybrid NN/HMM speech recognizer. It uses neural networks as vector quantizer that are trained according to the MMI objective function and discrete output HMMs. To allow a better comparison the same acoustic features as in the HTK system described above are obtained here. The system also uses ca. 2300 tied-state word-internal three state left-to right triphone HMMs. Each state models discrete emission probabilities of four VQ-streams. Thus four different MLP neural networks as vector quantizers are integrated into the system. One NN for the cepstral features (12 inputs), one for the power and its derivatives (3 inputs), one for the first (12 inputs) and one for the second derivatives (12 inputs). The NNs have 200 output nodes, they are trained on the MMI objective function. The system uses ca. 1.8 million adjustable parameters, details are given in Neukirchen and Rigoll (1997).

The third speech recognizer is a hybrid NN/HMM system of Cambridge University, described by Robinson (1994), that applies a neural network as a-posteriori estimator. The system uses cepstral coefficients plus signal power plus pitch as acoustic features. Quite simple structured monophone HMMs with a single emitting state (total: 61) are integrated in the system. The (scaled) emission probability density is modeled by a recurrent neural network that estimates monophone a-posteriori probabilities. The recurrent network has 61 output nodes and 256 different recurrent neurons that represent the current state of the NN, yielding ca. 90 thousand weights. The

Test set	continuous HMM	MMI-NN-VQ/HMM	recurrent NN/HMM
Feb'89	96,0% (95,5%)	96,3% (95,6%)	95,7% (95,0%)
Oct'89	95,4% (94,9%)	95,4% (94,5%)	94,8% (94,2%)
Feb'91	96,6% (96,0%)	96,7% (95,9%)	95,4% (94,4%)
Sep'92	93,6% (92,6%)	93,9% (92,5%)	91,5% (90,0%)
average	95,4% (94,7%)	95,6% (94,6%)	94,3% (93,4%)

Table 1: Comparison of RM SI word recognition rates (correct (accuracy))

neural network is trained by the backpropagation through time (BPTT) algorithm according to a relative entropy objective function.

As database for the experiments the speaker-independent part of the Resource Management (RM) corpus is used. This database consists of continuous spoken english sentences using ca. 1000 different words. For system training 3990 different sentences spoken by 109 different speakers are used. The recognition tests are performed on the four official DARPA test sets feb'89, oct'89, feb'91 and sep'92. For speech decoding a beam-guided viterbi search using the official DARPA word-pair grammar (perplexity ca. 60) is applied.

The word recognition rates for these three systems are shown in tab. 1. The results show that the first hybrid system using discrete triphone HMMs and the MMI neural network performs as well as the state-of-the-art continuous density system. The second hybrid system using the recurrent network as phoneme probability estimator performs by 1% (absolute) worse. But it has to be taken in account that such system only uses context-independent monophone models while the other systems get highly improved recognition rates by incorporating triphone models.

All in all, the hybrid approaches presented here offer some interesting alternatives concerning the modeling power and mathematical assumptions and it has been experimentally shown that these systems compare very well to other traditional speech recognizers.

References

BISHOP, C.M. (1995): Neural Networks for Pattern Recognition. *Oxford, Clarendon Press*

BRIDLE, J.S. (1990): Probabilistic Interpretation of Feedforward Classification Outputs, with Relationships to Statistical Pattern Recognition. *Neurocomputing: Algorithms, Architectures and Applications, Nato ASI Series, Springer, 227-236*

NEUKIRCHEN, C. and RIGOLL, G. (1997): Advanced training methods and new network topologies for hybrid MMI-Connectionist/HMM speech recognition systems. *Proc. IEEE ICASSP, Munich, 3257-3260*

ROBINSON, A.J. (1994): An Application of Recurrent Nets to Phone Probability Estimation. *IEEE Trans. Neural Networks, Vol. 5, No. 2, 298-305*

WOODLAND, P.C. and YOUNG, S.J. (1993): The HTK tied-state continuous speech recognizer. *Proc. Eurospeech, Berlin, 2207–2210*

Stochastic Modelling of Knowledge Sources in Automatic Speech Recognition

Hermann Ney

Lehrstuhl für Informatik VI, RWTH Aachen
University of Technology, D-52056 Aachen, Germany

Abstract: This paper gives an overview over the stochastic approach in automatic speech recognition. The Bayes decision rule along with its application to the speech recognition problem is discussed. There are five topics in stochastic modelling for speech recognition that are studied in more detail: the EM algorithm, the probabilistic interpretation of neural net outputs, the method of decision trees, the leaving-one-out method for language modelling and the maximum entropy approach to language modelling.

1 Introduction

During the last three decades, the performance of automatic systems for continuous speech recognition has been drastically improved. This progress has been achieved primarily by improving the statistical modelling techniques. This paper tries to illustrate the role of statistics in this context of automatic speech recognition by computer. Although we emphasize the *spoken* language, i.e. speech, over the *written* language, it should be stressed that many of the concepts presented are becoming more and more popular also for the processing of written language. The principal goal of statistics as used in speech recognition is to learn from observations and make predictions about new observations. This point of view puts more emphasis on the prediction of new observation than on the retrospective interpretation of given observations, which is maybe more along the mainstream statistics as it is traditionally found in textbooks.

In our applications, the statistical models are simplifications of complex dependencies in the real world of speech and language. Therefore in most cases, it is a mistake to assume that any such model is a true representation of the underlying processes for speech and language. What we require instead, however, is that the model is useful for predicting new observations. Often this requirement goes hand in hand with the desire to have a parsimonious description of the relevant dependencies in speech and language data. Unlike traditional statistics, our goal is to make intensive use of the computer for statistical modelling. Therefore there is a natural emphasis on algorithms that can be efficiently implemented on a computer.

2 Speech Recognition as Pattern Classification

In this section, we will point out why automatic speech recognition can be considered to be a pattern classification task *par excellence*. As a prototypical example of speech recognition, we consider

a dictation machine or 'automatic typewriter' that converts the acoustic signal in written text (Jelinek (1976), Ney et al. (1994)).

This speech recognition task has the following characteristic features:

- The classes to be recognized are exactly defined, namely the spoken words.

- It is a natural real-life task. There is no need to resort to artificial data because there are many business professionals like lawyers, medical doctors and other persons that produce suitable acoustic data in their everyday business work.

- There is a well defined performance criterion, which is the word error rate on *new* test data, i.e. on data that have not been seen by the system before. The word error rate is computed by comparing the recognized string of words with the actually spoken string of words and is obtained as the sum of the three types of recognition errors: word confusions, word deletions and word insertions.

However, automatic speech recognition is a complex and challenging task for several reasons:

- There is a high variability in the acoustic signal even if the same word is uttered twice by the same speaker. In addition, the way in which the acoustic realization of a sound is produced depends heavily on the phonetic context, i.e. on the sound before and after the sound under consideration. Furthermore, there is a distinct speaker dependence of the acoustic signal which makes speaker independent recognition particularly difficult.

- There is no fixed time scale for the acoustic signal. The speaking rate can vary drastically within the same utterance. There are no anchor points in the acoustic signal so that it is difficult and error prone to segment the signal in a preprocessing step.

- In the acoustic signal, word and sound boundaries do not exist as such. They can be determined reliably only *after* we know which words and sounds have been spoken.

- There is context and prior information that should be exploited for the recognition process. The sentences to be recognized are formed according to the syntactic and semantic constraints of the language used.

Although we limit ourselves to the 'automatic typewriter' in this paper, we would like to mention two closely related applications of stochastic modelling:

- a dialogue system that understands spoken natural language queries, asks for further information if necessary and produces an answer to the speaker's query; typical applications are inquiry systems for train schedule and air travel information (Pieraccini et al. (1993), Aust and Oerder (1994)). As an example of an operational system, we mention a prototype system for train schedule information (telephone ++49(241)604020) which works via telephone and in a speaker independent mode using a free dialogue.

- a translation system that translates a sentence from one language into another (Brown et al. (1993)).

3 Bayes Decision Rule

3.1 Principle

Knowing that speech recognition is a difficult task, we want to keep the number of misclassifications (of sounds, words or sentences) as small as possible. The corresponding formalism is provided by the so-called Bayes decision theory. To show its implications for speech and language processing, we consider the speech recognition problem in more detail (Jelinek (1976)). The starting point is the observed acoustic signal x_1^T, i.e. the sequence of signal samples x_t over time $t = 1, ..., T$, for which the underlying word sequence $w_1^N = w_1...w_N$ has to be determined. In order to minimize the number of recognition errors at the sentence level, we have to choose the sequence of words $[w_1^N]_{opt}$ according to the equation:

$$[w_1^N]_{opt} = \arg\max_{w_1^N} \left\{ Pr(w_1^N) \cdot Pr(x_1^T | w_1^N) \right\} .$$

This can be shown to be equivalent to the maximization of the posterior probability $Pr(w_1^N | x_1^T)$. However, the above formulation has the advantage that we obtain a factorization in two separate probability distributions which can be modelled and trained independently of each other. Strictly speaking, for continuous-valued observations, we have to use the term probability *density* rather than the term *probability* itself. Fig.1 shows the architecture that results from the Bayes decision theory; here we have already taken into account that, for a large vocabulary task, subword units like phonemes are used in connection with a pronunciation lexicon. Overall, we have the following crucial constituents of the statistical approach to speech recognition:

- the use of two separate probability distributions or *stochastic knowledge sources*:

- the language model or the prior probability distribution $Pr(w_1^N)$, which is assigned to each possible word sequence w_1^N and which ultimately captures all syntactic, semantic and pragmatic constraints of the language domain under consideration;
- the acoustic model or the class conditional probability distribution $Pr(x_1^T|w_1^N)$ which assigns a score as to how well the observations x_1^T match the hypothesized word sequence w_1^N.

- In addition to these two knowledge sources, we need a separate process which is referred to as a search or decision process. According to the Bayes decision rule, this search has to carry out the maximization of the product of the two probability distributions and thus ensures an optimal interaction of the two knowledge sources.

- There is a *guarantee* of the minimization of decision errors if we know the *true* probability distributions $Pr(w_1^N)$ and $Pr(x_1^T|w_1^N)$ and if we carry out a *full* search over all word sequences w_1^N.

Note that the Bayes decision rule has been applied to the *whole* sentence to be recognized rather than the individual words. The advantage then is that the prior information about the possible word sequences w_1^N can be exploited in the recognition process.

3.2 Implementation of the Statistical Approach

So far we have applied only the general framework of the Bayes decision theory, and we are still far away from the construction of a real system. The steps required for building a real operational system can be grouped in three categories:

- Search problem: In principle, the innocent looking maximization requires the evaluation of $10000^{10} = 10^{40}$ possible word sequences, when we assume a vocabulary of 10 000 words and a sentence duration of 10 words. This is the price we have to pay for a full feedback of the language model constraints, i.e. the high level knowledge, on the acoustic ('low-level') recognition. In such a way, however, it is guaranteed that there is no better way to take the decisions about the spoken words (for the given probability distributions $Pr(w_1^N)$ and $Pr(x_1^T|w_1^N)$. In a practical system, we of course use suboptimal search strategies which require much less effort than a full search, but nevertheless find the global optimum in virtually all cases.

- Modelling problem: The two probability distributions $Pr(w_1^N)$ and $Pr(x_1^T|w_1^N)$ are too general to be used in a table look-up approach, because there is a huge number of possible values x_1^T and w_1^N. Therefore we have to introduce suitable structures into the distributions such that the number of free parameters is drastically reduced by taking suitable data dependencies into account.

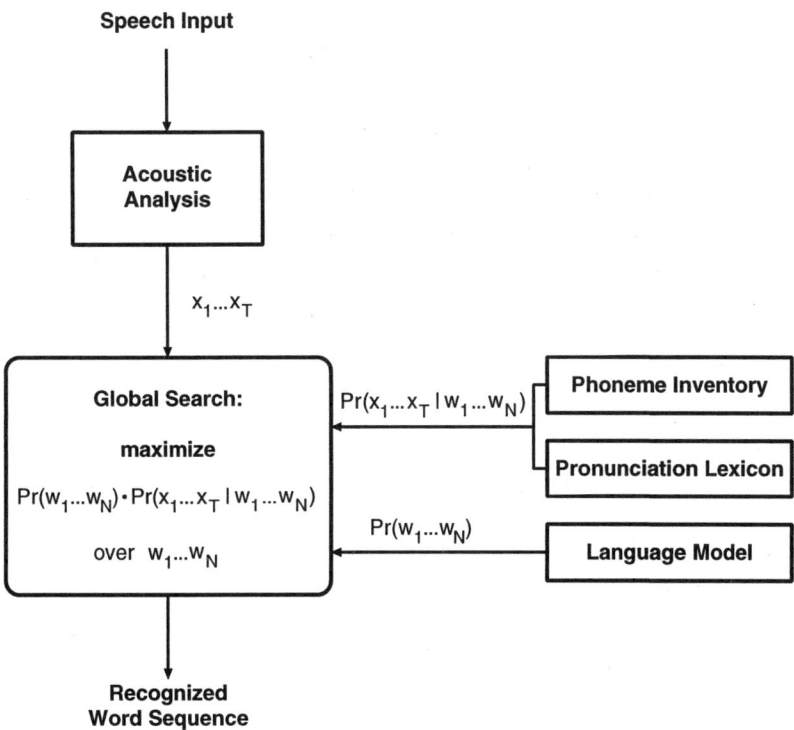

Figure 1: Bayes decision rule for speech recognition.

- Training problem: After choosing suitable models for the two distributions, there remain free parameters that have to be learned from a set of training observations, which in the statistical terminology is referred to as *parameter estimation*. For several reasons, especially for the mutual dependence of the parameters, this learning task typically results in a complex mathematical optimization problem the details of which depend on the chosen model and on the chosen training criterion (such as maximum likelihood, squared error criterion, discriminative criterion, minimum number of recognition errors, ...).

In conclusion, *statistics as such* does not solve the problems of automatic speech (and language) processing, but defines a basis on which we can found the solutions to the problems. In contradiction to a widely held belief, a statistical approach may very well require a specific model, and statistics helps us to make the best of a given model. Since undoubtedly we have to take decisions in the context of automatic speech and language processing, it can only be a rhetoric question of whether we should use statistical decision theory at all. To make a comparison with another field: in constructing a power plant, it would be foolish to ignore the principles of thermodynamics! For speech recognition, we briefly summarize the state of the art with respect to modelling:

- The acoustic signal x_1^T is too complex for direct modelling. Therefore, in almost all systems, a sequence of so-called short term spectral vectors is computed which describe the energy distribution over the frequency axis. There are variants such as spectral analysis by FFT (Fast Fourier Transform), cepstrum, LPC (Linear Predictive Coding), formants etc.

- For handling the problem of speaking rate variations, the so-called Hidden Markov models are widely and successfully used. Without them, the training of the associated probability distributions would be much more difficult. Only in simple situations like isolated word recognition can we do without them and use more complex static pattern matching such as neural networks.

- For large vocabularies of 10000 and more words, pronunciation lexica are used to describe the possible phoneme sequences. Such a pronunciation lexicon can be viewed as a compact representation of prior knowledge. In the spirit of Bayesian learning, of course, such lexica can be combined with a training sample.

- It is well known that phonemes are abstractions and that their acoustic realization depends heavily on the surrounding phonemes. In order to take this context dependency into account, context dependent models like diphones and triphones are often used.

- In language modelling, the currently dominating methods are based on using the frequencies of word bigrams and trigrams. There have been several attempts at introducing more linguistic structures into the language models, in particular by using stochastic context free grammars, but so far success has been moderate.

As to the search problem, the most successful strategies are based on either *stack decoding* or A^* search (Jelinek (1976)) and *dynamic programming beam search*. Over the last few years, there has been a lot of progress in structuring the search process to generate a compact *word lattice* (Ortmanns et al. (1997)).
To make this point crystal clear: The characteristic property of the statistical approach to speech and language processing is *not* the use of *Hidden Markov models* or *hidden alignments*. These methods are only the time-honoured methods and successful methods of today. The characteristic property lies in the systematic use of a probabilistic framework for the construction of models, in the statistical training of the free parameters of these models and in the explicit use of two knowledge sources for the decision making process.

3.3 Advantages of the Probabilistic Framework

For the 'low-level' description of speech and image signals, it is widely accepted that the probabilistic framework allows an efficient coupling between the observations and the models, which is often described by the buzz word 'subsymbolic processing'. But there is another advantage in using probability distributions, namely that they offer an explicit formalism for expressing hypothesis scores:

- The probabilities are directly used as scores: These scores are normalized, which is a desirable property: when increasing the score for a certain element in the set of all hypotheses, there must be one or several other elements whose scores are reduced at the same time.

- It is evident how to combine scores: depending on the task, the probabilities are either multiplied or added.

- Weak and vague dependencies can be modelled easily. Especially in (spoken and written) natural language, there are nuances and shades that require 'grey levels' between 0 and 1.

Even if we think we can manage without statistics, we will need models which always have some free parameters. Then the question is how to train these free parameters. The obvious approach is to adjust these parameters in such a way that we get optimal results (in terms of error rates or similar criteria) on a representative sample. So we have made a complete cycle and have reached the starting point of the statistical approach again!

When building an automatic system for speech or language, we should try to use as much prior knowledge as possible about the task under consideration. This knowledge is used to guide the modelling process and to enable improved generalization with respect to unseen data. Therefore in a good statistical approach, we try to identify the common patterns underlying the observations, i.e. to capture dependencies between the data in order to avoid the pure 'black box' concept.

4 Selected Topics in Stochastic Modelling

In this section, we will consider in more detail specific topics in stochastic modelling that have found widespread use in high-performance speech recognition systems: the EM algorithm, the interpretation of neural net outputs in terms of posterior probabilities, the decision tree approach, the leaving-one-out method, and the maximum entropy method.

4.1 Complex Models and the EM Algorithm

A widely used criterion for learning is the so-called maximum likelihood criterion, which can be formulated as follows. We are given a model $p(x|\lambda)$ with some unknown parameter which has to be learned or, in statistical terminology, *estimated* from training data $x_1...x_n...x_N$. The maximum likelihood criterion then considers the so-called likelihood function

$$\lambda \to \prod_{n=1}^{N} p(x_n|\lambda)$$

and maximizes it over the unknown parameter λ:

$$\lambda = \arg\max_{\lambda'} \prod_{n=1}^{N} p(x_n|\lambda') \quad .$$

Mathematically, it is often more convenient to use the *log-likelihood* rather than the likelihood itself. For a number of simple and popular models, this approach produces closed-form solutions which are often used intuitively without an explicit connection to the maximum likelihood method. We consider two typical cases:

- As an observation, we often have a high-dimensional vector made up from real-valued measurements. In these cases, typically a Gaussian model is used whose parameters are the mean vector and the covariance matrix. The maximum likelihood approach results in the *sample* average and the *sample* covariance matrix.

- For discrete events, for which we have no specific model distribution, we simply assume a separate outcome probability for each type of event. In this case, the maximum likelihood estimate is simply the relative frequency of each event.

In real-life data applications, we have to use more complex models for which no closed-form solutions for the maximum-likelihood criterion exist. Examples are:

- mixture distributions for multimodal distributions: for real data, distributions tend to have multiple maxima or *modes* as they are called in statistical terminology; in such cases, mixture distributions like weighted Gaussians are very useful.

- linear interpolation for smoothing, both in acoustic modelling and in language modelling: In cases when the size of the training set is small these estimates are not very reliable and have to be smoothed.

- the Hidden Markov models as they are widely used in speech recognition for the time alignment problem. Typically the models have a quite regular structure as shown in Fig. 2.

- stochastic context free grammars, which have received some recent interest in their *lexicalized* versions (Jelinek et al. (1992), Yamron et al. (1994), Pietra et al. (1994));

- alignment models for text translation (Brown et al. (1993));

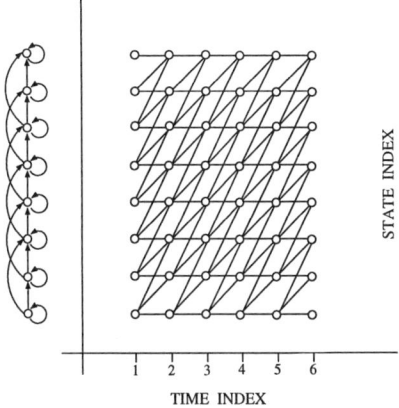

Figure 2: Hidden Markov model for nonlinear time alignment.

- models for language understanding (Pieraccini et al. (1993), Kuhn and de Mori (1994)).

As a specific example, we consider a mixture distribution which is made up from unimodal distributions. For the specification of a mixture distribution, we need:

- a set of so-called component densities $p(x_n|\vartheta_i)$, which have individual parameters $\vartheta_i, i = 1, ..., I$. E.g. in the case of a Gaussian distribution for component density i, the parameters are the mean vector μ_i and covariance matrix Σ_i.

- a set of non-negative mixture weights $c_i, i = 1, ..., I$, which must sum up to unity:

$$\sum_{i=1}^{I} c_i = 1 \ .$$

The mixture weight c_i specifies how much the density i contributes to the overall distribution.

We introduce the symbol λ to denote the whole set of unknown parameters c_i and ϑ_i:

$$\lambda \equiv \{c_i, \vartheta_i\} \ .$$

Thus we arrive at the following model for an observation x_n:

$$p(x_n|\lambda) = \sum_{i=1}^{I} c_i \, p(x_n|\vartheta_i) \ .$$

As usual, we are given a set of observations $x_1 \ldots x_n \ldots x_N$ for training. Optimizing the likelihood function for such a mixture distribution is a difficult mathematical problem. For mixture distributions and other complex models of distributions, there are no closed-form solutions. However there is an iterative procedure which is called the EM algorithm and which is very convenient for a computer implementation (Baum (1972), Dempster et al. (1977)). The EM algorithm is based on the notion of a (discrete) *hidden variable* which we will denote by the symbol y. In the case of mixture distributions, the hidden variable is the density index i which is *hidden* because we cannot observe the effect of a single density, but only the effect of all densities $i = 1, \ldots, I$. Similarly, in the case of a Hidden Markov model for time alignment, the hidden variable is the state sequence or time alignment path. In all these cases, we can rewrite the model distribution using the hidden variable:

$$p(x_n|\lambda) = \sum_y p(y, x_n|\lambda)$$
$$= \sum_y p(y|\lambda) \cdot p(x_n|y, \lambda) \quad .$$

For the hidden variable y, we will use a kind of posterior distribution whose natural definition is as follows:

$$p(y|x_n, \lambda) := \frac{p(y, x_n|\lambda)}{\sum_{y'} p(x_n, y'|\lambda)}$$
$$= \frac{p(y|\lambda)\, p(x_n|y, \lambda)}{\sum_{y'} p(y'|\lambda)\, p(x_n|y', \lambda)} \quad .$$

The derivation of the EM algorithm is easily presented by considering two sets λ and $\bar{\lambda}$ of parameter estimates, the idea being that $\bar{\lambda}$ is to be computed from λ in each iteration of the EM algorithm.

We use the so-called divergence inequality of information theory:

$$\sum_y p(y|x_n, \lambda) \cdot \log \frac{p(y|x_n, \lambda)}{p(y|x_n, \bar{\lambda})} \geq 0 \quad \forall\, \lambda, \bar{\lambda} \quad .$$

This inequality is easily proved using the inequality $\log z \leq z - 1$.

The key notion of the EM algorithm is to introduce an auxiliary function, the so-called $Q(.;.)$ function defined as follows:

$$Q(\lambda; \bar{\lambda}) := \sum_{n=1}^{N} \sum_y p(y|x_n, \lambda) \cdot \log p(x_n, y|\bar{\lambda}) \quad ,$$

By elementary manipulations using the above divergence inequality, we obtain the important inequality for the log-likelihood difference of the two

---

choose some initial values $\bar{\lambda}$
do for each iteration:

1. *update parameter*: $\lambda := \bar{\lambda}$

2. *expectation*: compute $Q(\lambda; \bar{\lambda})$ as expectation over y

3. *maximization*: $\arg\max_{\bar{\lambda}} \{Q(\lambda; \bar{\lambda})\}$

Figure 3: Illustration of the EM algorithm.

parameter estimates $\bar{\lambda}$ and λ:

$$\sum_{n=1}^{N} \log \frac{p(x_n|\bar{\lambda})}{p(x_n|\lambda)} \geq Q(\lambda; \bar{\lambda}) - Q(\lambda; \lambda) \quad .$$

This inequality forms the basis of the EM algorithm and says: In order to improve a given parameter estimate λ, compute the $Q(\lambda; \bar{\lambda})$ function and optimize it over $\bar{\lambda}$ to obtain a better estimate. Due to the inequality, the value of the log-likelihood function for the new parameter estimate will be improved. The concept of the EM algorithm is depicted in Fig.3. In a real implementation, the two steps, estimation and maximization, will be typically merged into a single one. The main advantage is the (relative) simplicity: there is no need to apply gradient search and to worry about the step size of the search. Note however that the EM algorithm has only a *local* convergence, and it is a separate issue as to how to find good guesses for the initial estimates to start with.

To illustrate how to apply the EM algorithm, we consider a mixture distribution as a concrete model distribution. For an observation $x_n, n = 1, ..., N$, we have the model:

$$\begin{aligned} p(x_n|\lambda) &= \sum_{i=1}^{I} p(x_n, i|\lambda) \\ &= \sum_{i=1}^{I} p(i|\lambda) \cdot p(x_n|i, \lambda) \\ &= \sum_{i=1}^{I} c_i \cdot p(x_n|i, \vartheta_i) \quad . \end{aligned}$$

As before, we abbreviate the set of unknown parameters by $\lambda \equiv (\{c_i\}, \{\vartheta_i\})$. For this model, we have the $Q(.;.)$ function:

$$Q(\lambda; \bar{\lambda}) = \sum_{n=1}^{N} \sum_{i=1}^{I} p(i|x_n, \lambda) \cdot \log\left[\bar{c}_i \cdot p(x_n, i|\bar{\vartheta}_i)\right]$$

$$\text{with} \quad p(i|x_n, \lambda) = \frac{c_i \cdot p(x_n|i, \vartheta_i)}{\sum_{i'} c_{i'} \cdot p(x_n|i', \vartheta_{i'})} .$$

To compute the new parameter estimates, we have to take the respective derivatives. For the mixture weights c_i, we have to observe the normalization constraint which is most conveniently done by using the method of Lagrange multipliers. Thus, we have the reestimation formula:

$$\bar{c}_i = \frac{1}{N} \sum_{n=1}^{N} p(i|x_n, \lambda)$$

$$= \frac{1}{N} \sum_{n=1}^{N} \frac{c_i \cdot p(x_n|i, \vartheta_i)}{\sum_{i'} c_{i'} \cdot p(x_n|i', \vartheta_{i'})} .$$

To derive the re-estimation formulae for ϑ_i, we have to make assumptions about the functional form of the component densities. For the case of Gaussian densities with mean vector μ_i and covariance matrix Σ_i, we obtain the reestimation formulae:

$$\bar{\mu}_i = \frac{\sum_{n=1}^{N} p(i|x_n, \lambda) \, x_n}{\sum_{n=1}^{N} p(i|x_n, \lambda)}$$

$$\bar{\Sigma}_i = \frac{\sum_{n=1}^{N} p(i|x_n, \lambda) \, [x_n - \bar{\mu}_i][x_n - \bar{\mu}_i]^T}{\sum_{n=1}^{N} p(i|x_n, \lambda)} ,$$

where the notation y^T stands for the transpose of the vector y. The interesting property of these reestimation formulae is that they can be interpreted in terms of the conventional maximum likelihood estimates for Gaussian distributions, where however each observation x_n contributes to the density i with a weight $p(i|x_n, \lambda)$. This interpretation was already given in (Duda and Hart (1973), pp. 194/195); however the local convergence was not known.

4.2 Interpretation of Neural Net Outputs

In this subsection, we will illustrate the role of the posterior probability in handling empirical observations. Typically, the posterior probability comes up in the framework of the Bayes decision rule. We are given the *true* probability distribution of (x, c), where x is the so-called observation vector and c is the class index for the $c = 1, ..., C$. Then it is always possible to derive from this joint probability to the class probabilities $p(c)$, the 'observation' probability $p(x)$, the class-conditional probabilities $p(x|c)$, and the posterior probability $p(x|c)$. To minimize the classification errors, we

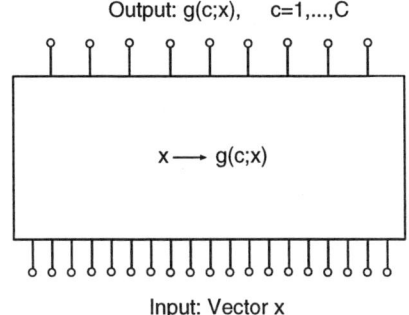

Figure 4: Illustration of a neural net with its output.

must use the Bayes decision rule. Having observed a vector x, we select the unknown class by:

$$x \to \arg\max_c \{p(c|x)\} \ .$$

We will now show that the same type of posterior probability comes up in the interpretation of the neural net outputs. Assuming a general structure for the neural network as shown in Fig. 4, the typical approach is to assume some ideal target outputs and measure the error between the actual network output and the ideal targets. These links between neural networks and posterior probabilities were already studied in the sixties (Aizerman et al. (1964), Patterson and Womack (1966)). Of course, the terminology and the framework were different; in particular, the mappings were called 'discriminant functions' rather than neural networks.

For a neural network with an arbitrary internal structure as shown in Fig. 4, we define the ideal outputs or targets using the Kronecker delta:

$$\delta(c, k) = \begin{cases} 1 & k = c \\ 0 & k \neq c \end{cases}$$

For a set of labelled training data $[x_n, c_n]$, $n = 1, \ldots, N$, we define the squared error criterion:

$$F(g) = \frac{1}{N} \sum_{n=1}^{N} \sum_{c=1}^{C} [g(c; x_n) - \delta(c, c_n)]^2 \ .$$

Note that the notation $F(g)$ explicitly shows the dependence on the estimate $g(c; x)$.

From the training data $[x_n, c_n]$, $n = 1, \ldots, N$, we can compute the

empirical distribution : $p_N(x, c)$.

For categorical and discretized measurements x_n, the empirical distribution is simply the histogram; for continuous-valued measurements x, the definition of the empirical distribution requires more care and a more sophisticated framework. However, for our needs, we can always imagine a discretization of the continuous-valued space by a sufficiently high resolution. By elementary manipulations, the error can be rewritten as follows (Ney (1995)):

$$F(g) = \int_x dx \sum_{c'=1}^{C} p_N(x,c') \sum_{c=1}^{C} [g(c;x) - \delta(c,c')]^2$$

$$= \int_x dx \, p_N(x) \sum_{c'=1}^{C} p_N(c'|x) \left(1 - \sum_c p_N^2(c|x) + \sum_c [p_N(c|x) - g(c;x)]^2\right).$$

Note that this result is totally independent of any assumptions about the form of the neural network. Furthermore the result does not depend on the type of search used to train the neural network. The error consists of two parts. The first part is independent of the network outputs $g(c;x)$ and depends only on the empirical distribution. The second part is the squared error between the estimates $g(c;x)$ and the posterior class probability $p_N(c|x)$ of the empirical distribution. By the choice

$$g(c;x) := p_N(c|x) \quad .$$

this second part disappears. Thus we have arrived at an interpretation of neural network outputs in terms of posterior probabilities. This link to classical pattern recognition is successfully used in a number of systems to model the emission distributions in Hidden Markov models for continuous speech recognition (Robinson (1994), Bourland and Morgan (1994)).

4.3 Decision Trees

The decision tree method is often referred to as CART which stands for "Classification And Regression Trees" as summarized in a book with the same title (Breiman et al. (1984)). The CART method uses a binary decision tree to model a conditional distribution. Denoting the conditional distribution by $p(y|x)$, we have to distinguish the two types of random variables:

- x: The *independent* variable, which stands for an observed or measured value and can take on either continuous (or discretized, also referred to as ordinal) or categorical values.

- y: The *dependent* variable, which is to be *predicted* by the CART method. Depending on the task to which the CART method is applied, the variable y may be a continuous value (as in classical regression) or the class index in a classification task (as in pattern recognition).

In the CART method, we typically distinguish three types of tasks:

- *classification*: given the observation x, find the unknown class y from which the observation x was generated;

- *probability estimation*: estimate the probability distribution $p(y|x)$ as a whole. E.g. in language modelling, the variable x is the conditioning history or sequence of predecessor words and the variable y is the word in the current position.

- *regression*: predict the variable y from the measurements x (nonlinear extension of linear regression); this task will not be considered here.

Given an observation x, we use the decision tree as follows. Starting at the root of the tree, we ask a yes-no question about the given observation x. Depending on the result, we follow either the left or right branch and ask again questions. This process is repeated until we reach a terminal node of the tree. In the case of a probability estimation task, there is a whole probability distribution $p(y|t)$ assigned to each terminal node t. In a classification task, this distribution can simply be reduced to the most likely class index y. Thus the characteristic property of the CART method is to use a binary decision tree for defining equivalence classes of the independent variable x. As a result, decision trees have the appealing property of being able to visualize the decision-making process and have the chance of being interpreted by a human expert.

To construct the decision tree, we need a set of training data

$$[x_n, y_n], \; n = 1, \ldots, N \quad .$$

For each node, a question has to be specified which is achieved by defining subsets over the set of observations x. Thus we can identify nodes and questions. So for a node t with left branch t_L and right branch t_R, we have:

$$t, t_L, t_R \subset \{x\} \quad ,$$

for which a binary question amounts to a binary split or partition:

$$t = t_L \cup t_R, \quad t_L \cap t_R = \emptyset \quad .$$

For these splits, not all possible questions are considered, but only certain types (Breiman et al. (1984)). Continuous variables are split by order, and categorical values by a binary partition of the possible values. Each candidate split is measured by the improvement in a so-called impurity function. For each observation (x_n, y_n) in the training data, we have to consider the probability of the conditional distribution $p(y_n|t)$, where t is the candidate split (or node) we are evaluating with $x_n \in t$. For each observation (x_n, y_n), we assume that somehow we can compute a suitable score

$$g(y_n|t) \quad \text{with} \quad x_n \in t \quad .$$

Assuming that this per-observation score is additive, we obtain the natural definition of a score or impurity function $G(t)$ for the node t:

$$G(t) := \sum_{n:x_n \in t} g(y_n|t) \;.$$

A popular impurity function is the so-called entropy criterion, which is obtained by using the negative *conditional likelihood*. To each node t, we assign a probability (density) distribution $p(y|t)$ and define as impurity function:

$$G(t) = -\sum_{n:x_n \in t} \log p(y_n|t) \;.$$

For a *discrete* variable y in a *modelfree* approach, this can be rewritten as:

$$G(t) = -\sum_{y} p(y|t) \log p(y|t) \;,$$

where now $p(y|t)$ is the *empirical* distribution over the observations sent down to node t. The important result then is that this splitting criterion is nothing else but the familiar (conditional) maximum likelihood criterion, where the binary tree is used to form equivalence classes for the unconditional variable x.

When splitting a node t into t_L and t_R, we have a change in the impurity function. The whole tree is grown by selecting the most effective split of each node. Having found the best split, we then select the best split for each of the successor nodes, and this process is repeated. Typically there is no stopping rule. Instead, a very large tree is constructed and then pruned from the bottom (Breiman et al. (1984)). Successful applications of the CART and related tree-based methods to speech and language include language modelling (Bahl et al. (1989)), language understanding (Kuhn and de Mori (1994)) and definition of generalized triphones in acoustic modelling (Young et al. (1994)).

4.4 Language Modelling and Leaving-One-Out

To illustrate the fundamental problem in language modelling, we consider a specific example, namely a bigram model. Conventional methods like the maximum likelihood method typically result in the relative frequencies as estimates for the bigram probabilities:

$$p(w|v) = \frac{N(v,w)}{N(v)} \;.$$

Here, (v, w) is the word bigram under consideration, and $N(v, w)$ and $N(v)$ are the numbers of observed word bigrams (v, w) and words v, respectively. Now assuming a vocabulary size of $W = 20000$ words, there are $W^2 = 400$

million possible word bigrams, but the training corpus consists rarely of more than 10 million words. As a result, the conventional probability estimate for each unseen event is zero, and no more than 2.5% of all bigrams can be observed in training. Using these conventional probability estimates, the recognition system would be unable to recognize any word sequence that contains an unseen word bigram.

To overcome these shortcomings of conventional probability estimates, we have to subtract probability mass from the relative frequencies and assign it to the unseen events. This is achieved by the leaving-one-out method which can be considered to be an extension of the cross-validation method (Duda and Hart (1993), Efron and Tibshirani (1993)). To illustrate this concept and avoid confusing details, we simplify the problem by considering *joint* probabilities. For a full description, see (Ney (1993)). The log-likelihood function for the leaving-one-out technique can be obtained as follows. The N observations are the *joint* events (v, w) that are obtained from the training text $w_1...w_n...w_N$ by isolating the word w_n and its predecessor word w_{n-1} in each of the N text positions. Here, we have combined all sentences into *one* long word sequence by interpreting the sentence end symbol as a special word of the vocabulary. We consider the process of removing an observation $(w_{n-1}, w_n) = (v, w)$ from the N observations and use it as holdout part. To describe this process, we denote the original count by $r = N(v, w)$ and define the *count* dependent quantities (for a count $r = 0, 1, ..., R$):

- n_r: number of classes, i.e. word bigrams, seen exactly r times;

- p_r: probability of any class seen exactly r times.

We have the following constraints:

$$\sum_{r=0}^{R} n_r p_r = 1 \quad \text{and} \quad \sum_{r=0}^{R} n_r r = N \quad .$$

For sake of clarity, we first write down the conventional log-likelihood function for the unknown probabilities $p_r, r = 0, ..., R$:

$$F(p_0, ..., p_R) = \sum_{r=0}^{R} r n_r \log p_r \quad ,$$

from which we obtain the usual estimates, i.e. the relative frequencies:

$$p_r = \frac{r}{N} \quad .$$

We now formulate the log-likelihood function in the leaving-one-out framework. After removing one observation as holdout observation, there are only $(r-1)$ observations of the same class left in the $(N-1)$ training observations. Therefore, we have to use the probability p_{r-1} rather than p_r. Observing that there are exactly $r \cdot n_r$ observations for each class with count r, we obtain the *leaving-one-out* log-likelihood function:

$$F(p_0, ..., p_{R-1}) = \sum_{r=1}^{R} r n_r \log p_{r-1} \quad,$$

where the probability p_R is supposed to be given. A straightforward optimization of this criterion over the unknown probabilities $p_r, r = 0, ..., R-1$ results in the formula:

$$p_r = \frac{1 - n_R p_R}{N} \cdot \frac{(r+1) n_{r+1}}{n_r} \quad.$$

Apart from the factor $(1 - n_R p_R)$ which is close to 1, this estimate for p_r is identical to the so-called Turing-Good estimate (Good (1953)). It is instructive to compute the total probability mass of unseen events:

$$n_0 p_0 = (1 - n_R p_R) \cdot \frac{n_1}{N} \quad,$$

which is zero for the conventional maximum likelihood approach. We see that this probability mass is basically given by n_1/N, i.e. the fraction of classes seen exactly once.

4.5 Maximum Entropy Approach to Language Modelling

The advantage of using the maximum entropy principle in language modelling is that the principle provides a well defined method for incorporating different types of dependencies into a language model (Rosenfeld (1994)). The starting point for the maximum entropy approach is to consider certain types of dependencies, so-called features, e.g. specific word bigrams or also long-distance co-occurrences (trigger and cache effect, see (Rosenfeld (1994)). For a word w in a given text position n and its history h, i.e. the predecessor words $w_{n-M}, ..., w_{n-1}$ with, say, $M = 100$, we define a feature function for each feature i:

$$f_i(h, w) \in \{0, 1\} \quad.$$

For each of these features, the assumption is that we know its frequency. Then the maximum entropy principle tells us that the most general distribution that satisfies these constraints as expressed by the corresponding frequencies has the following functional form (Bishop et al. (1975), pp. 83-87):

$$p_\Lambda(w|h) = \frac{\exp\left[\sum_i \lambda_i f_i(h, w)\right]}{\sum_{w'} \exp\left[\sum_i \lambda_i f_i(h, w')\right]} \quad,$$

where for each feature i we have a parameter λ_i and where we define: $\Lambda = \{\lambda_i\}$.

The important result of the maximum entropy principle is that the resulting model has a log–linear or exponential functional form. In the statistical terminology, the underlying sampling approach is referred to as a multinomial one (Bishop (1975), pp. 62-64). An important difference, however, is that we are considering *conditional* probabilities.

We consider the log-likelihood function $G(\Lambda)$ for a training corpus of running words $w_1, ..., w_n, ..., w_N$:

$$G(\Lambda) := \sum_{n=1}^{N} \log p_\Lambda(w_n|h_n) = \sum_{hw} N(h,w) \log p_\Lambda(w|h)$$

with the usual count definitions $N(h, w)$. To find the optimal set of parameters λ_i for maximum likelihood, or what is equivalent, minimum perplexity, we take the partial derivatives with respect to each of the parameters λ_i and set them to zero:

$$\frac{\partial G}{\partial \lambda_i} = \sum_{hw} N(h,w) \frac{\partial}{\partial \lambda_i} \log p_\Lambda(w|h) = 0 \ .$$

After some elementary manipulations, we obtain:

$$\frac{\partial G}{\partial \lambda_i} = - Q_i(\Lambda) + N_i = 0$$

with the Λ dependent auxiliary function $Q_i(\Lambda)$:

$$Q_i(\Lambda) := \sum_{hw} N(h) \, p_\Lambda(w|h) \, f_i(h,w)$$

and with the Λ independent feature counts N_i:

$$N_i := \sum_{hw} N(h,w) \, f_i(h,w) \ .$$

From the above equation, the unknown parameters λ_i can be found using the generalized iterative scaling algorithm (Darroch and Ratcliff (1972), Rosenfeld (1994)).

5 Conclusions

A counter argument that is often raised against the statistical approach is the following: These thousands or even millions of parameters cannot be learned by the system because inevitably the amount of training data is always too small. This illustrates a symptomatic misconception of the statistical approach: one of the most important concepts of statistics is the distinction between parameters and their estimates. For example, to a first approximation, we can identify probabilities with relative frequencies (in the case of discrete random variables) as computed from the training data, but this is only a first approximation. The art of statistical modelling is to introduce models and design statistical methods so that, even for very small corpora, we can estimate the unknown parameters of the models, e.g. by smoothing techniques in combination with cross validation. This distinction between model parameters and their estimates cannot be overemphasized: from the fact that there is a huge number of unknown parameters in the models and that they are difficult to estimate, it is wrong to draw the conclusion that the statistical approach fails. Even in the case of very sparse data, statistics helps us to make the best of the given boundary conditions. From the above, it becomes clear that in speech and language modelling we often have to enter new ground as far as the statistical methods are concerned, which is caused by the complexity of the models needed or the special boundary conditions like sparseness of training data.

References

AIZERMAN, M.A., BRAVERMAN, E.M. and ROZONOER, L.I. (1964): Theoretical Foundations of the Potential Function Method in Pattern Recognition Learning. *Automation and Remote Control, 25, 821-837*

AIZERMAN, M.A., BRAVERMAN, E.M. and ROZONOER, L.I. (1964): The Probability Problem of Pattern Recognition Learning and the Method of Potential Functions. *Automation and Remote Control, 25, 1175-1193*

AUST, H. and OERDER, M. (1994): A Real Time Prototype of an Automatic Inquiry System. *Int. Conf. on Spoken Language Processing,* Yokohama, Japan, 703-706.

BAHL, L.R., BROWN, P.F., de SOUZA, P.V. and MERCER, R.L. (1989): A Tree Based Statistical Language Model for Natural Language Speech Recognition. *IEEE Trans. on Acoustics, Speech and Signal Processing, 37, 1001-1008, 1989.*

BAUM, L.E. (1972): An Inequality and Associated Maximization Technique in Statistical Estimation of a Markov Process. *Inequalities, 3/1, 1-8.*

BISHOP, Y.M.M., FIENBERG, S.E. and HOLLAND, P.W. (1975): Discrete Multivariate Analysis. MIT press, Cambridge, MA.

BOURLAND, H. and MORGAN, N. (1994): Continuous Speech Recognition by Connectionist Statistical Methods *IEEE Trans. on Neural Networks, 4, No. 6, 893-909*

BREIMAN, L., FRIEDMAN, J.H., OHLSEN, R.A. and STONE, C.J. (1984): Classification And Regression Trees. Wadsworth, Belmont, CA.

BROWN, P.F., DELLA PIETRA, S.A., DELLA PIETRA, V.J. and MERCER, R.L. (1993): Mathematics of Statistical Machine Translation: Parameter Estimation. *Computational Linguistics, 19.2, 263-311.*

DARROCH, J.N. and RATCLIFF, D. (1972): Generalized Iterative Scaling for Log–Linear Models. *Annals of Mathematical Statistics, 43, 1470-1480.*

DEMPSTER, A.P., LAIRD, N.M. and RUBIN, D.B. (1977): Maximum Likelihood from Incomplete Data via the EM Algorithm. *J. Royal Statist. Soc. Ser. B (methodological), 39, 1-38.*

DUDA, R.O. and HART, P.E. (1973): Pattern Classification and Scene Analysis. John Wiley & Sons, New York.

EFRON, B. and TIBSHIRANI, R.J. (1993): An Introduction to the Bootstrap. Chapman & Hall, New York.

GOOD, I.J. (1953): The Population Frequencies of Species and the Estimation of Population Parameters. *Biometrika, 40, 237-264.*

JELINEK, F. (1976): Speech Recognition by Statistical Methods. *Proceedings of the IEEE.* 64, 532-556.

JELINEK, F. (1991): Self-Organized Language Modelling for Speech Recognition. In: A. Waibel, K.-F. Lee (eds): *Readings in Speech Recognition.* Morgan Kaufmann Publishers, San Mateo, CA, 450-506.

JELINEK, F., LAFFERTY, J. and MERCER, R.L. (1992): Basic Methods of Probabilistic Context Free Grammars. In: P. Laface, R. de Mori (eds.): *Speech Recognition and Understanding.* Springer, Berlin, 347-360.

KUHN, R. and DE MORI, R. (1994): Recent Results in Automatic Learning Rules for Semantic Interpretation. *Int. Conf. on Spoken Language Processing.* Yokohama, Japan, 75-78.

NEY, H. (1995): On the Probabilistic Interpretation of Neural Net Classifiers and Discriminative Training Criteria. *IEEE Trans. on Pattern Analysis and Machine Intelligence, PAMI-17, 2, 107-119.*

NEY, H., MARTIN, S. and WESSEL, F. (1997): Statistical Language Modelling by Leaving-One-Out. In: G. Bloothooft, S. Young (eds.): *Corpus-Based Methods in Speech and Language.* Kluwer Academic Publishers, Dordrecht, 174-207.

NEY, H., STEINBISS, V., HAEB-UMBACH, R., TRAN, B.-H. and ESSEN, U. (1994): An Overview of the Philips Research Szstem for Large-Vocabulary Continuous-Speech Recognition. *International Journal of Pattern Recognition and Artificial Intelligence, Special Issue on Speech Recognition for Different Languages, 8, 1, 33-70.*

ORTMANNS, S. NEY, H. and AUBERT, X. (1997): A Word Graph Algorithm for Large Vocabulary Continuous Speech Recognition. *Computer, Speech and Language, 11, 1, 43-72.*

PATTERSON, J.D., WOMACK, B.F. (1966): An Adaptive Pattern Classification Scheme. *IEEE Trans. on Systems, Science and Cybernetics, SSC-2, 62-67.*

PIERACCINI, R., LEVIN, E. and VIDAL, E. (1993): Learning how to Understand Language. *Third European Conference on Speech Communication and Technology.* Berlin, 1407-1412.

DELLA PIETRA, S., DELLA PIETRA, V., GILLET, J., LAFFERTY, J., PRINTZ, H. and URES, L. (1994): Inference and Estimation of a Long-Range

Trigram Model. *Second International Colloquium 'Grammatical Inference and Applications', Alicante, Spain, 78-92.*

ROBINSON, A.J. (1994): An Application of Recurrent Nets to Phone Probability Estimation. *IEEE Trans. on Neural Networks, 5, 2, 298-305.*

ROSENFELD, R. (1994): Adaptive Statistical Language Modeling: A Maximum Entropy Approach. Ph.D. Thesis, School of Computer Science, Carnegie Mellon University, Pittsburgh, PA, CMU-CS-94-138.

Yamron, J., CANT, J., DEMETDS, A., DIETZEL, T. and ITO, Y. (1994): The Automatic Component of the LINGSTAT Machine-Aided Translation System. *ARPA Human Language Technology Workshop, Plainsboro, NJ, Morgan Kaufmann Publishers, San Mateo, CA, 158-163.*

YOUNG, S.J., ODELL, J.J. and WOODLAND, P.C. (1994): Tree-Based State Tying for High Accuracy Acoustic Modelling. *ARPA Human Language Technology Workshop, Plainsboro, NJ, Morgan Kaufmann Publishers, San Mateo, CA, 286-291.*

Classification of Speech Pattern Using Locally Recurrent Neural Networks

H. Reininger, K. Kasper, H. Wüst

Institut für Angewandte Physik,
Johann Wolfgang Goethe-Universität Frankfurt am Main,
D-60054 Frankfurt am Main, Germany

Abstract: Subject of automatic speech recognition is the classification of speech pattern as phones, syllables or words. Speech is generated by a complex articulation process which is influenced by coarticulation effects and depends on speaker characteristics. Thus, static as well as dynamic aspects of the resulting speech signal must be captured during feature extraction. Optimum classification of speech pattern consisting of feature vectors can only be achieved if this representation of information is adequate for the chosen classification method. Here we present such a combination consisting of psychoacoustically oriented features and locally recurrent neural networks.

1 Locally Recurrent Neural Networks

Recurrent neural networks (RNN) as dynamic systems with universal approximation capability have the potential for optimum classification of speech pattern. They can be trained to classify sequences of feature vectors having different length without an additional algorithm like Viterbi algorithm for compensation of variations in the duration of speech utterances. However, the quadratic increase of the number of connection weights with the number of neurons in fully connected RNN leads to a very high computational complexity. Therefore, we introduced Locally Recurrent Neural Networks (LRNN) which have the computational power of RNN and also satisfy the constraints coming from efficient hardware realization (Kasper et al. (1995)).
A LRNN consists - as Figure 1 illustrates - of an input layer with a set $\mathcal{I}$ of N_I input neurons, a hidden layer with a set $\mathcal{H}$ of N_H hidden neurons, and an output layer with a set $\mathcal{O}$ of N_O output neurons. The interaction between the input and the hidden layer as well as between the hidden and the output layer are unidirectional. Furthermore, the concept of sparse connectivity is applied to the inter-layer connections. The neurons of the hidden layer are arranged on a 2-dimensional grid. A neuron j of the hidden layer is only connected to its local neighbours with indices $\mathcal{N}(j) \in \mathcal{H}$ and to the subset $\mathcal{I}(j)$ of the input neurons as well as to the subset $\mathcal{O}(j)$ of the output neurons. The recurrent connections of the hidden neurons are ending at the edges of the grid.

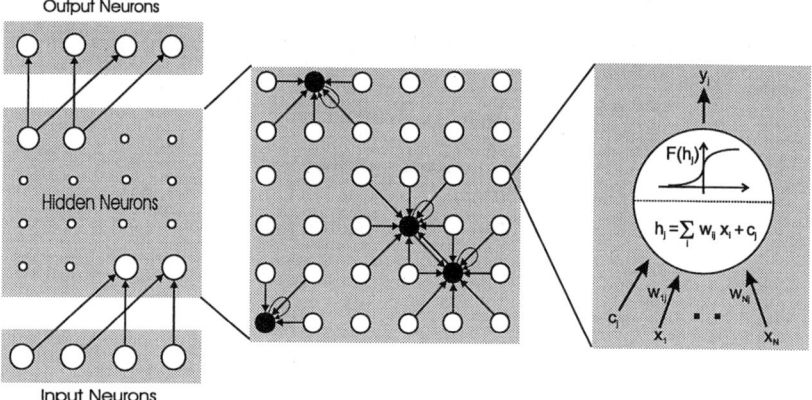

Figure 1: Structure of a LRNN.

The activity x_j of the hidden neuron j at time $t+1$ is given by

$$x_j(t+1) = \frac{1}{1 + \exp(-h_j(t+1))}$$

with the activation of neuron j at time $t+1$ according to

$$h_j(t+1) = \sum_{i \in \mathcal{N}(j)} w_{ij} x_i(t) + \sum_{i \in \mathcal{I}(j)} w_{ij} x_i(t) + T_j \quad .$$

$W = \{w_{ij}\}$ denotes the weight-matrix and T_j the threshold of neuron j. LRNN are trained by means of truncated back-propagation through time (BPTT) (Williams et al. (1990)).

The definition of the LRNN topology results in a regular structure and leads to an only linear growth of the number of weights with increasing number of neurons instead of the quadratic growth for fully connected neural networks. Especially, the regular structure is suitable for VLSI implementation and could not be achieved by unsupervised pruning methods.

2 Designing a LRNN for Word Recognition

2.1 Speech Data and its Presentation to LRNN

In first experiments, the way of feature presentation and the network training were optimized for speaker independent word recognition with LRNN. The vocabulary used in these simulation experiments comprised 23 German words, the 10 German digits, the word *zwo*, and 12 telephone command words. The speech signals were limited to telephone bandwidth and sampled with 8kHz. From these signals 12-dimensional feature vectors were extracted every 12 ms, each consisting of cepstral coefficients derived from LPC parameters and energy values. For the optimization of the LRNN parameters, feature vectors from 100 utterances of each word, spoken from different speakers, were used. Speaker independent recognition rates were measured on a set containing 100 utterances of each word from speakers not included in the training set.

Previous experiments have shown that without special modifications of a RNN or LRNN, only dependencies in the range of about 15 time steps could be learned with BPTT (Bengio et al. (1994)). Since the feature vectors are derived from the speech signal every 12 ms, one word consists of about 50 feature vectors. The discrimination of words could be performed more reliable if the complete feature sequence of a word can be taken into account. An effective solution with low complexity to this problem of learning long-term dependencies is to glue N_b consecutive feature vectors together to form a super-vector and use consecutive super-vectors as input to the LRNN. By appropriate choice of N_b it is possible to bring the length of a sequence of super-vectors down to a value below 15 which is in the range of learnable dependencies with BPTT. An additional advantage of this method is that the number of necessary network calculations per feature sequence is reduced by the factor of N_b. In simulation experiments it was found that for word recognition with LRNN a size of $N_b = 5$ gives the best recognition results.

2.2 Optimization of the LRNN Network Structure

The connectivity structure of a neural network, i.e. the density of connections and its regularity, determines mainly the cost for hardware implementation. Concerning a LRNN the number of connections between input and hidden layer, hidden and output layer as well as the size of the neighbourhood regions in the hidden layer have to be minimized.

By introducing a (m out of N) coding for the mapping of the output neurons onto the words of the vocabulary, the number of connections between hidden and output layer was drastically reduced. Only 7 instead of 23 output neurons are required, i.e. the number of connections is reduced to 30% (Kasper et al. (1996)). In order to get the classification result, the maximum search must be slightly modified to find not only the best but the $m = 2$ best output neurons.

Furthermore, the neighbourhood width n of the neurons in the hidden layer of a LRNN was optimized such that the same recognition rate as with a RNN was achieved. A RNN with $N_H + N_O = 176$ fully connected neurons, from which 7 were output neurons, reached the maximum recognition rate of 97.1% on the test data. This RNN has 41712 connections or weights, respectively. Table 1 shows the resulting recognition rates and the amount of weights for LRNN with 13x13 neurons in the hidden layer, which is the same amount of hidden neurons as in the RNN, 60 input neurons and 7 output

Table 1: Amount of weights (W_Σ) and word recognition rates R for different neighbourhood width n and for different reduction factors r of the inter-layer connection densities in case of $n = 5$.

n	W_Σ	$R(\%)$
0	11499	70.6
1	12699	88.3
2	14811	93.9
3	17571	95.1
4	20736	96.4
5	24099	96.9
6	27459	97.0

r	W_Σ	$R(\%)$
1/1	24099	96.9
1/2	18437	96.6
1/4	16551	96.3
1/5	15607	95.6

neurons as a function of n. At $n = 0$ the LRNN has no recurrent connections and is therefore similar to a multilayer perceptron with 169 hidden neurons, only a rather low recognition rate of 70% is achieved. Introducing recurrent connections to the nearest neighbours, i.e. LRNN with $n = 1$, leads to a significant increase of 18% in recognition rate. Obviously, recurrent connections in the hidden layer are substantial for exploiting the information contained in the dynamics of feature vectors. With increasing neighbourhood width the recognition performance increases significantly until $n = 5$, where the rate of the fully connected RNN is almost reached. This LRNN consists of only one half of the number of connections than the fully connected RNN.

To reduce the connection density between the input and the hidden layer as well as between the hidden and the output layer we introduced the concept of sparse connectivity. Table ?? shows the recognition rates for the LRNN with $n = 5$ at different reduction factors r which denotes the amount of the inter-layer connections relative to the number of the connections of fully connected layers. It could be seen that reductions up to $r = 1/4$ are possible without a significant loss in recognition performance. In total, by all these methods a LRNN results with 16551 weights which is nearly one third of the weights of the baseline RNN.

3 Robust Speech Recognition with LRNN Using Psychoacoustically Oriented Features

In further experiments we investigated whether the information represented by psychoacoustically oriented features could be exploited for robust speech recognition. Two feature extraction methods of this type were applied. One is JAH-RASTA. Here critical band energies are calculated every 10 ms. These energies are transformed with a noise adaptive mapping where the mapping coefficients are calculated from training utterances. The transformed energies are bandpass filtered. After loudness equalization and application of the power-law of hearing they are parameterized into 9 PLP-cepstral values (Koehler et al. (1994)).

The second method of feature extraction is based on an auditory perception model (PEMO) (Dau et al.(1996)). Here a gammatone filterbank consisting of 19 bandpass filters with center frequencies from 330-4000 Hz is used to split a speech signal in critical bands. Each frequency channel is half-wave rectified and lowpass filtered at 1 kHz to mimic the limiting phase-locking for auditory nerve fibers at high frequencies. Then an adaptive compression is performed to suppress slowly varying parts of the signal while retaining fast signal changes. Finally, an 8 Hz low-pass filter is applied to each bandpass signal to simulate the sluggishness of the auditory system in following rapid envelope fluctuations. From the resulting signals 19 coefficients are extracted every 10 ms. Figure 2 shows that PEMO derived features are sparse because they concentrate the information in relative few coefficients.

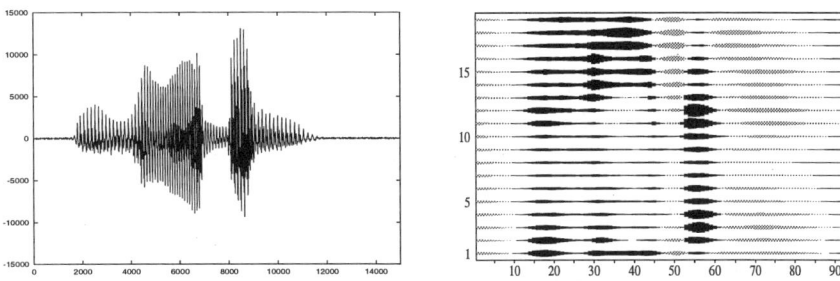

Figure 2: Speech signal and feature vectors derived with PEMO.

In order to compare the robustness of perceptually based preprocessing and LRNN we configured sytems using different preprocessing modules as well as scoring techniques. As features also 12 cepstral coefficients (LPC-CEP), derived every 10 ms via LPC analysis, and the short-term energy in combination with their temporal derivatives were considered. As alternative scoring technique continuous Hidden Markov Models (CHMM) were applied. Each HMM consisted of 8 states, organized in a left-to-right structure, and each state had 10 gaussian densities with diagonal covariance matrices.

The robustness of speech recognition was tested with additive background noise of different types and levels (SNR) as well as with recordings where the microphones and the telephone channel changed. As additive background noise white gaussian noise (WN), speech-simulating noise (SN), which was generated from a random superposition of words spoken by a male speaker,

Table 2: Speaker independent word recognition rates in per cent for the 10 German digits obtained different features and scoring techniques

Dimension	LPC-CEP 26		JAH-RASTA 9		PEMO 19	
NOISE	CHMM	LRNN	CHMM	LRNN	CHMM	LRNN
clean	97.0	96.6	98.2	98.2	97.4	98.1
WN 10 dB	10.1	10.0	80.4	86.6	45.6	80.1
WN 20 dB	17.6	11.3	95.4	94.3	73.3	95.1
SN 10 dB	32.8	41.5	79.6	78.6	48.3	84.6
SN 20 dB	91.0	80.1	96.0	94.0	77.2	96.5
CN 10 dB	20.3	30.0	74.9	81.4	46.8	89.4
CN 20 dB	58.6	72.9	96.2	94.3	75.6	97.2
TUBTEL	68.5	48.5	90.2	85.3	76.8	94.5

and recordings of noise on a construction site (CN) were used.

The vocabulary in these experiments consisted of the 10 German digits spoken by 200 different speakers. 100 utterances of each word were used for training and the remaining 100 utterances for testing the speaker-independent recognition performance. A second set of test data (TUBTEL) was applied in order to introduce a realistic noisy environment, which is in particular influenced by a convolutive type of noise. These data consisted of 117 utterances of each digit, spoken by different persons over dialed-up public telephone lines in the Berlin area (Schürer et al. (1995)).

The resulting recognition rates are given in Table 2. It can be seen that even without noise LPC-CEP give the lowest rates independent of the scoring technique. Furthermore, they are the most sensitive features. JAH-RASTA combined with CHMM for scoring leads to high recogniton rates comparable with the combination of PEMO and LRNN. For different noise types these two systems show similar results at a SNR of 20 dB. At the higher noise level of 10 dB, the PEMO/LRNN-recognizer outperforms the systems based on HMM. This higher robustness of the PEMO/LRNN-recognizer is even more obvious by the recognition rates achieved with TUBTEL. Obviously, scoring with LRNN takes the most advantage out of the perceptive representation of speech derived with the auditory model.

HMM are not able to achieve robustness with PEMO features. In order to analyze this effect in more detail we performed recognition experiments with modified PEMO feature sequences. In a first experiment, feature components were set to zero with magnitudes smaller than a certain threshold.

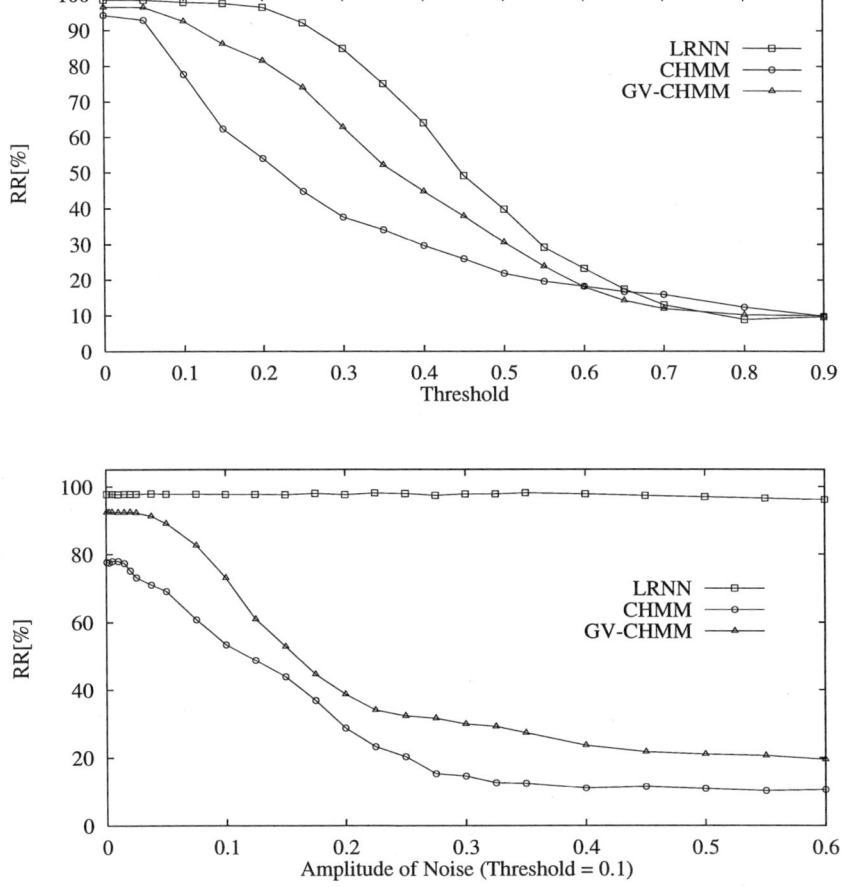

Figure 3: Analysis of PEMO based pattern classification.

Figure 3 shows the resulting recognition rates as function of the treshold for LRNN, HMM, and GV-HMM, a system where super-vectors consisting of 5 feature vectors are processed as one entity similar to the processing with LRNN. It can be seen that LRNN are very robust against this type of modification. Up to a threshold of 0.2 the LRNN recognition rate remains almost constant on a high level while the rate of the HMM recognizer has dropped below 60% recognition rate. The recognition rate of GV-HMM is higher than that of HMM but still significantly below that of LRNN.

In a second experiment, the feature components below the threshold were replaced by random noise. Figure 3 shows the influence of the noise amplitude on the recognition performance for a threshold of 0.1. Obviously, the noise has almost no influence on the performance of LRNN. In contrast to that, the recognition rates of the HMM systems decrease strongly even at very small noise amplitudes. These results indicate that during weight optimization LRNN learn to focus on characteristic speech pattern in a feature sequence which allow to discriminate the words of the vocabulary. Degradations of feature vectors not belonging to these patterns are of almost no influence on the word scores. HMM instead score each feature vector independently and with equal importance for the total word score. Thus, they are sensitive to distortions of any feature vector.

4 Conclusions

With the concept of LRNN it is possible to reduce the complexity of recurrent neural networks without affecting the recognition performance in a task of speaker independent word recognition. A (m out of N) coding of the number of output neurons, sparse inter-layer connectivity, and local connectivity in the hidden layer to the $n = 5$ nearest neighbours lead to a LRNN, which has only about one third of the weights as a RNN with the same recognition capability.

LRNN have the capability to exploit the robust and sparse representation of a speech signal obtained from the auditory model PEMO. Thus, LRNN in combination with PEMO is a promising concept for realizing a low complex speech recognition system with robust recognition performance. Currently, a VLSI-chip is designed for implementing a LRNN.

References

BENGIO, Y., SIMARD, P., FRASCONI, P. (1994): Learning Long-Term Dependencies With Gradient Descent is Difficult. *IEEE Trans. on Neural Networks,5, pp. 157-166*

DAU, T., PÜSCHEL, D., KOHLRAUSCH, A. (1996): A quantitative model of the effective signal processing in the auditory system: I. Model Structure. *J. Acoust. Soc. Am., 99(6), pp. 3615-3622*

KASPER, K., REININGER, H., WOLF, D., WÜST, H. (1995): A Speech Recognizer Based on Locally Recurrent Neural Networks. *In Proc. Int. Conf. on Artificial Neural Networks, vol. 2, pp. 15-20.*

KASPER, K., REININGER, H., WOLF, D., WÜST, H. (1996): Locally Recurrent Neural Networks for Efficient Realization of a Speech Recognizer. *Proc. EUSIPCO-96, Trieste (Italy), 1591-1594.*

KOEHLER, J., MORGAN, N., HERMANSKY, H., HIRSCH, G., TONG, G. (1994): Integrating RASTA-PLP into Speech Recognition. *Proc. IEEE Conf. on ASSP, Adalaide, pp. 421-424*

SCHÜRER et al. (1995): TUBTEL - Eine deutsche Telefon-Sprachdatenbank. *Studientexte zur Sprachkommunikation, Heft 12, pp. 183-187.*

WILLIAMS, J.W., PENG, J. (1990): An Efficient Gradient-Based Algorithm for On-Line Training of Recurrent Network Trajectories. *Neural Computation 2, pp. 490-501.*

Part 5

Knowledge and Databases

Information Gathering for Vague Queries Using Case Retrieval Nets

Hans-Dieter Burkhard

Inst. of Informatics
Humboldt University Berlin, D-10099 Berlin, Germany
e-mail: hdb@informatik.hu-berlin.de

Abstract: Case Retrieval Nets (CRNs) have been developed for the efficient and flexible retrieval of cases from large case bases in the context of Case Based Reasoning. The information access in CRNs is performed by a bottom-up spreading activation process according to similarity and relevance from query related nodes to case nodes. Special attention is put on the handling of vague queries in CRNs.

1 Introduction

Case Based Reasoning (CBR) Kolodner (1993) is an attempt to implement processes of reminding for reuse of previous experiences in similar situations. It requires efficient and flexible retrieval methods to search in the case base for those cases which can help to solve new problems. Usually, new problems do not exactly match the problems stored in the case base. Hence retrieval has to search for *similar* cases (which hopefully can be be adapted for the new case).

While pure data base queries are related to exact matches for all attributes, case base retrieval has to accept nearby matches as well. Even mismatches for some attributes might be acceptable. The found cases have to be *ranked* according to their similarity to the query: Especially this ranking is an important feature of CBR retrieval techniques. [1]

Related retrieval techniques from CBR are useful for information gathering, especially for vague queries (which can be considered as having nearby matches to the possible answers). We have implemented these techniques in applications for help-desk and assistance systems (for some prototypical implementations see http://www.informatik.hu-berlin.de/~lenz) like

- Customer support (find an appropriate answer to a customer's question from a collection of "frequently asked questions").

- Travel agency support (find appropriate answers for wishes like "... swimming in July for a reasonable price ... ", or find alternative offers replacing not available offers like " ... might choose Malta instead of Crete ... ") Lenz (1994).

---
[1] Data base queries could also accept values from certain intervals for each attribute. The amount of the found answers depends on the tuning of that intervals, which is left to the user. An appropriate ranking of answers can overcome theses needs, – it requires additional effort.

- Technical diagnosis (find similar problems from the past to get good arguments for the next steps in testing and repair) [?].

- Price calculation (find similar offers of real estates to make a guess) Lenz-Ladewig (1996).

The implementations are based on Case Retrieval Nets (CRNs) which were developed in our work on case based reasoning (cf. the references). CRNs allow a fast and flexible retrieval by a spreading activation process. It starts from initially activated "Information Entity" nodes according to the notions of the query. It leads to further nodes which stand for similar notions which could also be reminded for that query. Activations are then collected by case nodes, and the strength of activation gives the ranking of the cases.

The spreading activation process implements to some extend the idea from psychology (cf. e.g. Bartlett (1993), Anderson (1988), Kolodner (1993)) of *Reminding as reconstruction.*

A special benefit of this bottom-up retrieval technique is the efficient access to information for queries which do not exactly match the indexes under which the information was stored. The result of the retrieval is a ranking of information (cases, previous solutions, classifications, ...) according to their similarity and relevance for the query.

CRNs can implement attribute based classification methods like nearest neighbour approaches. But there is no need to have a fixed set of attributes, and CRNs can easily handle missing values (where e.g. decision trees may have problems). Queries may be only partially specified and may use vague notions. New information and new indexes can be added incrementally.

The paper is organized as follows: A short introduction to Case Based Reasoning is given in the following Section 2. Special emphasis is put on case retrieval techniques. Sections 3 explains the basic ideas of CRNs, and Section 4 gives a formal description of the basic CRN model with the spreading activation process. The treatment of vague notions in CRNs is discussed in section 5.

2 Basic ideas of Case Based Reasoning (CBR)

Human problem solving is guided to a great extend by experience. Concrete episodes are called cases. Generalization leads to "vertical" hierarchical structures: a concept describes on a "higher level" a set of related individuals of a "lower level". Cases may be seen as an "orthogonal" structuring, which combines individuals from different concepts only because of their combination in an episode. The underlying hypothesis of CBR is the repetition of events under similar circumstances. This leads to the ability of future directed behaviour without deeper domain knowledge, guided only by experience: A successful solution may be tried again in a similar problem situation (as well as an unsuccessful trial should be avoided in the future).

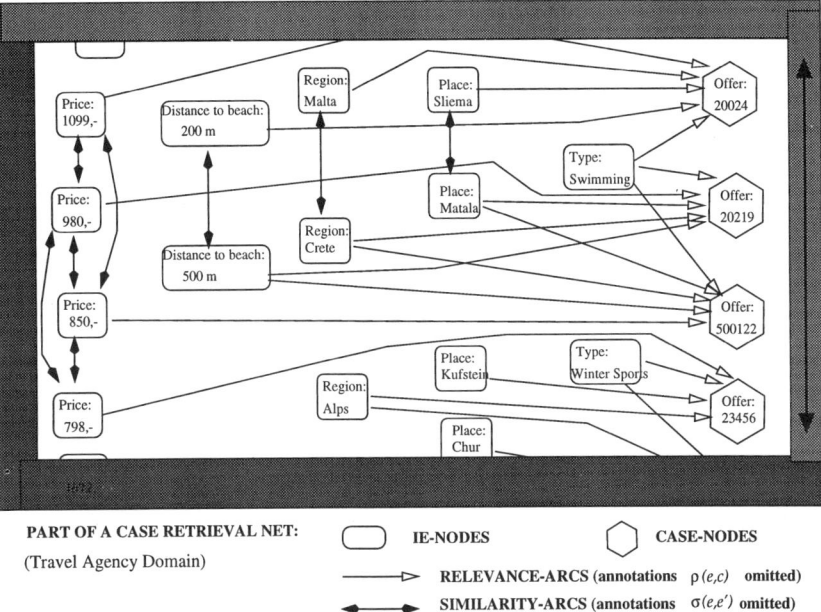

Figure 1: Example of a CRN in the TRAVEL AGENCY domain.

A central part of the CBR technique is the retrieval of "useful cases". As problem situations usually do not coincide in all aspects, CBR needs the possibility to retrieve *similar cases*, where *similarity* is meant to imply *usefulness* (utility). The aim of retrieval in CBR is the presentation of the most similar cases for a given query. That means, that a ranking of the cases in the case base has to be performed during the retrieval process.

Different retrieval methods have been proposed in the literature. The simplest one, the so-called "linear search", performs the comparison of a query with each case from the case base. Other approaches use decision trees. An extension of the well-known k-d-trees was worked out in Wess (1995), it uses a special technique to solve the problem of similar cases "behind the border" of a boundary plane. A special problem of all decision tree methods is the treatment of unknown values: It requires the search in different subtrees. A comparison of different methods can be found in Wess (1995), Goos (1994), and concerning CRN related techniques in Lenz and Burkhard (1996a).

3 Basic ideas of *Case Retrieval Nets*

The most fundamental item in CRNs are so-called *Information Entities* (IEs). They may represent any basic knowledge item, such as a particular attribute-value-pair, or a key word. The IEs play the role of indexes. They are defined under the view point of "relevant parts of cases to be used in reminding". They are integrated into the CRN as far as they appear in the cases of the case base, or in expected queries, respectively.

For the retrieval, the cases are simply considered as *sets of IEs*. The case base is a net with nodes for the IEs and additional nodes ("case descriptors") denoting the particular cases. The case descriptors may point to additional information (e.g. to a complete textual description of an episode).

IE nodes may be connected by *similarity arcs*, and a case node is reachable from its constituting IE nodes via *relevance arcs*. Given this structure, case retrieval is performed by

- *activating* the IEs given in the query case,

- *propagating* this activation according to similarity through the net of IEs, and

- *collecting* the achieved activation at the associated case nodes.

Different degrees of similarity and relevance may be expressed by arcs weights. The idea is illustrated for the TRAVEL AGENCY domain in Figure 1: A case is a special travel offer, denoted by a case descriptor, e.g. <Offer 20219>. It consists of a set of corresponding IEs giving the specification of that offer, in case of <Offer 20219> the IE nodes <Type:Swimming>, <Price:980,->, <Place:Matala>, <Region:Crete>, <Distance to beach:500 m> are connected with that case node. Asking for an offer in region Crete for swimming and not to far from the beach, the IE nodes <Type:Swimming>, <Distance to beach:200 m> and <Region:Crete> are initially activated. By similarity, the IE nodes <Region:Malta> and <Distance to beach:500 m> will be activated in the next step, but the amount of activation may depend on arc weights. Finally, the three offers <Offer 20024>, <Offer 20219>, <Offer 500122> will each get some activation. These final case node activations are computed from the incoming activations of IE nodes, which again may be weighted according to the relevance of an IE for case selection. The highest activated cases are proposed to the customer. Here the conflict arises whether the customer accepts a greater distance to the beach for being in Crete or if she changes to Malta. Special preferences may be expressed by initial weights, similarity weights and relevance weights, respectively. A first list of proposals might include both alternatives. Then, if the customer decides for Crete, an appropriate tuning of net parameters can prune all other offers in the future.

4 The formal model of *Case Retrieval Nets*

A formal description of *Case Retrieval Nets* in a basic version is given in the following (see Burkhard and Lenz (1996), for some more details). It can serve as a base for more extended models, and it allows a detailed investigation of the approach.

Definition 1
An Information Entity *(IE) is an atomic knowledge item in the domain, i.e. an IE represents the lowest granularity of knowledge representation, such as a particular attribute-value-pair. (Later on, in extended versions, IEs themselves may be structured, e.g. composed from "lower level" IEs).* □

Definition 2
A case *consists of a set of IEs. It is denoted by a unique case descriptor.* □

Definition 3
A Basic Case Retrieval Net (BCRN) *is given by* $N = [E, C, \sigma, \rho, \Pi]$ *with*

E *is the finite set of* information entities (IE) *("IE nodes"),*

C *is the finite set of* case descriptors *("case nodes"),*

σ *is the* similarity function

$$\sigma : E \times E \to \mathcal{R}$$

which describes the similarity $\sigma(e', e'')$ *between IEs* e', e'',

ρ *is the* relevance function

$$\rho : E \times C \to \mathcal{R}$$

which describes the relevance $\rho(e, c)$ *of the IE* e *for the case* c.

Π *is the set of* propagation functions π_n *for each node* $n \in E \cup C$ *with*

$$\pi_n : \mathcal{R}^E \to \mathcal{R}. \quad \square$$

An example of a graphical description is given by Figure 1.
The *"state"* of a BCRN is defined by the activation of the nodes:

Definition 4
An activation *of a BCRN* $N = [E, C, \sigma, \rho, \Pi]$ *is a function*

$$\alpha : E \cup C \to \mathcal{R}. \quad \square$$

The influence of an IE to the result of the case retrieval depends on its actual importance $\alpha(e)$ and its relevances $\rho(e, c)$ for the cases c (where π_c might express further preferences). Negative values can be used as an indicator for the rejection of cases containing that IE.
The dynamics of the retrieval process are described as changing activations:

Definition 5
Consider a BCRN $N = [E, C, \sigma, \rho, \Pi]$ *with* $E = \{e_1, ..., e_s\}$ *and let be* $\alpha_t : E \cup C \to \mathcal{R}$ *the activation at time* t.
The activation of IE nodes $e \in E$ *at time* $t + 1$ *is given by*

$$\alpha_{t+1}(e) = \pi_e(\sigma(e_1, e) \cdot \alpha_t(e_1), ..., \sigma(e_s, e) \cdot \alpha_t(e_s)),$$

and the activation of case nodes $c \in C$ *at time* $t + 1$ *is given by*

$$\alpha_{t+1}(c) = \pi_c(\rho(e_1, c) \cdot \alpha_t(e_1), ..., \rho(e_s, c) \cdot \alpha_t(e_s)). \quad \square$$

The propagation process for the basic model is a three-step process:

Step 1 – Query :
According to the query, the *primary scope of attention* is given by α_0 which is determined for all IE nodes as follows:

$$\alpha_{query}(e) = \begin{cases} 1 & : \text{ for IE nodes } e \text{ of the new problem} \\ 0 & : \text{ else} \end{cases}$$

For more subtle queries, α_0 might assign different weights to special IE nodes, and some *context* may be set as an initial activation for further nodes.

Step 2 – Similarity propagation between IE nodes :
The activation α_0 is propagated to all IE nodes $e \in E$ leading to an *extended scope of attention*:

$$\alpha_1(e) = \pi_e(\sigma(e_1, e) \cdot \alpha_0(e_1), ..., \sigma(e_s, e) \cdot \alpha_0(e_s)),$$

Step 3 – Relevance propagation from IE nodes to case nodes : The result of step 2 is propagated to the case nodes $c \in C$:

$$\alpha_2(c) = \pi_c(\rho(e_1, c) \cdot \alpha_1(e_1), ..., \rho(e_s, c) \cdot \alpha_1(e_s)).$$

For the 3-Step activation process we obtain the final activation $\alpha_N(c)$ at the case nodes c by combining the formulae from above:

$$\begin{aligned}\alpha_N(c) = \pi_c(& \rho(e_1, c) \cdot \pi_{e_1}(\sigma(e_1, e_1) \cdot \alpha_{query}(e_1), ..., \sigma(e_s, e_1) \cdot \alpha_{query}(e_s)) \\ & , ..., \\ & \rho(e_s, c) \cdot \pi_{e_s}(\sigma(e_1, e_s) \cdot \alpha_{query}(e_1), ..., \sigma(e_s, e_s) \cdot \alpha_{query}(e_s)))).\end{aligned}$$

Thus we can summarize the concept of case retrieval in the basic model of CRN:

> Consider a BCRN $N = [E, C, \sigma, \rho, \Pi]$ and the activation functions α_t as defined in Definitions 4 and 5. The result of the case retrieval for a given query activation α_0 is the *preference ordering* of cases according to decreasing activations $\alpha_N(c)$ of case nodes $c \in C$. □

The section is closed with a consideration of some standard techniques as an application field for CRN.

Case based systems as well as classification systems often use a fixed set of features/attributes $a_1, ..., a_k$ with values in $W_1, ..., W_k$ (such that the problems are described as feature vectors $[x_1, ..., x_n] \in W_1 \times ... \times W_k$, – e.g. as vectors of symptom values). Similarities between such vectors may be computed as the weighted sum of attribute similarities ("composite similarities"):

Definition 6
A similarity function
$$sim : (W_1 \times ... \times W_k) \times (W_1 \times ... \times W_k) \to \mathcal{R},$$
is called composite *if it is combined by a function* $\phi : \mathcal{R}^k \to \mathcal{R}$ *from feature similarity functions* $\sigma_i : W_i \times W_i \to \mathcal{R}$ *such that*
$$sim([x_1, ..., x_n], [y_1, ..., y_n]) = \phi(\sigma_1(x_1, y_1), ..., \sigma_k(x_k, y_k)). \qquad \square$$

The weighted sum of the feature similarities may serve as an example of a composite similarity function:
$$sim([x_1, ..., x_n], [y_1, ..., y_n]) = \sum_{i=1,...,k} g_i \cdot \sigma_i(x_i, y_i).$$

Composite similarities can be easily implemented by BCRNs. We consider the case where the functions π_n (collecting propagations in the nodes n) are specified as the sum of incoming (weighted) activations. Then we obtain for the steps from above:

$$\text{Step 2:} \quad \alpha(e) = \sum_{e'} \sigma(e', e) \cdot \alpha_{query}(e')$$

$$\text{Step 3:} \quad \alpha(c) = \sum_{e} \rho(e, c) \cdot \alpha(e)$$

And the resulting activation in the case nodes for a query α_{query} is given by

$$\alpha_N(c) = \sum_{e} \rho(e, c) \cdot \sum_{e'} \sigma(e', e) \cdot \alpha_{query}(e').$$

But while in the formula for the weighted sum from above the weights g_i are constant values, the relevances $\rho(e, c)$ in the net permit individual weights of incoming arcs for each case c.

5 Treatment of vague queries

Vague queries may come in several forms, e.g. as "linguistic terms" as in fuzzy theories ("cheap", "during summer") or as a vague value ("about 1000,- DM", "around July 1st"). Both notions could be interpreted using

- Fuzzy set theory (strength of membership of a concrete value to the fuzzy concept).

- Similarity (how similar is a concrete value to the given vague concept). In the CBR applications this means the strength for reminding a case with a concrete value (e.g. 950,- DM) when asking for "cheap" resp. "about 1000,- DM" offers.

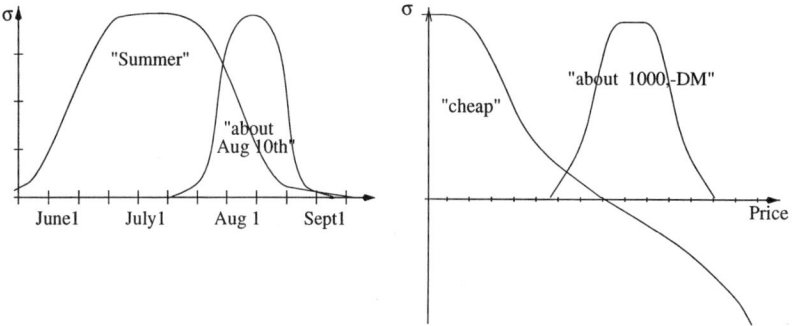

Figure 2: Similarity for vague notions.

We are interested in CBR, i.e. in the similarity approach. We consider the similarity σ_i for the i-th attribute (e.g. prices or time, respectively) to relate the vague notions to exact values (e.g. x for currency or t for time, respectively):

$$\sigma_i(cheap, x), \sigma_i(1000DM, x)$$
$$\sigma_i(summer, t), \sigma_i(July1st, t)$$

Note that for the vague values there is even no formal difference to the usage of similarity for concrete values (cf. Figure 2).

Similarity is used to express the power of reminding, especially negative values of similarity indicate the intention *not* to remind a related case (as depicted for "cheap" in the figure). Therefore the usage of similarity extends the usual notion of fuzzy membership. But we could interpret fuzzy membership functions as similarity functions (the similarity function σ_i for the linguistic term "summer" in the figure might come from a related characteristic function).

IE nodes for vague terms like "cheap" or "summer" can be included in a CRN just like other IE nodes. They are connected by related similarity arcs with the IEs for the concrete values of the cases. Initial activations are put on the IEs for vague notions if asked for. Problems may arise for vague values like "about y DM" because there are a lot of different possible values y. In many applications it is sufficient to permit only a limited number of such values (about 100,- , 200,- , 300,- ...).

But it is also possible to allow arbitrary vague values y in the query. There are different possibilities for implementation. We consider the problem for a query asking for a price of "about y DM". What we want to have is the following: For each IE node e_{price} denoting a related price x of a case in the CRN, the activation of e_{price} after the propagation of similarities (Step 2 from above) should be $\alpha_1(e_{price}) = \sigma_{price}(y, x)$ (where σ_{price} denotes the intended similarity between prices).

We can realize it with a single IE-node e_{query_price}. Differing from our considerations from above, the initial activation (Step 1) of this node is y (instead of 1), where y is the vague value given in the query ("about y DM").

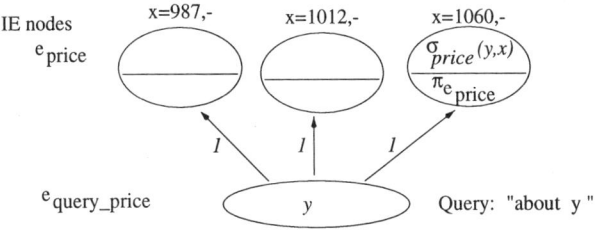

Figure 3: Implementation for vague notions.

The arc-weights between e_{query_price} and the IE nodes e_{price} are all fixed to $\sigma(e_{query\_price}, e_{price}) = 1$. The propagation functions in the IE nodes e_{price} are defined by $\pi_{e_{price}}(y) = \sigma_{price}(y, x)$ where x is the price denoted by the IE node e_{price}.

According to this construction, the initial activation at e_{query_price} is y in Step 1. This value y arrives as incoming activation at the nodes e_{price}, where it is transformed by $\pi_{e_{price}}$ to the intended value $\sigma_{price}(y, x)$ as the activation at e_{price} in Step 2 (cf. Figure 3).

6 Summary

Information gathering is a non-trivial task in a world of information overflow. Techniques are needed which are flexible and adaptable to the user's needs without great effort. Especially the *ranking* of information under more than only statistical view points is important. CRNs perform a ranking according to the relevance of indexes while considering even the mutual reference between indexes.

The technique of CRNs was developed for the retrieval of cases (experiences from the past) in Case Based Reasoning. Some ideas of CRNs in their recent stage of development have been presented in this article, together with a discussion of potential applications in the area of information gathering. Further extensions concern the implementation of concepts and rules Burkhard (1997), Lenz et al. (1996) and more sophisticated activation processes Burkhard and Lenz (1996), Lenz and Burkhard (1996), Lenz and Burkhard (1996a).

The last mentioned paper contains some early experimental results. Latest results have shown a retrieval time of about 6 seconds for a case base with 200 000 cases, where each case has 7 attribute values ("Last minute" travel overs, SPARC-20). Information gathering over a set of 700 documents with about 1 MByte text took about 1 second.

Acknowledgments. A great part in the development of the theory and the main work in the implementation of CRNs was done by Mario Lenz. The author wants to thank for this work and for all our discussions. Thanks for many fruitful discussions are also due to the colleagues in the field.

References

ANDERSON, J.R. (1988): A Spreading Activation Theory of Memory. In: A.M. Collins and E.E. Smith (eds.): *Readings in Cognitive Science*. Morgan Kaufmann, 137–145.

BARTLETT, R. (1932): Remembering: A study in experimental and social psychology. Cambridge University Press, London.

BURKHARD, H.-D. (1995): Case retrieval nets. Techn. report, Humboldt University, Berlin.

BURKHARD, H.-D. (1997): Cases, Information, and Agents. In: P. Kandzia, M. Klusch (eds.): *Cooperative Information Agents*. Proc. First Int. Workshop CIA'97. LNAI 1202, Springer, 64-79.

BURKHARD, H.-D. and LENZ, M. (1996): Case retrieval nets: Basic ideas and extensions. In: H.-D. Burkhard and M. Lenz (eds.): 4th German Workshop on CBR, Humboldt University Berlin, 103–110.

GOOS, K. (1994): Preselection strategies for case based classification. In: B. Nebel and L. Dreschler-Fischer (eds.): KI-94: *Advances in Case-Based Reasoning*. Springer, 1994.

KOLODNER, J.L. (1993): Case-Based Reasoning. Morgan Kaufmann, San Mateo.

LENZ, M. (1994): Case-based reasoning for holiday planning. In: W. Schertler, B. Schmid, A. M. Tjoa, and H. Werthner (eds.): *Information and Communications Technologies in Tourism*. Springer Verlag, 126–132.

LENZ, M. and LADEWIG, H. (1996): Fallbasierte Unterstützung bei der Immobilienbewertung. Wirtschaftsinformatik, 38(1), Schwerpunktheft *Fallbasierte Entscheidungsunterstützung*.

LENZ, M. and BURKHARD, H.-D. (1996): Lazy propagation in case retrieval nets. In: W. Wahlster (ed.): 12th ECAI 1996, John Wiley & Sons, 127–131.

LENZ, M. and BURKHARD, H.-D. (1996): Case Retrieval Nets: Basic Ideas and Extensions. KI-96: *Advances in Artificial Intelligence*. Proc. 20th Annual German Conference on AI, LNAI 1137, 227-239.

LENZ, M., BURKHARD, H.-D., and BRÜCKNER, S. (1996): Applying Case Retrieval Nets to Diagnostic Tasks in Technical Domains. In: I. Smith, B. Faltings (eds.): *Advances in Case-Based Reasoning*. Proc. of the Third European Workshop EWCBR-96. *Lecture Notes in Artificial Intelligence, 1168*, Springer, 219–233.

WESS, S. (1995): Fallbasiertes Problemlösen in wissensbasierten Systemen zur Entscheidungsunterstützung und Diagnostik. PhD thesis, Universität Kaiserslautern.

Characterizing Bibliographic Databases by Content - an Experimental Approach

M. Dreger, S. Göbel, S. Lohrum

Institut für Informatik,
Freie Universität Berlin, D-14195 Berlin, Germany

Abstract: With the growing number of bibliographic databases accessible online the user has to choose between numerous sources. For that content descriptions of the databases are necessary. In this paper we present an approach to describe bibliographic databases by content. It is based on classification profiles, which show the portion of a given database each class of a classification has. Approximations to these profiles can be gained automatically with a limited number of queries with characteristic terms for each class of a classification. A way to obtain characteristic terms is presented and the method is tested on different databases.

1 Introduction

The number of online databases is growing continuously and the user has access to a lot of information sources via the Internet. He has to choose between these various sources to select appropriate databases. It is therefore necessary to have content descriptions of the existing databases. Until now there have been few approaches to describe bibliographic databases by content. Moreover, most of them seek to compare a given set of databases, using a small set of queries, selected from experts or randomly, which have to be answered by each database (Jacso (1991), Marbach (1992), Martyn (1981), Tenopir (1982)). These small sample tests are inadequate and not appropriate to support a database selection for various user queries.

The approach described in this work is an attempt, to generate a description of bibliographic databases by content *automatically*. Moreover these descriptions support *automatic database selection*. In this approach a classification is used for describing the databases. The aim of the method is to gain a profile for each database, that can be used to measure how strong each class of the classification is represented. We call these profiles *classification profiles*. If every document in the database is classified, such a profile can be produced very easily by selecting the number of documents for each class of the classification. But there are no good methods for automatic classification of documents and intellectual classification is very expensive, so that there are a lot of databases that have no classified documents. For these databases our approach is a solution.

2 The Method

To select the appropriate databases for a given query the classification profile for each database is necessary. To obtain these profiles the following three steps are performed:

1. Using a classified database, characteristic terms for each class are selected.

2. The non classified databases are queried with the characteristic terms.

3. A classification profile is calculated for each database using the sizes of the result sets.

2.1 Getting Appropriate Search Terms

The basis for the following experiments is the database CompuScience[1]. Of the different categories of the document references in this database (FIZ Karlsruhe (1991)) we use

- title words (Title /TI),
- keywords (Supplementary Terms /ST) and
- authors' names (Author /AU).

For each class of the second level of the ACM Computing Classification System[2] used by CompuScience and for each of the three categories a list with all terms and the term frequencies is selected. For each term t and each class c the fraction of the frequency $freq(t,c)$ in the class c, and of the frequency $freq(t)$ in the whole database is calculated:

$$p(t,c) = \frac{freq(t,c)}{freq(t)} \qquad (1)$$

$p(t,c)$ is the conditional probability of a document belonging to the class c if it is described with the term t. The closer this value is to 1, the more characteristic the term t is for the class c.

2.2 The Number of Queries

The terms, which are the best for querying the non classified databases, are those, which have high probability values according to formula (1) and are frequent. Terms that are frequent in one database can be expected to occur in other databases, too. And the higher the probability values are the better

---

[1] http://www.zblmath.fiz-karlsruhe.de/cs/compueng.html
[2] http://www.acm.org/class/1991/cr91-intro.html

the results can be ascribed to a special thematical area. To minimize the necessary number of queries both criteria should be taken into consideration. This can be done with a weight $w(t, c)$, that is calculated for each term t as the product of its probability $p(t, c)$ and its frequency $freq(t, c)$ in the respective class c:

$$w(t,c) = p(t,c) \cdot freq(t,c) = \frac{freq(t,c)^2}{freq(t)} \qquad (2)$$

The terms with the highest weights are used to query the databases. In the following, these terms will be called *characteristic terms*. The first experiment described below shows that a small number of terms is sufficient to get a good approximation to the real profile.

2.3 Getting the Profiles

For databases with classified documents it is easy to get the profiles by selecting the number of references $freq(D, c)$ in each class of the classification. These frequencies give a profile that shows, whether a special thematical area is strong or weak in this database.

The described approach now shows, how to gain an approximated profile for non classified databases. These databases are queried with the characteristic terms for every class of the classification. Each category (title words, keywords and author names) is evaluated separately, provided that they exist in the database being queried. The result for each class c and n queries, each with one term t_i, is a set of sizes s_{t_i} of the result sets. The documents in the result set for a single term t_i belong to the corresponding class c with probability $p(t_i, c)$ calculated, as described in formula (1). So for every class c and database D, an estimator $e_n(D, c)$ can be calculated:

$$e_n(D, c) = \sum_{i=1}^{n} p(t_i, c) \cdot s_{t_i} \qquad (3)$$

The estimators for all classes together give a profile, that shows approximately how strong the different classes are in relation to each other.

3 Using the Profiles

Although the profiles show how strong the different classes in the database are, the sizes of the result sets must not be interpreted as the number of documents in the database for the corresponding class directly. They can only be used to compare the classes with each other. So it is possible to use the profiles to select those databases from a given set of thematically specialized databases, that are probably most appropriate to a given query. If the databases are not specialized thematically, but spread over all classes of a given classification like CompuScience, then one has to be careful drawing conclusions. In fact, even in such databases, the classes differ in size (see figure 2). This is because the number of publications differ in the various thematical areas. This can also be seen when the profiles of different years are compared. Areas corresponding to the research trend in a given year have more publications than those not corresponding. Because of this observation it is clear, that the terms, that are used to gain the profiles, have to be updated from time to time.

4 The Experiments

The experiments described in the following sections are designed to verify the effectiveness of our method. In the first experiment CompuScience itself is queried using the terms got as described in the sections 2.1 and 2.2. This first experiment shows, that only very few terms are needed to get a good approximation of the real classification profile. This result is not unexpected, because of the law of Zipf (Zipf (1949)) [3] and the law of Mandelbrot (Mandelbrot(1954, 1977)) [4] for the title words and keywords and the law of Lotka (Lotka (1926)) [5] for the authors' names (see also Egghe, Rousseau (1990)). Figure 1 shows a sample frequency diagram for the title words and a table with the most characteristic terms of the class H.3 (Information Retrieval) of CompuScience. In other classes the distributions are similar.

In the second experiment another database with classified documents is queried using the same terms to show that the approximated profile is close to the real profile. In this experiment it is to be expected that some terms with high weights in CompuScience do not occur in the other database.

The databases used in the third experiment are not classified, but they have a thematical focus. This is the application scenario the method is thought for. In the approximated profiles the foci are expected to be seen very clearly.

4.1 Getting Characteristic Terms

The basis of the experiments is the database CompuScience. Figure 2 shows, that not all classes of the Computing Classification of the ACM are represented equally in the database.

For some weak classes, it is not possible to find terms that both have a high probability and are frequent. For all classes it can be seen that often the terms with the highest probability values for title words and keywords are mistakes in writing or character sequences that make no sense. But these terms have low frequencies. Many of the most frequent terms are stop

---

[3] Given a list of all words of a text, in decreasing order of occurrence in the text, the product of the rank r of a word and the number of times j it occurs in the text is constant: $r \cdot j = C$.

[4] Derived from the same context, but with additional constants H and β: $j \cdot (1 + H \cdot r)^\beta = C'$.

[5] With $f(j)$ the number of authors with j publications: $f(j) = \frac{c}{j^\alpha}$, where $\alpha \approx 2$.

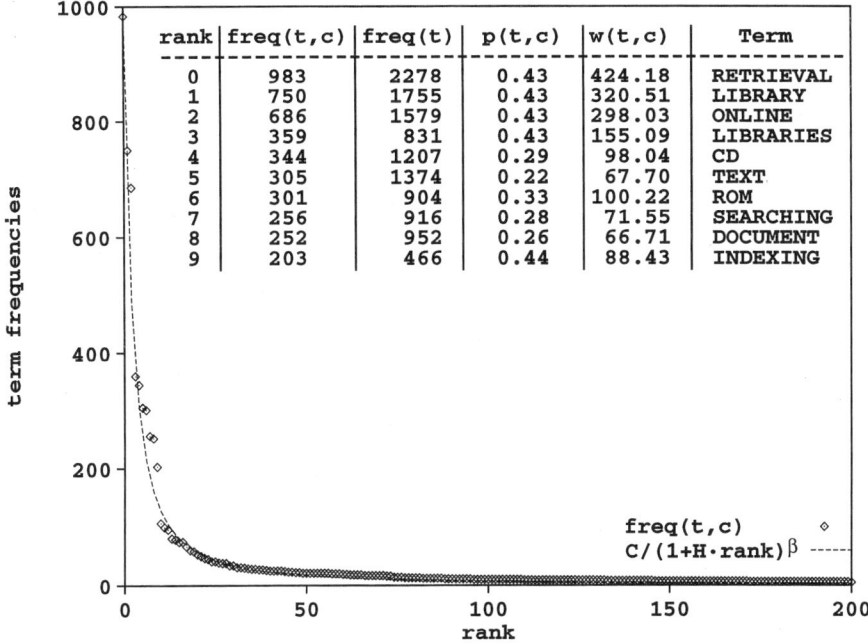

Figure 1: Title words in class H.3 (Information Retrieval) of CompuScience

words, that have a low probability in general. A threshold of 0.2 for the probability eliminates most of the stop words. As far as the authors' names are concerned, there are no stop words, but a threshold still makes sense to eliminate terms that are not appropriate to gain a profile, because they occur in too many classes.

For some classes it is not possible to find enough terms with a probability beyond the threshold. This is especially true of the general classes A.0, B.0 etc. and the miscellaneous classes A.m, B.m etc. Additionally these classes are very unspecific, so it makes no sense to take them into account for the experiments.

Authors' names are problematic. On the one hand the way of notation varies from one database to another or even within one database, e.g. the order of first names and surnames is different or first names are abbreviated or not. On the other hand there are different rules for the transcription of foreign names. Both kinds of variation are problematic for retrieval. The problem with the first kind of variation can be solved by taking only the surnames into account. But there is no solution to the transcription problem.

Using only surnames, some authors are not recognized being characteristic because of authors in other classes having the same surname. This sharpens the selection criterion for the authors' names.

4.2 First Experiment

In the first experiment CompuScience itself is queried with the characteristic terms to compare the approximated and the real profile. Figure 2 shows that the approximation with 20 or more terms per class is not significantly better than the one with only ten terms. Using more terms means, that the costs to gain the profiles rise. Therefore we decided to restrict the number of terms to ten for the following experiments.

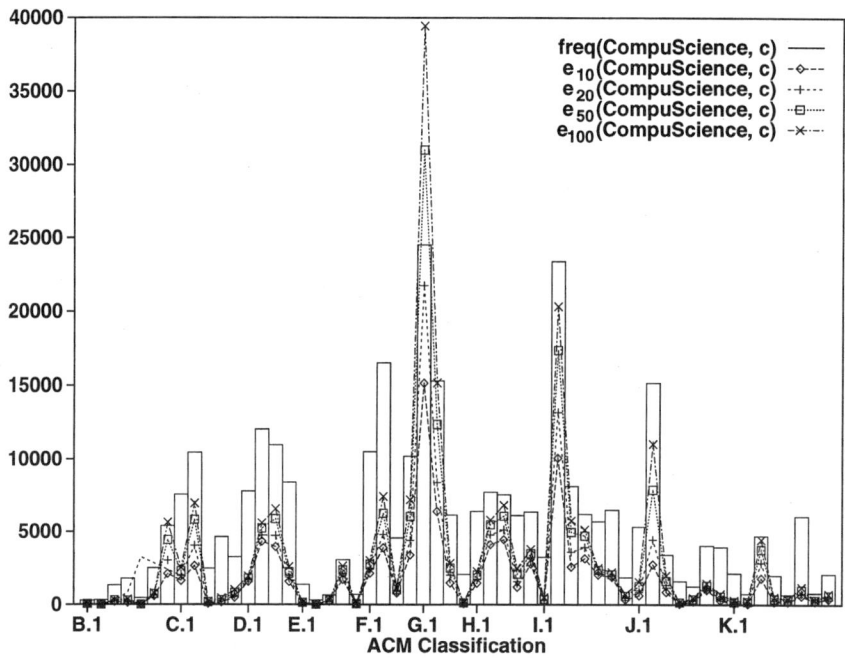

Figure 2: CompuScience Classification Profiles (Title Words)

Figure 3 shows the classification profiles for the different categories with the ten most characteristic terms. The figure shows, that the absolute values of the estimates gained with the authors' names are very low. This is because the number of publications a person is able to write during a lifetime is small. So, the number of documents written by few authors is also small. The estimates gained with the keywords are often higher than the real number of documents in the classes, because many documents are described with more than one of the characteristic keywords. These documents are then counted several times.

4.3 Second Experiment

The ACM Computing Archive CD-ROM (ACM (1993)) is used in the second experiment. The documents of this archive are classified, so it is possible to

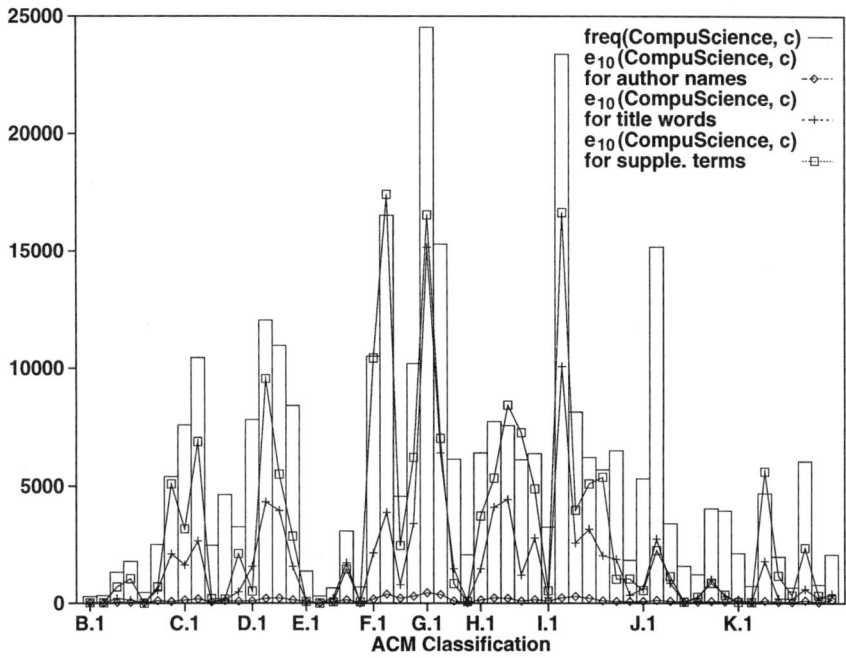

Figure 3: CompuScience Classification Profiles (10 Terms)

gain the real profile and compare it with the estimated one. When querying the database it happens that some of the characteristic terms from CompuScience are not present in the ACM database. For example, there are no German terms in the ACM database, as in CompuScience. Some authors' names are written differently because of different transcription rules.

Figure 4 shows for the title words that the graph produced with the estimates for the various classes follows the real profile with very few exceptions. This applies to the authors' names profile, too. There is no profile for the supplementary terms because there is no such category in this database.

This shows, that it is possible to gain the classification profiles of other databases with the terms from CompuScience.

4.4 Third Experiment

The third experiment is close to the application scenario the described method is created for. The used databases are not classified; but they have a thematical focus. Figure 5 shows the results for four BibTeX collections with foci in artificial intelligence, compilers, databases and theoretical computer science. They have been taken from The Collection of Computer Science Bibliographies[6]. It can be seen, that

---

[6]http://liinwww.ira.uka.de/bibliography/index.html

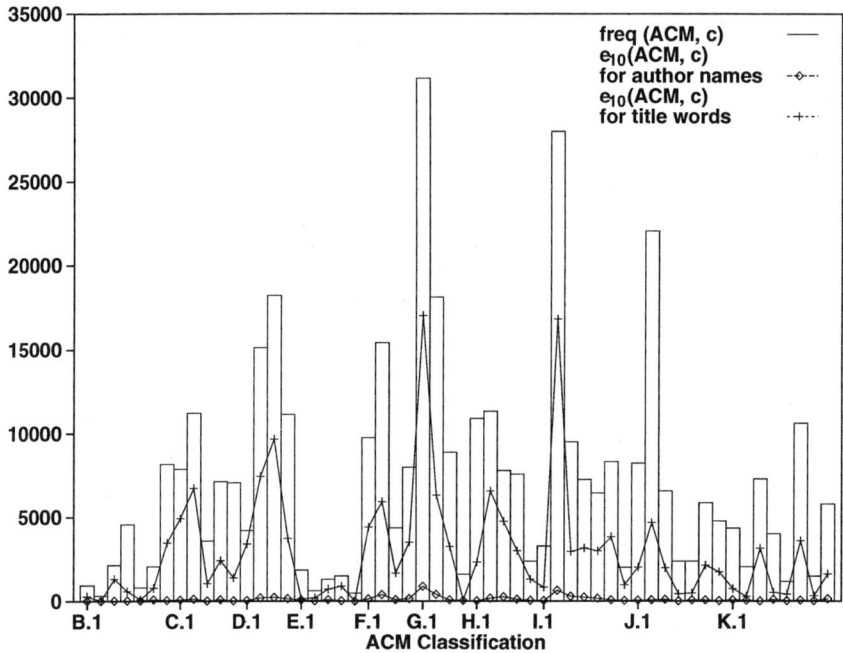

Figure 4: ACM Computing Archive (10 Terms)

- the AI collection has its foci in I (Computing Methodologies), especially I.2 (Artificial Intelligence), D (Software) and F (Theory of Computing),

- the compiler collection in D (Software), especially in D.3 (Programming Languages) and in F (Theory of Computing),

- the database collection in H (Information Systems), especially H.2 (Database Management)

- and the theory collection in F (Theory of Computation) and G (Mathematics of Computing).

That is exactly what was expected.

5 Conclusion and Outlook

The experiments show that the described method is a promising approach to characterize bibliographic databases by content, using classification profiles, which can be gained automatically. With an initial classified database it is possible to find characteristic terms that are appropriate to gain a good approximation of the real profiles of other databases automatically. To verify, that the method works in general, more experiments have to be done.

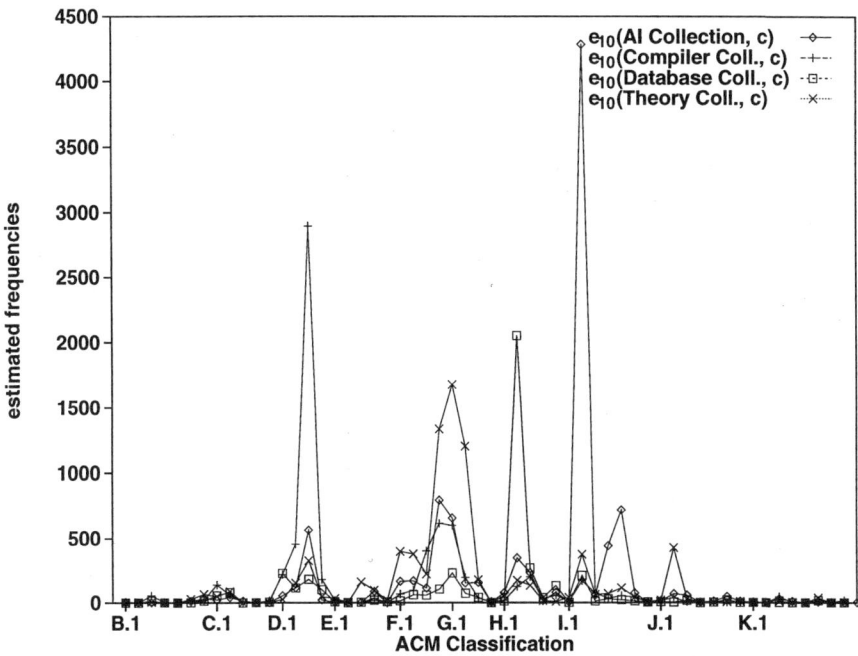

Figure 5: Computer Science Bibliographies (Title Words, 10 Terms)

Moreover, a detailed statistical analysis is necessary to evaluate the quality of the method. Another open research topic is the use of multiple classified databases to obtain the characteristic terms. For automatic database selection it would be helpful, to have quantitative estimators and not only qualitative ones that can only be interpreted in relation to those of the other classes of the same database.

References

ACM (1993): Computing Archive - Bibliography and Reviews from ACM. ACM Press, New York

EGGHE, L., ROUSSEAU, R. (1990): Introduction to Informetrics. Elsevier, Amsterdam

FIZ KARLSRUHE (1991): CompuScience - Database Description. STN International, Karlsruhe

JACSO, P. (1991): CD-ROM Software, Dataware and Hardware: Evaluation, Selection and Installation. Libraries Unlimited, Englewood

LOTKA, A.J. (1926): The frequency distribution of scientific productivity. *Journal of the Washington Academy of Sciences, 16, 317-323*

MANDELBROT, B. (1954): Structure formelle des textes et communication. Word, 10, 1-27

MANDELBROT, B. (1977): The fractal geometry of nature. Freeman, New York

MARBACH, J. (1992): Erfahrungen mit CD-ROM. Bewertungskriterien in Theorie und Praxis. 14. Online Tagung der Deutschen Gesellschaft für Dokumentation Frankfurt/Main 27.-30. April, 27–70

MARTYN, J., LANCASTER, F.W. (1981): Investigative Methods in Library and Information Science: an Introduction. Information Recources Press, Arlington

TENOPIR, C. (1982): Evaluation of Database Coverage: A Comparison of two Methologies. *Online Review 6, 423–441*

ZIPF, G.K. (1949): Human behavior and the principle of least effort. Addison Wesley, Cambridge

Medoc
Searching Heterogeneous Bibliographic and Text Databases

Kai Großjohann[1], Cornelia Haber[2], Ricarda Weber[2]

[1] Fachbereich Informatik, Lehrstuhl VI,
Universität Dortmund,
D-44221 Dortmund, Germany

[2] Institut für Informatik,
TU München, Arcisstraße 21
D-80290 München, Germany

Abstract: The Medoc system aims at providing Computer Science researchers and practitioners with information they need, on their desktops. On the one hand, this includes building a database of full text documents with browsing and navigation functions in addition to the usual search facilities. On the other hand, transparent access to heterogeneous full text and bibliographic databases is provided. The paper presented develops a document model needed to support all of the functions for the heterogeneous databases and sketches some methods for querying heterogeneous databases.

1 Introduction

Medoc (**M**ultimedia **e**lectronic **Doc**uments)[1] aims at improving the Computer Science related information search and retrieval of CS professionals, who should be able to search for and view literature from their desktop workstations or PCs. Medoc is a German digital library project. The project start was September 1995, and the duration is two years. It is led by a consortium consisting of the GI (Gesellschaft für Informatik, the German society for CS professionals), the FIZ Karlsruhe (database provider of technical scientific information, STN host), and the Springer Verlag (Heidelberg). The Medoc system is developed by ten universities and research institutes around Germany. The content is provided by twelve German and foreign publishing houses, and 24 universities and companies are pilot users. The project aims at collecting hands-on experience prior to starting up a commercial service after the end of the project.

The objective of the project, as mentioned above, is to enable CS students, researchers, and practitioners, to access information relevant to their work. The information provided comprises commercial products (such as books

---

[1]The Medoc Project is sponsored by the German Ministry for Education, Science, Research and Technology (no. 08 C 7829 6). The project's home page is http://medoc.informatik.tu-muenchen.de.

and journals) as well as non-commercial (such as technial reports), and it comprises documents in full text as well as bibliographic references, from commercial databases (FIZ) as well as from bibliographies around the Internet, such as the Databases and Logic Programming database maintained by Alf-Christian Achilles. We aim at providing access to about 50 books and 25 journals (full text), and at ten to fifteen bibliographic databases (see Brüggemann-Klein 96, MeDoc 96).

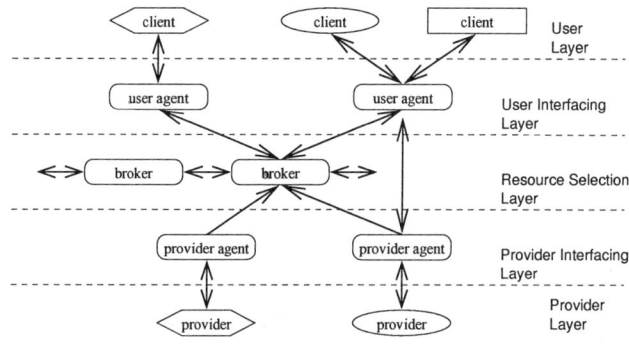

Figure 1: Architecture of the Medoc system

Figure 1 shows the architecure of the Medoc system. It is divided into five layers. Users contact the system using common Web browsers (*User Layer*). The *User Interfacing Layer* comprises the *User Agents* which transform user inputs into Medoc protocol messages and outputs from the Medoc system into a format understood by the clients used. The *Provider Selection Layer* comprises the *Brokers* which select the relevant databases (or providers) for a given user query, based on meta data about each database connected to the system. We use replication of Brokers for better availability and for performance reasons. The Provider Interfacing Layer consists of the *Provider Agents* which transform queries from the format used within the Medoc system into the format used by the provider system and results from the provider system into the format used within the Medoc system (see Boles et. al. (1996)).

A typical usage scenario would be as follows. Periodically, the Provider Agents extract meta data describing the content of the associated providers from the provider systems and send it to the broker. (See section 3.1 for more information what meta data is and how it is used.) A user issues a query to the system by filling out a form in her Web browser. The User Agent transforms this query into the format used by the Medoc system and sends it to the Broker. The Broker responds with a list of relevant providers. The User Agent sends the query to all the Provider Agents mentioned in that list.[2] They each respond with a list of document references. The User

---

[2] Actually, the User Agent might present this list to the user, who can then choose from the providers mentioned. This is configurable.

Agent merges the list of document references and presents it to the user, who can then browse the associated document, or have it delivered to her workstation, or navigate the provider the document comes from (see DrMü 96). (Some "documents" are bibliographic references from a bibliography, of course, so all the user will ever see is the bibliographic data. In this context, a document reference consists of some of the more important fields whereas the "document" is just a list of all fields of the bibliographic reference.)

Some of the providers mentioned in figure 1 are Medoc Full Text Servers which provide the greatest functionality among the providers: they offer browsing, document delivery, and navigation, too. In the following section, we will show how these functions can be supported with a document model and explains the rationale behind the document model we choose. In section 3, then, we show how the Broker selects the relevant providers for each query, and how different, heterogeneous, provider systems can be accessed. It is also shown how the document model developed in section 2 can be restricted to cover the functionality of bibliographic databases and extended to cope with heterogeneous databases. A summary concludes the paper.

2 Document Model

The Medoc Full Text Server has to provide special functionality due to the full text of documents being stored, and due to the diversity of documents with respect to structure and size. We support the functions of the Full Text Server with a document model, described below.

There are four requirements which the Full Text Server should fulfill: searching, browsing (within documents), navigation (between documents) and document delivery should be supported. Also, we assume that documents are hierarchically structured (into chapters, sections, subsections and so on) for easier perusal. We examine these four functions in more detail:

Searching We distinguish between searching the bibliographic information about documents from searching the full text of documents. Clearly, both kinds of search are potentially useful. For instance, even though the name of the author of a document appears in the full text, full text search is not sufficient to distinguish between those documents authored by John Smith, say, from those referring to John Smith. Moreover, allowing for searching with respect to the bibliographic field "publication year" enables the system to provide the "less than" and "greater than" operators which would be nearly impossible with full text search alone.

On the other hand, content-based searching is not very well supported with bibliographic fields alone.

In addition, we would like to support both kinds of query conditions to occur together in one query; it is plausible that users might want to search for "new" documents about some topic (this translates into a full text search combined with a condition with respect to the publication year), or that users might want to specify both the contents and the author when searching for a specific document.

The research in Information Retrieval has shown that systems that return a ranked list of documents exhibit better performance, so the Full Text Server should return ranked lists of documents for all queries, whether or not they refer to the full text.

There is one other point that needs to be raised because of the hierarchical structure of documents. Clearly, users do not want to be referred to the "Encyclopedia Britannica" when searching for something specific, nor do they want to be referred to a subsection of a book if they really need to read all of the book in order to satisfy their information need. Therefore, the Full Text Server should always return the smallest hierarchical unit of a document that satisfies a user's information need. If the query contains a condition referring to the full text, the size of the units returned should be minimized (most of the time, but not always). If, however, the user searches for "documents by John Smith" we would rather if the system returned the book instead of its chapters.

Browsing We define "browsing" as "following of explicit hyperlinks in the document". As this is a well-known feature exhibited by the Web we do not elaborate on this topic.

Navigation There are different kinds of navigation that we would like the Full Text Server to support.

1. Navigating according to the document hierarchy. As an example, consider a journal article. Given any journal article, the user might wish to see a list of articles in that journal issue, or in the whole volume, or a list of volumes of the journal. This would correspond to a navigation "up" in (towards the root of) the hierarchy. The opposite, corresponding to a list of sections of that article, should also be possible.

2. Navigating the dictionary (of a field). Documents are classified according to the ACM Computing Reviews classification scheme. Navigation in that hierarchy should be possible. For the "author" field, navigation in the dictionary means to get a list of author names, and for each author name, a list of documents by that author. Another attribute where navigation in the dictionary would be meaningful is the publication date: a list of all documents published in 1984, for instance. Navigation in the dictionaries of other fields works similarly.

3. Navigating between "like" documents. The meaning of "like" differs. Mainly, we think about bibliographic attributes: from a document or document reference it should be possible to get a

list of documents authored by the same person, or a list of documents from the same publisher, or a list of documents published in the same year, or a list of documents in the same class of the Computing Reviews classification scheme. Obviously, it would be nice to be able to navigate to "like" documents, then navigate the dictionary of a field.

Document Delivery We assume that each document is stored in one or more files. We further assume that the physical structure of a document (the division into files) does not correspond exactly to the logical structure of the document. A logical unit of a document may be only part of a file; a section would be only part of a file if the document is stored as PDF, each chapter in a file. Or, if a logical unit consists of several files, it may happen that a file occurs in several logical units (viz, the GIF logo on each HTML page). This discrepancy between the physical and the logical structure of documents is the main problem to be coped with. We solve this problem with a many-to-many relationship between logical units and physical units of documents.

We have developed a document model to support these four functions (see figure 2). The bibliographic data is stored in "LitItem" entities (each of which represents a document or a subdocument). The full text is stored in files, and there is a many-to-many relationship between LitItems and files. The hierarchical structure of documents is embodied in the part-of relationships between the different specializations of LitItem, shown in the lower half of the figure. Please refer to Haber (1996) for more details.

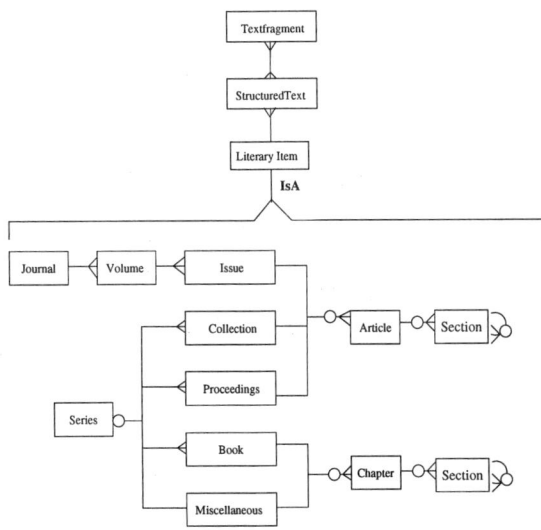

Figure 2: Document Model

3 External Databases

In the previous section, we have presented a document model that supports the functions of the Full Text Server. In this section we show how the document model can be adapted for dealing with heterogeneous provider systems. We begin with describing our approach to the provider selection problem.

3.1 Provider Selection

There are several providers that can be accessed using the Medoc system. There are different possibilities on how to enable the user to access them. The simplest way would be to just let the user connect to each system, but that is not a good idea as she would then have to deal with the idiosyncrasies of (the interface of) each system. The next step would be to provide a uniform interface to all systems, but the user still has to know which provider contains the information needed. It would be possible to broadcast the user's query to all providers connected but that is not feasible if the number of providers is too high (too many results returned), or if issuing a query to a provider costs money (too expensive), or if there are many users (too high a load on the servers of the providers, net load too high).

Therefore, it is important to have some mechanism for provider selection.

We use a decision-theoretic approach to provider selection. It is described in detail by Fuhr (1997). The basic idea is that we assume that the user issues a query and specifies the number of relevant documents she wishes to retrieve. For each combination of provider number of relevant documents to retrieve from that provider we estimate the cost. We then use a divide-and-conquer algorithm to optimize the total cost across all providers. In order to estimate the cost, an estimate of the number of relevant documents in a provider with respect to a query is needed.

A problem that has to be dealt with in calculating the cost for retrieving r relevant documents from provider i is that the user specifies the number of relevant documents whereas one can reasonably request from the system the total number of documents only. The relationship between these numbers is given by the *recall/precision curve*. *Precision* is the percentage of relevant documents among the retrieved documents whereas *recall* is the percentage of retrieved documents among the relevant documents.

There is a simple relationship between the recall/precision curve $P_i(R)$ and the number s_i of documents to retrieve from provider i:

$$r/s_i = P_i(R) = P_i(r/R_i)$$
$$s_i(r) = \frac{r}{P_i(r/R_i)}$$

where r the number of relevant documents requested by the user, and R_i the total number of relevant documents in provider i.

It seems reasonable to assume that the costs associated with retrieving r relevant documents from provider i can be divded into two parts, the system-specific costs and the user-specific costs. For the system-specific part, we assume a cost C_i^0 for processing a query, plus a per-document cost C_i^d, so the (system-specific) costs for retrieving k documents from provider i is

$$C_i^s(k) = C_i^0 + k \cdot C_i^d.$$

If we add to that the user-specific costs, a per-document cost C^R for reading a relevant and C^N for reading a non-relevant document, we get

$$\begin{aligned} C_i^r(r) &= C_i^s(s_i(r)) + rC^R + (s_i(r) - r)C^N \\ &= C_i^0 + r \cdot (C^R - C^N) + \frac{r}{P_i(r/R_i)}(C_i^d + C^N). \end{aligned}$$

In order to get the overall minimum cost, we have to optimize the following function

$$C^r(n) = \min_{\vec{u}} \sum_{i=1}^{l} u_i C_i^r(r_i)$$

with the additional criterium

$$n = \sum_{i=1}^{l} u_i r_i.$$

Here, $C^r(n)$ is the minimum cost for retrieving n relevant documents from the providers, l is the number of providers, and u_i is 1 if i is used, 0 otherwise. There is a divide-and-conquer algorithm that computes the optimum in $O(n \cdot l \cdot \log l)$ time.

A method for estimating the number of relevant documents for a provider with respect to a query is described in Fuhr (1997).

3.2 Query Transformation

In addition to the obvious fact that different provider systems speak different protocols there are a number of things that have to be considered when dealing with heterogeneous provider systems.

Attributes Different provider systems may use different attributes. The differences between attributes can be classified into *syntactic* and *semantic* differences. Syntactic differences (the "author" attribute is named "au" in one system and "21" in another[3]) are fairly easy to deal with by introducing a *canonical* attribute name and using a table to transform a query from the canonical attribute names to the ones

---

[3]Z39.50 uses numbers to identify attributes.

used by the provider system. Semantic differences (some system distinguishes between "primary author" and "coauthors" whereas another provider doesn't; still another provider might not even differentiate between authors and editors and have a less specific "originator" attribute only) are dealt with using an *attribute hierarchy*. The attribute hierarchy contains all attributes used in all providers and represents the semantic similarity between the attributes: the more general attributes can be found near the root, the most specific attributes are leaves of the hierarchy. An example for such a hierarchy is shown in figure 3.

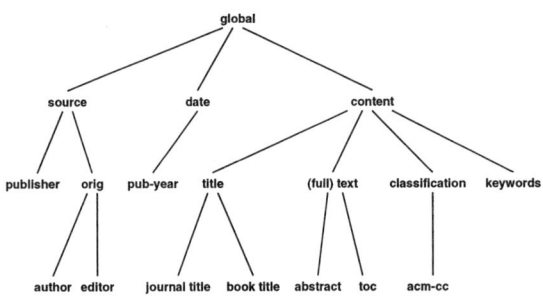

Figure 3: Example attribute hierarchy (excerpt)

Values The same value (from a semantic point of view) may have different syntactic representations for different providers. A prime example of this are proper names, which might be stored as "John Smith" in one system and "Smith, John" in a second, and "Smith, J." in still another provider.

Operators Different provider systems support different operators in their query languages. Mostly, this is because they offer syntactic operators that implement the same semantic operation in different ways. For example, the semantic operation "phrase search" may be implemented using linguistic facilities in one system, using proximity operators in another.

For query transformation, we use a stepwise process, based on four abstraction levels.[4] The *global schema* comprises all attributes of all provider systems and semantic operators. Users formulate their queries with respect to the global schema. It is provider independent. The *conceptual schema* differs from the global schema in that it includes the attributes actually supported by the provider system. It is provider specific. In transforming

---

[4]This is derived from the proven distinction between the global, or external, schema, the conceptual schema, and the physical schema, that is used by database management systems.

a query from the global to the conceptual schema, the attribute hierarchy mentioned above is used. The *physical schema* is also provider specific. Here, the semantic operators from the conceptual schema are replaced with the syntactic operators actually supported by the provider system. The query is still represented in the same format (or data structure) as in the other schemata. The transformation into the *protocol* used by the provider system deals with these differences.

4 Summary

In this paper we have presented a document model which allows us to represent both full text documents and bibliographic references such that bibliographic databases restricted to search functions can be supported as well as full text databases with additional advanced functions such as browsing, navigation, and document delivery. There is a working first prototype of the system, a second, extended, prototype is in the works.

References

BOLES, D., DREGER, M., GROSSJOHANN, K., LOHRUM, S. and MENKE, D. (1996): Architektur und Funktionalität des Medoc-Dienstes. *Technical Report.*

BOLES, D., DREGER, M. and GROSSJOHANN, K. (1996): Medoc Information Broker - Harnessing the Information in Literature and Full Text Databases. *Contribution to the NIR-Workshop of the SIGIR Conference at the ETH Zürich.*

BREU, M., BRÜGGEMANN-KLEIN, A., HABER, C. and WEBER, R. (1997): The Medoc Distributed Electronic Library - Accounting and Security Aspects. *Proceedings of the ICCC/IFIP Conference on Electronic Publishing '97 - New Models and Opportunities.*

BRÜGGEMANN-KLEIN, A. (1996): Medoc Pflichtenheft. *Technical Report.*

DREGER, M. and MÜLLER, P. (1996): IVS - Erster Prototyp. *Technical Report.*

FUHR, N. (1997), A Decision-Theoretic Approach to Database Selection in Networked IR. *Submitted for publication.*

MEDOC (1996): Medoc Full Text Digital Library For Computer Science. *Web Page: http://medoc.informatik.tu-muenchen.de*

Supervised Learning with Qualitative and Mixed Attributes

A Local Scaling Approach to Discriminate between Good and Bad Credit Risks

Harald Kauderer[1], Hans-Joachim Mucha[2]

[1] Daimler-Benz AG, Research and Technology, Evolutionary Systems F3S/E,
P.O. Box 23 60, D-89103 Ulm, Germany

[2] Weierstraß-Institut für Angewandte Analysis und Stochastik (WIAS),
Mohrenstraße 39, D-10117 Berlin, Germany

Abstract: Building classification tools to discriminate between good and bad credit risks is a supervised learning task which can be solved using different approaches (Graf and Nakhaeizadeh (1994)). In constructing such tools, generally, a set of training data, containing qualitative and quantitative attributes, is used to learn the discriminant rules. In real world of credit applications a lot of the available information about the customer and his behaviour of payment appears in qualitative, categorical attributes.
On the other hand many approaches of supervised learning require quantitative, numerical input variables to be processed in the learning algorithms. Qualitative attributes first have to be transformed into a numerical form, before they can be used for the learning process.
One very simple approach to handle that problem is to code each possible value of all qualitative categorical attributes in new, separate binary attributes. This leads to an increasing number of input variables, the learning process to build the rules gets more complicated. In particular neural networks need more time for training and often loose accuracy.
In this paper we consider different scaling approaches — here the number of variables does not increase — to transform categorical into numerical attributes (Nishisato (1994)). We use them as input variables to learn the discriminant rules and develop a method of *local* scaling to enhance accuracy and stability of the rules. Using real world credit data, we evaluate the different approaches and compare the results.

1 Introduction

Looking at the situation in credit business over the last several years we realise that things fundamentally changed: On the one hand a lot of companies (e.g. leasing companies, mail-order firms, service providers in cellular phone business, etc.) joined the credit market not belonging to the conventional circle of lenders (banks in general). All these companies rely on complete information about the credibility of their customers to be protected against loss in case of bad credit risks. On the other hand each credit lender plays on the market among other competitors, so there is a strong interest to decide on accepting or rejecting of (unknown) customers as immediately as possible. Credit scoring aims to develop an objective methodology leading to reproducible results to support credit officers.

In this paper we evaluate the effect of different scaling approaches on the performance of various supervised learning algorithms regarding the fact that a lot of these algorithms can not handle categorical attributes, directly. Due to this reason data transformation is necessary.

In section 2 we consider credit scoring as a classification problem and describe in summary different supervised learning algorithms that can deal with this problem. Section 3 discusses the alternative transformation methods, among them coding and scaling approaches. In section 4 we present and analyse our experimental results on a real credit domain. The last section is devoted to our conclusions.

2 Credit Scoring — A Classification Problem

The task of credit scoring can be described, formally, as a classification problem: Using the information the customer gives by filling out the credit application form (input variables) we have to categorize him into a certain predefined risk class (unknown output variable). On the other hand the class-membership of previous customers is well known and can be used in a classification model by learning both the information about the input and output values of each "old" customer. (Supervised Learning).

These classification models are often built with the help of conventional, multivariate statistics, but as Fig. 1 shows, there are also methods and algorithms developed in the field of artificial intelligence, e.g. machine learning and neural nets that offer appropriate solutions for the problem as well. (Michie et al. (1994), Graf and Nakhaeizadeh (1994)).

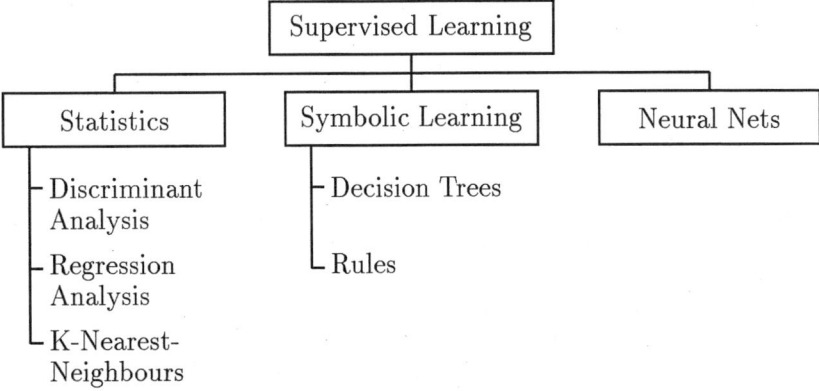

Fig. 1: *Alternative methods to handle credit scoring as classification task*

The question which supervised learning method can be used in a particular case depends on the characteristics of the available data. On the other hand not all data sets can be processed by all methods, directly. Mostly, some additional work has to be done in advance before the learning process begins (pre-processing).

Statistical methods as discriminant analysis and k-nearest-neighbours, for example, require numerical input attributes. This is the same for neural nets.

The data we consider in this paper come from a European service provider in cellular phone business. The data sets contain that information each new customer is asked for, when he applies for a phone card that enables him to use his phone. In principal, the card inserted in the phone can be characterised as a credit card and has the same functionality: The cost of each phone call is charged to the customer's account and after a period of time (normally one month) he gets a detailed phone bill he has to pay.

In our case the information the service provider gets to decide on the credibility of a new customer is qualitative. It means that most of the supervised learning methods mentioned above cannot be used directly for classification with exception of symbolic learning methods that are able to deal with both qualitative and numerical inputs. For all other cases, attributes with qualitative values first have to be transformed in a numerical continuous form.

In the next section we consider different approaches of data transformation and apply them to our data of cellular phone customers.

3 Data Transformation

Generally, data transformation methods applicable to our problem can be divided in two groups: Coding (Lautsch (1993)) and scaling approaches (Nishisato (1980, 1994)). The idea of coding is to transform the qualitative information in a numerical code, in general by adding new attributes to the original data set. Scaling approaches, on the other hand, reproduce the original information on a numerical scale of a certain range.

In the following discussion we concentrate on one coding- and three different scaling approaches and apply them to our raw data set.

3.1 Binary Coding

A very simple way to transform the information of a qualitative categorical attribute into numerals is to code the information in a certain number of binary (0,1) variables.

Assume we got a categorical attribute j with K different values. Then for each possible value x_{jk} a new binary variable J_k is generated. The new variable J_k is assigned with a '1', if the value of the original categorical attribute j in the data set i is x_{jk}, otherwise the value of J_k is '0'. This step has to be repeated for each data set i, for each categorical attribute j. At the end

of that procedure the original categorical attributes are removed from the database.
This procedure can be written down in the following pseudo code:

FOR EACH data set i
  FOR EACH categorical attribute j
    FOR EACH possible value x_{jk}
      CREATE new binary attribute J_k
      IF $x_{ij} = x_{jk}$
        THEN $J_{ik} := 1$;
        ELSE $J_{ik} := 0$;
      END; (*IF*)
    END; (*FOR*)
    ERASE categorical attribute j;
  END; (*FOR*)
END; (*FOR*)

Example:

customer	attrib1 (categ.)	attrib1 A (binary)	attrib1 B (binary)	attrib1 C (binary)	attrib1 D (binary)	attrib1 E (binary)
customer1	A	1	0	0	0	0
customer2	C	0	0	1	0	0
customer3	E	0	0	0	0	1
customer4	B	0	1	0	0	0
customer5	D	0	0	0	1	0
customer6	C	0	0	1	0	0
customer7	E	0	0	0	0	1
⋮	⋮	⋮	⋮	⋮	⋮	⋮
customerI	B	0	1	0	0	0

In the example shown above 5 new binary attributes have been generated for the 5 values (A,B,C,D,E) of the categorical attribute j, the information has been transferred in a binary code.

As we mentioned above, binary coding is a simple way to transform qualitative information into a numerical form. The main drawback of this method is that the number of attributes we have to process increases the more different values we got in the original data set. Using this approach, the number of attributes in our credit data rises from 16 categorical to 112 binary.

3.2 Univariate Scaling

Other possibilities to transform the given data sets into a numerical continuous form are provided by several scaling approaches. These methods transform each categorical value into one numerical continuous value, so that the number of attributes in the data matrix does not change. The main advantage of such approaches is that the arrangement of the categories on the numerical scale gets an interpretable sense. This point becomes clearer at the end of this section.

In our particular case, the customers of cellular phone services are divided in two risk classes 'good' and 'bad'. The class membership of 'old' customers is known and is a very useful information for the scaling process. A powerful scaling method is based on the dual scaling approach of Nishisato (1980, 1994). Generally, the dependencies between two categorical variables are analysed with the help of the corresponding contingency table. Considering our special case of only two categories in the class membership variable an attribute j with K categories is quantified in the following simple way (optimal scaling) (Mucha (1996)):

$$y_{jk} = \frac{p_{jk}^{good}}{p_{jk}^{good} + p_{jk}^{bad}}; \qquad k = 1, 2, ..., K$$

for: y_{jk} scale value of category k in attribute j

p_{jk}^{good} probability for being a *good* customer coming from category k of attribute j

p_{jk}^{bad} probability for being a *bad* customer coming from category k of attribute j

In real world applications, generally, the probabilities are unknown and have to be substituted by frequencies we observe in the training data set. In other words: We consider for each category k of an attribute j the quotient of good customers to all customers of that category as scale value for the category k.

Example: 100 customers, attribute j with categories k1, k2, k3

Contingency table:

j	k1	k2	k3	sum
good	20	15	10	45
bad	10	20	25	55
sum	30	35	35	100

Scale values:

$$y_{jk1} = \frac{0.2}{0.2+0.1} = 0.667$$

$$y_{jk2} = \frac{0.15}{0.15+0.2} = 0.429$$

$$y_{jk3} = \frac{0.1}{0.1+0.25} = 0.286$$

Note that the scale values get here an interpretable sense: The higher the scale value, the higher the share of good customers coming from a specific category k.

All scale values are situated in the interval [0;1], they become '0', if all customers coming from a category k of attribute j belong to the bad risk class ($p_{jk}^{good} = 0$), and '1', if all customers coming from a category k of attribute j belong to the good risk class ($p_{jk}^{bad} = 0$).

Another quite similar scaling method has been developed by Fahrmeir et al. (1984) as shown below:

$$y_{jk} = \begin{cases} \frac{p_{jk}^{good}}{p_{jk}^{bad}} - 1 & if \quad p_{jk}^{good} \geq p_{jk}^{bad} \\ 1 - \frac{p_{jk}^{bad}}{p_{jk}^{good}} & otherwise \end{cases}$$

This approach has, however, an obvious and essential drawback: If any probability is estimated as '0', the scale value for the category is undefined.

The third approach, in principle, is based on the optimal scaling approach as well. But in addition to that we first have a look on the contingency tables of each input attribute j and the class variable in order to detect strong dependencies.

Contingency table:

h	yes	no	sum
good	14 171	587	14 758
bad	**55**	1 563	1 618
sum	14 226	2 150	16 376

Relative frequencies:

h	yes	no	sum
good	86.54 %	3.58 %	90.12 %
bad	**0.34 %**	9.54 %	9.88 %
sum	86.88 %	13.12 %	100.0 %

In our data the attribute h is a strong separator between the two risk classes. If we exclude all data sets with value 'yes' in attribute h by estimating them as good customers, we get two obvious effects:

1. The number of cases we have to process in our learning algorithms decreases from 16 376 to 2 150 cases. The learning process speeds up.

2. The estimation of all excluded cases as good customers only induces an a priori error rate of 0.34 %.

In the next step we apply the optimal scaling method on the remaining data sets (here: 2 150) and get locally adapted scale values that are different from those we got using all 16 376 data sets. (Local scaling)

Applied to our data each scaling method returns a new data matrix containing 16, in case of local scaling 15 numerical input attributes and one (non-manipulated) categorical output variable (risk class). In contrast to the method of binary coding the number of attributes does not increase.

4 Experimental Results

For the evaluation of the data transformation methods discussed in the previous section we applied them to our real world credit data and used the

new numerical data sets to learn different classification models.
The raw data of 31 049 customers has been divided in a training data set of 16 376 examples for the learning process and in a test data set of 14 673 examples, we used for the performance evaluation on unseen cases.
Following classification methods have been used for our experiments:

- **C4.5** has been developed by Quinlan (1993) and belongs to the group of symbolic machine learning algorithms. C4.5 generates either a decision tree or a set of classification rules directly from a raw data set of both categorical and numerical attributes. Here we needed no data transformation at all.

- Linear discriminant analysis (**LDA**) and k-nearest-neighbours (**KNN**) belong to the group of classification methods coming from conventional multivariate statistics. We have used the versions implemented in SAS.

- **DIPOL** is a hybrid linear classifier developed by Schulmeister et al. (1997) combining the idea of pairwise linear regression with an optimisation by neural nets.

- As neural net (**NN**) we trained a full-linked backpropagation net of 112 input, 20 hidden and 2 output neurons in the case of binary coded data, in the case of the scaled data we chose 16 input, 4 hidden and 2 output neurons.

In a first step we determined the minimum error rate each classifier reached on the test data for the different data transformation approaches:

Supervised Learning Method	Error Rate				
	Raw data	Binary data	Scaled data		
			Fahrmeir	Nishisato	
				global	local
C4.5	4.59 %	4.93 %	5.01 %	4.99 %	4.57 %
LDA	–	5.70 %	5.70 %	5.70 %	4.57 %
KNN	–	6.20 %	5.46 %	5.17 %	5.07 %
DIPOL	–	5.09 %	4.79 %	4.68 %	4.57 %
NN	–	4.71 %	4.68 %	4.65 %	4.82 %

Comparing the error rates we observe that in most cases the optimal scaling approach (global and local) dominates the other data transformation methods, on binary data we rarely reached the results we got on scaled data. The local scaling approach mostly returned lower error rates than the global optimal scaling approach. Among the considered learning algorithms C4.5 and linear discriminant analysis processed on local scaled data showed the lowest error rate.

In a second step we observed the time each learning process spent to build a classification model. This criterion gets particularly important, if the classifier has to be updated from time to time caused by dynamic changes in real world data.

Supervised Learning Method	Time spent for learning process				
	Raw data	Binary data	Scaled data		
			Fahrmeir	Nishisato	
				global	local
C4.5	20 s	60 s	40 s	40 s	10 s
LDA	–	120 s	60 s	60 s	30 s
KNN	–	5 h	0.3 h	0.3 h	0.05 h
DIPOL	–	120 s	40 s	40 s	30 s
NN	–	5 h	1 h	1 h	0.3 h

Here, the essential drawback of the binary coding method is very obvious: Strongly increasing number of attributes slows down the learning process in a quite unacceptable way. In circumstances where the learning phase should be often repeated (for example, to adjust the learning parameters) the scaling approaches are more suitable.

5 Conclusion

In this paper we considered different approaches of data transformation and evaluated them on real world credit data by using several supervised learning methods.

In general, both the binary coding and the scaling approach offer appropriate solutions for transforming categorical in numerical data. Concerning the error rate the scaled data sets always reached better results than binary coded data sets. The advantage of scaling becomes, however more obvious, when we consider the learning time aspects. The increasing number of input attributes in binary data caused a heavy slow down of the learning processes. In comparision with global optimal scaling the local scaling approach reached further enhancements in error rate and learning time.

Acknowledgement

We thank Barbara Schulmeister for providing us the DIPOL classifier.

References

FAHRMEIR, L. and HAMERLE, A. (eds.) (1984): Multivariate Statistische Verfahren. De Gruyter Verlag, Berlin.

GRAF, J. and NAKHAEIZADEH, G. (1994): Credit Scoring Based on Neural and Machine Learning. In: Plantamura, Souček, Visaggio (eds.): *Frontier Decision Support Concepts: Help Desk, Learning, Fuzzy Diagnoses, Quality Evaluation, Prediction, Evolution.* John Wiley and Sons, New York

LAUTSCH, E. (1993): Binärdatenanalyse für Psychologen, Mediziner und Sozialwissenschaftler. Psychologie Verlags Union, Weinheim

MITCHIE, D.J, SPIEGELHALTER, D. M. and TAYLOR, C.C. (eds.) (1994): Machine Learning, Neural and Statistical Classification. Ellis Horwood, Chichester

MUCHA, H.-J. (1996): Distance Based Credit Scoring. In: Mucha, H.-J. and Bock, H.-H. (eds.): *Classification and Multivariate Graphics: Models, Software and Applications.* Report No. 10, Weierstrass Institute for Applied Analysis and Stochastics, Berlin

NISHISATO, S. (1980): Analysis of Categorical Data: Dual Scaling and ist Applications. University of Toronto Press, Toronto

NISHISATO, S. (1994): Elements of Dual Scaling: An Introduction to Practical Data Analysis. Lawrence Erlbaum Associates, Hillsdale

QUINLAN, J.R. (1993): C4.5: Programs for Machine Learning. CA: Morgan Kaufmann, San Mateo

SCHULMEISTER, B. and WYSOTZKI, F. (1997): DIPOL - A Hybrid Piecewise Linear Classifier. In: Nakhaeizadeh, G. and Taylor, C.C. (eds.): *Machine Learning and Statistics: The Interface.* John Wiley and Sons, New York

Part 6

Marketing

A Comparison of Traditional Segmentation Methods with Segmentation Based upon Artificial Neural Networks by Means of Conjoint Data from a Monte-Carlo-Simulation

H. Gierl, S. Schwanenberg

Lehrstuhl für Betriebswirtschaftslehre mit dem Schwerpunkt Marketing, Universität Augsburg, D-86159 Augsburg, Germany

Abstract: Simulated data are needed to compare traditional segmentation methods with segmentation by neural networks, because only under these circumstances the quality of reproduction between methods is comparable. Therefore conjoint data with differently distributed errors are created by a Monte-Carlo-Simulation. The results of a segmentation by neural networks are compared with those of a segmentation by traditional methods in order to reveal whether the introduced neural networks are capable of a better segmentation at all, respectively for which structure of the starting data the segmentation by neural networks appears to be particularly promising.

1 Introduction

The task of segmentation methods is to divide heterogeneous original data into homogeneous segments. Today, these methods are probably more important for the everyday work than ever. The registration of data is not difficult any more, it is mostly done within the company's computer information system that normally provides the data with a sufficient data level. Of much more interest is the best possible compression of the data, for example to single customer segments which can be contacted by several types of advertising.

Therefore, scientific research developed and tested different methods. The object of this study was to compare the results of a segmentation by neural networks with those of a segmentation by traditional methods.

It should be noted that (contrary to expectation) segmentation by neural networks tended to deliver inferior results compared to classification by the k-means procedure of the statistical package SPSS. That is why in the beginning no comparisons to other statistical methods were drawn. A judgement whether these sometimes unsatisfying results are based on the very carefully self-developed software is not possible. The complete lack of errors cannot be guaranteed for any software.

Since the available software-packages were not flexible enough or not usable on the only available Operating System DOS (SNNS, WinNN, Previa NeuralNet, Neural Planner, SPSS Neural Connection a.o.), a personal software was developed. To keep the computing-time under an acceptable limit was a second reason for the self-development of a specialized segmentation software.

2 Data Generation

In an article of Vriens/Wedel/Wilms (1996), different segmentation methods based on conjoint data were compared by means of simulated data sets. Refering to this article, appropriate original data was generated as follows: Selecting the conjoint-design and the number of simulated data, in this case for example

1. Number of data sets (persons): 200 persons were simulated.

   - Number of attributes: six attributes, each defined on three levels were simulated.
   - Number of profiles (evaluation objects): the simulation was based on a orthogonal 36 basic plan with 18 feature-combinations.
   - Number of segments: finally, the number of segments was set to four.

2. Within each segment the "real" partworths were fixed at random numbers in the interval (-1,7; 1,7) and (-1,0; 1,0), respectively, depending on the strength with which the segments should be distinguished.

3. Now random numbers drawn from a standard normal distribution with a variance of 0,05 and 0,10, respectively, were added to the partworths to simulate the heterogenity within each segment.

4. For each of the 18 profiles the true preference was computed out of the partworths.

5. Now another normal distributed random number was added to the preferences so that the error's variance in the preferences became 0,05 respectively 0,35.

To compare different segmentation methods it is better to use data generated this way than empirical data, because the true membership to a segment is known and thus the models' quality can be specified by the percentage of the correctly classified cases. Now the preferences simulated the way described above are used to form the segments.

3 Data Evaluation with Traditional Methods

As a first step different hierarchical clustering methods were used, as recommended by several authors (for example Bortz 1993, Ketchen / Shook

1996), to get the optimal number of segments. According to the elbow-criterion, the best solution is the number of clusters by which an increase in the number of clusters is not followed by a distinct improvement of the segmentation. The second step was to form the data-segments belonging to the optimal number of clusters by the non-agglomerating-hierarchical procedure k-means implemented in SPSS.

Results for different data-sets:

Partworths in Interval	Variance of the Partworths within the Segments	Variance of the Preferences' Error	Percentage of Correctly Classified Cases
(-1,7; 1,7)	5 %	5 %	100 %
(-1,7; 1,7)	10 %	5 %	96,5 %
(-1,7; 1,7)	10 %	35 %	**100 %**
(-1,0; 1,0)	10 %	35 %	**96 %**
(-0,75; 0,75)	10 %	35 %	**73 %***
(-1,0; 1,0)	0 %	0 %	100 %
*according to the elbow-criterion segmentation with k-means for three classes.			

Table 1: Results from evaluation with traditional methods

Obviously very good results are achieved with a combination of hierarchical and non-hierarchical methods for the data classification as described here. But it is conceivable that this proceeding delivers inferior results if the errors of the data sets are not normally distributed. It has also to be mentioned that the method's quality decreases (from 100 to 96 and 73 percent, respectively) when the segments become more similar.

4 Data Evaluation with Neural Networks

Now it was tried to do the data segmentation with a neural network with three levels, referring to Hruschka / Natter (1995). The construction of the net:

The quantity of the inner neurons is the same as the quantity of the segments to which the output data should be classified. The input neurons' only task is to transfer the input data to the inner neurons. In this study, the simulated preferences of the 18 different profiles are used as input data. The weighted input is transformed with an nonlinear function in the inner and the output nodes and then it is used as the input for the next layer or given as the networks output, respectively. In this study the tanh and the logistic function were used as nonlinear functions.

The preferences of the different profiles are placed at the network's disposal as expected output. Neural nets with a structure as described above that

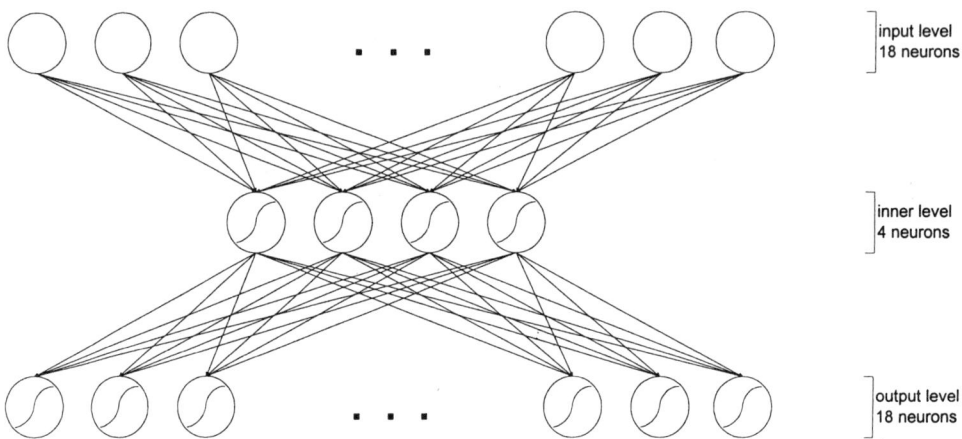

Figure 1: Neural Network with Feedforward-Architecture

should compress the data are also called Bottleneck-Nets.

For a more detailed description of the basics of neural networks refer to the relevant literature (Kratzer 1993, Zimmermann 1994, Lippmann 1987, Venugopal / Baets 1994).

The neural network was trained with the back-propagation training algorithm in which the error in the network is propagated back from the output to the input level. Then the network's weights are adjusted in opposit order. The weights' adjustment is done with a given learning rate in opposite direction to the negative gradient of the error function. The sum of squares of the deviation between the reproduced and the real output was used as error function.

When the learning phase was completed each data set was assigned to the segment (inner neuron) that had the highest activation concerning this input, i.e. the highest weighted input within the four inner nodes.

The method was modified in a way that the last weight adjustment, weighted with the momentum gain, was in addition included in the current adjustment. This technique is used to speed up the converging of the network if the error distribution is complicated (e.g. "bent valleys"). Therefore, the current searching direction is topped with the last searching direction. This is the standard back-propagation algorithm if the momentum gain is zero.

Furthermore, experiments with a controlled learning rate were done. The learning rate is increased and decreased step by step. The following different learning rate methods were implemented and tested:

- Multiply the learning rate by a element (0;1) always after m iterations, i.e. decrease the learning rate step by step.

- Increase the learning rate through multiplication by b element (0; un-

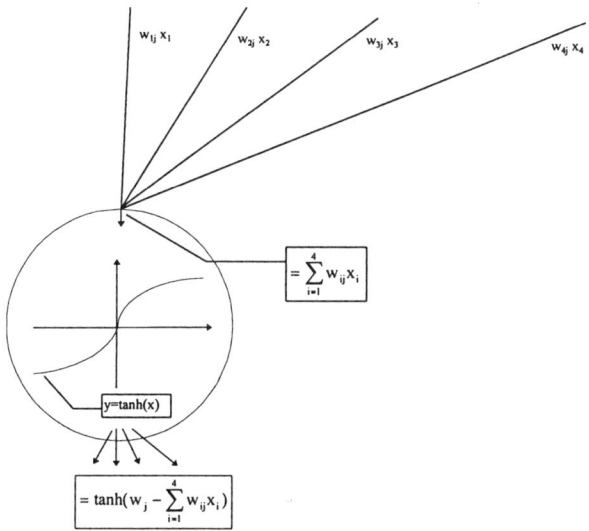

Figure 2: A Neuron's Working Method

endlich) always after m iterations if the error function declined, otherwise decrease through multiplication with a element (0;1).

The weights of the network were chosen randomly in a given interval at each program start. During the simulations it was observed that because of these different, randomly chosen initial weights the neural network was not able to find the optimum solution at each program pass. This is because of the possibly very complex "error-landscape" of the data. Thus it is a common problem that the error function remains in local minima. This can only partially be corrected by the controlled learning rate, the momentum gain, and a random selection of the training data sets. But even by these approaches it is not guaranteed to reach the global minimum. In the following table the intervals given for the quality result from ten program passes each.

- Number of Iterations: 1.000

- Learning rate: 0,1, decreased every 50 iterations by multiplication with 0,9

- Initial weights element (-0,1; 0,1)

It is obvious that at least with the software used here and the variation of the neural network's parameters it cannot be reliably guaranteed that the neural network reaches the global optimum. Unfortunately, more changes of the program were not possible in the brevity.

Partworths in Interval	Variance within Segments	Variance of the Error	Momentum Gain	Percentage of correctly Classified Cases
(-1,7;1,7)	5 %	5 %	0,6	67–100 %, Schnitt 79,3 %
(-1,7;1,7)	10 %	5 %	0,6	58–87 %, Schnitt 69,8 %
(-1,7;1,7)	10 %	35 %	0,6	60–83 %, Schnitt 74,2 %
(-1,0;1,0)	10 %	35 %	0,6	41–64 %, Schnitt 50,7 %
(-1,0;1,0)	0 %	0 %	0,6	49,5–100 %, Schnitt 72,5 %
(-1,7;1,7)	5 %	5 %	0,1	62–88,5 %, Schnitt 74,9 %
(-1,7;1,7)	10 %	5 %	0,1	63–88,5 %, Schnitt 78,5 %
(-1,7;1,7)	10 %	35 %	0,1	66–87,5 %, Schnitt 75,25 %
(-1,0;1,0)	10 %	35 %	0,1	44,6–54,6 %, Schnitt 49,4 %
(-1,0;1,0)	0 %	0 %	0,1	50–100 %, Schnitt 75 %

Table 2: Results of the evaluation with neural networks

5 K-Means versus Neural Networks

Now the first question is what can be concluded from the results shown. Definetely wrong would be the conclusion that neural networks are on principle not suitable for the segmentation or compression, respectively, of data. But it must be recognized that in the cases shown here already the traditional methods and procedures delivered in an obvious shorter time an excellent segmentation quality that even exceeded the quality of the neural net used. This was the reason why other data sets with bigger or other than normally distributed errors were not evaluated.

Moreover, the neural net has to accept the criticism that the step-by-step changing of the network parameters as carried out here, partly by means of the quality of earlier results, is on the one hand very time consuming and on the other hand not possible for real data. In these cases, an intended adaption of some parameters is not feasible.

6 Conclusion

Despite the criticism it does not appear to be hopeless to use artificial neural nets for the compression of data. But the partly effusive reports about the possibilities of neural networks cannot be understood.

In conclusion, different fields are mentioned that could perhaps achieve improvement for the results but that have not been or only partly been taken into consideration here:

- The assignment of data to the single segments is done here by means of the activation of the nodes. A data set is assigned to the segment or inner neuron, respectively, with the highest weighted input.

	Variance	Variance	Percentage of correctly Classified Cases	
Partworths in Interval	within Segments	of the Error	Hierarchical, followed by k-means	Neural Net
(-1,7; 1,7)	5 %	5 %	100 %	62–88,5 %, Schnitt 74,9 %
(-1,7; 1,7)	10 %	5 %	96,5 %	63–88,5 %, Schnitt 78,5 %
(-1,7; 1,7)	10 %	35 %	100 %	66–87,5 %, Schnitt 75,25 %
(-1,0; 1,0)	10 %	35 %	96 %	42,5–52,5 %, Schnitt 49,4 %
(-1,0; 1,0)	0 %	0 %	100 %	50–100 %, Schnitt 75 %

*according to the elbow-criterion segmentation with k-means for three classes.

Table 3: Comparison of the results

- Complete treatises on the possibilities of interpretation of the inner nodes were not done yet, therefore there are more findings possible in this field.

- Also in the field of controlling the learning rate there are still further improvements possible. For example a learning rate would be imaginable that depends directly on the changes in the error function.

- Also the searching direction does not need to be set by the negative gradient. For a fixed learning rate it could also be set in dependence of the reachable improvement of the quality of solution. Both aspects were only partly realised by the inclusion of a momentum gain.

- The pre-transformations of the original data should not be neglected. In this study the original data was transformed, partly standardized into the interval (0;1), partly transformed into normally distributed data or kept in the original version. The transformations had at least a clear influence on the time to learn. Whether they also influence the finding of the global minimum has to be investigated furtheron.

- Also the comparably new method of genetic algorithm in context with neural networks, where networks are developed by following the evolution theory, are, as stated by some authors, an interesting alternative for the field of data segmentation. They are based on the same network structure as introduced here, but they use genetic algorithm instead of back-propagation methods for learning.

References

BORTZ, J. (1993): Statistik für Sozialwissenschaftler. Berlin.

HRUSCHKA, H. and NATTER, M. (1995): Clusterorientierte Marktsegmentierung mit Hilfe künstlicher Neuraler Netzwerke. Marketing ZFP, Heft 4, 249-254.

KETCHEN, D. J. and SHOOK, C. L. (1996): The Application of Cluster-Analysis in Strategic Management Research: An Analysis and Critique. Strategic Management Journal, 441-458.

KRATZER, K. P. (1993): Neuronale Netze: Grundlagen und Anwendungen. Hanser, München, Wien.

LIPPMANN, R. P. (1987): An Introduction to Computing with Neural Nets. IEEE ASSP Magazine April 1987, 4-22.

VENUGOPAL V. and BAETS, W. (1994): Neural Networks & their Applications in Marketing Management. Journal of Systems Management, 9/94, 16-21.

VRIENS, M., WEDEL, M. and WILMS, T. (1996): Metric Conjoint Segmentation Methods: A Monte Carlo Comparison. Journal of Marketing Research, XXXIII, 73-85.

ZIMMERMANN, H. G. (1996): Neuronale Netze als Entscheidungskalkül. In: Rehkugler, H. and Zimmermann, H. G. (eds.): Neuronale Netze in der Ökonomie, Grundlagen und finanzwirtschaftliche Anwendungen. Franz Vahlen, München, 3-87.

Classification of Pricing Strategies in a Competitive Environment

M. Löffler, W. Gaul

Institut für Entscheidungstheorie und Unternehmensforschung,
Universität Karlsruhe (TH), Postfach 6980, D-76128 Karlsruhe, Germany

Abstract: The general structure of multiperiod price paths mainly depends on consumer characteristics, competitive reactions and restrictions which describe additional salient features of the underlying pricing situation. We present an approach which generalizes well-known price response functions in the area of reference price research and discuss price paths for important classes of competitive pricing strategies.

1 Reference price concept

There is intense research focussing on the concept of reference prices and managerial implications. A concise definition concerning reference prices is given by Kalyanaram, Winer (1995, p. G161): "The concept of a reference price is that it is an internal standard against which observed prices are compared." Reference prices can be understood as consumer specific, internal anchoring levels which are used to evaluate the actual market prices of products or services. A market price exceeding the corresponding reference price is perceived as loss and may on the aggregate level lead to an reduction in sales volume. The opposite effect is to be expected if a market price is below the corresponding reference price. The reference price concept and its different foundations are discussed in more detail, e.g., by Monroe (1990) and Nagle, Holden (1995).

In spite of the many different reference price operationalizations and formulations of price response functions there are some recommendations frequently mentioned as further research opportunities (see, e.g., Kalyanaram, Winer (1995)). Most of all it is suggested to incorporate more than one reference price in the description of pricing situations, to consider the possibility of a region of reduced price sensitivity, to allow for asymmetric gain resp. loss effects according to prospect theory (see Kahneman, Tversky (1979)), and to account for the other different behavioural theories underlying the reference price concept. An additional relevant aspect is that the formulation of pricing situations should allow for normative implications and managerial recommendations in the area of multi-period pricing decisions.

2 Example of a modified price response function

In the situation of a duopolistic market a price response function that considers the suggestions just mentioned is given by

$$\begin{aligned}
q_n = {} & q_n(p_n^{(r)}, \bar{p}_n^{(r)}, p_n, \bar{p}_n) = a - b \cdot p_n - c \cdot \bar{p}_n \\
& - d_1 \cdot 1\{p_n \leq p_n^{(r)} - \delta_1\}(p_n - p_n^{(r)} + \delta_1) \\
& - d_2 \cdot 1\{p_n > p_n^{(r)} + \delta_2\}(p_n - p_n^{(r)} - \delta_2) \\
& - e_1 \cdot 1\{p_n \leq \bar{p}_n - \epsilon_1\}(p_n - \bar{p}_n + \epsilon_1) \\
& - e_2 \cdot 1\{p_n > \bar{p}_n + \epsilon_2\}(p_n - \bar{p}_n - \epsilon_2) \\
& - f_1 \cdot 1\{\bar{p}_n \leq \bar{p}_n^{(r)} - \gamma_1\}(\bar{p}_n - \bar{p}_n^{(r)} + \gamma_1) \\
& - f_2 \cdot 1\{\bar{p}_n > \bar{p}_n^{(r)} + \gamma_2\}(\bar{p}_n - \bar{p}_n^{(r)} - \gamma_2), \quad n = 0, 1, \ldots, N,
\end{aligned} \quad (1)$$

with parameters $a, b, c, d_1, d_2, \delta_1, \delta_2, e_1, e_2, \epsilon_1, \epsilon_2, f_1, f_2, \gamma_1, \gamma_2 \in \mathbb{R}$, where

$$1\{x \geq y\} := \begin{cases} 1, & \text{if } x \geq y, \\ 0, & \text{otherwise,} \end{cases} \quad (2)$$

is the notation for the indicator function. q_n is the sales volume and p_n resp. $p_n^{(r)}$ are used for the market price resp. reference price of the product of the interesting enterprise in period n, where N denotes the planning horizon. The market price resp. reference price of the product of the competing enterprise is given by $\bar{p}_n$ resp. $\bar{p}_n^{(r)}$. The reference prices $p_n^{(r)}$, $\bar{p}_n^{(r)}$ and the market prices p_n, $\bar{p}_n$ are used in a prospect theory context (see Tversky, Kahneman (1991) for the multiattributed case). In addition, formulation (1) accounts for regions of reduced price sensitivity due to the parameters δ_1, δ_2 and γ_1, γ_2. Following a suggestion of Rajendran, Tellis (1994) the competitive price $\bar{p}_n$ is captured in the manner of a contextual reference price for p_n. Equation (1) is a piecewise linear price response function (as, e.g., the approach of Greenleaf (1995)). Note that q_n can be interpreted as attraction of the products under consideration and incorporated into an MCI-approach (MCI is the abbreviation for Multiplicative Competitive Interaction, see, e.g., Hruschka (1996)).

Formulation (1) is very flexible and incorporates some recently published contributions as special cases (see, e.g., Greenleaf (1995) with $c = 0$, $\delta_1 = 0$, $\delta_2 = 0$, $e_1 = 0$, $e_2 = 0$, $f_1 = 0$, $f_2 = 0$, Kopalle et al. (1996) with $\delta_1 = 0$, $\delta_2 = 0$, $e_1 = 0$, $e_2 = 0$, $f_1 = 0$, $f_2 = 0$, or Kopalle, Winer (1996) with $c = 0$, $\delta_1 = 0$, $\delta_2 = 0$, $e_1 = 0$, $e_2 = 0$, $f_1 = 0$, $f_2 = 0$). Most of these approaches do not take into account regions of reduced price sensitivity or ignore the fact, that the competitive price may serve as an anchor of price judgement and, therefore, has to be modelled adequately.

3 Classification of pricing strategies based on dynamic programming

In order to model the pricing situation described so far, dynamic programming was applied to a markov decision process formulation. A short description of the basic methodology is given in the appendix. Additional constraints, incorporated in the optimization via dynamic programming and discussed subsequently, can be used for classification issues. The following restrictions were considered:

$$\sum_{n=0}^{N-1} 1\{p_n \leq \sigma_{1,n}\} \leq \kappa_1, \qquad (3)$$

$$\sum_{n=0}^{N-1} 1\{p_n \leq \sigma_{2,n}\} \geq \kappa_2, \qquad (4)$$

$$\sum_{n=0}^{N-1} 1\{|p_n - p_{n-1}| \geq \sigma_{3,n}\} \leq \kappa_3, \qquad (5)$$

$$\sum_{n=0}^{N-1} 1\{|p_n - p_{n-1}| \geq \sigma_{4,n}\} \geq \kappa_4. \qquad (6)$$

In restriction (3), it is tried to cope that consumers often assume a positive correlation between the price of a product and its quality (see, e.g., Erevelles (1993)). For high-quality products it may be desirable to establish a quality category by means of a unique price tier. By inequality (3) it can be avoided to set more than κ_1 prices below the lower limit of this price tier, denoted by $\sigma_{1,n}$ in period n.

As the intention of price promotions is often to increase store traffic or to support the price image of underlying products (see, e.g., Monroe (1990)) a specified number κ_2 of promotional prices, i.e. prices which are lower than a lower price bound $\sigma_{2,n}$ in period n, can be prescribed by restriction (4).

If prices are reduced too often, consumers may not be willing any more to buy a product at the regular price (see, e.g., Kalwani, Yim (1992)) or may be unable to appreciate the amount of price reduction (e.g., Urbany et al. (1988)). If a product is perishable, consumers may become suspicious about the quality of the product. Therefore, price alterations should not be conducted too often, which can be modeled by inequality (5).

Authors like Rajendran, Tellis (1994) and Krishnamurthi, Raj (1991) stress the point to reach consumer segments of different price sensitivity by promotional activities. If it is intended to address different consumer segments, the number of price changes κ_4 should be large enough so that price alterations can be recognized as deal occasions by consumers with low price awareness or reduced willingness to switch the product. Constraint (6) can be used to tackle such a situation.

Together with the following three different classes of competitive pricing behaviour this opens a magnitude of possibilities for describing pricing situations.

In class 1, it is assumed that the competitor sets an everyday relatively high price near to p_{max}, a behaviour which is close to the pricing decisions of national brands. In class 2, the competitor is assumed to be very price aggressive and to set an everyday low price close to p_{min}, which is quite characteristic for private label brands or store brands. In class 3, the competing firm is assumed to directly copy the price settings of the profit maximizing enterprise. Pricing decisions of this kind are often observable (see, e.g., the recent price war in the area of forthnightly tv-magazines discussed by Rosenfeld (1996)).

Table 1: Classes of pricing strategies

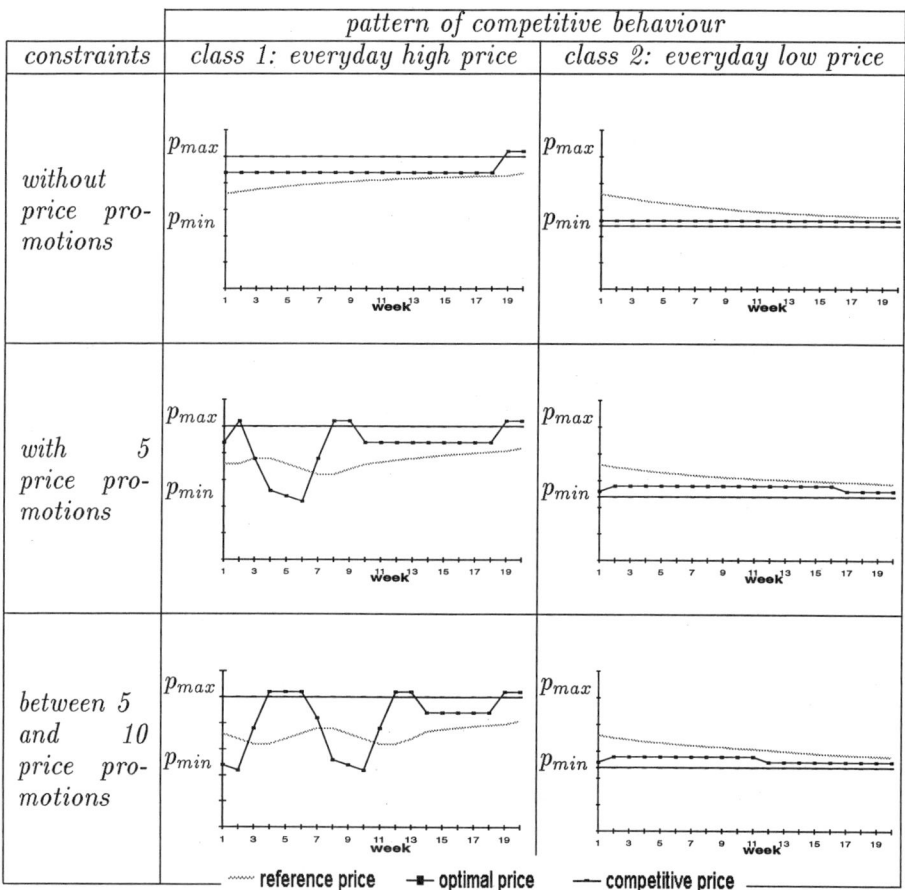

For all presented classes of competitive pricing behaviour profit maximization without additional constraints results in paths of nearly constant prices. Such optimal price paths are depicted by bold black dots in Tab. 1 together with reference and competitive prices.

In cases where exactly five or between five and ten price promotions are forced by the restrictions the results change significantly for class 1. In the situation of five to ten feasible price promotions, the price path is splitted into a phase with high price promotional activity at the beginning of the overall planning interval and a phase of relatively constant prices at the end. In periods 1, 2, and 3 and during periods 7 to 11 the profit maximizing enterprise conducts price promotions, i.e., selects a price which is lower than $\sigma_{2,n}$. Additionally, more than the minimum number of five price promotions are performed. Between these periods with price promotions the enterprise selects higher market prices in order to increase its reference price (periods 4 to 6) and to take advantage of a high reference price level in subsequent periods. At the end of the overall planning interval the profit maximizing enterprise selects prices which are near to p_{max} and therefore close to the price of the competing firm.

Table 1: Classes of pricing strategies (cont.)

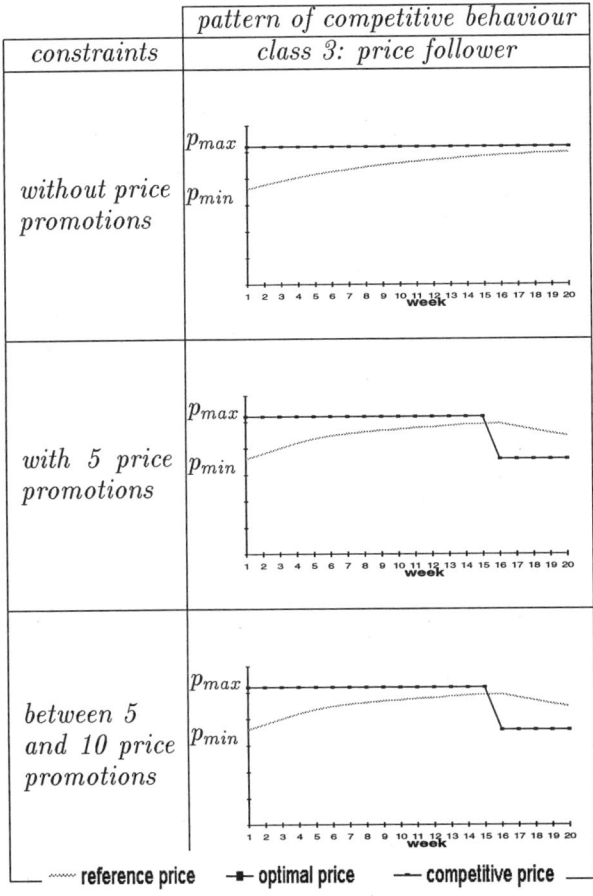

In class 2 of our scenario of competitive pricing behaviour the competitor is assumed to set an everyday low price. In cases with price promotions a comparison with the optimization results without constraints shows that the price paths change only slightly. In the first weeks of the overall planning interval the profit maximizing enterprise selects a market price which is below its reference price and close to the price of the competing firm. Accordingly, the reference price declines over time. In the last periods of the overall planning interval the profit maximizing enterprise lowers the market price. This increases the difference between its reference price and market price and, at the same time, decreases the difference between the prices of the competing brands, resulting in a last push with respect to the sales volume. During the overall planning interval the profit maximizing enterprise only sets the minimum number of price promotions. We observe a clear reluctance to set high market prices and to increase the own reference prices. The effects due to competitive prices seem to be more important than the effects due to reference prices.

A similar effect is observable in class 3. As the competitor selects the same market price as the profit maximizing enterprise, it is quite unfavourable to lower the market prices. Therefore, in the case of exactly five price promotions as well as in the situation, where the enterprise is allowed to conduct between five and ten price promotions, only the minimum number of promotional activities is selected. In both cases (exactly 5 price promotions resp. between 5 and 10 price promotions) the optimization with constraints results in identical optimal multiperiod price paths.

4 Conclusion and outlook

An extension with respect to the formulation of price response functions was presented. Additionally, restrictions for modeling pricing situations were introduced and the impact of such constraints on different classes of competitive pricing strategies was discussed. By application of dynamic programming to a markov decision process formulation remarkable changes of the structure of optimal multiperiod price paths could be observed.

Dependent on the information concerning the underlying class of pricing behavior, results of the kind mentioned before will influence the price setting behavior of enterprises in markets whose competitive structure can be described in terms of restrictions as exemplarily demonstrated in this contribution.

Appendix: Formulation of the pricing situation as markov decision process

Based on the above mentioned price response function a markov decision process is defined in order to derive optimal price paths for different classes of competitive pricing reactions. We need specifications for the state space S, the action space A, the reward function r, the transition probability law $\mathbf{p}$, the planning horizon N, and the terminal reward v_0.

Let p_{min}, p_{max} resp. $\bar{p}_{min}$, $\bar{p}_{max}$ denote thresholds for the underlying pricing situation and $s_n := (p_n^{(r)}, \bar{p}_n^{(r)})$ all possible combinations of reference prices of the two enterprises under consideration with

$$s_n \in S := \{[p_{min}, p_{max}] \cap \{0, 1/100, 2/100, \ldots\}\} \tag{7}$$
$$\times \{[\bar{p}_{min}, \bar{p}_{max}] \cap \{0, 1/100, 2/100, \ldots\}\}. \tag{8}$$

Possible actions $a_n := p_n$ are the price settings of the interesting enterprise with

$$a_n \in A := \{[p_{min}, p_{max}] \cap \{0, 1/100, 2/100, \ldots\}\}. \tag{9}$$

In order to specify the reward function r, we interpret q_n of equation (1) as attraction of the brand of the interesting enterprise and define in a similar manner $\bar{q}_n$ as attraction of the product of the competing enterprise. Using an MCI-approach, the market share of the interesting enterprise is given by

$$ms = ms(s_n, a_n, \bar{p}_n) = f(x) = \frac{q_n(x)}{q_n(x) + \bar{q}_n(x)} \tag{10}$$

with $x = (p_n^{(r)}, \bar{p}_n^{(r)}, a_n, \bar{p}_n)$. Now, the reward function r is specified as $r(s_n, a_n) := ms(s_n, a_n, \tilde{pr}_2(s_n)) \cdot mv_n \cdot (a_n - c_n)$ for the first and the second class and as $r(s_n, a_n) := ms(s_n, a_n, a_n) \cdot mv_n \cdot (a_n - c_n)$ for the third class of competitive pricing strategies. Here, c_n denotes the cost per unit of the product of the interesting enterprise, mv_n the volume of the market in period n, and $\tilde{pr}_2(s)$ the projection on the second component of a state $s \in S$.

In the example, the planning horizon N consists of 20 periods, the terminal reward v_0 is set equal to zero.

With an adequately specified transition probability law **p** one can define a density function on $(S^N, \mathcal{P}(S^N))$, where $\mathcal{P}(S^N)$ denotes the power set of S^N, see, e.g., Puterman (1994).

With the settings

$$\zeta_\nu := pr_\nu : S^N \to S, \quad \nu = 1, \ldots N, \tag{11}$$
$$\phi_0, \ldots, \phi_{N-1} \in F := \{f : S \to A\}, \tag{12}$$
$$\eta := (\zeta_\nu)_{\nu=1}^N, \quad \zeta_0 := s_0 \in S, \tag{13}$$

and the abbreviation pr_ν for the projection on component ν of S^N, the random N-period profit is given by

$$R_{(\phi_0,\ldots,\phi_{N-1})}(s_0, \eta) := \sum_{\nu=0}^{N-1} (1+\beta)^{-\nu} r(\zeta_\nu, \phi_\nu(\zeta_\nu)) + (1+\beta)^{-N} v_0(\zeta_N), \tag{14}$$

where β is the discount factor (in the example $\beta := 10\%$ p.a.).
With the notation mentioned before the profit maximizing enterprise has to solve

$$\max_{(\phi_0,\ldots,\phi_{N-1}) \in F^N} \leftarrow ER_{(\phi_0,\ldots,\phi_{N-1})}(s_0, \eta) \tag{15}$$

subject to restrictions (3) to (6).

References

EREVELLES, S. (1993): The price-warranty contract and product attitudes. *Journal of Business Research 27, 171–181.*

GREENLEAF, E. (1995): The impact of reference price effects on the profitability of price promotions. *Marketing Science 14, 82–104.*

HRUSCHKA, H. (1996): Marketing-Entscheidungen. Vahlen, München.

KAHNEMAN, D. and TVERSKY, A. (1979): Prospect theory: an analysis of decision under risk. *Econometrica 47, 263–291.*

KALWANI, M. and YIM, C. (1992): Consumer price and promotion expectation: an experimental study. *Journal of Marketing Research 19, 90–100.*

KALWANI, M., YIM, C., RINNE, H. and SUGITA, Y. (1990): A price expectations model of customer brand choice. *Journal of Marketing Research 17, 251–262.*

KALYANARAM, G. and LITTLE, J. (1994): An empirical analysis of latitude of price acceptance in consumer package goods. *Journal of Consumer Research 21, 408–418.*

KALYANARAM, G. and WINER, R. (1995): Empirical generalizations from reference price research. *Marketing Science 14, G161–G169.*

KOPALLE, P., RAO, A. and ASSUNÇÃO, J. (1996): Asymmetric reference price effects and dynamic pricing policies. *Marketing Science 15, 60–85.*

KOPALLE, P. and WINER, R. (1996): A dynamic model of reference price and expected quality. *Marketing Letters 7, 41–52.*

KRISHNAMURTHI, L. and RAJ, S. (1991): An empirical analysis of the relationship between brand loyalty and consumer price elasticity. *Marketing Science 10, 172–183.*

MONROE, K. (1990): Pricing. Making profitable decisions. 2nd. edition. McGraw Hill, New York.

NAGLE, T. and HOLDEN R. (1995): The strategy and tactics of pricing. A guide to profitable decision making. 2nd edition. Prentice-Hall Inc., Englewood Cliffs.

PUTERMAN, M. (1994): Markov decision processes. Wiley&Sons, New York.

RAJENDRAN, K. and TELLIS, G. (1994): Contextual and temporal components of reference price. *Journal of Marketing 58, 22–34.*

ROSENFELD, K. (1996): Programmie-Markt vor der Bewährung. *Horizont-Zeitung für Marketing, Werbung und Medien, 13(1996), 42–43.*

TVERSKY, A. and KAHNEMAN, D. (1991): Loss aversion and riskless choice: a reference dependent model. *Quarterly Journal of Economics 106, 1039–1061.*

URBANY, J., BEARDEN, W. and WEILBAKER, D. (1988): The effect of plausible and exaggerated reference prices on consumer perceptions and price search. *Journal of Consumer Research 15, 95–110.*

Predicting the Amount of Purchase by a Procedure Using Multidimensional Scaling: An Application to Scanner Data on Beer

A. Okada, A. Miyauchi

Department of Industrial Relations, School of Social Relations
Rikkyo (St. Paul's) University, 3 Nishi Ikebukuro
Toshima-ku, Tokyo 171, Japan

Abstract: A predicting procedure based on two multidimensional scaling methods, INDSCAL and PREFMAP, was applied to scanner data on a brand of beer and its competitive brands at a supermarket. The data, collected at the supermarket during the first 13 weeks after the introduction of the brand, were analyzed by the procedure to predict the amount of purchase of that brand and the competitive brands from weeks 14 to 39. The predicted market share of the brand in the category of beer between weeks 27 to 39 at the supermarket was close to the actual figure.

1 Introduction

Multidimensional scaling (MDS) has been used in various kinds of areas. One of very important areas of applying multidimensional scaling is marketing (Green et al. (1989)). In most applications of MDS on marketing, the purpose of utilizing MDS is to obtain a map; i.e., mapping products or consumers as points or vectors in a multidimensional space to evaluate and develop new concepts and products (Green et al. (1989), Roberts and Lilien (1993)). A map represented in a multidimensional space shows relationships among brands or between brands and consumers geometrically by means of interpoint distances or projections on vectors. In these applications of MDS on marketing, a map obtained by employing MDS generally represents these relationships at a single time point.

In the present paper, MDS is utilized to obtain a map which represents relationships among products as well as between products and consumers not at a single time point but at a series of time points. This makes it possible for us to utilize MDS in doing a prediction based on former time periods, which expand the horizon of utilizing MDS on analyzing marketing data. The purpose of the present paper is to apply a predicting procedure, based on two MDS methods, i.e., INDSCAL (Carroll and Chang (1970)) and PREFMAP (Carroll (1972)), to scanner data on a brand of beer named Drafty which was introduced into the Japanese market in 1995. The scanner data on Drafty and its competitive brands collected from a panel was analyzed by the procedure to predict the amount of purchase of Drafty and that of competitive brands.

2 Data

The scanner data, collected from all 56 households who bought Drafty and/or competitive brands at the supermarket during the first 13 weeks after it started to sell Drafty, consisted of the date of purchase, the amount of purchase of Drafty (number of cans), the total amount of purchase of competitive brands (number of cans and bottles), discount rate of Drafty, whether there was the end-aisle display of Drafty at that date, and whether the flyer of the supermarket at that date carried Drafty. The sum of purchases of other brands in the category of beer was recorded as the total amount of purchase of competitive brands. In the analysis the set of competitive brands was treated as if it was a single brand. Only the amount of purchase of Drafty and that of competitive brands were used in the analysis.

3 Method

The present procedure is fully described in Okada and Miyauchi (1996). Only the outline of the procedure is shown in steps (a) through (e) below.

(a) The amount of purchase of Drafty and competitive brands is tallied into the amount of purchase at each of weeks 1 through 13 for each household. A 56 x 26 table, where each row of the table shows the amount of purchase of Drafty and of competitive brands at each of 13 weeks of a household, is formed. The table is cluster analyzed to find clusters of households having homogeneous pattern of purchase of Drafty and competitive brands.

(b) Regarding Drafty at each of 13 weeks as 13 different objects and competitive brands at each of 13 weeks as 13 different objects, we have 26 objects. In each cluster, the square root of the sum of squared differences of the amount of purchase over constituent households of the cluster is calculated between any two of 26 objects to construct a dissimilarity matrix among 26 objects. The set of dissimilarity matrices is analyzed by INDSCAL.

(c) For each cluster the average amount of purchase of Drafty and that of competitive brands at each of 13 weeks are calculated, which are regarded as the magnitude of preference of that cluster to each of 26 objects, and are analyzed by PREFMAP to map each cluster as an (anti-)ideal point or vector in the common object configuration derived by INDSCAL. The formula, which relates distances between an (anti-)ideal point and objects (projections of objects on an ideal vector) to the amount of purchase, is given by PREFMAP.

(d) The orientation of dimensions of the common object configuration is inherently uniquely determined. This seems to suggest that each dimension of the common object configuration should have a close relationship with a characteristic or tendency which governs the purchase of Drafty and of competitive brands (cf. Arabie et al. p. 21 (1987)). The weight configuration shows the difference in importance of these characteristics among clusters. An equation, representing the trend of the characteristic or tendency corresponding to a dimension, is derived from coordinates of the dimension at weeks 1 through 13. Coordinates of the dimension at each week after 13 are predicted extrapolatively by the equation, which means that locations of Drafty and those of competitive brands at each week after 13 in the common object configuration are predicted.

(e) Substituting distances from the (anti-)ideal point to predicted locations of Drafty or to competitive brands (projections of predicted locations of Drafty or competitive brands on an ideal vector) into the formula given by PREFMAP at step (c), the amount of purchase of Drafty or that of competitive brands at each week after week 13 is predicted.

4 Results

The cluster analysis using k-means suggested three cluster result seems appropriate as the solution. Each cluster consists of 44, 11 and one household(s) respectively. A set of three dissimilarity matrices was analyzed by INDSCAL. The interpretation and the fitness suggested choosing the three-dimensional result as the solution (the variance accounted for was 76.7%). In Figure 1 the two-dimensional space of dimensions 1 and 2 of the three-dimensional common object configuration is shown (an anti-ideal point and ideal vectors are derived by using PREFMAP at the next step). Drafty at each of weeks 1 through 13 is represented by a circle, and competitive brands at each of weeks 1 through 13 is represented by a triangle. Table 1 shows the weight configuration of the INDSCAL solution, and suggests that dimension 1 has close relationship with cluster 1, dimension 2 has close relationship with cluster 2, and dimension 3 has close relationship with cluster 3.

Table 1: Weight configuration of the three-dimensional INDSCAL solution.

	Dim 1	Dim 2	Dim 3
Cluster 1	0.665	0.150	0.153
Cluster 2	0.029	0.874	0.085
Cluster 3	-0.000	0.006	0.998

Table 2 shows correlation coefficients between actual and predicted amount of purchases at weeks 1 through 13 for the ideal point and the ideal vector models given by PREFMAP, suggesting that the ideal point model is appropriate for cluster 1 while the ideal vector model is appropriate for clusters 2 and 3. Figure 1 shows the anti-ideal point representing cluster 1 and two ideal vectors representing clusters 2 and 3 in the two-dimensional space of dimensions 1 and 2 of the common object configuration. The projection of the ideal vector representing cluster 3 on the two-dimensional space is very small, and the ideal vector is almost parallel with dimension 3.

Table 2: Correlation coefficients between actual and predicted amount of purchases for ideal point model and ideal vector model of PREFMAP.

	Cluster 1	Cluster 2	Cluster 3
Ideal Point Model	0.691	0.990	1.000
Ideal Vector Model	0.626	0.990	1.000

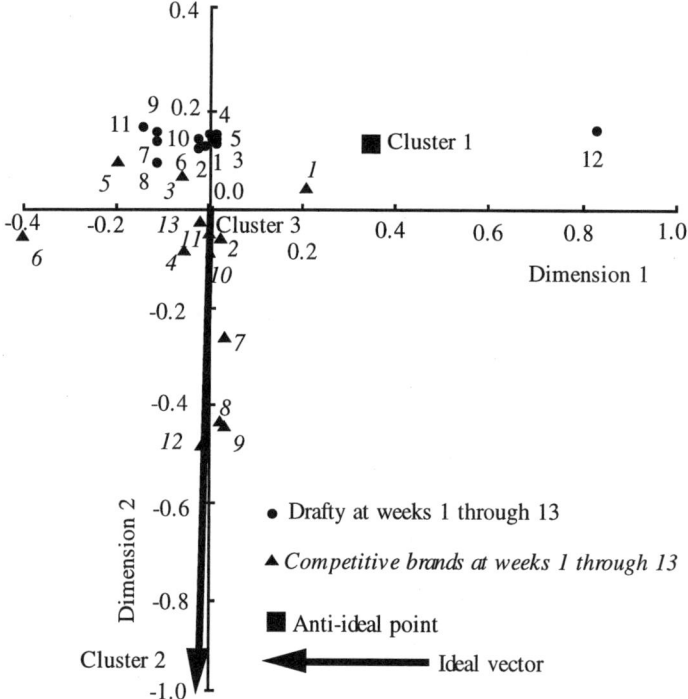

Figure 1: An anti-ideal point and ideal vectors in a two dimensional space of dimensions 1 and 2 of the common object configuration. Numbers besides circles or triangles represent week.

By using coordinates of either Drafty or competitive brands on a dimension at weeks 1 through 13, coefficients b and a which satisfy the equation

$$x = bt^a \qquad (1)$$

in a least squares sense are derived, where x denotes the coordinate of the dimension, and t (=1, 2, ..., 13) denotes week. Table 3 shows the derived coefficients. In deriving coefficients shown in Table 3, some coordinates (4 of 78 coordinates) which seem to conflict with the trend of the characteristic or tendency of the dimension were omitted. Equation (1) means that the characteristic or tendency corresponding to a dimension has the initial ($t = 1$) state b and tends to change with elasticity a. Coordinates of either Drafty or competitive brands on each dimension at weeks 14 through 39 are predicted by substituting 14, 15, ..., 39 into t of Equation (1) having b and a shown in Table 3.

Table 3: Derived coefficients.

	Dim 1		Dim 2		Dim 3	
	b	a	b	a	b	a
Drafty	0.006	-1.025	0.124	0.085	-0.151	0.020
Competitive Brands	-4.812	0.215	-0.022	0.974	5.989	-2.119

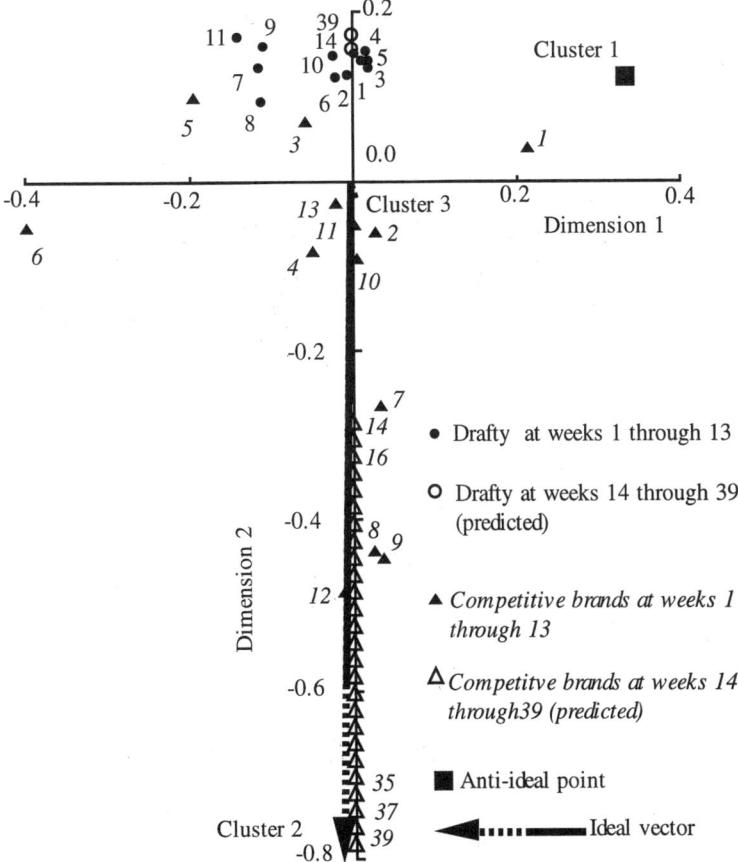

Figure 2: Predicted locations of Drafty and competitive brands at weeks 14 through 39. The arrowhead of the anti-ideal vector representing cluster 2 is

out of this figure. Numbers besides circles or triangles represent week.

Figure 2 shows predicted locations of Drafty and competitive brands at weeks 14 through 39 in the two-dimensional space of dimensions 1 and 2 of the common object configuration. Locations of Drafty at weeks 14 through 39 move slightly upward along dimension 2 (at the top of Figure 2). From weeks 14 to 39, distances between the anti-ideal point representing cluster 1 and locations of Drafty increase, and projections of locations on the ideal vector representing cluster 2 decrease. This causes the increase of the average amount of purchase of Drafty for cluster 1, and the decrease for cluster 2. Locations of competitive brands at weeks 14 through 39 move downward along dimension 2. From weeks 14 to 39, distances between the anti-ideal point representing cluster 1 and locations of competitive brands increase, and projections of locations on the ideal vector representing cluster 2 increase. This causes the increase of the average amount of purchase of competitive brands for clusters 1 and 2. The average amount of purchase of Drafty and of competitive brands for cluster 3 seems to be hardly affected, because the component of the ideal vector representing cluster 3 in the two-dimensional space is very small.

In the three-dimensional common object configuration, distances between the anti-ideal point representing cluster 1 and predicted locations of Drafty are almost unchanged from weeks 14 to 39, suggesting the average amount of purchase of Drafty for cluster 1 is almost unchanged in this period. Distances between the anti-ideal point representing cluster 1 and predicted locations of competitive brands increase from weeks 14 to 39, suggesting the increase of the average amount of purchase of competitive brands for cluster 1 in this period. Projections of the predicted locations of Drafty and of competitive brands from weeks 14 to 39 on the ideal vector representing cluster 2 decrease and increase respectively, suggesting the decrease of the average amount of purchase of Drafty and the increase of that of competitive brands for cluster 2. Both projections of the predicted locations of Drafty and of competitive brands from weeks 14 to 39 on the ideal vector representing cluster 3 decrease, suggesting the decrease of the average amount of purchase of Drafty and of competitive brands for cluster 3. Figure 3 shows the predicted average amount of purchase of Drafty and of competitive brands for cluster 1 at weeks 14 through 39.

Although the actual amount of purchase at each of weeks 14 through 39 is not disclosed, the actual market share of Drafty between weeks 27 and 39 in the category of beer at the supermarket was given to be 12.49%. The predicted market share calculated from the predicted average amount of purchase of Drafty and of competitive brands for each of three clusters was 9.8% at that period. The procedure was applied to another four brands introduced into the Japanese market in 1995 (Okada and Miyauchi (1996)). The predicted market share was close to the actual market share (actual market share 37.50% vs. predicted market share 35.3% ; 3.64% vs. 4.2%) for two brands, and completely different for one brand (1.36% vs. 24.4%).

The actual figure was not given for a brand.

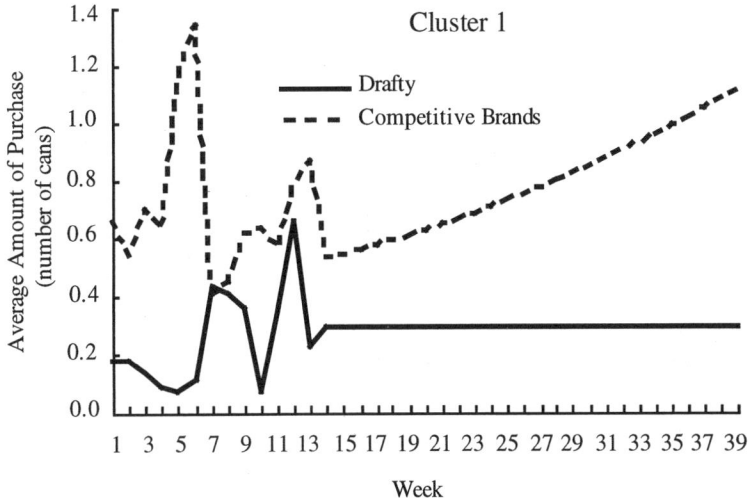

Figure 3: Predicted average amount of purchase of Drafty and of competitive brands for cluster 1 at weeks 14 through 39. The actual average amount of purchase is shown at weeks 1 through 13.

5 Discussion

A predicting procedure based on INDSCAL and PREFMAP was satisfactorily applied to scanner data on a brand of beer named Drafty and the competitive brands. The procedure is characterized by the ability that it can represent relationships among brands as well as between brands and clusters of consumers at a series of time points. Although the discrepancy between the predicted market share and the actual market share was small for Drafty and another two brands, it was large for one brand. The reason why the procedure failed to give a prediction close to the actual figure for one brand is not clear. The actual market share was based on the purchase between weeks 27 to 39, while the predicted market share was based on the data at the first 13 weeks. There is a possibility that the supermarket changed the treatment of the brand between weeks 14 and 26, e.g., reducing the length of the shelf allocated to it. If the amount of sale of the newly introduced brand was small for a couple of weeks, the length of the shelf allocated to it would be reduced in any supermarket.

Some shortcomings in the predicting procedure should be addressed (Okada and Miyauchi (1996)). In fitting the INDSCAL model the difference in the number of households in each cluster was ignored. In deriving coefficients b and a of Equation (1), some coordinates which seem to conflict with the trend of the characteristic or tendency of the dimension were omitted. An objective criterion to judge which coordinate should be omitted seems necessary. The predicted average amount of purchase can be negative or unreasonably large. In the present application the predicted average amount of purchase of Drafty for cluster 3 was negative at weeks 14 through 39. They were between -0.13 and -0.28 (number of cans), and were replaced with 0 in calculating the market share. An algorithm to bound the predicted value within some reasonable limit seems necessary. The stability of the prediction for different number of clusters and different dimensionality of the common object configuration should be examined.

The present data are regarded to be two time series, one for Drafty and the other for competitive brands, and might be able to be analyzed by multivariate time series. Multivariate time series can disclose the interaction between the amount of purchases of Drafty and competitive brands explicitly. While the present procedure cannot explicitly disclose the interaction, it can represent relationships among brands as well as between brands and clusters of consumers at each of 13 weeks geometrically. The present procedure can be used when the number of observation is too small for multivariate time series and requires no distributional assumption. It seems that the present procedure is versatile, although further comparisons with other methods of predicting the amount of purchase seem necessary to assess its usefulness.

References

ARABIE, P., CARROLL, J.D., and DeSARBO, W.S. (1987): *Three-way Scaling and Clustering*. Newbury Park, CA, Sage.

CARROLL, J.D. (1972): Individual differences and multidimensional scaling. In: R.N. Shepard, A.K. Romney, and S.B. Nerlove (eds.): *Multidimensional Scaling: Theory and Applications in the Behavioral Sciences Vol. 1 Theory*. Seminar Press, New York, 105–155.

CARROLL, J.D., and CHANG, J.J. (1970): Analysis of Individual Differences in Multidimensional Scaling. *Psychometrika, 35, 283- 319.*

GREEN, P.E., CARMONE, F.J., and SMITH, S.M. (1989): *Multidimensional Scaling: Concepts and Applications*. Allyn and Bacon, Boston.

OKADA, A. and MIYAUCHI, A. (1996): INDSCAL o Mochiita Yosoku no Ichi Hoho: Shin Seihin no Konyu Su Yosoku [A Forecasting Procedure Based on INDSCAL: Forecasting the Quantity of New Products Purchased]. *Shinrigaku Hyoron [Japanese Psychological Review], 39, 439-458.* (in Japanese)

ROBERTS, J.H., and LILIEN, G.L. (1993): Explanatory and predictive models of consumer behavior. In: J. Eliashberg and G.L. Lilien (eds.): *Handbooks in Operations Research and Management Science: Vol. 5 Marketing*. North Holland, Amsterdam, 27–82.

Author and Subject Index

The numbers given in this index refer to the first page of the respective papers

3-D Computer Vision	295
3-D Object Recognition	295
3-D-Space	277
Acoustic Model	313
Approximations	54
Architectural Aspects of Hypermedia Systems	205
Asymptotic Cramér-Rao Bound	182
Asymptotic Probability	54
Authoring on the Fly	213
Bauer, J.G.	287
Bayes' Classification	16
Bayesian Classifiers	295
Bayes Decision Theory	313
Bayesian Image Analysis	295
Bayes' Theorem	16
Bibliographic Databases	335, 365
Bildungsgesamtrechnung	3
Bilinear Clustering	172
Binary Coding	374
Binary Data	147
Bivariate Boxplot	93
Blien, U.	3
Böhning, D.	113
Boolean Regression	164
Branch-and-bound	164
Brehm, M.	123
Browsing	205, 245, 365
B-Spline	93
Burkhard, H.-D.	345
CART	313

Case Based Reasoning	345
Case Retrieval Nets	345
Categorical Data	132
Christlieb, N.	16
City-Block Distances	46
Classification	16, 374
Classification Profiles	335
Cluster	155
Clustering	101, 155
Clusters at Level d	35
Coincidence Graph	35
Communication	234
Competitive Structure	393
Conceptual Clustering	172
Conceptual Modelling	262
Conjoint Data	385
Connection	35
Content-Addressable Memory	245
Content Links	262
Contextual Correlation	277
Contingency Tables	132
Convex Hull	93
Corbellini, A.	93
Credit Scoring	374
Culture, Limitations of Access	234
Database	223
Database Selection	335
Data Dictionary	223
Data Mining	245
Data Transformation	374
Data Visualization	93
Decision Tree	313
Degree Distribution	35
Demographic Accounting	3
Design Effect	147

Design Matrices	192	Factorial Relative Risk	73
Design of Information Systems	262	Factorization	73
Dietz, E.	113	*Faßbinder, J.*	132
Digital Lecturing Board	213	Feature Logic	205
Digital Libraries	365	*Feger, H.*	24
Digital Spectra	16	FML	147
Disaggregation of Data	3	Formal Concept Analysis	277
Discriminative Training	287	Fulltext Retrieval	365
Disease Mapping	113	Fuzzy k-means Algorithm	101
Dissimilarities	46		
Distance	54	*Gaul, W.*	253, 393
Distances	46	*Gefeller, O.*	73, 193
Distributed Databases	365	Generalized Additive Model	62
Doberkat, E.-E.	205	*Geyer, W.*	213
Document Collection	245	Gibbs and Metropolis Sampling Algorithm	182
Document Map	245	*Gierl, H.*	385
Document Model	365	Global Optimization	295
DoDL	205	*Godehardt, D.*	35
Dreger, M.	335	*Godehardt, E.*	35, 54
Dynamic Modelling	192	*Göbel, S.*	335
Dynamic Partial Least Squares	192	Goodness-of-fit Test	35
Dynamic Path Model	192	*Graef, F.*	3
Dynamic Programming	393	Graph	54
		Graßhoff, G.	16
Eckert, A.	213	*Groenen, P.J.F.,*	46
Edge	35	*Großjohann, K.*	365
Effelsberg, W.	213	Guided Tour Link	262
Electronic Malls	253		
Electronic Publishing	270	*Haber, C.*	365
EM Algorithm	295, 313	*Harris, B.*	54
Entity-Relationship-Model	223, 262	Hausdorff Distance	139
ENTROP	3	Hazard Rate	139
Entropy Maximization	3	*Heiser, W.J.*	46
Entropy Projections	3	*Hejl, P.M.*	234
Epidemiology	155	Heterogeneity	113
Esswein, W.	223	Heterogeneous	3
Estimation of Tables	3	Heterogeneous Databases	365
Euclidean Distance	139	Heteroskedastic Models	182
Evolved Behavioral Strategies	234	Heteroskedastic Regression Model	182

Hidden Markov Models	304, 313, 335	Kaski, S.	245
		Kasper, K.	335
Hierarchic Clustering	172	Kauderer, H.	374
Hierarchy Tree	262	Kempe, W.	62
Hjort, N.L.	139	Kernel Density Estimators	62
HMM	287	Kernel Methods	139
Home Learning	213	Klein, T.	253
Honkela, T.	245	Knowledge	234
Horn Clauses	205	Kohonen, T.	245
Hornegger, J.	295	Kontextgestalt	277
Hox, J.	147	Krauth, J.	155
HTML	223		
Hybrid Systems	304	Labour Market	62
Hyperwave	270	Labour Supply	62
		Lag Operator	192
ICM-Algorithm	101	Lagus, K.	245
Ideal Point	401	Land, M.	73
Ideal Vector	401	Language Model	313
Incompatible and Incomplete Data	3	Latent Variable	113
		LDA	287
Index Link	262	Leaving-one-out	313
INDSCAL	401	Leenen, I.	164
Information Gathering	345	Lenz, K.	262
Information Overload	234	Likelihood Ratio Test	155
Information Retrieval	81, 87, 245	Liu, S.	182
Information Space	277	Löffler, M.	393
Information Systems	270	Logical Expressions	164
Integration Estimator	62	Lohrum, S.	335
Intelligent Agents	270	Low Complex Speech Recognition	335
Interaction	73		
Internet	253		
Internet as a Socio-Cultural System	234	Makedon, F.	81, 87
		Marginal Tables	132
Interval Graph	35, 54	Marketing	401
Isolated Vertices	35	Markov Chain Monte Carlo	182
		Markov Random Field Modeling	101
Jaworski, J.	35		
Jin, S.	182	Mathematical Classification	172
Joint Correspondence Analysis	132	Maurer, H.	270
		Maximum Entropy	313
		MBONE	213

MCE	287	*Oberweis, A.*	262
Meaning of Data	234	Object-Oriented Framework	205
Measurement Model	192	*Okada, A.*	401
Mechelen, I.V.	164	Online Effectiveness	253
Media, Maintopics	234	Online Pairwise Comparisons	253
Medical Information	277	Online Services	253
MeDoc	365	Online Survey	253
Meta-Analysis	113	*Owen, C.*	81, 87
Metropolis	182		
Meulman, J.J.	46	Page Link Model	262
Minimum Cost Rule	16	Partial Attributable Risk	73
Mirkin, B.	172	Participation of Women	62
Mixtures	54	Path Coefficients	192
Miyauchi, A.	401	Path Models	192
ML Estimator	182	*Paulus, D.*	295
Mucha, H.-J.	374	PLS	192
Multidimensional Scaling	46, 401	Poisson Distribution	54
Multilevel	147	*Polasek, S.*	182
Multimedia	81, 87	Pose Estimation	295
Multiperiod Price Paths	393	Posterior Probabilities	16
Multiple Correspondence Analysis	132	Power Plant Technology	277
Multiple Stream Analysis	81	Predicting Procedure	401
Multispectral Imagery	101	PREFMAP	401
Multivariate Outliers	93	*Preiser, U.*	277
Mutual Information	304	Price Promotions	393
		Price Response Function	393
		Probability Densities	304
Nelke, A.	16	Proportions	147
Neukirchen, Ch.	304	Prospect Theory	393
Neural Net Outputs	313	Psychoacoustically Oriented Features	335
Neural Networks	304, 385		
Ney, H.	313		
Niemann, H.	295		
Nonmetric City-Block MDS	46	Quasar Survey	16
Nonparametric Curve Estimation	139	Query Transformation	365
Nonparametric Mixture Distribution	113	Random Censorship	139
Nonparametric Regression	62	Random Coefficient	147
Normal Distributions	54	Random Stars	46
		Recurrent Neural Networks	335
		Redundancy	192

Reference Price	393	Speaker Independent Word Recognition	335
Regression Model	182	Specification of Hypermedia Systems	205
Reininger, H.	335		
Relative Entropy	3		
Relative Risk	73	Speech Recognition	287, 304, 313
Relevancy	234	Statistical Modeling	295
Remote Sensing	101	Statistical Object Recognition	295
Residual Variances	182	Stopping Criterion	46
Retrieval	345	Stress Function	46
Riani, M.	93	*Strohe, H.G.*	192
Rigoll, G.	304	Structural Links	262
RML	147	Structural Model	192
Robust Centroid	93	Structured Visualization	277
Robustness	335	Supervised Learning	374
		SYSTAT	46
Scaling	374		
Scanner Data	401	TCL/TK	87
Scan Statistic	155	Telephone Bandwidth	335
Schlemminger, A.	16	Teleseminar	213
Schwanenberg, S.	385	Teleteaching	213
Search Engines	277	Template Matching	16
Search Strategies	234	Term Frequencies	335
Segmentation	385	Text Document	245
Self-Organizing Map	245	Threshold	54
Selz, A.	223	Threshold Functions	35
Semantic Bandwidth Compression	81	Training Set	16
Sequential Relative Risks	73	Unsupervised Fuzzy Classification	101
SERM	223		
Shared Whiteboard	213	Upper Bound	155
Similarity	345		
Simulation	164, 385	Variable Window	155
Singular Value Decomposition	132	Vector Quantizer	304
Smoothing	46	Vertex	35
Software Engineering	205	Visual Error Criteria	139
Software Reengineering	277	VLSI Implementation	335
Sparse Connectivity	335		
Spatial Data	172		
Spatial Proximity	277	*Wartenberg, F.*	253
Spatial-Spectral Features	101	*Weber, R.*	365

Web Site Design	253
WEBSON Method	245
Weight Relations	192
Wiemker, R.	101
Word Category	245
World Wide Web	253, 262, 270
Wisotzki, L.	16
Wüst, H.	335
Zani, S.	93

Druck: Strauss Offsetdruck, Mörlenbach
Verarbeitung: Schäffer, Grünstadt